ALISON BING
JOHN A VLAHIDES

SAN FRANCISCO

CITY GUIDE

INTRODUCING SAN FRANCISCO

A cable car trundles along Hyde St, with Alcatraz (p62) in the background

Grab your coat and a handful of glitter, and you're good to go in San Francisco. Here antics usually reserved for holidays and disco theme nights erupt spontaneously, and when all that damp fog and sheer delight hits you, this town will give you goose bumps.

What with all the earthquakes and daydreamers, this peninsula keeps only a tentative hold on the planet, not to mention the continental US. But as any San Franciscan will point out, gravity is overrated anyway. With 43 hills and a population of free thinkers, crafty inventors and weirdos passing as normal, this city stubbornly refuses to be brought down to earth. Instead, reality is forced to rise to the occasion, with flocks of wild parrots taking to the treetops, ingenious meals by rising star chefs, and poets who just keep on riffing until their words take flight. San Francisco's stratospheric booms and crashing busts aren't for the faint of heart, but as anyone who's clung onto the side of a cable car will tell you, this town gives one hell of a ride.

SAN FRANCISCO LIFE

Many visitors have the same first reaction to San Francisco as to the *Mona Lisa*: can it really be so small? This seven-by-seven-mile peninsula looms much larger in the imagination than it does in reality. Earthquakes and capricious city rules that limit building higher than the tip of the Transamerica Pyramid have forced big-name architects to get creative with small-scale museums, resulting in Mario Botta's kaleidoscopic SFMOMA, Herzog & de Meuron's copper-clad MH de Young Memorial Museum oxidizing green to match Golden Gate Park, and Renzo Piano's wildflower-domed, Hobbit Moderne design for the California Academy of Sciences. But the city's most beloved architectural features are still its Victorian-style mansions, with their ice-cream colors and frosting flourishes. Whenever you find yourself on a hilltop, momentarily overwhelmed at the tooth-aching glory of all those confectionary houses, stick around: the fog will soon draw curtains on the westward expanse of Golden Gate Park and shrink the city to digestible size.

He probably didn't mean it as a compliment, but Rudyard Kipling's description of San Francisco as 'a mad city inhabited for the most part by perfectly insane people' is a century-old adage quoted by San Franciscans not with outrage but with unabashed pride. Insanity remains a relative term here, ranging from charmingly kooky characters like the blissed-out unicyclist sheathed in hot-pink Lycra to truly terrifying cult leaders like Jim Jones and Charles Manson. Yet with real estate prices hovering in the stratosphere for more than a decade, San Francisco has lately been more hospitable to wealthy eccentrics than starry-eyed artistes. While it's true that social conventions need not apply in San Francisco, this can be a mixed blessing: complete strangers will enthusiastically invite you to gourmet dinner parties or documentary premieres, only to flake out at the last minute, or spend the evening regaling you with paranoid conspiracy theories finely honed at San Francisco's 40-odd medicinal marijuana clubs.

But don't be too quick to dismiss those outlandish ideas, because San Francisco's willingness to consider all possibilities has made it a world capital of technology, cuisine, poetry, biotechnology, gay liberation, graphic novels, skateboarding, urban ecology, street art, documentary film and (believe it, babydoll) drag queendom. Despite their slacker reputations, San Franciscans hold more patents per capita than any other US city, and read more books and rack up many more degrees than other Americans. The city has been working up quite a reputation for compassion, too, creating new models for AIDS care, family homeless shelters, and more nonprofits than any other US city.

You can blame SF for any number of temptations: chocolate bars, designer jeans, martinis, TV broadcasts, online shopping and LSD. But don't believe the hype that there's something unusual in the water here – that would be too easy an explanation for San Francisco. No, it's in the air. Under the aromas of Pacific salt and perpetually blooming flowers, you'll notice a tantalizing whiff of unlimited possibility. Breathe in, and brace yourself: other towns may surprise you, but only in San Francisco will you surprise yourself.

The LGBT Pride Parade (p247) is San Francisco's biggest party

EMBARCADERO & THE PIERS

Cover the waterfront in San Francisco and you'll encounter canoodling sea lions, ruthless Space Invaders and escapees from Alcatraz. Top shimmering bay views with a local specialty dating from the Gold Rush: chocolate.

➊ Sea Lions at Pier 39
Watch free slapstick comedy from SF's resident marine mammals (p66)

➋ Musée Mécanique
Feed Ms Pac-Man and guillotine the guilty with spare change (p66)

➌ Alcatraz
Plot your own prison break from the notorious island jail (p62)

DOWNTOWN & CIVIC CENTER

Get giddy atop staggeringly high hills scaled by creaking cable cars, at top-floor galleries transformed by breakthrough art installations, and in flagship stores piled to the rafters with limited-edition sneakers and SF's own Levi's.

❶ San Francisco Opera
Levitate in your seat as SF's divas hit high notes (p222)

❷ Asian Art Museum
Travel half the world through this standout art collection (p76)

❸ Cable Cars
Jump up and hang on to Andrew Hallidie's vintage contraptions (p74)

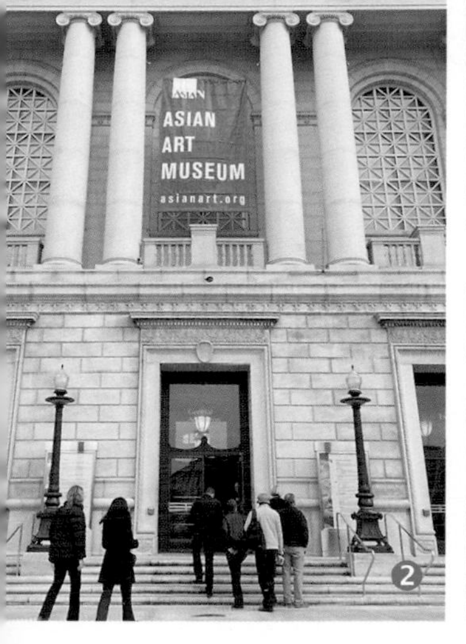

CHINATOWN

Revolutions, gold rushes, earthquakes, bootlegger gun battles: the true stories of Chinatown's 44 alleyways make action flicks by favorite son Bruce Lee seem tame. Today Chinatown is family-friendly – but watch out for killer salt-and-pepper calamari.

❶ Waverly Place
Spot temple balconies along SF's most soulful back alley (p83)

❷ Spofford Alley
Eavesdrop on mah-jong marathons in SF's revolutionary alleyway (p83)

❸ Li Po
Booze like a Beat poet beside the gold Buddha (p197)

❶ **City Lights Bookstore**
Get lit at SF's free-speech landmark and home of the Beats (p146)

❷ **Caffe Trieste**
Take espresso at the ultimate bohemian hangout (p198)

❸ **Coit Tower & Telegraph Hill**
Discover hidden cottages, sculpture gardens and wild parrots along stairway walks (p88)

NORTH BEACH

Get lost and find bliss in backstreets full of poetry, vintage finds and focaccia hot from a 100-year-old oven. Inspiration comes easy in sidewalk cafes serving espresso to Francis Ford Coppola's crew, and in mural-lined alleyways with poetry underfoot.

➊ Diego Rivera Gallery
See SF from the great Mexican muralist's perspective (p93)

➋ Grace Cathedral
Spot science, mysticism and social conscience in the Episcopalian architecture (p93)

➌ Literary Locations
Discover the real-life locales that inspired Kerouac, Maupin and Coolbrith (p93)

RUSSIAN & NOB HILLS

For lunch with a side of adrenaline, haul picnics to hilltop parks with staggering views and the names of poets. Wander past side streets straight out of books by Kerouac and Maupin, and find your own happy endings downhill in Polk Gulch boutiques and dive bars.

THE MARINA & THE PRESIDIO

Hip boutiques and award-winning dining in a former cow pasture, and kite-flying and public nudity at a former army base: yep, sounds like San Francisco. For thrills with chills, stick around to watch the fog parade over Golden Gate Bridge.

❶ Golden Gate Bridge
Bike across the bay on this marvel of art deco engineering (p104)

❷ Union Street Boutiques
Update your decor and your look in under three blocks (p150)

❸ Exploratorium
Boggle the brain with weird science and freaky technology (p102)

SOMA

Lurking in the long shadows of SoMa warehouses and skyscrapers is the breakthrough Yerba Buena arts district, SF's hottest nightlife, and start-ups quietly kicking off the next tech boom. Get here now, and you can say you saw it happening.

❶ South Park
See the next tech boom coming from SF's grassy knoll (p113)

❷ Stud
Make the scene at SF's hot, hunky, historic gay bar (p245)

❸ Contemporary Jewish Museum
Explore multifaceted contemporary Jewish culture in Daniel Libeskind's postmodern landmark (p112)

1

2

THE MISSION & POTRERO HILL

Street art and bargain eats are never far from cutting-edge galleries and organic bistros in the Mission, where the underground hits the mainstream. Mingle with families and hipsters bonding over murals, tacos and innovative nonprofits.

3

1 La Taqueria
Devour killer SF-Mex among Mission families and off-duty food critics (p183)

2 El Rio
Get down and funky at SF's most multiculti, pan-sexual club (p243)

3 826 Valencia
Score eye patches, literature and lard at SF's writing nonprofit (p118)

1 F Line Streetcar
Hit the Castro or go both ways on SF's swinging-est streetcar (p305)

2 Castro Theatre
Applaud the Wurlitzer and boo villains at SF's movie palace (p124)

THE CASTRO & NOE VALLEY

Somewhere over the rainbow you'll find the Castro, SF's history-making, boundary-bending gay neighborhood. There's no better place to be out and about at Bette Davis movies, community-minded boutiques, neighborhood parks and thumping clubs where only shoes are required.

THE HAIGHT

Make love and a fashion statement, not war, in the flashback-friendly Haight. Free spirits are still drawn to the site of the Summer of Love by street musicians, psychedelic Victorians, book and movie cooperatives, vintage clothing, microbrews and pot clubs (sorry dude, prescription required).

1 Amoeba Music
Hear free concerts and binge on CDs at SF's indie-music superstore (p158)

2 Bound Together Anarchist Book Collective
Plot revolutions and/or organic gardens at Haight's volunteer-run bookstore (p156)

3 Alamo Square
Strike a pose alongside Postcard Row's va-va-voom Victorians (p130)

GOLDEN GATE PARK & THE AVENUES

Picnic among bison, bonsai and far-out artwork in SF's bodacious backyard. Everything San Francisco really needs is here: potent coffee, great bookstores, fabulous greenery and enough bargain eateries to satisfy hardcore Ocean Beach surfers.

1 MH de Young Memorial Museum
Admire artistry from California to Zimbabwe inside sleek, copper-clad galleries (p139)

2 Namu
Discover modern Korean cuisine with local, organic ingredients (p188)

3 Ocean Beach
Beachcomb by day and have bonfires at night along SF's misty beachfront (p138)

OTHER NEIGHBORHOODS

Shock SF natives with your knowledge of the city's best-kept secrets, hidden in smaller neighborhoods off the tourist track. Japantown, Hayes Valley and the Tenderloin don't have any big, glitzy landmarks – but if you hit these highlights, you'll find they have plenty of soul.

❶ Japantown

Take in the Cherry Blossom Festival (p21) in April and sample the jazz at Yoshi's (p211) and the culinary delights at Tataki (p177) year-round

❷ Heart of the City Farmers Market

Go local and seasonal for less every Wednesday and Sunday in the Tenderloin (p169)

❶ Sausalito
Laze sunny days away among houseboats and waterfront cafes (p280)

❷ Muir Woods
Find primordial bliss among giant old-growth redwoods (p277)

❸ Santa Cruz
Ride the waves or rickety roller coasters in Surf City, USA (p296)

BEYOND SF

Enchanting though it is, San Francisco is surprisingly easy to leave. Cross the Golden Gate Bridge and enter a world where sailboats drift, wine flows and sun filters through 300ft redwoods – or follow Hwy 1 to Santa Cruz, home of California surf culture.

CONTENTS

THE AUTHORS

Alison Bing

Over 15 years in San Francisco, Alison has done everything you're supposed to do in the city and many things you're not, including falling in love on the 7 Haight bus and gorging on Mission burritos before Berlioz symphonies. Alison holds degrees in art history and international diplomacy – respectable diplomatic credentials she regularly undermines with opinionated culture commentary for radio, newspapers, foodie magazines, and books, including Lonely Planet's *California*, *USA*, *Coastal California*, *California Trips*, *San Francisco* and *San Francisco Encounter*.

Alison coauthored the Neighborhoods and Excursions chapters, and wrote the Shopping and Eating chapters.

ALISON'S TOP SAN FRANCISCO DAY

Roll out of bed and down Haight St for a coffee. Check out what's new/old in vintage fashion, what classic CD someone's ex vindictively sold at Amoeba Music (p158), and what favorite author is reading at the Booksmith (p224). Then head to Golden Gate Park (p139) to find the most aggressive blooms in the Dahlia Garden and the fiercest mask in the Oceania wing of the MH de Young Memorial Museum (p139). Follow Andy Goldsworthy's simulated earthquake cracks in the sidewalk back out to the sunshine, and wander up to Clement St for dim sum and a browse at Green Apple Books (p160) and Park Life (p160). Hit Genki (p190) for tapioca bubble tea before hopping the Downtown-bound 38 Geary. Troll Gallery Paule Anglim (p73) for shows by local and international artists before heading to Mission St for a peek at Catharine Clark Gallery (p109), Yerba Buena Center for the Arts (p219) and the latest photography show at SFMOMA (p108). When a growling stomach threatens to drown out gallery conversation, take BART to 24th St and La Taqueria (p183) for the perfect *pollo asada* burrito with chipotle salsa. Wash this down with a happy hour *mojito* at Medjool Sky Terrace (p201), watching the sun restore glamour to faded Mission cinema marquees. Window-shop up Valencia St to the Roxie (p221) for a film or documentary. Discuss at length over salted caramel ice cream from Bi-Rite Creamery (p182) before calling it a night. Early risers get the Early Girl tomatoes at the farmers market (p169).

John A Vlahides

John A Vlahides lives in San Francisco. He co-hosts the TV series *Lonely Planet: Roads Less Traveled,* on National Geographic Adventure. He is also co-founder of the California travel site 71miles.com. John studied cooking in Paris with the same chefs who trained Julia Child, and is a former luxury-hotel concierge and member of the prestigious Les Clefs d'Or, the international union of the world's elite concierges. He spends free time singing with the San Francisco Symphony, sunning on the nude beach beneath the Golden Gate Bridge, skiing the Sierra Nevada and touring California on his motorcycle.

John coauthored the Neighborhoods and Excursions chapters and wrote the Drinking, Nightlife, Arts, Sports & Activities, GLBT and Sleeping chapters.

LONELY PLANET AUTHORS

Why is our travel information the best in the world? It's simple: our authors are passionate, dedicated travellers. They don't take freebies in exchange for positive coverage so you can be sure the advice you're given is impartial. They travel widely to all the popular spots, and off the beaten track. They don't research using just the internet or phone. They discover new places not included in any other guidebook. They personally visit thousands of hotels, restaurants, palaces, trails, galleries, temples and more. They speak with dozens of locals every day to make sure you get the kind of insider knowledge only a local could tell you. They take pride in getting all the details right, and in telling it how it is. Think you can do it? Find out how at **lonelyplanet.com**.

Sherpas probably won't be necessary, but you should still come prepared for high adventure in the hills of San Francisco. With 43 hills stretching the imagination and the calf muscles, this town will leave you breathless – keep a few bucks handy for the cable car. Otherwise, you don't need all that much cash to have a good time here: there are free events, street fairs, concerts and parades throughout the year, and plenty of cheap eats and boutique bargains to go around. But if you're here to splurge, San Francisco's top-notch dining establishments, art galleries and hotel-top bars will lighten your load as surely as Miss Piggot and her thieving barmaids did to their customers nightly during the Gold Rush – only these days, you're less likely to wake up on a ship bound for Argentina with a skipper barking at you to swab the decks.

Red velvet ropes and black-tie dress aren't San Francisco's style: entry to SF's hottest restaurants, clubs and events is almost always open to all on a first-come, first-served basis, though a feather boa may come in handy. You'll want to reserve ahead online, especially in summer, for film festivals and theater, or dinner in the city's trendiest restaurants. With so much to do, the challenge is not overbooking; this is one city where spontaneity is well rewarded.

WHEN TO GO

Little-known fact: the Summer of Love actually kicked off here in January of 1967, and once you've spent a chilly summer's day in San Francisco you'll understand how the hippies might've gotten confused even without the help of hallucinogens. Entire June days are spent shivering in a fog bank, with temperatures hovering around 55°F. Determined picnickers huddle over their barbecue grills in Golden Gate Park, while just across the bay, tanned Berkeley locals are rocking their Birkenstocks without socks. It would hardly seem fair, except for the many street fairs and nonstop parades that make San Francisco in summer the place to be, and worth the high-season hotel rates.

Early fall is the best of all possible worlds in San Francisco, when summer really arrives (never mind the calendar), neighborhood street fairs are still in full swing, California's seasonal cuisine is at its flavor-bursting best and hotel rates unaccountably drop. By October, Wine Country cools off enough at night to appreciate a peppery zinfandel and a Calistoga mud bath. Most of the year the consistent San Francisco forecast makes easy money for local meteorologists: a high of about 55°F to 70°F during the day, with fog burning off in the morning and rolling back into town in the late afternoon. Tote a sweater or coat at all times, or you'll be forced to commit the ultimate San Francisco fashion crime and sheepishly sport one of those $12 fleece pullovers with the Golden Gate Bridge embroidered on it.

FESTIVALS & EVENTS

Professional paraders, raging exhibitionists and homecoming queens of all kinds won't want to miss the glut of annual street fairs that kicks off with Pride month (known elsewhere as June) and ends with the gleeful partying skeletons of Día de los Muertos in November. However, if you must come in the rainier, chillier months from December through to March, don't despair, because there's still plenty to celebrate, both indoors and out: dance-along Nutcracker Suites, tiny-tot kung-fu classes marching in adorably inept formation in the Lunar New Year parades, throngs rocking Astroturf jackets at public art gallery openings, and the improbable incessant blooming of Golden Gate Park. Not-to-be-missed events are listed below.

January

DINE ABOUT TOWN

www.sfdineabouttown.com

Over 100 of San Francisco's best restaurants offer set-price lunch and dinner specials with local seasonal treats, including Dungeness crab cakes galore.

February

INDEPENDENT FILM FESTIVAL

☎ 415-820-3907; www.sfindie.com

Cinephiles binge on over 100 indie films, documentaries, animated films and short films over two weeks in early February.

NOISE POP

www.noisepop.com

Winter blues be gone: discover your new favorite indie band and catch rockumentary premieres, crafty concert gear and rockin' gallery openings at get-to-know-you venues; third week of February.

LUNAR NEW YEAR PARADE

☎ 415-986-1370; www.chineseparade.com

Chase through town the 200ft dragon, lion dancers, toddler kung-fu classes and frozen-smile runners-up for the Miss Chinatown title, as lucky red envelopes and fireworks fall from the sky like a February drizzle.

March

ST PATRICK'S DAY PARADE

☎ 415-661-2700; www.sfstpatricksdayparade.com

Since 1851, the luck and libations of the Irish have been liberally enjoyed in SF in mid-March. Renegade paraders ditch the official route and leap on booze trolleys with revelers whose entire vocabulary seems suddenly reduced to 'Erin Go Bragh!' and 'Woo-hoo!'

ANARCHIST BOOK FAIR

http://sfbookfair.wordpress.com

Rise up and read freely at Golden Gate Park's County Fair Building on the third weekend in March. Meet radical comic book artists, swap DIY tips for organic farming and web design, and find inspiration for your own manifesto.

ASIAN AMERICAN FILM FESTIVAL

☎ 415-863-0814; www.asianamericanmedia.org

Two-hundred filmmakers debut features and documentaries at Sundance Kabuki Cinema (p221) during the third week in March.

April

PERPETUAL INDULGENCE IN THE PARK

☎ 415-820-9697; www.thesisters.org

Easter Sunday is all indulgence, all day in Mission Dolores Park (p118): there's an Easter-egg hunt in the morning for the kiddies, followed by a bitchin' Bonnet Contest and the Hunky Jesus Contest, for those who prefer their messiahs with some muscle tone.

CHERRY BLOSSOM FESTIVAL

☎ 415-563-2313; www.nccbf.org

Japantown blooms and booms with *taiko* drums, homegrown hip-hop, shrines and sunshine in mid-April. Foodies are drawn here from a 10-block radius by April breezes carrying the scent of food-stall yakitori, tempura, and *gyoza* (dumplings).

SAN FRANCISCO INTERNATIONAL FILM FESTIVAL

☎ 415-561-5000; www.sffs.org

The nation's oldest film festival is still looking stellar after more than 50 years, with two weeks of star-studded premieres from the end of April to early May. Get tickets early and pace yourself: the longest-running film fest in the country is a marathon event, with 325 films (from countries as disparate as Denmark and Iran), 200 directors, and sundry actors and cinephile crowds subsisting almost entirely on popcorn at the Sundance Kabuki Cinema HQ (p221).

May

CINCO DE MAYO

☎ 415-256-3005; www.sfcincodemayo.com

On the first weekend of May, Mexican independence and Chicano pride come to Civic Center and Mission Dolores Park, complete with fantastic Aztec feather headdresses, gleaming lowriders, revolutionary speeches, chipotle chili beer and much more. *¡Que viva!*

KABOOM!

www.kfog.com/kaboom; Pier 30/32

KFOG radio station gets the jump on July 4, with fireworks choreographed to the Ramones, kids' activities and headliners like Los Lonely Boys supported by Scottish singer-songwriter sensation KT Tunstall. Take public transit to avoid traffic before and after the fireworks, which attract crowds up to 350,000 on the second Saturday of May. Tickets cost $20.

BAY TO BREAKERS

☎ 415-359-2800; www.baytobreakers.com

Many run costumed, others naked, some scared from Embarcadero to Ocean Beach on the third Sunday in May. Around 65,000 people run the race – though a few runners dressed as salmon run upstream from the finish line to the beginning. Race registration costs $44 to $48.

CARNAVAL

☎ 415-826-1401; www.carnavalsf.com

Brazilian, or just faking it with a wax and a tan? Get head-dressed to impress and shake your tail feathers in the Mission on the last weekend of May, and brave the inevitable fog – you might be surprised where it's possible to get goose bumps.

June

NORTH BEACH STREET FAIR

☎ 415-989-6426; http://sfnorthbeach.org/nbfestival

Swing dancing, pizza-tossing and sidewalk drawings worthy of Leonardo have taken over the streets of North Beach mid-June for 50 years and counting. Get your pets blessed by a priest and sample juicy Italian sausages hot off the grill – *che bella*.

HAIGHT ASHBURY STREET FAIR

☎ 415-661-8025; www.haightashburystreetfair.org

Free music on two stages, macramé and tie-dye galore, and plenty of dubious brownies surreptitiously for sale: all that's missing is the free love. Takes place every mid-June since 1978, when Harvey Milk helped make the first Haight fair happen.

GAY & LESBIAN FILM FESTIVAL

☎ 415-703-8650; www.frameline.org

Here, queer and ready for a premiere for three decades, yet it doesn't look a day over 29. This is the oldest GLBT film fest anywhere and, as regular crowds of 60,000 will tell you, consistently the best. Over two weeks in the second half of June, more than 225 films launch new talents from more than 25 countries, drawing celebs like Rosie O'Donnell and John Waters, and raucous crowds that talk back to the screen.

PINK SATURDAY & DYKE MARCH

www.sfpride.org, www.dykemarch.org

Around 50,000 LBGT women parade from Dolores to Castro Sts, kicking off SF's largest all-ages street party on the last Saturday of June. Party admission is free to all, though donations are collected by the Sisters of Perpetual Indulgence to defray Port-a-Potty and cleanup costs.

PRIDE PARADE

☎ 415-864-0831; www.sfpride.org

Come out wherever you are: SF goes wild for GLBT pride on the last Sunday of June, with half a million people, seven stages, tons of glitter and ounces of bikinis. The crowd roars for newlyweds, PFLAG (Parents and Friends of Lesbians and Gays), men and women in uniform, and, let's be honest, pretty much anyone tossing beads or candy their way – so get out there and join the parade.

July

INDEPENDENCE DAY

July 4 explodes with fireworks even in summer fog, celebrating San Francisco's dedication to life, liberty and the pursuit of happiness no matter the climate – economic, political or meteorological.

MISSION CREEK MUSIC & ARTS FESTIVAL

www.mcmf.org

The city finally breaks a summer sweat in mid-July thanks to 150-plus Bay Area bands as well as art shows and dance premieres at several ideal venues, including Café du Nord/ Swedish American Hall (p212), Rickshaw Stop (p213) and Adobe Books & Backroom Gallery (p152), plus free shows in McLaren Park.

AIDS WALK

www.aidswalk.net/sanfran

Until AIDS takes a hike, you can: this 10km fundraiser benefits 43 AIDS organizations and happens on the third Sunday in July. When San Francisco was hit by the AIDS epidemic more than 20 years ago, the city wiped away its tears and took to the streets, raising $65 million to date to fight the pandemic and support those living with HIV. Hundreds of thousands of walkers are treated to free ice cream, live music and applause from passersby along the route.

August

SAN FRANCISCO JEWISH FILM FESTIVAL

☎ 415-621-0556; www.sfjff.org

The world's premier Jewish film festival will leave you *kvelling* (welling up with pride) at the end of July/early August at the Castro Theatre (p220) and other venues around the bay. Expect the unexpected from this festival, from Muslim-Jewish love stories from Kazakhstan to documentaries directed by Natalie Portman.

September

FRINGE FESTIVAL

www.sffringe.org

More outrageous theatrical antics in SF than usual hit the stage in late September, at discount prices. Book ahead, or chance it at the Exit Theater's (p225) box office.

ARAB FILM FEST

☎ 415-564-1100; www.aff.org

The Roxie Cinema (p221) shows Middle Eastern films in the second week of September, including 75 features and shorts. For over a decade, this showcase has explored a world of ideas, from feminism to fishing, in ground-breaking new cinema from Lebanon to Morocco.

OPERA IN THE PARK

☎ 415-864-3330

Opera divas sing their hearts out gratis at Sharon Meadow in Golden Gate Park (p139) on the first Sunday of the opera season (the second Sunday in September), just as they did in SF after the 1906 earthquake to lift the city's spirits – and more than a century later, a heartfelt aria still begins fall with a grace note.

FOLSOM STREET FAIR

☎ 415-777-3247; www.folsomstreetfair.com

Work those leather chaps and enjoy public spankings for local charities on the last weekend of September. To answer the obvious question in advance: yes, people do actually get pierced and tattooed down there, but it's probably best not to stare unless you're prepared to strip down and compare.

SF SHAKESPEARE FESTIVAL

☎ 415-422-2221; www.sfshakes.org

The play's the thing in the Presidio, outdoors and free of charge on sunny September weekends. Kids' summer workshops are also held for junior Juliets and budding Bards, culminating in performances throughout the Bay Area.

October

CASTRO STREET FAIR

☎ 415-841-1824; www.castrostreetfair.org

Drag royalty rules the stage, punk rockers fill the mosh pit and rainbow flags fly above the fray on the first weekend of October.

LITQUAKE

☎ 415-750-1497 www.litquake.org

Stranger-than-fiction literary events take place in the second week of October, with bestselling and cult-hit authors spilling true stories at lunch readings and trade secrets over drinks at the legendary Lit Crawl.

HARDLY STRICTLY BLUEGRASS FESTIVAL

www.strictlybluegrass.com

The west goes wild for free bluegrass and rock with a twang in Golden Gate Park (p139), with three days and three stages of bluegrass legends on the first weekend of October. Recent headliners include Emmylou Harris, Billy Bragg, Nick Lowe and the legendary Earl Scruggs.

SF JAZZ FESTIVAL

☎ 415-788-7353; www.sfjazz.org

Horns and minds are blown from late September to late November in SF as jazz greats share the bill with newcomers, from Brazilian bossa chanteuse Gal Costa and jazz-tap impresario Savion Glover to jazz ukelele upstart Jake Shimabukuro and powerhouse drummer Cindy Blackman.

LOVEVOLUTION

www.sflovevolution.org

The first weekend of September, all you need is love – that, and over 100 DJs Downtown. Join the parade of art cars and surreal floats, or join the psychedelic dance party at Civic Center that makes Burning Man look like a dress rehearsal.

ALTERNATIVE PRESS EXPO

www.comic-con.org/ape

Meet the demented masterminds behind your favorite cult-hit comics, and score original Chris Ware sketches and Lark Pien books prepublication, as well as precious signed, limited-edition handmade comic books by the Bay Area's next Daniel Clowes, Adrian Tomine or R Crumb.

November

DÍA DE LOS MUERTOS (DAY OF THE DEAD)

☎ 415-821-1155; www.dayofthedeadsf.org; November 2

Zombie brides, Aztec dancers in full feather regalia and dancing skeletons party like there's no tomorrow, leading the parade of happy mourners down 24th St and paying their respects to community altars to the dead along the way.

TRANNY FEST

www.trannyfest.com

Cross-dress and transgress with the best on the first weekend in November, with a film festival and all-star performances; tickets cost $8.

GREEN FESTIVAL

www.greenfestivals.org

The lights may be low-watt fluorescents, but the bright ideas are positively blinding in mid-November at this landmark three-day showcase for the latest in green cuisine, technology and sustainable thinking. Events include workshops and talks with 150 eco-luminaries, such as Alice Waters, performances by the likes of Chuck D, eco-fashion shows, organic beer and wine tastings, and 400 leading green businesses. Tickets cost $15 per day or $25 for all three days; proceeds support SF food banks and pioneering fair-trade nonprofit Global Exchange.

UN-THANKSGIVING DAY

Un-make colonial history at the Alcatraz sunrise ceremony with Native leaders and supporters, held on the third Thursday of November every year since 1975. The celebration commemorates the 19-month Native occupation of Alcatraz, and pays homage to indigenous traditions around the bay and beyond.

December

CELEBRATION OF CRAFTSWOMEN

☎ 415-431-1180; www.celebrationofcrafts women.org

Get crafty with unique handmade gifts in support of a worthy cause at this Women's Building (p119) fundraiser, held on the last weekend of November/first weekend of December.

DANCE ALONG NUTCRACKER

☎ 415-255-1355; www.sflgfb.org/show.html

Do you tutu? Dance to the *Nutcracker Suite*, performed with booty-shaking verve by the Lesbian/Gay Freedom Band at the Yerba Buena Center for the Arts (p219) on the first weekend of December.

KUNG PAO KOSHER COMEDY

www.koshercomedy.com

A cherished SF holiday tradition: Jewish comedy on Christmas at a Chinese restaurant. Tickets cost $42 with cocktails and egg rolls, or $62 with dinner, featuring kosher walnut prawns and Kung Pao chicken.

COSTS & MONEY

The cost of living in San Francisco is high, though in general you get what you pay for – inventive, fresh cuisine, stimulating cultural events, fine art and strong drink. But many of the best things about San Francisco are gratis: natural beauty, street festivals, park strolls, gallery openings and idle conversation. Others are damn near free, and you'll only have to part with a few bucks for a steaming bowl of Vietnamese noodles, a vintage fashion statement, tickets to take the N-Judah metro line all the way to the beach, or happy hour in Mission dive bars. With some resourcefulness you can live well beyond your means here, with set-price lunches, same-day or standing-room-only tickets to the theater or opera, and killer sales racks at chi-chi boutiques – see the Eating (p164), Arts (p218) and Shopping (p142) chapters for details.

In case you haven't already heard from some San Franciscan kvetching about the as-

HOW MUCH?

Cup of coffee $1.30 (small American drip coffee)

Gallon of gas $2.79 to $3.45 (find the cheapest gas stations at www.sanfrangasprices.com)

Burrito $5 to $7 (even a cent more is cause for foodie uprisings)

Movie ticket $11 to $13 (look for bargain matinees and double features)

Pint of local microbrew draft beer $3.50 to $5 (plus $1 for SF's signature sassy bartenders)

Liter of bottled water $1.69 (which locals seldom pay, because SF's tap water comes from Yosemite and is better than bottled)

Cable-car ride $5 (one-way adult, or $10 all day)

Souvenir T-shirt $12 (comes with mockery by locals gratis)

Spirits & speech Free (offer only good for San Francisco)

Love A bargain at any price (just ask the hippies)

ADVANCE PLANNING

Two months before you go Book your reservations at Chez Panisse (p274) or French Laundry (p285), and start walking – you'll want to work up an appetite and enough stamina to handle SoMa gallery crawls by day and Mission bar-hopping by night.

Three weeks before you go Book your cruise to Alcatraz (p62) and a Chinatown Alleyway Tour or Precita Eyes Mission Mural Tour (p312). Sign up for classes to get into the swing of things at Circus Center Trapeze (p235) and get properly sloshed at Cav Wine Bar (p203).

One week before you go Relax: it's not too late to get tickets for the American Conservatory Theater (p225) or San Francisco Symphony (p223) matinees, find out who's playing at SF's hot music venues at www.sfbg.com and score tickets online at TIX Bay Area (p225). For the pick of this week's events, check out http://laughingsquid.com/squidlist/events, www.thrillist.com and http://sf.flavorpill.net.

One day before you go See what San Franciscans are buzzing about at www.sfgate.com and www.sfbg.com, find out at www.indybay.org/sf if there's an upcoming protest worth shouting about, and look into www.somalit.com/newsletter.html for literary events where you can suavely schmooze with your favorite authors. Join SF shenanigans already in progress at http://sfbay.craigslist.org/act, from citywide treasure hunts to cross-dressing cheerleader squads.

tronomical price of local real estate, accommodation will be your biggest cost in SF. Hostels and B&Bs are best to keep your rates under $100 – be wary of hotels listed 'in the theater district' that are actually deep in the hard heart of the Tenderloin and function as live-in hotels for the city's transient population. Splashing out for a five-star hotel will get you bay views and kind of an inconvenient perch atop Nob Hill, so opt for a smart boutique hotel if you want to be in the center of the action.

Unless you have places to be and biotech business deals to broker, car rental isn't usually worth the price and mental taxation. Basic rental starts at around $48 per day without insurance, plus there are gas prices to consider. Metered street parking often runs $4 for a couple of hours (when you can even find it, let alone free street parking), and $30 fines will haunt you if you arrive even a few minutes past your limit. Overnight parking is often $35, unless you can get it validated by your hotel. By comparison, an average taxi fare runs $12 and a Muni ticket costs $2, but a car may be handy for excursions along the coast and around Wine Country.

Check out p312 for more on money, p314 for taxes, and the inside front cover for tipping info.

INTERNET RESOURCES

To take SF by storm, do what the locals do: go online to these indispensable sites to find out what's happening where.

www.7x7.com The newest, trendiest restaurants, bars, boutiques and more.

www.cookhereandnow.com Free local and seasonal food events and weekly updates on what's in season in SF.

www.craigslist.org Find a job, apartment rental, a German-speaking poker party, free furniture or that hottie you spied on the 22 Fillmore bus via Missed Connections.

www.dailycandy.com The latest hot spots for drinking, shopping, seeing and being seen.

www.flavorpill.com The flavor of the week in SF movie premieres, art openings, music lectures and more.

www.indybay.org Left Coast news, protest listings, fundraisers and causes galore.

www.laughingsquid.com/squidlist/events Fair warning about bizarre, offbeat events happening around the Bay Area daily.

www.sfbg.com *San Francisco Bay Guardian's* website offers hot tips on local theater, art, events, movies and sex habits.

www.sf.eater.com The lowdown on the SF food and nightlife scene: restaurant openings, drinking deals and juicy gossip on SF star chefs.

www.sfgate.com The online version of the *San Francisco Chronicle*, with news and comprehensive event listings.

www.sfist.com Blog with irreverent take on San Francisco news and politics.

www.somalit.com/newsletter.html LitGuide covers events, workshops and the last word on the SF literary scene.

www.stretcher.org Art reviews, interviews and more.

www.thebaybridged.com Music podcast featuring local talents and event listings.

www.thedelimagazine.com/sf Tasty tidbits about the Bay Area indie-rock scene.

www.thrillist.com Blog on the new and now in SF: bars, bands, shops, restaurants, events.

HISTORY

COWBOYS ON A MISSION

San Francisco is one dinner party where most of the guests arrived rather rudely late. When Spanish cowboys brought 340 horses, 302 head of cattle and 160 mules to graze here in 1776, the area we know as San Francisco already had a standing dinner date with local Native Americans that went back over 14,300 years. Early California cuisine included shellfish, bear meat, edible flowers and acorn-flour bread, and when the seasons changed, the Native Ohlone moved their dinner venue further up or down the coast. The arrival of unexpected guests Captain Juan Bautista de Anza, Father Francisco Palou and their livestock met with no apparent resistance initially, until the Spaniards began to demand more than dinner.

The new arrivals expected the locals to build them a mission, and to take over its management within 10 years. In exchange, the Ohlone were allowed one meager meal a day, which didn't always materialize, and a place in God's kingdom – which came much sooner than expected for many, due to the smallpox the Spanish brought with them. Introduced diseases decimated the Ohlone population by almost three-quarters during the 50 years of Spanish rule in California.

While some Ohlone managed to escape the short life of obligatory construction work and prayer, others were caught, returned to the adobe barracks and punished. By 1845, the 6700 local converts seemed much less keen on managing the mission than expected by optimistic Spanish priests, and scandalized their captors with the local custom of wearing nothing under traditional fur capes. The mission settlement never really prospered. The sandy, scrubby fields were difficult to farm, fleas were a constant irritation, and the 20 soldiers who manned the local Presidio army encampment were allotted only one scanty shipment of provisions per year. The mass graves of Ohlone under the Misión San Francisco de Asís give a tragic note of truth to what is today its more common name: Mission Dolores (Mission of the Sorrows, p115).

Spain wasn't especially sorry to hand over the troublesome settlement to the newly independent nation of Mexico, but Mexico soon made this colony a profitable venture with a bustling hide and tallow trade at Yerba Buena Cove, where the Financial District now stands. Yankee trappers arrived to make their fortunes, and the trading post became a desirable destination for freed African Americans after Mexico outlawed slavery in Alto California.

Meanwhile, US-Mexico relations steadily deteriorated, made worse by rumors that Mexico was entertaining a British buy-out offer to take California off its hands. News was slow to arrive from Washington, DC, and Mexico City, leaving locals in a state of wary uncertainty. US commodore Thomas Catesby Jones actually invaded Monterey on the assumption that the US and Mexico were at war; two days later he realized his mistake, hastily apologized and returned to his ships. The Mexican-American War broke out for real in 1846, and dragged on for two years before ending with the Treaty of Guadalupe Hidalgo. This treaty formally ceded California and the present-day southwestern states to the USA – a loss that was initially reckoned by missionizing Church fathers in souls, but within months could be counted in ingots.

June 1776

Captain Juan Bautista de Anza and Father Francisco Palou descend on SF with cattle and settlers. With Ohlone conscripts, they set up a military outpost and build the Misión San Francisco de Asís (now Mission Dolores).

1835

An emissary of President Andrew Jackson makes a formal offer of $500,000 to buy Northern California, but Mexico testily refuses, and tries to sell California as a package deal to England.

1846

The Mexican-American War breaks out, and drags on for two years, with much posturing but little actual bloodshed in California.

'GOLD! GOLD! GOLD!'

Say what you will about Sam Brannan: the man knew how to sell a story. In 1848, the real-estate speculator and Mormon tabloid publisher of the *California Star* published sensational news of a find 120 miles from San Francisco at Sutter's Mill, where sawmill employees had taken to gold-panning duty after flakes had surfaced downstream. Brannan had his reasons for publishing what was then pure speculation as fact: he was hoping it would excite some interest back East in some swampland he was trying to sell, not to mention scooping rival San Francisco newspaper the *Californian*. San Franciscans ignored Brannan's bluster at first, preoccupied with news of the handover of California to the US from Mexico. To prove his point, Brannan traveled to Sutter's Fort, where news of the find was verified under conditions of strict secrecy. Brannan kept his word for about a day. Upon his arrival, he ran through the San Francisco streets, brandishing a vial of gold flakes and shouting, 'Gold! Gold! Gold on the American River!'

But Brannan's plan backfired. Within weeks San Francisco's population shrank to 200, as every able-bodied individual headed to the hills to pan for gold. Both newspapers folded; there was no one around to read, write or print them. Good thing Brannan had a backup plan: he'd bought every available shovel, pick and pan, and opened a general store near Sutter's Fort. Within its first 70 days, Brannan & Co had sold a whopping $36,000 in equipment – about $949,000 in today's terms. Initially Brannan charged big-spending Mormon buyers a special tax he claimed was for the church. But, when Mormon founder Brigham Young reportedly requested a cut for the church, Brannan retorted that he'd like a receipt from God.

Luckily for Brannan's profit margins, other newspapers around the world weren't that scrupulous about getting their facts straight either, hastily publishing stories of 'gold mountains' near San Francisco. Within months, boatloads of prospectors arrived from Europe, Australia and China, and another 40,000 prospectors trudged through snow and mud overland, eager to scoop up their fortunes on the hillsides. Sailors in sight of San Francisco abandoned ship and swam ashore, emptying damp pockets at mining supply stores. Prices for mining supplies shot up tenfold, and Brannan was raking in $150,000 a month, almost $4 million in today's terms. Food wasn't cheap, either: a dozen eggs could cost as much as $10 in San Francisco in 1849, the equivalent of $272 today.

A tent city rose up along San Francisco's waterfront comparable in size to the actual city. By 1850, the year California was fast-tracked for admission as the 31st state in the Union, San Francisco's population had shot up from 800 a year earlier to an estimated 25,000. But for all the new money in town, it wasn't exactly easy living. The fleas were still a problem and the rats were getting worse – but at least there were plenty of distractions.

Most of the early prospectors (called '49ers, after their arrival date) were men under the age of 40, and to keep them entertained – and fleece the gullible out of their earnings – some 500 saloons, 20 theaters and numerous venues of ill repute opened in the space of just five years. Miners with dreams of a millionaire's welcome back home usually had to wait for weeks in San Francisco for a departing ship, giving them plenty of time to blow all their earnings in the city's casinos and bordellos.

A buck might procure whiskey, opium or one of the women frolicking on swings rigged from saloon ceilings – publicly revealing they weren't wearing bloomers, 150 years before Britney Spears. At the gaming tables, luck literally was a lady: women card dealers were known to deal winning hands to those who engaged their back-room services. In 1851, visiting French journalist (and noted brothel expert) Albert Benard de Russailh reported, 'There are also some honest women in San Francisco, but not very many.'

1848

Gold is discovered near present-day Placerville by mill employees. Sometime San Francisco newspaper publisher and full-time big mouth Sam Brannan lets word out, and the Gold Rush is on.

1850

With hopes of solid-gold tax revenues, the US hastily dubs California the 31st state.

1851

Gold discovery in Australia leads to cheering in the streets of Melbourne and panic in the streets of San Francisco as the price for California gold plummets. Brawls, arson and phony arrests of Australians ensue.

OUTCASTS AMONG OUTCASTS

Con men, visionaries, crackpots, adventurers, fugitives and anyone with nothing to lose: there was a place for everyone in San Francisco in 1849. For a couple of flush years, Chinese, Peruvians, Hawaiians, Australians, Chileans, Native Americans, Irish and Mexicans panned for gold side by side, boozed together and slept in close quarters. But as gold became harder to find, backstabbing became more common – sometimes literally.

'Gold fever' was a malady with extreme symptoms. Take for example Joshua Norton: he arrived in 1849 from South Africa with $40,000, made a fortune, lost it all through speculation, and disappeared. In 1859 he returned to San Francisco a changed man, wearing theatrical gold-braided military attire and grandly proclaiming himself 'Emperor of the United States and Protector of Mexico.' San Francisco newspapers published Emperor Norton's proclamations over 21 years, including decrees dissolving the Democratic and Republican parties, commanding the building of suspension bridges spanning the bay (considered one of his craziest ideas), and outlawing use of the term 'Frisco' upon penalty of a $25 fine (payable to the Emperor, naturally). Police saluted him in the streets, and some local establishments accepted banknotes issued by the 'Imperial Government of Norton.' When the Emperor's adopted stray dog Bummer departed for that great doghouse in the sky, Mark Twain wrote the epitaph: 'He died full of years, and honor, and disease, and fleas.'

As Emperor Norton learned the hard way, prospectors who did best arrived early and got out quick. Those who stayed too long either lost fortunes searching for the next nugget or became targets of resentment. Successful Peruvians and Chileans were harassed and denied renewals to their mining claims, and most left California by 1855. Native Californian laborers who had helped the '49ers strike it rich were also denied the right to hold claims.

Even though San Francisco earned its notoriety with freewheeling lawlessness, Australian newcomers were singled out as criminals, whether or not they actually hailed from penal colonies. From 1851 to 1856, San Francisco's self-appointed 'Vigilance Committee' tried, convicted and hung suspect 'Sydney Ducks' in hour-long proceedings that came to be known as 'kangaroo trials.' The *San Francisco Herald* caricatured the Australian waterfront neighborhood called Sydney-Town with undisguised venom: 'The upper part of Pacific Street, after dark, is crowded by thieves, gamblers, low women, drunken sailors, and similar characters, who resort to the groggeries that line the street, and there spend the night in the most hideous orgies. Every grog shop is provided with a fiddle, from which some half-drunken creature tortures execrable sounds, called by way of compliment, music.' Australian boarding houses were torched six times by arsonists from 1849 to 1851, so when gold was found in Australia in 1851, many were ready to head home; Australians who stayed were promptly blamed for the ensuing California gold panic.

RAILROADS & RIOTS

Along with Australians, Chinese – the most populous group in California by 1860 – were at the receiving end of misplaced resentment. Frozen out of mining claims, many Chinese instead opened service-based businesses that survived when all-or-nothing mining ventures went bust – incurring further antipathy among miners. In 1870, San Francisco became the first US city to pass ordinances restricting housing and employment options for anyone born in China.

1861–65

While the US Civil War divides North from South back East, SF perversely profits in the West. Industry is diverted from factories burdened by the war effort, and SF's rakes and ruffians find honest work.

May 10, 1869

The Golden Spike is nailed in place, completing the first transcontinental railroad linking the West and East Coasts. The event is reported blow-by-blow using San Franciscan David Brooks' invention, the telegraph, in the world's first real-time communication.

1873

When a nervous driver declines to test the braking power of Andrew Hallidie's 'wire rope railway,' aka cable car, Hallidie jumps into the driver's seat and steers the car downhill as crowds cheer.

SPEAK OF THE DEVIL

Go ahead and call Ambrose Bierce a cynic: you might be too if you'd reported on Barbary Coast shenanigans for more than a decade, ditched your newspaper job to seek and not quite find your fortune as a prospector in Deadwood, and worked as a lobbyist for Machiavellian San Francisco mining magnate George Hearst. Bierce's satirical 1868–1911 columns yielded his 1911 book *The Devil's Dictionary,* where he provided disambiguation for key terms as used in San Francisco. To wit:

- acquaintance, *n*: a person whom we know well enough to borrow from, but not well enough to lend to.
- brandy, *n*: a cordial composed of one part thunder-and-lightning, one part remorse, two parts bloody murder, one part death-hell-and-the-grave and four parts clarified Satan.
- bride, *n*: a woman with a fine prospect of happiness behind her.
- impunity, *n*: wealth.
- telephone, *n*: an invention of the devil which abrogates some of the advantages of making a disagreeable person keep his distance.
- tenacity, *n*: a certain quality of the human hand in its relation to the coin of the realm.
- vote, *n*: the instrument and symbol of a freeman's power to make a fool of himself and a wreck of his country.
- zeal, *n*: a certain nervous disorder afflicting the young and inexperienced.

Not coincidentally, this law served the needs of local magnates looking for cheap labor to build the first cross-country railroad. There were few other takers for treacherous railroad work, given a job description that, if truthful, might have read thusly: must dangle off cliffs in rickety baskets, light sticks of dynamite in rock crevices and yell like hell to be yanked to safety prior to detonation; salary negligible, benefits include sporadic meals and prisonlike bunkhouse accommodation under armed guard in cold, remote mountain camps. With little other choice in legitimate employment, an estimated 12,000 Chinese laborers were blasting through the Sierra Nevada at the height of railroad construction.

Upon completion of the railroad, most Chinese laborers settled in San Francisco, increasingly confined to Chinatown. But there would be no respite for the weary workers. After being accused of taking low-paid, dangerous dockworker jobs no one else wanted, Chinese San Franciscans were attacked in the 1877 anti-Chinese riots. This violence troubled Emperor Norton, who in one instance reportedly stood between the attackers and their intended targets, and recited the Lord's Prayer until the rioters dispersed.

Any hope that the general populace – composed almost entirely of recent immigrants at the time – would follow the Emperor's example and reject xenophobia was dashed when California's discriminatory anti-Chinese laws were extended nationwide in 1882. The US Chinese Exclusion Act prevented new immigration from China, and barred Chinese from citizenship until 1943. The passage of the Exclusion Act also spurred parallel Japanese exclusion laws, with 100 ordinances limiting citizenship, marriage, immigration and property rights for Japanese San Franciscans.

From 1910 to 1940, new arrivals from Asia were redirected to the Angel Island immigration station (p282), where they were detained and interrogated for months or even years, pending official verification of parentage by a US citizen and/or a bribe to an immigration official of at least $1000 (about $20,000 in today's terms). Most of the 175,000 Asian immigrants detained at Angel Island were eventually deported, though a few escaped their bleak imprisonment by

1882

The US Chinese Exclusion Act suspends new immigration from China. These racially targeted laws stay on the books until 1943, setting the tone for similar measures in Canada, Australia and New Zealand.

April 18, 1906

A massive earthquake levels entire blocks of SF in 47 seconds flat, setting off fires that rage for three days. Survivors start rebuilding while the town is still smoldering, at an astonishing rate of 15 buildings per day.

1910

Angel Island opens as the West Coast immigration station. Over the next 30 years, 175,000 arrivals from Asia are subjected to months or years of interrogation, deprivation, medical examinations and a prisonlike existence.

suicide. More than 100 poems of despair, regret and outrage were carved into the walls of the immigration station, such as this one summarizing the Angel Island experience: 'America has power, but not justice/In prison, we were victimized as if we were guilty/Given no opportunity to explain, it was really brutal.'

KEEPING THE WEST WILD

As gold, silver and railroad money flowed into San Francisco, the city grew. It didn't exactly blossom at first, though – public works were completely neglected, and heavily populated sections of the city were mired in muck. Eventually the debris-choked waterfront filled in, streets were graded and paved, and scores of fancy French restaurants opened to educate the palates of the nouveau riche. A financial district shot up along Montgomery and California Sts to manage all this new money, and the lawyers' offices that cropped up alongside Jackson Sq saloons provided less deadly (if more costly) ways to resolve disputes. As soon as Andrew Hallidie made the formidable crag accessible by cable car in 1873, Nob Hill started sprouting mansions for millionaires, including the 'Big Four' railroad barons: Leland Stanford, Collis P Huntington, Mark Hopkins and Charles Crocker. The Gold Rush was officially over; the land rush was on.

Wherever there was green in the city, real-estate speculators saw greenbacks. Developers cleverly repackaged the marshy cattle-grazing pastures of the Mission District and Cow Hollow, selling them as residential districts. San Francisco's outlaw prospectors were lured into a state approaching respectability, settling into new neighborhoods far from the red-light districts and dutifully paying property taxes and police bribes. No wonder San Francisco's cynic-in-chief Ambrose Bierce dryly defined the 'out-of-doors' c 1881 as follows: 'That part of one's environment upon which no government has been able to collect taxes. Chiefly useful to inspire poets.'

Some idealistic San Franciscans were determined to preserve the city's natural splendors, even at the risk of attracting poets. The city's first park was established in 1867, when squatters were paid to vacate the area now known as Buena Vista Park (p128). The early urban environmentalist and Parks Superintendent John McLaren took charge of tree planting, and the hilltop park opened to sunset-seekers, fitness buffs and amorous advances by 1894.

Through local activism (see the boxed text, p32), the natural wonders that surrounded San Francisco became more accessible to the public. Populist millionaire Adolph Sutro decided that every working stiff should be able to escape Downtown tenements for the sand dunes and sunsets of Ocean Beach, made possible for a nickel on his public railway. Sutro's idea proved wildly popular, and by way of thanks he was elected mayor in 1894. Naturalist John Muir came through San Francisco in 1868, but quickly left with a shudder for Yosemite. However, the early environmentalist organization he founded, the Sierra Club, would eventually find its major backers in San Francisco. The unspoiled wilderness Muir and his organization successfully lobbied to protect includes one of San Francisco's most popular escapes: Muir Woods (p277).

Just as Bierce predicted, all this non-taxable nature inspired the inevitable poetry. Bierce's own protégé, 'the uncrowned king of Bohemia' George Sterling sang San Francisco's praises in such corny, heartfelt panegyric as 'City by the Sea,' 'The Evanescent City' and 'The Cool, Grey City of Love.' Fittingly, he too has a panoramic park named in his honor (p91).

1914

The Red Light Abatement Act prohibits dancing in the city's 2800 bars; police arrest female barkeeps, burlesque dancers and prostitutes. Dancehall regulars don't take kindly to soda-pop and waltzes, so the scene soon retreats to speakeasies.

1915

Scrappy post-quake San Francisco challenges other US cities to win the coveted role as host to the Panama-Pacific International Exposition. San Francisco cements its reputation as showplace for new technology, outlandish ideas and the arts.

1927

After a year of tinkering, 21-year-old Philo Farnsworth captured an image in a machine, and transmitted the first successful TV broadcast of...a straight line. In years since, audiences have been treated to marginally more interesting images.

DOUBLE DISASTER

No stranger to earthquakes, fires and other calamities, San Francisco was determined to be more prepared for disaster in the 20th century than it had been in the 19th. The city learned the hard way about seismic retrofitting: makeshift buildings often collapsed in minor tremors. Water wasn't readily available, and in one fire in 1851 an entire 20-block radius was burned but for one building doused with a handy warehouse-worth of vinegar. Public funds were set aside for a citywide system of water mains and fire hydrants, but at the time, city leaders were more concerned with lining their pockets than structural overhauls. Abe Ruef, the city's notorious political boss, and his hand-picked mayor, Eugene Schmitz, were eventually indicted on charges of extorting huge sums of money from whorehouses.

To attract more legitimate business, San Francisco needed to redirect attention from its notorious waterfront fleshpots and focus attention on its comparatively underexposed assets. The city was determined to be in the vanguard of the 'city beautiful' urban planning movement, and commissioned Chicago architect Daniel Burnham to give San Francisco a beaux arts makeover to rival Baron Haussmann's Paris. This elaborate plan had just been finalized in April 1906 when disaster struck – twice.

On April 18, 1906, a quake estimated at a terrifying 7.8 to 8.3 on today's Richter scale struck the city. For 47 seconds, the city emitted unholy groans and crashes as streets buckled, windows popped and brick buildings imploded. Wooden structures snapped into firewood were set ablaze by toppled chimneys, and ruptured gas mains spread the fire.

In a matter of minutes, San Franciscans discovered just how many corners had been cut on government building contracts. Unreinforced civic structures – even City Hall – collapsed in ruins. Since fire hydrants and water mains hadn't been maintained, there was no way to contain fires Downtown. The sole functioning water source was a fountain donated to the city by opera prodigy Lotta Crabtree, the belle of San Francisco's Bella Union (see the boxed text, p35).

Assembly lines were formed to haul buckets of water from Lotta's Fountain (p72) to combat Downtown blazes, but the water couldn't reach the crest of steep Nob Hill fast enough. Mansions with priceless Old Master and Impressionist art collections went up in smoke; inhabitants were lucky to escape with their lives. Lotta's Fountain would become a meeting place for dazed survivors seeking news of children, family and neighbors gone missing; descendants of 1906 earthquake survivors still meet there each April 18.

Federal support was brought in to rescue the flaming city and restore order. Under the direction of General Frederick Funston, firebreaks were created by dynamiting entire city blocks. But instead of containing the conflagration, the explosions set off new fires. Firefighters couldn't haul equipment and water through the rubble-choked streets, so in a city surrounded by water on three sides, fires continued to rage. Homeless citizens took refuge atop Potrero Hill and Buena Vista Park, and watched their city and its dreams of grandeur go up in smoke.

After three days and two nights, most of the city was reduced to a smoldering black heap. The death toll mounted to an estimated 3000 people, plus an unknown number of prostitutes kept under lock and key. More than a third of the 300,000 people living in the city at the time were left homeless. Thousands of people left San Francisco for good, convinced its glory days were over.

1934

A West Coast longshoremen's strike ends with 34 San Francisco strikers and sympathizers shot and 40 beaten by police. A mass funeral procession and citywide strike follow, and longshoremen win historic concessions.

1937

After four years of dangerous labors in the treacherous Pacific tides, San Francisco's engineering marvel, the Golden Gate Bridge, is complete. The US Navy had proposed a black-and-yellow-striped concrete bridge, which SF ignored.

February 1942

Executive Order 9066 mandates the relocation of 120,000 Japanese Americans to internment camps. The Japanese American Citizens League takes the case against internment to courts, culminating in the 1964 Civil Rights Act and 1988 presidential apology.

GOLDEN GATE PARK: A TALE OF CORRUPTION, GAMBLING & HUGS

In 1865 the citizens of San Francisco submitted a petition to the Board of Supervisors for an ambitious park project. In 1869, 1017 acres of dune stretching west of the city were set aside for a park, and Frederick Law Olmstead was commissioned to design the project. But it would take a tenacious young civil engineer, William Hammond Hall, decades to see Golden Gate Park (p139) through to fruition, fending off speculators, gamblers and corrupt politicians at every turn.

He briefly quit his job in disgust in 1886, after the 'Big Four' railroad barons – Leland Stanford, Collis P Huntingdon, Mark Hopkins and Charles Crocker – lobbied City Hall to convert the park into a racetrack lined with tract homes. The park hosted a casino and carnival attractions for the 1893 Midwinter's Fair, and Hammond Hall had to fight to get the park returned to its intended purpose. Luckily City Hall was too busy lining its own pockets to fund the ambitious racetrack plan, and the park had already proved too popular with the public to be sequestered for private use.

On a single sunny day in 1886, almost a fifth of the city's entire population made the trip to the park. Though a San Francisco newspaper of the day cautioned that its scenic benches led to 'excess hugging,' the people loved their park, and effectively defended it from private development.

THE SHOW MUST GO ON

San Francisco had learned one thing from its experience with catastrophe: how to stage a comeback. The city was rebuilt at an astounding rate of 15 buildings a day. A city plan was concocted to relocate Chinatown to less desirable real estate in Hunter's Point, but the Chinese consulate refused to relocate, as did the temples of Waverly Place (p83) and several gun-toting merchants. No longer would Chinatown serve as a convenient den of iniquity for the slumming socialites of Nob Hill: Look Tin Eli and a consortium of Chinatown community leaders ousted opium dens and brothels, and hired notable architects to rebuild the district as a crowd-pleasing tourist destination with a signature Chinatown deco look.

The rest of Downtown was brought back to its feet not by City Hall, but by die-hard entertainers. All but one of San Francisco's 20 historic theaters had been completely destroyed by the earthquake and subsequent fire, but theater tents were soon set up amid the rubble. The smoke wafting across makeshift stages wasn't a special effect when the surviving entertainers began marathon performances to keep the city's spirits up – but it wasn't hard to bring down the house when buildings were still collapsing all around them.

In a show of popular priorities, San Francisco's theaters were rebuilt long before City Hall's grandiose Civic Center was completed. Most of the Barbary Coast had gone up in flames (with the notable, highly flammable exception of Hotaling's whiskey warehouse; see p75) and was destined to be rebuilt as a major port, so the theater scene and most of its red-light entourage decamped to the Tenderloin. Built in 1907, soon after the earthquake, the Great American Music Hall (p212) still shows the determined flamboyance of post-earthquake San Francisco, with carved gilt decor recalling golden days of yore and scantily clad frescoed figures hinting at other possible backstage entertainments.

San Francisco's more highbrow entertainments of opera and classical music began a glorious second act, despite the fact that the world's most famous tenor, Enrico Caruso, vowed never to return to the city after the quake had jolted him out of bed at the Palace Hotel (p252). Soprano Luisa Tetrazzini ducked out of a 1911 squabble over her talents between Oscar Hammerstein

1957

City Lights Bookstore wins a landmark ruling against book banning over the publication of Allen Ginsberg's *Howl,* and free speech and free spirits enjoy a reprieve from McCarthyism.

1959

Mayor George Christopher authorizes crackdowns on cruising areas and gay bars and starts a blacklist of gay citizens.

January 21–23, 1966

The Trips Festival is organized by techno-futurist Stewart Brand, featuring author and prankster-in-chief Ken Kesey, the Grateful Dead, Janis Joplin, plus sundry Native American activists and Hells Angels, and oodles of LSD.

and New York's Metropolitan Opera to return to San Francisco, and gave a free performance at Lotta's Fountain for an audience of 250,000 – virtually every last man, woman and child in San Francisco.

San Francisco's greatest comeback performance was the 1915 Panama-Pacific International Exposition, in celebration of the completion of the Panama Canal. Resourceful San Franciscans used earthquake rubble to fill 635 marshy acres of the Marina, and hired famous architects to build elaborate pavilions showcasing San Francisco's Pacific Rim connections, exotic foods and forward thinking. Crowds gasped at the glowing Tower of Jewels, mysteriously lit with strategically placed electric footlights, and a parade of the latest, greatest inventions, including the world's first steam locomotive, a color printing press and a prototype personal typewriter (at 14 tons, a far cry from a laptop).

When the party ended, Bernard Maybeck's Palace of Fine Arts (p102) was the one temporary exhibit San Franciscans couldn't bear to see torn down. The structure was recast in concrete in the 1960s and in the spirit of the Expo it now hosts the Exploratorium (p102), San Francisco's hands-on museum of weird science.

THE LEFT COAST

With new piers and the fanfare of the Panama Expo, San Francisco became the major West Coast port, but the morning lineup at the docks told another story. Only longshoremen known for toughness, speed and readiness to pay bribes were hired to unload heavy cargo onto perilously slippery docks from 8am to midnight. And they did this for pay that hardly put dinner on the table. On May 9, 1934, longshoremen gathered down by the piers and, one by one, refused work.

As shiploads of food spoiled dockside in the summer sun, shipping companies frantically scoured first the bay, then ports all along the West Coast for substitute dockworkers. No one was available: San Francisco's longshoremen had coordinated their strikes with 35,000 workers all along the West Coast. They held out for an unprecedented 83 days, until police, hired guns and finally the National Guard forcibly ended the strike, killing two longshoremen. In the ensuing riots, 34 strikers and sympathizers were shot and another 40 beaten.

In a silent funeral procession that marched down Market St on July 9, thousands of San Franciscans stood shoulder to shoulder with longshoremen. Word of a general strike spread throughout the city, and for four days even San Francisco's nightclubs and movie palaces were closed in solidarity and draped in black. The ship owners met the longshoremen's demands, cementing San Francisco's reputation as the organizing headquarters of the 'Left Coast.'

When WWII brought a shipbuilding boom to town, women and 40,000 African American arrivals claimed key roles in San Francisco's workforce. But with misplaced anxiety about possible attacks from the Pacific, Japanese San Franciscans became convenient targets for public animosity. Two months after the attack on Pearl Harbor, President Franklin Delano Roosevelt signed Executive Order 9066 ordering the relocation of 120,000 Japanese Americans to internment camps. The San Francisco–based Japanese American Citizens League immediately challenged the grounds for internment, and lobbied tirelessly for more than 40 years to overturn Executive Order 9066, gain symbolic reparations for internees, and restore the community's standing with a formal letter of apology signed by President George HW Bush in 1988.

October 1966

In Oakland, Huey Newton and Bobby Seale found the Black Panther Party for Self-Defense, a militant black-power group that called Vietnam 'the white man's war' and demanded 'Land, Bread, Housing, Education, Clothing, Justice and Peace.'

January 14, 1967

The Summer of Love kicks off with the Human Be-In, with blowing of conch shells and minds, draft cards used as rolling papers, free performances by the Grateful Dead, and Allen Ginsberg naked as usual.

June 5, 1968

Presidential candidate, former US attorney general, civil rights ally and antipoverty campaigner Robert Kennedy is fatally shot after winning the California primary – a turning point for political disillusionment and armed separatist struggle ahead.

BEATS: FREE SPEECH, FREE SPIRITS

Members of the armed services dismissed from service for homosexuality and other 'subversive' behavior during WWII were discharged onto the streets of San Francisco, as if that would teach them a lesson. Instead, the new arrivals found themselves at home in the low-rent, laissez-faire neighborhoods of North Beach and the Haight. So when the rest of the country took a sharp right turn with McCarthyism in the 1950s, rebels and romantics headed for San Francisco – including one Jack Kerouac. By the time *On the Road* was published in 1957 chronicling his westward journey, the motley crowd of writers, artists, dreamers and unclassifiable characters Kerouac called 'the mad ones' had found their way to like-minded San Francisco.

San Francisco didn't always take kindly to the nonconformists derisively referred to in the press as 'beatniks,' and police and poets were increasingly at odds on the streets of North Beach. Officers tried to fine 'beatnik chicks' for wearing sandals, only to be mercilessly taunted in verse by the self-styled African American Jewish anarchist, street corner poet Bob Kaufman. Poet Lawrence Ferlinghetti and manager Shigeyoshi Murao of City Lights Bookstore (p146) were arrested for 'willfully and lewdly' printing Allen Ginsberg's magnificent, incendiary epic poem *Howl*. But artistic freedom prevailed in 1957, when City Lights won its landmark ruling against book banning.

Ginsberg's generation of 'angel-headed hipsters burning for the ancient heavenly connection' experimented freely with art, radical politics, marijuana and one another, flouting 1950s social-climbing conventions and blatantly defying Senator Joe McCarthy's alarmist call to weed out 'communists in our midst.' When McCarthy's House Un-American Activities Committee (HUAC) convened for the fourth time in San Francisco in 1960 to expose alleged communists, UC Berkeley students organized a disruptive, sing-along sit-in at City Hall. After police turned fire hoses on the protesters, thousands of San Franciscans rallied, and HUAC split town, never to return. It was official: the sixties had begun.

FLOWER POWER

San Francisco would continue to be a testing ground for freedom of expression in the years to come, as comedian Lenny Bruce uttered the F-word on stage and burlesque dancer Carol Doda bared it all for titillated audiences in North Beach clubs. But neither jokes nor striptease would pop the last button of conventional morality in San Francisco – that was a job for the CIA. In a pronounced lapse in screening judgment, the CIA hired a writer named Ken Kesey to test psychoactive drugs intended to create the ultimate soldier. Instead, they had unwittingly inspired Kesey to write the novel *One Flew Over the Cuckoo's Nest,* drive psychedelic busloads of Merry Pranksters across country, and introduce the city to LSD and the Grateful Dead at the legendary Acid Tests.

After the Civil Rights movement anything seemed possible, and for a while it seemed that the freaky force of free thinking would stop the unpopular Vietnam War. At the January 14, 1967 Human Be-In in Golden Gate Park, trip master Timothy Leary urged a crowd of 20,000 to dream a new American dream and 'turn on, tune in, drop out.' Free music rang out in the streets, free food was provided by the Diggers and LSD by Owsley Stanley, free crash pads were found all over the Haight, and free love transpired on some very dubious free mattresses. For the duration of the Summer of Love – weeks, months, even a year, depending who you talk to and how stoned they were at the time – it seemed possible to make love, not war.

But a chill soon settled over San Francisco, and for once it wasn't the afternoon fog. Civil rights hero Martin Luther King Jr was assassinated on April 8, 1968, followed by the fatal shooting

1969

The first link is made via computer between Stanford Research Institute and UCLA via ARPANET. Within a few years an unsolicited group message about politics is sent across the network, and spam is born.

November 20, 1969

Native American activists land on the island of Alcatraz, and symbolically claim it as partial reparation for broken treaties. The occupation holds out against authorities for 19 months, until FBI agents oust the activists in 1971.

December 6, 1969

A free concert at Altamont Speedway organized as a West Coast Woodstock goes tragically wrong when Hells Angels on bodyguard duty turn on the performers and audience. Four people die.

CIAO, BELLA

Between the 1906 fire and 1914 Red Light Abatement Act, the curtains closed on many of the Barbary Coast's boldest, bawdiest revues – including the celebrated Bella Union. The theater managed to reincarnate itself several times between 1849 and the 1906 fire, with the help of sensational advertising: 'As Sweet and Charming Creatures As Ever Escaped a Female Seminary. Lovely Tresses! Lovely Lips! Buxom Forms! at the BELLA UNION. And Such Fun! If You Don't Want to Risk Both Optics, SHUT ONE EYE.' Despite such enticements, its post-fire revival as the Imperial Music Hall flopped. The bill that over the years featured risqué comedy, serious stagings of Charles Dickens tales, scandalous can-can dancing, arias by opera diva Lotta Crabtree, and the agonizingly tuneless comic singer Big Bertha was reduced to a penny arcade and wax museum – a kind of Musée Mécanique (p66) meets Ripley's Believe It Or Not! Museum. But the traditions established by the Bella Union continue to this day, in the vaudeville burlesque of Beach Blanket Babylon (p206), soaring arias at the San Francisco Opera (p222), and buskers of varying abilities that turn San Francisco's sidewalks into ever-changing street theater revues.

of Robert Kennedy on June 5, right after he'd won California's presidential primary. Radicals worldwide called for revolution, and separatist groups like Oakland's own Black Panther Party for Self-Defense took up arms. Meanwhile, recreational drug-taking was turning into a thankless career for many, a distinct itch in the nether regions was making the rounds, and still more busloads of teenage runaways were arriving in the ill-equipped, wigged-out Haight. The Haight Ashbury Free Clinic (p311) helped with the rehabbing and the itching, but the disillusionment seemed incurable when Hell's Angels turned on the crowd at a free Rolling Stones concert at Altamont, and beat protestors in Berkeley.

Many idealists headed 'back to the land' in the bucolic North Bay, jumpstarting California's organic farm movement. A dark streak emerged among those who remained, including young Charles Manson, the Symbionese Liberation Army (better known post-1974 as Patty Hearst's kidnappers) and an evangelical egomaniac named Jim Jones, who would command 900 followers to commit mass suicide in 1978. By the time Be-In LSD supplier Owsley Stanley was released from a three-year jail term in 1970, the party seemed to be over. But in the Castro, it was just getting started.

PRIDE

By the 1970s, San Francisco's gay community was fed up with police raids, done with Haight squats and ready for music with an actual beat. In 1959, after an opponent had accused then-mayor George Christopher of allowing San Francisco to become 'the national headquarters of the organized homosexuals,' Christopher authorized crackdowns on cruising areas and gay bars and started a blacklist of gay citizens. Never one to be harassed or upstaged, WWII veteran and drag star José Sarria became the first openly gay man to run for public office in 1962, in protest of police harassment of gay citizens of San Francisco. He won 5600 votes. Undaunted, he declared himself Absolute Empress of San Francisco, the widow and true heir of Emperor Norton.

When local media joined the growing criticism of the continuing raids, the crackdown stopped – a feat not achieved for years elsewhere, until New York's 1969 Stonewall protests. Meanwhile, San Francisco gays had ditched hetero hippies in the Haight, headed over the hills to Victorian fixer-uppers in the Castro, and proceeded to make history to a funky disco beat.

By the mid-1970s, the rainbow flag was flying high over gay businesses, restaurants and homes in out-and-proud Castro. The sexual revolution had arrived, and gay San Francisco came out of

April 16–17, 1977

The Apple II is introduced in San Francisco at the first West Coast Computer Faire by Steve Jobs and Steve Wozniak, and stuns the crowd with its speed (1MHz) and memory capacity (up to 48KB of RAM).

1977

Harvey Milk becomes the first openly gay man to be elected to public office in the US. As San Francisco Supervisor, Milk sponsors a gay-rights bill and trend-setting 'pooper-scooper' ordinance before his murder by Dan White.

November 18, 1978

After evading taxes by moving his People's Temple from San Francisco to Guyana, cult leader Jim Jones has US Congressman Leo Ryan and four journalists killed, then commands 900 heavily sedated followers to commit suicide.

the closet and frolicked in gay clubs and bathhouses on Polk St and in South of Market (SoMa). San Francisco author Armistead Maupin's *Tales of the City* serial in the *San Francisco Chronicle* fictionalized the eye-opening adventures of new arrivals on the city's swinging scene in real time. Gay San Francisco had its own chroniclers, anthems ('Over the Rainbow,' 'I'm Coming Out,' 'I Will Survive') and businesses; now all it needed was an elected representative.

The Castro was triumphant when Castro camera-store owner Harvey Milk became the nation's first openly gay man to become an elected official – but as Milk himself predicted, his time in office would be cut short by an act of extremist violence. Dan White, a washed-up politician hyped on Hostess Twinkies, fatally shot Milk and then-mayor George Moscone in 1978. The charge was reduced to manslaughter due to the infamous 'Twinkie Defense' faulting the ultrasweet junk food, sparking an outpouring of public outrage that came to be called the 'White Riot.' But White was deeply disturbed, and committed suicide a year after his 1984 release.

By then San Francisco had other matters weighing heavily on its mind. A strange illness began to appear in local hospitals, and seemed to be hitting the gay community especially hard. The first cases of AIDS reported in 1981 were initially referred to as GRID, Gay-Related Immune Deficiency, and a social stigma became attached to the virus. But San Francisco health providers and gay activists rallied to establish global standards for care and prevention, with vital early HIV/AIDS initiatives funded not through federal agencies, but with tireless local fundraising efforts. Despite significant progress on treatment for HIV/AIDS, legal authorization for unmarried partners to make lifesaving medical decisions remained a stumbling block.

Civil rights organizations, religious institutions and GLBT organizations increasingly popped the question: why couldn't same-sex couples get married too? Early backing came from the Japanese American Citizens League, which in 1994 publicly endorsed marriage for same-sex couples as a civil right. A decade later and just 45 days into his term in office, San Francisco mayor Gavin Newsom took the unprecedented step of authorizing same-sex weddings in San Francisco, just in time for Valentine's Day, 2004.

The first couple to be married were Phyllis Lyon and Del Martin, a San Francisco couple who had spent 52 years together. California courts ultimately halted the weddings and voided theirs and 4036 other San Francisco same-sex marriage contracts, but Lyon and Martin weren't dissuaded: they married again on June 18, 2008, with Mayor Newsom personally officiating. Del Martin passed away in August at age 83, her wife by her side. In November 2008, California voters passed Proposition 8, asserting that only marriages between a man and a woman would be legally recognized. Phyllis Lyon commented, 'It may not be while I'm alive, but eventually it will work out that if two people want to get married, they can get married and it won't matter to whom.'

SAN FRANCISCO 3.0

Industry dwindled steadily in San Francisco after WWII, as Oakland's port accommodated container ships and the Presidio's military presence tapered off. But onetime military-industrial tech contractors found work in a stretch of scrappy tech firms south of San Francisco, in an area known today as Silicon Valley. When a company called Hewlett-Packard, started in a South Bay garage, introduced the 9100A 'computing genie' in 1968, a generation of unconventional thinkers and tinkerers took note.

Ads breathlessly gushed that Hewlett-Packard's 'light' (40lb) machine could 'take on roots of a fifth-degree polynomial, Bessel functions, elliptic integrals and regression analysis' – all

1981

The first cases of AIDS are identified and misnamed GRID, Gay-Related Immune Deficiency. The disease has taken 25 million lives, but early intervention in SF instituted prevention measures and established global standards of care and treatment.

1989

Hundreds of sea lions inexplicably haul out on the yacht slips near Pier 39; state law and wildlife officials grant them squatters' rights, and the rebel beach bums soon become San Francisco's favorite mascots.

October 17, 1989

The Loma Prieta earthquake hits 6.9 on the Richter scale and a freeway in SF and part of the Bay Bridge collapse in 15 seconds, killing 41. The seismic retrofitting of the bridge would take 20 years to complete.

for the low, low price of $4,900 (about $29,000 today). Consumers didn't quite know what to do with such a computer, until its potential was explained in simple terms by Stewart Brand, an early LSD tester for the CIA with Ken Kesey and organizer of the first Trips Festival in 1966. In his 1969 *Whole Earth Catalog,* Brand reasoned that the technology governments used to run countries could empower ordinary people. That same year, UCLA professor Len Kleinrock proved Brand right, sending the first rudimentary email from a computer in Los Angeles to another at Stanford. The message he typed was 'L,' then 'O,' then 'G' – at which point the computer crashed.

The next wave of California techies was determined to create a personal computer that could compute and communicate without crashing. When 21-year-old Steve Jobs and Steve Wozniak introduced the Apple II at the first West Coast Computer Faire in 1977, techies were abuzz about the memory (4KB of RAM!) and the microprocessor speed (1 MHz!) – today's gigabytes of RAM, gigahertz processor speeds and online downloads would have seemed unbelievable. The Mac II originally retailed for the equivalent today of $4300, or, if you wanted to get really fancy with 48KB of RAM, more than twice that amount. This was a staggering investment for what still seemed like a glorified calculator/typewriter – and even if these computers could talk to one another, pundits reasoned, what would they talk about?

Billions of web pages later, it turns out computers had plenty to say. By the mid-1990s an entire industry boomed in SoMa warehouses, as start-up ventures rushed to be the first to put news, dates, politics, fashion and, yes, sex online. But, while investors wanted information to be expensive, users preferred it to be free. When venture capital funding dried up, multimillion-dollar sites shriveled into online oblivion.

The paper fortunes of the dot-com boom disappeared on one nasty NASDAQ-plummeting day, March 10, 2000, leaving service-sector employees and 26-year-old former vice-presidents alike without any immediate job prospects. City dot-com revenues vanished; a 1999 FBI probe revealed that a sizable windfall ended up in the pockets of real-estate developers. Real-estate prices have yet to return to earth, despite the 2008 mortgage crisis.

But true to shape-shifting form, San Francisco has morphed again with Web 2.0 start-ups and social media ventures like San Francisco–based Twitter and Palo Alto's Facebook. Recession has slowed the flow of venture capital, but in shiny new glass towers in Mission Bay, biotech start-ups are still hanging out their shingles. Biotech is nothing new here: in 1976, an upstart company called Genentech was founded over beer at a San Francisco bar, then got to work cloning human insulin and introducing the hepatitis B vaccine. California voters approved a $3 billion bond measure in 2004 for stem cell research, and by 2008, California had become the biggest funder of stem cell research, with Mission Bay as its designated headquarters. With the US in recession, it seems impossible that San Francisco could initiate another boom – but if history is any indication, the impossible is almost certain to happen in San Francisco.

ARTS

Logic is insufficient to really understand San Francisco: for that, you'll need art. This town has plenty of it, and a superabundance of creative friction where tectonic plates collide. Poetry fights the law and wins; new technology rubs up against old-school craftsmanship; and Victoriana, high modernism and California Arts and Crafts clash in the best possible way. You can hardly throw a pebble in this town without hitting a writer, though it might get you cursed in verse.

March 10, 2000

After the NASDAQ index peaks at double its value a year earlier, the dot-com bubble pops and share prices drop. By 2001, San Franciscans can no longer get ice cream and videos ordered online delivered in an hour...pity.

February 12, 2004

Defying California's same-sex marriage ban, SF mayor Gavin Newsom licenses 4037 same-sex marriages. Courts declare the marriages void, but the civil rights challenge stands.

November 4, 2008

California voters approve Proposition 8. Opponents of the measure included President Obama, Amnesty International, *San Francisco Chronicle*, Apple, Google and a wide majority of SF voters.

Since 1970, San Francisco has consistently stayed in the top five US cities for the caliber and sheer number of fine artists, musicians, dancers and independent filmmakers – a point of local pride you'll no doubt hear repeated on your visit.

When San Francisco's latest creative foray doesn't quite work, ouch, you'll know it – but when it all comes together, you'll swear you feel a tremor underfoot as reality is cut loose from its mundane moorings. In its most shining moments, this town lives up to San Francisco poet laureate Lawrence Ferlinghetti's words in 'The Changing Light': 'And in that vale of light/the city drifts/anchorless upon the ocean.'

SAN FRANCISCO REQUIRED READING

Poetry

- *Howl and Other Poems* by Allen Ginsberg – each line of Ginsberg's epic title poem is an ecstatic improvised mantra, chronicling the waking dreams of the generation that rejected postwar conformity.
- *Time and Materials* by Robert Hass – these Pulitzer Prize–winning poems by the Berkeley-based US poet laureate don't seem to have been written so much as released onto the page, where every word takes to the air like a seagull.
- *A Coney Island of the Mind* by Lawrence Ferlinghetti – this slim 1958 collection by San Francisco's poet laureate is an indispensable doorstop for the imagination, letting fresh air and ideas circulate.

Nonfiction & Memoir

- *Slouching Towards Bethlehem* by Joan Didion – like hot sun through San Francisco fog, Didion's 1968 essays burn through the hippie haze to reveal glassy-eyed teenage revolutionaries adrift in the Summer of Love.
- *On the Road* by Jack Kerouac – the book Kerouac banged out on one long scroll of paper in a San Francisco attic over a couple of sleepless months of 1951 woke up America.
- *San Francisco Stories: Great Writers on the City* edited by John Miller – 150 years of San Francisco impressions. Jack London's 1906 earthquake reports, Jack Kerouac's attempts to hold a Downtown day job, Anne Lamott's send-up of pretentious cafes and more.
- *Hell's Angels: A Strange and Terrible Saga* by Hunter S Thompson – this spare-no-details insider take on the outlaw Bay Area motorcycle club invented gonzo journalism and scandalized the nation.
- *The Electric Kool-Aid Acid Test* by Tom Wolfe – his florid style is dated, but Wolfe had extraordinary presence of mind to capture tuning in, turning on and dropping out with Ken Kesey, the Merry Pranksters, the Grateful Dead and Hell's Angels.

Fiction

- *Tales of the City* by Armistead Maupin – the 1976 *San Francisco Chronicle* serial follows true San Francisco characters: pot-growing landladies of mystery, ever-hopeful Castro club-goers and wide-eyed Midwestern arrivals.
- *The Man in the High Castle* by Philip K Dick – the bestselling Berkeley sci-fi writer presents the ultimate what-if scenario: imagine San Francisco c 1962 if Japan and Nazi Germany had won WWII.
- *The Joy Luck Club* by Amy Tan – the stories of four Chinese-born women and their American-born daughters are woven into a textured history of immigration and aspiration in San Francisco's Chinatown.
- *The Maltese Falcon* by Dashiell Hammett – in this classic noir novel, private eye Sam Spade risks his reputation on a case involving an elusive redhead, a gold statuette, the Holy Roman Empire and an unholy cast of thugs.
- *Martin Eden* by Jack London – San Francisco's first literary star started out as the Prince of the Oyster Pirates, a waterfront bad boy who got by on his wits in this semi-autobiographical account.

Graphic Novels

- *Ghost World* by Daniel Clowes – the Oakland-based graphic novelist's sleeper hit follows recent high-school grads Enid and Rebecca as they make plans, make do, grow up and grow apart.
- *Long Tail Kitty* by Lark Pien – San Francisco cartoonist/architect Pien brings the poetry of *The Little Prince* and the charm of Hayao Miyazaki's *Spirited Away* to her long-tailed tales of a heavenly cat.
- *American Born Chinese* by Gene Yang – a young-adult graphic novel with smarts and heart, combining Monkey King fables with two teenagers' stories of assimilation and alienation.

LITERATURE

Bookish flirts and over-the-shoulder-readers, you've come to the right city. You'll find a city full of people who become coquettish when they see a favorite author being read, and have kinked necks from craning to read the books of fellow bus riders. The way to a San Franciscan's heart is definitely through the books they adore. San Francisco buys more books per capita than any other US city, hoards three times as many library books as the national average, and has more writers per capita than any other US city. So should you invite a date over, expect those bookshelves to be scrutinized, and plant some suitably local titles on your shelves.

To cover your bases, a solid local bookshelf should include plenty of poetry (Beat authors obligatory), some satire, a graphic novel and a noir, nonfiction essays about the San Francisco scene, and at least one novel by a Bay Area author. San Francisco's Kenneth Rexroth popularized haiku here back in the 1950s, and San Franciscans still enjoy nothing more than a few well-chosen words – the fog seems to lift with a few solar syllables supplied by Berkeley-based US poet laureate Robert Hass. Ambrose Bierce and Mark Twain set the San Francisco standard for sardonic wit early on, but recently, Bay Area graphic novelists like Daniel Clowes have added a twist to this tradition with finely drawn, deadpan behavioral studies. For more, don't miss the Cartoon Art Museum (p109).

People-watching rivals reading as a preferred San Francisco pastime, and close observation of antics that would seem bizarre elsewhere pays off in stranger-than-fiction nonfiction – hence Hunter S Thompson's gonzo journalism and Joan Didion's core-shaking truth-telling. Many San Franciscans seem like characters in a novel, and the reverse is also true. After a few days here, you might feel like you've seen Armistead Maupin's bright-eyed, corn-fed Castro newbies, Dashiell Hammet's mysterious redheads, and Amy Tan's American-born daughters explaining slang to their Chinese-speaking moms.

But San Francisco's literary tradition doesn't just hang out on book shelves. Allen Ginsberg's ecstatic readings of *Howl* continue to inspire slam poets at Litquake (p23) and spoken-word nights at Edinburgh Castle (p196), and Beat authors like Kerouac freed up generations of monologuists at the Marsh (p226) and Make-Out Room (p213) from the tyranny of tales with morals and punctuation.

The local zine scene has been the underground mother lode of riveting reading since the '70s brought punk, a DIY ethic and V Vale's groundbreaking *RE/Search* to San Francisco. The San Francisco Main Library (p79) has amassed a collection of 'zines, but to see the latest check out the Alternative Press Expo (p23) and Needles & Pens (p153). The most successful local 'zine of all, *McSweeney's,* is the doing of Dave Eggers, who achieved first-person fame with *A Heartbreaking Work of Staggering Genius* and generously sunk the proceeds into 826 Valencia (p118), a nonprofit publisher and writing program for teens. *McSweeney's* also publishes an excellent map of literary San Francisco so you can walk the talk.

VISUAL ARTS

If you usually think of art as painting and sculpture, San Francisco will come as a visual shock. The streets vibrate with murals, graffiti and political protest that flows right into galleries. Besides stellar traditional photography shows, most sights you'll see in San Francisco galleries and museums defy easy categorization, and wall tags often unhelpfully describe works as 'mixed media' or 'new media.' What does this mean, exactly? Could be some combination of video, performance art, installations, interactive art, and other media too novel and/or weird to be named yet. Take for example an interactive work by San Francisco artist John Slepian shown at Catharine Clark Gallery (p109): a hairy rubber nub swaddled in blankets, programmed to sob disconsolately until you pick it up and pat its posterior. Forget admiring Old Masters from afar: here you're invited to burp the art.

Photography

Of all the visual art forms, photography is the one that punched San Francisco's ticket to art stardom. Back when photography was still a new medium and widely dismissed by most museums and galleries as too literal and commercial to have artistic value, Bay Area photographers ignored the naysayers and occupied themselves with masterworks that put photography on the art-world map. Always fascinated by technical novelty and willing to take a gamble, San

Franciscans started collecting photographs avidly in the 19th century. As a result of local interest and key donations from private collectors, San Francisco Museum of Modern Art (SFMOMA; p108) has amassed one of the world's best photography collections, and frequently exhibits the work of local artists past and present.

Pioneering 19th-century photographer Pirkel Jones saw expressive potential in California landscape photography, but it was SF native Ansel Adams' photos of Northern California's sublime wilds and his accounts of photography in Yosemite in the 1940s that would draw legions of camera-clutching visitors to San Francisco. Adams founded Group f/64 with Seattle-based Imogen Cunningham and Edward Weston, who also kept a studio in SF and made frequent visits from his permanent base in nearby Carmel. Instead of using the 19th-century tricks of soft focus and tinting, f/64 favored 'straight' photography – pictures that were matter-of-fact yet evocative, like Weston's famous shot of a single green pepper that looks like two lovers entwined.

Dorothea Lange spent many of her most productive years based in San Francisco, photographing Californians grappling with the hardship of the Great Depression and WWII. While she is best known for her searing photographs of desperate Dust Bowl farmers, such as *Migrant Mother, Nipoma, California, 1935,* her images of Japanese Americans forced to leave their San Francisco homes for WWII internment camps have the aching impact of a body blow. This legacy of cultural critique is kept alive today in the full-color suburban dystopias of Larry Sultan and Todd Hido. Hido's desolate tract homes eerily lit by car taillights look like crime scenes in the making, while Sultan's 'In the Valley' series shows sunny California suburbs serving as backdrops for bored porn stars awaiting their extra-close-ups. The work of all these photographers can be found at SFMOMA and 49 Geary (p73).

top picks

MUST-SEE GALLERIES

- **49 Geary** (p73)
- **77 Geary** (p73)
- **Catharine Clark Gallery** (p109)
- **Gallery Paule Anglim** (p73)
- **Luggage Store Gallery** (p79)
- **Creativity Explored** (p119)
- **Ratio 3** (p120)

Social Commentary

The social realist movement of the 1930s had a major impact on San Francisco, and original work by muralist Diego Rivera graces several interiors in the city, including the San Francisco Art Institute's Diego Rivera Gallery (p93). The Depression-era Work Projects Administration (WPA) sponsored other painters who worked in the mural tradition, and you'll find fine examples at Coit Tower (p88) and Rincon Center. Their bold figures and leftist leanings are reprised in works by Mission muralistas from the 1970s to today; Precita Eyes (p313) offers tours of some of the most historic, or you can wander along Clarion Alley (p119) and Balmy Alley (p118) on your own time. Another artist you may begin to recognize from his many San Francisco public works is Beniamino Bufano, whose smooth, rounded granite and steel structures include a tribute to Chinese revolutionary Sun Yat-sen in Chinatown's St Mary's Square (p84) and patron saint of the everyman St Francis of Assisi (p65).

To offset all this serious, high-minded revolutionary art, San Francisco artists have brought the art scene crashing back down to earth with gutsy, irreverent satire. In the '70s Tom Marioni scandalized gallery audiences who were expecting highbrow entertainment with performances where he would urinate from a ladder and drink beer (not necessarily in that order). Tony Labatt's disco balls dangling from his nether regions pretty much summed up the '70s era of Travolta testosterone, and Mads Lynnerup's vigilant camo-clad surveillance of San Francisco from the sunroof of a cardboard-armored SUV seems a fitting response to today's 'orange alerts.' Provocative performances by these and other artists can be witnessed at Yerba Buena Center for the Arts (p219) and New Langton Arts (p113). Political satire is not a passing fad here, and San Francisco provocateur Enrique Chagoya serves comic relief piping hot for those economic crisis hunger pangs with his cans of 'Mergers, Acquisitions and Lentils' soup at Electric Works (p113).

Abstract Thinking

Art schools in San Francisco attracted major abstract expressionist talents during the vibrant postwar period, when Clyfford Still, David Park and Elmer Bischoff taught at the San Francisco Art Institute. Still and Park splintered off from antiseptic mainstream abstraction to become leading proponents of the somewhat misleadingly named Bay Area Figurative Art, an elemental style often associated with San Francisco painter Richard Diebenkorn's fractured, color-blocked landscapes and the luminous, slippery figures of Oakland painter Nathan Oliveira.

San Francisco's Wayne Thiebaud tilted Sunset street grids into giddy Bay Area abstract cityscapes, but the abstract artist who made the biggest impact on the San Francisco landscape in terms of sheer scale is Richard Serra, as you can see in the rooftop sculpture garden at SFMOMA (p108). With their massive scale, Serra's spare metal shapes begin to take on other dimensions: a prow of a ship, say, or a Soviet factory second. To see what Bay Area abstractions have morphed into lately, check out 49 Geary (p73), 77 Geary (p73), Ratio 3 (p120) and Hosfelt Gallery (p113).

High Concept, High Craft

San Francisco's peculiar dedication to craft and personal vision can get obsessive. Consider *The Rose,* the legendary painting Beat artist Jay DeFeo began in the 1950s and worked on for eight years, layering it with 2000lb of paint until a hole had to be cut in the wall of her apartment to forklift it out. Ruth Asawa also began weaving her suspended wire cocoon sculptures back in the 1950s, finding sublime proportions and mind-altering light refractions in base metal. Lines of people waiting for the elevator to the MH de Young Memorial Museum tower (p139) pass the time marveling at Asawa's sculpted otherworldly organisms: jellyfish within onion domes within mushrooms. But perhaps the most famous example of obsession is Matthew Barney, who was raised in San Francisco and made his definitive debut at SFMOMA with his *Cremaster Cycle* videos. Barney seems to delight in making life and art unnecessarily difficult for himself, choosing Vaseline as his major medium and tethering himself for the recent *Drawing Restraint* – but it's hard to argue with the mesmerizing results.

Today's smart, craft-conscious contemporary Bay Area art owes equal debts of gratitude to the detail orientation of early-20th-century California Arts and Crafts and the discipline of late-1960s painting. But David Hockney–style pristine, poolside Southern Californian aesthetics never quite worked in San Francisco, with its love of rough-and-readymade '50s Beat collage, '60s psychedelic Fillmore posters, earthy '70s funk and beautiful-mess punk and '80s graffiti culture.

Despite all these competing influences, many standout Bay Area artworks don't seem labored at all. Anna Von Mertens covers army-cot-like beds with gorgeously discomfiting quilts, stitched with abstract patterns drawn from mushroom cloud explosions, WWII bombing raids and September 11 radar-screen readings. Substituting urban myth with urban truth, Felipe Dulzaides has replaced Nike billboards with blown-up photos of the tattered-chain basketball hoops seen in the streets below. Artists Ann Chamberlain and Ann Hamilton coordinated 200 volunteers to collage an entire wall at the San Francisco Main Library with 50,000 cards from the old card catalog, each card with commentary handwritten in one of a dozen locally spoken languages. Works by these and other rising art stars can be spotted at Jack Hanley Gallery (p120), Catharine Clark Gallery (p109) and the SF Arts Commission Gallery (p79).

Street Smarts

Like atoms in a radioactive substance, California DIY craftiness, skate culture and art-schooled finesse combined and collided in the late '90s in a distinctly San Francisco style. It's now known as 'Mission School' for its storytelling muralista sensibilities and graffiti-tag urgency. The Mission School professor emeritus was the late Margaret Kilgallen, whose closely observed character studies blended hand-painted street signage, comic-book pathos and a miniaturist's attention to detail. Clare Rojas expanded on these principles with splashy wall paintings, featuring looming, clueless California grizzly bears and tiny, fierce figures.

Other Mission School work is rougher around the edges: Chris Johansen's crowds of shy hipsters are drawn in endearingly awkward style, and Barry McGee's assemblages include piles of found bottles painted with freckled, feckless characters and jumpy animations shown on beat-up TVs.

Some Mission School art is fairly derided as the faux-naive work of stoned MFAs, but when its earnestness works, it hits you where it counts. Mission School artists make the scene at Luggage Store Gallery (p79), Eleanor Harwood Gallery (p119) and Jack Hanley Gallery (p120).

New Media

The technological expertise of the Bay Area is hard to match, and it's no surprise that local artists are putting it to creative use. But some of the most compelling new media artists don't show off with lots of bells and whistles, as in Rebecca Bollinger's grouped sketches of images found through a single keyword search on the web. Frame by frame, using specially modified software, Kota Ezawa turned the OJ Simpson trial into the multi-channel cartoon animation it actually was.

There's a new strain of anti-interactive art, too. Since the early '80s, Silicon Valley artist Jim Campbell has been building motherboards to misbehave – in one case, a running figure freezes as soon as it senses the slightest motion in the gallery, and like a frightened doe will resume activity only if you stay stock still. There's a certain silent-movie slapstick humor to Scott Snibbe's projections: it's a plain square on the wall until approached, when it suddenly recoils like a sensitive jungle fern. These and other intriguing new media works are featured at SFMOMA (p108), Catharine Clark Gallery (p109) and Hosfelt Gallery (p113).

MUSIC

You'll have to excuse San Francisco DJs if they seem a little schizophrenic: it takes an extremely eclectic collection to cover SF's varied musical tastes. Classical, opera and bluegrass have weathered earthquakes, fires and fickle audiences in San Francisco. In the alleyways of Chinatown, you can still hear the heartstring-plucking sounds of Chinese zithers and the boom of drums practicing for lion dances, and the Mission brings on the big, brassy fanfare of salsa and Latin ska bands. Music that started here never really went away, so you can hear it all: folk music and bebop that were the soundtrack of San Francisco in the '50s; '60s psychedelic rock and alt-rock; disco anthems that emerged from '70s bathhouse club culture; and electronica and DJ mash-ups that put all those mainframes and Moog machines sitting around in Silicon Valley to use in the '80s and '90s. Today you can take your pick – see The Arts (p221) and Nightlife (p210) chapters for more on the music scene.

Classical Music & Opera

The San Francisco Symphony (p223) has rated among the finest interpreters of classical music since conductor Michael Tilson Thomas was wooed away from the London Symphony Orchestra to take up the baton here in 1995. Thomas' innovative programming combines American and Russian composers, full-throttle Mahler and Beethoven, and some genuinely odd experimental music. These days, even the obligatory Mid-Summer Mozart and holiday Sing-Along *Messiah* crowd-pleasers seem somehow fresher. New York critics grouse that their city's renowned music scene now seems comparatively staid, and they're right – on the bright side, they can always load up on San Francisco Symphony CDs at Amoeba (p158). Thomas and the San Francisco Symphony record regularly, producing several Grammy-winning recordings and a number two hit in the Billboard charts with *S&M,* an album recorded with San Francisco heavy-metal powerhouse Metallica.

The San Francisco Opera (p222) is the USA's second-largest opera company. But while New York's Metropolitan Opera is larger in size and reputation, SF takes big, bold risks. You'd never guess San Francisco's opera roots go back to the 19th century from its more avant-garde productions, such as *Dangerous Liaisons, Harvey Milk* and *Dead Man Walking*. The company has seen its share of megawatt divas: Leontyne Price made her debut here and performed with the company during the 1950s, and the recent recurring favorite is Renée Fleming, whose dulcet tones you may recognize from more than a dozen CDs and *The Lord of the Rings* movie soundtrack. The latest excitement is new musical director Nicola Luisotti, who hails from Puccini territory in Tuscany and worked at Venice's fabled La Fenice before conducting breakthroughs at the Met and London's Royal Opera. His first order of business in SF: resurrecting Puccini's California Gold Rush opera *The Girl of the Golden West,* with star tenor and anointed Pavarotti successor Salvatore Licitra. After drastic public funding cutbacks, the company has been forced to scale back its programming, but to broaden the audience, tickets are now available for $50, among the lowest-priced anywhere in the opera world.

Rock

Fire up those lighters, but don't go calling for 'Freebird' as an encore. The San Francisco rock of choice lately is preceded by the prefix alt-, as in 'alternative to radio pap.' At Mission, Potrero and Polk Gulch venues and free music extravaganzas like the Mission Creek Music Festival, bands new on the scene earn their following the old-fashioned way: throwing down onstage like they're auditioning for a spot in heaven next to Joe Strummer (late, great front man of the Clash and pantheistic San Francisco rock idol). Metalheads need no introduction to the mighty Metallica, the perpetually hard-rocking innovators and triumphant survivors of a genre slowly smothered in the '80s by its own hair and binding leather pants. You might also hear blast-from-the-past rockabilly, popularized by crooner Chris Isaak (of 'Wicked Game' fame, often spotted out of cowboy attire surfing at Ocean Beach) and kept alive and swinging by relentless Lindy-hoppers in Golden Gate Park.

And to think that before you arrived, you thought San Francisco's rock scene had ODed long ago, along with Jerry Garcia, Janis Joplin, Jimi Hendrix, various Doors and most of Jefferson Airplane. Fair enough. San Francisco has the ignominious distinction of being a world capital of rocker drug overdoses, ranking right up there with Rome. You could do a macabre tour of the Haight to see all the places Janis nearly met her maker, passing by 32 Delmar St, where Sid Vicious went on the heroin bender that finally broke up the Sex Pistols (p130).

But no drug was powerful enough to kill Grateful Dead guitarist Jerry Garcia, who survived decades beyond any medically explicable life expectancy, only to die in rehab in 1995. Memorials left the Haight awash in homemade candle wax and tears scented vaguely of patchouli, and flowers are still often left near the former home of the Grateful Dead (p128) on Ashbury St. The Grateful Dead refused to die though, and the song remains the same on now-digitized mix tapes traded among Deadheads like currency. The band continues to gain new fans as jam bands like Phish keep their signature rambling, shambling rock sound going, and Jerry's former band mates still periodically tour under the name the Dead.

Baby boomers have kept the sound of San Francisco in the '60s alive and profitable for decades, as they replaced their worn-out records with 8-tracks, then cassettes, then CDs, and now MP3s. Give it a good listen, and you'll concede the hippies were onto something (as opposed to merely on something). After Joan Baez and Bob Dylan had their Northern California fling, folk turned into folk rock, and Jimi Hendrix turned the American anthem into a tune suitable for an acid trip. When Janis Joplin and Big Brother & the Holding Company applied their rough musical stylings to 'Me and Bobby McGee,' it was like applying that last necessary pass of sandpaper to the sometimes clunky, wooden verses of folk. Jefferson Airplane held court at the Fillmore, turning Lewis Caroll's opium-inspired children's classic into the psychedelic anthem 'White Rabbit' with singer Grace Slick's piercing wail.

The '60s were quite a trip, but the '70s weren't a let-down either, at least musically speaking. Crosby, Stills, Nash & Young splintered, but Neil Young keeps 'rockin' in the free world' from his ranch just south of San Francisco with his earnest, bluesy whine. Through Young's continued advocacy, the annual **Bridge School Benefit** (www.bridgeschool.org/events.html) for physically impaired youth in Mountain View attracts folkie greats like Simon & Garfunkel and Bonnie

SAN FRANCISCO'S TOP THREE MUSICAL CRIMES

Many egregious offenses were perpetrated by the Bay Area on unsuspecting listeners, particularly during the 1970s and '80s (though really, where isn't that true?), but these three top any local list:

- 'She's a Beauty' (1983) – the Tubes were headquartered in SF in the '70s during their 'White Punks on Dope' heyday, when they opened for Iggy Pop and Led Zeppelin, but then they had to go and spoil their indie track record with the inane and infernally catchy hit. Talk about going down the Tubes...
- 'Hip to Be Square' (1986) – so declared Marin County's Huey Lewis & the News, but actually, it wasn't. Not even in Marin.
- 'When the Lights Go Down in the City' (1978) – power balladeers Journey unleashed mulleted, high-pitched anthems on an unsuspecting world in the '70s, and to this day no other ode to San Francisco lodges itself as distressingly in the brain as Steve Perry's screechy vocals: 'When the lights go down in the city/And the sun shines on the Bay/Oh I wanna be they-eee-yah in my city...' You know you've gone soft on SF when you start to sing along (ahem).

Raitt, as well as marquee names like Dave Matthews Band, Pearl Jam and Beck. Since the 1970s, California-born, longtime Marin resident Tom Waits has been singing in a gruff, after-hours voice with a permanent catch in the throat, giving the world some idea what folk might sound like if it spent a decade working jangly honky-tonks across the West. Mission-born, lifelong San Franciscan Carlos Santana turned out '70s hits with a sexy guitar moan and Latin backbeat, including 'Black Magic Woman,' 'Evil Ways' and 'Oye Como Va' – and made a roaring crossover pop comeback with his Grammy-winning 1999 *Supernatural* and 2005 *All That I Am,* featuring fellow San Franciscan Kirk Hammett of Metallica.

Funk & Hip-Hop

The '60s were perhaps best summed up by freaky-funky, racially integrated San Francisco supergroup Sly and the Family Stone in their creatively spelled 1969 number-one hit: 'Thank You (Falettinme Be Mice Elf Agin).' San Francisco's '70s funk was mostly reverb from across the bay in Oakland, where Tower of Power worked a groove with taut horn arrangements. All this trippy funk worked its way into the DNA of the Bay Area hip-hop scene, spawning the jazz-inflected free-form Charlie Hunter Trio and the infectious wokka-wokka baseline of rapper Lyrics Born. Oakland's MC Hammer was an '80s crossover hip-hop hitmaker best known for inflicting harem pants on the fashion world, though his influence can be felt in the bouncing, hyperactivity of E-40. Political commentary and pop hooks became an East Bay hip-hop signature with the breakaway Billboard-chart hits of Michael Franti and Spearhead, Blackalicious and the Coup.

But the Bay Area is still best known as the home of arguably the world's most talented and notorious rapper of all: Tupac Shakur. He became a victim of his own success in Las Vegas in 1996, when an assailant out to settle the increasingly violent East Coast/West Coast gangsta rap rivalry fatally shot him. San Francisco rapper San Quinn got his start opening for Tupac but takes a less hard line, remixing the 1967 Mamas and the Papas hit 'San Francisco (Be Sure to Wear Flowers in Your Hair)' into his 'San Francisco Anthem' and adding a bougie twist: 'We got the cable car/but my car got cable.'

Punk

London may have been more political and Los Angeles more hardcore, but San Francisco's take on punk was just weirder. The New Wave and punk scene took root in San Francisco in the late 1970s, and Dead Kennedys frontman Jello Biafra ran for mayor in 1979 with a platform written on the back of a bar napkin: ban cars, set official rates for bribery and force businesspeople to dress as clowns. With a motto 'There's Always Room for Jello,' he received 6000 votes; his political endorsement is still highly prized in mayoral races.

Biafra was the ringleader of a three-ring circus in the '70s that included the Avengers (founded by San Francisco Art Institute grad Penelope Houston), Crime (whose 1976 song 'Hotwire My Heart' was the first US punk single, later covered by Sonic Youth), and noise/punk innovators Flipper (formed from the remains of Negative Trend, which also yielded post-punk dub masters Toiling Midgets). Post-punk kicked off locally with Marin's precocious proto–New Waver Todd Rundgren and power-popping Flamin' Groovies, whose 1976 cult-hit album *Shake Some Action* critics call the first New Wave album. But for oddity it's hard to top art-rockers the Residents, whose identities remain unknown after three decades and 60 records' worth of strange sounds, all while wearing giant eyeballs over their heads.

Search & Destroy was San Francisco's poorly photocopied and totally riveting chronicle of the '70s punk scene as it happened from 1977 to 1979, starting with an initial run financed with $100 from Allen Ginsberg and Lawrence Ferlinghetti, and morphing into V Vale's seminal 'zine *RE/Search* in the 1980s.

Today, punk's not dead in the Bay Area – in fact, it's getting mainstream radio play. The East Bay's one-two punch of ska-inflected Rancid and Berkeley's Green Day brought punk staggering out of the underground and blinking into the glare of the mass-media spotlight in the mid-'90s. Recorded in three weeks, Green Day's *Dookie* yielded three number-one singles for the group and the first of several Grammys for the band. When the acoustic Green Day ballad 'Time of Your Life' was featured in the last episode of the sitcom *Seinfeld,* the punk world sneered in unison, but the group won back admiration in 2004 with the dark social critique of *American Idiot.* Since the early success of their gold album *Punk in Drublic*, San Francisco–based NOFX avoided Green Dayish derision by staying on an independent label and recording an exceedingly sloppy show at Slim's (p214) called *I Hear They've Gotten Worse Live*! – winning mosh-pit props from their punk base and racheting up their record sales to $6 million without the help of a sitcom.

Punk continues to evolve in San Francisco, with queercore success of Pansy Division, the brass-ballsiness of Latin ska-punk La Plebe, and all-girl, all-badass rockers the Donnas. It may not be 'traditional' punk (isn't that an oxymoron anyway?), but it's very San Francisco.

Jazz

Ever since house bands and player pianos pounded out ragtime hits to distract Barbary Coast audiences from bar-room brawls and gunshots, San Francisco has had a romance with jazz. Today, the SF Jazz Festival (p23) is among the nation's best jazz festivals, attracting the leading innovators, interpreters and improvisers.

For decades, the city was besotted with bebop and West Coast jazz innovated by the legendary Dave Brubeck Quartet in the 1950s. Brubeck's groovy, mathematically complex rhythmic shifts, combined with Paul Desmond's supercool bossa nova saxophone style, had San Francisco hep-cats finger-snapping their approval, and made *Time Out* one of the best-selling jazz albums of all time. Bebop had its disciples among the Beats, and such is the continued devotion to the work of John Coltrane in particular that he's revered as a saint at the African Orthodox Church of St John Coltrane (p98). San Francisco's '50s jazz scene saw recordings by Miles Davis and frequent tour stops by Billie Holliday, and it's memorably chronicled in Kerouac's *On the Road*.

Starting in the '60s, the SF jazz scene exploded into a kaleidoscope of styles. Devotees of trumpeter Don Cherry followed his work with Ornette Coleman's avant-garde ensemble, while Dixieland band Turk Murphy developed a following with roots jazz fans. At the legendary Yoshi's (p211) and other jazz clubs around town (p210), tempos shift from Latin jazz to klezmer, acid jazz to swing. Local jazz innovators like Broun Fellinis regularly share the bill with hip-hop groups at local clubs and street festivals, and jazz traditionalists have shared the bill at Hardly Strictly Bluegrass Festival (p23). Even listeners not familiar with jazz will recognize the work of native San Franciscan Vince Guaraldi, whose score for *A Charlie Brown Christmas* has become the beloved antidote to cloying Christmas carols.

CINEMA & TELEVISION

The local film and TV industry is frequently referred to as 'Hollywood North' – and ooh, how they hate that. San Francisco doesn't do sitcoms, though many pretend to take place here (the city is hereby absolved of all responsibility relating to the Olsen twins and the cheesy '80s *Full House*), and only the odd *MythBusters* episode, Food Network show or HGTV home-design special bother to do location shooting here. What the city does do are standout public TV programs at powerhouse PBS station KQED and local ethnic media programs in dozens of languages, ranging from Persian to Portuguese. The local film industry would prefer to keep a respectable distance from Los Angeles so that it can concentrate on making documentary films and Sundance contenders, minus the paparazzi and studio-mandated happy endings.

Well, it's a little late for that. The Bay Area has been home to big-name directors and producers and a liberal sprinkling of movie stars since the 1970s, and there's no reason to expect that this will change anytime soon. American Zoetrope, the production company of *Godfather* auteur Francis Ford Coppola and producer of Sofia Coppola films such as *Lost in Translation*, is headquartered in North Beach's historic Columbus Tower, where a ground-floor bistro also sells Coppola wines and bland Italian food – though you might order dessert just to say with a smirk, 'I'll take the cannoli.' Coppola's tenants in the tower include filmmaker Wayne Wang (*Chan is Missing*, 1982; *Smoke*, 1995; *Because of Winn Dixie*, 2006) and Sean Penn, director and Academy Award–winning actor for his title role in 2008's *Milk*. Philip Kaufman, director of *Invasion of the Body Snatchers* (1978), *The Right Stuff* (1983) and *The Unbearable Lightness of Being* (1988), also lives and frequently works in San Francisco. Just across the bay, in Berkeley, is the company headquarters of producer Saul Zaentz, who has won three Oscars, for *One Flew Over the Cuckoo's Nest* (1975), *Amadeus* (1984) and *The English Patient* (1997).

SAN FRANCISCO'S MUST-SEE MOVIES

Comedy Classics

- *City Lights* (1931) – filmed in San Francisco by star-director Charlie Chaplin, this poetic silent masterpiece has SF's landmark bookstore (p146) named in its honor.
- *Harold and Maude* (1971) – the ultimate May-December romance features metaphorically apt SF locations: the eternal spring of the Conservatory of Flowers and the fabulous ruin of the Sutro Baths.
- *Tales of the City* (1993) – PBS' most popular miniseries stars Laura Linney unraveling a modern mystery amid the swinging SF '70s disco scene.

Mysteries

- *Maltese Falcon* (1941) – Dashiell Hammett's classic noir tale features Humphrey Bogart as tough-talking private dick Sam Spade.
- *Vertigo* (1958) – the Golden Gate Bridge sets the stage for dizzying drama when acrophobic Jimmy Stewart watches Kim Novak leap into the bay at Fort Point.
- *The Game* (1997) – packing more twists than Lombard St, Michael Douglas plays a deadly game with Sean Penn.

Documentaries

- *The Times of Harvey Milk* (1984) – this Oscar-winning documentary recounts city supervisor Milk's rise as a gay community leader and his murder alongside Mayor Moscone by deranged former supervisor Dan White – an assassination Milk had eerily predicted.
- *The Cockettes* (2002) – follow the glittering trail of SF's gender-bending, psychedelic performance group that became a 1970s pop-culture phenomenon in this Sundance Grand Jury Prize winner.
- *Jonestown: The Life and Death of People's Temple* (2006) – with rare footage and first-hand interviews, relatives and survivors recall the principles and practices of the Bay Area cult that committed mass suicide in 1978.

Cops & Robbers

- *Bullitt* (1968) – the plot has something to do with underworld kingpins, but it's all about supercool Steve McQueen's GTO flying over the crest of Nob Hill in hot pursuit and landing in SoMa (hence that editing Oscar).
- *Dirty Harry* (1971) – think you can mess with flinty detective Clint Eastwood? Go ahead: make his day.
- *Zodiac* (2007) – a real-life whodunit, David Fincher's star-studded film tracks the mounting obsession of reporters, detectives and Bay Area citizens with finding the 1970s Zodiac Killer.

Local Drama

- *The Conversation* (1974) – in Francis Ford Coppola's tense drama, surveillance expert Gene Hackman spies on an unwitting couple from the Westin St Francis Hotel (p252), only to get stalked himself by Harrison Ford and Robert Duvall.
- *Patty Hearst* (1988) – Natasha Richardson stars in writer/director Paul Schrader's account of Patty's plight, making her conversion from heiress to revolutionary bank robber weirdly relatable.
- *Milk* (2008) – minutes into Gus Van Sant's beguiling biopic, you can see why Sean Penn won an Oscar for his moving portrayal of charismatic Milk; look for cameos by SF locations, GLBT activists and 1970s pop culture references.

Even after 35 years, the force is still with the Bay Area's biggest movie mogul, George Lucas. Say what you will about his latest ventures (ouch, those *Star Wars* prequels…) but his films *American Graffiti* (1973), *Star Wars* (1977) and *Raiders of the Lost Ark* (1981) are among the most influential and profitable films ever made. What's more, Lucas' sound and special effects companies seem to have a hand in every big-budget film coming out of Hollywood, racking up numerous Academy Awards for technical achievement. A statue of Yoda stands in front of the Presidio's Letterman Digital Arts Center, the official front office for Industrial Light & Magic and LucasArts. Lucas still maintains his cloaked-in-secrecy Skywalker Ranch in Marin County, where Skywalker Sound is headquartered.

San Francisco tantalizes movie buffs with thousands of film premieres and classic revivals each year, thanks to plucky independent cinemas and a packed calendar of annual film festivals.

As a shooting location, San Francisco's filmography is checkered with perfectly dreadful rom-coms, in the apparent hope that such a picturesque backdrop might detract from such fatally flawed setups as Mark Ruffalo falling for Reese Witherspoon in a coma *(Just Like Heaven)*, or Jennifer Aniston falling for the geezer who seduced her mom and grandma *(Rumor Has It)*. To see San Francisco in some of its better star turns before you arrive, check out opposite. For classic noir films set in SF, see the boxed text, p219.

THEATER

Before San Francisco was a foodie town, or a tech town, or even much of a town at all, it was the West Coast's home of independent theater. Sure, there are still major productions destined for the lights of Broadway and London – the American Conservatory Theater (p225) sees to that, with breakthrough productions by Tony Kushner *(Angels in America)*, Robert Wilson and William S Burroughs *(Black Rider)*, Tom Stoppard *(Arcadia)* and David Mamet *(Oleanna, November)*.

For better or for worse, depending on how likely a tune is to haunt you, San Francisco also serves as the proving ground for musicals such as *Rent* and *Phantom of the Opera* in the grand Downtown theaters such as the Curran and the Orpheum. One homegrown musical event is *Beach Blanket Babylon* (p206), a drag spoof now into its third decade. But San Francisco's true claims to dramatic fame are the sights seen nightly in the city's small theater spaces, where (for a change) you really don't know what will happen next.

In the 1960s several cutting-edge companies opened in San Francisco, and the scene has staked its claim on the public imagination ever since. San Francisco's answer to Glasgow is the annual Fringe Festival at the Exit Theater (p225) and the boundary-pushing Theater Artaud. Magic Theatre (p225) gained a national reputation in the '70s, when Sam Shepard was the theater's resident playwright, and it's still one of the city's most important theaters. The Magic continues to stage works like Shepard's 2006 political satire *The God of Hell* and premieres by such established playwrights as Edna O'Brien and David Mamet, but also provides a platform for rising stars like Betty Shamieh and Josh Kornbluth.

top picks

PERFORMING ARTS VENUES

- San Francisco Symphony (p223)
- SF Opera at War Memorial Opera House (p222)
- Yerba Buena Center for the Arts (p219)
- San Francisco Performances at Herbst Theater (p222)
- Intersection for the Arts (p225)

For the past few years, novelist Denis Johnson of *Jesus' Son* fame has been a playwright at Intersection for the Arts (p225), the plucky multi-use space whose tiny theater showcases brave new worlds, playwrights and ideas. For a listing of theaters, see p224.

If you can't splash out for tickets, even at half-price in Union Square (see the boxed text, p225, for details), do not despair, gentle theater-goer: free street theater happens to be a San Francisco specialty. Beyond its spontaneous sidewalk scenes and quasi-daily protests, the city offers free Shakespeare (see p23) and traveling shows around town by the San Francisco Mime Troupe (p223). No, not that kind of mime – think *The Simpsons* with a leftist bent, a dose of kabuki kitsch, and just enough burlesque to make sure you're paying attention. Troupe founder RG Davis won a free speech case way back in 1962, and ever since, the Troupe has been gleefully trying (and sometimes succeeding) to get itself arrested and get audiences on their feet (whichever happens first).

DANCE

Never afraid of kicking up its heels and making grand gestures that show off its knickers, San Francisco has been dancing since the Barbary Coast days – notwithstanding an attempt to ban dance during San Francisco's blessedly brief flirtation with Victorian respectability just after the 1906 earthquake leveled the city's entertainment venues. From burlesque to ballet and all shades of modern, San Francisco so enjoys dance in all its permutations that its premier holiday event is the Dance Along Nutcracker (p24).

The city is home to the nation's oldest professional ballet company, formed in 1933 to keep heels and spirits lifted. The San Francisco Ballet (p218) quickly established a reputation for excellence, with George Ballanchine himself advising then-director Willam Christensen and setting the tone for the company. In 1944, San Francisco mounted the nation's first full-length versions of the *Nutcracker Suite* and *Swan Lake,* now widely regarded as signature pieces. Meanwhile, San Francisco's independent ballet companies seek ever more creative ways to break the traditional mold, like Savage Jazz, which does ballet to jazz music.

In modern dance, New York once again gets the credit for innovations that started in San Francisco. Widely credited with originating modern dance, Isadora Duncan (1877–1927) was born just a few blocks west of Union Square and grew up in Oakland before scandalizing and delighting dance fans from Manhattan to Europe. An alley near her birthplace, off Taylor St between Post and Geary Sts, now bears her name. Today, some of the city's more renowned companies, like Oberlin Dance Collective (p218) and Liss Fain Dance, combine raw Western physicality with San Francisco ingenuity. For a listing of dance companies, see p218.

ARCHITECTURE

Never a city to conform to expectations, San Francisco boasts a plethora of eclectic architecture, offering unexpected delights for visitors and endless challenges for architects charged with creating new buildings consistent with existing historic structures. The question is, which ones to match? A trip across town or even down the block will bring you face to facade with the region's Spanish and Mexican heritage, East Asian influences, California Arts and Crafts, high modernism and Victoriana movements, plus its own hodge-podge homegrown style. The roofline is as erratic and charming as a crooked smile, and bay windows often function as impromptu altars, often featuring ceramic owls, political endorsements, macramé and action figures in compromising positions.

Little is left of San Francisco's original Ohlone style beyond the grass memorial hut you'll see in the graveyard of the Spanish Mission Dolores (p115) and the wall of the original *presidio* (military post; p104), both built in adobe with Ohlone labor. With the Gold Rush came hasty deforestation and construction, with buildings slapped together from ready-made sawn timber components. Prefabricated houses arrived from Australia and the East Coast, a harbinger of the postwar prefab, and architect-designed, eco-prefab was innovated in the Bay Area during the 1990s.

San Francisco first distinguished itself architecturally not with grand civic buildings – in the Barbary Coast days, City Hall was located at the bawdy Jenny Lind Theater – but with residences for the nouveau riche. As San Francisco evolved from a temporary settlement to a permanent town, rows of Victorian houses were built. These wooden row houses were variations on a theme, using a similar underlying structure and floor plan but often with wildly different embellishments and eye-catching paint jobs.

The mid-19th century was the culmination of the European Age of Discovery, bringing with it renewed fascination with the civilizations of yore. The Victorian era was also a time of colonial conquest, and Victorians liked to imagine themselves as the purveyors of culture and the true inheritors of such great civilizations as ancient Rome, Egypt and the Italian Renaissance. They incorporated imagery from these cultural high-water marks into their houses, giving fresh-out-of-the-box San Francisco a certain globe-trotting, anachronistic instant culture. Homes were decorated to the hilt with stylistic flourishes from multiple eras, and cluttered with exotic souvenirs from distant colonies alongside objets d'art reflecting the cultural origins and fascinations of the owners. This rococosmopolitan look was as popular in its day as spare modernism is today, applied equally to lavish Nob Hill mansions and to waterfront bordellos and gambling houses. Regular fires, minor quakes and newly minted fortunes kept contractors busy replacing and expanding homes, not to mention tricking them out with the latest flourishes and mod cons such as electricity.

The 1906 quake and fire destroyed many of the city's 19th-century treasures, and eliminated much of its kitschy excess. But many styles of Victorian-era buildings can still be found around the city: the strict, long-windowed brick Italianates, the gabled Gothic Revivals, the delicate Eastlakes. But none match the sheer exuberance of the Queen Annes, first built here in the 1880s and 1890s. Architects pulled out all the stops on Queen Anne homes, bedecking them with balconies, towers, turrets, chimneys, bay windows and gables. The Haas-Lilienthal House (p98) is a fine example of this period's design. The most ornate and picturesque Victorian homes are found in neighborhoods that were spared the destruction of 1906, such as Pacific Heights (where many Painted Ladies have sadly been painted white for commercial sale) and the Haight (where some of the largest are now rehab facilities). Post-quake Edwardian architecture is generally less ornate than the earlier styles; the Mission and Castro have some well-preserved examples. Some attractive oversize Victorians are now B&Bs, so you too can live large in the swanky San Francisco digs of yore; see p250.

San Francisco's public and commercial buildings were comparatively modest initially. While Chicago and New York were raising skylines to new heights, fear of quakes arrested high-rise development in San Francisco. Only after steel-frame buildings stood the test of the 1906 earthquake did larger, higher steel-framed buildings begin to appear Downtown. Willis Polk was among the city's busiest architects; one of his best-known works is the Hallidie Building (see the boxed text, below).

The city always had aspirations to rival the capitals of Europe, and commissioned architect Daniel Burnham to build a grand Civic Center in the classicizing beaux arts or 'city beautiful' style. But this Pacific Rim city also felt a pull in other geographical directions, incorporating the Spanish and Aztec influences of Mexico into Mission High School (p120) and financial institutions along Sansome St. The 1920s brought the mission revival style, a nostalgic look back at the state's Spanish heritage. Julia Morgan became the first licensed female architect in California, and rose to fame with a precocious postmodern style that drew from a number of different cultural traditions, with her over-the-top Spanish-Gothic-Greek design for Hearst Castle, Italian-by-way-of-Meiji-Japan brick Zen Center (p132) and tastefully restrained pagoda-topped brick Chinatown YWCA (now the home of the Chinese Historical Society of America Museum; p83). Distinctive Chinatown deco became a cornerstone of Chinatown's redevelopment initiative after the 1906 quake, when a forward-thinking group of merchants led by Look Tin Eli undertook consultations with a cross-section of architects and held

BUILDINGS I LOVE (& LOVE TO HATE) *David Crotty, Bay Area architect*

Why should the Painted Ladies and Transamerica Pyramid get all the attention? Some of the most interesting buildings in the city – for better or worse – don't appear on any postcards.

- Federal Building (2007, Thom Mayne; Map pp110–11; 7th & Mission Sts) – this building is just plain badass. Its 18-story-high perforated metal sunscreen helps the building consume less than half the energy target for new federal buildings. Goes to show you can be environmentally sensitive without being enviro-wimpy.
- Crown Zellerbach Building (1959, SOM; Map pp70–1; 1 Bush St) – stand on Market St and you can fully understand how the building works. The tall dark tower is the 'core,' with elevators and services, leaving the glassy rectangle for unobstructed office space. Simple and elegant.
- Ferry Building (1898, renovated 2003, SMWM; Map p63; Embarcadero & Market St) – the renovators understood how to take advantage of this dusty old building by opening it up to the sky and water. Architecture isn't always about the building itself.
- MH de Young Memorial Museum (2005, Herzog & de Meuron; Map pp136–7; Golden Gate Park) – controversial, academic, beautiful and self-important, this rusty battleship marks SF's entrance into architectural relevance.
- Hallidie Building (1918, Willis Polk; Map pp70–1; 130 Sutter St) – might not look like much, but this was the first curtain wall building in the USA. The skin of the building sits in front of the structure like a curtain in front of a window, allowing the glass wall to sit uninterrupted by columns and creating a much lighter-looking building.
- SFO International Terminal (2004, SOM; Map p265) – check out the slick interiors and curvy, sexy exterior. This is the right way to enter our city.
- Yerba Buena Gardens (opened 1993; Map pp110–11; 3rd & Mission Sts) – stand in the garden and you can see stunning buildings on four sides: God, art and shopping – all in great buildings! This complex shows successful design on large and small scales.
- AT&T Park (2000, HOK Sport; Map pp110–11; 3rd & King Sts) – the architects had such great success in Baltimore they decided to do it again (and again and again). This brick park is a crowd-pleaser and a fun place to see a ballgame, but the *Leave It to Beaver* architecture is a lost opportunity.
- Marriott Hotel (1989, DMJM; Map pp110–11; 55 4th St) – locals call it the Jukebox, and we hate it. The ugliest building in SF screams for attention with its clumsy massing and flashy materials. Have a drink on the top floor of the hotel so you can see the city with this monster out of view.

rudimentary focus groups to produce a consistent, crowd-pleasing, modern *chinoiserie* look that would attract tourists.

Meanwhile across the bay, Berkeley-based architect Bernard Maybeck was reinventing England's Arts and Crafts movement with distinctly down-to-earth California sensibilities, cutting out frills in favor of harmonious geometry. Population growth and the movement to the suburbs inspired the California bungalow, a small, simple single-story design derived from summer homes favored by British officers serving in India. California Arts and Crafts proved equally applicable to cottages and to earthy ecclesiastical structures like San Francisco's Swedenborgian Church (p103).

SF's ornate Victorian sensibility was quickly being superseded by toned-down, but no less beautiful architecture. By this time most of the city's flatlands had been fully built up, so housing construction headed for the hills. As a result, the best places to see post-Victorian residential architecture are in hilly neighborhoods such as Diamond Heights and Twin Peaks. Art deco emerged from a 1920s fascination with machines and movement, yielding the futuristic, streamlined design aesthetic that gives the Golden Gate Bridge (p104) its wow factor.

The Depression years of the 1930s and the following WWII era brought a bonanza of WPA murals to town, but very little heavy construction. With the exclamation-point exception of Coit Tower (p88), the city skyline scarcely changed until the early 1960s, when Downtown suddenly started to soar skyward. Before the '60s, San Francisco had been known as the 'white city' because of its vast swaths of white stucco surfaces. But as engineers figured out how to build up without risk of complete tragedy in an earthquake, the Financial District rose skyward with acres of glass and steel to become thoroughly Manhattanized, with one notable San Francisco quirk: the Transamerica Pyramid (p71).

Recent construction has focused on Mission Bay around AT&T Park, as San Francisco braces itself for an expected boom in biotech and another wave of internet start-ups. This time, developers are determined to make the money-making outer reaches of SoMa attractive to businesses but also livable, with slots for shops, condos, restaurants and cafes to lend the area that 'Main Street Retail' quality. These carefully designed 'urban villages' seek to manufacture a sense of community in San Francisco's latest attempt at instant culture, though they're considerably more bland than the city's earlier Victorian attempt. If the plan succeeds in creating communities, it could drastically reduce the need for cars and provide a key alternative to the after-five desertification of Downtown and soulless bedroom communities. But critics argue that in a high-cost town like San Francisco, the economics of such projects tend to attract impersonal chain stores and high-priced retailers, leaving little room for affordable homegrown businesses and cultural institutions.

Meanwhile, in San Francisco neighborhoods best known for their vivid Victorian mansions and bay windows, some radical new architectural ideas are afoot. Amid graceful old homes, starkly modern forms are taking shape with modernist planes of steel and glass plus the organic materials favored by California Arts and Crafts. The exteriors of these new constructions can seem minimal to the point of forbidding, but the interior spaces make the most of air and light, with high ceilings and open-plan living areas. An indoor-outdoor flow linking living quarters to private patios and gardens provide the ready access to nature that makes San Francisco so livable. Detractors take issue with the striking outward appearances, which almost always clash with neighboring homes. But even hardcore Victorian preservationists concede that the old 'railroad style' interiors with small rooms lining a long, narrow corridor can be cramped, inhospitable and downright unsociable. Besides, this is San Francisco: love it or hate it, eclectic comes with the territory.

ENVIRONMENT & PLANNING

CLIMATE

Here's your year-round forecast for San Francisco: cool in the morning until the fog burns off, with afternoon temperatures reaching between 55°F and 70°F, then dropping as the sun sets or the fog rolls in, whichever happens first. Chances of precipitation are slight (though more likely from December to March) and the likelihood of temperatures topping 80°F even slimmer (though spring through fall and the odd February, you can always hope). Not bad, really, as long as you don't mind constantly dressing in layers and throwing some kind of fabulous coat or wrap over your obligatory parade ensemble – a feather boa can begin to seem mighty practical.

If you're coming to San Francisco expecting endless summer and bikinis galore, think again. That's San Francisco's rival city-state of Los Angeles down south that you've got in mind, and San Franciscans will show no compassion if you whine through chattering teeth about how this is supposed to be *C-C-California*. Consider yourself forewarned about the summer fog, which can lower temperatures and raise goose bumps in a hurry. The day might start out hot, but when inland summer heat draws the fog in from the sea, temperatures plummet and the wind picks up. San Franciscans take consolation in mild winters, when the contrast between land and sea temperatures is less extreme, the fog less frequent and the weather more reliable.

Microclimates add a touch of magic realism to San Francisco: when it's foggy and drizzling in the outer reaches of the Sunset, it may be bright and sunny in the Mission. The sunniest spots in town are nestled in the protective cover of hills, and you can witness clouds bounding through low-lying areas like Golden Gate Park and wander into hairdo-altering wind tunnels on the eastern shore of the bay. If you don't like the weather in one part of the city, try hopping on Muni for a different climate. You can feel the climate shift on east–west routes like the N-Judah, from windswept reaches of Downtown through the sunny pocket of Duboce Park and the Castro to the often foggy, blustery Ocean Beach. North–south routes such as the 22 Fillmore can take you from a misty Marina to a quick peek over the clouds in Pacific Heights, before descending to a hazy Haight, through the sunny Mission and Potrero, and all the way to a windswept waterfront.

THE LAND

Think of San Francisco as the thumbnail of a 30-mile-long peninsula that sticks up like a thumb into the Pacific Ocean and the San Francisco Bay, trying to hitch a ride off continental US. But more than its sparkling stretches of waterfront, the city's pride and worth-the-climb joy are its hills. The most spectacular panoramas are atop Nob and Russian Hills, rising above Downtown just a few blocks from Union Square and the Financial District to offer sweeping views of the Pacific, Golden Gate Bridge, Alcatraz, the Downtown skyline and across the bay to Berkeley and Oakland. Telegraph Hill sprouts up between North Beach and the bay, adding a touch of urban wilderness to panoramic views, with stairway gardens and wild parrots. Potrero Hill rises up from the flatlands of SoMa to overlook the industrial waterfront of China Basin and the Downtown skyline. Pacific Heights offers glimpses of the Presidio and Golden Gate Bridge between tony mansions and well-kept parks. Twin Peaks shelters the Castro and Mission from the foggy avenues to the west, while Buena Vista Park gives a bird's-eye view of Victorians in the Castro and the Haight.

For less arduous walks, try wandering close to the water, west of the Haight or SoMa. The waterfront is flat in the Marina, along the Embarcadero, and all the way down through Hunter's Point; much of the bay front is formed by landfill. SoMa and the Mission District are also mostly flat, as are the Sunset and Richmond Districts, and these flatlands are mostly reclaimed areas with filled-in streams, swamps and flattened sand dunes. There is a downside to these easygoing, low-slung areas: they're particularly vulnerable during earthquakes, when the soft ground underneath makes streets buckle and houses shift off their foundations. Sure makes a little huffing and puffing up bedrock seem worthwhile.

GREEN SAN FRANCISCO

In a place surrounded by so much natural beauty, environmentalism comes easily. This is one town where you can eat, sleep and cavort using sustainable means; the GreenDex in the index lists the best options in all of these categories and more. The US may be a two-party system, but in San Francisco the Green Party is a power player, introducing innovative emissions-reductions and municipal power measures. San Franciscans actually use the public transportation system, and some use green-minded car-sharing programs in lieu of owning a vehicle (see p306). San Franciscans have effectively defended parks and green spaces against development schemes for more than a century (see the boxed text, p32), and even reclaimed acres of military bases and industrial sites as green space. The city already has one of California's most successful curbside recycling programs, and as of 2010, mandates compost waste for reuse. Creative reuse has been big here ever since Beat artists starting turning junk into collages and assemblages in the '50s, and you too can get in on the artistic recycling action at SCRAP (p153).

One area of continued environmental concern is the San Francisco Bay, which is part of the West Coast's largest estuary and has become increasingly fragile in recent years. Much of the city's storm-water runoff goes directly into the bay, so you'll notice stenciled warnings on city sidewalks prohibiting the pouring of pollutants down the gutter. But shipping, recreational boating, fishing and bayside farming and industry have also taken their toll on the shallow bay and the wetlands that line it. Salmon are among the first fish to be affected by changes in water quality, and in 2008 the prized Pacific chinook salmon, once abundant in the Sacramento River and previously found running through the bay, were suddenly unable to survive as far as the Golden Gate Bridge. As the Bay Area's population continues to grow, added measures will be needed to protect the region's signature natural feature: its tributaries and aquaculture.

URBAN PLANNING & DEVELOPMENT

In poll after poll, the number-one concern in San Francisco is traffic. Add residential vehicles to increasing commuter traffic from the East and South Bays, and you're looking at a compelling case for additional improvements to intercity public transportation. There is a consultative body of Bay Area governments that supposedly addresses this sort of thing, but it lacks the power and finances to get much done.

Housing shortages in the city itself are being met with new construction, mostly in the SoMa area. The vast avenues of warehouses in this part of town are gradually being converted or replaced with small, smartly designed and inevitably expensive loft spaces. SoMa and the bayside slope of Potrero Hill are characterized by long, monotonous blocks, with parks few and far between. Recent development nearer the bay has started to address these shortcomings, integrating some greenery into future building plans. Extensions of the once-limited streetcar system, with new lines along the Embarcadero and 3rd St, are also helping to draw these communities more closely into the city's broader fabric, reducing commuter reliance on cars.

High-density housing is a fine green idea to conserve resources and contain sprawl, but the problem of parking in San Francisco remains. San Francisco may be a compact city, but the same cannot always be said about the cars that roam its streets, and street parking is perennially at a premium. Take public transportation Downtown and you may save yourself half an hour looking for parking at either end of your trip, not to mention saving parking garage fees and the environment.

GOVERNMENT & POLITICS

The City and County of San Francisco is a peculiar creature with a single body run by different minds, which sometimes makes it futuristically forward-thinking and other times as unruly as a many-headed monster. The city government consists of a mayor and an 11-member Board of Supervisors, which is headed by a president. At any given time, the board is internally conflicted and/or at odds with the mayor, which makes open meetings lively and occasionally soul-searching affairs worth sitting in on. Like the mayor, the supervisors serve four-year terms and are limited to two terms.

Although the city has an active multiparty system in which Greens and other independents do get elected, San Francisco tends to vote overwhelmingly Democratic, and it's not uncommon for the mayor and all 11 supervisors to be affiliated with the Democratic Party. The Board of Supervisors also tends to reflect the city's diverse population – women, gay, lesbian, transgender, Chinese, Latino and African American candidates have all been voted onto the board. There are pockets of conservatives in the city, but for the most part they keep a low profile.

MEDIA

NEWSPAPERS & MAGAZINES

The *San Francisco Chronicle* is the Bay Area's number-one daily, with one of the nation's largest newspaper circulations – but perhaps not for long. Its website, www.sfgate.com, has been among the top five US news sites on the internet, yet since its purchase by Hearst Newspapers in 2000, the *Chron* has been losing money. The paper has been recently redesigned in a smaller format, and while it continues to show some chutzpah with investigative journalism and outspoken columnists, it's now heavily padded with soft news. Its future remains uncertain.

The city's most prominent locally owned free weekly, the *Bay Guardian,* is a prime source of local news, although its zealous muckraking can be tiresome even to the most devoted local politicos. Most readers flip to the extensive arts and entertainment reviews and features, and the sex-advice column. While not locally owned, *SF Weekly* offers decent news and entertainment listings and entertaining profiles. The *Bay Area Reporter* is a free weekly by, for and about the GLBT community, offering a community-minded take on local politics, a handy calendar of events and decent entertainment listings.

The magazine *7x7* (a reference to the city's size in miles) and its website (www.7x7.com) are good bets for food and drink listings, shopping and fashion coverage, plus inexplicable society-page coverage (as if anyone here really cares). *San Francisco* magazine is a slick monthly that's surprisingly stodgy in its recommendations, but has some interesting reportage on local arts, culture and politics.

RADIO & TV

Nearly 100 radio stations in the Bay Area broadcast hip-hop, classic rock and alt-rock, country and western, jazz, classical, Mexican *banda,* news, talk, sports, evangelism and college esoterica. Bright spots on the dial include multiple public radio stations, with original programming and the usual NPR standbys – it's the soundtrack you'll hear in many San Francisco cars, homes and workplaces. TV consists of the usual national network affiliates, ethnic media in multiple languages and a proliferation of cable stations. The most truly original local programming is found on KQED (channel 9), the PBS affiliate.

FASHION

If San Francisco had its own unisex national costume, here's what it would include: fly kicks or funky low-heeled shoes to manage those hills; jeans of course, invented here by Levi Strauss 150 years ago and getting more overpriced by the minute; a whimsical and/or controversial T-shirt, or possibly a vintage Western shirt; a sweater and/or coat of some kind, which remains inexplicably unbuttoned even in the chilliest fog; and a backpack, handbag or man-bag, holding big books and exceedingly small techno-gadgets. That said, there's no designated underground-culture uniform here; trucker hats, ironic T-shirts, white belts and skinny jeans are far too mass-marketed and one-size-fits-all for SF's sub-subcultures (see the boxed text, above). The most double-take-inducing, original fashion is spotted by night, especially at Downtown art galleries, Mission bars, Haight haunts or SoMa clubs.

Yet if you ask how long it took to pull that look together, most San Franciscans will swear they got dressed in 10 minutes, and if you compliment some article of clothing, you'll probably be told what a bargain it was. San Franciscans do their utmost not to be

SF'S MIXED FASHION SIGNALS

You may think you can tell a subculture at a glance, but SF has its own set of dress codes that don't conform to fashion norms elsewhere. The same fashion statement can signify more than one SF subculture, for example:

- Skinny jeans: Mission punk guitarist or Marina soccer mom
- Combat boots with backpack: Haight anarchist or Castro clubgoer
- Sleeves of tattoos: Downtown bike messenger or SoMa software engineer
- Statement jewelry: Pacific Heights socialite or Tenderloin drag queen
- Fleece vest: Crissy Field yuppie or Berkeley radical

confused with Los Angeles' fashion victims, and like to think they've got more important things to worry about – such as protesting wars, attaining enlightenment and finishing that documentary film. Natural, low-maintenance beauty is the norm, or at least the goal – San Franciscans prefer to conserve their effort for drag, Burning Man and promising Saturday nights. Cutting-edge salons provide the stylish yet effortless cuts and outrageous color. Except for piercings and tattoos, San Franciscans don't often pain themselves for fashion.

Dressing off the rack is only for the fashion-impaired in San Francisco, where DIY is the dominant ethic. The ultimate San Francisco fashion statement is a one-off made by hand, preferably your own. Vintage shops, local boutiques and indie designers are the preferred sources for readymade style, and the savvy regularly trawl the sales racks on SF's most boutique-studded streets: Haight, Valencia, Hayes, upper Grant, Fillmore, Union and Polk. There's no shame in admitting you got some staples at trendy, cheap H&M (p143) – everyone loves a sweet deal – but otherwise locals are loath to patronize chain stores. Some people will claim political reasons (support local designers, the economy, fellow workers of the world etc, etc) but the real reason is individualist vanity. Many San Franciscans would rather spend Friday night at home than be caught at a party in the same Gap sweater as three other people. But since most rules are made to be broken in SF, even the most independent-minded fashionistas will sneak down to Union Square and the mall for after-holiday and end-of-summer sales.

Some things are worth splashing out for, especially costumes and local designers – no one wants to miss out on the next local sensation to follow Derek Lam and Peter Som. San Francisco dotes on its homegrown designers, including ADS Hats, Delilah Crown, Upper Playground, Mabel Chong, Loyal Army Clothing, Dema, Claudia Kussano and Sunhee Moon. Residents Apparel Gallery is a collective of local designers cutting out the middleman to give you the best prices, while Mingle, Mission Statement, Ooma, Candystore Collective, Velvet da Vinci and Doe offer a tantalizing range of local and indie designers. See the Shopping chapter (p142) for store listings.

NEIGHBORHOODS

top picks

- **Alcatraz** (p62)
- **Chinatown alleyways** (p81)
- **San Francisco Museum of Modern Art** (p108)
- **California Academy of Sciences** (p140)
- **Ferry Building** (p64)

What's your recommendation? www.lonelyplanet.com/san-francisco

NEIGHBORHOODS

> 'the city is about the size of California's thumb and packs in under a million people even in high-tourist season, yet there is something here for everyone'

Don't believe San Francisco's false modesty on a map. Yes, the city is about the size of California's thumb and packs in under a million people even in high-tourist season, yet there really is something here for everyone. 'Eclectic' doesn't begin to describe a town where you can begin your day with a leisurely breakfast of huevos rancheros (ranch-style eggs) in the morning Mission sun, picnic on Italian panini among parrots and poets on a North Beach stairway garden, get goose bumps watching the fog roll in from the Pacific on a Presidio nude beach, dine Downtown on wildly inventive cuisine inspired by California's cornucopia of produce, and end up the next morning still partying at 5am with SoMa clubsters of indeterminate sexual orientation in a universal groove. City streets are ethnic enclaves that are difficult to define and never entirely exclusive: largely Latin American 24th St is also Southeast Asian, lesbian and arty hipster, while Clement St highlights include authentic Irish bars, Taiwanese and Thai restaurants and Japanese convenience stores.

Since the Gold Rush, Embarcadero and the Piers has been the point of entry for new arrivals, and it's where you'll enjoy gourmet treats, sea-lion antics, old-school video games and getaways to and from Alcatraz. Your next stop is Downtown for art galleries, swanky hotels, first-run theaters, a mall full of brand names and XXX cinemas. Civic Center and the Tenderloin is quite the urban conundrum: great performances and Asian art treasures on one side, dive bars, soup kitchens and bargain *banh mi* (Vietnamese sandwiches) on the other. On the main streets of Chinatown, dumplings and rare teas are served under pagoda roofs, but in its historic back alleys there's temple incense, mah-jong tile clatter and long-ago echoes of revolution. In North Beach wild parrots circle overhead, while the idle chatter in Italian cafes and bohemian bars below runs from soccer to filmmaking over the sound of opera on the jukebox. Russian and Nob Hills are the stomping grounds of eccentric millionaires and hardcore urban hikers alike, with cable cars delivering customers to hilltop bars and haute cuisine.

When you see sushi picnics in the fountains, cutting-edge fashion in starchy Victorian storefronts and rock at the legendary Fillmore, you'll know you've arrived in Japantown and Pacific Heights. Just uphill are chic boutiques in a former cow pasture and organic dining along the waterfront of the Marina and the Presidio, where you'll encounter Shakespeare, Yoda and public nudity at a former army base. Some are drawn to South of Market (SoMa) for high technology, others for high art, but everyone gets down and dirty on the dance floor.

The best way to enjoy the Mission is with a book in one hand and a burrito in the other, amid murals, sunshine and the usual crowd of documentary filmmakers and novelists. Silicon Valley refugees take to Potrero Hill, while barflies and artists lurk in the valley below. Rainbow flags gaily wave their welcome to party boys, career activists and leather daddies in the Castro. Meanwhile, over the hill in Noe Valley, megastrollers brake for bakeries and boutiques, and lesbians load up on uberchic footwear and baby togs.

Hippies reminisce and punks lose their sneers in the Haight, land of flower-power souvenirs, anarchist comic books, free concerts and skateboards. Fashionistas raid boutiques for local designs as Zen monks drift past on the sidewalks of Hayes Valley. Out in the Richmond, the Sunset and Golden Gate Park, hardcore surfers and gourmet adventurers find a home where the buffalo roam, and the MH de Young's tower rises above it all.

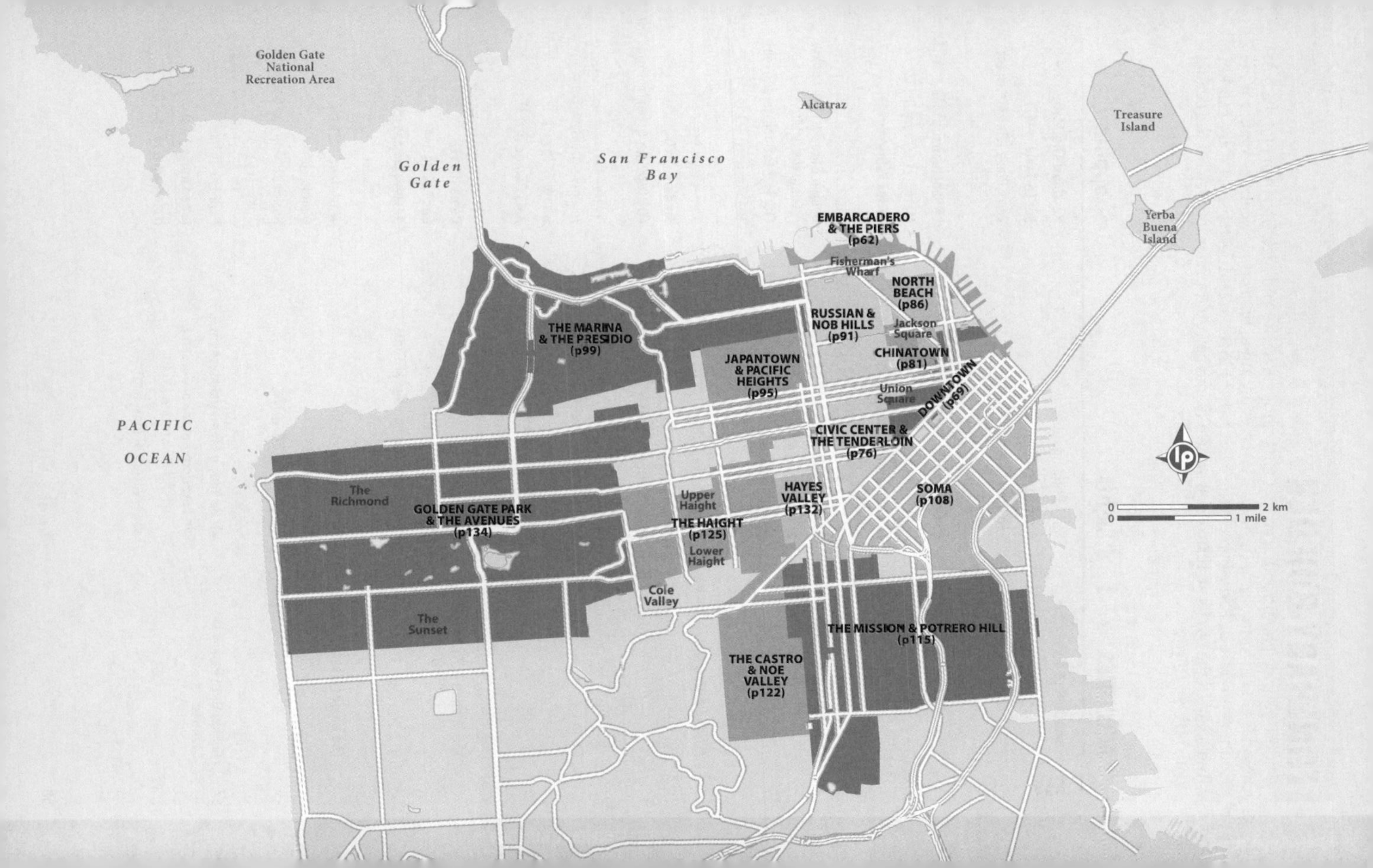
Golden Gate National Recreation Area
Alcatraz
Treasure Island
Golden Gate
San Francisco Bay
Yerba Buena Island
EMBARCADERO & THE PIERS (p62)
Fisherman's Wharf
NORTH BEACH (p86)
RUSSIAN & NOB HILLS (p91)
Jackson Square
THE MARINA & THE PRESIDIO (p99)
JAPANTOWN & PACIFIC HEIGHTS (p95)
CHINATOWN (p81)
Union Square
DOWNTOWN (p69)
PACIFIC
OCEAN
CIVIC CENTER & THE TENDERLOIN (p76)
The Richmond
GOLDEN GATE PARK & THE AVENUES (p134)
Upper Haight
THE HAIGHT (p125)
HAYES VALLEY (p132)
SOMA (p108)
0
2 km
0
1 mile
Lower Haight
Cole Valley
The Sunset
THE MISSION & POTRERO HILL (p115)
THE CASTRO & NOE VALLEY (p122)

ITINERARY BUILDER

Choose your neighborhood; scan its sights, shops, eateries and nightlife; then plot the best possible course from one to the next. Maybe you want to break into Alcatraz? Snaffle Wine Country produce at Ferry Plaza Wine Merchant? Linger over delectables at Gary Danko? Run away to the circus at Teatro Zinzanni? Or maybe you'd prefer to stray off the beaten path? It's up to you.

AREA / ACTIVITIES	Sights	Shopping
Embarcadero & the Piers	**Ferry Building** (p64) **Alcatraz** (p62) **Sea lions at Pier 39** (p66)	**Recchiuti Chocolates** (p142) **Sur La Table** (p142) **Ferry Plaza Wine Merchant** (p142)
Downtown	**49 Geary** (p73) **& 77 Geary** (p73) **Gallery Paule Anglim** (p73) **Transamerica Pyramid & Redwood Park** (p71)	**Le Sanctuaire** (p144) **Margaret O'Leary** (p143) **Britex Fabrics** (p144)
Chinatown & North Beach	**Spofford Alley** (p83) **Ross Alley** (p84) **Coit Tower** (p88)	**Golden Gate Fortune Cookie Company** (p145) **City Lights Bookstore** (p146) **101 Music** (p147)
Russian & Nob Hills	**Diego Rivera Gallery** (p93) **Sterling Park** (p91) **Grace Cathedral** (p93)	**Velvet da Vinci** (p148) **Studio** (p147) **City Discount** (p148)
SoMa	**San Francisco Museum of Modern Art** (p108) **Cartoon Art Museum** (p109) **Museum of the African Diaspora** (p112)	**Jeremy's** (p151) **Isda & Co** (p151) **Rolo Garage** (p151)
The Mission & Potrero Hill	**Clarion Alley** (p119) **826 Valencia** (p118) **Precita Eyes Mission Mural Tours** (p313)	**Dema** (p152) **Good Vibrations** (p153) **Needles & Pens** (p153)
The Haight & Hayes Valley	**Alamo Square** (p130) **Zen Center** (p132) **Buena Vista Park** (p128)	**Wasteland** (p158) **Gimme Shoes** (p160) **Residents Apparel Gallery** (p159)
Golden Gate Park & the Avenues	**MH de Young Memorial Museum** (p139) **San Francisco Botanical Garden & Strybing Arboretum** (p140) **Conservatory of Flowers** (p140)	**Park Life** (p160) **Green Apple Books** (p160) **New May Wah** (p160)

HOW TO USE THIS TABLE

The table below allows you to plan a day's worth of activities in any area of the city. Simply select which area you wish to explore, and then mix and match from the corresponding listings to build your day.

Eating	Drinking/ nightlife	Off the beaten path
Ferry Plaza Farmers Market (p169) **Gary Danko** (p167) **Boulette's Larder** (p168)	**Punch Line** (p206) **Teatro Zinzanni** (p207) **Buena Vista Café** (p194)	**Forbes Island** (p167) **Angel Island** (p282) **Tiburon** (p280)
Aqua (p169) **Bocadillos** (p171) **farmerbrown** (p171)	**American Conservatory Theater** (p225) **Warfield** (p214) **Pied Piper Bar** (p195)	**Gitane** (p170) **Glide Memorial United Methodist Church** (p74)
Jai Yun (p173) **City View** (p174) **Ristorante Ideale** (p175)	**Li Po** (p197) **Specs'** (p197) **Caffe Trieste** (p198) **Top of the Mark** (p198)	**Chinatown Alleyway Tours** (p313) **Good Luck Parking Garage** (p84)
Acquerello (p176) **Za** (p176) **Swan Oyster Depot** (p176)	**Tonga Room** (p198) **Bigfoot Lodge** (p198) **EndUp** (p208)	**Jack Kerouac Alley** (p88) **Jack Kerouac's Love Shack** (p93) **Macondray Lane** (p94)
Patisserie Philippe (p179) **Tu Lan** (p180) **Boulevard** (p178)	**Eagle Tavern** (p243) **Cat Club** (p208) **Elbo Room** (p212)	**Lumiere Theater** (p221) **Catharine Clark Gallery** (p109) **Rainbow Grocery** (p180)
Range (p180) **Bi-Rite** (p182) **Delfina** (p180)	**Lexington Club** (p243) **Roxie Cinema** (p221) **Toronado** (p202)	**Electric Works** (p113) **Galería de la Raza** (p120) **SCRAP** (p153)
Rosamunde Sausage Grill (p186) **Little Star Pizza** (p185) **Suppenküche** (p187)	**Triple Crown** (p215) **Red Vic Movie House** (p221) **Plough & the Stars** (p204)	**Wild Side West** (p245) **African Orthodox Church of St John Coltrane** (p98) **Madrone** (p202)
Aziza (p188) **Genki** (p190) **Taiwan Restaurant** (p189)	**540 Club** (p203) **Trad'r Sam's** (p204)	**Noc Noc** (p202) **Columbarium** (p138) **Java Beach Café** (p204) **Louis** (p189)

GREATER SAN FRANCISCO

MAP INDEX

Golden Gate
Doyle Dr
Lagoon
11
Lombard St
Lincoln Blvd
Baker Beach
The Presidio National Park
Presidio Golf Course
Alta Plaza Park
Mountain Lake Park
California St
Bush St
Geary Blvd
Park Presidio Blvd
University of San Francisco
Turk St
25th Ave
The Richmond
Balboa St
Masonic Ave
Upper Haight
14
4
Ocean Beach
Fulton St
Spreckels Lake
Golden Gate Park
Golden Gate Municipal Golf Course
Great Hwy
Buena Vista Park
Lincoln Way
Cole Valley
7th Ave
The Sunset
Grand View Park
Mt Sutro
Clarendon Ave
Laguna Honda
Twin Peaks
Twin Peaks
Sunset Reservoir
Sunset Heights Park
Upper Great Hwy
Sunset Blvd
19th Ave
Portola Dr
McCoppin Square
Taraval St
Glen Canyon Park
Vicente St
Mt Davidson
Aqua Surf Shop
Parkside Square
San Francisco Croquet Club
Stern Grove
San Francisco Zoo
Sloat Blvd
Monterey Blvd
Skyline Blvd
Harding Park Municipal Golf Course
San Francisco State University
Junipero Serra Blvd
Balboa Park
Ocean Ave
Lake Merced
Brooks Park

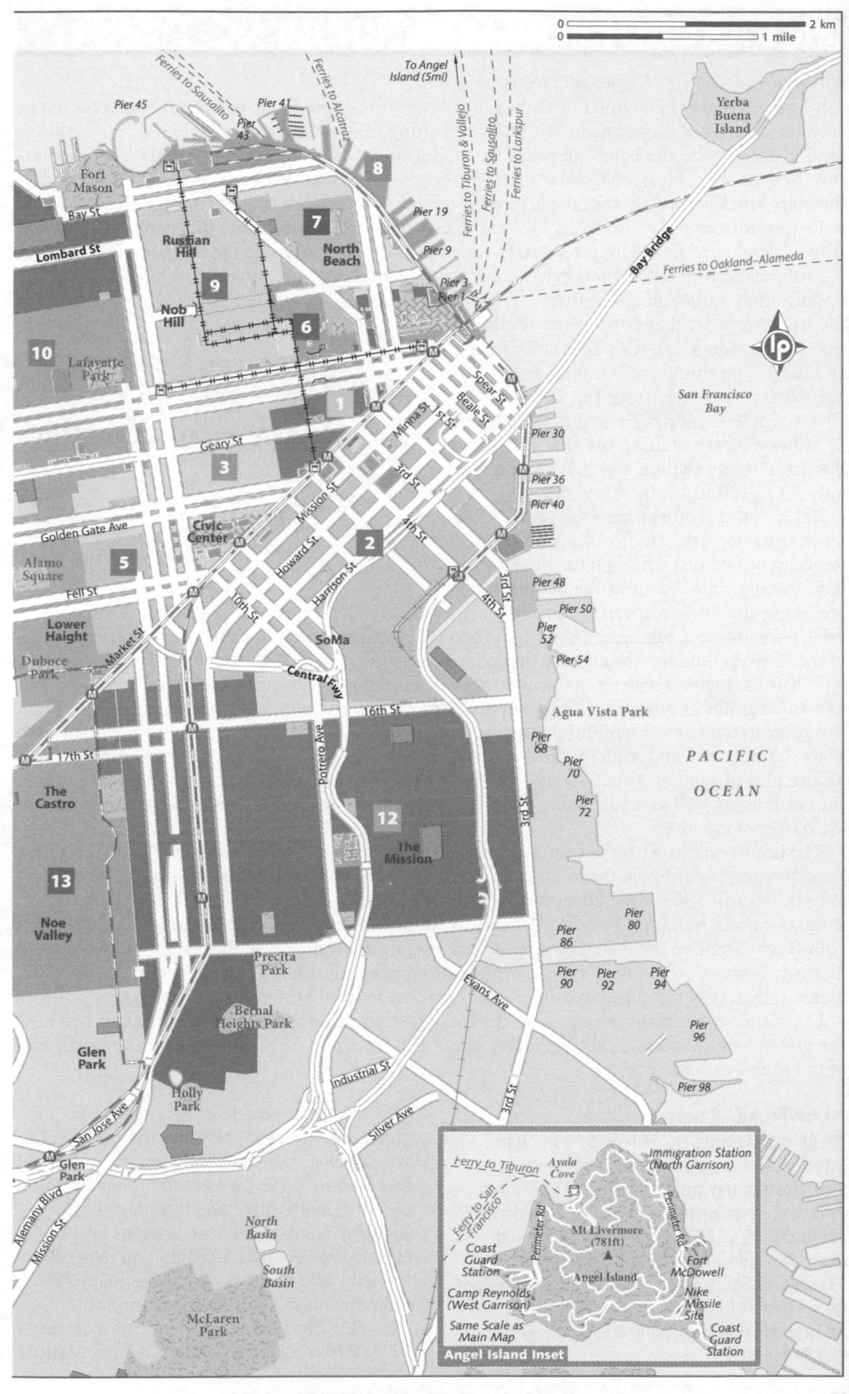
0 2 km
0 1 mile
To Angel Island (5mi)
Ferries to Sausalito
Ferries to Alcatraz
Ferries to Tiburon & Vallejo
Ferries to Sausalito
Ferries to Larkspur
Pier 45
Pier 41
Pier 43
Yerba Buena Island
Fort Mason
Bay St
Lombard St
Russian Hill
North Beach
Pier 19
Pier 9
Bay Bridge
Ferries to Oakland–Alameda
Pier 3
Pier 1
Nob Hill
Lafayette Park
Spear St
Beale St
Minna St
1st St
San Francisco Bay
Pier 30
Geary St
3rd St
Pier 36
Pier 40
Mission St
Golden Gate Ave
Civic Center
Howard St
4th St
Alamo Square
Harrison St
Fell St
Pier 48
3rd St
4th St
Pier 50
Pier 52
10th St
Lower Haight
Market St
SoMa
Pier 54
Duboce Park
Central Fwy
16th St
Agua Vista Park
Pier 68
17th St
Potrero Ave
Pier 70
PACIFIC OCEAN
The Castro
Pier 72
3rd St
The Mission
Noe Valley
Pier 80
Pier 86
Precita Park
Pier 90
Pier 92
Pier 94
Evans Ave
Bernal Heights Park
Pier 96
Glen Park
Industrial St
Holly Park
Pier 98
3rd St
San Jose Ave
Silver Ave
Glen Park
Alemany Blvd
Mission St
North Basin
South Basin
McLaren Park
Ferry to Tiburon
Ayala Cove
Immigration Station (North Garrison)
Ferry to San Francisco
Perimeter Rd
Perimeter Rd
Mt Livermore (781ft)
Coast Guard Station
Fort McDowell
Angel Island
Camp Reynolds (West Garrison)
Nike Missile Site
Same Scale as Main Map
Coast Guard Station
Angel Island Inset
1
2
3
5
6
7
8
9
10
12
13

EMBARCADERO & THE PIERS

Drinking p194; Eating p167; Shopping p142; Sleeping p251

San Francisco may be defined by its bay, but only sundry sea lions, sailors and exercise freaks spend a majority of their time in San Francisco along Embarcadero and the Piers. You'll still see local seafood specialties hauled in near Pier 45, but since San Francisco's old wharves are too narrow for container ships, most seafaring traffic heads directly to the port at West Oakland. Today, the piers function as a point of departure for ferries and pleasure cruises through the bay to the notorious former prison island of Alcatraz (below), the overgrown former immigration station at Angel Island (p282) or the hippie houseboats and millionaire mansions of Sausalito (p280).

Embarcadero and the Piers have their ways of making you slow down and stay awhile. Foodies may forget all about their ferries in the movable feast that is the Ferry Building (p64), and gamers can lose all track of time at Musée Mécanique (p66) testing their skill against classic games from the 1880s to the 1990s. Anglers and danglers sit at the edge of Broadway Pier, watching the tide ebb from the surprisingly shallow bay, which averages only 6ft to 10ft in depth at low tide.

But for most visitors there's too much going on in the rest of the city to stay here, as Otis Redding put it, 'just sittin' on the dock of the Bay/wasting time.' Most of the people you'll see along the Embarcadero are moving at a brisk pace, jogging, biking and skating. When the overhead freeway along the Embarcadero fell in the 1989 earthquake, the city decided not to block these waterfront views with a new freeway, and instead created a waterfront boulevard wide enough to accommodate streetcars, bike lanes and street gangs of power-walking yuppies from the luxury lofts that sprang up nearby. When the cops aren't around, you might also see renegade skateboarders appear from nowhere to skate the rails and dodge pier pylons.

The plot of sand at Aquatic Park (p67) on the north shore of the bay sports its share of idle suntan fans, as well as a surprising number of swimmers willing to brave the frigid waters of the bay even in winter.

The Embarcadero skirts the central waterfront, beginning at South of Market (SoMa) at AT&T Park, passing Downtown, the Financial District and North Beach before reaching Fisherman's Wharf. Back in 1849 when adventurers and miners arrived here, most of this area was under water. A steady buildup of sludge, debris, docks, saloons, and ships abandoned by crews with gold fever extended the waterfront east, and a retaining wall was built to keep the piers from drifting. Fisherman's Wharf moved from Embarcadero and Union St to its current location, where Italian fishermen began doing brisk business in local Dungeness crab.

Levi Strauss originally set up shop for his new denim dungarees in the Mission, but now the global headquarters of his legendary jeans empire are in Levi's Plaza, near the north end of the Embarcadero.

top picks

EMBARCADERO & THE PIERS

- Alcatraz (left)
- Ferry Building (p64)
- Sea lions at Pier 39 (p66)
- Musée Mécanique (p66)
- USS Pampanito (p66)

ALCATRAZ off Map p63

☎ Alcatraz Cruises 415-981-7625; ticket info http://alcatrazcruises.com, park info www.nps.gov/alcatraz; day tickets adult/child under 5yr/child 5-11yr/senior/family (2 adults, 2 children) $26/free/16/24.50/79, night tours adult/child under 5yr/child 5-11yr/child 12-17yr/senior $33/free/19.50/30.50/32; call center 8am-7pm, ferries depart from Pier 33 every half hour 9am-3:55pm, night tours 6:10pm & 6:45pm; F to Pier 33 for ferry

Alcatraz: for almost 150 years, the name has given the innocent chills and the guilty cold sweats. Over the years it's been the nation's first military prison, a forbidding maximum-security penitentiary and disputed territory between Native American activists and the FBI. No wonder that first step you take off the ferry and onto 'the Rock' seems to cue ominous music: dunh-dunh-dunnnnh!

It all started innocently enough back in 1775, when Spanish lieutenant Juan Manuel

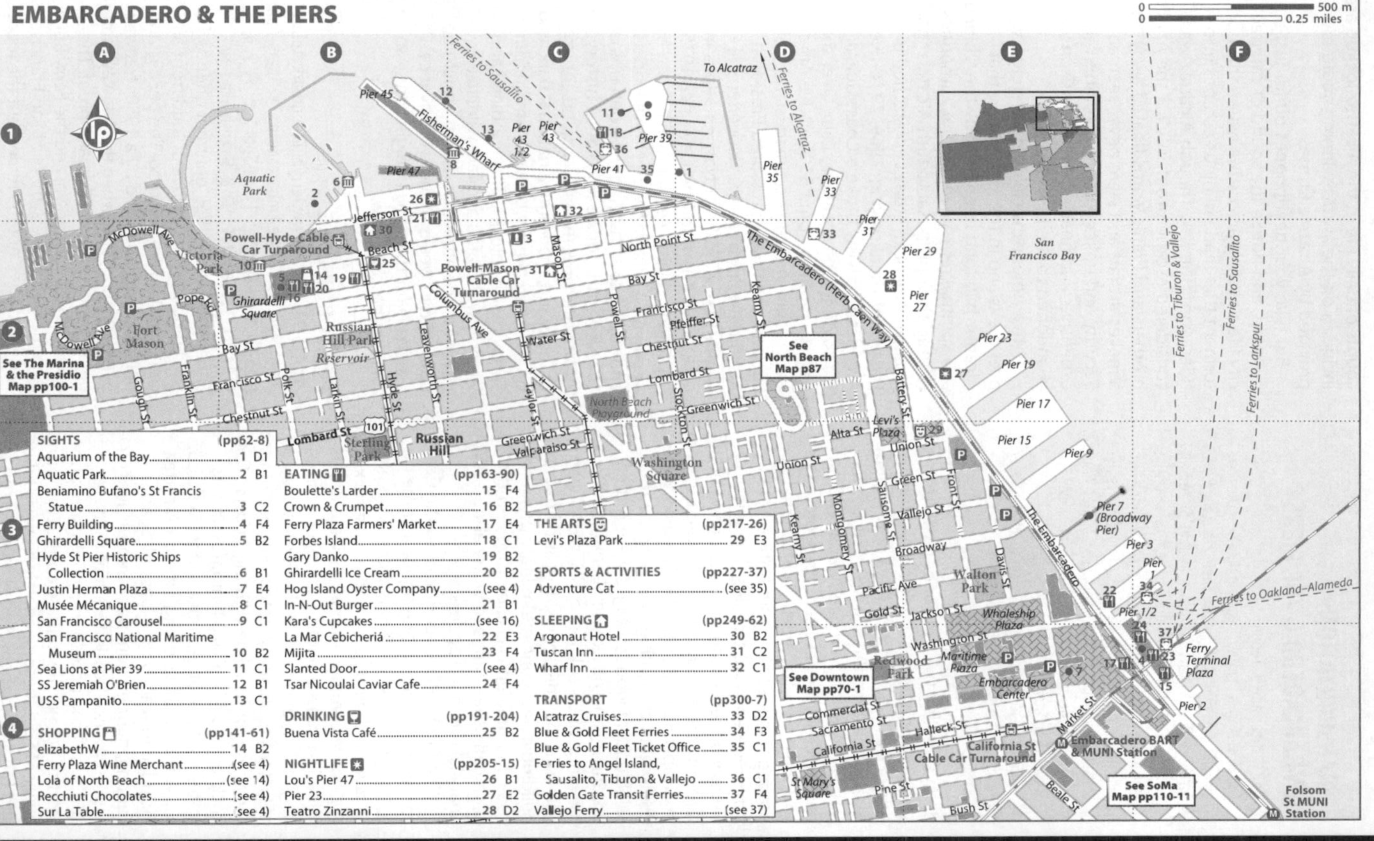
EMBARCADERO & THE PIERS
0 500 m
0 0.25 miles
To Alcatraz
Ferries to Alcatraz
Ferries to Sausalito
Ferries to Tiburon & Vallejo
Ferries to Larkspur
Ferries to Oakland–Alameda
San Francisco Bay
Aquatic Park
Fisherman's Wharf
Pier 45
Pier 47
Pier 43 1/2
Pier 43
Pier 41
Pier 39
Pier 35
Pier 33
Pier 31
Pier 29
Pier 27
Pier 23
Pier 19
Pier 17
Pier 15
Pier 9
Pier 7 (Broadway Pier)
Pier 3
Pier 1
Pier 1/2
Pier 2
Ferry Terminal Plaza
Victoria Park
Fort Mason
Ghirardelli Square
Russian Hill Park
Reservoir
Russian Hill
Sterling Park
North Beach Playground
Washington Square
Levi's Plaza
Walton Park
Whaleship Plaza
Maritime Plaza
Redwood Park
Embarcadero Center
St Mary's Square
Powell-Hyde Cable Car Turnaround
Powell-Mason Cable Car Turnaround
California St Cable Car Turnaround
Embarcadero BART & MUNI Station
Folsom St MUNI Station
The Embarcadero (Herb Caen Way)
The Embarcadero
McDowell Ave
Pope Rd
Jefferson St
Beach St
North Point St
Bay St
Francisco St
Pfeiffer St
Chestnut St
Lombard St
Greenwich St
Valparaiso St
Union St
Green St
Vallejo St
Broadway
Pacific Ave
Jackson St
Gold St
Washington St
Commercial St
Sacramento St
California St
Halleck St
Pine St
Bush St
Market St
Beale St
Alta St
Gough St
Franklin St
Polk St
Larkin St
Hyde St
Leavenworth St
Columbus Ave
Taylor St
Water St
Mason St
Powell St
Stockton St
Kearny St
Montgomery St
Sansome St
Battery St
Front St
Davis St
See The Marina & the Presidio Map pp100-1
See North Beach Map p87
See Downtown Map pp70-1
See SoMa Map pp110-11
SIGHTS (pp62-8)
Aquarium of the Bay 1 D1
Aquatic Park 2 B1
Beniamino Bufano's St Francis Statue 3 C2
Ferry Building 4 F4
Ghirardelli Square 5 B2
Hyde St Pier Historic Ships Collection 6 B1
Justin Herman Plaza 7 E4
Musée Mécanique 8 C1
San Francisco Carousel 9 C1
San Francisco National Maritime Museum 10 B2
Sea Lions at Pier 39 11 C1
SS Jeremiah O'Brien 12 B1
USS Pampanito 13 C1
SHOPPING (pp141-61)
elizabethW 14 B2
Ferry Plaza Wine Merchant (see 4)
Lola of North Beach (see 14)
Recchiuti Chocolates (see 4)
Sur La Table (see 4)
EATING (pp163-90)
Boulette's Larder 15 F4
Crown & Crumpet 16 B2
Ferry Plaza Farmers' Market 17 E4
Forbes Island 18 C1
Gary Danko 19 B2
Ghirardelli Ice Cream 20 B2
Hog Island Oyster Company (see 4)
In-N-Out Burger 21 B1
Kara's Cupcakes (see 16)
La Mar Cebichería 22 E3
Mijita 23 F4
Slanted Door (see 4)
Tsar Nicoulai Caviar Cafe 24 F4
DRINKING (pp191-204)
Buena Vista Café 25 B2
NIGHTLIFE (pp205-15)
Lou's Pier 47 26 B1
Pier 23 27 E2
Teatro Zinzanni 28 D2
THE ARTS (pp217-26)
Levi's Plaza Park 29 E3
SPORTS & ACTIVITIES (pp227-37)
Adventure Cat (see 35)
SLEEPING (pp249-62)
Argonaut Hotel 30 B2
Tuscan Inn 31 C2
Wharf Inn 32 C1
TRANSPORT (pp300-7)
Alcatraz Cruises 33 D2
Blue & Gold Fleet Ferries 34 F3
Blue & Gold Fleet Ticket Office 35 C1
Ferries to Angel Island, Sausalito, Tiburon & Vallejo 36 C1
Golden Gate Transit Ferries 37 F4
Vallejo Ferry (see 37)

TRANSPORTATION: EMBARCADERO & THE PIERS

BART Embarcadero station
Bus Most Market St Muni lines terminate near the Ferry Building. The 49 skirts the north shore along the Piers.
Streetcar F streetcars run down Market St to San Francisco Bay, then follow the northern curve of the Embarcadero to Fisherman's Wharf. The N-Judah line runs underground down Market St, then follows the Embarcadero south to AT&T Park. The T goes from the Embarcadero station past AT&T Park, down 3rd St past Dog Patch.
Parking There are parking lots south of the Ferry Building at Pier 2 and at Embarcadero Center.

de Ayala sailed the *San Carlos* past the 12-acre island he called Isla de Alcatraces (Isle of the Pelicans). In 1859 a new post on Alcatraz became the first US West Coast fort, and soon proved handy as a holding pen for Civil War deserters, insubordinates and those who had been court-martialed. Among the prisoners were Native American scouts and 'unfriendlies,' including 19 Hopis who refused to send their children to government boarding schools where speaking Hopi and practicing their religion were punishable by beatings. By 1902 the four cell blocks of wooden cages were rotting, unsanitary and otherwise ill-equipped for the influx of US soldiers convicted of war crimes in the Philippines. The army began building a new concrete military prison in 1909, but upkeep was expensive and the US soon had other things to worry about: WWI, financial ruin and flappers.

When the 18th Amendment to the Constitution declared selling liquor a crime in 1922, rebellious Jazz Agers weren't prepared to give up their tipple – and gangsters kept the booze coming. Authorities were determined to make a public example of criminal ringleaders, and in 1934 the Federal Bureau of Prisons took over Alcatraz as a prominent showcase for its crime-fighting efforts. 'The Rock' averaged only 264 inmates, but its roster read like an America's Most Wanted list. A-list criminals doing time on Alcatraz included Chicago crime boss Al 'Scarface' Capone, dapper kidnapper George 'Machine Gun' Kelly, hot-headed Harlem mafioso and sometime poet 'Bumpy' Johnson, and Morton Sobell, the military contractor found guilty of Soviet espionage along with Julius and Ethel Rosenberg. Today, first-person accounts of daily life in the Alcatraz lockup are included on the award-winning audio tour provided by Alcatraz Cruises.

But take your headphones off for just a moment, and notice the sound of carefree city life traveling across the water: this is the torment that made perilous escapes into rip tides worth the risk. Though Alcatraz was considered escape-proof, in 1962 the Anglin brothers and Frank Morris floated away on a makeshift raft and were never seen again. Security and upkeep proved prohibitively expensive, and finally the island prison was abandoned to the birds in 1963.

Native Americans claimed sovereignty over the island in the '60s, noting that Alcatraz had long been used by the Ohlone as a spiritual retreat, yet federal authorities refused their proposal to turn Alcatraz into a Native American study center. Then on the eve of Thanksgiving, 1969, 79 Native American activists broke a Coast Guard blockade to enforce their claim. Over the next 19 months, some 5600 Native Americans would visit the occupied island. Public support eventually pressured President Richard Nixon to restore Native territory and strengthen self-rule for Native nations in 1970. Each Thanksgiving Day since 1975, an 'Un-Thanksgiving' ceremony has been held at dawn on Alcatraz, with Native leaders and supporters showing their determination to reverse the course of colonial history.

After the government regained control of the island, it became a national park, and by 1973 had already become a major draw. Today the cell blocks, 'This Is Indian Land' water-tower graffiti and rare wildlife are all part of the attraction. Tickets should be booked two weeks or more in advance – especially for the popular night tour – so plan your escape now.

FERRY BUILDING Map p63

☎ 415-983-8000; www.ferrybuildingmarketplace.com; Market St & the Embarcadero; 🕑 10am-6pm Mon-Fri, 9am-6pm Sat, 11am-5pm Sun; 🚌 2, 6, 7, 9, 14, 21, 31, 66, 71, F; 🚌 & 🚇 Embarcadero

Other towns have their gourmet ghettos, but San Francisco puts its love of food front and center at the Ferry Building. The once-grand port was overshadowed by a 1950s freeway overpass until 1989, when the freeway turned out to be less than earthquake-proof. The overpass was torn down, and the Ferry Building emerged as the symbol of San Francisco's pride and joy – not the ferries, but the food.

Like a grand salute, the Ferry Building's trademark 240ft tower greeted dozens of ferries daily after its inauguration in 1898. But once the Bay Bridge and Golden Gate Bridge provided more convenient ways to cross the bay in the 1930s, ferry traffic subsided. Then the overhead freeway obscured the building's grand facade and car fumes turned it ashen. Only after the 1989 earthquake did city planners come to their senses and notice what they'd been missing: with its grand halls and bay views, this was the perfect place to stop for a bite.

Even before building renovations were complete, the Ferry Plaza Farmers' Market (p169) began operating out front on the sidewalk. While some complain the prices are higher here than at other farmers markets, there's no denying this one offers seasonal, gourmet treats and local specialty foods not found elsewhere. Artisanal goat cheese, fresh-pressed California olive oil, wild boar and organic vegetables soon captured the imagination of SF's professional chefs and semiprofessional eaters.

Today the gourmet action continues indoors, where select local shops sell wild-harvested mushrooms, gold-leaved chocolates, sustainably farmed oysters and caviar from Marin, and other temptations. Standout restaurants provide further reasons to miss that ferry: shaking beef at Slanted Door (p168) and fresh fish tacos at Mijita (p169). For retailers, see p142; for restaurants, check out p168.

You can still catch a ferry here (p302), and on that rare warm, sunny day, it might qualify as a highlight of your visit. Ferries go to Jack London Sq in Oakland (p268) and to Sausalito and Tiburon in Marin County (p280). To get to Napa, hop on the Vallejo ferry here and transfer to the Napa Valley Vine bus at the Vallejo terminal.

JUSTIN HERMAN PLAZA Map p63

Market St & the Embarcadero; 🚌 2, 6, 7, 9, 14, 21, 31, 32, 66, 71, F; 🚌 & 🚆 Embarcadero

The plaza across from the Ferry Building may not be much to look at – what's Vaillancourt Fountain supposed to be, anyway, a cubist large intestine? – but for years Justin Herman has been popular with lunchtime concert-goers, Critical Mass protesters, ice-skaters at the outdoor rink in winter, and internet daters screening their dates from behind the fountain's wall of water.

BENIAMINO BUFANO'S ST FRANCIS STATUE Map p63

cnr Taylor & Beach Sts; 🚌 15, 37, 49, F

A winsome statue of SF's favorite saint by its favorite sculptor – so what's it doing in a parking lot? Technically this was only a model for Bufano's massive black granite St Francis in Grace Cathedral, but there's something so SF about this version with exposed toes hanging ten like a surfer. When looking for wharfside parking, divine guidance is mighty handy.

FISHERMAN'S WHARF

Where once Italian fishermen in Genoese feluccas trapped unsuspecting sealife, San Francisco traps unwitting tourists. Hapless hordes trawl the boardwalks here shivering in their 'I escaped from Alcatraz' T-shirts, attempting to walk off meals of gloppy clam chowder served in sourdough bread bowls – until a notorious 'Bush Man' of Pier 39 lurking behind some eucalyptus branches jumps out, roars 'Ugga bugga!,' startles unsuspecting passersby into dropping their soup, then hits them up for change. On Fisherman's Wharf, it's better to come prepared: hit specific attractions before heading to the Ferry Building for far more inventive, digestible seafood.

Sea lions laze the day away sunbathing and posing for photo ops on Pier 39, where an aquarium, carousel and carnival-style attractions keep little kids wide-eyed. Many of the ships you'll see docked on Pier 45 are actually museums, giving naval-gazers a chance to check out tall ships, submarines and WWII warships. Bring your quarters to consult the spooky mechanical fortune tellers and save the world from space invaders at Musée Mécanique (p66). Most Fisherman's Wharf sights worth seeing are on the Embarcadero or Jefferson St.

The wharf is on the city's northern shore, where Columbus Ave and the Embarcadero converge, with North Beach to the south. Immediately to the west is Ghirardelli Square, a former chocolate factory that's currently being reinvented with boutiques, sweet shops, a tearoom and wine-tasting rooms. To heed the siren call of Marina boutiques and the natural wonders of the Presidio beyond, head west on Bay St. For dinner, head down the Embarcadero to the Ferry Building (p168), or splash out for sumptuous multicourse meals at nearby Gary Danko (p167).

SEA LIONS AT PIER 39 Map p63

California Welcome Center 415-981-1280; www.pier39.com; Pier 39, Beach St & the Embarcadero; Jan-Jul & whenever else they feel like it; 15, 37, 49, F

Beach bums took over San Francisco's most coveted waterfront real estate in 1990 and have been making a public display of themselves ever since, canoodling, belching, scratching their naked backsides and gleefully shoving one another off the docks. Naturally these unkempt squatters became San Francisco's favorite mascots, and since California law requires boats to make way for marine mammals, yacht owners have to relinquish valuable slips to accommodate as many as 1300 sea lions who 'haul out' onto the docks between January and July, and whenever else they feel like sunbathing.

MUSÉE MÉCANIQUE Map p63

415-346-2000; www.museemechanique.org; Shed A, Pier 45; admission free; 10am-7pm Mon-Fri, to 8pm Sat, Sun & holidays; 47, F; Powell-Mason, Powell-Hyde;

Sinister, freckle-faced Laughing Sal has creeped out kiddies for over a hundred years, but don't let this manic mannequin deter you from what is the best arcade west of Coney Island. A few quarters lets you start bar brawls in coin-operated Wild West saloons, peep at belly dancers through a vintage Mutoscope, feed the insatiable Ms Pac-Man and get your fortune told by an eerily lifelike wooden swami.

USS PAMPANITO Map p63

415-775-1943; www.maritime.org/pamphome.htm; Pier 45; adult/child under 6yr/child over 6yr/senior/family (2 adults, 4 children) $9/free/4/5/20; 9am-6pm Sun-Thu, to 8pm Fri & Sat Oct 14-May 23, 9am-8pm Thu-Tue, to 6pm Wed May 24-Oct 13; 19, 32, F; Powell-Hyde

Talk about a survivor: this WWII-era US Navy submarine completed six wartime patrols, sunk six Japanese ships (including two carrying British and Australian POWs), battled three others and lived to tell the tale. Submariners' stories of tense moments in underwater stealth mode will have you holding your breath – caution claustrophobics – and all those cool brass knobs and mysterious hydraulic valves make 21st-century technology seem way overrated.

AQUARIUM OF THE BAY Map p63

415-623-5300, 888-732-3483; www.aquariumofthebay.com; Pier 39; adult/senior & child $15.95/8; 9am-8pm daily summer, 10am-6pm Mon-Fri, to 7pm Sat & Sun rest of year; 49, F;

Watch sharks circle overhead, manta rays skate shyly by and seaweed sway all around, as conveyer belts guide you through glass tubes right into the bay. Not for the claustrophobic, perhaps, but the thrilling fish-eye view of San Francisco leaves kids and parents wide-eyed and humming *Little Mermaid* tunes.

HYDE STREET PIER HISTORIC SHIPS COLLECTION Map p63

415-561-7100; www.nps.gov/safr; Pier 45, 499 Jefferson St at Hyde St; adult/child under 16yr $5/free; 9:30am-5pm Oct-May, to 7pm Jun-Sep; 19, 32, F; Powell-Hyde

'Aye, she's a beauty,' you'll growl like a true salty dog once you've visited any of the four historic Bay Area boats currently open as museums along Hyde St Pier – especially elegant 1891 schooner *Alma* and the steamboat *Eureka,* the world's largest ferry c 1890. For more mariner action, check out the toylike, steam-powered paddle-wheel tugboat *Eppleton Hall* and the magnificent triple-masted, iron-hulled *Balclutha,* an 1886 British vessel that brought coal to San Francisco and took grain back to Europe via the dreaded Cape Horn.

SS JEREMIAH O'BRIEN Map p63

415-544-0100; www.ssjeremiahobrien.com; Pier 45; adult/child under 6yr/child 6-14yr/senior $8/free/4/5; 9am-4pm; 19, F; Powell-Hyde

Hard to believe this 10,000-ton beauty was turned out by San Francisco's ship workers in under eight weeks, and harder still to imagine how she dodged U-boats on a mission delivering supplies to Allied forces on D-Day. Of 2,710 Liberty Ships launched during WWII, this is the only one still fully operational. For steamy piston-on-piston, 2700HP action, visit during 'steaming weekends' (usually the third weekend of each month) or check the website for upcoming four-hour cruises.

SAN FRANCISCO CAROUSEL Map p63

California Welcome Center 415-981-1280; www.pier39.com; Pier 39, Beach St & the Embarcadero; admission $3; 11am-7pm; F;

Your chariot awaits to whisk you and the kiddies past the Golden Gate Bridge, Alcatraz and other SF landmarks hand-painted on this Italian carousel twinkling with 1800 lights at the bayside end of Pier 39. The old-timey organ carnival music is loud enough to drown out the inevitable tiny tot clinging for dear life to a high-stepping horsey.

SAN FRANCISCO NATIONAL MARITIME MUSEUM Map p63

☎ 415-561-7000; www.maritime.org; 900 Beach St; 🚌 19, 49; 🚋 Powell-Hyde

This quirky museum shaped like a streamlined art deco luxury liner was initially a casino and public bathhouse when built by the Depression-era Works Project Administration (WPA) in 1939. The museum is currently closed while its interior is restored to ship-shape, but you can still appreciate the exterior decor: entryway slate carvings by celebrated African American artist Sargent Johnson, and toad and seal sculptures glimpsed on the back veranda by SF's own Beniamino Bufano.

GHIRARDELLI SQUARE Map p63

☎ 415-775-5500; www.ghirardellisq.com; 900 North Point St; 🕑 10am-9pm daily summer, 10am-9pm Mon-Sat, to 6pm Sun rest of year; 🚌 19, 49; 🚋 Powell-Hyde; ♿

Willy Wonka would tip his hat to Domingo Ghirardelli (*gear*-ar-deli), whose business became the West's largest chocolate factory in 1893. After the company moved to the East Bay, two sweet-talking developers reinvented the factory as a mall and landmark ice-cream parlor in 1964. Today, the square is entering its third incarnation as a boutique luxury timeshare/spa complex with wine-tasting rooms – care for a massage and some merlot with your Ghirardelli chocolate sundae? The square is already looking spiffy, with local boutiques such as elizabethW (p142) and a branch of Lola of North Beach (p147), along with the charming tearoom Crown & Crumpet (p167) and tempting branch of Kara's Cupcakes (p178).

AQUATIC PARK Map p63

Hyde St; 🚌 19, 49; 🚋 Powell-Hyde

Eccentricity along Fisherman's Wharf is mostly staged, but here it's the real deal: extreme swimmers dive from the concrete beachfront into the blood-curdling waters of the bay in winter, weirdos mumble conspiracy theories on the grassy knoll of panoramic Victoria Park, and wistful tycoons stare off into the distance and contemplate sailing far away from their Blackberries.

BARBARY COAST Walking Tour

1 Hyde St Pier Historic Ships Collection (opposite) Start your tour of SF's waterfront as a Gold Rush sailor pulling into port would have seen it: from the deck of a 19th-century ship.

2 Sea Lions (opposite) As you cover the waterfront, take a detour by Pier 39 to watch sea lions take over the yacht marina, canoodling and belching in public like sailors.

3 Levi's Plaza This pleasant plaza would've been muddy sludge 150 years ago, when Levi Strauss began making his tough denim pants in San Francisco. Without his copper-riveted pockets, lucky miners would've had nowhere to stash their gold nuggets – and Barbary Coast saloon-keepers would've fleeced them that much faster.

4 Old Ship Saloon Instead of abandoning the good ship *Arkansas* in 1851, enterprising Joseph Anthony built a bar around it at 298 Pacific Ave. Sailors drank here at their own risk, knowing this bar was notorious for drugging customers, who woke up miles from shore, shanghaied into service on a crew.

5 Gold St Prospectors who struck it rich in the Gold Rush headed directly to this brick-lined alleyway, where finds were evaluated at the assay office. Thieves, swindlers and pimps were never far behind.

6 Barbary Coast Bohemia When the block of buildings at 708–720 Montgomery St was rebuilt after the 1906 fire, it became even more notorious than during its Barbary Coast days.

WALK FACTS

Start Hyde St Pier Historic Ships Collection
End Ferry Building
Distance Three miles
Time Three hours, not including photo-op stops
Exertion Easy
Fuel stop Slanted Door

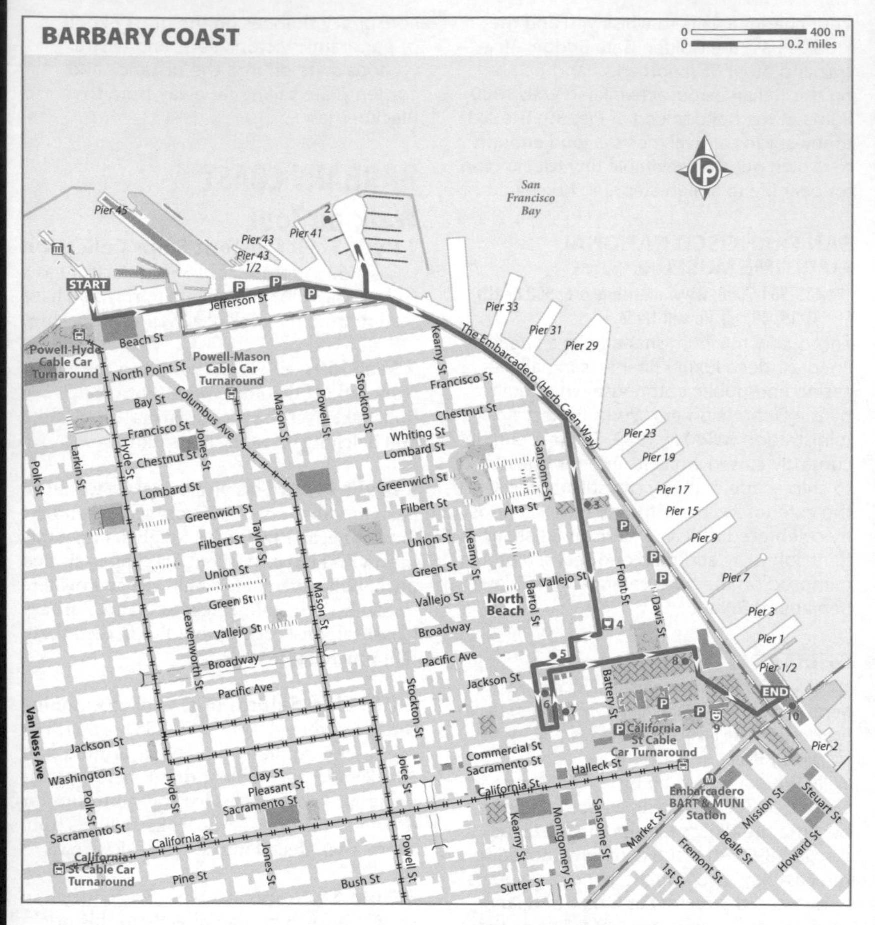

In 1925, artists moved into studios here and stayed for 35 years; Diego Rivera worked here when he was in town. Housed at 710 Montgomery St was the legendary Black Cat bar, which won a landmark 1951 California Supreme Court case that allowed gays to congregate in bars.

7 Transamerica Redwood Park (p71) Alongside the distinguishing feature of SF's skyline is a grove of 80 redwood trees, where occasional free concerts are held and there are kitschy/creepy bronze statues of cackling children and frogs leaping from lily pads in the fountain.

8 Whaleship Plaza Ships left to rot by prospecting sailors came in handy to shore up SF's waterfront; at least two whaling ships are underfoot here.

9 Justin Herman Plaza (p65) Daredevil skaters, crafts vendors and protesters do their best to distract visitors from a fountain that looks like the site of an industrial accident.

10 Ferry Building (p64) The long-vacant 1898 ferry hub was gutted and spiffed up in 2001 to become a gourmet-food emporium and upscale farmers market, with gourmet stalls and acclaimed restaurants such as **Slanted Door** (p168).

DOWNTOWN

Drinking p194; Eating p169; Shopping p143; Sleeping p251

Like a gold miner's grin, Downtown is full of character but a little crooked. Where once sailors abandoned their ships in search of gold, stock brokers now speculate on Asian markets and the US dollar. The neighborhood that once parted new arrivals from their gold nuggets with hundreds of saloons, gambling dens and waterfront brothels has mostly lost its con-artist touch, except for friendly bets at a few sports bars and savvy junior copywriters cadging drinks at champagne lounges. But the biggest scammers are hotels that boast of a location in 'the theater district,' and on arrival turn out to be squalid residential affairs, conveniently located near methadone clinics and massage parlors. To tell the real boutique hotels from the pretenders, consult p251.

The seductive spirit of yore is kept alive in designer showrooms and art galleries that will tempt the last dollar out of you. Otherwise, despite its reputation as a shopping paradise, Downtown mostly offers the usual chains and a few department stores. Once named for the ladies of the night who worked the block, Maiden Lane has since gone upscale and plays hostess to the likes of Chanel and Marc Jacobs.

Despite all the drinking and dining establishments in the area, only a few tempt San Franciscans to stay Downtown after work. Fleur de Lys (p171) and Aqua (p169) are among the few restaurants that rise to locals' exacting standards for inventiveness – for culinary kicks, most people instead head to SoMa. Locals don't frequent Downtown hotel bars, but when relatives are visiting they'll make an exception for the swanky stylings of the Clock Bar (p194) or the Starlight Room (p215).

top picks

DOWNTOWN

- Galleries at 49 Geary (p73) and 77 Geary (p73)
- Sunday gospel services at Glide Memorial (p74)
- Cable cars (p74)
- Market St flatirons (p74)
- St Francis Hotel Glass Elevators (p74)

Downtown San Francisco may have lost its bite since the Barbary Coast days, but it's still best admired from atop Russian or Nob Hills or looking backwards from Crissy Field (p105). The irregular-shaped buildings stick out at odd angles, lorded over by the pointy Transamerica Pyramid (p71).

Running diagonally through San Francisco's tidy east–west grid is Market St, creating angular intersections and a series of V-shaped flatiron buildings. North of Market between 4th and 5th Sts is the Powell St cable-car turnaround, often surrounded by a religious type warning against fornication, and squadrons of competitive chess players and tap dancers. Follow Powell St two blocks north to Union Square for department stores and grand hotels. Along the southern edge of Union Square runs Geary St, which heads east to galleries and west to theaters and more dubious amusements. Southwest of Union Square is the Tenderloin. The Financial District starts east at Kearny and Market Sts, and runs east to the bay and north to the Transamerica Pyramid. East of Columbus Ave and south of Broadway is Jackson Square, where once many a sailor's lucky streak ended.

FINANCIAL DISTRICT

The Financial District may not loom as large as Wall Street, but until the late 1990s this was the historic financial capital of the American West, dating back to the mid-19th century. Los Angeles has lately supplanted San Francisco for high finance, but Montgomery St remains home to big-name brokerage houses and banks.

The Mex-deco, pseudo-Mayan banking buildings along Sansome St near Sacramento St are monuments to money-making enterprises that have become ever more abstract. Once fortunes were made in gold nuggets, then came shipping and railroad holdings, then (ever so briefly) dot-com stock certificates, and now digital readouts of fluctuations in technology and Asian markets.

By day the hustle is palpable. Taxis discharge briefcase-toting venture capitalists, narrowly missing kamikaze bike-messengers, who swerve dangerously near hot-coffee-bearing stockbrokers.

In the Financial District you'll spot the last people in San Francisco who actually wear suits to work, other than restaurant hosts, hoteliers and gangsters.

By 5pm the sidewalks are filled with power-brokers loosening ties and lining up for express buses, eager to distance themselves from work. By 7pm, the Financial District abruptly becomes a ghost town.

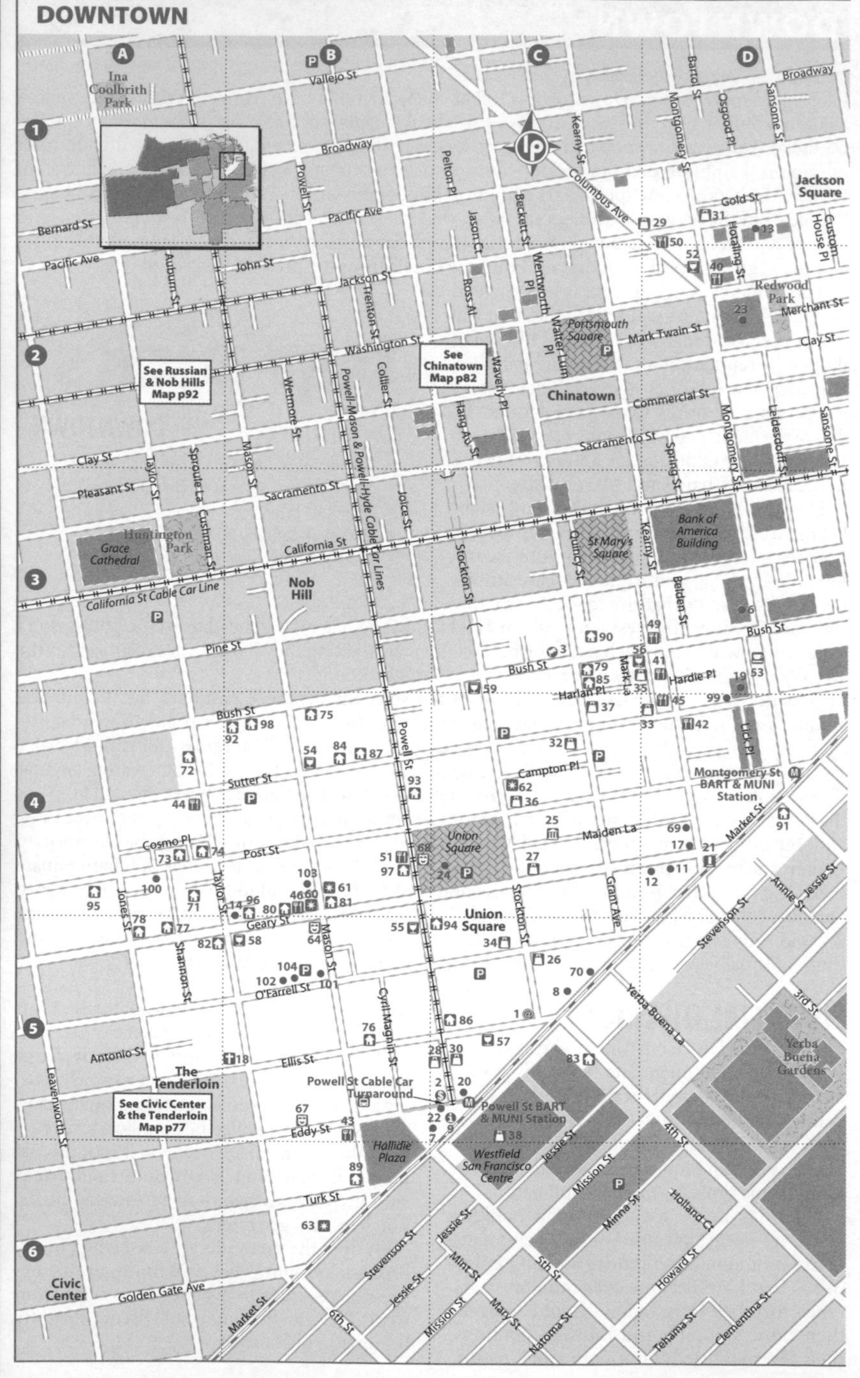
DOWNTOWN
A
B
C
D
1
2
3
4
5
6
Ina Coolbrith Park
Vallejo St
Broadway
Bartol St
Montgomery St
Osgood Pl
Sansome St
Kearny St
Powell St
Pelton Pl
Columbus Ave
Jackson Square
Gold St
Bernard St
Pacific Ave
Jason Ct
Beckett St
Hotaling St
Custom House Pl
John St
Jackson St
Trenton St
Ross Al
Wentworth Pl
Waverly Pl
Walter Lum Pl
Redwood Park
Merchant St
Auburn St
Portsmouth Square
Mark Twain St
Clay St
Washington St
See Chinatown Map p82
See Russian & Nob Hills Map p92
Chinatown
Commercial St
Wetmore St
Powell-Mason & Powell-Hyde Cable Car Lines
Collier St
Hang Ah St
Leidesdorff St
Sacramento St
Spring St
Mason St
Taylor St
Sproule La
Cushman St
Pleasant St
Joice St
Huntington Park
Grace Cathedral
California St
Stockton St
Quincy St
St Mary's Square
Bank of America Building
Nob Hill
California St Cable Car Line
Belden St
Pine St
Bush St
Mark La
Hardie Pl
Harlan Pl
Lick Pl
Sutter St
Campton Pl
Montgomery St BART & MUNI Station
Maiden La
Market St
Cosmo Pl
Post St
Union Square
Grant Ave
Jones St
Geary St
Stevenson St
Annie St
Jessie St
Shannon St
O'Farrell St
Yerba Buena La
3rd St
Cyril Magnin St
Antonio St
Ellis St
The Tenderloin
Powell St Cable Car Turnaround
Powell St BART & MUNI Station
Yerba Buena Gardens
Leavenworth St
See Civic Center & the Tenderloin Map p77
Eddy St
Hallidie Plaza
Westfield San Francisco Centre
4th St
Mission St
Turk St
Minna St
Holland Ct
Civic Center
Golden Gate Ave
6th St
Mint St
Mary St
5th St
Natoma St
Howard St
Tehama St
Clementina St

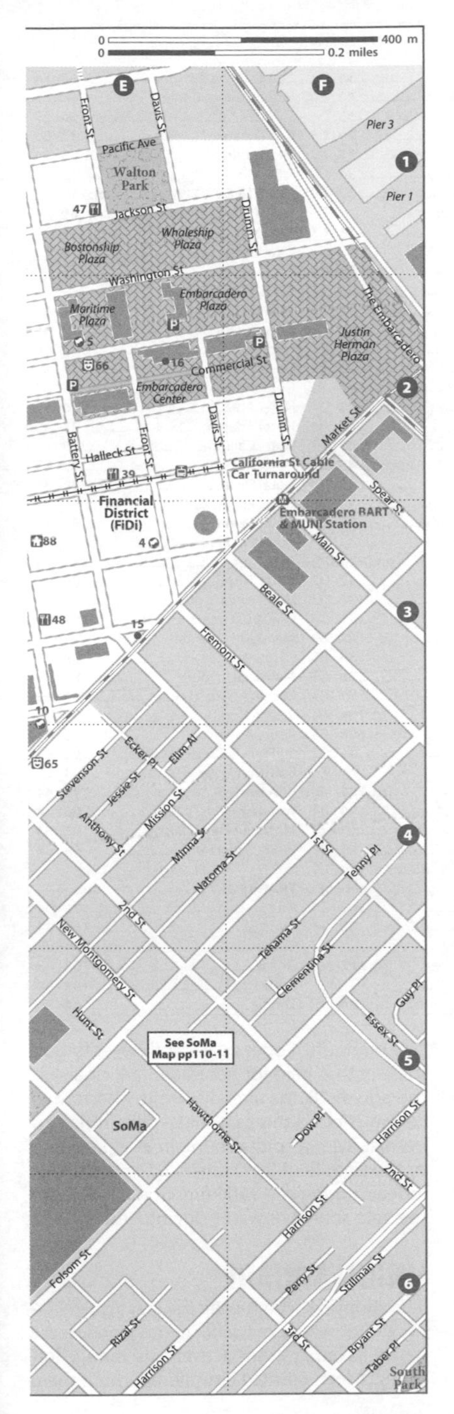

TRANSAMERICA PYRAMID & REDWOOD PARK Map pp70–1

600 Montgomery St; admission free; 9am-6pm Mon-Fri; 1, 15, 41; & Embarcadero

The defining feature of San Francisco's skyline was built during the Jet Age, atop the wreck of a whaling ship abandoned in the 1849 Gold Rush, on the site of a saloon frequented by Mark Twain and the newspaper office where Sun Yat-sen drafted his Proclamation of the Republic of China.

Architect William Pereira maximized light in the narrow streets below with his pyramid design, but even before its 1972 inauguration his pointy office tower was derided as 'Pereira's Prick.' Critics claimed Pereira's background in Hollywood special effects was too apparent in the 853ft streamlined tower, which looked ready for blastoff.

But others pointed out that the quirky landmark was perfectly suited to SF, and even those who still love to hate the building adore Redwood Park, the half-acre stand of redwood trees at its base.

Another redeeming feature was the view – note the past tense. Since September 11, the viewing platform at the tip of the pyramid has been closed to visitors 'for security reasons.' But if you're determined to get virtually queasy witnessing the slight half-foot sway at the top of the Pyramid in a strong wind, you can do so by visiting the virtual observation deck.

EMBARCADERO CENTER Map pp70–1

415-772-0700; www.embarcaderocenter.com; Sacramento St; admission free; 10am-5pm; 1; & Embarcadero; California

If this really is San Francisco's answer to Lincoln Center, that's one round for New York. These skyscrapers joined by an overhead walkway form an urban sprawl of a mall, and the upper office floors have nothing to recommend them beyond the crowd-pleasing Embarcadero Center Cinema (p221), the indie movie multiplex whose concessions counter is consistently rated the city's best.

PALACE HOTEL Map pp70–1

415-512-1111, 800-325-3535; www.sfpalace.com; 2 New Montgomery St; & Montgomery St

The city's most storied hotel opened in 1875, and was gutted during the 1906 earthquake and fire. Opera star Enrico Caruso was staying here that day, and reportedly ran into the street, swearing he'd never return to

DOWNTOWN (pp70-1)

INFORMATION

Apple Store 1 C5
Bank of America 2 C5
French Consulate 3 C3
Irish Consulate 4 E3
New Zealand Consulate 5 E2
San Francisco Chamber of Commerce 6 D3
San Francisco Convention & Visitors Bureau 7 C5
San Francisco School of Bartending 8 C5
San Francisco Visitor Information Center 9 C5
UK Consulate 10 E3
US Post Office .... (see 34)

SIGHTS (pp69-75)

49 Geary 11 D4
77 Geary 12 D4
AP Hotaling Warehouse 13 D1
Bohemian Club 14 B4
Crown Zellerbach Building 15 E3
Embarcadero Center 16 E2
Gallery Paule Anglim 17 D4
Glide Memorial United Methodist Church 18 B5
Hallidie Building 19 D3
James Flood Building 20 C5
Lotta's Fountain 21 D4
Palace Hotel .... (see 91)
Powell St Cable Car Turnaround 22 C5
Transamerica Pyramid & Redwood Park 23 D2
Union Square 24 C4
Westin St Francis Hotel Glass Elevators .... (see 97)
Xanadu Gallery: Folk Art International 25 C4

SHOPPING (pp141-61)

Barneys 26 C5
Britex Fabrics 27 C4
DSW 28 C5
Eden & Eden 29 D1
Folk Art International .... (see 25)
H&M 30 C5
Japonesque 31 D1
Le Sanctuaire 32 C4
Loehmann's 33 D4
Macy's 34 C5
Margaret O'Leary 35 C3
Original Levi's Store 36 C4
Shotwell Boutique 37 C4
Westfield San Francisco Centre 38 C5

EATING (pp163-90)

Aqua 39 E2
Bocadillos 40 D2
Boxed Foods 41 D3
Bread and Cocoa 42 D4
farmerbrown 43 B5
Fleur de Lys 44 A4
Gitane 45 D4
Katana-ya 46 B4
Kokkari 47 E1
Mixt Greens 48 E3
Muracci's Curry 49 D3
Pickles 50 D1
Restaurant Michael Mina 51 B4

DRINKING (pp191-204)

Bubble Lounge 52 D2
Caffe Amici 53 D3
Cantina 54 B4
Clock Bar .... (see 97)
Gold Dust Lounge 55 B5
Irish Bank 56 C3
John's Grill 57 C5
Pied Piper Bar .... (see 91)
Redwood Room 58 B5
Tunnel Top Bar 59 C3

NIGHTLIFE (pp205-15)

Biscuits & Blues 60 B4
Punch Line .... (see 5)
Ruby Skye 61 B4
Starlight Room .... (see 93)
TIX Bay Area .... (see 68)
Vessel 62 C4
Warfield 63 B6

THE ARTS (pp217-26)

American Conservatory Theater 64 B5
Commonwealth Club 65 E4
Embarcadero Center Cinema 66 E2
Exit Theater 67 B5
TIX Bay Area 68 B4

SPORTS & ACTIVITIES (pp227-37)

Bella Pelle Skin Studio 69 D4
True Massage & Wellness 70 C5

SLEEPING (pp249-62)

Adelaide Hostel 71 A4
Amsterdam Hotel 72 A4
Andrews Hotel 73 A4
Dakota Hotel 74 A4
Golden Gate Hotel 75 B4
Hotel Abri 76 B5
Hotel Adagio 77 A5
Hotel California 78 A5
Hotel des Arts 79 C3
Hotel Diva 80 B4
Hotel Frank 81 B4
Hotel Monaco 82 A5
Hotel Palomar 83 C5
Hotel Rex 84 B4
Hotel Triton 85 C3
Hotel Union Square 86 C5
Larkspur Hotel 87 B4
Mandarin Oriental Hotel 88 E3
Metropolis Hotel 89 B6
Orchard Garden Hotel 90 C3
Palace Hotel 91 D4
Petite Auberge 92 B4
Sir Francis Drake Hotel 93 B4
Stratford Hotel 94 C5
USA Hostels 95 A4
Warwick Regis 96 B4
Westin St Francis Hotel 97 B4
White Swan Inn 98 B4

TRANSPORT (pp300-7)

AAA 99 D4
Avis 100 A4
Budget 101 B5
Dollar 102 B5
Hertz 103 B4
Thrifty 104 B5

San Francisco. The current building opened in 1909. Ten years later, Woodrow Wilson gave his League of Nations speech here, and in 1923 US President Warren G Harding died upstairs. Visit the lobby by day to see the opulent Garden Court and its luminous stained-glass domed ceiling, then pop into the Pied Piper Bar (p195) to see Maxfield Parrish's mural of the Pied Piper.

LOTTA'S FOUNTAIN Map pp70–1

Market St at Kearny St; 5, 6, 7, 15, 21, 31, 38, 71, F; & Montgomery St

Lotta Crabtree made a killing as San Francisco's diminutive opera diva, and never forgot the city that paid for her trademark cigars. At the age of 28, the already-wealthy performer commissioned this cast-metal pillar thrice her size with a spigot fountain as a present to the people of San Francisco – a useful gift indeed during the 1906 fire, when it became the sole source of water Downtown.

UNION SQUARE

The shoppers who throng the area usually ignore Union Square itself, and no wonder: the newly paved grounds actively discourage loitering. Mean-spirited city planners built them that way lest visitors get too comfortable and forget that the unifying theme of Union Square is shopping – the pro-Union Civil War rallies that gave the plaza its name are long forgotten. Now the 1850-plaza-turned-1950s-patio sits atop a parking garage, bordered by chain hotels and department stores, and bedizened with a few gold-, silver- and bronze-clad mimes working their decades-old 'living statues' schtick.

But perch awhile on a skinny bench or grab a coveted seat at the cafe in the square, and you'll find that people-watching is what separates San Francisco from other cities. Theater-goers debate the merits of the latest Tom Stoppard and David Mamet productions, attempting to hear each other over drummers banging on buckets. Down Geary St, gallerists gingerly load bubble-wrapped sculptures into waiting hybrid SUVs. Nob Hill society dames in dark glasses duck into Maiden Lane spas for facials, or into Sutter St doctors' offices for Botox, while giddy teens and their worn-out parents shop for school clothes and prom dresses at Macy's and the behemoth Westfield San Francisco Centre further down 4th St.

49 GEARY Map pp70–1

☎ San Francisco Art Dealers Association 415-788-9818; www.sfada.com; 49 Geary St; admission free; galleries 10:30am-5:30pm Tue-Fri, 11am-5pm Sat; 5, 6, 7, 15, 21, 31, 38, 71, F, J, K, L, M, N; & Montgomery St

Pity collectors silently nibbling endive in austere Chelsea galleries – at 49 Geary, openings mean unexpected art, goldfish-shaped crackers and outspoken crowds. Four floors of galleries feature standout international and local works including eclectic, eye-popping photography ranging from the 19th to 21st centuries at Fraenkel Gallery to sculptor Seth Koen's crocheted minimalist pieces at Gregory Lind. Beat the crowds on weekdays for quieter contemplation. (For top gallery picks, see the boxed text, p75.)

TRANSPORTATION: DOWNTOWN

BART Montgomery St station serves the Financial District; Powell St serves Union Square.

Bus Market St Muni lines serve Downtown, as does the 38 Geary bus.

Cable car All lines run through Downtown. The Powell St lines link Union Square to Chinatown, North Beach, Russian Hill and Fisherman's Wharf. The California St line links the Financial District with Nob Hill.

Metro The J, K, L, M and N metro lines run under Market St.

Streetcar F streetcars run above Market St.

Parking Street parking is difficult. The lot at Stockton and Sutter Sts is convenient to the Financial District and Union Square. The lot at 5th and Mission Sts is convenient to Union Square.

77 GEARY Map pp70–1

77 Geary St; admission free; 10:30am-5:30pm Tue-Fri, 11am-5pm Sat; 5, 6, 7, 15, 21, 31, 38, 71, F, J, K, L, M, N; & Montgomery St

The most intriguing art usually appears in what looks like the wrong place, and 77 Geary's unmarked entryway is no exception. Get seduced on the mezzanine by the minimalism of Patricia Sweetow Gallery (www.patriciasweetowgallery.com) and shaken up on the 2nd floor by the political art of Togonon Gallery (www.togonongallery.com). For beauty with brains, see Marx & Zavattero (www.marxzav.com) next door for David Hevel's neo-baroque, middle-America-meets-Hollywood taxidermy sculptures and Paul Mullins' tragic-comic exploration of rural contentment. Sensitive meets sensational at Rena Bransten Gallery (www.renabranstengallery.com), featuring shows such as Hung Liu's mirage-like portraits of found ancestors, and collaged stills from 'unwatchable' movies by a man who should know: *Polyester* cult sensation John Waters.

GALLERY PAULE ANGLIM Map pp70–1

☎ 415-433-2710; www.gallerypauleanglim.com; 14 Geary St; admission free; 10am-5:30pm Tue-Fri, to 5pm Sat; 5, 6, 7, 15, 21, 31, 38, 71, F, J, K, L, M, N; & Montgomery St

Here you'll find marquee names like Tony Oursler, whose video projections of distorted faces grumble and squeak in the corner. But works by local upstarts threaten to steal the show, including Ala Ebtekar's paintings of soldiers and storm clouds gathering on ancient Iranian prayer scriptures, and Bull Miletic's video views of San Francisco from the perspective of a flitting butterfly.

UNION SQUARE Map pp70–1

intersection of Geary, Powell, Post & Stockton Sts; 5, 6, 7, 21, 31, 38, 71, F, J, K, L, M, N; & Powell St; Powell-Mason, Powell-Hyde

Louis Vuitton is more top-of-mind than the Emancipation Proclamation, but this plaza, bordered by brand-name retailers, was named after pro-Union Civil War rallies held here 150 years ago. A misguided renovation paved the place and installed benches narrow enough to keep junkies from nodding off, turning this once-lovely park into a prison exercise yard. Redeeming features include Emporio Rulli Caffè, the half-price theater-ticket booth (see p225) and stellar people-watching.

GLIDE MEMORIAL UNITED METHODIST CHURCH Map pp70–1

415-674-6090; www.glide.org; 330 Ellis St; celebrations 9am & 11am Sun; 27, 31, 38, F, J, K, L, M, N; & Powell St

'Go ahead!' shouts the lady in the wheelchair as the rainbow-robed ex-con closes his eyes to hit a high note. The 100-member Glide gospel choir is kicking off another Sunday celebration, and the welcome is warm for whoever walks (or rolls) through the door – the 1500-plus congregation includes gays, lesbians, transsexuals, single-parent families and many who'd once lost all faith in faith. After the celebration ends, the radical Methodist congregation keeps the inspiration coming, providing a million free meals a year and housing for 52 formerly homeless families – now that's hitting a high note.

POWELL STREET CABLE-CAR TURNAROUND Map pp70–1

cnr Powell & Market Sts; & Powell St;

'Wire-rope railway' was a name that didn't inspire confidence in Andrew Hallidie's invention in the 1870s, when crowds steered clear of his rickety wooden trolleys on their early downhill runs. More than a century later, the two cable-car lines from this terminus seem more like carnival rides than commuter transport – and therein lies the appeal.

Pause for a moment at Powell and Market Sts, and you'll notice cable-car operators leaping out, getting a good grip on the trolley and slooowly turning it around by hand on a revolving wooden platform. As technology goes, this seems pretty iffy. Cable cars can't go in reverse, emit labored mechanical grunts on uphill climbs and require burly brakemen and bionic brakewomen to lean hard on the handbrake to keep from careening down Nob Hill at alarming speed.

But SF has always been a town of risk-takers, and locals casually leap on and keep their balance like pro surfers – you can tell SF novices from their white knuckles and death grips on slippery wooden benches.

WESTIN ST FRANCIS HOTEL GLASS ELEVATORS Map pp70–1

415-397-7000; www.westin.com; 335 Powell St; Powell-Mason, Powell-Hyde;

For a bird's-eye view of Union Square, head for the front desk (in the new building), find the glass-walled tower elevators in the corner and soar 32 stories high for drop-dead vistas. Shhh! Don't tell 'em we told you.

BOHEMIAN CLUB Map pp70–1

415-884-2400; 624 Taylor St; 2, 3, 4, 27; Powell-Mason, Powell-Hyde

The most storied, secretive club in all San Francisco was founded in the 19th century by bona fide bohemians, but they couldn't afford the upkeep and allowed the ultra-rich to join. Now the roster lists an odd mix of power elite and famous artists: apparently both George W Bush and Bob Weir are current members. On the Post St side of the club's ivy-covered brick wall, look for the plaque honoring Gold Rush–era author Bret Harte, which depicts characters from his works. On the extreme right is 'The Heathen Chinee.' It's not a racist attack – quite the opposite – but a reference to the eponymous 1870 satirical poem Harte wrote *mocking* anti-Chinese sentiment in Northern

SF'S SEE-THROUGH BUILDINGS

Market St cuts a diagonal across San Francisco's tidy east–west street grid, leaving both flanks of four attractive, triangular flatiron buildings exposed to view. Among the XXX cinemas surrounding Golden Gate Ave, Taylor and Market Sts, you'll find the lacy, white flatiron featured as broody Brad Pitt's apartment in the film *Interview with a Vampire*. On a more respectable block above the Powell St cable-car turnaround is the stone-cold silver fox known as James Flood Building (opposite), a flinty character that has seen it all: fire, earthquakes and the Gap's attempts to bring back bell bottoms at its ground-floor flagship store. Flood's opulent cousin is the 1908 Phelan at 760 Market St, where the ground floor offers a glimpse of people making online love connections on the display computers at CompUSA. That adorable little slip of a building on the block at 540 Market St is the 1913 Flatiron Building, whose sunny disposition outshines all the overwrought bank buildings along nearby Sansome St.

ART FOR FOGGY DAYS

When clouds swallow the Transamerica Pyramid, don't despair: there are indoor sights galore, packed inside galleries within a few blocks of each other – and admission is free. Hop the elevator at 49 Geary (p73) to the top floor, and work your way down four floors of contemporary art galleries. Look for these highlights:

- 5th floor – Gregory Lind (mind-warping painting and sculpture), Haines Gallery (sublime traditional and new media) and Robert Koch Gallery (high-impact, large-scale photography)
- 4th floor – Stephen Wirtz Gallery (absorbing photography and installations) and Steven Wolf Fine Art (further adventures in dadaism)
- 3rd floor – Fraenkel Gallery (photography masterworks)
- 2nd floor – Mark Wolf Contemporary (bold graphics, bold statements)

Ready for more? Head next door to 77 Geary (p73) for two more floors:

- Mezzanine – Patricia Sweetow Gallery (memorable minimalism)
- 2nd floor – Marx & Zavattero Gallery (risk-taking concept meets careful craft), Rena Bransten Gallery (big names, big ideas) and Togonon Gallery (social commentary)

Then head across the street to Gallery Paule Anglim (p73), then down a block to Mission St for Catharine Clark Gallery (p109) and SF Camerawork (p112). Recap on your favorites over a drink at artistically inclined 111 Minna (p215).

California. Ironically upon publication the poem had the opposite effect and became a rallying cry against Chinese immigration. Things are seldom what they seem at the Bohemian Club. Google 'Bohemian Grove' and read the Wikipedia entry.

XANADU GALLERY: FOLK ART INTERNATIONAL Map pp70–1

☎ 415-392-9999; www.folkartintl.com; 140 Maiden Lane; admission free; 🕑 10am-6pm Tue-Sat; 🚌 & Ⓜ Powell St

Shrink the Guggenheim and plop it inside a brick box with a sunken Romanesque archway, and there you have Frank Lloyd Wright's 1949 Circle Gallery Building, which since 1979 has been the home of Xanadu Gallery. The nautilus shell ramp in the atrium leads you on a world tour of high-end folk art, from Fijian war clubs to mounted nose ornaments from the Andes.

JAMES FLOOD BUILDING Map pp70–1

cnr Market & Powell Sts; 🚌 & Ⓜ Powell St

This 1904 stone building survived the 1906 quake and retains much of its original character, notwithstanding the ground-level Gap flagship. Upstairs are long, labyrinthine halls lined with frosted-glass doors, just like in a noir movie – and that's no coincidence. Back in 1921 the San Francisco office of the infamous Pinkerton National Detective Agency hired a young PI named Dashiell Hammett, now better known as the author of the 1930 noir classic *The Maltese Falcon*.

JACKSON SQUARE

Local advertising agencies and antiques dealers are far more subtle about wheedling money from unsuspecting consumers than were the previous occupants of this former dock area, where notorious saloon owner Shanghai Kelly and madam Miss Piggot once conked new arrivals on the head and delivered them to ships in need of crew. Despite their efforts, many ships were abandoned as sailors left to seek their fortune in San Francisco.

Along the former waterfront bounded by Washington St, Columbus Ave, Pacific Ave and Sansome St, Italianate buildings with tall windows and cast-iron shutters were erected to house whiskey dealers, loan offices, lawyers and other necessary Barbary Coast evils. Architects and gallery owners liked the high ceilings and low rents, and successfully lobbied for historic status for the Jackson Square area in 1971. Since then, many of the elegant storefronts have been taken over by upscale design showrooms.

AP HOTALING WAREHOUSE Map pp70–1

451-455 Jackson St; 🚌 10, 12, 15

'If, as they say, God spanked the town/For being over-frisky,/Why did He burn His churches down/And spare Hotaling's whiskey?' The snappiest comeback in SF history was this saloon-goers' retort after Hotaling's 1866 whiskey warehouse survived the 1906 earthquake and fire, which many considered divine retribution for Barbary Coast debauchery. A bronze plaque with this ditty still graces the resilient Italianate building.

CIVIC CENTER & THE TENDERLOIN

Drinking p195; Eating p171; Shopping p145; Sleeping p256

At the beginning of the 20th century, San Francisco aspired to become the Paris of the Pacific, with the beaux-arts Civic Center as its pride and glory. One earthquake, a fire, an ill-conceived fountain and a ton of gold leaf later, San Francisco is still pretty far off the mark – for better and for worse. On the plus side, the grand plaza lined with peculiar gnarled trees that stubbornly refuse to bloom has turned out to be the ideal spot for massive antiwar demonstrations, skirt-twirling Cinco de Mayo fiestas and Pride parades far too raucous for Par-*ee* (however gay it may claim to be). Meanwhile, many of the city's finest chefs operate restaurants in the neighborhood, catering to crowds chattering with the thrill of great performances at Davies Symphony Hall (p223), the War Memorial Opera House (p222) and Herbst Theater (p224). On the downside, the aforementioned fountain is often mistaken for the open-air urinal it resembles, and the shopping carts of the indigent in front of City Hall (p78) stand as a seemingly permanent rebuke to the dot-com windfall squandered on the gleaming gold dome, c 1999.

For all San Francisco's European aspirations, the city is sorely lacking European public services. Hence the overburdened Tenderloin, one of the few areas in town (and indeed the state of California) to provide a full range of nonprofit services for the city's homeless families, impoverished elderly, disabled veterans, recovering substance abusers and others in need. The upscale lounge-bars that have landed here of late seem oddly placed, since the Tenderloin sidewalk scene is a rather ominous cautionary tale for casual girls-night-out cocktails. There are some brighter spots on the horizon, in particular the nonprofit Luggage Store Gallery (p79), which brightens dark alleys with murals by former artists who emerged from these city streets. An excellent farmers market in otherwise desolate United Nations Plaza (p80) brings a much-needed fresh outlook to the neighborhood twice weekly.

Some Vietnamese families who were first relocated to the Tenderloin after the Vietnam War have put down roots here and run such legendary local restaurants as Pagolac (p173), Saigon Sandwich Shop (p173) and Tu Lan (p180). City Hall has optimistically attempted to repackage Larkin St as 'Little Saigon.' While we love the new gateway to Little Saigon at Eddy and Larkin Sts – two matching granite-and-marble columns on either side of the street, topped with winged dragons – the moniker still seems something of a slight to Saigon, given the neighborhood's down-and-out vibe. Nonetheless, scrappy community nonprofits and tiny Tet (Vietnamese lunar new year) celebrations show that community can crop up in the unlikeliest places.

Ultimately, many of the neighborhood's best features aren't Parisian at all. The light-drenched San Francisco Main Library (p79) is stocked with an eclectic selection of books in multiple languages beloved by San Francisco's polyglot residents. The former main library building was transformed by popular vote and popular Italian architect Gae Aulenti into a spectacular Asian Art Museum (below) worthy of a city that faces Asia, not Europe.

Civic Center stretches from Franklin St, where the Symphony, Opera House and War Memorial buildings begin, eastward past the United Nations Plaza and the red-light marquees of Market St to 6th St, aka San Francisco's Skid Row. Grit ends and glam begins east of Mason St, and SoMa kicks in around Folsom St west of 5th St.

top picks

CIVIC CENTER & THE TENDERLOIN

- SF Symphony at Davies Symphony Hall (p223)
- Asian Art Museum (left)
- SF Opera at War Memorial Opera House (p222)
- Opposition politics at City Hall (p78)
- Luggage Store Gallery (p79)

ASIAN ART MUSEUM Map p77

☎ 415-581-3500; www.asianart.org; 200 Larkin St; adult/child under 12yr/student & child 13-17yr/senior $12/free/7/8, 1st Sun of month free, after 5pm Thu $5; 10am-5pm Tue-Sun, to 9pm Thu Feb-Sep; 5, 6, 7, 21, 31, 71, F, J, K, L, M, N; & Civic Center;

The largest collection of Asian art outside Asia covers 6000 years and thousands of miles of terrain. A trip through the galleries

CIVIC CENTER & THE TENDERLOIN
0 400 m
0 0.2 miles
Nob Hill
The Tenderloin
Union Square
See Downtown Map pp70-1
See Japantown & Pacific Heights Map p96
See SoMa Map pp110-11
Alcazar Theatre
Old Federal Building
Opera Plaza
State Building
Courthouse
Veterans Building
City Hall Rotunda
Civic Center Plaza
United Nations Plaza
Federal Building
Civic Center BART & MUNI Station
Powell St BART & MUNI Station
Powell St Cable Car Turnaround
Hallidie Plaza
Van Ness MUNI Station
Pine St
Austin St
Bush St
Fern St
Sutter St
Post St
Cosmo Pl
Hemlock St
Daniel Burnham Ct
Geary St
Cedar St
O'Farrell St
Myrtle St
Antonio St
Ellis St
Olive St
Eddy St
Willow St
Turk St
Eddy St
Larch St
Elm St
Golden Gate Ave
Redwood St
McAllister St
Ash St
Fulton St
Grove St
Ivy St
Hayes St
Linden St
Fell St
Hickory St
Oak St
Lily St
Page St
Rose St
Haight St
Franklin St
Gough St
Octavia Blvd
Van Ness Ave
Polk St
Larkin St
Hyde St
Leavenworth St
Jones St
Shannon St
Taylor St
Mason St
Powell St
Dale Pl
Breen Pl
Market St
12th St
Brady St
Stevenson St
Jessie St
Mission St
Julia St
Minna St
Natoma St
Howard St
Laskie St
Sumner St
Rausch St
Langton St
Moss St
Russ St
5th St
6th St
7th St
8th St
EATING (pp163-90)
Café Asia 9 B3
Dottie's True Blue Café 10 C2
Fish & Farm 11 C2
Heart of the City Farmers Market 12 C3
Jardinière 13 A4
Lahore Karahi 14 C2
Millennium 15 C1
Pagolac 16 B3
Saigon Sandwich Shop 17 B3
Shalimar 18 C2
INFORMATION
Civic Center Post Office 1 B3
San Francisco Main Library (see 5)
SIGHTS (pp76-80)
Asian Art Museum 2 B3
City Hall 3 B4
Luggage Store Gallery 4 D3
San Francisco Main Library 5 B4
SF Arts Commission Gallery 6 A4
United Nations Plaza 7 C3
SHOPPING (pp141-61)
Kayo Books 8 C1
DRINKING (pp191-204)
Bambuddha Lounge (see 39)
Edinburgh Castle 19 B2
Ha-Ra 20 B2
Hemlock Tavern 21 A1
Koko Cocktails 22 A2
Lush Lounge 23 B2
Rye 24 C2
NIGHTLIFE (pp205-15)
Great American Music Hall 25 B2
Mitchell Brothers O'Farrell Theater 26 B2
Rickshaw Stop 27 A4
THE ARTS (pp217-26)
AMC Van Ness 14 28 A2
Café Royale 29 C1
City Arts & Lectures (see 30)
Herbst Theater 30 A4
San Francisco Ballet (see 32)
San Francisco Opera (see 32)
San Francisco Symphony 31 A4
War Memorial Opera House 32 A4
GAY & LESBIAN (pp239-48)
Aunt Charlie's 33 D3
Deco Lounge 34 B3
Gangway 35 B2
New Conservatory Theater 36 B5
SLEEPING (pp249-62)
HI San Francisco City Center 37 B2
Hotel Vertigo 38 B1
Phoenix Hotel 39 B3
Steinhart Hotel & Apartments 40 B1
TRANSPORT (pp300-7)
American Automobile Association 41 B4

is a treasure-hunting expedition, from racy Rajasthan palace miniatures to the largest collection of Japanese sculptural baskets outside Japan to the jewel-box gallery of Chinese lustrous jade – just don't bump into those priceless Ming vases.

To give some idea of Asia's virtuosity, the museum has amassed 17,000 prime examples of the region's ingenuity and artistry. Consider the diplomatic back-bends curators had to do to put such a diverse collection into proper perspective. Where the UN falters, the Asian succeeds in bringing Taiwan, China and Tibet together, uniting Pakistan and India, and striking a harmonious balance among Japan, Korea and China. Granted, the Chinese collection takes up two wings and South Asia only one, but that healthy cultural competition has served to encourage donations of South Asian artifacts lately – mighty clever, those curators. Given the city's 150-year history as North America's gateway to Asia, the collection is also quintessentially San Franciscan, drawing on longstanding local ties and distinguished local collections.

The building itself is another feat of diplomacy. Italian architect Gae Aulenti's clever repurposing of the old San Francisco Main Library building left intact the much-beloved granite bas-relief on the building's face, the entryway's travertine arches and the polished stone staircase inside. She also created two new indoor plazas on either side for oversize sculpture installations and demos by artists.

You begin your tour of the collection by taking a single-file escalator up to the top floor. The curatorial concept is to follow the geographical path of Buddhism through Asia from the top floor down, beginning on the 3rd floor with India, and then – wait, isn't that Iran, followed by the Sikh kingdoms, then Indonesia? By the time you've cruised past 3000-plus Zoroastrian artifacts and splendid Balinese shadow puppets, all theological quibbles will yield to astonishment – and possibly exhaustion. If museums wear you out fast – or you're short on time – either find art from your favorite Asian country or head directly for the Chinese collections (the jade and bronze are particularly impressive).

As if the constantly rotating collection wasn't enough, the Asian also emphasizes educational programs that keep pan-generational crowds thronging the place. Hands-on workshops for kids and evening lectures with noted art historians are boons for parents and couples on date night. Check the calendar.

Make a day of it with lunch at Café Asia (p173), where sunny days mean *bento* (boxed meals) on the balcony terrace. One Thursday every other month, from 5pm to 9pm, the hipsters are in charge with Matcha, an urban-contemporary event series with a changing lineup but always music and cocktails. Think DJs spinning Japanese hip-hop, tattoo artists giving live demos, sake-makers pouring tastings, and crafty types making Chinese paper lanterns to ward off hungry ghosts.

CITY HALL Map p77

☎ 415-554-4000, tour info 415-554-6023, art exhibit line 415-554-6080; www.ci.sf.ca.us/cityhall; 400 Van Ness Ave; admission free; 8am-8pm Mon-Fri, tours 10am, noon & 2pm; 5, 19, 21, 49; & Civic Center;

That mighty beaux-arts dome pretty much covers San Francisco's grandest ambitions and fundamental flaws. Designed by John Bakewell and Arthur Brown Jr in 1915 to top Paris for flair and outsize the capitol building dome in Washington, DC, the dome was a little unsteady until its retrofit after the 1989 earthquake, when ingenious technology enabled the dome to swing on its base without raising alarm.

TRANSPORTATION: CIVIC CENTER & THE TENDERLOIN

BART Civic Center is the main BART stop for both areas; Powell St station also serves the Tenderloin.

Bus All Market St Muni lines stop at Civic Center and at various points in the Tenderloin; the northern end of the Tenderloin is also accessed by buses 1, 2, 3, 4, 5, 19, 38, 47 and 49; Civic Center is accessible via Van Ness Ave buses 47 and 49.

Streetcar The aboveground F streetcar makes stops at Civic Center and in the Tenderloin, and underground streetcars J, K, L, M and N all stop at Civic Center and Van Ness Ave (along the western edge of Civic Center).

Parking Public parking is available at the garage at 5th and Mission Sts.

The gold leafing on the dome's exterior is a reminder of dot-com-era excess. But from the inside, the splendid rotunda has ringing acoustics, and if that dome could talk, it would tell of triumph and tragedy.

Anti-McCarthy sit-in protesters were hosed off the grand staircase in 1960, but finally ran McCarthy out of town; Harvey Milk was assassinated here in 1978; and the cheers heard around the world in 2004 were from families and friends of the 4037 same-sex couples who celebrated their marriages here, thanks to Mayor Newsom's short-lived challenge to California state marriage law. Take the elevator one flight down to discover intriguing public art exhibits, which range from photographs of senior subcultures to art by the blind.

Free docent tours of City Hall meet at the tour kiosk near the Van Ness entrance, but City Hall is best seen in action. If you want insight into how San Francisco government works – or doesn't, as the case may be – the Board of Supervisors meets Tuesdays at 2pm in City Hall; check the agenda and minutes online. Theoretically, visitors may be removed for 'boisterous' behavior, but this being San Francisco, democracy in action can get pretty rowdy without fazing seen-it-all security guards.

SAN FRANCISCO MAIN LIBRARY

Map p77

☎ 415-557-4400; http://sfpl.lib.ca.us; 100 Larkin St; 10am-6pm Mon & Sat, 9am-8pm Tue-Thu, noon-6pm Fri, noon-5pm Sun; admission free; 5, 6, 7, 21, 31, 71, F, J, K, L, M, N; & Civic Center;

In the early 1990s, every bookish citizen in SF was excited about plans to build a new main library, which had previously been located in what is now the Asian Art Museum. The old building had myriad problems keeping up with technology, and the museum needed a new home for its burgeoning collection. Sounds like a perfect fit, right? Wrong. Critics, such as acclaimed author Nicholson Baker, have accused the library of thowing away many books to accommodate the its new architecture. Claims that the library administration contradicts.

Despite the controversy, the project has on many levels been a success the vast skylight dome sheds plenty of light through the building. And this being San Francisco, the library actively appeals to broad audiences – to wit the African American Center, Chinese Center, the James C Hormel Gay & Lesbian Center and the Center for San Francisco History. Besides its eclectic collection of San Franciscans and (some of) their favorite books, the library quietly boasts an excellent high-profile author-reading and lecture series, plus intriguing ephemera exhibits in the 6th-floor Skylight Gallery.

Artistic touches include Alice Aycock's spiral staircase between the 5th and 6th floors, and artist Ann Chamberlain's 2nd-floor wallpaper made of cards from the old card catalog, with running commentary provided by 200 San Franciscans. Just don't go looking for all those books listed on the cards.

LUGGAGE STORE GALLERY Map p77

☎ 415-255-5971; www.luggagestoregallery.org; 1007 Market St; admission free; noon-5pm Wed-Sat; 5, 6, 7, 21, 31, 71, F, J, K, L, M, N; & Civic Center

A dandelion pushing through cracks in the sidewalk, this plucky nonprofit gallery has brought signs of life to one of the toughest blocks in the Tenderloin for more than 20 years. The art that sprawls out across the spacious 2nd-floor gallery rises above the street without losing sight of it – this space was the launching pad for renowned graffiti satirists.

Two Luggage Store regulars you might recognize around town are Rigo, who did the 'One Tree' mural that looks like a one-way sign by the 101 Fwy on-ramp in SoMa, and Brazilian duo Ogemeos, who did the mural of a defiant kid holding a lit firecracker atop the gallery building. With such oddly touching works, poetry nights and monthly performing-arts events, this place puts the tender in the Tenderloin.

SF ARTS COMMISSION GALLERY

Map p77

☎ 415-554-6080; www.sfacgallery.org; 401 Van Ness Ave; admission free; noon-5pm Wed-Sat; 5, 42, 47, 49, F, J, K, L, M, N; Van Ness

Get in on the next art movement at this lobby-level public gallery featuring international perspectives and local talents. You never know what you might find. As well as hanging shows and hosting receptions in its gallery, the commission also sponsors wide-ranging works, such as a recent sound sculpture in the rotunda of City Hall. Very cool. Drop by to hear what's doing now.

UNITED NATIONS PLAZA Map p77

Market St btwn Hyde & Leavenworth Sts; 6am-midnight; 5, 6, 7, 14, 21, 31, 71, F, J, K, L, M, N; & Civic Center

This vast brick-paved triangle commemorates the signing of the United Nations charter in San Francisco. It offers a clear view of City Hall, sundry Scientologists drumming up converts, and the odd drug deal in progress. Thankfully, a wonderful farmers market (415-558-9455) provides a fresher perspective on the Tenderloin, every Wednesday and Sunday from about 7am to 5pm.

CHINATOWN

Drinking p197; Eating p173; Shopping p145; Sleeping p256

Chinatown cropped up within a year of the 1849 Gold Rush, and how it survived since then is even more amazing. At first it wasn't exclusively Chinese at all, but a bachelor community of Mexican, American, European, African American and Chinese miners who bunked, prospected and caroused side by side. Women who entered these streets automatically surrendered their reputations, and those who did might make a living as a prostitute behind the iron-clad doors of Ross Alley (p84) or prosper as a madam. Working conditions were often harsh, and in 1852 San Francisco's first labor strike was orchestrated by the Chinatown guild of masons.

top picks

CHINATOWN

- **Waverly Place** (p83)
- **Spofford Alley** (p83)
- **Portsmouth Square** (p83)
- **Chinese Historical Society of America Museum** (p83)
- **Chinese Culture Center** (p84)

But the solidarity didn't last. When gold prices came crashing down with the discovery of gold in Australia, miners down on their luck turned their irrational resentments on resident Australians and Chinese. Australian lodging houses were burned to the ground, anti-Chinese riots broke out and Chinese miners' and farmers' land claims were rendered null and void. In 1870 San Francisco passed its first law restricting housing and employment for anyone born in China, creating tough competition for space and legitimate work in these increasingly cramped quarters. Restrictions on marriage and family immigration turned Chinatown into a community of bachelors and 'paper sons' claimed as relatives in order to get around exclusion laws.

Most services in Chinatown were provided not by the city but by *tongs*, neighborhood family associations whose headquarters you can still see in Waverly Place (p83). Meanwhile, white landlords, police and even the mayor looked the other way as long as they benefited from brothels, opium dens, gambling houses and bootlegging operations. Police ignored plumes of fragrant smoke escaping subterranean opium dens on Duncombe Alley, but when a white person was spotted emerging from the alley, every Chinese person in sight was rounded up on 'corruption' charges. After the red-light Commercial St caught fire in 1906, Chinese brothels were replaced by white run 'parlor houses.'

Officials planned to oust Chinese residents and develop this prime property after the fire, but the Chinese consulate and rifle-toting Chinatown merchants persuaded the city otherwise. Instead, Chinatown residents reclaimed their neighborhood and held temple services in the smoldering ruins. Chinatown businessmen led by Look Tin Eli pooled funds to reinvent the area as the tourist attraction you see today, with pagoda-style roofs and dragon lanterns lining shopping streets. Grant Ave soon began a brisk business in tchotchkes for the tourist trade and beer for Beat poets, with Stockton St to the north supplying Chinatown locals with fresh produce, roast duck, herbal remedies and dumplings galore. Some 41 historic alleyways are packed into Chinatown's 22 blocks.

Chinatown is now a major economic boon to the city as one of its top tourist attractions, but many residents scrape by on less than $10,000 a year – hardly the 'Gold Mountain' suggested by the name for San Francisco in Cantonese, though fortunes are made daily at Golden Gate Fortune Cookie Company (p145). Better-off residents tend to leave Chinatown, new arrivals move in, and the cycle begins anew. Each night as the crowds of visitors thin out and the sun sets on Chinatown, the strains of a Chinese orchestra rise from Spofford Alley (p83) and ballroom dancers convene in social halls to glide across the floor and past all the odds.

Dragon's Gate (p84) marks the grand entry of Chinatown on Grant Ave, which runs parallel to Stockton St. Both head uphill through the heart of Chinatown on their way from Union Square to North Beach. To the east, Kearny St divides Chinatown from the Financial District, while North Beach overlaps Chinatown at Broadway.

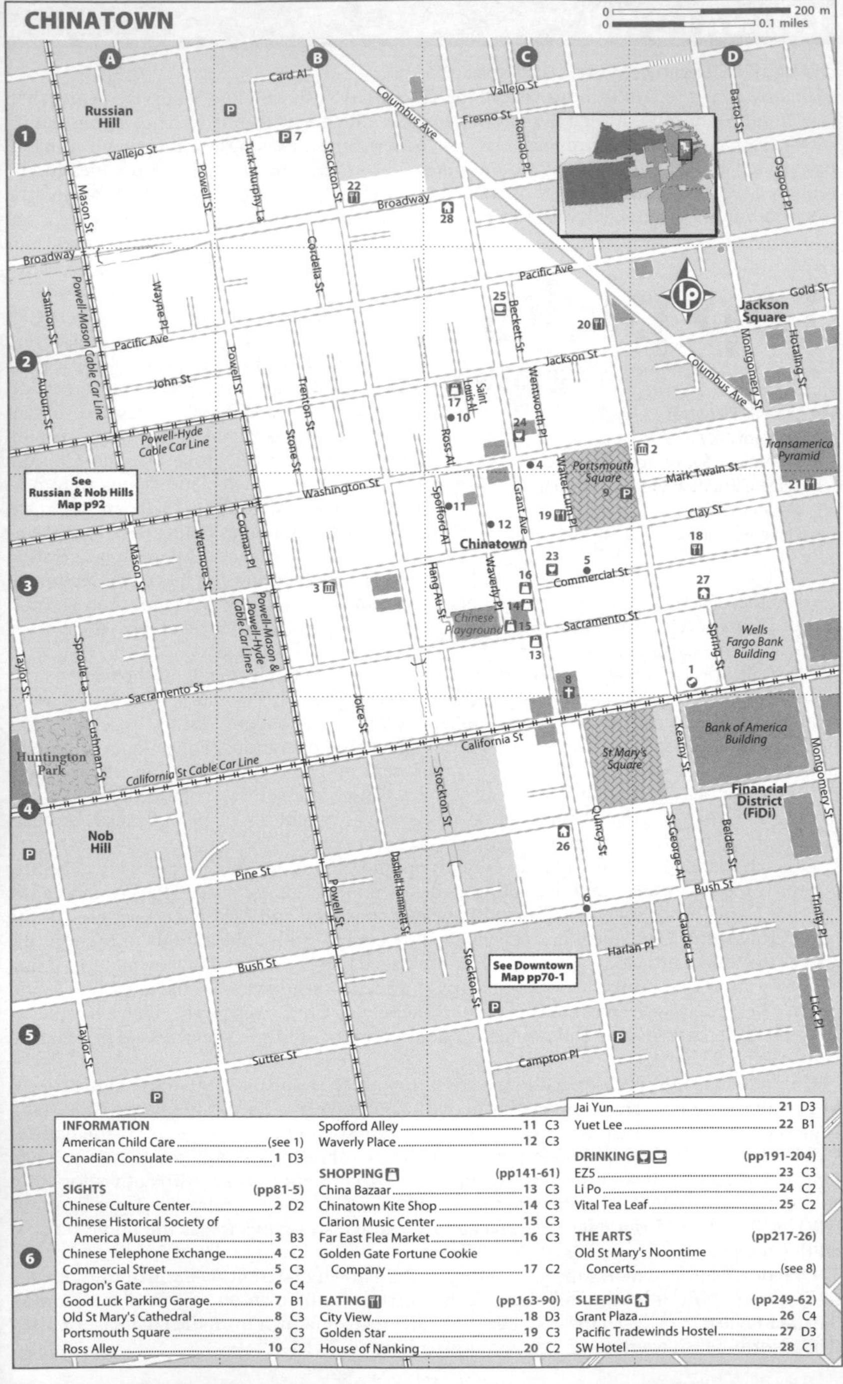
CHINATOWN
0 200 m
0 0.1 miles
A
B
C
D
1
2
3
4
5
6
Russian Hill
Card Al
Vallejo St
Fresno St
Columbus Ave
Romolo Pl
Bartol St
Osgood Pl
Mason St
Powell St
Turk-Murphy La
Stockton St
Broadway
Cordelia St
Pacific Ave
Gold St
Jackson Square
Beckett St
Salmon St
Powell-Mason Cable Car Line
Wayne Pl
John St
Jackson St
Trenton St
Saint Louis Al
Wentworth Pl
Montgomery St
Hotaling St
Auburn St
Powell-Hyde Cable Car Line
Stone St
Ross Al
Walter Lum Pl
Portsmouth Square
Mark Twain St
Transamerica Pyramid
See Russian & Nob Hills Map p92
Washington St
Spofford Al
Grant Ave
Clay St
Chinatown
Wetmore St
Codman Pl
Hang Au St
Waverly Pl
Commercial St
Powell-Mason & Powell-Hyde Cable Car Lines
Chinese Playground
Sacramento St
Wells Fargo Bank Building
Spring St
Taylor St
Sproule La
Joice St
Huntington Park
Cushman St
California St Cable Car Line
California St
St Mary's Square
Kearny St
Bank of America Building
Financial District (FiDi)
Nob Hill
Quincy St
St George Al
Belden St
Pine St
Dashiell Hammett St
Bush St
Claude La
Harlan Pl
Trinity Pl
See Downtown Map pp70-1
Lick Pl
Sutter St
Campton Pl

INFORMATION
American Child Care (see 1)
Canadian Consulate 1 D3

SIGHTS (pp81-5)
Chinese Culture Center 2 D2
Chinese Historical Society of America Museum 3 B3
Chinese Telephone Exchange 4 C2
Commercial Street 5 C3
Dragon's Gate 6 C4
Good Luck Parking Garage 7 B1
Old St Mary's Cathedral 8 C3
Portsmouth Square 9 C3
Ross Alley 10 C2
Spofford Alley 11 C3
Waverly Place 12 C3

SHOPPING (pp141-61)
China Bazaar 13 C3
Chinatown Kite Shop 14 C3
Clarion Music Center 15 C3
Far East Flea Market 16 C3
Golden Gate Fortune Cookie Company 17 C2

EATING (pp163-90)
City View 18 D3
Golden Star 19 C3
House of Nanking 20 C2
Jai Yun 21 D3
Yuet Lee 22 B1

DRINKING (pp191-204)
EZ5 23 C3
Li Po 24 C2
Vital Tea Leaf 25 C2

THE ARTS (pp217-26)
Old St Mary's Noontime Concerts (see 8)

SLEEPING (pp249-62)
Grant Plaza 26 C4
Pacific Tradewinds Hostel 27 D3
SW Hotel 28 C1

WAVERLY PLACE Map p82

1, 30, 45; California, Powell-Mason, Powell-Hyde;

There was no place to go but up in Chinatown after 1870, when local laws limited where Chinese San Franciscans could live and work. Temples were built atop the barber shops, laundries and neighborhood associations lining Waverly Pl, making their presence known with brightly painted balconies festooned with flags and lanterns.

Tien Hou Temple (hours vary) atop 125 Waverly Pl was built in 1852, and the altar miraculously survived the 1906 earthquake and fire to become a symbol of community endurance. Drop by and pay your respects; entry is free, but it's customary to leave an offering for temple upkeep.

CHINESE HISTORICAL SOCIETY OF AMERICA MUSEUM Map p82

415-391-1188; www.chsa.org; 965 Clay St; adult/senior/child 6-17yr $3/2/1, 1st Thu of month free; noon-5pm Tue-Fri; 1, 30, 45; California, Powell-Mason, Powell-Hyde;

Picture what it was like to be Chinese in America during the Gold Rush, transcontinental railroad construction or the Beat heyday at the nation's largest Chinese American historical institute. Intimate vintage photos, an 1880 temple altar and personal artifacts are seen alongside the Daniel KE Ching collection of thousands of vintage advertisements, toys and postcards conveying Chinese stereotypes. Temporary art shows are across the courtyard in this graceful 1932 landmark building, built as Chinatown's YWCA by Julia Morgan of Hearst Castle fame.

SPOFFORD ALLEY
Map p82

1, 15, 30, 45; California, Powell-Mason, Powell-Hyde;

Sun Yat-sen once plotted the overthrow of China's Manchu dynasty here at number 36, and during Prohibition, this was the site of turf battles over local bootlegging and protection rackets. Spofford has mellowed with age; it's now lined with senior community centers. But the action still starts around sundown, when a Chinese orchestra strikes up a tune, the clicking of a mah-jong game begins, and beauty parlor owners and florists use the pretense of sweeping their doorsteps to gossip.

PORTSMOUTH SQUARE Map p82

733 Kearny St; 1, 15, 41, 45; California;

Since apartments in Chinatown's old brick buildings are small, Portsmouth Sq is the neighborhood's living room. The square is named after John B Montgomery's sloop, which pulled up near here in 1846 to stake the US claim on San Francisco, but the presiding deity at this park is the Goddess of Democracy, a bronze replica of the statue made by Tiananmen Square protesters in 1989.

First light is met with outstretched arms by tai-chi practitioners. By afternoon toddlers rush the playground slides, and tea crowds collect at the kiosk under the pedestrian bridge to joke and dissect the day's news. The checkers and chess played on concrete tables in gazebos late into the evening aren't mere games, but 365-day obsessions, come rain or shine. Chinese New Year brings a night market to the square, featuring Chinese opera, calligraphy demonstrations and cell-phone charms of the goddess Guan Yin for better reception. Bronze plaques dot the perimeter of the historic square, noting the site of San Francisco's first bookshop and elementary school and the bawdy Jenny Lind Theater, which with a few modifications became San Francisco's first City Hall.

CHINESE TELEPHONE EXCHANGE
Map p82

743 Washington St; 1, 15, 30, 45; California

This triple-decker tiled pagoda caused a sensation in 1894 not for its looks, but its smarts: to connect callers to the right person, switchboard operators had to speak fluent English and five Chinese dialects and memorize at least 1500 Chinatown residents by name, residence and occupation. The switchboard was open 365 days a year, and the manager and assistant managers lived onsite.

Since anyone born in China was prohibited by law from visiting San Francisco

TRANSPORTATION: CHINATOWN

Bus Lines 30 and 45 run up Stockton St from Union Square; bus 15 runs along Kearny St, while bus 1 runs along California St.

Cable car The Powell-Mason St line links Union Square to Chinatown; the California St line runs through Chinatown on its ascent to Nob Hill.

Parking Street parking is impossible; try your luck at the public Good Luck Parking Garage (p84).

throughout the 1882–1943 Chinese Exclusion era, this switchboard was the main means of contact with family and business partners in China. The exchange operated until 1949, and the landmark was bought and restored by Bank of Canton in 1960.

CHINESE CULTURE CENTER Map p82

☎ 415-986-1822; www.c-c-c.org; 3rd fl, Hilton Hotel, 750 Kearny St; gallery free (donation requested), tours adult/child $25/20; 10am-4pm Tue-Sat; 1, 15, 41

You can see all the way to China on the 3rd floor of the Hilton inside this cultural center, which hosts exhibits of traditional Chinese arts and such breakthrough contemporary shows as the Present Tense Biennial. For this show, held in odd-numbered years, 30-plus artists from across the Bay Area give their personal takes on Chinese culture, from Cui Fei's Chinese calligraphy that's painstakingly sculpted from bent twigs to Thomas Chang's monumental photographs of a miniaturized Great Wall at a Florida theme park.

Kid-friendly, docent-led Chinese Heri tage Walks guide visitors through the living history and mythology of Chinatown in two hours; tours are available by reservation with a two-person minimum. For more first-hand experiences of Chinese culture, check the center's schedule of Mandarin classes, poetry readings, movies and genealogy services.

DRAGON'S GATE Map p82

intersection of Grant Ave & Bush St; 1, 15, 30, 45; California;

Enter the Dragon archway and you'll find yourself on the once-notorious street known as Dupont in its red-light heyday. Sixty years before the family-friendly overhaul of the Las Vegas Strip, Look Tin Eli and a group of forward-thinking Chinatown businessmen pioneered the approach here in Chinatown, replacing seedy attractions with more tourist-friendly ones.

After consultation with architects and community groups, Dupont was transformed into Grant Ave, with Deco-Chinoiserie dragon lamps and tiled pagoda rooftops, and police were reluctantly persuaded to enforce the 1914 Red Light Abatement Act in Chinatown. By the time this gate was donated by Taiwan in 1970 grandly proclaiming that 'everything in the world is in just proportions,' Chinatown finally had a main street that did the community greater justice.

OLD ST MARY'S CATHEDRAL Map p82

☎ 415-288-3800; www.oldsaintmarys.org; 660 California St; 11am-6pm Mon-Tue, 11am-7pm Wed-Fri, 9am-6:30pm Sat, 9am-4:30pm Sun; 1, 15, 30, 45; California, Powell-Mason, Powell-Hyde;

Many thought it a lost cause, but California's first cathedral, inaugurated in 1854, tried for decades to give San Francisco some religion – despite its location in brothel central. Hence the stern admon ition on the church's brick clock tower: 'Son, observe the time and fly from evil.'

Eventually the archdiocese abandoned attempts to convert Dupont St whoremongers and handed the church over to a Chinese community mission run by the activism-oriented Paulists. During WWII, the church served the US military as a recreation center and cafeteria. The 1906 fire destroyed one of the district's biggest bordellos directly across from the church, making room for St Mary's Square. Today, skateboarders do tricks of a different sort on the park's rails and benches, under the watchful eye of Beniamino Bufano's 1929 pink granite and steel statue of Sun Yat-sen.

ROSS ALLEY Map p82

1, 30, 45; Powell-Mason, Powell-Hyde;

The colorful murals lining Ross Alley hint at the colorful characters that once roamed SF's oldest alleyway, which has been known variously as Mexico, Spanish and Manila St after the ladies who once staffed its notorious back-parlor brothels. More recently, Ross Alley has been occasionally pimped out to Hollywood production companies as the picturesque backdrop for sequels like *Karate Kid II* and *Indiana Jones and the Temple of Doom*.

GOOD LUCK PARKING GARAGE Map p82

735 Vallejo St; 1, 15, 30, 45; California, Powell-Mason, Powell-Hyde

Each parking spot at this garage comes with fortune-cookie wisdom stenciled onto the asphalt: 'You have already found your true love. Stop looking.' These omens are brought to you by artist Harrell Fletcher and co-conspirator Jon Rubin, who also gathered the vintage photographs of local residents' Chinese and Italian ancestors that grace the entry tiles like heraldic emblems.

COMMERCIAL STREET Map p82

742 Commercial St; 1, 15, 41, 45; California;

Back when the red lights of Commercial St could be seen down by the waterfront, this strip provided many provocative answers to the age-old question: what do you do with a drunken sailor? Conveniently located across Portsmouth Sq from San Francisco's City Hall, this hot spot caught fire in 1906. The city banned its 25¢ Chinese brothels in favor of white-run 'parlor houses,' where basic services were raised to $3 – watching cost $10 at the faux-French Parisian Mansion. Today that much gets you a couple of hot dishes – of dumplings, that is, at **City View** (p174).

CHINATOWN RAMBLE

Walking Tour

1 Dragon's Gate (opposite) Enter the Dragon, heading through the green, tile-topped gate with its triple portals, past Grant Ave souvenir shops and dragon lamps.

2 St Mary's Square (opposite) Glimpse skaters practicing revolutionary moves beneath Beniamino Bufano's statue of Sun Yat-sen, who plotted the overthrow of China's Manchu dynasty not far from here.

3 Waverly Place (p83) Off Sacramento St are the flag-festooned balconies of Chinatown's historic temples, which have survived earthquakes, fires and politicians. In San Francisco author Amy Tan's bestselling novel *The Joy Luck Club*, a Chinese mother names her American-born daughter after this history-making street.

4 Spofford Alley (p83) Stop and listen to clicking mah-jong tiles, a Chinese orchestra warming up and beauticians gossiping indiscreetly over blow-dryers. Generations ago, you might have overheard here the whispers of Sun Yat-sen and his conspirators at number 36 plotting the 1911 overthrow of China's last dynasty, or gunfire blasts during 1920s bootlegger turf wars.

5 Golden Gate Fortune Cookie Company (p145) Enter mural-bedecked Ross Alley, where you can get your fortune while it's hot, folded into a warm cookie on vintage machines at Golden Gate Fortune Cookie Company.

6 Portsmouth Square (p83) Check out historical markers ringing San Francisco's Gold Rush–era town square, strike a pose next to the Tiananmen Goddess of Democracy, or even challenge regulars to a game of pick-up chess.

7 Commercial Street (opposite) Pause to picture what the view from here must've been like 150 years ago, when ships were abandoned to rot at piers and red lights lured sailors along ramshackle docks to Commercial St.

8 City View (p174) Feast on plump dumplings shaped like Chinese gold ingots, and you'll feel like you struck it rich in Chinatown.

WALK FACTS

Start Dragon's Gate
End City View
Distance One mile
Time 40 minutes
Exertion Moderate
Fuel stop City View

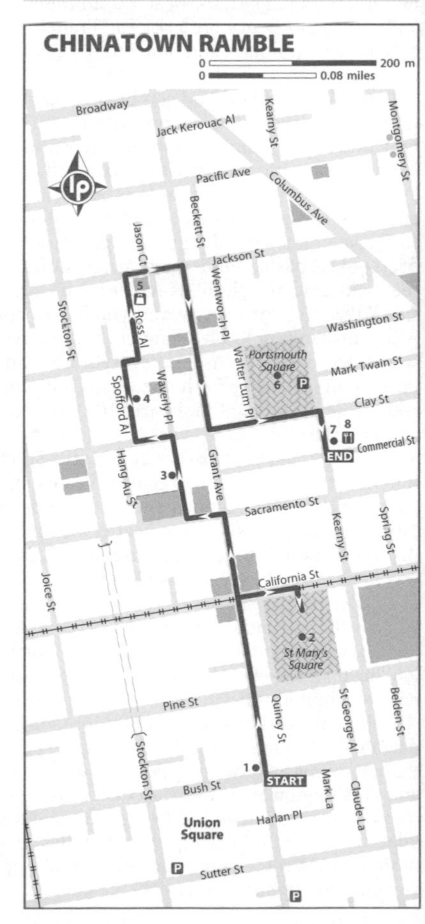

NORTH BEACH

Drinking p197; Eating p174; Shopping p146; Sleeping p257

Standing at the apex of the Filbert Street Steps, you can understand what Italian fishermen and Beat poets saw in North Beach: tough climbs and giddy vistas, a place with more sky than ground, an area that was civilized but never entirely tamed. The fishermen and poets are mostly gone now, but wild hawks and parrots have taken their place, circling above the neighborhood as though waiting, as poet Lawrence Ferlinghetti once put it, 'for a rebirth of wonder.'

Or maybe they're just looking for a parking spot. The North Beach parking situation is so dire that locals tend to avoid the entire neighborhood at weekends, missing out on conspiracy theory one-upmanship at Specs' (p197), Sean Penn sightings at Tosca Cafe (p197) and Italian accordion sing-alongs at Caffe Trieste (p198). They also miss out on serious finds in the boutiques along upper Grant Ave, including rare records, one-of-a-kind fashions by local designers, and 19th-century love letters still in their glassine envelopes (p146).

But true to North Beach fashion, there is poetry even in parking misfortune. On foot, you'll notice alleyways named after Beat writers, such as Jack Kerouac Alley (p88) and Bob Kaufman Alley (p89). To discover these and other authors' works and stranger-than-fiction biographies, you can't beat the Beat Museum (p89) and City Lights Bookstore (p146), San Francisco's literary landmark and home to the Beat movement.

Often the neighborhood gets by on cheerfully inauthentic Italian charm, with restaurant touts attempting to grab the attention of passersby with an emphatic 'Ciao, bella!' Works every time – everyone is just vain enough to respond to *bella*. But too often such restaurants serve disappointingly bland, overcooked pasta, while many cafes along the main drag of Columbus Ave serve unforgivably weak espresso. But veer off onto a quiet side street and enter a cafe and you'll hear the soft consonants of Tuscan-accented Italian. A few upstanding locales staunchly resist the California impulse to throw goat cheese and sun-dried tomato pesto onto everything, and maintain authentic recipes that make Italian immigrants nostalgic for home. Ristorante Ideale (p175), Liguria Bakery (p175), Cinecittá (p175) and the deli counter at Molinari (p175) transport taste buds to that other peninsula, minus the cost of airfare.

top picks

NORTH BEACH

- City Lights Bookstore (p146)
- Coit Tower (p88)
- Filbert Street Steps (p88)
- Molinari (p175)
- Caffe Trieste (p198)

You won't find an actual beach in North Beach – the nearest these days is in Aquatic Park (p67). But the intrepid will discover natural beauty atop Telegraph Hill. The dramatic cliff was formed when a ruthless 19th-century entrepreneur decided to quarry here – never mind that explosions rattled the neighbors – and only after a chunk of the stone hill was gone did City Hall demand that the dynamiting stop. Staircases and garden-lined pedestrian boardwalks became the best way to navigate the sheer rock faces of Telegraph Hill, and all the bucolic splendor drew a flock of escapee pet parrots here into a kind of hippie bird commune. Capping this already surreal scene is the enormous nozzle of Coit Tower (p88), commissioned in the 1930s by the eccentric honorary firefighter Lillie Hancock Coit. North Beach may have its commercial downsides, but looking up from your salami sandwich at the parrots circling that great fire hose in the sky, you have to admit: this neighborhood elevates you out of the fog of everyday life.

Columbus Ave bends sharply off Montgomery St at the edge of the Financial District and cuts diagonally through North Beach. Despite what the Columbus Ave touts may tell you, most of the best dining and shopping is off Columbus along side streets such as narrow upper Grant Ave and Washington St. Midway up Columbus, Broadway joins North Beach to the Embarcadero on the east, Chinatown just to the west and Russian Hill via the Broadway Tunnel. Although Filbert St and other equally steep parallel streets will get you to the top of Telegraph Hill, a more indirect route along stairways breaks up the strenuous trek with views that will make you glad you came this way.

NORTH BEACH

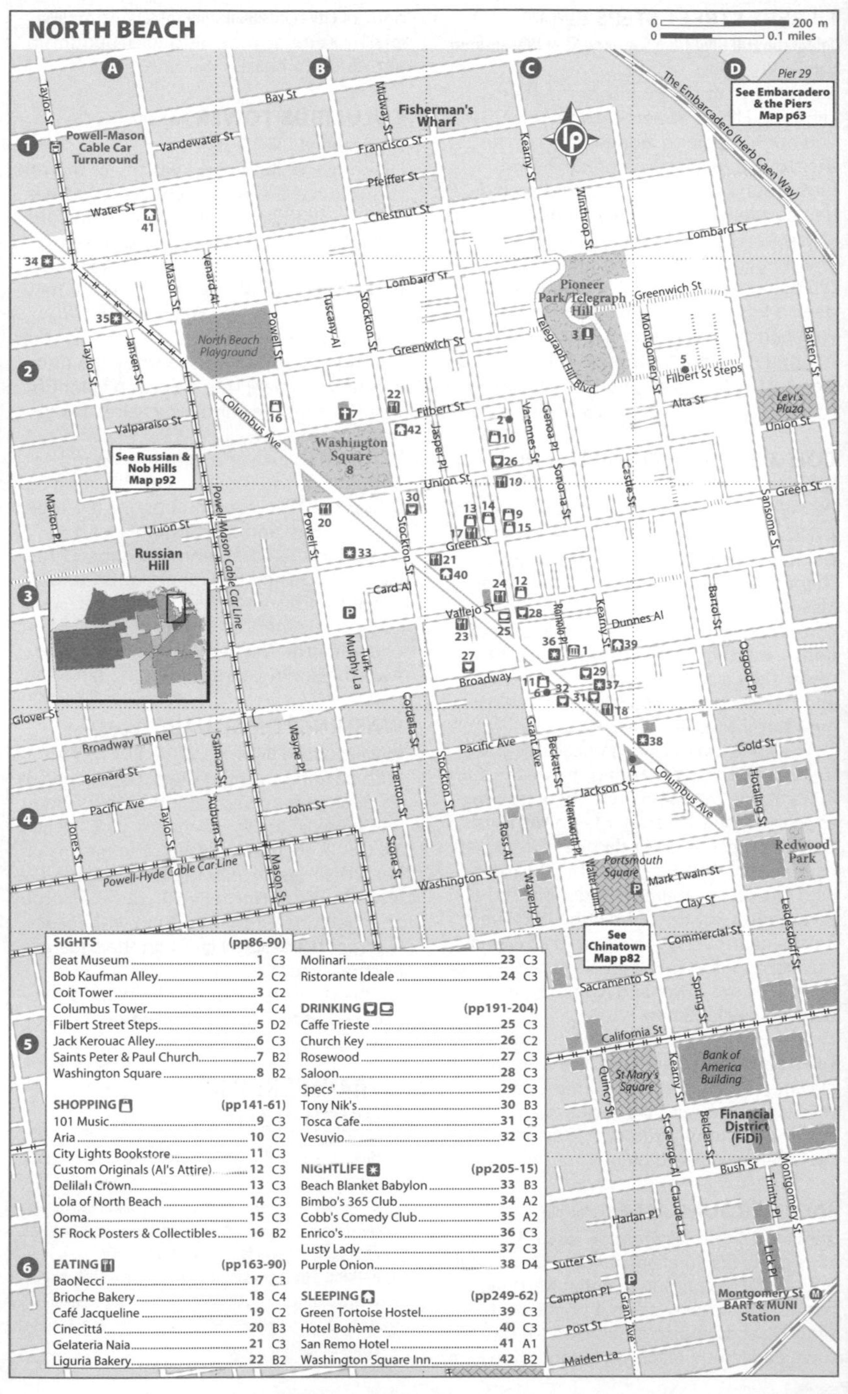

SIGHTS (pp86-90)

Beat Museum	1	C3
Bob Kaufman Alley	2	C2
Coit Tower	3	C2
Columbus Tower	4	C4
Filbert Street Steps	5	D2
Jack Kerouac Alley	6	C3
Saints Peter & Paul Church	7	B2
Washington Square	8	B2

SHOPPING (pp141-61)

101 Music	9	C3
Aria	10	C2
City Lights Bookstore	11	C3
Custom Originals (Al's Attire)	12	C3
Delilah Crown	13	C3
Lola of North Beach	14	C3
Ooma	15	C3
SF Rock Posters & Collectibles	16	B2

EATING (pp163-90)

BaoNecci	17	C3
Brioche Bakery	18	C4
Café Jacqueline	19	C2
Cinecittá	20	B3
Gelateria Naia	21	C3
Liguria Bakery	22	B2
Molinari	23	C3
Ristorante Ideale	24	C3

DRINKING (pp191-204)

Caffe Trieste	25	C3
Church Key	26	C2
Rosewood	27	C3
Saloon	28	C3
Specs'	29	C3
Tony Nik's	30	B3
Tosca Cafe	31	C3
Vesuvio	32	C3

NIGHTLIFE (pp205-15)

Beach Blanket Babylon	33	B3
Bimbo's 365 Club	34	A2
Cobb's Comedy Club	35	A2
Enrico's	36	C3
Lusty Lady	37	C3
Purple Onion	38	D4

SLEEPING (pp249-62)

Green Tortoise Hostel	39	C3
Hotel Bohème	40	C3
San Remo Hotel	41	A1
Washington Square Inn	42	B2

FILBERT STREET STEPS Map p87

Telegraph Hill Blvd from Sansome St or Washington Sq; 39

Somewhere in the middle of the steep climb up Filbert Street Steps to Coit Tower, you might begin to wonder if it's worth the trouble. Well, take a breather and look around. Already you're passing hidden cottages along a wooden boardwalk called Napier Lane, sculpture tucked in among gardens flowering year-round, and sweeping vistas of the Bay Bridge. If you need a few words of encouragement, the wild parrots in the trees have been known to interject a few choice words that your gym instructor would probably get sued for using.

COIT TOWER & TELEGRAPH HILL Map p87

415-362-0808; Telegraph Hill Blvd; adult/senior & child $3.75/2; 10am-6:30pm; 39

Go ahead and snicker at the wacky hose-shaped concrete projectile that eccentric Ms Lillie Hancock Coit left a third of her considerable fortune to build – everyone does – but the climb here is no joke, the tower's dedication to firefighters is heartfelt and the views inside the tower will win you over to Lillie's point of view.

The heiress had some radical ideas (see the boxed text, opposite), and the tower built in her name in 1934 has plenty of its own, as seen in the worker-glorifying **WPA murals** that line the lobby. For decades after their completion, the murals and the 25 artists who worked on them were denounced as communist. But the red-baiting backfired: for the controversy they ignited as well as the artistic effort involved, San Franciscans embraced the tower and its murals as a beloved city landmark.

After climbing the Greenwich St or Filbert St Steps to get here, the wait for the elevator is well worth it. From the top of the tower, you can take in panoramic views and spot colorful flocks of parrots turning the treetops red and blue.

JACK KEROUAC ALLEY Map p87

btwn Grant & Columbus Aves; 15, 30, 41

Fans of *On the Road* and *Dharma Bums* will appreciate how fitting it is that Kerouac's namesake alleyway offers a poetic and slightly seedy shortcut between Chinatown and North Beach via favorite Kerouac haunts **City Lights Bookstore** (p146) and **Vesuvio** (p198) – Kerouac took his books, Buddhism and drink to heart.

COLUMBUS TOWER Map p87

916 Kearny St; 15, 30, 41

Like most SF landmarks worthy of the title, this one has a seriously checkered career. Built by shady political boss Abe Ruef in 1905, the building was finished just in time to be reduced to its steel skeleton in the 1906 earthquake and fire. The new copper cladding was still shiny in 1907 when not-so-honest Abe was convicted of bribing city supervisors, and by the time he emerged bankrupt from San Quentin State Prison, the cupola was already oxidizing green.

Towering artistic aspirations found a home here, too. The Grammy-winning folk group the Kingston Trio bought the tower in the 1960s, and the Grateful Dead recorded in the basement. Since the 1970s it has been owned by Francis Ford Coppola, and film history has been made here by Coppola's American Zoetrope, *The Joy Luck Club* director Wayne Wang and Academy Award–winning actor/director Sean Penn.

WASHINGTON SQUARE Map p87

Columbus Ave & Union St; 15, 30, 41, 45

Wild parrots, tai chi masters, nonagenarian churchgoing *nonnas* (grandmothers) and Ben Franklin are the company you'll keep on this lively patch of lawn. The parrots keep their distance in the treetops, but like anyone else in North Beach, they can probably be bribed into friendship with focaccia from **Liguria Bakery** (p175) on the square's northeast corner.

The 1897 statue of Ben Franklin is a non sequitur, and the taps below his feet

TRANSPORTATION: NORTH BEACH

Bus Lines 30 and 45 run up Stockton St from Union Square; buses 15 and 41 run along Columbus Ave.
Cable car The Powell-Mason St line skirts the top of North Beach – get off at Vallejo or Green Sts and walk about three blocks to Columbus Ave.
Parking Street parking is remotely possible, but a waste of time. Try your luck first at the public Good Luck Parking Garage (p84), on Vallejo St between Powell and Stockton Sts.

THE FIERY, FEISTY HEIRESS

In 19th-century San Francisco, fire engines were usually pulled by horses, but they had to be pushed up steep inclines by firefighters, who until 1866 were well-to-do volunteers. There were some 16 squads in all, and No 5 had the advantage of being urged on by its mascot, the self-appointed fire cheerleader and eccentric heiress Lillie Hancock Coit. She was the ultimate groupie: she could drink, smoke and play cards as well as any off-duty firefighter, rarely missed a fire or a firefighter's funeral, and even had the firehouse emblem embroidered on her bedsheets. Eventually she split town to join the bohemian scene in Paris, but she left $5000 (about $50K today) in her will to each firefighter in the No 5 company, and funds to construct the monument to the city's firefighters now known as **Coit Tower** (opposite).

falsely advertise mineral water from Vichy, France – yet another example of a puzzling public artwork courtesy of a certifiable SF eccentric, Henry D Cogswell, who made his fortune fitting miners with gold fillings.

BEAT MUSEUM Map p87

☎ 1-800-537-6822 (1-800-KER-OUAC); www.thebeatmuseum.org; 540 Broadway; admission $5; 10am-6pm Mon & Tue, to 10pm Wed-Sun; 15, 30, 41, 45

The Beat goes on, and on – OK, so it rambles a little – at this truly obsessive collection of SF literary-scene ephemera c 1950–69. The banned edition of Allen Ginsberg's *Howl* is the ultimate free-speech trophy, and the 1961 check Jack Kerouac wrote to a liquor store has a certain dark humor, but some items are head-shakers: did those Kerouac bobble-head dolls and yo-yos ever really go into mass production?

Enter the museum through a turnstile in the back of the store, grab a ramshackle reclaimed theater seat redolent with the accumulated odors of pot and pets, and watch fascinating films about the Beat era's leading musicians, artists, writers, politicos and undefinable characters. Upstairs there are shrines to individual Beats with first-hand remembrances and artifacts, and first editions of books that expanded the American outlook to include the margins. Downstairs in the store, you can buy poetry chapbooks and limited-run editions of obscure Beat titles you won't find elsewhere, and entry to this part is free.

SAINTS PETER & PAUL CHURCH Map p87

☎ 415-421-0809; www.stspeterpaul.san-francisco.ca.us; 666 Filbert St; admission free; 7:30am-4pm; 15, 30, 41, 45

Wedding cake was the apparent inspiration for this 1924 triple-decker cathedral with its lacy white towers, and in its downtime between masses in Italian and Chinese, the church pulls a triple wedding shift on Saturdays. Joe DiMaggio and Marilyn Monroe had their wedding photos taken here, though they weren't permitted to marry in the church because both had been divorced (they got hitched at City Hall instead).

True to North Beach literary form, there's poetry by Dante in a glittering mosaic inscription over the grand triple entryway: 'The glory of Him who moves all things/ penetrates and glows throughout the universe.' How very Ginsberg-meets-the-Beatles.

BOB KAUFMAN ALLEY Map p87

off Grant Ave near Filbert St; 15, 30, 41, 45

What, you mean your hometown doesn't have a street named after an African American Catholic-Jewish-voodoo anarchist Beat poet who refused to speak for 12 years? The man revered in France as the 'American Rimbaud' was a major poet who helped found the legendary *Beatitudes* magazine in 1959 and a spoken-word bebop jazz artist who was never at a loss for words, yet he felt compelled to take a Buddhist vow of silence after John F Kennedy's assassination that he kept until the end of the Vietnam War.

Kaufman's life was hardly pure poetry: he was a teenage runaway, periodically found himself homeless, was occasionally jailed for picking fights in poetry with police, battled methamphetamine addiction with varying success and once claimed his goal was to be forgotten. Yet like the man himself, this hidden alleyway in his honor is offbeat, streetwise and often profoundly silent.

NORTH BEACH BEAT

Walking Tour

1 City Lights Bookstore (p146) At the home of Beat poetry and free speech, get some lit to inspire your journey into the heart of literary North Beach – Lawrence Ferlinghetti's *San Francisco Poems* is a good bet.

2 Caffe Trieste (p198) Order a potent espresso, check out the opera on the jukebox and slide into the back booth where Francis Ford Coppola allegedly wrote his first draft of *The Godfather*. This place has been beloved since 1956, with the local characters and bathroom wall poetry to prove it.

3 Washington Square (p88) Pause to admire parrots in the treetops and octogenarians' smooth tai chi moves below: pure poetry in motion.

4 Liguria Bakery (p175) Focaccia hot from a hundred-year-old oven makes a worthy pit stop for ravenous readers.

5 Bob Kaufman Alley (p89) This quiet alley renamed for the legendary street-corner poet, who broke a 12-year vow of silence when he walked into a North Beach cafe and recited 'All Those Ships That Never Sailed': 'Today I bring them back/Huge and transitory/And let them sail/Forever.'

6 Beat Museum (p89) Don't be surprised to hear a Dylan jam session by the front door, or see Allen Ginsberg naked in documentary footage screened inside the museum: the Beat goes on here in rare form.

7 Specs' (p197) Begin your literary bar crawl here amid merchant-marine memorabilia, tall tales, choice words worthy of a sailor and a glass of (what else?) Anchor Steam.

8 Vesuvio (p198) Jack Kerouac once blew off Henry Miller to go on a bender here; try the house brew and see if you have the will to continue this walking tour…

9 Jack Kerouac Alley (p88) It's poetic justice that this mural-covered byway is named for the *On the Road* author, since this is where he was tossed after a raucous night at Vesuvio. Kerouac's words embedded in the alley seem to sum up North Beach nights: 'The air was soft, the stars so fine, and the promise of every cobbled alley so great…'

10 Li Po (p197) Follow the literary lead of Kerouac and Ginsberg and end your night in a vinyl booth at Li Po, with another beer beneath the gold Buddha's forgiving gaze.

WALK FACTS

Start City Lights Bookstore
End Li Po
Distance 1.5 miles
Time Two hours
Exertion Easy
Fuel stops Caffe Trieste, Liguria Bakery, Specs', Vesuvio, Li Po

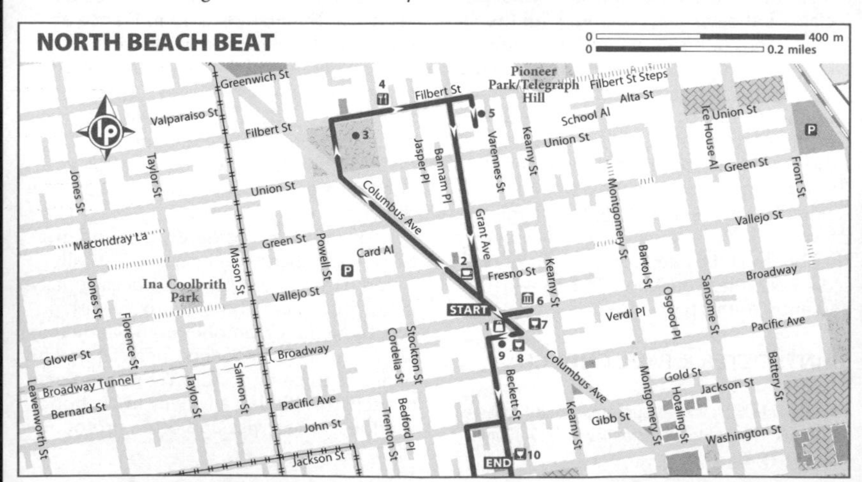

RUSSIAN & NOB HILLS

Drinking p198; Eating p175; Shopping p147; Sleeping p257

Many a San Francisco fortune has been made on two words: what if? This is the question 19th-century inventor Andrew Hallidie asked himself as he gazed upward at the windswept 338ft crag of Nob Hill, which no one in their right mind wanted to climb after a long day's work Downtown. Much to the dismay of Nob Hill hermits inhabiting shotgun shacks, Hallidie found the ideal solution to the seemingly insurmountable problem. By the 1870s Hallidie's cable car provided easy access to breathtaking views on the summit of Nob Hill, which soon after became prime real estate, with the hill's crest covered in mansions.

top picks

RUSSIAN & NOB HILLS

- **Sterling Park** (below)
- **Grace Cathedral** (p93)
- **Diego Rivera Gallery** (p93)
- **Cable Car Museum** (p94)

But nature had other 'what if' scenarios in store: earthquake and fire. Without a windbreak between them, almost all the fine Nob Hill mansions were destroyed when the 1906 earthquake struck and the subsequent fire swept uphill. Today, elegant, tight-lipped Nob Hill is something of a non sequitur in nonconformist San Francisco – but you have to give it credit for reinvention and retaining a little mystery. Nob Hill is big on swanky old hotels, boys' clubs and secret societies. The thrice-rebuilt Grace Cathedral (p93) has also retained an air of intrigue, with its indoor and outdoor labyrinths. But for truly arcane fascination, two Nob Hill institutions are tied for top place: mysterious Masonic Auditorium (p94), with glowing esoteric symbols in its stained-glass windows, and the tiki-riffic Tonga Room (p198).

Adjacent Russian Hill also became accessible with Hallidie's cable car, but more greenery was kept intact between Russian Hill's more modest homes and flats. Today, the garden stairway walks of Russian Hill are lined with minuscule playgrounds for tots who brave the climb, and hidden cottages with major literary merits. In 1952 Jack Kerouac manically wrote *On the Road* in a tiny Russian Hill shack he shared with Neal and Carolyn Cassady in a convoluted free-love triangle, and Armistead Maupin modeled the setting of his bestselling novel *Tales of the City* on Russian Hill's Macondray Lane (p94). Visitors intent solely on a joyride down zigzagging Lombard St miss out on some of the city's best-kept secrets in Russian Hill, including a mural of the city by Diego Rivera in the Diego Rivera Gallery (p93) at San Francisco Art Institute.

The downhill slide of Russian and Nob Hills known as Polk Gulch made no secret of its male-bonding rituals, and by the 1960s it had become gay San Francisco's main drag (in more ways than one). Since then upper Polk St has almost detached itself from its out-and-proud history, with swanky restaurants and boutiques, but lower Polk, Hyde and Larkin Sts still have gay bars, hustlers, funky vintage shops, low-cost housing and grit. Polk Gulch makes for an adventurous bar crawl.

STERLING PARK Map p92

www.rhn.org/pointofinterestparks.html; Greenwich & Hyde Sts; 19, 41, 45, 47, 49, 76; Powell-Hyde;

'Homeward into the sunset/Still unwearied we go,/Till the northern hills are misty/With the amber of afterglow.' Poet George Sterling's 'City by the Sea' is almost maudlin – that is, until you watch the sunset over the Golden Gate from the hilltop park named in his honor.

Sterling was a great romancer of all San Francisco had to offer, including nature, idealism, free love and occasionally opium, and was frequently broke. But as the toast of the secretive, elite **Bohemian Club** (p74), San Francisco's high society indulged the poet in all his eccentricities, including carrying a lethal dose of cyanide as a reminder of life's transience. Broken by his ex-wife's suicide and the loss of his best friend, novelist Jack London, the 'King of Bohemia' apparently took this bitter dose in 1926 inside his apartment in the club. Within two years his influential friends had this park – with zigzagging paths and stirring, Sterling views – named after him.

If you're not left breathless by these hilltop views, play tennis on the adjacent public court named after San Francisco's Alice

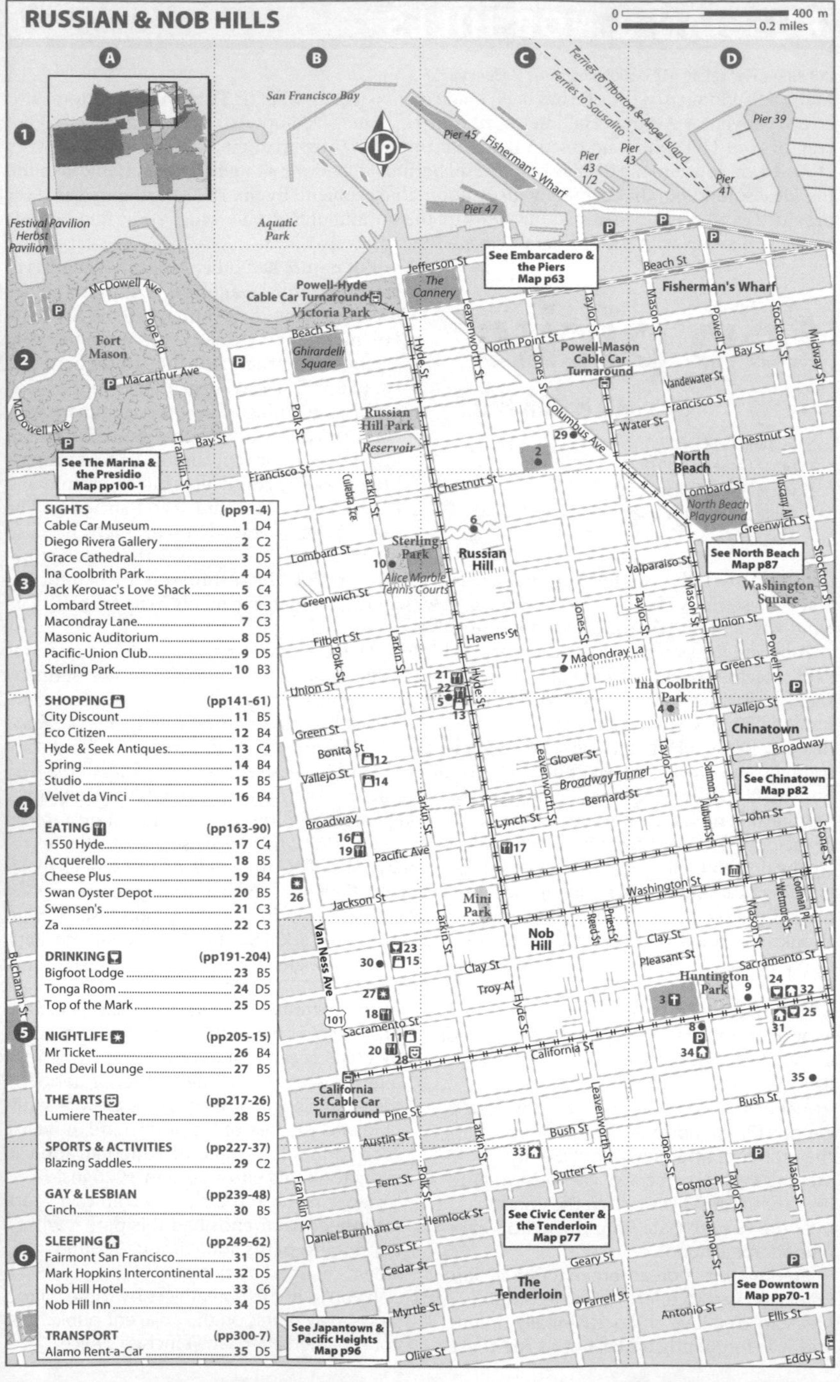
RUSSIAN & NOB HILLS
0 400 m
0 0.2 miles
A
B
C
D
1
2
3
4
5
6
San Francisco Bay
Ferries to Tiburon & Angel Island
Ferries to Sausalito
Pier 39
Pier 45
Fisherman's Wharf
Pier 43 1/2
Pier 43
Pier 41
Pier 47
Festival Pavilion
Herbst Pavilion
Aquatic Park
See Embarcadero & the Piers Map p63
Jefferson St
Beach St
Fisherman's Wharf
Powell-Hyde Cable Car Turnaround
The Cannery
Victoria Park
McDowell Ave
Pope Rd
Fort Mason
Macarthur Ave
Ghirardelli Square
North Point St
Powell-Mason Cable Car Turnaround
Bay St
Vandewater St
Francisco St
Water St
Chestnut St
Columbus Ave
Russian Hill Park
Reservoir
North Beach
Lombard St
North Beach Playground
Greenwich St
See The Marina & the Presidio Map pp100-1
Franklin St
Polk St
Culebra Tce
Larkin St
Hyde St
Leavenworth St
Jones St
Taylor St
Mason St
Powell St
Stockton St
Midway St
Tuscany Al
Sterling Park
Russian Hill
Alice Marble Tennis Courts
Valparaiso St
See North Beach Map p87
Washington Square
Union St
Filbert St
Havens St
Macondray La
Green St
Ina Coolbrith Park
Vallejo St
Chinatown
Broadway
Bonita St
Glover St
Broadway Tunnel
Bernard St
See Chinatown Map p82
Salmon St
Auburn St
John St
Stone St
Lynch St
Pacific Ave
Washington St
Wetmore St
Codman Pl
Jackson St
Mini Park
Nob Hill
Reed St
Priest St
Clay St
Pleasant St
Sacramento St
Huntington Park
Troy Al
Van Ness Ave
California St
California St Cable Car Turnaround
Pine St
Bush St
Austin St
Sutter St
Fern St
Cosmo Pl
Shannon St
Hemlock St
See Civic Center & the Tenderloin Map p77
Daniel Burnham Ct
Post St
Geary St
Cedar St
The Tenderloin
O'Farrell St
See Downtown Map pp70-1
Myrtle St
Antonio St
Ellis St
See Japantown & Pacific Heights Map p96
Olive St
Eddy St
Buchanan St
SIGHTS (pp91-4)
Cable Car Museum 1 D4
Diego Rivera Gallery 2 C2
Grace Cathedral 3 D5
Ina Coolbrith Park 4 D4
Jack Kerouac's Love Shack 5 C4
Lombard Street 6 C3
Macondray Lane 7 C3
Masonic Auditorium 8 D5
Pacific-Union Club 9 D5
Sterling Park 10 B3
SHOPPING (pp141-61)
City Discount 11 B5
Eco Citizen 12 B4
Hyde & Seek Antiques 13 C4
Spring 14 B4
Studio 15 B5
Velvet da Vinci 16 B4
EATING (pp163-90)
1550 Hyde 17 C4
Acquerello 18 B5
Cheese Plus 19 B4
Swan Oyster Depot 20 B5
Swensen's 21 C3
Za 22 C3
DRINKING (pp191-204)
Bigfoot Lodge 23 B5
Tonga Room 24 D5
Top of the Mark 25 D5
NIGHTLIFE (pp205-15)
Mr Ticket 26 B4
Red Devil Lounge 27 B5
THE ARTS (pp217-26)
Lumiere Theater 28 B5
SPORTS & ACTIVITIES (pp227-37)
Blazing Saddles 29 C2
GAY & LESBIAN (pp239-48)
Cinch 30 B5
SLEEPING (pp249-62)
Fairmont San Francisco 31 D5
Mark Hopkins Intercontinental 32 D5
Nob Hill Hotel 33 C6
Nob Hill Inn 34 D5
TRANSPORT (pp300-7)
Alamo Rent-a-Car 35 D5

Marble, the 1930s tennis champ who recovered from tuberculosis to win Wimbledon and serve as a US secret agent among the Nazis during WWII. Sure puts a little post-tennis panting into perspective, doesn't it?

DIEGO RIVERA GALLERY Map p92

☎ 415-771-7020; www.sfai.edu; 800 Chestnut St; admission free; 🕑 9am-7:30pm; 🚌 30; 🚋 Powell-Mason

No, you're not seeing double: Diego Rivera's 1931 *The Making of a Fresco Showing a Building of a City* is a trompe l'oeil fresco within a fresco, showing the artist himself as he pauses to admire his work, as well as the work in progress that is San Francisco.

The fresco takes up an entire wall in the Diego Rivera Gallery at the San Francisco Art Institute, on your left through the entryway courtyard. For a memorable 3-D San Francisco vista, head down the corridor to the terrace cafe for espresso and panoramic bay views.

LOMBARD STREET Map p92

1000 block btwn Hyde & Leavenworth Sts; 🚋 Powell-Hyde; 🚸

You've seen its eight switchbacks in a thousand photographs. The tourist board has dubbed this 'the world's crookedest street,' which is factually incorrect. Vermont St in Potrero Hill deserves this street cred, but Lombard is (much) more scenic, with its red-brick pavement and lovingly tended flowerbeds. It wasn't always so bent; before the automobile it lunged straight down the hill.

TRANSPORTATION: RUSSIAN & NOB HILLS

Bus Bus 45 runs along Union St in Russian Hill. Bus 1 runs along Clay and Sacramento Sts in Nob Hill. Polk Gulch is accessible via bus 19, and is one block from Van Ness Ave buses 47 and 49.

Cable car The Powell-Hyde St line skirts the downtown side of Nob Hill, then doglegs to Hyde St, which takes it up Russian Hill. The Powell-Mason St line traces the Downtown side of Nob and Russian Hills. The California St line scales Nob Hill through the heart of the neighborhood.

Parking Street parking can be found by diligently circulating and then pouncing on the first available spot. There's a public lot on Taylor St, opposite the Huntington Hotel.

Don't try anything funny. The recent clampdown on renegade skaters means that the Lombard St thrills featured in Tony Hawk's Pro Skater video game will remain strictly virtual, at least until the cops get slack. Until 2008, every Easter Sunday for seven years adults had arrived at the crest of Lombard St toting plastic toy tricycles for the annual Bring Your Own Big Wheel Race. But after vehement complaints from killjoy residents, the art prankster organizers moved their toy-joyride to – where else? – Vermont St. Check www.jonbrumit.com/byobw.html for the latest.

INA COOLBRITH PARK Map p92

Vallejo St; 🚋 Powell-Mason

On the San Francisco literary scene, all roads eventually lead to Ina Coolbrith, California's first poet laureate; colleague of Mark Twain and Ansel Adams; mentor of Jack London, Isadora Duncan, George Sterling and Charlotte Perkins Gilman; and lapsed Mormon (she kept secret from her bohemian posse that her uncle was Mormon prophet Joseph Smith). The tiny park is a fitting honor, long on romance and exclamation-inspiring vistas. Climb past gardens, decks and flower-framed apartment buildings and, as the fog blows in, listen for the whooshing wind in the treetops.

JACK KEROUAC'S LOVE SHACK Map p92

29 Russell St; 🚌 19, 41, 45, 47, 49, 76; 🚋 Powell-Hyde

This modest house on a quiet alley was the source of major literature and major drama from 1951 to 1952, when Jack Kerouac shacked up with Neal and Carolyn Cassady and their baby daughter to pound out his 120ft-long scroll draft of *On the Road*. Jack and Carolyn became lovers at her husband Neal's suggestion, but Carolyn frequently kicked them both out – though Neal was allowed to move back for the birth of their son John Allen Cassady (named for Jack, and Allen Ginsberg).

GRACE CATHEDRAL Map p92

☎ 415-749-6300; www.gracecathedral.org; 1100 California St; except for services, suggested donation for adult/child $3/2; 🕑 7am-6pm Mon-Fri, 8am-6pm Sat, 8am-7pm Sun, services 8:30am & 11am (with choir) Sun; 🚌 1, 27; 🚋 California

This Episcopal church has been rebuilt three times since the Gold Rush, and the current French-inspired, reinforced concrete cathedral took 40 years to complete.

But Grace keeps pace with the times. Its commitment to pressing social issues is embodied in its AIDS Memorial Chapel, which has a bronze altarpiece by artist-activist Keith Haring. Here his signature figures are angels taking flight – especially powerful imagery as this was his last work before death by AIDS in 1990.

Grace's spectacular stained-glass windows include a series dedicated to human endeavor, including one of Albert Einstein uplifted in a swirl of nuclear particles. Day and night you'll notice people absorbed in thought while walking the outdoor, inlaid stone labyrinth, meant to guide restless souls through three spiritual stages: releasing, receiving and returning. Check the website for events at the indoor labyrinth, which include meditation services and yoga.

MACONDRAY LANE Map p92

btwn Taylor & Leavenworth Sts; 41, 45; Powell-Mason

This scenic route down from Ina Coolbrith Park via a steep stairway and gravity-defying wooden cottages is so charming that it looks like something out of a novel. And so it is: Armistead Maupin used this as the model for Barbary Lane in his *Tales of the City* series.

MASONIC AUDITORIUM Map p92

415-776-4702; www.masonicauditorium.com; 1111 California St; 10am-3pm Mon-Fri; 1; California

Conspiracy theorists, jazz aficionados and anyone exploring immigrant roots should know about Masonic Auditorium. Built as a temple to freemasonry in 1958, the building regularly hosts top jazz acts, such as Wynton Marsalis and the Lincoln Center Jazz Orchestra, and the Preservation Hall Jazz Band. And every other Tuesday morning it hosts mass US-citizenship swearing-in ceremonies.

If you're looking for confirmation that California is run by a secret club, well, here you have it: many of the nation's founding fathers were Freemasons, including George Washington, and the same can be said about California's. It's all captured in the modernist stained-glass windows, which supposedly depict founders of Freemasonry in California and their accomplishments – that is, if you can decipher the enigmatic symbols and snippets of fabric embedded in the glass. The frieze below the windows has soil and gravel samples from all 58 California counties, plus Hawaii for some reason known only to those in on the secret handshake. Downstairs a visitors center and art displays reveal some of the society's intriguing secrets.

CABLE CAR MUSEUM Map p92

415-474-1887; www.cablecarmuseum.org; 1201 Mason St; admission free; 10am-6pm Apr-Sep, to 5pm Oct-Mar; Powell-Mason, Powell-Hyde;

Grips, engines, braking mechanisms…if terms like these warm your gearhead heart, you will be completely besotted with the Cable Car Museum, housed in the city's still-functioning cable-car barn. See three original 1870s cable cars and watch as cables glide over huge bull wheels – as awesome a feat of physics now as when the mechanism was invented by Andrew Hallidie in 1873.

PACIFIC-UNION CLUB Map p92

1000 California St; 1; California

The only Nob Hill mansion to survive the 1906 earthquake and fire is a squat neoclassical brownstone, which despite its grandeur lacks architectural imagination. Today it's a private men's club. The exclusive membership roster lists newspaper magnates, both Hewlett and Packard of Hewlett-Packard, several US secretaries of defense and government contractors (insert conspiracy theory here).

Democrats, people of color and anyone under 45 are scarce on the published list, but little else is known about the 800-odd, all-male membership: members can be expelled for leaking information. Cheeky cross-dressing protesters have pointed out that there's no specific ban on transgender/transvestite visitors supping in its main dining room or walking through the front door – privileges denied women. Give it a try and report back, won't you?

JAPANTOWN & PACIFIC HEIGHTS

Drinking p198; Eating p176; Shopping p148; Sleeping p258

Porcelain kitties wave from every countertop here, but like the floating town in Hayao Miyazaki's *Spirited Away,* picturesque Japantown is also the site where trials have been endured and legends made. Retro Japan Center (p97) looks like it's torn from a 1960s Japanese leisure travel brochure, but actually San Francisco's Japanese community dates back to at least the 1860s – not that it's been an easy 150 years. First there were California's anti-Asian exclusion laws passed in the 1870s, limiting employment and marriage for San Franciscans born in Japan. Then came the 1906 earthquake and fire, when local Japanese fled to an area of lower Pacific Heights that came to be known as Nihonjinmachi, or 'Japanese people's town,' starting businesses, schools, temples and newspapers. Second- and third-generation Japanese San Franciscans had already gained citizenship and joined the US armed forces to fight the Axis powers (including Japan) by 1942, when President Roosevelt signed Executive Order 9066, mandating the removal of residents of Japanese heritage, including US citizens.

top picks

JAPANTOWN & PACIFIC HEIGHTS

- Kabuki Springs & Spa (p237)
- Yoshi's (p211)
- Sundance Kabuki Cinema (p221)
- Japan Center (p97)
- Benkyodo (p177)

Japantown's approximately 7000 residents were rounded up and sent to internment camps, bringing only what they could carry. Long-term residents and US citizens alike endured cramped living conditions under armed guard and, to add insult to injury, were required to sign loyalty oaths under threat of deportation to Japan. Japanese Americans immediately took their civil rights case to the courts and, for almost 40 years, fought for reparations and an official letter of apology from the US government (finally delivered by President George HW Bush). Japanese American GIs finished tours of duty in WWII to find they often didn't have a home to return to, and many Japanese Americans were resettled by the government in makeshift Japantown apartments, downhill from Victorian family homes they'd once owned.

All of this would be hard to imagine from looking at today's 'Little Osaka,' where stores are cheerfully crammed with panda-shaped staplers and iron teapots, and sushi and karaoke bars greet diners with '*Konichiwa!*' Yoshi's p211) has brought jazz back south of Geary, and there's even the Japanese anime-themed Hotel Tomo (p258). The most obvious dramas here unfold in ikebana window displays, Sundance Kabuki Cinema (p221) and *taiko* drumming demonstrations during the Cherry Blossom Festival (p21). Yet the community is as active as ever, holding protests against treatment of US prisoners in Guantanamo Bay and co-hosting Ramadan celebrations with the city's Arab American and South Asian Muslim population. No wonder the octogenarians at Kabuki Springs & Spa (p237) seem so sprightly.

Uphill from Japantown, Pacific Heights seems to lead a charmed existence, with Victorians miraculously spared from the 1906 earthquake and fire, panoramic hilltop parks, high-end restaurants and designer boutiques. Alta Plaza and Lafayette Parks offer stunning views along Pacific Heights' northern ridge, surrounded by outrageous Victorians, whose original vibrant paint jobs have been painted over with more saleable shades of white, gray and beige. Coincidentally enough, these colors are also a fair reflection of the ethnic makeup of the neighborhood, which in multiculti SF is often derisively referred to as 'Specific Whites.' But behind those stately doors, weekly séances and ambient-music concerts are held, and pug parades are held in Alta Plaza Park the first Sunday of the month from 1pm to 4pm. Never underestimate SF's colorful eccentricity.

Japantown is west of Franklin St, east of Divisadero St, and below California to Geary Sts, where it merges with the historically African American Fillmore district. Some gorgeous Victorian homes survive around Japantown; spot a few along Pine and Bush Sts. Japantown is south of Pacific Heights, which in turn is south of the Marina and the bay. Wide Geary St runs from Downtown art galleries past Japan Center (p97) with its Peace Pagoda (p97). Boutique-packed Fillmore St runs north–south through Japantown and Pacific Heights, while California St runs from the Financial District through Nob Hill to the heart of Pacific Heights, and onward to the Richmond.

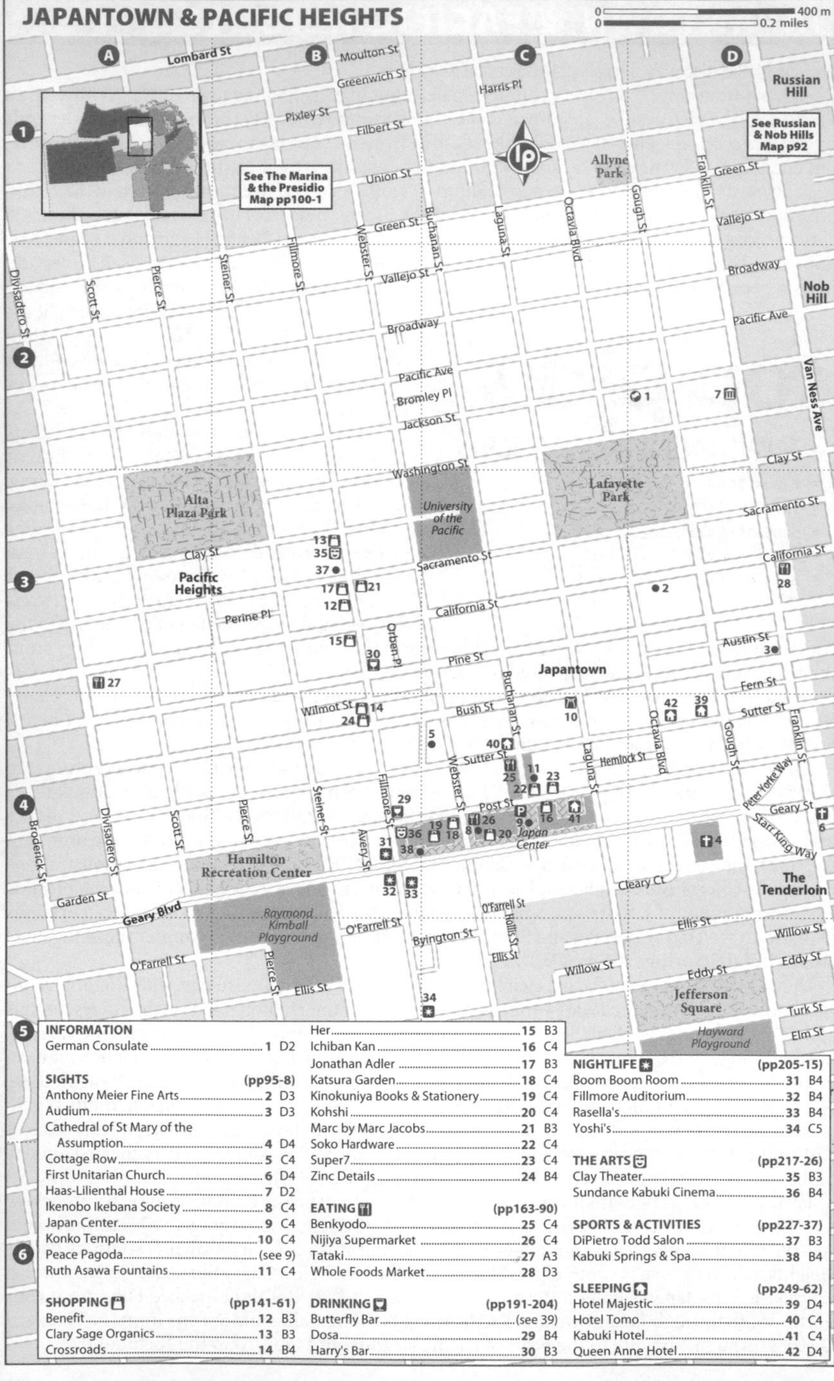
JAPANTOWN & PACIFIC HEIGHTS
0 400 m
0 0.2 miles
A
B
C
D
1
2
3
4
5
6
Lombard St
Moulton St
Greenwich St
Harris Pl
Pixley St
Filbert St
Union St
Green St
Vallejo St
Broadway
Pacific Ave
Bromley Pl
Jackson St
Washington St
Clay St
Sacramento St
California St
Perine Pl
Pine St
Austin St
Fern St
Wilmot St
Bush St
Sutter St
Hemlock St
Post St
Geary St
Geary Blvd
Starr King Way
Peter Yorke Way
Cleary Ct
Garden St
O'Farrell St
Byington St
Ellis St
Willow St
Eddy St
Turk St
Elm St
Divisadero St
Scott St
Pierce St
Steiner St
Fillmore St
Webster St
Buchanan St
Laguna St
Octavia Blvd
Gough St
Franklin St
Van Ness Ave
Orben Pl
Avery St
Hollis St
Broderick St
Russian Hill
See Russian & Nob Hills Map p92
See The Marina & the Presidio Map pp100-1
Allyne Park
Nob Hill
Alta Plaza Park
University of the Pacific
Lafayette Park
Pacific Heights
Japantown
Japan Center
Hamilton Recreation Center
Raymond Kimball Playground
The Tenderloin
Jefferson Square
Hayward Playground
INFORMATION
German Consulate 1 D2
SIGHTS (pp95-8)
Anthony Meier Fine Arts 2 D3
Audium 3 D3
Cathedral of St Mary of the Assumption 4 D4
Cottage Row 5 C4
First Unitarian Church 6 D4
Haas-Lilienthal House 7 D2
Ikenobo Ikebana Society 8 C4
Japan Center 9 C4
Konko Temple 10 C4
Peace Pagoda (see 9)
Ruth Asawa Fountains 11 C4
SHOPPING (pp141-61)
Benefit 12 B3
Clary Sage Organics 13 B3
Crossroads 14 B4
Her 15 B3
Ichiban Kan 16 C4
Jonathan Adler 17 B3
Katsura Garden 18 C4
Kinokuniya Books & Stationery 19 C4
Kohshi 20 C4
Marc by Marc Jacobs 21 B3
Soko Hardware 22 C4
Super7 23 C4
Zinc Details 24 B4
EATING (pp163-90)
Benkyodo 25 C4
Nijiya Supermarket 26 C4
Tataki 27 A3
Whole Foods Market 28 D3
DRINKING (pp191-204)
Butterfly Bar (see 39)
Dosa 29 B4
Harry's Bar 30 B3
NIGHTLIFE (pp205-15)
Boom Boom Room 31 B4
Fillmore Auditorium 32 B4
Rasella's 33 B4
Yoshi's 34 C5
THE ARTS (pp217-26)
Clay Theater 35 B3
Sundance Kabuki Cinema 36 B4
SPORTS & ACTIVITIES (pp227-37)
DiPietro Todd Salon 37 B3
Kabuki Springs & Spa 38 B4
SLEEPING (pp249-62)
Hotel Majestic 39 D4
Hotel Tomo 40 C4
Kabuki Hotel 41 C4
Queen Anne Hotel 42 D4

JAPAN CENTER Map p96

www.sfjapantown.org; 1625 Post St; 10am-midnight; 2, 3, 4, 22, 38

Entering this oddly charming mall is like walking onto a 1960s Japanese movie set – the fake-rock waterfall, indoor wooden pedestrian bridges, rock gardens and curtained wooden restaurant entryways have hardly aged a day since the mall's grand opening in 1968. If not for the anachronistic Tare Panda cell-phone charms and Harajuku fashion mags displayed at Kinokuniya Books & Stationery (p148), Japan Center would be a total time warp.

PEACE PAGODA Map p96

Peace Plaza, Japan Center; 2, 3, 4, 22, 38

When San Francisco's sister city of Osaka, Japan, made a gift of Yoshiro Taniguchi's five-tiered concrete stupa to the people of San Francisco in 1968, the city seemed stupa-fied what to do with the minimalist monument, and kept clustering boxed shrubs around its stark nakedness. But with some well-placed cherry trees and low, hewn-rock benches in the plaza, the pagoda is finally in its element au naturel.

RUTH ASAWA FOUNTAINS Map p96

Buchanan Pedestrian St; 2, 3, 4, 22, 38

Sit inside the fountain, splash around and stay awhile: celebrated sculptor and former WWII internee Ruth Asawa designed these fountains to be lived in, not observed from a polite distance. Bronze origami dandelions sprout from polished-pebble pools, with benches built right in for *bento*-box picnics. On rare warm days along this wind-tunnel pedestrian block, kids frolic and weary shoppers enjoy footbaths under the dandelions.

TRANSPORTATION: JAPANTOWN & PACIFIC HEIGHTS

Bus The 38 follows Geary St from Downtown to Japantown. Bus 1 runs up California St to Pacific Heights. Bus 22 runs the length of Fillmore St on its way from the Mission to the Marina.

Cable car The California St line terminates at Van Ness Ave, from where you can take a strenuous seven-block trek up to Fillmore St.

Parking Street parking, while limited, can usually be found on quieter residential streets. There's a parking garage at Japan Center.

ANTHONY MEIER FINE ARTS Map p96

415-351-1400; www.anthonymeierfinearts.com; 1969 California St; by appointment; 1, 2, 3, 4, 22

The toast of international art fairs, Anthony Meier specializes in abstract thinking from major museum artists and emerging talents, from Richard Tuttle's shape-shifting abstract assemblages to lacy, ethereal collages made of transparent office tape by San Francisco's own Rosana Castrillo Diaz.

IKENOBO IKEBANA SOCIETY Map p96

415-567-1011; Japan Center, 1625 Post St; 2, 3, 4, 22, 38

Even shoppers hell-bent on iron teapots and *maneki neko* (waving kitty) figurines stop and stare at the arrangements in the windows here. This is the oldest and largest society outside Japan for ikebana, the Japanese art of flower arranging, and has the displays to prove it: a curly willow branch tickling a narcissus under its chin in an abstract *jiyubana* (freestyle) arrangement, and a traditional seven-part *rikka* landscape featuring pine and iris.

COTTAGE ROW Map p96

off Bush St btwn Webster & Fillmore Sts; 2, 3, 4, 22, 38

Take a detour to days of yore when San Francisco was a sleepy seaside fishing village, before houses got all uptight, upright and Victorian. Easygoing 19th-century California clapboard cottages hang back along a brick-paved pedestrian promenade and let plum trees and bonsai take center stage. The homes are private, but the mini-park is public and ideal for a sushi picnic.

KONKO TEMPLE Map p96

415-931-0453; www.konkofaith.org; 1909 Bush St; 8am-6pm Mon-Sat, to 3pm Sun; 2, 3, 4, 22

Inside the low-roofed, high-modernist temple, you'll find a handsome blond-wood sanctuary with a lofty beamed ceiling, vintage photographs of Konko events dating back 70 years, and friendly Reverend Joanne Tolosa, who'll greet you, answer any questions about the temple or its Shinto-based beliefs, and then leave you to your contemplation. On New Year's Day, the temple invites visitors to jot down a remembrance, regret and wish on a slip of paper to affix to a tree, and receive a blessing with sacred rice wine.

SAN FRANCISCO'S UNORTHODOX RELIGIOUS ARCHITECTURE

Geary Ave is San Francisco's major east–west thoroughfare, and you'll notice some of its most prominent churches along or near this artery. A US post office now stands on the Geary St location of Jim Jones' People's Temple, which was leveled after the tragedy in Jonestown (p34). In the neighborhood, these churches stand out of the landscape:

First Unitarian Church (Map p96; ☎ 415-776-4580; www.uusf.org; 1187 Franklin St; services 11am Sun; 38, 49) Low-down and rough around the edges aren't usually meant as compliments, and they're not usually applied to a church. But George Percy's down-to-earth 1888 design for a cathedral in rough-hewn stone was considered appropriate by the progressive Universalists, whose current church committees include a pagan interest group and gay marriage advocacy. The 1970–74 annex built by Callister Payne & Rosse is a modernist eye-catcher that's conceptually consistent with the older structure: a low, concrete-slab building that makes no secret of its construction. The design for the annex owes an obvious debt to Frank Lloyd Wright's Unity Temple in Oak Park, Illinois, as well as local Japanese influences appropriate to its location at the edge of Japantown.

Cathedral of St Mary of the Assumption (Map p96; ☎ 415-567-2020; www.stmarycathedralsf.org; 1111 Gough St; admission free; 6:45am-12:10pm Mon-Fri, 6:45am-5:30pm Sat, 7:30am-1pm Sun; 38, 49) You might assume from afar that this 1971 concrete cathedral is a ship's prow or witch's hat. This behemoth started out as a modest proposal by a local architecture firm, but the archbishop read architectural criticism in his spare time and hired MIT guru Pietro Belluschi and Italian engineer Pier-Luigi Nervi to construct this sci-fi Catholic landmark. Say what you will about the exterior, but the honeycomb ceiling has great acoustics for organ recitals.

African Orthodox Church of St John Coltrane (Map pp126–7; ☎ 415-673-7144; www.coltranechurch.org; 1286 Fillmore St; mass noon-3pm Sun; 21, 22, 24) Cymbals shudder, and the bassist plucks the opening notes of 'A Love Supreme.' The liturgy has begun just as it has every Sunday since 1971, and the entire congregation joins in the three-hour devotional jam session. As Coltrane once said: 'Damn the rules; it's the feeling that counts.' Overseeing the celebration from mesmerizing icons on the wall is the musician venerated here as St John Will-I-Am Coltrane, shown with flames leaping from his saxophone.

HAAS-LILIENTHAL HOUSE Map p96

☎ 415-441-3004; www.sfheritage.org/house.html; 2007 Franklin St; adult/senior & child $8/5; noon-3pm Wed & Sat, 11am-4pm Sun; 1, 12, 19, 27, 47, 49

A grand Queen Anne–style Victorian with its original period splendor c 1882, this family mansion looks like a Clue game come to life – Colonel Mustard could definitely have committed murder with a rope in the dark-wood ballroom, or Miss Scarlet with a candlestick in the red-velvet parlor. One-hour tours are led by volunteer docents whose devotion to Victoriana is almost cultish.

AUDIUM Map p96

☎ 415-771-1616; www.audium.org; 1616 Bush St; admission $15; performances 8:30pm Fri & Sat, arrive by 8:15pm; 1, 2, 3, 4, 22

Sit in total darkness as Stan Shaff plays his hour-plus compositions of sounds emitted by his sound chamber, which sometimes degenerate into 1970s sci-fi sound effects before resolving into oddly endearing Moog synthesizer wheezes. The Audium was specifically sculpted in 1962 to produce bizarre acoustic effects and eerie soundscapes that only a true stoner could enjoy for two solid hours in the dark – you know who you are.

THE MARINA & THE PRESIDIO

Drinking p199; Eating p177; Shopping p150; Sleeping p258

Wandering through boutique-lined streets, past a yacht harbor and onward to pine-sheltered beaches, it's hard to imagine just how forbidding and stinky this place once was. Since the Presidio was turned into a national park in 1996, it has looked more like it did in the mid-19th century, when both the Presidio and the Marina were mostly wilderness. Not many people wanted to be downwind from the Marina back in those early days, when inland breezes carried the stench of cattle, moonshine stills, drying fish and most of Northern California's dirty laundry. Now the Marina is strictly top-drawer and dry-cleaned, with sales reps and ad execs descending in all their front-office finery at happy hour.

San Francisco's official motto is still 'Oro in Paz, Fierro in Guerra' (Gold in Peace, Iron in War), but these days San Francisco is much more leisurely than iron-willed. At the north end of the Marina is Fort Mason, where, since the 1970s, former military warehouses have hosted avant-garde theater, art fairs, community nonprofits and fine organic vegetarian dining. The wooded Presidio coastline beyond is dotted with kites, surfers and nudists where once there were fighter planes, gunboats and cannons – the battle-hardened officers who once bunked here would probably have scoffed at camo-clad bird-watchers and yoga headstands in their midst. But for decades now, the only wars going on here have been of the interstellar variety, in George Lucas' Presidio screening room. For all its military installations, San Francisco proper hasn't actually seen much military action since the 18th century, so it's fitting that Fort Mason and the Presidio have relaxed and are giving peace a chance.

top picks

THE MARINA & THE PRESIDIO

- **Golden Gate Bridge** (p104)
- **Crissy Field** (p105)
- **Exploratorium** (p102)
- **Baker Beach** (p105)
- **Greens** (p177)

The Marina is a stretch of flatland between Fort Mason to the east and the Presidio to the west, with the eponymous yacht marina to the north and motel-lined Lombard St running along the south. Fort Mason is a dense collection of military buildings and barracks wedged in between the Marina and Fisherman's Wharf, within blocks of the Powell-Hyde cable-car turnaround. Chestnut St is the main commercial strip of the Marina, and most businesses can be found between Fillmore and Divisadero Sts. Fillmore St runs south past a cluster of bars and restaurants to Union St and the strip of land at the base of Pacific Heights known as Cow Hollow.

The Presidio is the vast stretch of green that caps the northwest corner of the San Francisco peninsula, with Hwy 1 running north–south through the center and Doyle Dr running east–west. Both streets take you to the Golden Gate Bridge (p104) and a glorious stretch of coastline popular for hiking, jogging, biking and bird-watching.

THE MARINA & COW HOLLOW

The Marina may be populated by clean-cut, sporty types, but it has plenty of dirty little secrets. Back during the Gold Rush, a lagoon just south of Lombard St gave washerwomen a local livelihood: attempting to remove accumulated months of soil from miners' jeans and sailors' whites. By the 1880s the water had turned so foul it would only have made clothes dirtier, and prison chain gangs were brought in to fill in the polluted lagoon. Dairy farming was the next neighborhood enterprise, with cattle being fed leftovers from SF's whiskey stills. Poor hygiene soon ended this drunken bovine venture, but the name for the Union St gulch stuck: Cow Hollow.

Most of the Marina materialized after the 1906 earthquake, when San Francisco was looking to stage a comeback. The waterfront marshland was filled in with rubble to create the grounds for the 1915 Panama-Pacific International Exposition, ostensibly commemorating the completion of the Panama Canal while craftily announcing that San Francisco was once again open for business. When the expo was over, most of the displays came down, but San Francisco romantics attached to Bernard Maybeck's picturesque plaster Palace of Fine Arts (p102) insisted that it be rebuilt in concrete for future generations to enjoy.

Real-estate speculation began, and the makeshift Marina soon took on the look of

THE MARINA & THE PRESIDIO

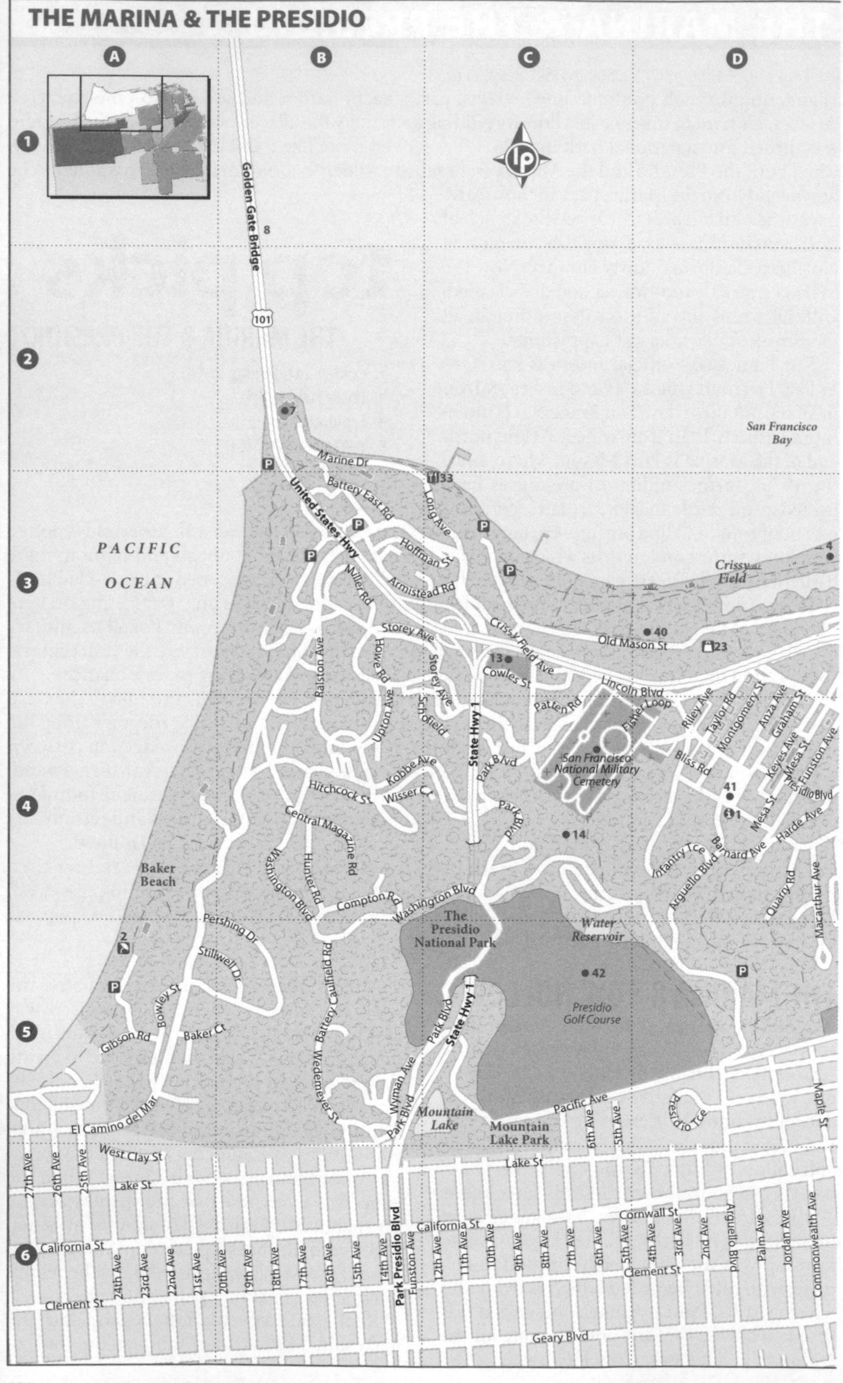

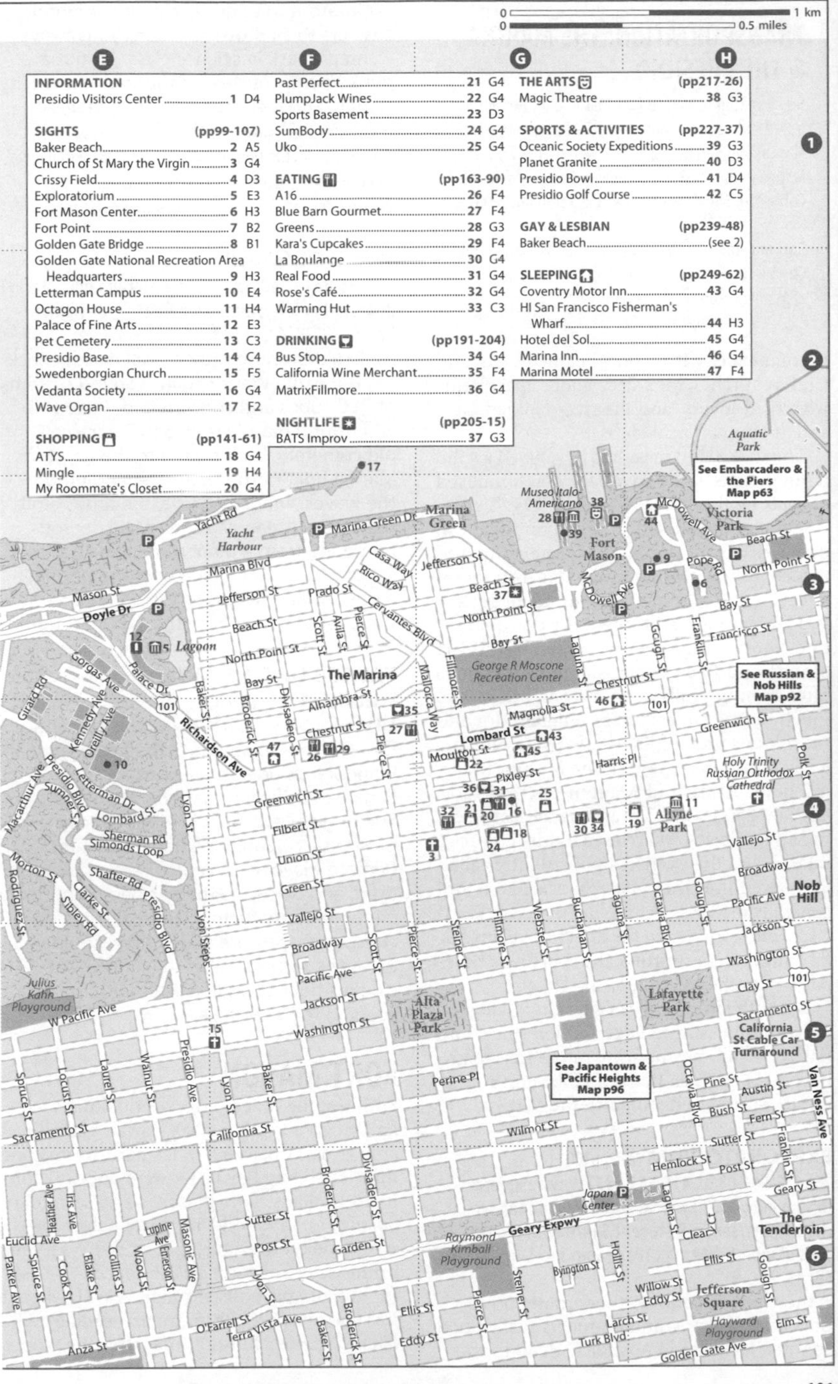
0 1 km
0 0.5 miles
E
F
G
H
1
2
3
4
5
6
INFORMATION
Presidio Visitors Center 1 D4
SIGHTS (pp99-107)
Baker Beach 2 A5
Church of St Mary the Virgin 3 G4
Crissy Field 4 D3
Exploratorium 5 E3
Fort Mason Center 6 H3
Fort Point 7 B2
Golden Gate Bridge 8 B1
Golden Gate National Recreation Area Headquarters 9 H3
Letterman Campus 10 E4
Octagon House 11 H4
Palace of Fine Arts 12 E3
Pet Cemetery 13 C3
Presidio Base 14 C4
Swedenborgian Church 15 F5
Vedanta Society 16 G4
Wave Organ 17 F2
SHOPPING (pp141-61)
ATYS 18 G4
Mingle 19 H4
My Roommate's Closet 20 G4
Past Perfect 21 G4
PlumpJack Wines 22 G4
Sports Basement 23 D3
SumBody 24 G4
Uko 25 G4
EATING (pp163-90)
A16 26 F4
Blue Barn Gourmet 27 F4
Greens 28 G3
Kara's Cupcakes 29 F4
La Boulange 30 G4
Real Food 31 G4
Rose's Café 32 G4
Warming Hut 33 C3
DRINKING (pp191-204)
Bus Stop 34 G4
California Wine Merchant 35 F4
MatrixFillmore 36 G4
NIGHTLIFE (pp205-15)
BATS Improv 37 G3
THE ARTS (pp217-26)
Magic Theatre 38 G3
SPORTS & ACTIVITIES (pp227-37)
Oceanic Society Expeditions 39 G3
Planet Granite 40 D3
Presidio Bowl 41 D4
Presidio Golf Course 42 C5
GAY & LESBIAN (pp239-48)
Baker Beach (see 2)
SLEEPING (pp249-62)
Coventry Motor Inn 43 G4
HI San Francisco Fisherman's Wharf 44 H3
Hotel del Sol 45 G4
Marina Inn 46 G4
Marina Motel 47 F4
Aquatic Park
See Embarcadero & the Piers Map p63
Museo Italo-Americano
Marina Green
Yacht Harbour
Fort Mason
Victoria Park
Lagoon
The Marina
George R Moscone Recreation Center
See Russian & Nob Hills Map p92
Holy Trinity Russian Orthodox Cathedral
Allyne Park
Nob Hill
Alta Plaza Park
Lafayette Park
California St Cable Car Turnaround
Julius Kahn Playground
See Japantown & Pacific Heights Map p96
Japan Center
Raymond Kimball Playground
Jefferson Square
Hayward Playground
The Tenderloin
Marina Blvd
Marina Green Dr
Yacht Rd
Mason St
Doyle Dr
Richardson Ave
Lombard St
Geary Expwy
Van Ness Ave
Golden Gate Ave

TRANSPORTATION: THE MARINA & THE PRESIDIO

Bus Bus 30 gets you to Fort Mason and the Marina from Union Square. Buses 42, 47 and 49 serve Fort Mason from Van Ness Ave. The 28 bus goes from the Marina to the Presidio and Golden Gate Bridge.
Cable car The Powell-Hyde line terminates three blocks from Fort Mason.
Parking Ample parking in the Presidio, especially Crissy Field. There are two lots in Fort Mason and one at Marina Green.

permanence, with wood-beamed Arts and Crafts churches, Mex-deco adobe apartments with tiled foyers, and the ritzy Golden Gate and St Francis yacht clubs.

The shaky land mass had developed a solid reputation as a safe haven for new-moneyed arrivals by the 1980s, when the 1989 Loma-Prieta earthquake left millions of dollars in damages. Again the Marina cleaned up and turned its luck around, and today its tranquil streets reveal nothing of its turbulent past.

The Marina is still where the city quarantines most of those wispy-haired California blonds and beefy, back-slapping frat boys often seen in Hollywood movies, but not so much on the streets of San Francisco – and most locals prefer it that way. Some categorically refuse to set foot in the Marina watering holes Armistead Maupin referred to as 'breeder bars,' which are among the last places in San Francisco where men loudly compare salaries and the women are insistently called 'girls' well into their 40s. 'So Marina' is not generally meant as a compliment in San Francisco, often snarled in the direction of anyone flashing cash or unironically sporting a baseball cap in the Mission or the Haight.

But with more local designers supplying the Marina with cutting-edge fashion sense and flashy new money pouring into other neighborhoods, such as Potrero Hill, soon it may not be so easy to distinguish the Marina.

EXPLORATORIUM Map pp100–1

☎ 415-561-0360, 415-563-7337; www.exploratorium.edu; 3601 Lyon St; adult/child under 4yr/child 4-12yr/senior & student $14/free/9/11, 1st Wed of month free; 10am-5pm Tue-Sun; 28, 30, 43, 76;

Is there a science to skateboarding, do robots have feelings, and do toilets really flush counterclockwise in Australia? Head to the Exploratorium to get fascinating scientific answers to all those questions you always wanted to ask in science class. Try out a punk hairdo courtesy of the static-electricity station, and feel your way – in darkness – through the maze of the highly recommended Tactile Dome (☎ 415-561-0362; incl general admission $17); patrons must be over seven years old, and reservations are required.

WAVE ORGAN Map pp100–1

☎ 415-561-0360; www.exploratorium.edu; Marina Boat Harbor jetty; admission free; daylight hours; 28, 43, 76;

An Exploratorium project well worth checking out is the Wave Organ, a sound system of PVC tubes and concrete pipes capped with found marble from San Francisco's old cemetery, built right into the tip of the Marina Boat Harbor jetty. Depending on the waves, winds and tide, the tones emitted by the organ can sound like nervous humming from a dinnertime line chef or spooky heavy breathing over the phone in a slasher film. Access to the organ is free, but a bit of a hike from the Exploratorium.

PALACE OF FINE ARTS Map pp100–1

Palace Dr; 28, 30, 43, 76

Like a fossilized party favor, this romantic, fake Greco-Roman ruin is the memento San Francisco decided to keep from the 1915 Panama-Pacific International Exposition. The original was built in wood, burlap and plaster by celebrated Berkeley architect Bernard Maybeck as a picturesque backdrop, and by the 1960s was beginning to crumble. The structure was recast in concrete, so that future generations could gaze up at the rotunda relief to glimpse 'Art Under Attack by Materialists, with Idealists Leaping to her Rescue.'

FORT MASON

Sitting at the water's edge overlooking yachts, enjoying your organic vegetarian black-bean chili from Greens (p177), it's hard to imagine these sparkling bay views were once off-limits to civilians. Fort Mason was a secondary Spanish fort and residential area before the US Army took it over during the Civil War. This prime waterfront acreage continued to be used for military purposes through WWII, when it was the transport hub for troops heading to the Pacific theater. But not long after the troops had come home, speculation began about the warehouses occupying prime real estate: would they be razed to make room for luxury condos, or commercial high rises, or more yachts? While competing private interests lobbied, San Francisco's scrappy nonprofits and arts centers quickly staked their claim to Fort Mason as a public-access space that still hosts the city's best arts, food and events. Long-term residents include the Magic Theatre (p225), the longtime home base of Pulitzer Prize–winning playwright Sam Shepard, the Golden Gate National Recreation Area (below) and the Museo Italo-Americano.

FORT MASON CENTER Map pp100–1

☎ 415-441-3400; www.fortmason.org; Bay & Franklin Sts; 🚌 22, 28, 30, 43, 47, 49

San Francisco takes subversive glee in turning military installations into venues for nature, fine dining and out-there experimental art – evidence, Fort Mason. The military mess halls are gone, replaced by vegan-friendly Greens (p177), a restaurant run by a Zen community. Warehouses now host cutting-edge theater at Magic Theatre (p225) and improvised comedy workshops at BATS (p206), and the dockside Herbst Pavilion has art fairs and craft fairs in its arsenal – see the website for upcoming performances and events.

GOLDEN GATE NATIONAL RECREATION AREA HEADQUARTERS

Map pp100–1

☎ 415-561-4700; www.nps.gov/goga; Bldg 204, Fort Mason; admission free; 🕑 8:30am-4:30pm Mon-Fri; 🚌 22, 28, 30, 43, 47, 49

Find out everything a hard-core hiker needs to know about accessing the outer reaches of the Golden Gate National Recreation Area (GGNRA), including the Presidio, Alcatraz, Fort Point, Fort Funston, the Cliff House, Muir Woods and the Marin Headlands. This is the park's HQ and visitors center, and offers a wealth of maps and information about camping, hiking and other programs for these and other national parks in the Pacific West region (including Yosemite).

SWEDENBORGIAN CHURCH Map pp100–1

☎ 415-346-6466; www.sfswedenborgian.org; 2107 Lyon St; admission free; 🕑 hours vary; 🚌 1, 24, 43

Radical ideals in the form of distinctive buildings make beloved SF landmarks; this standout 1894 example is the collaborative effort of 19th-century Bay Area progressive thinkers, such as naturalist John Muir, California Arts and Crafts leader Bernard Maybeck and architect Arthur Page Brown.

Church founder Emanuel Swedenborg was an 18th-century Swedish theologian, a scientist and an occasional conversationalist with angels, who believed that humans are spirits in a material world unified by nature, love and luminous intelligence – a lovely concept, embodied in an even lovelier building. Enter the church through a modest brick archway, and pass into a garden sheltered by trees from around the world. Inside, nature is everywhere, in the hewn-maple chairs, mighty madrone trees that support the roof, and the scenes of Northern California that took muralist William Keith 40 years to complete.

CHURCH OF ST MARY THE VIRGIN

Map pp100–1

☎ 415-921-3665; www.smvsf.org; 2325 Union St; admission free; 🕑 9am-5pm Sun-Fri; 🚌 23, 43, 45

You might expect to see this rustic Arts and Crafts building on the slopes of Tahoe instead of Pacific Heights, but this Episcopal church is full of surprises. The structure dates from 1891, but the church has kept pace with its progressive-minded parish, with homeless community outreach and 'Unplugged' all-acoustic Sunday services led by hip young reverend Jennifer Hornbeck.

VEDANTA SOCIETY Map pp100–1

☎ 415-922-2323; www.sfvedanta.org; 2963 Webster St; 🚌 41, 45, 47, 49, 76

Meandering through the Marina, you'll pass Mexican-inspired art deco, Victorian mansions, generic bay-windowed boxes – and hello, what's this? A riotous 1905 mishmash of architectural styles, with red turrets representing major world religions and the Hindu-inspired Vedanta Society's organizing principle: 'the oneness of existence.' The society founded a new temple in 1959, but its architectural conundrum remains. The only thing missing is a finger pointing at the moon, with a caption reading 'Thou art that.'

OCTAGON HOUSE Map pp100–1

☎ 415-441-7512; 2645 Gough St; admission $3 (donation appreciated); 🕑 noon-3pm on 2nd & 4th Thu & 2nd Sun of month, closed Jan; 🚌 45

Crafty architects are always trying to cut corners on their clients, and here architect

William C McElroy succeeded. This is one of the last examples of a brief San Franciscan vogue for octagonal houses in the 1860s, when it was believed that houses catching direct sunlight from eight angles were good for your health. Three afternoons a month you can peruse the collection of colonial antiques and peek inside a time capsule McElroy hid under the stairs.

THE PRESIDIO

The Presidio is a quintessentially San Franciscan playland of nude beaches, free Shakespeare and spectacular views of the Golden Gate Bridge (right), but it wasn't always so welcoming. After it became a Spanish military harbor in 1776, any boat entering the San Francisco Bay would have to pass the Presidio's trigger-happy cannons and gunboats. News of peace treaties took a long time to reach this distant outpost, so ships that failed to hoist a known friendly flag or a white one of surrender could expect to be boarded and seized, if not blown up.

During the Gold Rush the US naval presence in the Presidio seems to have been more concerned with unofficial toll-collecting than keeping the peace, largely ignoring even direct orders from Washington, DC, to impose order on a city increasingly run by vigilantes and corrupt cops. To be fair, it was hard enough keeping sailors from going AWOL and joining the Gold Rush themselves, let alone ordering them to risk their lives in civil strife soon overshadowed by the US Civil War. Relics from the Civil War can be seen at Fort Point (p106), the three-story fort that took eight years to build and had 126 cannons that saw not one day of military action. Mostly the installation served to intimidate. During the Exclusion era, the Presidio enforced US law directing boats carrying Chinese and Japanese nationals to Angel Island (p282) for months or even years of 'processing,' consisting of detainment, quarantine and interrogation prior to likely deportation.

For the duration of WWII, the Presidio became a key base of operations for the Allied Pacific campaign and a port of call for sailors and soldiers dispatched here for R&R in San Francisco's Barbary Coast. The Presidio base continued to be in use during the Cold War as a bulwark against communism across the Pacific in China, Korea and Vietnam, despite widespread public antipathy towards McCarthyism in San Francisco. In 1960 thousands of locals protested the interrogations of UC Berkeley professors and students by McCarthy's House Un-American Activities Committee, which was disrupted by the first-ever sit-in and abruptly concluded its proceedings in City Hall, never to return. But the Cold War, too, had its casualties. The fates of many veterans can be seen in the veterans hospital complex in the Presidio, not to mention Downtown, where a recent survey indicated that veterans account for at least half the entrenched homeless population.

In 1996 the Presidio was repurposed as public parkland, and most of the military buildings have since been turned over to nonprofits, low-income housing and *Star Wars* filmmaker George Lucas. He was granted special dispensation to move his for-profit Industrial Light & Magic special-effects production studio here, with the promise of new jobs, then decided to offshore most of the work anyway. Only some off-limits front offices, a private screening room and a bronze Yoda statue remain out front.

GOLDEN GATE BRIDGE Map pp100–1

☎ 415-556-1693 Fri-Mon; www.goldengate.org; Fort Point Lookout Marine Dr; southbound car $6, car pools (3 or more passengers) admission free btwn 5-9am & 4-6pm; 🚌 28, 29, Golden Gate Transit buses; 🚼

Strange but true: the elegant suspension bridge painted a signature shade called 'International Orange' was almost nixed by the navy in favor of concrete pylons and yellow stripes. Joseph B Strauss correctly gets heaps of praise as the engineering mastermind behind this marvel, but without the aesthetic intervention of architects Gertrude and Irving Murrow and the incredibly quick work of daredevil workers, this 1937 landmark might have been just another traffic bottleneck.

The project first proposed in a proclamation by beloved local eccentric Emperor Norton in the 19th century began to become a reality in the 20th, when ferries began to seem impractical to accommodate traffic to and from the North Bay. The War Department didn't want to take any chances with the ships passing through the Golden Gate, so safety and solidity were its primary goals – but a green light was given to the counterproposal by Strauss and the Murrows for a subtler deco span and color that harmonized with the natural environment. Before the War Department could

CROSSING THE BRIDGE

- Bike it – follow the 49-Mile Dr signs along Lincoln Blvd through the Presidio to the parking lot right before the toll plaza. Beyond the lot is a paved bike path, which begins just past a sign showing a map of Fort Point; it takes you under the bridge and around to the sidewalk on the westbound side, which is reserved for bikes only. You can cross on bike 24 hours a day.
- Gear up and hoof it – walking along the eastern sidewalk in street clothes can be downright unpleasant, since wind and exhaust fumes tend to detract from the natural beauty, and the Pacific can only be glimpsed through traffic. But hardy walkers who come prepared in windbreakers and warm clothes need not be deterred. From the Fort Point Lookout a pathway leads up to the toll plaza, then it's 1.7 miles across. Go during off-peak hours to minimize your exhaust intake, and bus it back if the 3.4-mile round-trip seems too much. Note: pedestrian access in summer is open 5am to 9pm, shorter in winter.
- Catch the bus – the most convenient way to cross the bridge is by car, but it'll cost you $6 coming back into SF, unless you're carpooling during rush hour. The 29 Muni runs from the Sunset to the Fort Point Lookout and the toll plaza (which is on the SF side); the 28 Muni runs from 19th Ave just to the toll plaza. Or take any Marin County–bound Golden Gate Transit bus (routes 70 and 80 run frequently; $3.30 one-way) – the fastest, most comfortable way to reach the bridge from Downtown – and get off at the toll plaza. To actually cross the bridge by bus without penetrating deep into Marin (as GG Transit buses do), take the 76 Muni (Sundays only) to the Marin Headlands (p277).

insist on an eyesore, laborers dove into the treacherous riptides of the bay and got the bridge underway in 1933. Just four years later workers balanced atop swaying cables to complete what was then the longest suspension bridge in the world at nearly 2 miles long, and the 746ft suspension towers were higher than any construction west of New York.

Today, Brooklyn still tries to debate who has the more beautiful bridge, but for San Franciscans that argument was won 70 years ago, and the only debatable point is where to get the best vantage point on their beloved bridge. Cinema buffs believe Hitchcock had it right: seen from below at **Fort Point** (p106), the bridge induces a thrilling case of *Vertigo*. Fog aficionados prefer the lookout at Vista Point in Marin, on the north side of the bridge, to watch gusts rush through the bridge cables. **Crissy Field** (right) is a key spot to appreciate the whole span, with windsurfers and kite-fliers to add action to your snapshots. Unlike the Bay Bridge, the Golden Gate Bridge provides access to cyclists and pedestrians (see the bicycling tour, p106).

The picture-perfect Golden Gate has a surprisingly dark side: the bridge is San Francisco's number-one suicide site. A suicide-prevention net is being studied to curb the numbers, which now top 1000 (for the latest, see www.ggbsuicidebarrier.org). Few live, though an 18-year-old woman survived a jump in 1988 only to commit suicide from the same spot two months later. A German stunt man made the jump in 1980 with the intention of surviving. He didn't, and it's safe to say that Tarzan swings are not among the best ways to cross the bridge (see the boxed text, above).

CRISSY FIELD Map pp100–1

☎ 415-561-7690; www.crissyfield.org; btwn Mason St & Golden Gate Promenade; bus 28, 30, 43, 76

War is definitely for the birds in this military-airstrip-turned-nature-preserve. Where military aircraft once zoomed in for a landing, bird-watchers now huddle in the silent rushes of a reclaimed tidal marsh. Joggers pound beachside trails that were once oil-stained asphalt, and the only security alerts are raised by puppies suspiciously sniffing surfers. On foggy days, stop by the certified-green **Warming Hut** (p178) or **Crissy Field Center** (603 Mason St; hours 9am-5pm) to browse regional nature books and thaw out over fair-trade coffee.

BAKER BEACH Map pp100–1

hours sunrise-sunset; bus **28**

Picnic amid the sheltering pines, fish among the rocks or frolic nude – you know, all the usual stuff you do on a military base. Spectacular views of Golden Gate Bridge and the Lincoln Golf Course remind you you're still in the city, but don't let that make you self-conscious – out here, among locals, no one's going to notice a few tan lines. Mind the currents and the c-c-cold water.

PRESIDIO BASE Map pp100–1

☎ 415-561-4323; www.nps.gov/prsf; ⌚ center 9am-5pm, park dawn-dusk; 🚌 43, 76

Explore that splotch of green on the map between Baker Beach and Crissy Field, and you'll find a parade grounds, Yoda, a centuries-old adobe wall and a pet cemetery. What started out as a Spanish fort built by conscripted Ohlone in 1776 is now a treasure hunt of oddities.

Begin your adventures by heading across the parade grounds at Moraga to get a trail map at the visitors center (Moraga Ave near Arguello Blvd) in the old Officers' Club (verify location ahead of time; it's slated to move), or take advantage of rock-star photo ops among the decrepit barracks. This is where Jerry Garcia began and ended his ignominious military career by going AWOL nine times in eight months before twice being court-martialed and co-founding the Grateful Dead. Fans of the maudlin and macabre hike directly to the Pet Cemetery off Crissy Field Ave, where handmade tombstones mark the final resting places of military hamsters who've completed their final tour of duty. Head east of the parade grounds towards the Palace of Fine Arts and you'll come across the Letterman Campus, home to nonprofits and *Star Wars* filmmaker George Lucas, whose offices require a special pass – but you can pay your respects to the Yoda statue out front.

FORT POINT Map pp100–1

☎ 415-556-1693; Marine Dr; admission free; ⌚ 10am-5pm Fri-Sun; 🚌 28

Fort Point is the result of an eight-year makeover from small Spanish fort to triple-decker US military fortress. The fort was completed with 126 cannons in 1861, just in time to protect the bay against certain invasion by Confederate soldiers during the Civil War...or not, as it turned out. Without firing a single shot, Fort Point was abandoned in 1900 and became neglected once the Golden Gate Bridge was built over it. (Engineers added an extra span just to preserve it.)

Alfred Hitchcock saw deadly potential in Fort Point, and shot the trademark scene from *Vertigo* of Kim Novak leaping from the lookout to certain death into the bay...or not, as it turned out. Fort Point has since given up all pretense of being deadly, and now provides a gift center, Civil War displays and panoramic viewing decks.

FREEWHEELING OVER THE BRIDGE

Bicycling Tour

1 San Francisco National Maritime Museum (p67) A 1939 creation of WPA workers and once a public bathhouse, its deco design gives off a stylish luxury-liner guise – complete with a bridge, tubular steel railings and portholes. The building is crawling with public art – look for the fish-tile mosaic and polished toad and seal.

2 Marina Green Fashion-conscious joggers, Frisbee throwers and kite-fliers congregate here on weekends. A right turn bisects the two boat marinas, and at the end is the curious Wave Organ (p102), a 'musical' sculpture that sounds something like a clogged toilet.

3 Palace of Fine Arts (p102) Sprawl on the grass (if it's sunny) or check out how your voice echoes inside this flashback to the 1915 Panama-Pacific International Expo. Languidly pose for photos like a god or goddess under the Greco-Roman arches reflected in the pond.

4 Exploratorium (p102) Hop off the bike for a bit and exercise your senses in this dark, wacky, one-of-a-kind museum. After you've been through the Seeing Gallery, Listen Station and Tactile Dome, gear up for even more stimulation.

5 Crissy Field (p105) Watch windsurfers and kite-boarders attempt what is probably the windiest beach in SF. Take the Golden Gate Promenade, a foot-and-bike path that skirts the field to Fort Point and the Warming Hut.

6 Warming Hut (p178) Fuel up on organic sandwiches, fair-trade coffee and pastries at the Warming Hut, at the base of the bridge. Afterwards, backtrack to Long Ave and hang a sharp right up steep Lincoln St to the mouth of the Golden Gate Bridge.

RIDE FACTS

Start San Francisco National Maritime Museum
End Pier 41
Distance Eight miles
Time Two to four hours
Exertion Ascending 246ft to the bridge is tiring
Fuel stop Warming Hut

FREEWHEELING OVER THE BRIDGE

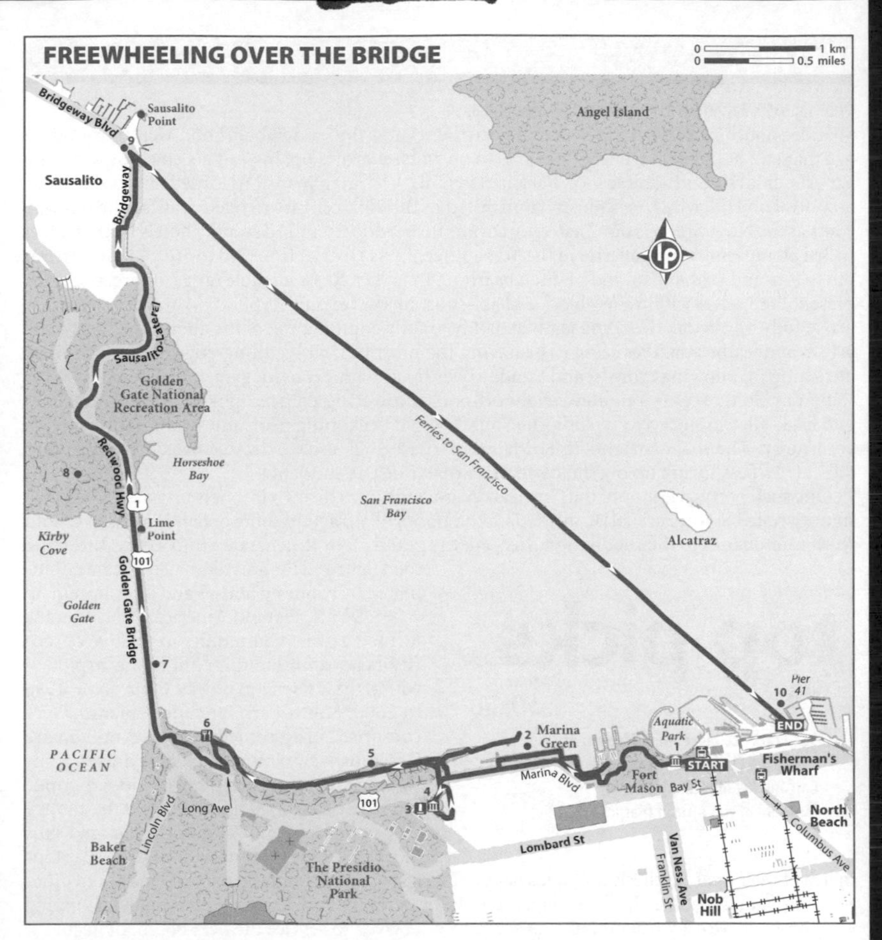

7 Golden Gate Bridge (p104) With everyone craning their necks, it's no surprise that bicycles sometimes collide with pedestrians. Keep your eyes peeled. You'll be grateful you've packed a lightweight windbreaker if the fog blows in when you're halfway across. Those who haven't get wet and chilled to the bone.

8 Marin Headlands (p277) You can lock your bike here and hike into the tempting green hills – the steep, winding Coastal Trail leads to Rodeo Beach (5 miles). Or just enjoy the views and pedal past.

9 Sausalito (p280) This elite hamlet in a bay-view setting is almost too cutesy, but it's worth strolling when your legs need a stretch. Get drinks on the sunny deck at Paradise Bay (☎ 415-331-3226; 1200 Bridgeway).

10 Pier 41 You can take the ferry from Sausalito back to Pier 41 at Fisherman's Wharf.

SOMA

Drinking p199; Eating p178; Shopping p151; Sleeping p259

Wander *So*uth of *Ma*rket St (hence the acronym) and find a neighborhood well into middle age that still hasn't decided what it wants to be when it grows up; instead it's enjoying a rowdy, experimental second adolescence. Back in its youth, Victorian mansions lorded over SoMa from atop Rincon Hill, which was mostly dynamited in the 20th century to make way for the freeway overpasses. Now, SoMa is dominated by corporate headquarters and swanky hotels from the bay to 3rd St, museums and galleries in the Yerba Buena Arts District from 3rd to 5th, Skid Row from 6th to 8th, and leather bars and nightclubs from 9th to Van Ness. A whole range of career options present themselves within a few blocks: khaki-sporting Gap executive, SFMOMA-celebrated video artist, full-time drunk, weekend leather-daddy, or any combination of the above. Currently, the artists and leather-daddies seem to be having the most fun, with cutting-edge gallery openings attracting overflowing crowds, and Sunday beer busts with exposed, gym-toned pecs.

By day SoMa seems a motley neighborhood of towering edifices, poker-faced warehouses and back-alley motorcycle-repair joints, but by night beckoning neon and strobe lights provide continuity. The real constants in SoMa are parties: drag-show extravaganzas, DJ nights and fetish fests that spring up overnight and disappear just as suddenly.

One such party in honor of the Crimean War victory was thrown in a new upscale gated community called South Park (p113), in 1855, in the hopes of attracting some of San Francisco's Gold Rush millionaires to the subdivision. Instead, the grand affair degenerated into a cake-throwing food fight and the area ultimately became dominated by rooming houses and longshoremen. After WWII, Filipino American war veterans formed a quiet community in relative obscurity here, until the dot-com boom exploded within these few short blocks. From about 1996 to 2000, South Park lunchtime picnics were comprised of 20-something paper-millionaire CEOs furtively plotting their next moves, while risk-drunk venture capitalists sipped coffee in nearby cafes. Then in late 2000 the money evaporated like mid-afternoon fog, and employees were sent home with company laptops in lieu of their final paychecks. Now it's happening again (sort of) with Twitter, MySpace and other new companies that are playing it cooler. Locals know South Park for discount designer shopping and some noteworthy restaurants that somehow survived to service the next boom: biotech.

top picks

SOMA

- **San Francisco Museum of Modern Art** (below)
- **Catharine Clark Gallery** (opposite)
- **Cartoon Art Museum** (opposite)
- **Museum of the African Diaspora** (p112)

Those shiny glass-clad towers just south of South Park represent Mission Bay, the newest addition to SoMa and the promised home of a biotech industry that's been slower to arrive than expected because of cuts in federal spending. The area is eerily empty except when commuters arrive at CalTrans station or there's a game on at AT&T Park (p228). A walkway around the backside of the park provides a free glimpse of games in progress and a rowdy crowd of baseball fans.

Market St is the northern boundary of SoMa, which stretches from Van Ness Ave to the bay on the east. All of SoMa's streets crisscross at oblique angles, and if you follow them towards Potrero and the Mission, all of them bend in a true southerly direction. These bends are your cue that you're leaving the South of Market area, and Central Skyway over Division St forms an overhead border. Nearly every street in SoMa is wide and one-way, with long city blocks sometimes broken up by alleyways. Foggy days are best spent in the galleries and museums clustered around Yerba Buena Arts District, and pretty much any kind of nightlife that strikes your fancy (straight, gay, trans, leather, loud, kinky) can be found around Folsom and Harrison Sts between 8th and 11th Sts.

SAN FRANCISCO MUSEUM OF MODERN ART Map pp110–11

☎ 415-357-4000; www.sfmoma.org; 151 3rd St; adult/child under 13yr/student & senior $15/free/9, 6-8:45pm Thu half-price, 1st Tue of month free; 11am-5:45pm Mon-Tue & Fri-Sun, to 8:45pm Thu, from 10am Jun-Sep; 6, 7, 14, 21, 31, 71, F, J, K, L, M, N; & Montgomery St

San Francisco Museum of Modern Art (SFMOMA) was destined from the start in

1935 to be an eclectic, unconventional museum. But when it moved into architect Mario Botta's light-filled brick box in 1995, it became clear just how far this museum was prepared to push the art world. The new museum showed its backside to New York and leaned full-tilt towards the western horizon, taking risks on then-unknowns like Matthew Barney and his poetic videos involving industrial quantities of Vaseline, and Olafur Eliasson's outer-space installations that distort all sense of reality. Finally SFMOMA had room to launch international traveling shows by squeegee-wielding German painter Gerhardt Richter and great postwar Japanese photographers such as Shomei Tomatsu and Daido Moriyama. The 1995 reopening coincided with the tech boom, and new media art took off in the SFMOMA galleries at roughly the same time as new technologies in nearby South Park.

Collectors took notice of this new direction, and donations and promised gifts have begun transforming SFMOMA's holdings to a multistory collection with room for emerging niches: video art, conceptual architecture, wall-drawing installations and relational art. But one constant is SFMOMA's standout photography collection, which got the jump-start on other museums with works by Ansel Adams, Edward Weston, Robert Frank, Dorothea Lange and William Klein, and has continued acquiring compelling contemporary works to keep the collection fresh.

There are regular, free gallery tours, but exploring on your own gives you the thrill of discovery, which is what this museum is about. The 3rd-floor photography galleries are the place to begin, then up through the 4th- and 5th-floor major-contemporary exhibits, catching your breath outdoors at the 5th-floor rooftop sculpture garden. From here, work your way down through the galleries via the dramatic stairwell to espresso and strawberry-rhubarb crisp at the ground-floor cafe. Tack on additional time for the excellent SFMOMA shop.

If you can't swing the admission price, wander into the main atrium for free and see the vibrant comic-book historical murals of Monticello, by Kerry James Marshall, for a quick hit of the MoMa's curatorial vision.

TRANSPORTATION: SOMA

Bus Buses run up and down most streets. The 30 and 45 lines run down 4th St from Union Square. The 14 runs to the Mission District along Mission St.
Cable car The Powell St turnaround is at Market St, just two blocks from Yerba Buena Gardens.
Streetcar All of the Market St streetcars serve the upper part of SoMa. The N and T lines head south along the Embarcadero.
Parking The garage at 5th and Mission Sts is one block from Yerba Buena Gardens. Street parking can be surprisingly difficult, especially near nightclubs.

CATHARINE CLARK GALLERY Map pp110–11

☎ 415-399-1439; www.cclarkgallery.com; 150 Minna St; admission free; noon-6pm Tue-Sat; 6, 7, 14, 21, 31, 71, F, J, K, L, M, N; & Montgomery St

Catharine Clark has an astronomer's ability to detect art stars in the making and chart radical new directions. No material is too political or risqué here: witness Travis Somerville's altered-photo altars of smiling suburban California high-school students in Ku Klux Klan hoods, or Masami Teraoka's paintings of geishas and Venus goddesses banding together like superheroines to fend off wayward priests. Don't miss the video/new media room, featuring works such as Julia Page's snicker-inducing video collage of US presidential offspring.

CARTOON ART MUSEUM Map pp110–11

☎ 415-227-8666; www.cartoonart.org; 655 Mission St; adult/child under 6yr/child 6-12yr/student & senior $6/free/2/4, 1st Tue of month is 'pay what you wish' day; 11am-5pm Tue-Sun; 6, 7, 14, 21, 31, 71, F, J, K, L, M, N; & Montgomery St

Comics fans need no introduction to the permanent collection here – think John Romita's amazing *Spiderman* cover drawings, or Edward Gorey's sketches for *Gashlycrumb Tinies,* starting with 'A is for Amy who fell down the stairs/B is for Basil assaulted by bears…'

Founded on a grant from Bay Area cartoon legend Charles M Schultz of *Peanuts* fame, this bold museum isn't afraid of the dark, racy or political, including R Crumb drawings from the '70s and a show not so long ago featuring painfully funny cartoon satires of the US from Middle Eastern newspapers. Lectures and openings are rare opportunities to mingle with comic legends, Pixar studio heads and obsessively knowledgeable collectors.

SOMA

INFORMATION
- American Express ... 1 F2
- Australian Consulate ... 2 E2
- Brainwash ... (see 49)
- Japanese Consulate ... 3 F2
- Lyon-Martin Women's Health Services ... 4 B5
- Mexican Consulate ... 5 F3

SIGHTS (pp108-14)
- AT&T Park ... 6 G4
- California Historical Society Museum ... 7 E3
- Cartoon Art Museum ... 8 F3
- Catharine Clark Gallery ... 9 F3
- Contemporary Jewish Museum ... 10 E3
- Crown Point Press ... 11 F3
- Electric Works ... 12 D4
- Federal Building ... 13 D4
- Hosfelt Gallery ... 14 E4
- Jack London's Birthplace ... 15 G4
- Marriott Hotel ... 16 E3
- Museum of Craft and Folk Art ... 17 E3
- Museum of the African Diaspora ... 18 E3
- New Langton Arts ... 19 D5
- San Francisco Museum of Modern Art ... 20 F3
- SF Camerawork ... 21 E3
- South Park ... 22 G4
- Victoria Manalo Draves Park ... 23 E5
- WPA Murals at Rincon Annex Post Office ... 24 G1
- Yerba Buena Gardens ... 25 E3
- Zeum ... 26 E3

SHOPPING (pp141-61)
- Gama-Go ... 27 D5
- General Bead ... 28 D4
- Goodwill 'As Is' Shop ... 29 C5
- Isda & Co ... 30 G4
- Jeremy's ... 31 G3
- Madame S & Mr S Leather ... 32 D5
- Rolo Garage ... 33 C5
- San Francisco Flower Mart ... 34 F5
- SFMOMA Museum Store ... (see 20)

EATING (pp163-90)
- Boulevard ... 35 G1
- Butler & the Chef ... 36 G4
- Delancey Street ... 37 H3
- Island Earth Farmers Market ... 38 E3
- Patisserie Philippe ... 39 E6
- Rainbow Grocery ... 40 C6
- Salt House ... 41 F2
- Sentinel ... 42 E2
- Split Pea Seduction ... 43 D4
- Tropisueño ... 44 E3
- Tu Lan ... 45 D4
- Waterbar ... 46 H2

DRINKING (pp191-204)
- 83 Proof ... 47 F2
- Bloodhound ... 48 D5
- Brainwash ... 49 D5
- Butter ... 50 D6
- City Beer Store & Tasting Room ... 51 D5
- House of Shields ... 52 F2
- Mars Bar ... 53 E5
- Medici Lounge ... 54 C5
- Zeitgeist ... 55 B6

NIGHTLIFE (pp205-15)
- 111 Minna ... 56 F2
- 1015 Folsom ... 57 E4
- Annie's Social Club ... 58 E4
- Anu ... 59 D3
- Cat Club ... 60 D5
- Club Havana at Jelly's ... 61 H5
- Club Six ... 62 D4
- DNA Lounge ... 63 D6
- EndUp ... 64 E4
- Harlot ... 65 F2
- Hotel Utah ... 66 F4
- Mezzanine ... 67 D3
- Mighty ... 68 E6
- Paradise Lounge ... 69 D5
- Qoöl ... (see 56)
- Shine ... 70 C5
- Slim's ... 71 C6
- Supperclub ... 72 F3
- Temple ... 73 F2
- Thursday Night Live at the Eagle ... (see 85)

THE ARTS (pp217-26)
- AMC Loews Metreon 16 ... 74 E3
- Climate Theater ... (see 54)
- Counterpulse ... 75 C5
- Yerba Buena Center for the Arts ... 76 E3

SPORTS & ACTIVITIES (pp227-37)
- Bakar Fitness & Recreation Center ... 77 G6
- Barber Lounge ... 78 E4
- City Kayak ... (see 81)
- Embarcadero YMCA ... 79 G1
- It's Yoga ... 80 E4
- Spinnaker Sailing ... 81 H4
- Yerba Buena Center Ice Skating & Bowling ... 82 E3

GAY & LESBIAN (pp239-48)
- Blow Buddies ... 83 E4
- Chaps II ... 84 D5
- Eagle Tavern ... 85 C6
- GLBT Historical Society ... (see 8)
- Gold's Gym ... 86 D6
- Hole in the Wall ... 87 D5
- Honey Soundsystem ... (see 69)
- Ladies Night ... 88 F4
- Lone Star ... 89 D5
- Powerhouse ... 90 D5
- Stud ... 91 D5

SLEEPING (pp249-62)
- Americania Hotel ... 92 D4
- Good Hotel ... 93 D4
- Hotel Vitale ... 94 G1
- Mosser Hotel ... 95 E3
- St Regis Hotel ... (see 9)
- W Hotel ... 96 F3

TRANSPORT (pp300-7)
- Autoreturn ... 97 E5
- Dubbelju ... 98 F4
- Golden Gate Transit ... (see 99)
- Transbay Terminal ... 99 F2

See Civic Center & the Tenderloin Map p77

See Hayes Valley Map p133

See The Mission & Potrero Hill Map pp116-17

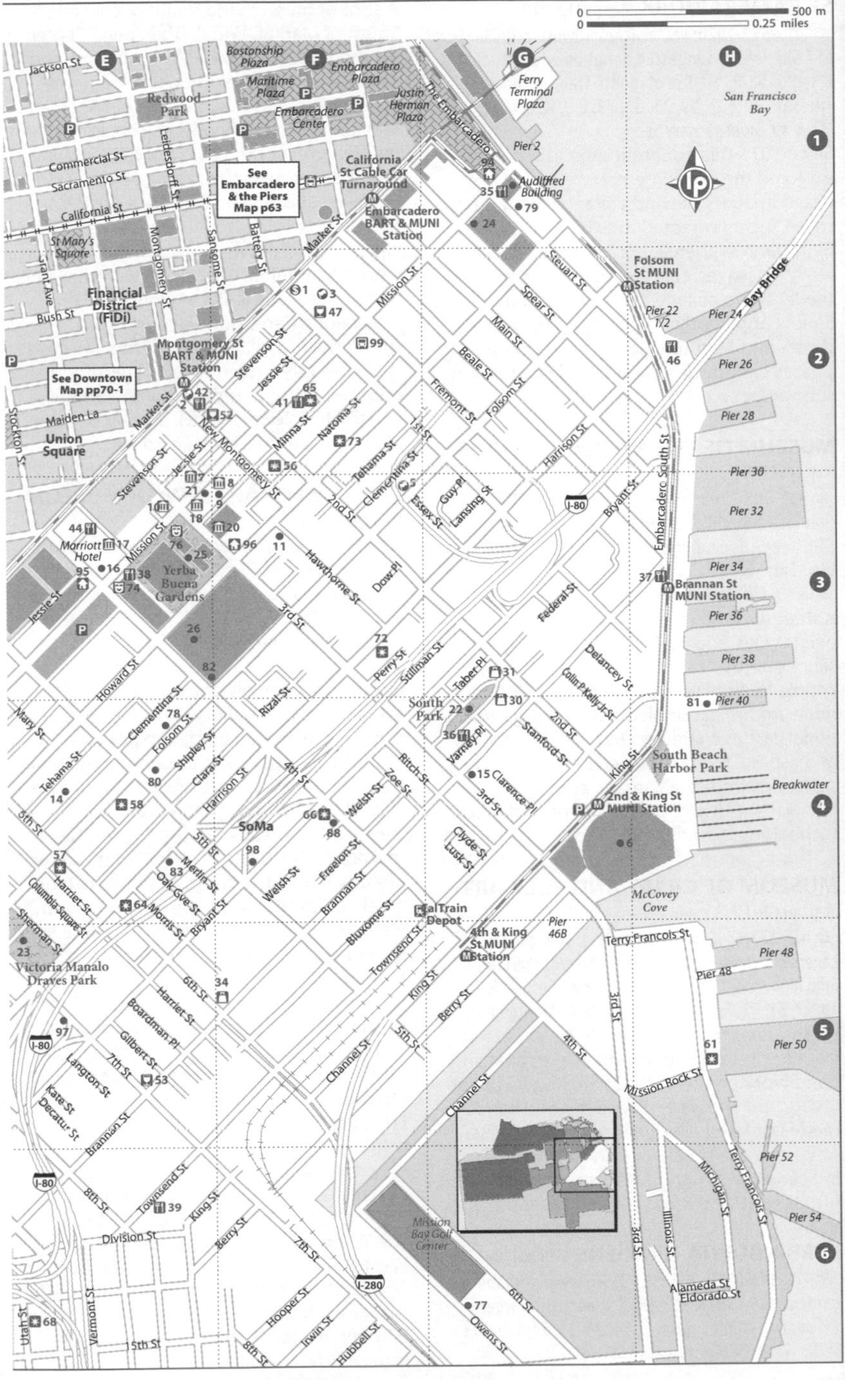
0 500 m
0 0.25 miles
Jackson St
Bostonship Plaza
Embarcadero Plaza
Maritime Plaza
Redwood Park
Justin Herman Plaza
Embarcadero Center
The Embarcadero
Ferry Terminal Plaza
San Francisco Bay
Pier 2
Commercial St
Sacramento St
California St
Leidesdorff St
See Embarcadero & the Piers Map p63
California St Cable Car Turnaround
Embarcadero BART & MUNI Station
Audiffred Building
St Mary's Square
Montgomery St
Sansome St
Battery St
Market St
Grant Ave
Financial District (FiDi)
Bush St
Mission St
Steuart St
Spear St
Folsom St MUNI Station
Bay Bridge
Pier 22 1/2
Pier 24
Main St
Montgomery St BART & MUNI Station
Stevenson St
Jessie St
Beale St
Pier 26
See Downtown Map pp70-1
Fremont St
Folsom St
Maiden La
Stockton St
Union Square
Natoma St
Minna St
New Montgomery St
1st St
Harrison St
Pier 28
Tehama St
Clementina St
Embarcadero South St
Pier 30
Guy Pl
Lansing St
Essex St
2nd St
Bryant St
I-80
Pier 32
Marriott Hotel
Yerba Buena Gardens
Hawthorne St
Dow Pl
Pier 34
Brannan St MUNI Station
Federal St
Pier 36
3rd St
Perry St
Stillman St
Delancey St
Pier 38
Howard St
Taber Pl
Colin P Kelly Jr St
Pier 40
Rizal St
South Park
Mary St
Varney Pl
Stanford St
South Beach Harbor Park
Shipley St
Clara St
King St
Breakwater
Tehama St
Ritch St
Zoe St
Clarence Pl
2nd & King St MUNI Station
4th St
Welsh St
5th St
SoMa
Clyde St
Lusk St
Merlin St
Freelon St
McCovey Cove
Harriet St
Oak Gve St
Morris St
Bryant St
Brannan St
CalTrain Depot
Columbia Square St
Bluxome St
Pier 46B
Sherman St
Townsend St
4th & King St MUNI Station
Terry Francois St
Victoria Manalo Draves Park
6th St
Pier 48
Boardman Pl
Berry St
Gilbert St
5th St
Pier 50
Langton St
7th St
Channel St
Mission Rock St
Kate St
Decatur St
Brannan St
Michigan St
Pier 52
8th St
Townsend St
Mission Bay Golf Center
Illinois St
Pier 54
Division St
7th St
I-280
Alameda St
Eldorado St
6th St
Utah St
Vermont St
Hooper St
Irwin St
Owens St
15th St
Hubbell St

SF CAMERAWORK Map pp110–11

☎ 415-512-2020; www.sfcamerawork.org; 2nd fl, 657 Mission St; suggested donation adult/student & senior $5/2, 1st Tue of month free; noon-5pm Tue-Sat; 6, 7, 14, 21, 31, 71, F, J, K, L, M, N; & Montgomery St

Since 1974 this nonprofit organization has explored the experimental world of photo-based imagery beyond vintage black and white, including rotating exhibits such as Binh Danh's ethereal portraits developed directly on leaves, Lars Laumann's conspiracy-theory video collage of Morrissey from the Smiths apparently predicting Princess Diana's death, and Matthew Geiger's composite photos capturing commuter tide patterns in subways.

MUSEUM OF THE AFRICAN DIASPORA

Map pp110–11

☎ 415-358-7200; www.moadsf.org; 685 Mission St; adult/child under 12yr/student & senior $10/free/5, Tue admission free; 11am-6pm Wed-Sat; 6, 7, 14, 21, 31, 71, F, J, K, L, M, N; & Montgomery St

A three-faced divinity by Ethiopian icon painter Qes Adamu Tesfaw, a stereotype in silhouette by American Kara Walker, a regal couple by British sensation Chris Ofili: this museum has assembled a standout international cast of characters to tell the epic story of diaspora. Memorable recent shows include selections from the Bamako photography biennial and 'Africa.Dot.Com,' a show of digital technology in traditional African arts.

MUSEUM OF CRAFT AND FOLK ART

Map pp110–11

☎ 415-227-4888; www.mocfa.org; 51 Yerba Buena Lane; adult/under 18yr/senior $5/free/4; 11am-6pm Mon, Tue, Thu, Fri, to 5pm Sat & Sun; 6, 7, 14, 21, 31, 71, F, J, K, L, M, N; & Montgomery St

Vicarious hand cramps are to be expected from a trip to this museum, where amazing handiwork comes with fascinating backstories. Recent shows explored historic handmade ukuleles, four generations of African American quilt makers, and parallel lines in Scandinavian and Californian modernist furniture. It also leads craft workshops.

YERBA BUENA GARDENS Map pp110–11

☎ 415-541-0312, 415-820-3550; www.yerbabuenagardens.com; 3rd & Mission Sts; admission free; sunrise-10pm; 6, 7, 14, 21, 31, 71, F, J, K, L, M, N; & Montgomery St

A spot of green in the swath of concrete South of Market. With Yerba Buena Center for the Arts and SFMOMA on one side and the Metreon on the other, this is a prime spot for sun and downtime in between art and a movie. Free noontime concerts in summer feature world music, hip-hop and jazz. The show-stopping centerpiece is Houston Cornwell and Joseph De Pace's sleek Martin Luther King Jr Memorial Fountain, a wall of water that runs over the Reverend's immortal words: '…until justice rolls down like waters and righteousness like a mighty stream.'

A pedestrian bridge over Howard St links the popular esplanade to its tagalong kid sister, an often overlooked playground and entertainment complex that includes the worthwhile **Zeum** (opposite), a small bowling alley and ice rink, and a carousel.

CONTEMPORARY JEWISH MUSEUM

Map pp110–11

☎ 415-344-8800; www.thecjm.org; 736 Mission St; adult/under 18yr/senior & student $10/free/8, after 5pm Thu $5; 11am-5pm Fri-Tue, 1-8pm Thu; 6, 7, 14, 21, 31, 71, F, J, K, L, M, N; & Montgomery St

That upended brushed-steel box balancing improbably on one corner isn't a sculpture but a gallery for the Contemporary Jewish Museum, a major new San Francisco landmark that opened in 2008 but had been around since 1984. Before Daniel Libeskind signed on to design New York's much-debated September 11 memorial, his design for this museum was already causing a stir in SF, with its blue-steel cladding and shape drawn from the Hebrew word *l'chaim*, 'to life' – a fine idea in theory, but one best appreciated from a helicopter.

The steel structure incorporates the brick facade of the Jesse St Power substation, an 1881 industrial structure rather oddly ornamented with cream-colored cherubs and garlands. Some architectural critics call it creative adaptive reuse, others call it pure hodgepodge. Either way, the exhibits inside are impeccably curated, compelling and heavy-hitting. Recent shows have included Warhol's Jews: Ten Portraits Reconsidered – their West Coast premier – and vintage Russian Jewish theater posters from 1919 to 1949, the years when Marc Chagall joined forces with avant-garde theater people in the former Soviet Union.

ZEUM Map pp110–11
415-820-3320; www.zeum.org; 221 4th St; adult/child under 2yr/student & child $10/free/8; 1-5pm Wed-Fri, 11am-5pm Sat & Sun, 11am-5pm daily summer; 30, 45; & Powell St
No velvet ropes or hands off here: kids have the run of the place, with high-tech displays that double dare them to make their own music videos, claymation movies and soundtracks. Jump right into a live-action video game, and sign up for workshops with the Bay Area's superstar animators, techno-wizzes, robot-builders and belly dancers.

HOSFELT GALLERY Map pp110–11
415-495-5454; 430 Clementina St; admission free; 11am-5:30pm Tue-Sat; 27, 30, 45, F, J, K, L, M, N; & Powell St
Trancelike states are often induced by Hosfelt, where visitors step from gritty SoMa sidewalks into dreamy, meticulously detailed interior worlds. Close inspection of Russell Crotty's giant orbs reveals nocturnal landscapes painstakingly sketched with a Bic pen, and Marco Maggi's minutely carved stacks of office paper make paperwork seem sublime.

SOUTH PARK Map pp110–11
enclosed by 2nd, 3rd, Bryant & Brannan Sts; 10, 30, 45, 76, N, T
'Dot-com' was the word on the street here in the mid-'90s, when venture capitalists plotted website launches in parkside cafes with tattooed 20-something techies. But speculation is nothing new to South Park, which was planned by a real-estate speculator in the 1850s as a bucolic gated community.

Though the South Park development itself never quite took off, a plaque on an office building around the corner at 601 3rd St marks the **birthplace of Jack London**, esteemed author of *The Call of the Wild, White Fang* and many other popular adventure stories. Otherwise the neighborhood retreated into obscurity, and Filipino American war veterans formed a quiet community here until the dot-com boom. Nowadays it seems even the birds in the trees are twittering about another South Park venture, founded here after the dot-com bust: Twitter.

NEW LANGTON ARTS Map pp110–11
415-626-5416; www.newlangtonarts.org; 1246 Folsom St; admission free; noon-6pm Tue-Sat; 12, 19, F, J, K, L, M, N; & Civic Center
Strange is the norm at New Langton, where artists have done odd and occasionally unprintable things since 1975. This nonprofit is where Tony Labat stepped into the boxing ring with his critics and Harrell Fletcher distributed newspapers by teen reporters he'd commissioned to collect good news from their neighbors. Don't miss the Musée d'Honneur Minuscule, a window box in the entryway featuring small, ambitious works, such as Jill Sylvia's tiny cityscape made from accountants' ledger paper.

ELECTRIC WORKS Map pp110–11
415-626-5496; www.sfelectricworks.com; 130 8th St; admission free; 11am-6pm Tue-Fri, to 5pm Sat; 5, 6, 7, 14, 21, 31, 71, F, J, K, L, M, N; & Civic Center
In the gallery/printmaking studio that calls itself 'The Land of Yes,' anything is possible – including Marcel Dzama's gangs of vampire toddlers and Sandow Birk's modern take on Dante's *Inferno,* starring traffic-jammed LA as hell and San Francisco as a foggy purgatory. Also, it's an affordable alternative to museum stores, and sales from some print editions benefit nonprofits.

CALIFORNIA HISTORICAL SOCIETY MUSEUM Map pp110–11
415-357-1848; www.californiahistoricalsociety.org; 678 Mission St; adult/child under 5yr/senior & student $3/free/1; noon-4:30pm Wed-Sat; 6, 7, 14, 21, 31, 71, F, J, K, L, M, N; & Montgomery St
Get the lowdown on California history at this exhibition space devoted entirely to the state's history. Portions of the museum's vast collection – think half-a-million-plus photographs, paintings by famous Californians and myriad ephemera and artifacts – are showcased in exhibits that rotate every 18 months. You might see Jack London's flask or then-and-now shots of famous California sights in century-old paintings hung beside contemporary photographs of the same place.

Bibliophiles: don't miss the old-fashioned **research library** (noon-5pm Wed-Fri), which puts rare books, photos and manuscripts right in your hand. The library has the definitive collection on the American Civil Liberties Union and the People's Temple, among other California-centric subjects. Call ahead if you want to research a specific topic so staff can pull the appropriate materials from the vault.

CROWN POINT PRESS Map pp110–11

415-974-6273; www.crownpoint.com; 20 Hawthorne St; admission free; 10am-6pm Mon-Sat; 10, 12, 14, 30, 45, 76

Bet you didn't think anyone could capture Chuck Close's giant portraits, Wayne Thiebaud's Pop Art pastries, or Australian Aboriginal artist Dorothy Napangardi's dreamings on paper. Yet here they are: color woodcut portraits produced by carving and printing 51 separate blocks of wood; cream-pie tinged pale-blue within glass pastry cases, captured in a color gravure; and salt tracings of Mina Mina in mesmerizing sugar-lift etchings. Such are the mysterious powers of Crown Point Press printmakers, who work with artists to turn singular visions into large-scale paper multiples.

WPA MURALS AT RINCON ANNEX POST OFFICE Map pp110–11

101 Spear St; admission free; 2, 7, 14, 21, 71, F, J, K, L, M, N; & Embarcadero

Russian-born painter Anton Refregier won the Works Project Administration's largest commission to depict the history of Northern California in 1941, but WWII intervened. When Refregier began again in 1945, he was lobbied by interest groups to present their version of history, and it took three years and 92 changes to make everyone happy. The murals were deemed 'communist' by McCarthyists in 1953, but they're now protected as a National Landmark.

FEDERAL BUILDING Map pp110–11

Mission & 7th Sts; 5, 6, 7, 14, 21, 31, 71, F, J, K, L, M, N; & Civic Center

The revolutionary green design of this new government office building by 2005 Pritzker Architecture Prize winner Thomas Mayne means huge savings in energy consumption, not to mention taxpayer dollars. The ingenious layout eliminates internal political battles over corner offices, providing direct sunlight, natural ventilation and views for 90% of work stations. Detractors claim it looks like a too-tall fortress designed to remind plucky SF who's really boss. Regardless, it's a significant and much-needed addition to the otherwise bland, sometimes ugly, SoMa skyline.

VICTORIA MANALO DRAVES PARK Map pp110–11

Folsom St, btwn 6th & 7th Sts; 12, 19, 27;

A welcome patch of green in a sea of concrete, this lovely 2-acre park is the perfect spot for a picnic in SoMa – little ones love the slide and jungle gym. Good landscaping, a community garden and interesting art – including laser-etched steel murals – give reason to linger. There's also a public bathroom, one of few in the neighborhood.

ON THE HORIZON: DOWNTOWN'S NEW SKYLINE

Until the 1970s, SF skyscrapers topped out below 20 stories. Then came the boom. New towers started popping up around Montgomery St. Some, like the Transamerica Pyramid (p71), were met with mixed approval. When the Bank of America Building – the first non-white skyscraper in SF – went up at 555 California St, San Franciscans dubbed the amorphous sculpture at its base 'the black heart of the banker.' The final straw was Fontana Apartments, which rose on the waterfront, east of Van Ness Ave, blocking Russian Hill residents' bay views. Locals went ballistic. 'No Manhattanization of San Francisco' became the rallying cry, and for decades development stopped.

Twenty years later, the dot-com boom of the late '90s sparked huge real-estate demand, and before anyone could shout Manhattan, land had been quietly re-zoned. Massive new towers began springing up South of Market. In the old days SoMa was all light-industrial buildings, with box cars parked on Harrison St. No self-respecting straight person would be caught dead here after dark. To see what it looked like, head to 12th St between Howard and Folsom Sts and find the rusting corrugated-metal building on the east side of the street.

Now walk to Mission St and look east. Behold the new Downtown. At 888 Howard St (at 5th St), the Intercontinental Hotel draws criticism for its Miami-blue glass that doesn't match the pewter-gray SF sky. Locals call it the 'Listerine Bottle.' And then there's One Rincon Hill, directly at the foot of the Bay Bridge, which looks like a giant ionizing air filter, loudly proclaiming that all height-restriction bets are off.

It's not all bad news. Some of the interplays between past and present are visually arresting, such as on the plaza in front of the Contemporary Jewish Museum (p112) – SoMa's smartest architectural adaptation of an old building, a former power station from 1881. Skyscrapers lord over it on three sides, including the Marriott Hotel (aka the Jukebox) to the west. Adjacent stands the demure red-brick 1851 St Patrick's Church, and behind rises the ornate crown of the 1869 Humboldt Bank Building, now dethroned by the surrounding monolithic towers of the new Downtown.

THE MISSION & POTRERO HILL

Drinking p200; Eating p180; Shopping p152; Sleeping p260

You never know who you'll bump into next in the Mission, and the graveyard at Mission Dolores (below) is a historical case in point. Piled atop the mass graves of the Ohlone who built the first mission here in 1776 are the skeletons of Spanish Mexican priests and colonial overlords, alongside the bones of Italian, Scots Irish and Australian adventurers lured here not by God, but by gold. Within blocks of this historic spot, famous authors are busy helping teens with their homework at 826 Valencia (p118), curators and developmentally disabled artists are mounting their next breakthrough gallery show at Creativity Explored (p119) and graffiti artists are touching up murals in Clarion Alley within full view of the Mission police station (p119).

San Franciscans love to show off the Mission as proof that ideals can actually work in practice, and are itching for you to ask the obvious: what kind of neighborhood is this, anyway? This is a trick question. Latinos, lesbians, foodies, ravers, career activists, chichi designers, punks, prostitutes and suits all play featured roles in the Mission's ensemble act.

Further east, Potrero Hill has become a bedroom community for Google execs and Mission Bay biotech pioneers, with art and culinary schools springing up in warehouses downhill. Though Mission and Potrero change from one block and one day to the next, there is one noteworthy constant: even when the rest of the city is shivering in fog, locals will be squinting in the sunshine on front stoops here.

top picks

THE MISSION & POTRERO HILL

- **Murals in Balmy Alley** (p118) **and Clarion Alley** (p119)
- **826 Valencia** (p118)
- **Creativity Explored** (p119)
- **Intersection for the Arts** (p225)
- **California College of the Arts** (p119)

All this creative community flux wasn't achieved overnight. When rich industrialists lost their mansions here in the 1906 quake, they abandoned the area to Irish and Italian immigrants. Central American and Mexican immigrants arrived from the 1920s through the 1970s, and Southeast Asians in the 1980s. Murals expressing outrage at US policy in Central America in Balmy Alley (p118) also took on women's issues, especially with the arrival of lesbian activists and the Women's Building (p119) in the 1970s, while streetwise graffiti artists like Barry McGee and Andrew Schoultz kept the neighborhood's independent spirit alive as the Mission and Potrero broke out in a rash of dot-commers in the '90s. Tech money still mingles uneasily with gang activity and Mission Dolores devotion with nightly bar antics, but like many Mission murals, it all makes chaotic, surreal sense – you just have to be here.

The Mission is a flat area bounded by hills on three sides, with Castro and Noe Valley to the west, Potrero Hill to the east and Bernal Heights to the south. Mission St was once San Francisco's 'miracle mile' of deco cinemas and Sunday strollers, and though most of the cinemas are now occupied by 99 Cent stores, faded marquees remain and Latino families still stroll Mission St dressed for church on Sundays. On parallel Valencia St, former appliance storefronts are now prime locations for hip restaurants, local designers and vintage boutiques. The street known as El Corazón de la Mission (the heart of the Mission) is 24th St, with its bodegas, mural-covered alleyways and taquerias (taco restaurants).

Potrero Hill is divided from the Mission by a couple of streets and several income brackets, but on the downward slope of Potrero off 3rd St between 18th and 22nd Sts, galleries, bars and reasonable restaurants are springing up among the shipyards in an area known as the Dogpatch. Downhill among the warehouses clustered around 16th St are furniture designers, the San Francisco Center for the Book (p119) and the California College of the Arts (p119).

MISSION DOLORES Map pp116–17

☎ 415-621-8203; www.missiondolores.org; 3321 16th St; adult/senior & child $5/3, audio tour $5; 9am-4pm Nov-Apr, to 4:30pm May-Oct; 14, 22, 33, 49, J; 16th St Mission

The city's oldest building and its namesake, the Misión San Francisco de Asis, was founded in 1776 and rebuilt in 1782 with conscripted Ohlone labor in exchange for a meal a day – note the ceiling patterned after

THE MISSION & POTRERO HILL

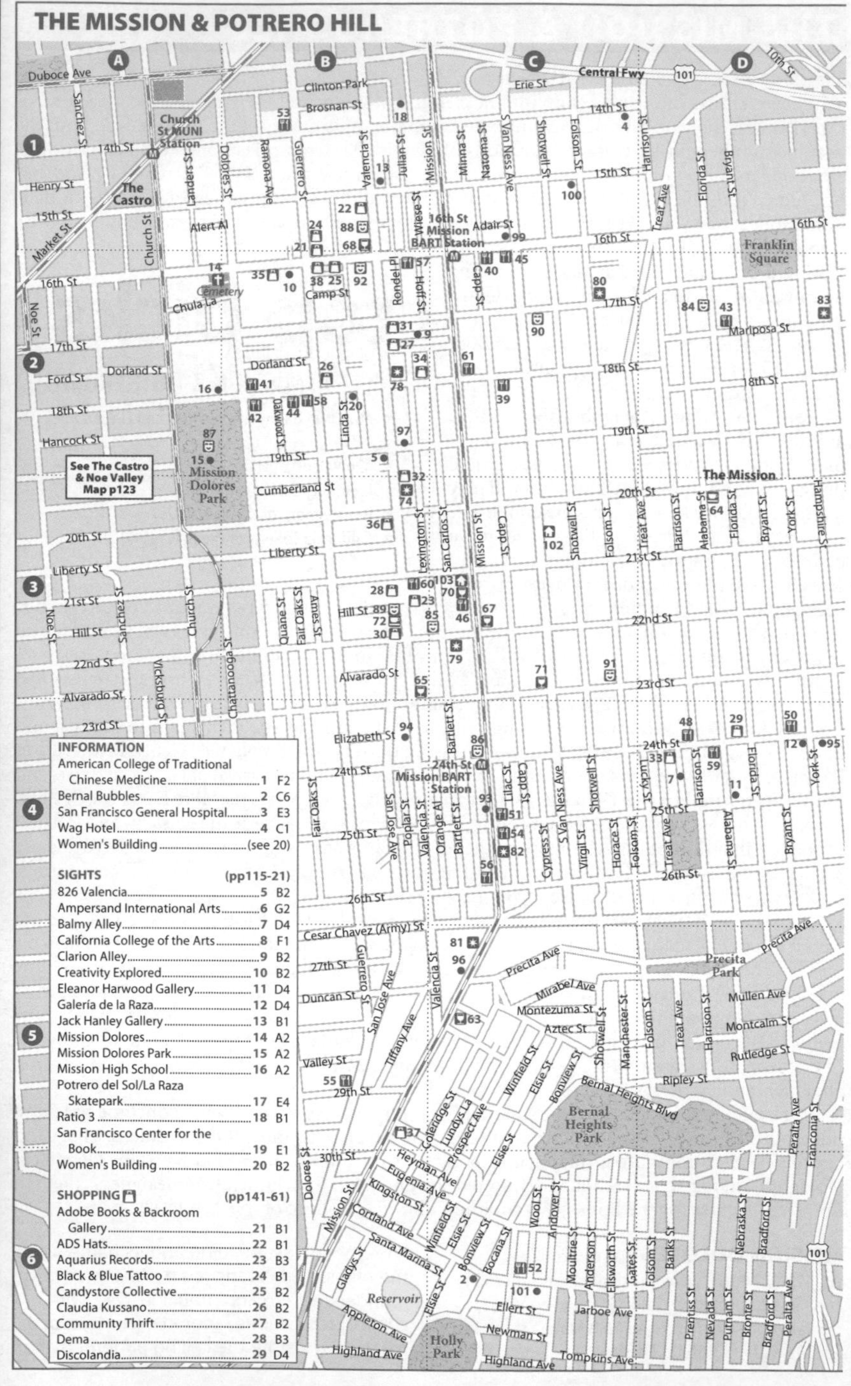

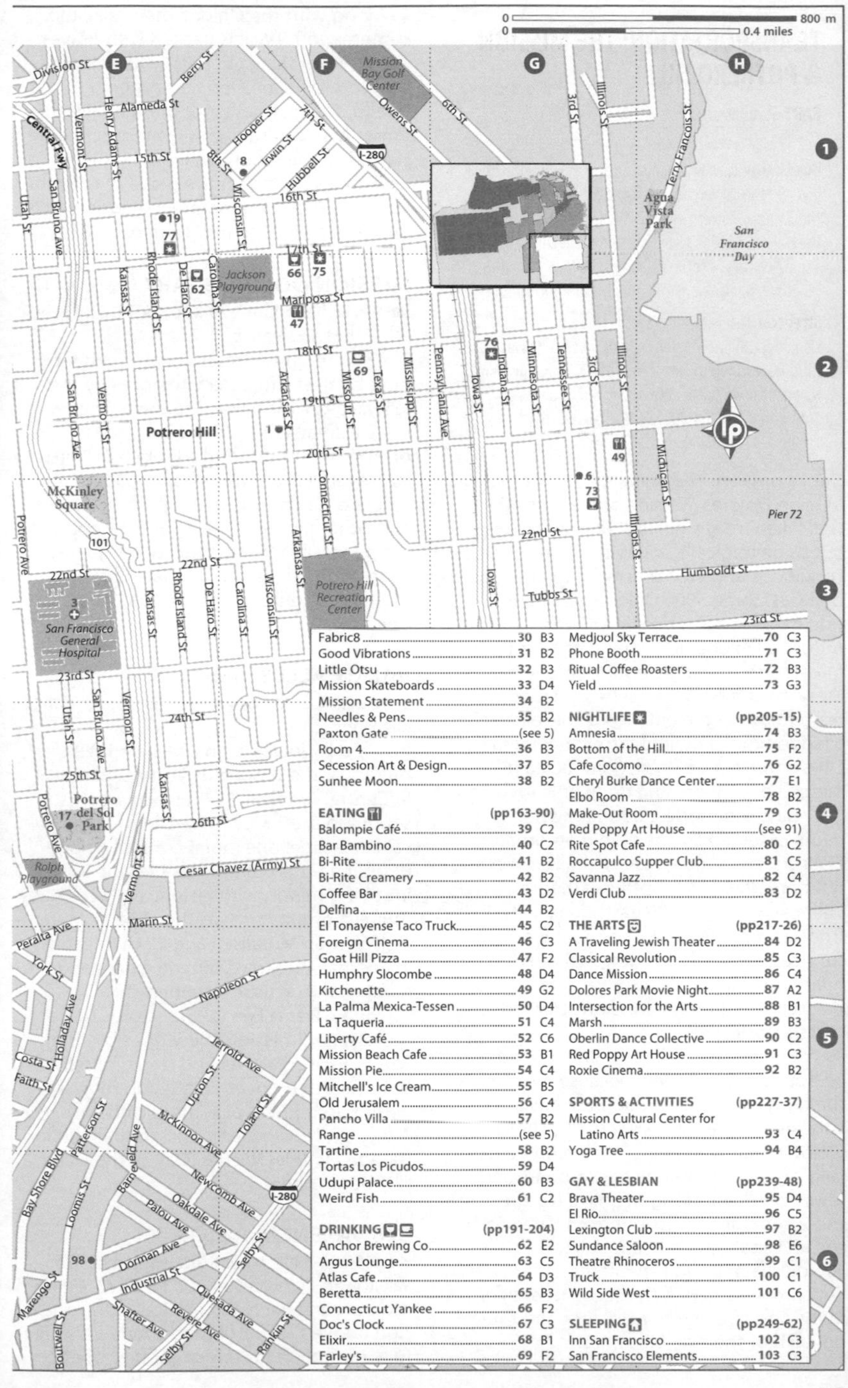
0
800 m
0
0.4 miles
E
F
G
H
1
2
3
4
5
6
Division St
Berry St
Alameda St
Central Fwy
Vermont St
Henry Adams St
15th St
8th St
Hooper St
Irwin St
7th St
Hubbell St
16th St
Owens St
6th St
Mission Bay Golf Center
I-280
3rd St
Illinois St
Terry Francois St
Agua Vista Park
San Francisco Bay
Utah St
San Bruno Ave
Wisconsin St
Kansas St
Rhode Island St
De Haro St
Carolina St
Jackson Playground
17th St
Mariposa St
18th St
19th St
20th St
Arkansas St
Missouri St
Texas St
Mississippi St
Pennsylvania Ave
Iowa St
Indiana St
Minnesota St
Tennessee St
Michigan St
Potrero Hill
McKinley Square
Connecticut St
22nd St
Pier 72
Humboldt St
Tubbs St
23rd St
Potrero Ave
101
San Francisco General Hospital
Potrero Hill Recreation Center
24th St
25th St
26th St
Potrero del Sol Park
Rolph Playground
Cesar Chavez (Army) St
Marin St
Peralta Ave
York St
Holladay Ave
Napoleon St
Jerrold Ave
Costa St
Faith St
Upton St
Toland St
McKinnon Ave
Patterson St
Bay Shore Blvd
Loomis St
Barneveld Ave
Newcomb Ave
Oakdale Ave
Palou Ave
Dorman Ave
Industrial St
Selby St
Quesada Ave
Revere Ave
Shafter Ave
Rankin St
Marengo St
Boutwell St
Fabric8 ....30 B3
Good Vibrations 31 B2
Little Otsu 32 B3
Mission Skateboards 33 D4
Mission Statement 34 B2
Needles & Pens 35 B2
Paxton Gate ....(see 5)
Room 4 ....36 B3
Secession Art & Design 37 B5
Sunhee Moon 38 B2
EATING (pp163-90)
Balompie Café 39 C2
Bar Bambino 40 C2
Bi-Rite 41 B2
Bi-Rite Creamery 42 B2
Coffee Bar 43 D2
Delfina 44 B2
El Tonayense Taco Truck 45 C2
Foreign Cinema 46 C3
Goat Hill Pizza 47 F2
Humphry Slocombe 48 D4
Kitchenette 49 G2
La Palma Mexica-Tessen 50 D4
La Taqueria 51 C4
Liberty Café 52 C6
Mission Beach Cafe 53 B1
Mission Pie 54 C4
Mitchell's Ice Cream 55 B5
Old Jerusalem 56 C4
Pancho Villa 57 B2
Range ....(see 5)
Tartine 58 B2
Tortas Los Picudos 59 D4
Udupi Palace 60 B3
Weird Fish 61 C2
DRINKING (pp191-204)
Anchor Brewing Co 62 E2
Argus Lounge 63 C5
Atlas Cafe 64 D3
Beretta 65 B3
Connecticut Yankee 66 F2
Doc's Clock 67 C3
Elixir 68 B1
Farley's 69 F2
Medjool Sky Terrace 70 C3
Phone Booth 71 C3
Ritual Coffee Roasters 72 B3
Yield 73 G3
NIGHTLIFE (pp205-15)
Amnesia 74 B3
Bottom of the Hill 75 F2
Cafe Cocomo 76 G2
Cheryl Burke Dance Center 77 E1
Elbo Room 78 B2
Make-Out Room 79 C3
Red Poppy Art House ....(see 91)
Rite Spot Cafe 80 C2
Roccapulco Supper Club 81 C5
Savanna Jazz 82 C4
Verdi Club 83 D2
THE ARTS (pp217-26)
A Traveling Jewish Theater 84 D2
Classical Revolution 85 C3
Dance Mission 86 C4
Dolores Park Movie Night 87 A2
Intersection for the Arts 88 B1
Marsh 89 B3
Oberlin Dance Collective 90 C2
Red Poppy Art House 91 C3
Roxie Cinema 92 B2
SPORTS & ACTIVITIES (pp227-37)
Mission Cultural Center for Latino Arts 93 C4
Yoga Tree 94 B4
GAY & LESBIAN (pp239-48)
Brava Theater 95 D4
El Rio 96 C5
Lexington Club 97 B2
Sundance Saloon 98 E6
Theatre Rhinoceros 99 C1
Truck 100 C1
Wild Side West 101 C6
SLEEPING (pp249-62)
Inn San Francisco 102 C3
San Francisco Elements 103 C3

TRANSPORTATION: THE MISSION & POTRERO HILL

BART Stations at 16th and 24th Sts serve the Mission.

Bus Line 14 runs along Mission St from Downtown. Bus 49 follows Van Ness Ave and Mission St, while the 33 links Potrero and the Mission to the Castro, the Haight, Golden Gate Park and the Richmond. The 22 connects Potrero Hill and the Mission to the Haight, Japantown, Pacific Heights and the Marina.

Streetcar The J streetcar passes through the Mission, stopping at Mission Dolores Park on its way from Downtown to Noe Valley. The T Muni line from Downtown via SoMa stops along 3rd St between 16th and 22nd, in Potrero's Dogpatch district.

Native baskets. The building's nickname, Mission Dolores (Mission of the Sorrows), was taken from a nearby lake, but it turned out to be tragically apt. With harsh living conditions and little resistance to introduced diseases, some 5000 Ohlone died in mission measles epidemics in 1814 and 1826. A replica Ohlone hut commemorates their mass burial in the graveyard, among early Mexican and European settlers. Recent restorations in the old mission have revealed a hidden mural behind the altar painted by Ohlone artisans: a small, grim sacred heart, pierced by a sword and dripping with blood.

Today, the modest adobe mission is overshadowed by the adjoining ornate Churriguera-esque basilica, built in 1913 after an 1876 brick Gothic cathedral collapsed in the 1906 earthquake. The front doors are usually open only during services, so to get inside you'll need to head into the small entryway shop, pass through the original mission structure and cross a courtyard.

Your eyes may take a moment to adjust once you're inside, because most of the light is filtered through the basilica's splendid stained-glass windows. The choir windows show St Francis beaming beatifically against an orange background, and lower windows along the nave feature the 21 California missions from Santa Cruz to San Diego and mission builders Father Junípero Serra and Father Francisco Palou. Seven panels depict the *Seven Sorrows of Mary,* one above the main door and three on each of the side balconies.

Along with the Ohlone memorial, the cemetery out back is packed with graves dating from the Gold Rush. Alongside mission founders are Don Luis Antonio Arguello, the first governor of Alta California under Mexican rule, and Don Francisco de Haro, first mayor of San Francisco. Hitchcock fans looking for the grave of Carlotta Valdes will be disappointed: the tomb was only a prop for the film *Vertigo*.

MISSION DOLORES PARK Map pp116–17

Dolores St, btwn 18th & 20th Sts; 14, 22, 33, 49, J; 16th St Mission;

The site of quasi-professional Castro tanning contests, free performances by the San Francisco Mime Troupe (see the boxed text, p223), a small kids' playground, free movies on summer nights and a Hunky Jesus Contest (p21) every Easter, this sloping park is also beloved for its year-round political protests and other favorite local sports. Flat patches are generally reserved for soccer games, candlelight vigils and ultimate Frisbee, and the tennis courts and basketball hoops are open to all.

BALMY ALLEY Map pp116–17

btwn 24th & 25th Sts; 9, 27, 33, 48; 24th St Mission

Inspired by local Diego Rivera and WPA murals, and outraged by US foreign policy in Central America, Mission activist artists set out in the 1970s to transform the political landscape, one mural-covered garage door at a time. Balmy Alley became a site for inquiring minds, with historic early works by muralist groups such as the Mujeres Muralistas (Women Muralists) and Placa (meaning 'mark-making') transforming fences and garages into artistic statements.

Today, Precita Eyes (p313) restores these murals, commissions new ones by rising San Francisco artists and leads muralist-led tours that cover 75 Mission murals within an eight-block radius of Balmy Alley. On November 1, the annual Mission parade Día de los Muertos (Day of the Dead; p23) begins here.

826 VALENCIA Map pp116–17

415-642-5905; www.826valencia.com; 826 Valencia St; noon-6pm; 14, 26, 33, 49;

'No buccaneers! No geriatrics!' warns the sign above the vat of sand where kids gleefully rummage for buried pirates' booty.

The treasures are theirs for the taking, if they offer barter for it at the front counter – a song, perhaps, or a knock-knock joke.

This eccentric nonprofit Pirate Supply Store selling eye patches, scoops from an actual tub o' lard, and *McSweeney's* literary magazines is the front for a nonprofit offering free writing workshops and tutoring for youth, plus the occasional adult program on starting a magazine and scripting video games (check website for listings). Step behind the velvet curtain into the Fish Theater, where a bug-eyed puffer fish is immersed in Method acting. The ichthyoid antics may not be quite up to Sean Penn standards, but as the sign says, 'Please don't judge the fish.'

CLARION ALLEY Map pp116–17

btwn 17th & 18th Sts, off Valencia St; 🚌 14, 22, 26, 33, 49; Ⓜ 16th St Mission

Trial by fire is nothing compared to Clarion Alley's street-art test: unless a piece is truly inspired, it's going to get peed on or painted over. Very few pieces survive for years – Andrew Schoultz's mural of gentrifying elephants displacing scraggly birds, a silhouette of kung-fu-fighting female anarchists that makes Charlie's Angels look like chumps, and a trompe l'oeil escalator. Incontinent art critics seem to have taken over the east end of the alley – pee-eew! – so the less aromatic, more intricate murals are on the west.

CREATIVITY EXPLORED Map pp116–17

☎ 415-863-2108; www.creativityexplored.org; 3245 16th St; donations welcome; 🕑 10am-3pm Mon-Fri, until 7pm Thu, 1-6pm Sat; 🚌 14, 22, 33, 49, J; Ⓜ 16th St Mission

Brave new worlds are captured in celebrated artworks that have appeared in museum retrospectives, major collections, even on Marc Jacobs clutches (see p148) – all by local developmentally disabled artists. Intriguing themed shows reveal fresh perspectives on themes ranging from jazz to alien life forms, and openings are joyous celebrations with the artists and their families.

CALIFORNIA COLLEGE OF THE ARTS

Map pp116–17

☎ 1-800-447-1278; www.cca.edu; 1111 8th St at 16th St; admission free; 🕑 gallery 11am-7pm Tue & Thu, to 6pm Wed, Fri & Sat; 🚌 19, 22, 33

A generous endowment and big-name curators allow the Wattis Institute to take on ambitious, sweeping shows like 'Americana: 50 States, 50 Months, 50 Exhibitions,' which runs through 2012 in a high-concept road trip from Alabama to Wyoming. Head across the courtyard and upstairs to PLAySPACE (🕑 3-7pm Tue-Thu, noon-2pm Sat Sep-May), an experimental exhibition space curated by MFA candidates in the college's curatorial studies program. Intriguing recent PLAySPACE shows explored luxury in the post-bling era, and real and reproduced Bay Area soundscapes.

SAN FRANCISCO CENTER FOR THE BOOK Map pp116–17

☎ 415-565-0545; www.sfcb.org; 300 De Haro St; admission free; 🕑 10am-5pm Mon-Fri; 🚌 19, 22, 33

Anyone who can't get enough of the sound and smell of a freshly cracked book will achieve a whole new level of obsession with these displays of elaborate Coptic binding and wooden typesetting machines. One recent exhibit showcased the creative process of acclaimed book illustrators, from David Macaulay *(The Way Things Work)* to Caldecott Medal winner Chris Raschka *(Hello, Goodbye Window)*. The center offers classes, so you can learn to make your own books that fit into matchboxes, pop up into cityscapes and unfold into prison guard towers.

WOMEN'S BUILDING Map pp116–17

☎ 415-431-1180; www.womensbuilding.org; 3543 18th St; 🚌 14, 26, 33, 49, J; Ⓜ 16th St Mission

The nation's first female-owned-and-operated community center has been quietly doing good work with 170 women's organizations since 1979, but the 1994 addition of the *Maestrapeace* mural showed this building for the landmark that it truly is. An all-star team of muralistas covered the building with the icons of female strength, from Mayan and Chinese goddesses to modern trailblazers, including Rigoberta Menchu, Hanaan Ashrawi and former US surgeon general Dr Jocelyn Elders.

ELEANOR HARWOOD GALLERY

Map pp116–17

☎ 415-867-7770; www.eleanorharwood.com; 1295 Alabama St; admission free; 🕑 1-5pm Thu-Sat; 🚌 9, 27, 33, 48; Ⓜ 24th St Mission

Hidden on a residential Mission side street is this treasure-box showcase for Bay Area talents, from emerging sensations like James Chronister's oil portraits painted dot by dot, tattoo-style with a tiny brush, to breakthrough stars like US Venice Biennale artist Emily Prince, whose daily drawings form poignantly personal catalogs: all the hats in her house, say, or all the US soldiers killed in Iraq.

POTRERO DEL SOL/LA RAZA SKATEPARK Map pp116–17

www.sfgov.org; 25th & Utah Sts; 9, 27, 33, 48; 24th St Mission

An isolated, scrubby park that had been abandoned to gangs became NorCal's hottest urban skatepark in 2008 with support from the city's Park and Rec department. Day and night under strategically placed lights, newbies and pros blast ollies off the hip of these concrete bowls. The downsides: the bathroom is often off-limits due to misuse or stench, and graffiti on the concrete can make for a slippery ride. Go before you hit your flow, and wait for a clean area of the bowl to bust big moves. For gear, hit up Mission Skateboards (p153).

RATIO 3 Map pp116–17

415-821-3371; www.ratio3.org; 1447 Stevenson St; admission free; 11am-6pm Wed-Sat; 14, 22, 33, 49; 16th St Mission

Art-fair buzz begins in San Francisco exactly where it should, down a back alley with a dog barking bloody murder as you wait anxiously to be buzzed into an unfinished loft space with raw wood floors and pristine white walls. Artists here are regularly covered in Artforum and wind up at Miami Basel, and a recent show featured graduates of the Mission School moving into abstraction: a geometric panel assemblage by graffiti auteur Barry McGee looked like a super-flat Frank Stella, and Jose Alvarez' square of blue feathers mounted on black mica was a dazzling Aztec Rothko.

JACK HANLEY GALLERY

Map pp116–17

415-522-1623; www.jackhanley.com; 395 Valencia St; admission free; 11am-6pm Tue-Sat; 14, 22, 33, 49; 16th St Mission

Furious scribblers and meticulous daydreamers will relate to Chris Johansen's crowds of shy hipsters, Michele Blade's metaphysical meteor showers and Keegan McHargue's hyper-doodled dudes sprouting antlers. Collectors often snap up works before shows open, so see them now before they disappear into Manhattan penthouses.

GALERÍA DE LA RAZA

Map pp116–17

415-826-8009; www.galeriadelaraza.org; 2857 24th St; admission free; noon-6pm Wed-Sat, to 7pm Tue; 9, 27, 33, 48; 24th St Mission

Art never forgets its roots at this showcase for Latino art since 1970. Witness Salvadoran Victor Cartagena's *Invisible Nation* installation of found ID photos, a group show exploring SF's Latin gay culture and David Bacon's portraits of indigenous Mexican migrant laborers. On the gallery wall outside is the Digital Mural Project, a billboard featuring slogans like 'Trust Your Struggle' instead of the usual cigarette advertisements.

AMPERSAND INTERNATIONAL ARTS

Map pp116–17

415- 285-0170; www.ampersandintlarts.com; 1001 Tennessee St at 20th St; admission free; noon-5pm Thu-Fri & by appointment; 22, 33, T

Curator Bruno Mauro really takes his work home with him: since 1999, his live/work Dogpatch loft studio has doubled as an installation space for Bay Area and international galleries (there's a sister space in Paris). Recent shows have featured Ellen Babcock's mysterious melting glacier caves made of salvaged Styrofoam, and Andrew Vogt's wall-mounted found-wood sculptures that look like old-fashioned contraptions and are carefully crafted to appear as though they're falling apart.

MISSION HIGH SCHOOL

Map pp116–17

415-241-6240; 3750 18th St; 14, 22, 33, 49, J; 16th St Mission

San Francisco's most spectacular bell tower is the churrigueresque tiled tower of Mission High, built in the mission revival style from 1925 to 1927. This is one place where you might actually want to see a high-school musical – the theater has a glorious gold-leafed dome with deco chandeliers. The multiculti student body here is mostly African American and Latino, and its famous alumni include Maya Angelou and Carlos Santana.

MISSION ART TRAMP

Walking Tour

1 Clarion Alley (p119) Once favored by heroin addicts, this alley still sometimes reeks with the stench of a just-missed urinal. But since the Clarion Alley Mural Project was founded in 1992, almost every inch of wall and garage door here has been covered with art – some by San Francisco street artists who have gone on to museum shows, including Barry McGee and Chris Johansen. Only the strong art survives peeing, tagging and overpainting here and in neighboring Sycamore Alley.

2 Generator Adorning the side of an apartment building on the corner of Lexington and 18th Sts, this collaboration by Andrew Schoultz and Aaron Noble shows a Seussian metropolis of tall buildings twisting around birdhouses, capturing the competition for space in gentrifying SF neighborhoods. You may recognize the theme and bird motifs from a Schoultz mural over on Clarion Alley.

3 Women's Building (p119) *Maestrapeace* covers two sides of this four-story structure, created in 1993–94 by seven local muralistas with a team of community collaborators.

4 826 Valencia (p118) Stop by the Pirate Supply Store to browse the selection of glass eyes, peg-leg oil and publications by local authors, or just go with the Dadaist flow of puffer-fish performances in the Fish Theater.

5 Balmy Alley (p118) Following the lead of Mexican muralists Diego Rivera and José Clemente Orozco, local muralistas address current social and political themes in styles that range from social realism to hallucinogenic.

6 Eleanor Harwood Gallery (p119) End your adventure with new discoveries at this gallery championing local artists with dreamy, obsessive visions. The gallery makes the international art fair circuit, but saves the best for home. If you can't live on art alone, do what starving Mission artists do: head to nearby **Tortas Los Picudos** (p182) for a Mexico City–style stuffed sandwich with all the fixings.

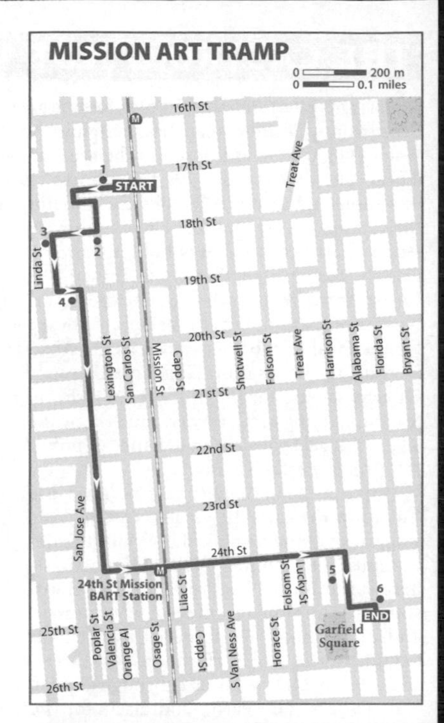

WALK FACTS

Start Clarion Alley
End Eleanor Harwood Gallery
Distance 1.5 miles
Time 1½ hours
Exertion Easy
Fuel stop Tortas Los Picudos

THE CASTRO & NOE VALLEY

Drinking p202; Eating p183; Shopping p155; Sleeping p260

This frumpy Scandinavian-Irish neighborhood became a glamorous symbol of gay freedom when Haight hippies flocked to the area, attracted by cheap rent, freer love and music with a beat. The time was the '70s, the soundtrack was disco, and in the sunny Castro, the weight of a thousand secrets lifted like the morning fog. Seedier, more outrageous gay scenes also thrived in Polk Gulch (near Civic Center) and on Folsom St south of Market, but the Castro stood apart because it was bold, business savvy and politically organized. In front of 575 Castro St is a plaque that marks this spot as the one-time camera store of Harvey Milk, the Castro entrepreneur who became the first openly gay man elected to public office in the US. Near the Castro branch of the public library is a stretch of 16th St renamed José Serría Court for the local icon better known as the Absolute Empress of San Francisco, who led patrons in rousing choruses of 'God Save Us Nelly Queens' at the height of the gay-bashing, fear-mongering McCarthy era, and threw the city's first gala gay balls in defiance of police raids on gay establishments.

When a mysterious illness ravaged the Castro in the early 1980s, loss cast its long shadow over the neighborhood. But the determined intervention of HIV/AIDS activists here saved untold lives, establishing global standards for humane, life-saving treatment and prevention. The Imperial Court balls begun by Her Royal Highness José Serría and a 10km AIDS Walk (p22) through Golden Gate Park became early fundraisers for the fight against AIDS, supplying essential monies not forthcoming from public coffers and providing a model other cities soon followed to show their support for the fight against AIDS. The Castro's response continues to prove to the world that model citizens do not always hide behind picket fences or come in a standard-issue uniform. To support this heroic effort, visit Under One Roof (p156) and the Human Rights Campaign (p241).

top picks

THE CASTRO & NOE VALLEY

- **Castro Theatre** (p124)
- **Corona Heights Park** (p124)
- **F line Streetcar** (p304)
- **Under One Roof** (p156)

Today, the rainbow flag flies high over the neighborhood, and the Castro flexes its political muscle. With backing from local organizations, more openly gay officials were elected in the first decade of the 21st century than at any time in US history. Good times are always on the bill at the landmark Castro Theatre (p124) and the neighborhood's many bars and cafes (for top picks, see p241).

The Castro's orientation? Gay, of course, with a smattering of straight couples with babies thrown in for shock value. The Castro was formerly known as Eureka Valley and sits at the base of Twin Peaks. The corner of Castro and Market Sts forms the main crossroads of the district, with more shops and restaurants along Market St to Church St and cafes along 18th St. To ogle picture-perfect, Queen Anne–style Victorian cottages, head uphill on 18th and 19th Sts below Upper Market and Twin Peaks.

Follow Castro St south to Noe Valley, one of the most family-friendly spots in San Francisco. Though it is distinctly yuppie, a significant number of lesbian and gay families and the odd stray Mission hipster keep it from seeming too much like a stodgy Connecticut suburb. Mommy stereotypes were made to be broken by the chic boutiques along 24th St, where nary a high-waisted jean or lumpy sweater can be found. And while the food and bars are better in the Mission, Noe Valley cafes are an ideal spot to park a stroller and while away a sunny day.

Noe Valley is just over the hill from the Castro, around 24th St between Castro and Church Sts. The main drag is 24th St, bordered by residential streets with lots of pretty, pale Victorian housing. On Church St the restaurants and shops continue until the last stop on the J Church line around 29th St.

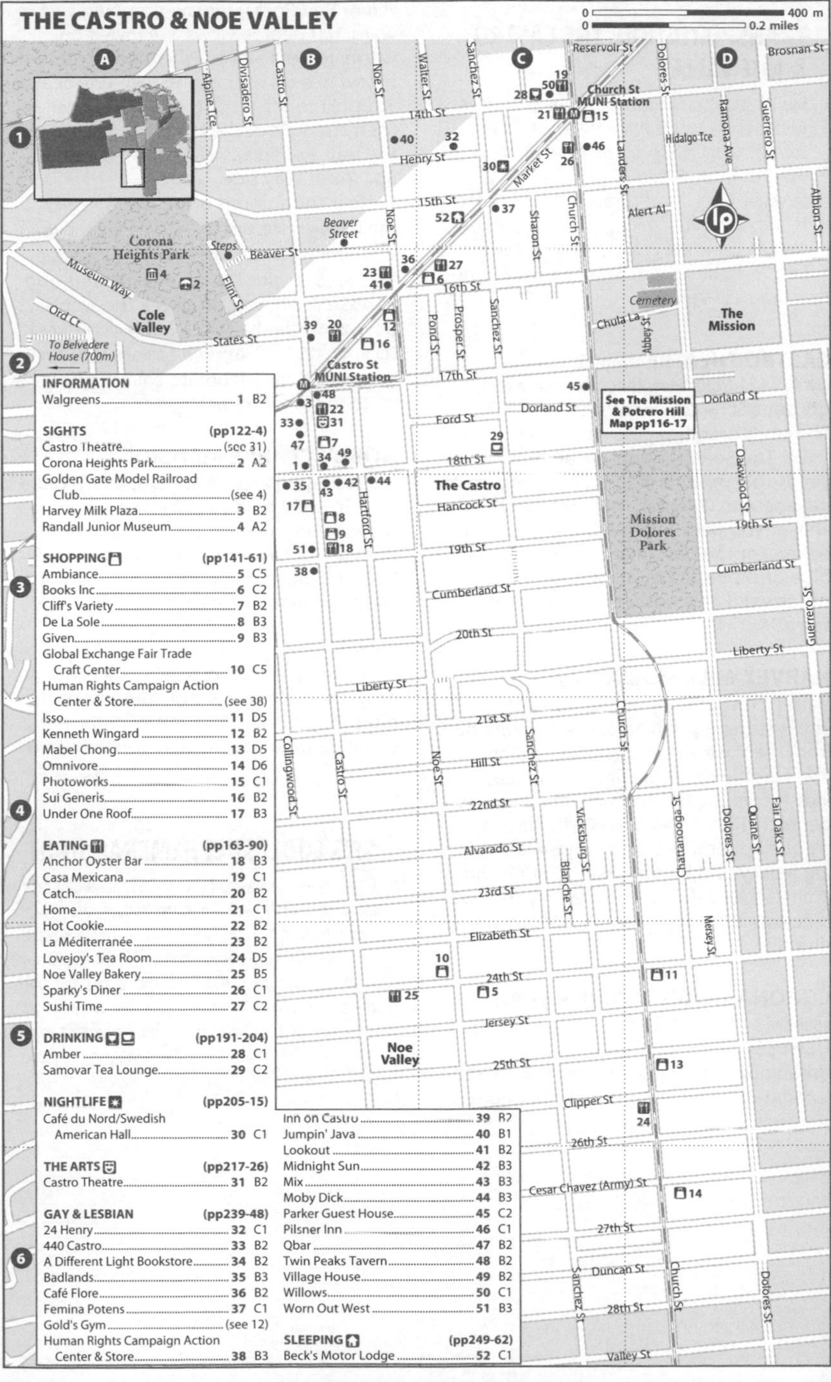
THE CASTRO & NOE VALLEY
0 400 m
0 0.2 miles
INFORMATION
Walgreens 1 B2
SIGHTS (pp122-4)
Castro Theatre (see 31)
Corona Heights Park 2 A2
Golden Gate Model Railroad Club (see 4)
Harvey Milk Plaza 3 B2
Randall Junior Museum 4 A2
SHOPPING (pp141-61)
Ambiance 5 C5
Books Inc 6 C2
Cliff's Variety 7 B2
De La Sole 8 B3
Given 9 B3
Global Exchange Fair Trade Craft Center 10 C5
Human Rights Campaign Action Center & Store (see 38)
Isso 11 D5
Kenneth Wingard 12 B2
Mabel Chong 13 D5
Omnivore 14 D6
Photoworks 15 C1
Sui Generis 16 B2
Under One Roof 17 B3
EATING (pp163-90)
Anchor Oyster Bar 18 B3
Casa Mexicana 19 C1
Catch 20 B2
Home 21 C1
Hot Cookie 22 B2
La Méditerranée 23 B2
Lovejoy's Tea Room 24 D5
Noe Valley Bakery 25 B5
Sparky's Diner 26 C1
Sushi Time 27 C2
DRINKING (pp191-204)
Amber 28 C1
Samovar Tea Lounge 29 C2
NIGHTLIFE (pp205-15)
Café du Nord/Swedish American Hall 30 C1
THE ARTS (pp217-26)
Castro Theatre 31 B2
GAY & LESBIAN (pp239-48)
24 Henry 32 C1
440 Castro 33 B2
A Different Light Bookstore 34 B2
Badlands 35 B3
Café Flore 36 B2
Femina Potens 37 C1
Gold's Gym (see 12)
Human Rights Campaign Action Center & Store 38 B3
Inn on Castro 39 B2
Jumpin' Java 40 B1
Lookout 41 B2
Midnight Sun 42 B3
Mix 43 B3
Moby Dick 44 B3
Parker Guest House 45 C2
Pilsner Inn 46 C1
Qbar 47 B2
Twin Peaks Tavern 48 B2
Village House 49 B2
Willows 50 C1
Worn Out West 51 B3
SLEEPING (pp249-62)
Beck's Motor Lodge 52 C1
Corona Heights Park
Cole Valley
To Belvedere House (700m)
Castro St MUNI Station
Church St MUNI Station
The Castro
The Mission
Mission Dolores Park
Noe Valley
Cemetery
See The Mission & Potrero Hill Map pp116-17
Market St
Castro St
Noe St
Church St
Sanchez St
Dolores St
14th St
15th St
16th St
17th St
18th St
19th St
20th St
21st St
22nd St
23rd St
24th St
25th St
26th St
27th St
28th St
Cesar Chavez (Army) St
Valley St

TRANSPORTATION: THE CASTRO & NOE VALLEY

Bus The 24 passes through the Castro on its way from Pacific Heights and the Haight to Noe Valley. The 33 links the Castro to the Mission, the Haight, Golden Gate Park and the Richmond.

Streetcar The K, L and M lines run under Market St, with stops at Castro St. The F streetcar does the same on the surface of Market St. The J line runs from Downtown and stops on the edge of the Castro at Church and Market Sts.

CASTRO THEATRE Map p123

☎ 415-621-6120; www.thecastrotheatre.com; 429 Castro St; 🚌 24, 33, Castro St

The city's grandest cinema opened in 1922. The Spanish-Moorish-ish exterior yields to a mishmash of styles inside, from Italianate to Oriental. Ask nicely and staff will let you peak inside without buying a ticket. For the best images of the blinking blue-and-pink lights, shoot from across the street. For programming information, see p220.

HARVEY MILK PLAZA Map p123

Market & Castro Sts; 🚌 24, 33, F, Castro St

The first thing you'll notice as you emerge from the Castro St Muni station is a huge, irrepressibly cheerful rainbow flag. Gay kids too young for the bars sit on the wall beneath; look closer and you'll notice a plaque honoring the man whose lasting legacy to the Castro is civic pride and political clout. The ugly plaza may soon be redesigned to give Harvey more of a starring role.

CORONA HEIGHTS PARK Map p123

bounded by 16th St & Roosevelt Way; 🚌 24, 37, F, Castro St

Urban hikers scramble up the rocky, 520ft summit of Corona Heights (aka Museum Hill or Red Rocks) for jaw-dropping eastward 180-degree views. We love it on warm, fogless nights, when the city unfurls below in a carpet of light. Take tiny Beaver St uphill to the steps through the bushes, then cut right of the tennis courts and up the trail. For an easier hike, enter via the Roosevelt Way side.

Near the summit is the family-ready **Randall Junior Museum** (☎ 415-554-9600; www.randallmuseum.org; admission free; ⏰ 10am-5pm Tue-Sat; 👶), with live-animal exhibits and hands-on workshops (check the web); downstairs is the **Golden Gate Model Railroad Club** (☎ 415-346-3303; www.ggmrc.org; ⏰ 10am-4pm Sat; 👶), an elaborate collection of vintage Lionel trains.

NOBBY CLARKE MANSION

250 Douglass St, at Caselli Ave; 🚌 24, 33, F, Castro St

Built in 1892 by a wealthy attorney who recognized the weather was sunnier in this part of town than atop fashionable Nob Hill, this gorgeous turreted mansion went uninhabited after its construction: Snob Hill socialites dubbed the house 'Nobby Clarke's Folly,' and his wife refused to move in. It served briefly as a hospital; now it's an apartment building. Spot the disco ball in the top-turret window and you'll definitely know that you're not on Nob Hill.

SF'S COOLEST EPHEMERAL SIGHT

If you're in the Castro or Noe Valley on a summer afternoon when the fog starts rolling over Twin Peaks, look up at Sutro Tower, that enormous Erector Set–like radio tower atop the peaks. As the clouds ascend its base and reach the cross-pieces near the top, the tower magically transforms into a two-masted schooner sailing across a sea of fog. And then it vanishes as fast as it appeared, like a Wagnerian ghost ship. Gorgeous.

THE HAIGHT

Drinking p202; Eating p185; Shopping p156; Sleeping p261

Was it the fall of 1966 or the winter of '67? As the San Francisco saying goes, if you can remember the Summer of Love, man, you probably weren't here. The fog was laced with Nag Champa incense and burning draft cards, entire days were spent contemplating Day-Glo posters advertising psychedelic rock at the Fillmore (p212), and on the Haight end of Golden Gate Park, Hippie Hill reverberated with the vibrations of naked Beat poets blowing conch shells and some Grateful Dead song that remained the same for decades.

Flashbacks are a given in the Haight, which still has its swinging '60s tendencies. Only a very mysterious, very local illness could explain the number of neighborhood medical marijuana clubs, and tie-dyes and ideals have never entirely gone out of fashion here, hence the Bound Together Anarchist Book Collective (p156), the cooperative indie Red Vic Movie House (p221), and the Haight Ashbury Food Program (p128) serving anyone in need with hot meals and job training. Some '60s memories are better left behind: habits were kicked in the neighborhood's many rehabs, and many an intimate itch has been mercifully treated gratis at the Haight Ashbury Free Clinic (p311). To relive the highlights of the era, a short walk (p130) will take you past the former flophouses of the Haight's most famous and infamous residents, and locations of some of the decade's most defining moments.

Since the '60s, the hedonist Haight has cultivated a surprisingly serious rep for leftist politics (the Green Party candidate for supervisor is usually the incumbent), and the Upper Haight specializes in skateboarding, potent coffee, radical literature and retail therapy for rebels. The neighborhood's upwardly mobile strivers seem to be mostly sequestered in Cole Valley, where you'll find upscale restaurants and brunch joints, baby-carriage traffic jams, sidewalks that are actually cleaned up after dogs, and residents who can get testy before downing their first double nonfat latte and brioche in the morning. The Lower Haight has better bars, more economic and ethnic diversity, and a pot-club kind of mellow occasionally disrupted by recent gang activity northeast of Fillmore and Haight Sts.

Whether you're a hippie born too late, punk born too early, or a weirdo who passes as normal, the Haight is here to claim you as its own. But like any leftist entity, the Haight has its splinter factions. Alamo Sq is the Lower Haight/Fillmore hilltop park bordered by Hayes, Scott, Fulton and Steiner Sts, and fringed with Victorians seemingly made for postcards. The Upper Haight blends into Western Addition from Divisadero St to Stanyan St north of Fell St – but hipster eateries and nightspots are attempting to rebrand the corridor around Divisadero St south of Geary Blvd as 'NoPa,' before Divisadero ascends uphill and upscale north of Geary into Pacific Heights.

The Haight runs from Haight and Octavia Sts up to Golden Gate Park at Stanyan St. West of Divisadero St, the Upper Haight features head shops, cafes, vintage clothes and used CDs. Across Divisadero, the Lower Haight is big on hairdressers, bars, skater gear and, um, gardening supply shops, south of Alamo Sq. Cole Valley is south of the Upper Haight along Cole St, up towards 17th St. The Panhandle, a narrow strip of park between Fell and Oak Sts, forms a handle to Golden Gate Park's long pan and forms the northern border to the Haight.

top picks

THE HAIGHT

- **Alamo Square** (p130)
- **Red Vic Movie House** (p221)
- **Haight Ashbury Food Program** (p128)
- **Buena Vista Park** (p128)
- **Magnolia Brewpub** (p185)

UPPER HAIGHT

Weekends are quite a scene in the Upper Haight, what with oldsters reliving their glory days trailed by teenage relatives pretending not to know them, suburban punks who smell far too strongly of daddy's aftershave to panhandle convincingly, and Harajuku hipsters dragging suitcases full of prime vintage attire for resale in Tokyo. But also in the mix are a few locals, cafe regulars who greet one another by name, and street musicians who play a mean banjo. Brave the crowds for used CDs and free concerts at Amoeba Music (p158), radical comics at Bound To-

THE HAIGHT

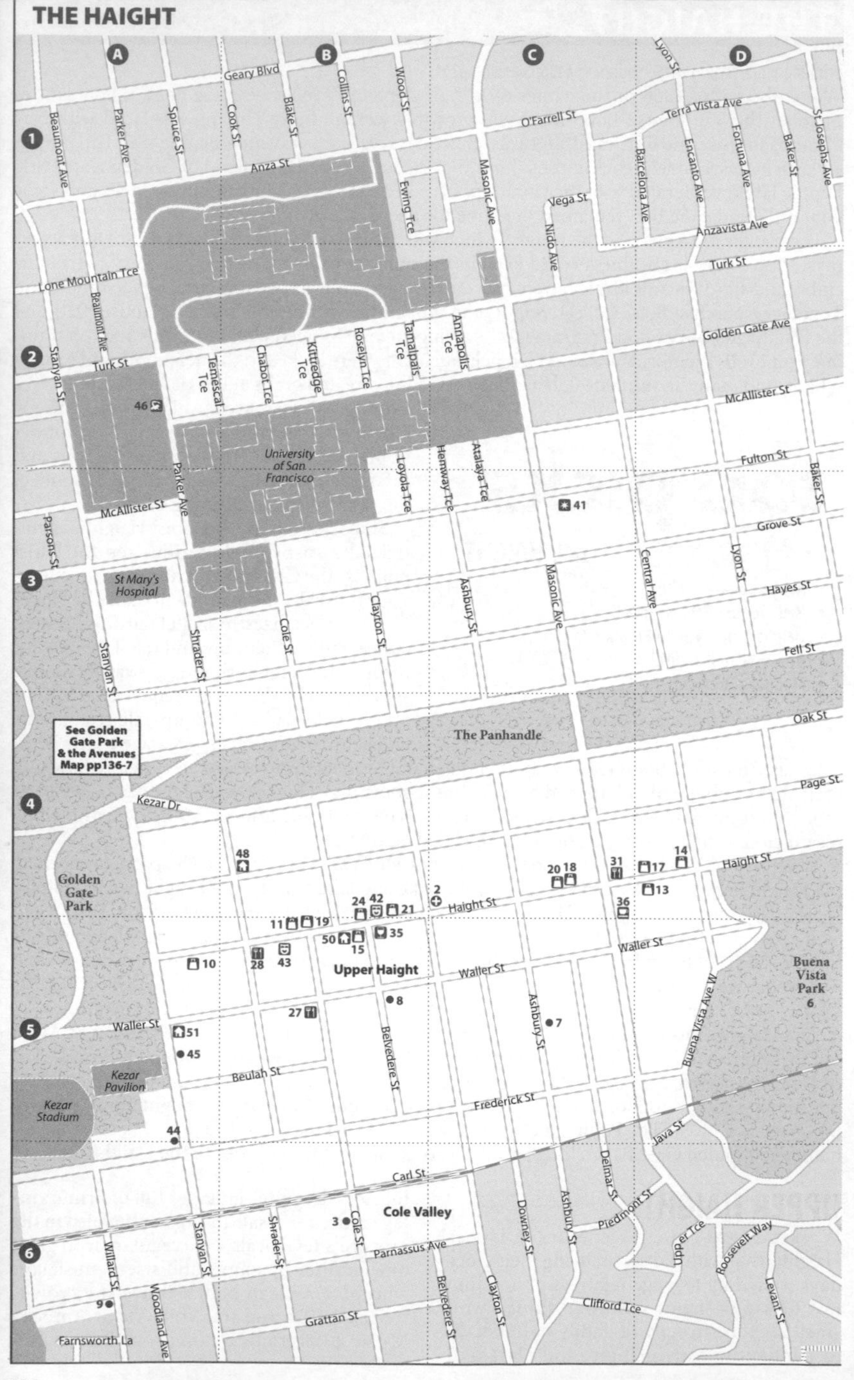

A
B
C
D
1
2
3
4
5
6
Geary Blvd
O'Farrell St
Terra Vista Ave
Lyon St
Beaumont Ave
Parker Ave
Spruce St
Cook St
Blake St
Collins St
Wood St
Masonic Ave
Barcelona Ave
Encanto Ave
Fortuna Ave
Baker St
St Josephs Ave
Anza St
Ewing Tce
Vega St
Nido Ave
Anzavista Ave
Turk St
Lone Mountain Tce
Golden Gate Ave
Stanyan St
Turk St
Temescal Tce
Chabot Tce
Kittredge Tce
Roselyn Tce
Tamalpais Tce
Annapolis Tce
McAllister St
University of San Francisco
Loyola Tce
Hemway Tce
Atalaya Tce
Fulton St
McAllister St
Parsons St
Grove St
St Mary's Hospital
Central Ave
Hayes St
Shrader St
Cole St
Clayton St
Ashbury St
Fell St
See Golden Gate Park & the Avenues Map pp136-7
The Panhandle
Oak St
Page St
Kezar Dr
Golden Gate Park
Haight St
Upper Haight
Waller St
Buena Vista Park
Buena Vista Ave W
Belvedere St
Beulah St
Kezar Pavilion
Kezar Stadium
Frederick St
Java St
Carl St
Cole Valley
Delmar St
Downey St
Piedmont St
Parnassus Ave
Upper Tce
Roosevelt Way
Levant St
Willard St
Woodland Ave
Clifford Tce
Grattan St
Farnsworth La

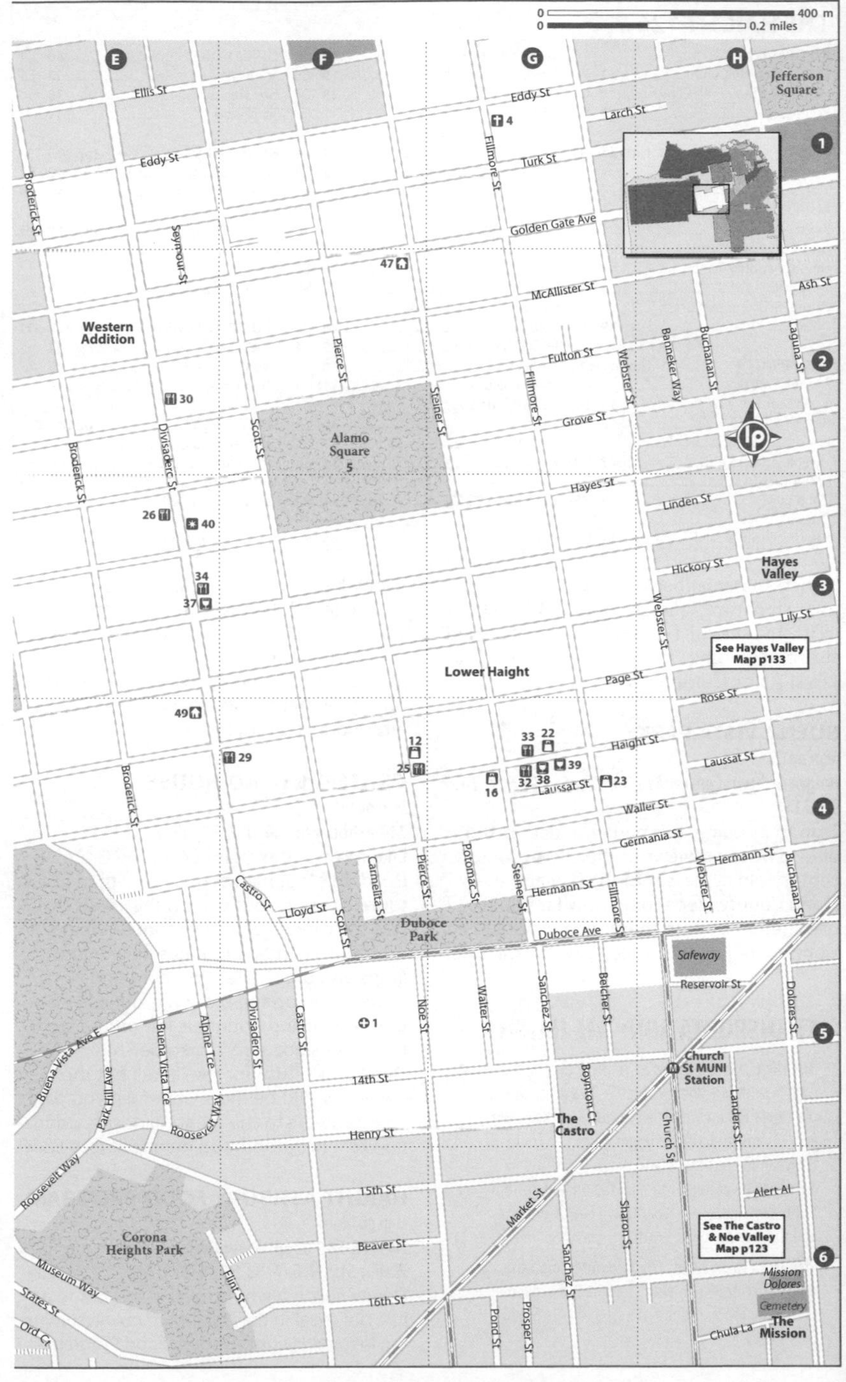

0 400 m
0 0.2 miles
E
F
G
H
Jefferson Square
Ellis St
Eddy St
Larch St
Turk St
Golden Gate Ave
McAllister St
Ash St
Fillmore St
Broderick St
Seymour St
Western Addition
Pierce St
Fulton St
Webster St
Banneker Way
Buchanan St
Laguna St
Steiner St
Grove St
Scott St
Alamo Square
5
Divisadero St
Hayes St
Linden St
Hickory St
Hayes Valley
Lily St
See Hayes Valley Map p133
Lower Haight
Page St
Rose St
Haight St
Laussat St
Waller St
Germania St
Hermann St
Castro St
Lloyd St
Carmelita St
Potomac St
Duboce Park
Duboce Ave
Safeway
Reservoir St
Walter St
Sanchez St
Belcher St
Dolores St
Noe St
Alpine Tce
Buena Vista Tce
Buena Vista Ave E
Park Hill Ave
14th St
Boynton Ct
Church St MUNI Station
Landers St
Roosevelt Way
Henry St
The Castro
Church St
15th St
Alert Al
Market St
Sharon St
Corona Heights Park
Beaver St
See The Castro & Noe Valley Map p123
Museum Way
Flint St
States St
16th St
Pond St
Prosper St
Mission Dolores
Cemetery
The Mission
Ord Ct
Chula La

THE HAIGHT 126-7

INFORMATION

Davies Medical Center ... **1** F5
Haight Ashbury Free Clinic ... **2** C4
Pharmaca ... **3** B6

SIGHTS (pp125-31)

African Orthodox Church of St John Coltrane ... **4** G1
Alamo Square ... **5** F2
Buena Vista Park ... **6** D5
Grateful Dead House ... **7** C5
Haight Ashbury Food Program ... **8** B5
Hunter S Thompson Crash Pad ... **9** A6

SHOPPING (pp141-61)

Amoeba Music ... **10** A5
Aqua Surf Shop ... **11** B5
Bluebird ... **12** F4
Bound Together Anarchist Book Collective ... **13** D4
Braindrops ... **14** D4
Coco-Luxe ... **15** B5
Doe ... **16** G4
Express Photo & Mail ... **17** D4
Goorin Brothers Hats ... **18** C4
Loyal Army Clothing ... **19** B5
Piedmont Boutique ... **20** C4
SFO Snowboarding & FTC Skateboarding ... **21** B4
Trunk ... **22** G4
Upper Playground ... **23** G4
Wasteland ... **24** B4

EATING (pp163-90)

Axum Cafe ... **25** F4
Bar Crudo ... **26** E3
Cole Valley Cafe ... **27** B5
Escape from New York Pizza ... **28** B5
Little Chihuahua ... **29** F4
Little Star Pizza ... **30** E2
Magnolia Brewpub ... **31** C4
Rosamunde Sausage Grill ... **32** G4
Uva Enoteca ... **33** G4
Ziryab ... **34** E3

DRINKING (pp191-204)

Alembic ... (see 30)
Aub Zam Zam ... **35** B5
Coffee to the People ... **36** C4
Madrone ... **37** E3
Noc Noc ... **38** G4
Toronado ... **39** G4

NIGHTLIFE (pp205-15)

Independent ... **40** E3
Poleng Lounge ... **41** C3

THE ARTS (pp217-26)

Booksmith ... **42** B4
Red Vic Movie House ... **43** B5

SPORTS & ACTIVITIES (pp227-37)

American Cyclery ... **44** A5
Avenue Cyclery ... **45** A5
Koret Pool ... **46** A2

SLEEPING (pp249-62)

Chateau Tivoli ... **47** F2
Inn 1890 ... **48** B4
Metro Hotel ... **49** E4
Red Victorian Bed, Breakfast & Art ... **50** B5
Stanyan Park Hotel ... **51** A5

gether Anarchist Book Collective (p156), your own signature vintage look at Wasteland (p158), and surreal T-shirts featuring stir-fried shrimp shouting 'Party like a wok star!' at Loyal Army Clothing (p157).

BUENA VISTA PARK

Map pp126–7

Haight St btwn Central Ave & Baker St; 🚌 6, 7, 24, 33, 71

True to its name, this park founded in 1867 offers sweeping views of the city beyond century-old cypresses to the bay and even Marin County, depending how far you're prepared to hike up the steep hill. When SF went up in flames in 1906, this was the safe spot where San Franciscans found refuge, and watched the town smolder; on your way downhill, take Buena Vista Ave West to spot Victorian mansions that date from that era. Technically the park closes at sunset, but the romantic views sometimes inspire after-hours cruising.

TRANSPORTATION: THE HAIGHT

Bus The 6, 7 and 71 lines all connect the Haight with Downtown along Market St. Bus 43 connects the Upper Haight with the Presidio and the Marina, and 33 runs through the Upper Haight en route between the Richmond and the Mission. The 22 links the Lower Haight to the Mission and Potrero Hill to the south, and Japantown, Pacific Heights and the Marina to the north.

Streetcar The N heads from Downtown all the way to Ocean Beach, with stops at Duboce Park in the Lower Haight and at Carl and Cole Sts in Cole Valley.

GRATEFUL DEAD HOUSE

Map pp126–7

710 Ashbury St; 🚌 6, 7, 33, 37, 71

Like most of the members of the Grateful Dead, this Victorian sports more than just a touch of gray – but back in the 1960s this was the candy-colored flophouse where Jerry Garcia and bandmates blew minds, amps and brain cells. The mom-and-pop flower shop up the block has done brisk business selling bouquets left on the steps here ever since Jerry's membership in the Dead took a turn for the literal, but the new owners would be most Grateful if you paid your respects to the great man with a donation to a neighborhood nonprofit (see below).

HAIGHT ASHBURY FOOD PROGRAM

Map pp126–7

☎ 415-566-0366; www.thefoodprogram.org; 1525 Waller St; 🚌 6, 7, 33, 37, 43, 71, N

Flower children who arrived in the '60s to a free hot meal in the Haight are now returning the favor at Haight Ashbury Food Program.

MAKING QUEEN VICTORIA BLUSH

The city's signature architectural style is usually called 'Victorian,' but demure Queen Victoria would surely blush to see the eccentric architecture perpetrated in her name in San Francisco. True Victorians tend to be drab, stately, earth-toned structures – nothing like San Franciscan 'Painted Ladies' with candy-jar color palates, lavish gingerbread woodworking dripping off steeply peaked roofs, and gilded stucco garlands swagging huge, look-at-me bay windows. Only a fraction of the older buildings you'll see in SF were built during Victoria's 1837–1901 reign, and the rest are cheerfully inauthentic San Franciscan takes on a vaguely Anglo-Continental style.

Of the 19th-century buildings that survived the 1906 fire and earthquake, many belong to other architectural categories.

- Italianate (1860s–1880s): around Jackson Sq, you can still see original Italianate brick buildings with elevated false facades capped with jutting cornices, a straight roofline and graceful arches over tall windows.
- Stick (1880s): in the Lower Haight and Pacific Heights, you'll notice some squared-off Victorians built to fit side-by-side in narrow lots, usually with flat fronts and long, narrow windows.
- Queen Anne (1880s–1910): Alamo Sq has several exuberant examples built in wood with fish-scale shingle decoration, rounded corner towers and decorative bands to lift the eye skyward.
- Edwardian (1901–1914): most of the 'Victorians' you'll see in San Francisco are actually from the post-fire Edwardian era, and Art Nouveau, Asian-inspired, and Arts and Crafts details are the giveaway. You'll notice the stained-glass windows and false gables in homes in the inner Richmond and Castro.

Hippie idealism meets 21st-century street smarts here, where everyone gets a healthy meal and a second chance through retraining. If you volunteer to serve a meal or contribute to job training programs, you'll help them prove the Summer of Love isn't over yet.

LOWER HAIGHT

Skateboards are the preferred method of transportation on the downhill slide from the Upper to Lower Haight, though it's not for the faint of heart – but then the same could be said for the Lower Haight in general. The high density of bars and medicinal marijuana clubs tends to define the neighborhood scene, though there are some quality cheap eats in the area and some amazing Victorians on Laussat Alley, including a Rasta house painted red, gold and green. When value, a central location and down-to-earth attitude counts, head to the Lower Haight for food, drink and homeboy hoodies at Upper Playground (p157).

COLE VALLEY

A motley collection of young professionals and their families reside in this area, united by a common tax bracket, a shared passion for espresso drinks and not much else. Hard to believe this staid, upwardly mobile neighborhood was the mid-'60s haunt of Hunter S Thompson and the Hells Angels who crashed his parties. These days most of the excitement in Cole Valley comes from the opening of a new eatery and the occasional baby-stroller traffic jam.

HUNTER S THOMPSON CRASH PAD

Map pp126–7

318 Parnassus Ave; 🚌 6, 37, 43, 71, N

How this building survived Hunter S Thompson's tenancy here in the mid-'60s is anyone's guess. On the otherwise unremarkable bay-windowed facade, you might notice the odd bullet hole – mementos of parties that invariably degenerated into Hell's Angels orgies and shoot-outs. Gonzo journalism was born when the inimitable Thompson narrowly survived to tell the tale in his book *Hell's Angels: The Strange and Terrible Saga of the Outlaw Motorcycle Gang,* and state his motto: 'When the going gets weird, the weird turn pro.'

NOPA & DIVISADERO

Between the Upper and Lower Haight is a buffer zone along Divisadero St. This neighborhood is caught between Cole Valley financial aspirations and a Lower Haight respect for street cred. NoPa restaurants and bars seem conflicted: wanting to attract both a cool, young crowd as well as customers who can afford to leave a decent tip. The main reasons to come here are an odd streak of shops along Divisadero between Fell and Haight Sts, plus some tasty (if not exactly cheap) eats from Ziryab (p185), Bar Crudo (p185) and Little Star Pizza (p185).

WESTERN ADDITION & ALAMO SQUARE

Aim your camera at Alamo Square Park and the picturesque Victorians lining streets nearby, and your camera trigger-finger is bound to get overworked by all the quaint photo ops. For the obligatory touch of San Francisco eccentricity, walk to the crest of the hill by the public bathrooms to see flowers planted in stray shoes. Western Addition doesn't have much more to recommend it to visitors, beyond more Victorians and offbeat cafes.

ALAMO SQUARE Map pp126–7

Hayes & Scott Sts; 21, 22, 24

The finest restaurants in town can't provide views as spectacular as the picnic tables atop Alamo Square Park facing Steiner St's Postcard Row, a row of pastel Victorian 'Painted Lady' houses with gingerbread detailing and frosting flourishes that may leave you craving dessert. The city skyline looms in the background, and from the corner of Steiner and Fulton Sts you can glimpse City Hall. On the crest of the hill, check out the old shoes creatively reused as planters. On foggy days, you may want to wear a parka – as you can guess from the wind-sculpted pines, it can get a tad blustery up here.

HAIGHT FLASHBACK

Walking Tour

1 Buena Vista Park (p128) Start your trip back in time with panoramic city views that inspired Victorians to make scandalously bold romantic moves c 1867, and moved surviving San Franciscans to tears after the fire of 1906.

2 Richard Spreckels Mansion The most impressive spot on Buena Vista Ave West, number 731 has a reputation for celebrity that goes back a century. Jack London lived here while writing *White Fang;* San Francisco's resident cynic Ambrose Bierce spent his last years here (see p29); Graham Nash took up residence here in the '70s; most recently, the place was bought by actor Danny Glover.

3 Magnolia Brewpub (p185) Heading west on Haight St, you can't miss this corner microbrewery and organic eatery named after a Grateful Dead song, which hippies may dimly recognize as the site of the infamous Drogstore Café. Pull up a seat at the communal table for a bite and/or a sampler of beer – with any luck, Arrogant Bastard will be on tap.

4 Bound Together Anarchist Book Collective (p156) Across Haight St, you may recognize Emma Goldman and Sacco and Vanzetti in the *Anarchists of Americas* mural – if you don't, staff can provide you with some scholarly treatises or biographical comics by way of introduction.

5 1235 Masonic Ave At this address, you might once have glimpsed the Simbionese Liberation Army. This was once a safehouse where the SLA is believed to have held Patty

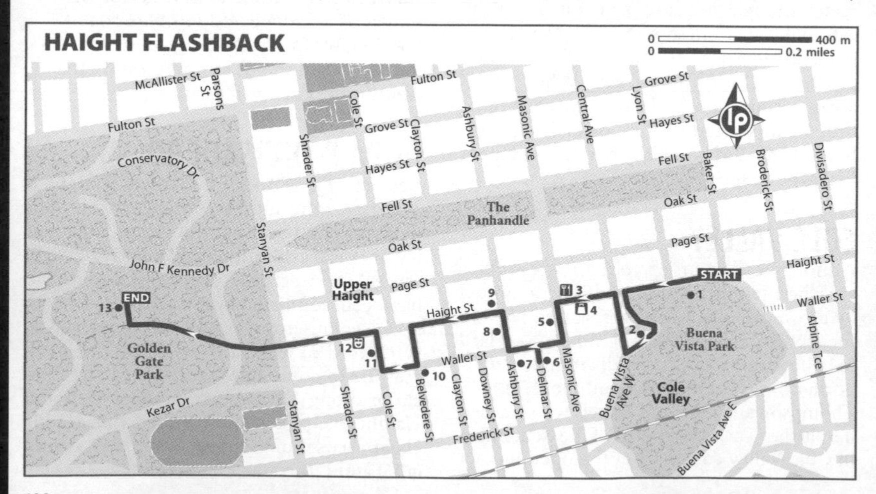

WALK FACTS

Start Buena Vista Park
End Golden Pate Park
Distance 1.3 miles
Time 1½ hours
Exertion Moderate
Fuel stop Magnolia Brewpub

Hearst, the kidnapped heiress turned revolutionary bank robber.

6 32 Delmar St Turning right off Masonic Ave onto Waller St, you'll notice a narrow lane leading uphill. Number 32 was the site of the 1978 Sid Vicious overdose that finally broke up the Sex Pistols. Under new ownership, this building betrays no trace of its rock 'n' roll past – as Johnny Rotten said at the band's last-ever gig in San Francisco, 'Ever get the feeling you've been cheated?'

7 Grateful Dead House (p128) Pay your respects to the former flophouse of Jerry Garcia, Bob Weir and Pigpen, plus sundry Deadheads at 710 Ashbury St. In October 1967, antidrug cops raided the house and arrested everyone in it (Garcia wasn't home).

8 635 Ashbury St Down the block from the Dead, this is one of many known San Francisco addresses for Janis Joplin, who had a hard time hanging onto leases in the 1960s – but, as she sang, 'Freedom's just another word for nothin' left to lose.'

9 4:20 Clock At the corner of Haight and Ashbury, you'll notice that the clock overhead always reads 4:20, better known in 'Hashbury' as International Bong Hit Time.

10 Haight Ashbury Food Program (p128) Back on Waller St, swing by the nonprofit that serves up hot meals and fresh starts to anyone in need. With helping hand or modest donation, visitors can help the Food Program keep the spirit of the Summer of Love alive.

11 635 Cole St Another innocuous-looking building with a dark past, this apartment building once housed Charles Manson, the cult leader behind the 'Helter Skelter' murder of Sharon Tate – but on the corner, a rainbow mural serves to lighten the mood.

12 Red Vic Movie House (p221) Check out the schedule of this worker-owned collective movie house, which regularly screens cult classics, surf documentaries and premieres by local filmmakers.

13 Hippie Hill in Golden Gate Park Follow the erratic beat of the drum circle to 'Hippie Hill,' where free spirits have gathered since the '60s to tune in, turn on, and attempt to hit a workable groove.

HAYES VALLEY

Drinking p203; Eating p186; Shopping p158; Sleeping p261

Beyond the concrete solemnity of Civic Center lies funky Hayes Valley, where old Victorian storefronts are anachronistic showcases for cutting-edge local designers and upstart chefs. This is the neighborhood that's been waiting to happen for decades. For years the pace of urban renewal here was as slow as local traffic, stuck under the remnants of a freeway ramp that fell in the 1989 earthquake. But now that Octavia Blvd has provided a pleasant thoroughfare through the neighborhood, under-the-radar local boutiques with killer sales racks and worthy upstart restaurants like Bar Jules (p186) and next-door Suppenküche (p187) are getting some dedicated foot traffic, and landmark California bistro Jardinièr (p172) stays busy before, during and after symphony performances. Whether so many hopeful young entrepreneurs can keep pace with rents is anyone's guess, and sporadic gang-related violence at the projects up the hill between Webster and Fillmore Sts is another looming concern. But the neighborhood seems determined to take a cue from the saffron-robed residents at the Zen Center (below) and transcend its current circumstances.

top picks

HAYES VALLEY

- Zen Center (left)
- Cav Wine Bar (p203)
- Polanco (p158)
- Gimme Shoes (p160)

Small yet high-maintenance Hayes Valley is securely tucked between the Lower Haight and Civic Center like a prized Chihuahua. It has just two distinguishing landmarks, the Zen Center and Octavia Blvd. But in general, you'll know you've been in Hayes Valley when you find yourself holding a receipt that's much more than you expected for something you never knew you needed, like sculpted-heel Chie Mihara boots at Gimme Shoes (p160), French passionfruit macaroons from Paulette Macarons (p187), or hair pomade that smells good enough to eat from Nancy Boy (p158). The boundaries are roughly Franklin St to the east, Laguna St to the west and Market St on the south, and you could easily trawl all five square blocks of it before a performance at the symphony (p223) or a visit to the nearby Asian Art Museum (p76).

ZEN CENTER Map p133

☎ 415-863-3136; www.sfzc.org; 300 Page St; 9:30am-12:30pm & 1:30-5pm Mon-Fri, 8:30am-noon Sat; 6, 7, 21, 22, 71

No, this isn't a spa, but rather an active spiritual retreat since 1969 for the largest Buddhist community outside Asia. The graceful landmark building was designed by Julia Morgan, California's first licensed female architect, who earned her reputation as a savvy cross-cultural architect with the Spanish-Greek Hearst Castle and the Chinatown YWCA (now the Chinese Historical Society of America Museum; see p83). Here Morgan has created a seamless Italianate-Japanese style without resorting to kitsch, providing plenty of interior light for illumination. The center is open to the public for visits, meditation (see website for meditation schedule) and workshops, and also offers overnight stays by prior arrangement for intensive meditation retreats.

TRANSPORTATION: HAYES VALLEY

BART Civic Center BART is four blocks east of Hayes Valley.

Bus The number 21 heads from Downtown along Hayes St to Golden Gate Park, and the 49 runs up Van Ness Ave along the eastern edge of Hayes Valley. Market St buses 6, 7 and 71 stop along the south end of Hayes Valley, while bus 5 passes along the north side.

Streetcar The N and J lines stop at Van Ness station on Market St.

Parking Street parking is usually available, and there's a public lot underneath the City Hall plaza.

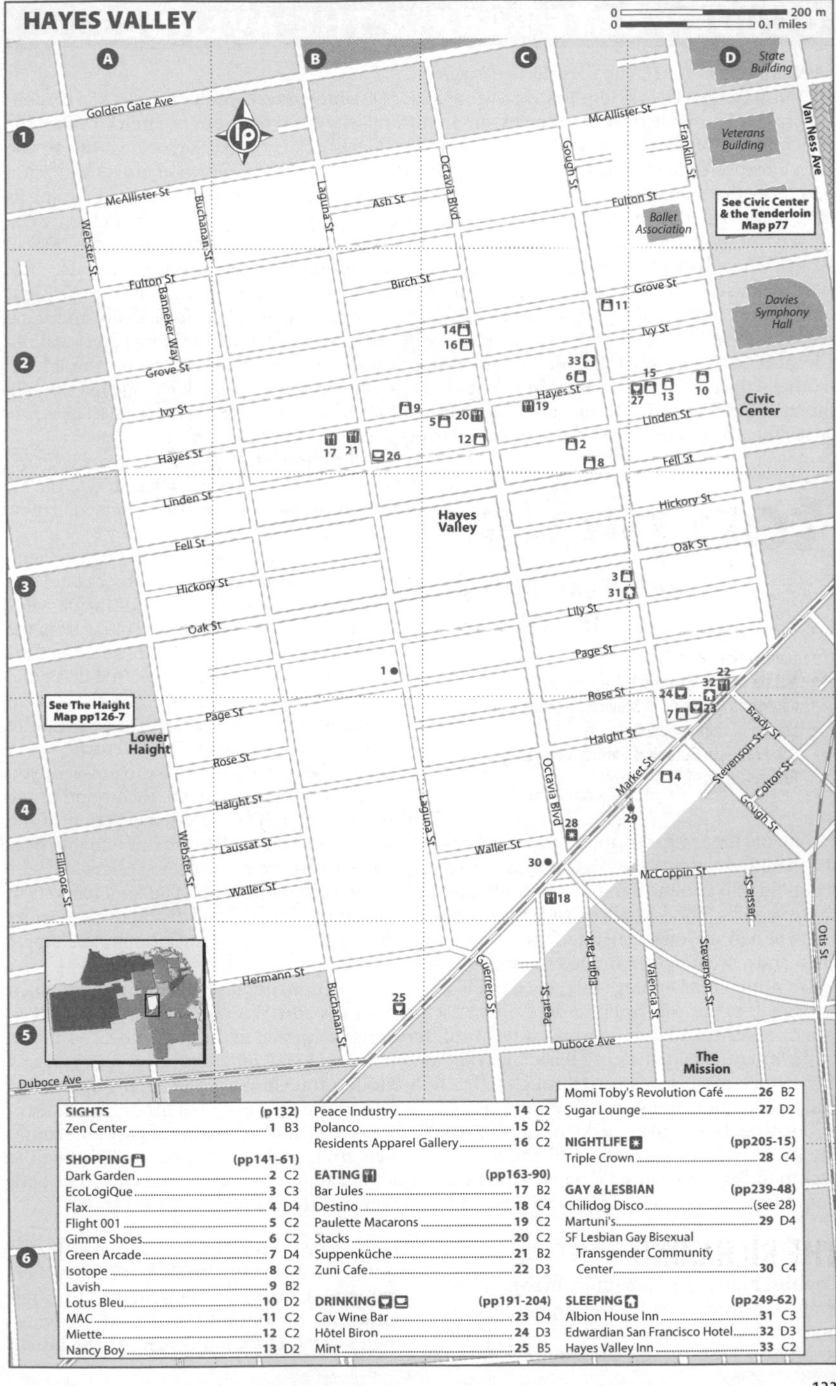
HAYES VALLEY
0 200 m
0 0.1 miles
State Building
Veterans Building
Ballet Association
Davies Symphony Hall
Civic Center
Hayes Valley
Lower Haight
The Mission
See Civic Center & the Tenderloin Map p77
See The Haight Map pp126-7
Golden Gate Ave
McAllister St
Fulton St
Grove St
Ivy St
Hayes St
Linden St
Fell St
Hickory St
Oak St
Lily St
Page St
Rose St
Haight St
Laussat St
Waller St
Hermann St
Duboce Ave
McCoppin St
Ash St
Birch St
Webster St
Buchanan St
Banneker Way
Laguna St
Octavia Blvd
Gough St
Franklin St
Van Ness Ave
Fillmore St
Market St
Brady St
Stevenson St
Colton St
Jessie St
Otis St
Guerrero St
Pearl St
Elgin Park
Valencia St
SIGHTS (p132)
Zen Center 1 B3
SHOPPING (pp141-61)
Dark Garden 2 C2
EcoLogiQue 3 C3
Flax 4 D4
Flight 001 5 C2
Gimme Shoes 6 C2
Green Arcade 7 D4
Isotope 8 C2
Lavish 9 B2
Lotus Bleu 10 D2
MAC 11 C2
Miette 12 C2
Nancy Boy 13 D2
Peace Industry 14 C2
Polanco 15 D2
Residents Apparel Gallery 16 C2
EATING (pp163-90)
Bar Jules 17 B2
Destino 18 C4
Paulette Macarons 19 C2
Stacks 20 C2
Suppenküche 21 B2
Zuni Cafe 22 D3
DRINKING (pp191-204)
Cav Wine Bar 23 D4
Hôtel Biron 24 D3
Mint 25 B5
Momi Toby's Revolution Café 26 B2
Sugar Lounge 27 D2
NIGHTLIFE (pp205-15)
Triple Crown 28 C4
GAY & LESBIAN (pp239-48)
Chilidog Disco (see 28)
Martuni's 29 D4
SF Lesbian Gay Bisexual Transgender Community Center 30 C4
SLEEPING (pp249-62)
Albion House Inn 31 C3
Edwardian San Francisco Hotel 32 D3
Hayes Valley Inn 33 C2

GOLDEN GATE PARK & THE AVENUES

Drinking p203; Eating p187; Shopping p160; Sleeping p262

All those Golden Gate Bridge postcards and talk of Downtown restaurants are part of a diabolical ploy by San Franciscans to direct your attention away from the western stretch of the city, which they'd prefer to keep to themselves. Golden Gate Park is the city's glorious wild streak, with unexpected landscape features like pagan altars, bonsai forests, redwood groves and bison paddocks that make New York's Central Park look entirely too staid and orderly. Free spirits have congregated here for decades over roller disco, mass protests, drumming circles, tai chi, lawn bowling and free concerts, including opera, bluegrass and rock. At the Sunset end is Ocean Beach, where surfers brave walls of water and ritual bonfires blaze in purpose-built pits.

If the park had decent espresso and burritos, locals might never leave. But in plain sight on opposite sides of the park are some of the city's most reasonably priced, drool-inducing restaurants in the Richmond and Sunset. Anyone downwind of neighborhood eateries along Clement St, Geary Blvd, Balboa St and Irving St doesn't need to be told to try these local haunts – the tantalizing smell of fresh cooking is all the direction needed. No one likes to talk much about places like Namu (p188), San Tung (p190), Dragonfly (p188), Kabuto (p188) or Aziza (p188), for fear of creating competition for coveted seats and inflating prices.

But it's too late: the veil of secrecy is lifting over the fog belt. The park has drawn the attention of visitors with the spectacular new home for the California Academy of Sciences (p140), built by legendary architect Renzo Piano (of Paris' George Pompidou Center fame) and capped with a living roof of California wildflowers. Across the Music Concourse from the Academy of Sciences is another celebrated architectural landmark: the sleek MH de Young Memorial Museum (p139), cleverly clad in oxidizing copper by Pritzker Prize–winning Swiss architects Herzog & de Meuron.

top picks

GOLDEN GATE PARK & THE AVENUES

- **Golden Gate Park** (p139)
- **MH de Young Memorial Museum** (p139)
- **California Academy of Sciences** (p140)
- **Legion of Honor** (opposite)
- **San Francisco Botanical Garden & Strybing Arboretum** (p140)

Don't believe locals who try to persuade you there's nothing to see in the Richmond or the Sunset, either. The eclectic collection of the Legion of Honor (opposite), the bunny memorials at the Columbarium (p138), the surf hangout near the sand dunes at the N Judah terminus, the ruins of Sutro Baths (opposite) and the spectacular views from the walk around Land's End are all only-in-San-Francisco moments. The food markets in these neighborhoods could provide inspiration for a lifetime of meals, and distinctive souvenirs are to be had at Mollusk (p161) surf shop, Park Life (p160), Wishbone (p161), Kamei Restaurant Supply (p161) and a seemingly unlimited number of stores specializing in cheapo trinkets.

It's difficult to begrudge this area its well-deserved attention, because great pains were taken to bring it to life. Mayor Frank McCoppin's wild idea for a park was ahead of its time in 1866, when western sand dunes seemed utterly uninteresting compared to the gold and silver mines in the mountains to the east. Tenacious William Hammond Hall took on the project, and saw San Francisco's beloved park through to fruition. Modest tract homes soon sprang up nearby, and transplanted immigrant communities thrived alongside the park's botanical transplants.

Bordered by the green parkland of the Presidio to the north and a freeway tangle to the south, the long blocks of the Richmond and Sunset Districts stretch right to the ocean. Splitting the Richmond and the Sunset cleanly is the near perfect rectangle of Golden Gate Park. The park bumps up against the Haight in the east and runs west to Ocean Beach.

THE RICHMOND

Populist millionaire and future mayor of San Francisco Adolph Sutro was determined to make the city's western beaches accessible to all San Franciscans. He built a railway in the 1890s that for just a nickel transported hardworking locals away from their cramped Downtown tenements, through the future Richmond District, to the wide-open stretch of Ocean Beach. At the beach,

Sutro was struck with an idea for an elaborate swimming and entertainment complex that wouldn't be private like the exclusive gentlemen's clubs of 'Snob Hill,' but open to the public for a modest fee. The Sutro Baths and Cliff House would be built and rebuilt after fires and disuse, and today all that is left of Sutro's democratic notion of leisure is an overpriced restaurant and a splendid ruin. But the Richmond District retains Sutro's original populist sensibility, as a seaside neighborhood that is accessible to all, for the price of a public transit ticket.

COASTAL TRAIL Map pp136–7

sunrise-sunset; 28, N

Suit up and hit your stride on the 9-mile Coastal Trail, starting at Fort Funston and wrapping around the Presidio paralleling Lincoln Blvd to end at Fort Mason. The 4 miles of sandy Ocean Beach will definitely work those calves and numb your toes – yep, the water's about that cold year-round. Casual strollers will prefer to pick up the trail near Sutro Baths, head around Land's End for a peek at Golden Gate Bridge, and then duck into the **Legion of Honor** (below) at Lincoln Park.

LEGION OF HONOR Map pp136–7

415-750-3600; www.famsf.org/legion/index.asp; Lincoln Park; adult/child under 12yr/teen/senior $10/free/6/7, $2 discount with Muni transfer, 1st Tue of month free; 9:30am-5:15pm Tue-Sun; 1, 2, 18, 38;

Never doubt the unwavering resolve of a nude model. The Legion was a gift to San Francisco from Alma de Bretteville Spreckels, a sculptor's model who married well and decided to create a fitting artistic tribute to Californians killed in France in WWI. Today, the Legion still 'honors the dead while serving the living' with blockbuster exhibitions, mixing crowd-pleasing shows of Egyptian art and Fabergé eggs with Max Klinger's obscure, macabre 19th-century Waking Dream etchings.

The collection spans medieval to 20th-century European art, including many works by the Impressionists and the Achenbach Foundation for Graphic Arts, one of the premier collections of works on paper in the US. In honor of 'Big Alma's' early career, the museum also has a sizable collection of sculpture by Auguste Rodin and Henry Moore.

LINCOLN PARK Map pp136–7

415-221-9911; Clement St; admission free; sunrise-sunset; 1, 2, 18, 38

John McLaren took time out from his day job as Golden Gate Park's superintendent for 56 years to establish lovely Lincoln Park. A well-tended walking path covers a surprisingly rugged, bucolic stretch of coast from the Cliff House to the Legion of Honor, part of the 9-mile Coastal Trail. Terrific views of the Golden Gate are a highlight of the half-hour hike from Land's End to the Legion – and it's worth it, fog or no fog. Pick up the trailhead near the remains of the Sutro Baths.

SUTRO BATHS Map pp136–7

sunrise-sunset; 5, 18, 31, 38

All good things must come to an end, but the Sutro Baths make a particularly splendid ruin. In its heyday, Victorian dandies and working stiffs converged here for a bracing bath and workout in itchy wool rental swimsuits. Mining magnate and populist mayor Adolph Sutro built hot and cold indoor pools to accommodate 25,000 frolicking unwashed masses in 1896, but the masses apparently preferred dirt, and the place was finally closed in 1952. Follow the path through the sea-cave archway at low tide for an end-of-the-world view of Marin.

CLIFF HOUSE Map pp136–7

415-386-3330; www.cliffhouse.com; 1090 Point Lobos Ave; admission free; 18

Populist millionaire Adolph Sutro imagined this place as a working-man's paradise, and in 1863 it already provided a much-needed escape from the tenements and tawdriness of Downtown. But by 1869 Sutro's dream had expanded the Cliff House to an elegant eight-story resort with art galleries, dining rooms and an observation deck. It miraculously survived the 1906 earthquake, only to be destroyed by fire the following year. The 1909 replacement didn't match the original, and was mostly popular for its bar and restaurant.

The latest attempt to reclaim former glory was in 2004, when a $19 million facelift turned the Cliff House into an upscale (read: overpriced) restaurant with all the charm of a fast-food outlet. Sutro would not be pleased, though two of the area's popular attractions remain: views

GOLDEN GATE PARK & THE AVENUES

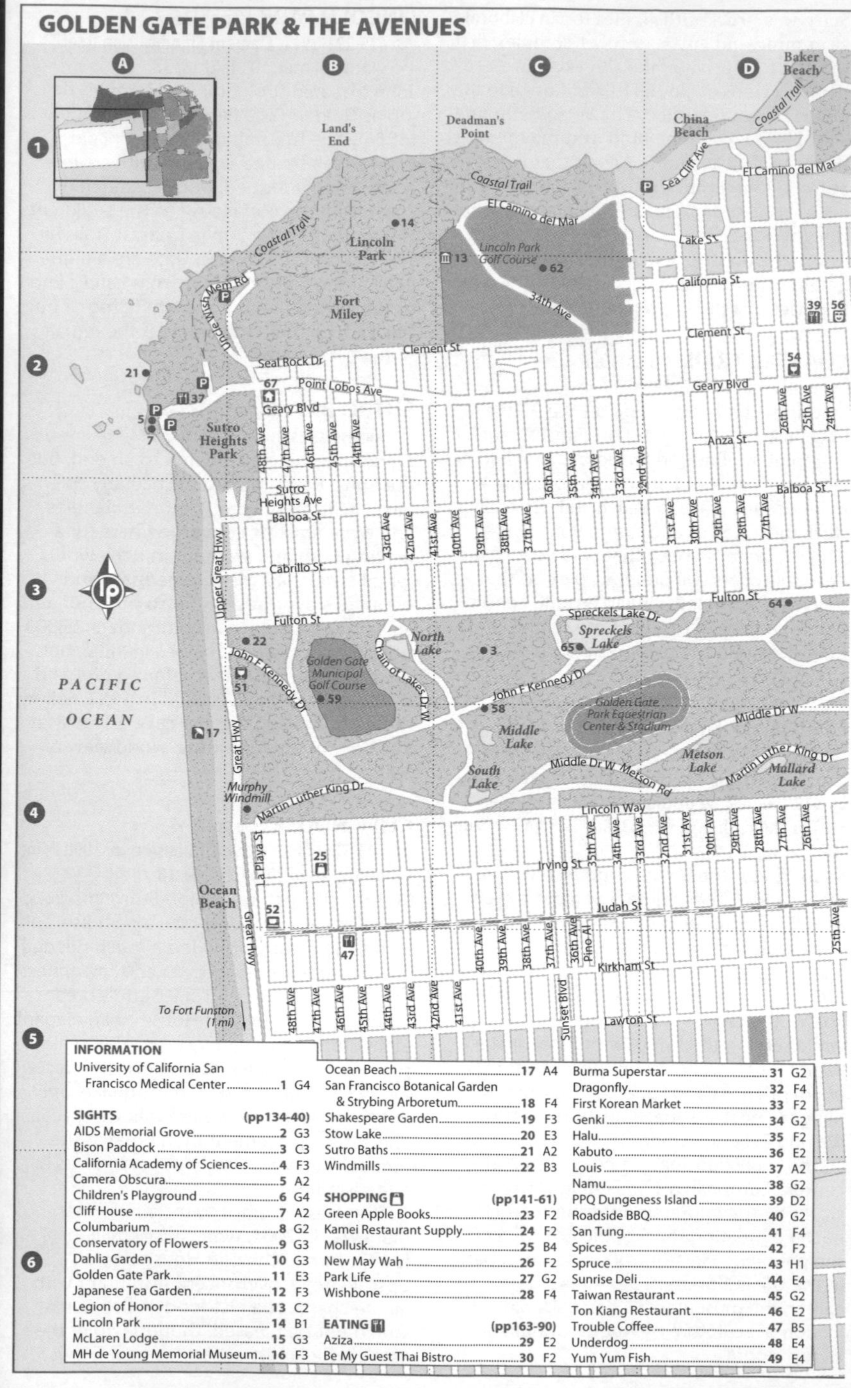

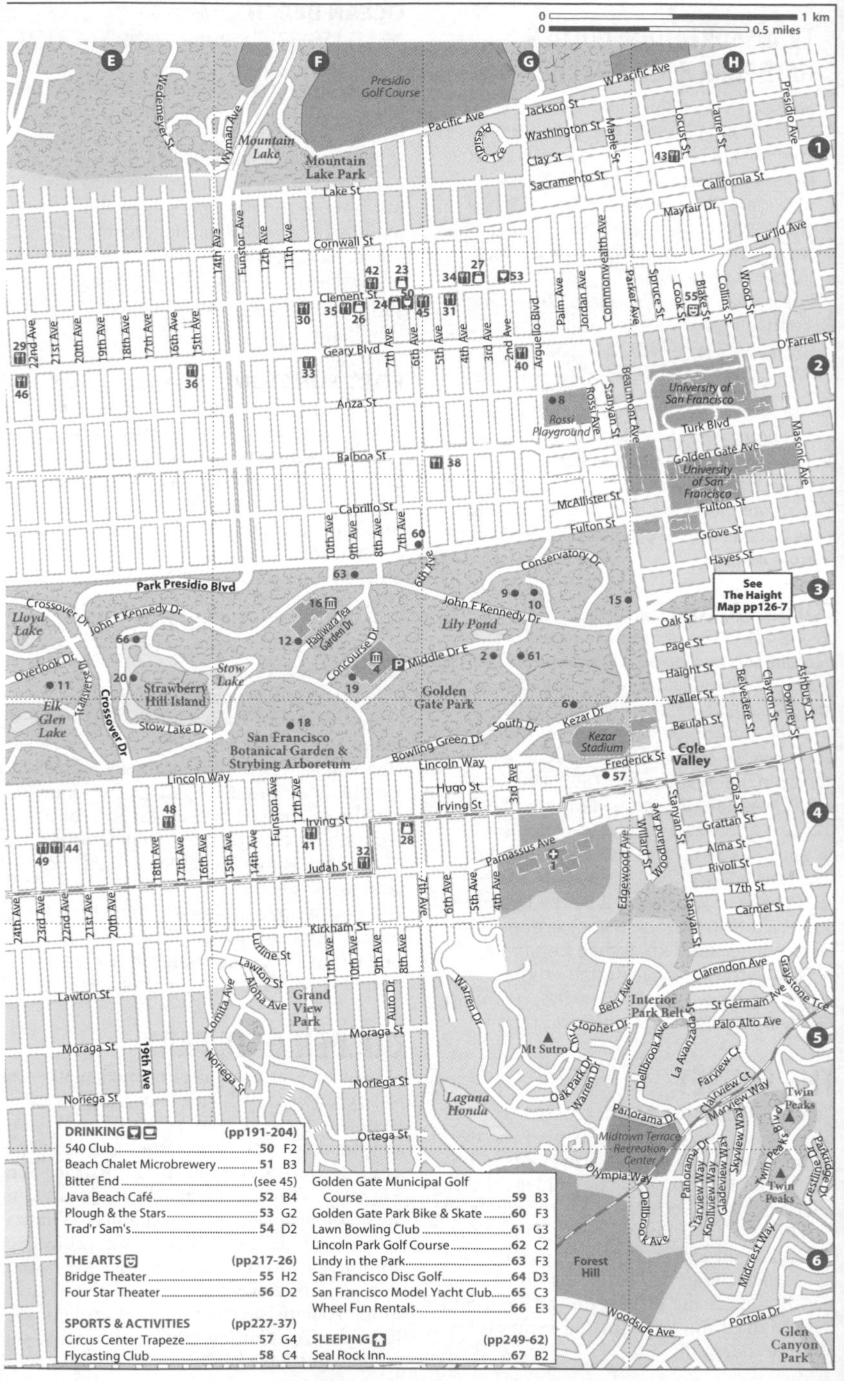
0 1 km
0 0.5 miles
E
F
G
H
1
2
3
4
5
6
Presidio Golf Course
Mountain Lake
Mountain Lake Park
Lake St
W Pacific Ave
Pacific Ave
Jackson St
Washington St
Clay St
Sacramento St
California St
Mayfair Dr
Euclid Ave
Cornwall St
Clement St
Geary Blvd
O'Farrell St
Anza St
Balboa St
Cabrillo St
Fulton St
McAllister St
Turk Blvd
Golden Gate Ave
Grove St
Hayes St
University of San Francisco
Rossi Playground
Park Presidio Blvd
Crossover Dr
John F Kennedy Dr
Lloyd Lake
Overlook Dr
Elk Glen Lake
Strawberry Hill Island
Stow Lake
Stow Lake Dr
Hagiwara Tea Garden Dr
Concourse Dr
Middle Dr E
Conservatory Dr
Lily Pond
Golden Gate Park
San Francisco Botanical Garden & Strybing Arboretum
Bowling Green Dr
South Dr
Kezar Dr
Kezar Stadium
Lincoln Way
Frederick St
Cole Valley
See The Haight Map pp126-7
Oak St
Page St
Haight St
Waller St
Beulah St
Hugo St
Irving St
Judah St
Parnassus Ave
Kirkham St
Lawton St
Moraga St
Noriega St
Ortega St
Grand View Park
Mt Sutro
Interior Park Belt
Clarendon Ave
St Germain Ave
Palo Alto Ave
Laguna Honda
Midtown Terrace Recreation Center
Panorama Dr
Olympia Way
Twin Peaks
Forest Hill
Woodside Ave
Portola Dr
Glen Canyon Park
19th Ave
DRINKING (pp191-204)
540 Club 50 F2
Beach Chalet Microbrewery 51 B3
Bitter End (see 45)
Java Beach Café 52 B4
Plough & the Stars 53 G2
Trad'r Sam's 54 D2
THE ARTS (pp217-26)
Bridge Theater 55 H2
Four Star Theater 56 D2
SPORTS & ACTIVITIES (pp227-37)
Circus Center Trapeze 57 G4
Flycasting Club 58 C4
Golden Gate Municipal Golf Course 59 B3
Golden Gate Park Bike & Skate 60 F3
Lawn Bowling Club 61 G3
Lincoln Park Golf Course 62 C2
Lindy in the Park 63 F3
San Francisco Disc Golf 64 D3
San Francisco Model Yacht Club 65 C3
Wheel Fun Rentals 66 E3
SLEEPING (pp249-62)
Seal Rock Inn 67 B2

TRANSPORTATION: GOLDEN GATE PARK & THE AVENUES

Bus Numbers 1 and 38 run from Downtown to the Richmond. Buses 5 and 21 head from Downtown along the north edge of Golden Gate Park. Bus 71 hooks around Golden Gate Park on the Sunset side, while number 2 runs the length of Clement St from Arguello Blvd past the Legion of Honor.

Streetcar The N train runs from Downtown, through the Sunset to Ocean Beach.

Parking There's a small lot near the MH de Young Memorial Museum in Golden Gate Park; otherwise, curb-side parking is available in the park.

of sea lions blithely frolicking among the seagull guano on Seal Rock, and the Camera Obscura (☎ 415-750-0415; www.giantcamera.com; 1090 Point Lobos Ave; admission $3; 11am-sunset), a Victorian invention that projects the sea view outside onto a parabolic screen inside a small building.

COLUMBARIUM Map pp136–7

☎ 415-771-0717; www.neptune-society.com; 1 Loraine Ct btwn Stanyan St & Arguello Blvd (off Anza St); 8am-5pm Mon-Fri, 9:30am-3pm Sat & Sun; 5, 21, 31, 33, 38

The ancient Roman innovation of memorial buildings for cremated remains came in handy in San Francisco in 1898, when real estate was already hitting a premium on the seven-by-seven peninsula. The neo-classical Columbarium was abandoned to raccoons and mushrooms from 1934 until 1979, when it was rescued by the Neptune Society, a cremation advocacy group. The restored, resplendent domed Columbarium is lined with Art Nouveau stained-glass windows and more than 5000 niches, honoring dearly beloved friends, dogs and rabbits.

THE SUNSET

The area south of the park down to Sloat Blvd (which runs past Stern Grove) and west from Stanyan St to the ocean is known as the Sunset District, a mostly residential area filled with pastel-colored stucco homes built between the 1930s and the 1950s. Since those days, the Sunset has earned a reputation for its ethnic eateries and surf hangouts. Ocean Beach bounds the district on the west, and Lake Merced and Fort Funston await exploration to the south.

OCEAN BEACH Map pp136–7

☎ 415-556-8371; sunrise-sunset; 5, 23, 31, 38, 48, 71, N

Bikinis, Elvis sing-alongs and clambakes are not the scene here – think more along the lines of wetsuits, pagan rituals and s'mores (toasted marshmallow treats). Bonfires are permitted in the artist-designed fire pits, but be sure to follow park rules about fire maintenance and alcohol (not allowed) or you could get fined. On rare sunny days the waters may beckon, but only hardcore surfers and sea lions should brave these riptides.

FORT FUNSTON off Map pp136–7

☎ 415-561-5505; Skyline Blvd; 6am-9pm

The grassy dunes of Fort Funston give you some idea what the Sunset looked like before it was paved over in the early 20th century. The fort is protected as part of the Golden Gate National Recreation Area, and it attracts butterflies and migrating birds. The park is a defunct military installation, and you can still see a WWII gun battery where 146-tonne guns point out to sea, and remains of Nike missile silos near where the parking lot is now.

Left to its own devices, the hardy non-native succulent known as ice plant has taken over in this windswept area, but the National Park Service is gradually replacing ice plants with native plants such as dune sagebrush, coastal buckwheat and sand verbena. One of the most thrilling aspects of the park is that hang gliders launch and land from there.

If you're driving, bicycling or walking here, follow the Great Hwy south and turn right on Skyline Blvd; the entrance to the park is past Lake Merced, on the right-hand side.

GOLDEN GATE PARK

When San Francisco first dreamed up its wild idea, even Frederick Law Olmstead, the celebrated architect of New York's Central Park, was daunted by the prospect of transforming 1017 acres of dune into park. Instead, San Francisco's green scheme fell to a young but surprisingly tenacious civil engineer William Hammond Hall, who steered the project to completion (for the full story, see the boxed text, p32). Instead of hotels and casinos, Hammond Hall insisted on botanical gardens, the Japanese Tea Garden (p140) and boating on scenic Stow Lake (p140).

The park does have its outlandish attractions, including carnivorous plants and outer-space orchids in the 1879 Conservatory of Flowers (p140). But even in Hammond's wildest dreams, he might not have imagined the park's newest attractions: architect Renzo Piano's 2008 landmark LEED-certified California Academy of Sciences (p140) houses Pierre the Penguin and 38,000 other weird and wonderful animals under a 'living roof' of California wildflowers, and Herzog & de Meuron's sleek, copper-clad MH de Young Memorial Museum (right) is oxidizing green to blend into the park.

GOLDEN GATE PARK Map pp136–7

☎ 415-831-2700; McLaren Lodge park headquarters cnr Fell & Stanyan Sts; admission free; 24hr; 5, 7, 21, 31, 33, 71, N

When San Franciscans refer to 'the park,' there's only one that gets the definite article: Golden Gate Park. Everything San Franciscans hold dear is here: free spirits, free music, redwoods, Frisbee, protests, fine art, bonsai and buffalo. Check out the range of attractions listed below, or just follow your bliss from east to west.

On the northeast end of the park, you'll find **Dahlia Garden** and the sheltered, contemplative valley of the **AIDS Memorial Grove**, while on the southeast side is a **children's playground** (under renovation at the time of writing). On your way west towards 9th Ave, you'll pass by a baseball diamond with pagan altars on the hill behind. As you near the Academy of Sciences, you'll spot the entry to the **Shakespeare Garden**, featuring 150 plants mentioned in Shakespeare's writings. Towards Martin Luther King Dr you'll pass the **Polo Fields**, where the 1967 Human Be-In took place and free concerts are still held in summer. With a windbreaker and will-power you'll reach the western edge of the park, where quixotic **bison** stampede in their paddock towards the upright Dutch and dilapidated Murphy **windmills**, with Ocean Beach beyond.

Sporty and not-so-sporty types will appreciate the range of outdoor activities available in the park: an archery range, baseball and softball diamonds, fly-casting pools, greens for lawn bowling, a horse-shoe pitch, four soccer fields and 21 tennis courts. But the big draw here for athletes are the miles of trails for biking, jogging and horse-riding through the park's natural splendors. To accommodate the masses that descend on the park any given Sunday, John F Kennedy Dr is closed to motor vehicles east of Crossover Dr (around 8th Ave), where the skateboarders, in-line skaters and unicyclists come out in force. Saturdays from June to October the park is also closed to traffic along John F Kennedy Dr.

To plan a picnic, protest or some other event in the park and get detailed park maps, check in at **McLaren Lodge** (cnr Fell & Stanyan Sts; 8am-5pm Mon-Fri) at the eastern entrance of the park, under the splendid cypress that's the city's official tree. For information about free park walking tours, call **Friends of Recreation & Parks** (☎ 415-263-0991).

MH DE YOUNG MEMORIAL MUSEUM

Map pp136–7

☎ 415-750-3600; www.famsf.org/deyoung; 50 Hagiwara Tea Garden Dr; adult/child under 12yr/college student & child 13-17yr/senior $10/free/6/7, $2 discount with Muni transfer, 1st Tue of month free; 9:30am-5:15pm Tue-Sun, until 8:45pm Fri mid-Jan–Nov; 5, 21, 44, 71, N;

You'd think the art would be upstaged by Swiss architects Herzog & de Meuron (of Tate Modern fame) and their sleek building, with its copper cladding oxidizing green to become part of the scenery, the facade perforated in a seemingly abstract pattern drawn from aerial photography of the park. But this landmark collection of arts and fine crafts from around the world puts California's own artistic pursuits into global perspective, and hides a surprise around every corner – don't miss 19th-century Oceanic ceremonial masks and stunning Central Asian rugs from the 11,000-plus textile collection. Blockbuster temporary shows range from Tutankhamen's treasures to Dale Chihuly's bombastic glass sculpture, but the real gems here are rotating-collection highlights like a coffin shaped like a cocoa pod by Ghanian artist Kane Kwei, and Masami Teraoka's 1977 wry commentary on globalization: a geisha eating Baskin & Robbins vanilla ice cream. Special collections are downstairs, and the museum shop offers two floors of shopping temptation.

The 144ft twisting medieval-style armored tower is the one feature of the building that seems incongruous with the park setting, but though you might expect to see vats of oil boiling on the top floor, instead there are spectacular views on clear days to the Pacific and Golden Gate Bridge, and yes, another bookstore. Access to the tower viewing room is free, and worth the wait for the elevator by Ruth Asawa's mesmerizing filigreed pods.

CALIFORNIA ACADEMY OF SCIENCES

Map pp136–7

☎ 415-379-8000; www.calacademy.org; 55 Music Concourse Dr; adult/child under 6yr/child 7-11yr/senior & child 12-17yr $24.95/free/14.95/19.95; 9:30am-5pm Mon-Sat, 11am-5pm Sun; 5, 21, 44, 71, N

Finally the California Academy of Sciences has a museum suited to its fascinating collection of 38,000 natural wonders and the occasional freak of nature. Under the wildflower-covered 'living roof' of Renzo Piano's LEED-certified green building, butterflies flutter through a four-storey glass rainforest dome, a rare white alligator stalks a swamp, and Pierre the Penguin paddles his massive new tank in the African Hall. In the basement aquarium, kids duck inside a glass bubble to enter an eel forest, find Nemos in the tropical-fish tanks and squeal to pet starfish in an aquatic petting zoo. The views here are sublime: you can glimpse into infinity in the Planetarium or ride the elevator to the roof for panoramas over Golden Gate Park. Displays throughout the main floor explain conservation issues affecting California's ecosystem, and you can actually eat those words – the cafeteria sells treats made with local, organically grown ingredients. For an even wilder scene, check the schedule for Thursday evenings when the academy is open late and cocktails are served.

CONSERVATORY OF FLOWERS

Map pp136–7

☎ 415-666-7001; www.conservatoryofflowers.org; Conservatory Dr West; adult/child 5-11yr/senior & child 12-17yr $5/1.50/3; sunrise-sunset; 5, 7, 21, 33, 71;

Flower power is alive and well inside this grand Victorian greenhouse, where orchids sprawl out like bohemian divas, lilies float contemplatively in ponds and carnivorous plants give off odors that smell exactly like insect belches. The original 1878 structure is newly restored and the plants are thriving.

SAN FRANCISCO BOTANICAL GARDEN & STRYBING ARBORETUM

Map pp136–7

☎ 415-661-1316; www.strybing.org; Martin Luther King Dr; admission free; 8am-4:30pm Mon-Fri, 10am-5pm Sat, Sun & holidays; 5, 21, 44, 71, N

There's always something blooming in these 70-acre gardens, which cover a world of vegetation from South African savannah to New Zealand cloud forest. The Garden of Fragrance is designed for appeal to the visually impaired, and the California native-plant section explodes with color when the wildflowers bloom in early spring, right off the redwood trail. Free arboretum tours take place daily; for details, stop by the bookstore inside the entrance.

JAPANESE TEA GARDEN Map pp136–7

☎ 415-831-2700; Hagiwara Tea Garden Dr; adult/child & senior $3.50/1.25, green tea & fortune cookies $2; 8:30am-6pm Mar-Oct, to 5pm Nov-Feb; 5, 21, 44, 71, N;

Have your moment of Zen in the Zen Garden, or while enjoying green tea under a pagoda, watching kids ogle doll-sized bonsais that are pushing 100 years. These bonsai are a credit to the dedicated gardeners of the Hagiwara family, who returned from WWII Japanese American internment camps to discover their prized bonsai had been sold. The Hagiwaras spent the next two decades tracking down the trees, and returned the bonsai grove to its rightful home.

STOW LAKE Map pp136–7

☎ 415-752-0347; sunrise-sunset; 28, 44

The mini-resort in the center of the park is Stow Lake, with a picturesque island called Strawberry Hill for short but steep and sweaty hikes. Huntington Falls tumble down the hill into the lake, near a romantic Chinese pavilion that fairly begs for soap-opera scenes. Pedal boats, row boats and electric motor boats are available at the **boathouse** (☎ 415-752-0347; per hr paddleboats/canoes/rowboats $24/20/19, surrey bikes $20-35, tandem bikes $12, bikes $6-8; rentals 10am-4pm). Boats must have at least one person 16 or older aboard, and you can bring dogs on rowboats.

SHOPPING

top picks

- **City Lights Bookstore** (p146)
- **Under One Roof** (p156)
- **Velvet da Vinci** (p148)
- **Park Life** (p160)
- **Wasteland** (p158)
- **Needles & Pens** (p153)
- **Loyal Army Clothing** (p157)
- **Global Exchange Fair Trade Craft Center** (p155)

SHOPPING

All those catchy playlists, psychedelic parlors, vast poetry collections and fabulous outfits don't just pull themselves together, you know – San Franciscans had to get out there and shop for it all. At the risk of annoying any locals who'd like to keep their style secrets and sweet deals to themselves, San Francisco's key stops for originality and value are listed in this chapter.

When you want something really unique, scan this chapter for the tags Local Designer or Local Maker, which mark stores selling San Francisco specialties. To score souvenirs that do SF and the environment a favor, check the GreenDex index. But in inventive, independent-minded San Francisco, the best souvenirs are the ones you make yourself: for inspiration and supplies, look for venues tagged with DIY in this chapter.

OPENING HOURS

Most stores are open daily from 10am or 11am to 6pm or 7pm. Some shops are closed Sunday, or have limited hours. In the Haight and the Mission, stores can be slack about opening promptly – or at all. Department stores keep later hours, often staying open until 8pm or 9pm.

EMBARCADERO & THE PIERS

ELIZABETHW

Map p63 — Beauty Products, Local Maker

☎ 415-351-2800; www.elizabethw.com; 900 North Point St; ⌚ 10am-6pm Mon-Thu & Sun, to 8:30pm Fri & Sat; 🚌 2, 7, 21, 71, F, J, K, L, M, N; 🚌 & 🚇 Embarcadero

Thermometers permanently hover around 70°F in San Francisco, but local scent-maker elizabethW supplies the tantalizing aromas of changing seasons without the sweaty brows or frozen toes. Sweet Tea smells like a Georgia porch in summertime, Vetiver like autumn in Maine. For a true SF fragrance, Leaves is as audaciously green as Golden Gate Park in January.

FERRY PLAZA WINE MERCHANT

Map p63 — Food & Drink

☎ 415-391-9400; www.fpwm.com; 1 Ferry Plaza; ⌚ 11am-8pm Mon, 10am-8pm Tue-Wed, 10am-9pm Thu-Fri, 8am-9pm Sat, 10am-7pm Sun; 🚌 2, 7, 21, 71, F, J, K, L, M, N; 🚌 & 🚇 Embarcadero

Stock up on California wines after you've sipped a few – start with viogniers, work your way to cabs, and swish and spit when you only want to taste. Savvy staff describe wines in a fun, informative way, making sure a fine time is had by all. The bar is jammed on Saturdays, but otherwise staff will take the time to suggest pairings and exciting new releases.

RECCHIUTI CHOCOLATES

Map p63 — Food & Drink, Local Maker

☎ 415-834-9494; www.recchiuticonfections.com; 1 Ferry Bldg; ⌚ 10am-7pm Mon-Fri, 8am-6pm Sat, 10am-5pm Sun; 🚌 2, 7, 21, 71, F, J, K, L, M, N; 🚌 & 🚇 Embarcadero

No San Franciscan can resist Recchiuti: Pacific Heights parts with old money for its *fleur de sel* caramels; Noe Valley's child foodie prodigies prefer S'more Bites to the campground variety; and the Mission splurges on chocolates designed by developmentally disabled artists from Creativity Explored (p119) – part of the proceeds benefit the nonprofit gallery.

SUR LA TABLE

Map p63 — Housewares

☎ 415-262-9970; www.surlatable.com; 1 Ferry Bldg, most classes at 77 Maiden Lane; ⌚ 9am-7pm Mon-Fri, 8am-7pm Sat, 10am-6pm Sun; 🚌 2, 7, 21, 71, F, J, K, L, M, N; 🚌 & 🚇 Embarcadero

Can't fathom life without an espresso maker and citrus reamer? You'll never need to, thanks to these understanding salespeople. For the hippie gourmet, there's a windowsill grow-light for sprouting, ahem, herbs, and for the young aspiring chef,

CONSUMER TAXES

When you're tallying up the grand total of all those bargains, don't forget the 9.5% sales tax tacked onto every item sold. Sorry, this isn't refundable to visitors like the European VAT (value-added tax).

CLOTHING SIZES

Women's clothing

Aus/UK	8	10	12	14	16	18
Europe	36	38	40	42	44	46
Japan	5	7	9	11	13	15
USA	6	8	10	12	14	16

Women's shoes

Aus/USA	5	6	7	8	9	10
Europe	35	36	37	38	39	40
France only	35	36	38	39	40	42
Japan	22	23	24	25	26	27
UK	3½	4½	5½	6½	7½	8½

Men's clothing

Aus	92	96	100	104	108	112
Europe	46	48	50	52	54	56
Japan	S		M	M		L
UK/USA	35	36	37	38	39	40

Men's shirts (collar sizes)

Aus/Japan	38	39	40	41	42	43
Europe	38	39	40	41	42	43
UK/USA	15	15½	16	16½	17	17½

Men's shoes

Aus/UK	7	8	9	10	11	12
Europe	41	42	43	44½	46	47
Japan	26	27	27½	28	29	30
USA	7½	8½	9½	10½	11½	12½

Measurements approximate only; try before you buy

a cupcake-frosting set. The Ferry Building location features free demos; evening classes at the Maiden Lane store on knife skills, seasonal California cuisine and more cost $79 to $89.

DOWNTOWN

FOLK ART INTERNATIONAL

Map pp70–1 Arts & Crafts

☎ 415-392-9999; www.folkartintl.com; 140 Maiden Lane; 10am-6pm Tue-Sat; & Powell St

Squeeze the Guggenheim spiral into a brick box with a sunken Romanesque archway, and there you have Frank Lloyd Wright's 1949 Circle Gallery Building, which since 1979 has been the home of Folk Art International. Strategically located in niches along the ramp is a carefully curated collection of Thai neck cuffs and pre-Columbian fertility figurines that casually command the entire room.

EDEN & EDEN

Map pp70–1 Clothing & Accessories, Housewares

☎ 415-983-0490; www.edenandeden.com; 560 Jackson St; 10am-7pm Mon-Fri, 10am-6pm Sat, noon-6pm Sun; 15, 30, 41, 45

Quirkiness is an SF style trademark that can either be achieved through an MFA program or a quick stop at Eden & Eden. Everything you might dream up after diligent study of pop art is already here: a necklace that looks like a giant zipper, shaggy-haired orange tea cozies, a cushion that says 'blahblahblah,' and hideous apartment buildings on elegant bone-china plates.

H&M Map pp70–1 Clothing & Accessories

☎ 415-986-4215; www.hm.com; 150 Powell St; 10am-9pm Mon-Sat, 11am-8pm Sun; 5, 6, 7, 21, 31, 71, F, J, K, L, M, N; & Powell St; Powell-Mason & Powell-Hyde

What IKEA is to home furnishing, H&M is to fashion: suspiciously affordable, perpetually crowded, not really made for the long haul and perfect for parties. With limited-edition runs and special collections by designers like splashy British colorist Matthew Williamson (and lesser ones like, oof, Madonna) you won't have to worry that your closet looks exactly like everyone else's – unless you bought it at IKEA. There are several outlets in town, but the one on Powell St is the biggest, with a vast men's section.

LOEHMANN'S

Map pp70–1 Clothing & Accessories

☎ 415-982-3215; www.loehmanns.com; 222 Sutter St; 9am-8pm Mon-Sat, 11am-7pm Sun; 15, 30, 41, 45

The most revealing Downtown fashion choice isn't what shoes you wear, but which floor you choose in this discount designer superstore. North Beach artists drift to the middle floor for almost-free Free People smocks; Pacific Heights charity fundraisers hit the top floor for discounted Prada shirtdresses; and gift shoppers converge around 40%-off red-tagged Kate Spade clutches in main-floor accessories. Pace yourself: women's shoes and an impressive men's section are across the street.

MARGARET O'LEARY

Map pp70–1 Clothing & Accessories, Local Designer

☎ 415-391-1010; www.margaretoleary.com; 1 Claude Lane; 10am-5pm Tue-Sat; 1, 15, 30; California

Ignorance of the fog is no excuse in San Francisco, but should you confuse SF for LA (the horror!) and neglect to pack the obligatory sweater, Margaret O'Leary will sheathe you in knitwear, no questions asked. The San Francisco designer's specialties are warm, whisper-light cardigans in cashmere, organic cotton or eco-minded bamboo yarn.

ORIGINAL LEVI'S STORE

Map pp70–1 Clothing & Accessories

☎ 415-501-0100; www.us.levi.com; 300 Post St; 10am-9pm Mon-Sat, to 6:30pm Sun; 2, 3, 4, 30, 38, 45; & Powell St; Powell-Mason & Powell-Hyde

The flagship store in Levi Strauss' hometown sells classic jeans that fit without fail, plus limited-edition pairs made of tough Japanese selvage and eco-organic cotton denim. Start with the impressive discount racks (30% to 60% off), but don't hold out for sales – denim fanatics Tweet their finds here, so rare lines like 1950s prison-model denim sell out fast. Shout out to fellow shorties: they'll hem your jeans here for $10.

SHOTWELL BOUTIQUE

Map pp70–1 Clothing & Accessories

☎ 415-399-9898; www.shotwellsf.com; 320 Grant Ave; 11am-5pm Mon-Sat, noon-6pm Sun; 1, 15, 30; California

SF fashion vanguardians could shop for decades for a look achieved in an afternoon at Shotwell: purple-rimmed '80s sunglasses, Surface to Air low-tops, a '70s fedora, draped tank from Society for Rational Dress over Cheap Monday jeans, and locally designed bling. Unlike other Downtown boutiques, there are good selections of menswear and vintage under $25, plus a $5 jewelry bin.

BARNEYS Map pp70–1 Department Store

☎ 415-268-3500; www.barneys.com; 77 O'Farrell St; 10am-7pm Mon-Wed, Fri & Sat, 10am-8pm Thu, 11am-6pm Sun; 5, 6, 7, 21, 31, 71, F, J, K, L, M, N; & Powell St; Powell-Mason & Powell-Hyde

The high-end New York fashion staple known for its inspired window displays and near-lethal 70% off sales has hit the West Coast, just in time for the recession. Year-round, Barneys showcases emerging designers; well-priced, well-fitted sportswear on its Co-op label; and exclusive eco-conscious lines by Philip Lim, Theory, and its own affordable Green Label, focusing on clean lines with a clean conscience.

MACY'S Map pp70–1 Department Store

☎ 415-397-3333; www.macys.com; 170 O'Farrell St; 10am-9pm Mon-Thu, 10am-11pm Fri, 9am-11pm Sat, 11am-7pm Sun; 5, 6, 7, 21, 31, 71, F, J, K, L, M, N; & Powell St; Powell-Mason & Powell-Hyde

Five floors of name brands, plus a basement food court with oddly sour smells. The men's department is across the street so they won't have to worry their pretty little heads about where to find boxer briefs and Kenneth Cole shirts, while women have to brave the perfume police and fend off slightly insulting free makeover offers just to check out the shoe sale (totally worth it).

WESTFIELD SAN FRANCISCO CENTRE

Map pp70–1 Department Store

☎ 415-512-6776; http://westfield.com/sanfrancisco; 865 Market St; most shops 10am-8:30pm Mon-Sat, 11am-7pm Sun; 5, 6, 7, 21, 31, 71, F, J, K, L, M, N; & Powell St; Powell-Mason & Powell-Hyde;

Wait, is this suburbia? Sure looks like it inside this nine-level chain-store city, with Bloomingdale's and Nordstrom, plus 400 other retailers and a movie theater. Supposedly there's a 'distinctive boutique' concept to this mall, which translates to same amount of stuff crammed into smaller stores. Best/only reasons to brave this behemoth: post-holiday sales, H&M's Spanish cousin Mango, bathrooms (including lounges with changing tables for women and families) and a respectable basement food court.

BRITEX FABRICS Map pp70–1 DIY

☎ 415-392-2910; www.britexfabrics.com; 146 Geary St; 10am-6pm Mon-Sat; 2, 3, 4, 30, 38, 45; & Powell St; Powell-Mason & Powell-Hyde

No reality design show can compare with the four floors of nonstop fashion drama at Britex. First floor: designers bicker over who gets first dibs on caution-orange chiffon. Second floor: glam rockers dig through a velvet goldmine. Third floor: Hollywood stylists squeal 'To die for!' over '60s Lucite buttons. Top floor: fake fur flies and remnants roll as costumers prepare for Burning Man, Halloween and your average SF weekend.

LE SANCTUAIRE Map pp70–1 Food & Drink

☎ 415-986-4216; www.le-sanctuaire.com; 5th fl, 315 Sutter St; by appointment 10:30am-4:30pm Mon-Fri; 2, 3, 4, 30, 38, 45; Powell-Mason & Powell-Hyde

Mad scientists, thrill seekers and professional chefs are buzzed in speakeasy-style to this culinary curiosity shop selling anchovy juice, spherifiers to turn fruit into caviar, salt for curing meats, and of course that hallmark of molecular gastronomy: foaming agents. Check the website for classes on making smoked watermelon with vacuum sealers and using liquid nitrogen to make powdered lard – too bad suspending disbelief using gellants isn't on the schedule.

JAPONESQUE

Map pp70–1 Housewares, Arts & Crafts

☎ 415-391-8860; 824 Montgomery St; 10:30am-5:30pm Tue-Sat, 11am-5pm Sun; 10, 12, 15

Wabi-sabi is not something you smear on sushi but the fine appreciation for organic forms and materials you can experience first-hand at Japonesque. Owner Koichi Hara stocks antique Japanese bamboo baskets and raku ceramics alongside Ruth Rhoten's molten silver vases and Hiromichi Iwashita's graphite-coated, chiseled-wood panels that look like bonfire embers.

DSW Map pp70–1 Shoes

☎ 415-445-9511; www.dswshoe.com; 111 Powell St; 9am-9pm Mon-Sat, to 8pm Sun; 5, 6, 7, 21, 31, 71, F, J, K, L, M, N; & Powell St; Powell-Mason & Powell-Hyde

The basement clearance section is where recovering shoe hounds come once they've sworn that they've bought their last pair for the season. Diligent research has uncovered 40% to 60% off Marc Jacobs flats, Betsy Johnson wedges and an inexplicable bonanza of limited-edition Pumas.

top picks

FASHION STRIPS

- North Beach – Grant Ave from Columbus Ave to Filbert St (p146).
- Hayes Valley – Hayes St between Laguna and Franklin Sts (p158).
- Pacific Heights – Fillmore St between Clay and Sutter Sts (p148).
- The Haight – Haight St from Shrader to Fillmore Sts (p156).
- Noe Valley – 24th St between Castro and Church Sts (p155).

CIVIC CENTER & THE TENDERLOIN

KAYO BOOKS Map p77 Books

☎ 415-749-0554; www.kayobooks.com; 814 Post St; 11am-6pm Thu-Sat; 2, 3, 4, 27, 38, 76

Juvenile delinquents will find an entire section dedicated to their life stories here, where vintage pulp fiction, true crime and erotica titles ending in exclamation points (including the succinct *Wench!)* induced John Waters to endorse this place on NPR. You might find a first edition Dashiell Hammet gumshoe caper, a wayward nun's tale filed under Catholic Guilt, or *Women's Medical Problems* in the Bizarre Nonfiction section.

CHINATOWN

GOLDEN GATE FORTUNE COOKIE COMPANY Map p82 Food & Drink

☎ 415-781-3956; 56 Ross Alley; admission free; 8am-7pm; 30,45; Powell-Mason, Powell-Hyde

You too can say you made a fortune in San Francisco after visiting this bakery, where cookies are stamped out on old-fashioned presses and folded while hot – just as they were back in 1909, when they were invented in San Francisco for the Japanese Tea Garden (p140). You can make your own customized cookies, or pick up a bag of the risqué 'French' fortune cookies – no need to add 'in bed' at the end to make these interesting.

CHINA BAZAAR Map p82 Gifts

☎ 415-391-6369; 667 Grant Ave; 10am-10pm; 1, 9, 30, 45; California, Powell-Mason, Powell-Hyde

Wire racks are perilously overloaded with bargain novelty items in no discernible order, except for the tiki section, which will add some aloha to your home bar. Just when you thought home decor couldn't get any cheaper, check out the ceramics sale section downstairs.

CHINATOWN KITE SHOP Map p82 Gifts

☎ 415-989-5182; www.chinatownkite.com; 717 Grant Ave; 10am-6pm; 1, 9, 30, 41, 45; California, Powell-Mason, Powell-Hyde

Be the star of Crissy Field and wow any kids in your life with a fierce 6ft-long flying shark, a flying panda bear that looks understandably stunned, or 'Pink Floyd,'

top picks

NON-TOURISTY SF SOUVENIRS

- City Lights Bookstore (right) Beat poetry.
- Electric Works (p113) Limited-edition local art.
- Bi-Rite (p182) Locally made chocolates.
- Loyal Army Clothing (p157) Happy fog T-shirt.
- Doe (p157) Golden State necklace.

the goofy pink flamingo (shouldn't that be a pig, really?). Pick up a papier-mâché two-person lion dance costume, and invite a date to bust some ferocious moves with you next lunar new year.

FAR EAST FLEA MARKET Map p82 Gifts

☎ 415-989-8588; 729 Grant Ave; 10am-10pm; 1, 9, 30, 45; California, Powell-Mason, Powell-Hyde;

The shopping equivalent of crack, this bottomless store is dangerously cheap and certain to make you giddy and delusional. Of course you can get that sale samurai sword through airport security! There's no such thing as too many bath toys, paper lanterns and bobble-headed Edgar Allen Poe action figures! Step away from the dollar Golden Gate snow globes while there's still time…

CLARION MUSIC CENTER Map p82 Music

☎ 415-391-1317; www.clarionmusic.com; 816 Sacramento St; 11am-6pm Mon-Fri, 9am-5pm Sat; 1, 9, 30, 45; California, Powell-Mason, Powell-Hyde

The minor chords of the *erhu* (Chinese string instrument) will pluck at your heartstrings as you walk through Chinatown's alleyways, and here you can try your hand at the bow yourself with a superior student model. With the impressive range of African congas and Central American marimbas and gongs, you could become your own multi-culti one-man band. Check the website for concerts, workshops and demonstrations by masters.

NORTH BEACH

ARIA Map p87 Antiques & Collectibles

☎ 415-433-0219; 1522 Grant Ave; 11am-6pm Mon-Sat, noon-5pm Sun; 15, 30, 41, 45

This shop has all the makings of a Tom Waits song: wartime French love letters returned to senders, anatomical drawings of the heart, castle keys lost in gutters a century ago, a wax mannequin arm raised in ghostly salute. Hours are erratic whenever owner/chief scavenger Bill is out treasure-hunting.

SF ROCK POSTERS & COLLECTIBLES

Map p87 Antiques & Collectibles

☎ 415-956-6749; www.rockposters.com; 1851 Powell St; 10am-6pm Tue-Sat; 15, 30; Powell-Mason

Anyone who hazily remembers the '60s may recall long-lost bands (and brain cells) in this trippy temple to the rock gods. Nostalgia isn't cheap, so expect to pay hundreds or even thousands for first-run psychedelic Fillmore concert posters featuring Big Brother and the Holding Company or the Grateful Dead, but you can still find deals on handbills for the Dead Kennedys, Talking Heads and Black Sabbath.

CITY LIGHTS BOOKSTORE

Map p87 Books

☎ 415-362-8193; http://citylights.com; 261 Columbus Ave; 10am-midnight; 15, 30, 41, 45

'Abandon all despair, all ye who enter,' orders the sign by the door to City Lights written by founder and San Francisco poet laureate Lawrence Ferlinghetti. This commandment is easy to follow upstairs in the sunny Poetry Room, with its piles of freshly published verse, a designated Poet's Chair, and literary views of laundry strung across Jack Kerouac Alley. Poetic justice has been served here since 1957, when City Lights won a landmark ruling against book banning, and went on to publish Lenny Bruce, William S Burroughs, Angela Davis and Tahar Ben Jelloun, among others. When you abandon despair, you make more room for books.

CUSTOM ORIGINALS (AL'S ATTIRE)

Map p87 Clothing & Accessories, Local Designer

☎ 415-693-9900; www.alsattire.com; 1314 Grant Ave; 11am-7pm Mon-Sat, noon-6pm Sun; 15, 30, 41, 45

Hepcats and slick chicks get their duds at Al's, where vintage styles are reinvented in rocker gabardine, noir-novel twill and philosophical tweeds. Prices aren't exactly bohemian, but recent finds in the sales rack include men's thin-lapel jackets and halter dresses that would make Marilyn Monroe gnash her teeth in envy. Ask about custom orders for weddings and other shindigs.

DELILAH CROWN

Map p87 Clothing & Accessories, Local Designer

☎ 415-765-9060; www.delilahcrown.com; 524 Green St; 11am-6:30pm Tue-Sat, noon-5pm Sun; 15, 30, 41, 45

The crowning touches to SF style are the screen-printing, pin-tucking and vintage fabrics used in owner Kristina De Pizzol's silver-crown-label designs: patch-pocket skirts with contrasting stitching, yellow shifts with vintage orange buttons, and mushroom-silkscreened T-shirts. Baby mini-tunics and gypsy skirts make tiny tots look like the charming end results of the Summer of Love.

OOMA

Map p87 Clothing & Accessories, Local Designer

☎ 415-627-6963; www.ooma.net; 1422 Grant Ave; 11am-7pm Tue-Sat, noon-5pm Sun; 15, 30, 41, 45

Feel-good style is what Objects of My Affection is all about: ticklish coral waterfall earrings, springy Poetic License wedges, and locally made, sweatshop-free Del Forte organic denim. Better still, most items are in the affordable double-digit range, including laser-cut wood bubble earrings by local designer Molly M.

LOLA OF NORTH BEACH

Map p87 Gifts, Stationery

☎ 415-781-1817; www.lolaofnorthbeach.com; 1415 Grant Ave; 11am-6:30pm Mon-Sat, to 5:30pm Sun; 15, 30; Powell-Mason

Answers to all your SF gifting quandries, from creative souvenirs (ticket stub album for all those cool-looking SF museum tickets) to Silicon Valley baby showers ('my dad's a geek' onesies), plus California-made soy candles that smell like sunshine.

101 MUSIC Map p87 Music

☎ 415-392-6369; 1414 Grant Ave; 10am-8pm Tue-Sat, noon-8pm Sun; 15, 30, 41, 45

You'll have to bend over those bins to let DJs and hardcore collectors pass (and, hey, wasn't that Carlos Santana?!), but among the $5 to $10 discs are obscure releases *(Songs for Greek Lovers)* and original recordings by Oscar Peterson, Janis Joplin and, oh yes, Pat Benatar. At the sister shop at 513 Green St, don't bonk your head on the vintage Les Pauls, and check out the sweet turntables that must've cost some kid a year's worth of burger-flipping c 1978.

RUSSIAN & NOB HILLS

HYDE & SEEK ANTIQUES

Map p92 Antiques & Collectibles

☎ 415-776-8865; 1913 Hyde St; noon-6pm Tue-Sat; 19, 41, 45; Powell-Hyde

Like the home of a long-lost eccentric aunt, this tiny storefront is full of surprises: a briefcase that opens to reveal a full tartan bar, a Danish-design silver calla lily, a Native basket more tightly wound than your boss – all at reasonable prices.

SPRING

Map p92 Beauty Products, Housewares

☎ 415-673-2065; www.astorecalledspring.com; 2162 Polk St; 11am-6pm Tue-Sun; 19, 41, 45, 47, 49, 76; Powell-Hyde

Spring has sprung a fresh new idea: housework shouldn't mean an instant headache from noxious cleaning fumes. Instead, this store thoughtfully provides all the nontoxic lemon and lavender products you need to clean up your home and your environmental act. The bamboo-fiber bedding is pricey, but Caldrea cleansers and Farmaesthetics soaps in 'sweet pea' and 'cornmeal chamomile' smell scrumptious and are priced to move.

ECO CITIZEN

Map p92 Clothing & Accessories

☎ 415-614-0100; www.ecocitizenonline.com; 1488 Vallejo St; 11am-7pm Mon-Sat, noon-6pm Sun; 1, 19, 47, 49

Idealism meets street chic in this boutique of ecofriendly, fair-traded fabulousness, from ultraglam gold hemp jeans to Vivienne Westwood T-strap heels made of nontoxic PVC (recyclable onsite). Prices are reasonable and sales a steal – $50 could get you a fair-trade cashmere dress or SF-made Turk+Taylor organic cotton jacket. The faucet charm necklace made from reclaimed silver is truly lucky – its purchase helps support clean water initiatives.

STUDIO

Map p92 Gifts, Local Designer

☎ 415-931-3130; www.studiogallerysf.com; 1815 Polk St; 11am-8pm Wed-Fri, to 6pm Sat & Sun; 1, 19, 47, 49, 76; California

Maybe shopping is a substitute for Prozac after all – especially that silver necklace in the shape of a serotonin molecule. Spiff up your pad with locally made arts and crafts at bargain prices, such as Mike Farruggia's altered street sign that cautions 'Beware the Pompitous,' Chiami Sekine's collages of birds tweeting instead of bloggers, and Monique Tse's fat-free cupcakes made of blown glass.

CITY DISCOUNT

Map p92 Housewares

☎ 415-771-4649; 1542 Polk St; 10am-6pm; 1, 19, 47, 49, 76; California

Bargains never tasted so sweet: heart-shaped Le Creuset casseroles, frighteningly effective Microplane graters, Brika espresso makers and other specialty gourmet gear, all at 30% to 50% off the prices you'd pay downtown. Hard-to-find appliance replacement parts, parchment paper and cooking tips are all readily available from dedicated foodie counter staff.

VELVET DA VINCI

Map p92 Jewelry

☎ 415-441-0109; www.velvetdavinci.com; 2015 Polk St; noon-6pm Tue-Sat, to 4pm Sun; 12, 19, 47, 49, 76; Powell-Hyde

You can actually see the ideas behind these handcrafted gems: Lynn Christiansen puts her food obsessions into a purse that looks like whipped cream, and Enric Majoral's Mediterranean meditations yield rings that appear to be made of sand. Shows here reveal brilliance behind the baubles; during the Ethical Metalsmiths' 'Radical Jewelry Makeover,' the public was invited to bring broken trinkets to be recycled into new jewelry, with sales supporting a campaign for responsible sourcing practices.

JAPANTOWN & PACIFIC HEIGHTS

BENEFIT

Map p96 Beauty Products, Local Maker

☎ 415-567-0242; 2117 Fillmore St; 10am-7pm Mon-Wed, 9:30am-7pm Thu & Fri, 9am-6:30pm Sat, 10am-6pm Sun; 1, 2, 3, 4, 22

Get cheeky with BeneTint, the dab-on liquid blush made from roses, or raise some eyebrows with Brow Zings tinted brow wax – they're two of Benefit's signature products invented in San Francisco by the twin-sister team. Surgery is so LA: in SF, overnight Angelinas swear by LipPlump and Lindsay Lohan dark-eye-circles are cured with Ooh La Lift.

CLARY SAGE ORGANICS

Map p96 Beauty Products, Clothing & Accessories

☎ 415-673-7300; www.clarysageorganics.com; 2241 Fillmore St; 10am-7pm Mon-Sat, 11am-6pm Sun; 1, 3, 12, 22, 24

To top off your spa day at Kabuki Springs & Spa (p237), Clary Sage will outfit you with effortlessly flattering tunics made from organic Californian cotton, organic plant-based cleansers and lotions with light, delectable scents, and homeopathic flower-essence stress remedies.

KINOKUNIYA BOOKS & STATIONERY

Map p96 Books, Stationery

☎ 415-567-7625; 1581 Webster St; 10:30am-8pm; 2, 3, 4, 22, 38

Like warriors in a showdown, the bookstore, stationery and manga divisions of Kinokuniya compete for your attention. Only you can decide where your loyalties lie: with stunning photography books and Harajuku fashion mags upstairs, vampire comics downstairs, or the stationery department's *washi* paper, supersmooth Sakura gel pens and pig notebooks with the motto 'what lovely friends*they will bring happy.'

HER

Map p96 Clothing & Accessories

☎ 415-923-9628; www.her-sf.com; 2053 Fillmore St; 11am-7pm Tue-Sat, noon-5pm Sun; 1, 2, 3, 4, 22

Count on Her for universally flattering Ella Moss dresses and pencil skirts that skim your curves. You could get the star treatment with a personal shopper from Her dispatched to your home, but then you'd miss the smoking-hot sales rack for deals of up to 70% off.

MARC BY MARC JACOBS

Map p96 Clothing & Accessories

☎ 415-447-9322; www.marcjacobs.com; 2142 Fillmore St; 11am-7pm; 1, 2, 3, 4, 22

The USA's hippest designer usually charges prices to match, but here alongside the $800 satchels and $300 flip-flops are bins of accessories under $25: $6 chunky resin bangles, $14 yellow belts and limited-edition $24 clutches with funky designs by SF's own Creativity Explored (p119).

SUPER7

Map p96 Clothing & Accessories, Local Designer

☎ 415-409-4701; www.super7store.com; 1628 Post St; ⏰ noon-7pm Mon-Thu, noon-8:30pm Fri, 11am-8:30pm Sat, 11am-7pm Sun; 🚌 2, 3, 4, 38

After tiresome T-shirt trends of self-promotion ('Porn Star') and retro-irony ('Virginia is for Lovers'), it's a shock to find piles of limited-edition T-shirts this original. 'Superterrific Animal Friendlies' announces one Super7 T-shirt with an unlikely superhero team of cuddly owls, bats and monkeys; 'Martial Art Garfunkel' proclaims another, with the 'Mrs Robinson' crooner striking a karate pose. Godzilla fans cannot miss the selection of rare action figures here.

SOKO HARDWARE

Map p96 DIY, Housewares

☎ 415-931-5510; 1698 Post St; ⏰ 9am-5:30pm Mon-Sat; 🚌 2, 3, 4, 22, 38

Cover all your San Francisco contingencies: window wipes (for fog), duct tape (for earthquakes), paper lanterns (to disguise those awkward Victorian chandeliers) and a rice cooker (because soggy rice is a culinary crime in SF). Ikebana, bonsai, tea ceremony and Zen rock-garden supplies are all here at fair prices.

KATSURA GARDEN

Map p96 Flowers & Gardens

☎ 415-931-6209; 1581 Webster St; ⏰ 10am-5:30pm Mon-Sat, 11am-5pm Sun; 🚌 2, 3, 4, 22, 38

When you're in the mood for a little something special, try a bonsai. Katsura Garden can set you up with a miniature juniper that looks like it grew on a windswept molehill, or a stunted maple that will shed five tiny, perfect red leaves this autumn.

ICHIBAN KAN Map p96

Gifts

☎ 415-409-0472; 22 Peace Plaza, Suite 540; ⏰ 10:30am-8pm; 🚌 2, 3, 4, 22, 38

Really, it's a wonder you got this far in life without penguin soy-sauce dispensers, chocolate-covered pretzelS 'Men's Pocky,' extra-spiky Japanese hair wax, soap dishes with feet, and the ultimate in gay gag gifts, the handy 'Closet Case' – all for under $5.

KOHSHI

Map p96 Gifts

☎ 415-931-2002; www.kohshisf.com; 1737 Post St, Suite 335; ⏰ 11am-7pm Tue-Sun

Let's be honest: San Francisco fog smells better when gently scented by Japanese incense. Here you'll find fragrant sticks for every purpose, from long-burning sandalwood for meditation to cinnamon-tinged Gentle Smile to atone for laundry left too long, plus lovely gift ideas: gentle charcoal soap, cups that look like crumpled paper, and purple Daruma figurines for making wishes.

JONATHAN ADLER

Map p96 Housewares

☎ 415-563-9500; www.jonathanadler.com; 2133 Fillmore St; ⏰ 11am-7pm Mon-Sat, noon-6pm Sun; 🚌 1, 2, 3, 4, 22

Vases with handlebar mustaches and cookie jars labeled 'Quaaludes' may seem like holdovers from a Big Sur bachelor pad c 1974, but they're the latest snappy interior inspirations from California pop potter (and *Top Design* judge) Jonathan Adler. Don't worry whether that leather pig footstool matches your mid-century couch – as Adler says, 'Minimalism is a bummer.'

ZINC DETAILS

Map p96 Housewares

☎ 415-776-2100; www.zincdetails.com; 1905 Fillmore St; ⏰ 11am-7pm Mon-Sat, noon-6pm Sun; 🚌 2, 3, 4, 22, 38

Pacific Heights chic meets Japantown mod at Zinc Details, with orange lacquerware salad-tossers, a Rondo sake dispenser that looks like a Zen garden boulder, and bird-shaped Alessi soy dispensers. If you can't find what you need here, try up the street at Zinc's 2410 California St location.

CROSSROADS

Map p96 Vintage Clothing & Accessories

☎ 415-775-8885; www.crossroadstrading.com; 1901 Fillmore St; ⏰ 11am-7pm Mon-Thu, 11am-8pm Fri & Sat, noon-7pm Sun; 🚌 1, 2, 3, 4, 22

Pssst, fashionistas: you know those designers you see lining Fillmore St? Many of their creations can be found used at Crossroads for a fraction of retail, thanks to Pacific Heights clotheshorses who tire of clothes fast and can't be bothered to hang onto receipts. That's why this Crossroads store is better than the other ones in the city (including Market and Haight Sts). For even better deals, trade in your own old stuff and browse the half-price rack.

THE MARINA & THE PRESIDIO

PAST PERFECT

Map pp100–1 Antiques & Collectibles

☎ 415-929-7651; 2230 Union St; 🕑 11am-7pm; 🚌 22, 41, 45

So this is how Pacific Heights eccentrics fill up those mansions: Fornasetti face plates, Danish teak credenzas and Lucite champagne buckets. The store is a collective, so prices are all over the place – some sellers apparently believe their belongings owe them back rent, while others are happy just to unload their ex's mother's prized spoon collection.

SUMBODY

Map pp100–1 Beauty Products, Local Maker

☎ 415-775-6343; www.sumbody.com; 2167 Union St; 🕑 10am-6pm Mon-Wed, to 7pm Thu-Sat, to 6pm Sun; 🚌 22, 41, 45

Tans are too LA; in SF everyone is after that dewy, fogged-in-for-months fresh face. This Sebastopol-based company uses natural ingredients like rice bran and honey in the aptly named Rice & Shine facial wash, kava kava in the narcolepsy-inducing Knockout Bath Melt, and coconut cream in sea-salt scrubs that leave you as emollient as a Pier 39 sea lion.

MINGLE

Map pp100–1 Clothing & Accessories, Local Designer

☎ 415-674-8811; www.mingleshop.com; 1815 Union St; 🕑 11am-7pm Mon-Fri, 10:30am-7pm Sat, 11am-7pm Sun; 🚌 41, 45, 47, 49, 76

To break up the khaki monotony of the Gap and wrest free of H&M trends, get out there and Mingle with SF designers. Local designers keep this boutique stocked with hot Cleopatra-collar dresses, mod ring-buckled bags and plaid necklaces, all for less than you'd pay for Marc Jacobs on mega-sale. Men emerge from Mingle date-ready in dark tailored denim and black Western shirts with white piping – the SF version of a tux.

MY ROOMMATE'S CLOSET

Map pp100–1 Clothing & Accessories

☎ 415-447-7703; www.myroommatescloset.com; 3044 Fillmore St; 🕑 11am-6:30pm Mon-Fri, 11am-6pm Sat, noon-5pm Sun; 🚌 22, 28, 41, 43, 45

All the half-off bargains and none of the clawing dangers of a sample sale. You'll find cloudlike Catherine Malandrino chiffon party dresses, executive-office Diane Von Furstenburg wrap dresses, and designer denim at prices approaching reality.

UKO

Map pp100–1 Clothing & Accessories

☎ 415-563-0330; 2070 Union St; 🕑 11am-6:30pm Mon-Sat, noon-5:30pm Sun; 🚌 22, 28, 41, 43, 45

Laser-cut, draped and micro-pleated are the fashion-forward signatures of Uko's inventive garments for men and women. Get bonus fashion IQ points for clever jackets with hidden pockets-within-pockets, Cop-Copine wrap skirts with oddly flattering flaps, and silver drop earrings that add an exclamation point to your look.

PLUMPJACK WINES

Map pp100–1 Food & Drink, Local Makers

☎ 415-346-9870; www.plumpjack.com; 3201 Fillmore St; 🕑 11am-8pm Mon-Fri, to 8pm Sat, to 6pm Sun; 🚌 22, 28, 41, 43, 45

Discover a new favorite organically grown California vintage under $30 at the distinctive wine boutique that won former owner Mayor Gavin Newsom respect from even Green Party gourmets. A more knowledgeable staff is hard to find anywhere in SF, and they'll set you up with the right bottles to cross party lines.

ATYS

Map pp100–1 Housewares

☎ 415-441-9220; www.atysdesign.com; 2149b Union St; 🕑 11am-6:30pm Mon-Sat, noon-6pm Sun; 🚌 22, 41, 45

Tucked away in a courtyard, this design showcase offers version 2.0 of essential household items: a mirrored coat rack, a rechargeable flashlight that turns a wineglass into a lamp, and a zero-emissions solar-powered toy airplane.

SPORTS BASEMENT

Map pp100–1 Sporting Goods

☎ 415-437-0100; www.sportsbasement.com; 610 Old Mason St; 🕑 9am-9pm Mon-Fri, 8am-8pm Sat & Sun; 🚌 15

All you triathletes who desperately need your gait analyzed or your kiddies outfitted with rental snowboards, you've come to the right place – and so have all you slackers looking to cadge a free coffee or hot cider in the Presidio. This 70,000 sq ft of sports and camping equipment was once a US Army PX, which is why you'll find hiking boots near the Fresh Produce sign.

SOMA

SFMOMA MUSEUM STORE

Map pp110–11 Books, Gifts

☎ 415-357-4000; www.sfmoma.org/museumstore; 151 3rd St; ⌚ 10am-6:30pm Mon-Wed & Fri-Sun, to 9:30pm Thu; 🚌 6, 7, 14, 21, 31, 71, F, J, K, L, M, N; 🚌 & Ⓜ Montgomery St

Design fetishists may have to be pried away from the glass shelves and display cases, which brim with porcelain carafes shaped like logs, chirping bird pencil-clip holders and watches with a face to match Mario Botta's black-and-white SFMOMA facade. Contemporary art books will keep aspiring collectors absorbed for hours, and kids will be entranced by William Wegman's video of dogs spelling out the alphabet.

GAMA-GO

Map pp110–11 Clothing & Accessories, Local Designer

☎ 415-626-0213; www.gama-go.com; 335 8th St; ⌚ noon-6pm Mon-Fri, to 5pm Sat & Sun; 🚌 12, 19, F, J, K, L, M, N; 🚌 & Ⓜ Civic Center

Every one of SF-designer Gama-Go's products seems calibrated to hit the fascination nerve: a bacon-printed billfold, T-shirts with owls balancing on dandelions, and a brown hoodie with a rampaging baby-blue Bigfoot. Gama-Go is distributed nationally, but here in the showroom you'll find 70% off last season's lines and $30 Mysterious Fortune grab-bags of sample and discontinued goods.

ISDA & CO

Map pp110–11 Clothing & Accessories, Local Designer

☎ 415-512-1610; www.isda-and-co.com; 21 S Park Ave; ⌚ 10am-6pm Mon-Sat; 🚌 10, 15, 30, 76, N, T

Sharp SF urban professionals aren't born into casual Friday elegance – they probably clawed their way up through racks of pin-tucked jackets and tie-front cardigans at this local designer outlet. Colors are mostly variations on a charcoal-gray theme, but the lean silhouette is shamelessly flattering.

JEREMY'S

Map pp110–11 Clothing & Accessories

☎ 415-882-4929; www.jeremys.com; 2 S Park St; ⌚ 11am-6pm Mon-Sat, to 5pm Sun; 🚌 10, 15, 30, 76, N, T

No South Park excursion would be complete without swapping stories about your all-time-best bargains from Jeremy's. Runway modelling, window displays and department store customer returns translate to jaw-dropping bargains on major designers for men and women. Men's stuff gets picked over faster, but you could score a skinny Jil Sander suit at half off if you work fast. Try before you buy – returns are possible for store credit, but only within seven days.

ROLO GARAGE

Map pp110–11 Clothing & Accessories

☎ 415-355-1122; www.rolo.com; 1235 Howard St; ⌚ 11am-7pm Mon-Sat, noon-6pm Sun; 🚌 12,19, F, J, K, L, M, N; 🚌 & Ⓜ Civic Center

You'd go out tonight, but you haven't got a stitch to wear? Rolo Garage fixes that old excuse at 30% to 60% off retail price for club-ready menswear, including artfully distressed G-Star jeans, a French military jacket by SF's own Nice Collective, a stag shirt so everyone is clear on your single status, and sunglasses for tomorrow morning.

MADAME S & MR S LEATHER

Map pp110–11 Costumes & Fetish Wear

☎ 800-746-7677; www.madame-s.com; 385 8th St; ⌚ 11am-7pm; 🚌 12, 19, F, J, K, L, M, N; 🚌 & Ⓜ Civic Center

Only in San Francisco would an S&M superstore outsize Home Depot, with such musts as suspension stirrups, latex hoods and, for that special someone, a chrome-plated codpiece. If you've been a very bad puppy, there's an entire department catering to you here, and gluttons for punishment will find home decor inspiration in Dungeon Furniture.

top picks

SF FOODIE SUPPLIES

- **Omnivore** (p155) Signed cookbooks.
- **Ferry Plaza Farmers' Market** (p169) Andante cheeses and Marin Sun Farms boar.
- **Kamei Restaurant Supply** (p161) Amuse-bouche plates.
- **Le Sanctuaire** (p144) Molecular gastronomy makings.
- **PlumpJack Wines** (opposite) Local wines under $30.

SAN FRANCISCO FLOWER MART

Map pp110–11 Flowers & Gardens

☎ 415-781-8410; www.sfflmart.com; 640 Brannan St; 10am-3pm Mon-Sat; 27, 42, N

When you're in San Francisco, in love, and in the doghouse, do what the locals do: bring armloads of relentlessly cheerful sunflowers, bask in forgiveness and never let on that you got them cheap at the Flower Mart. Many of the 80 flower and plant vendors offer seasonal flowers grown locally, not flown in, so you can enjoy your greenery the green way.

GENERAL BEAD Map pp110–11 Jewelry, DIY

☎ 415-255-2323; www.genbead.com; 637 Minna St; 10am-5pm Tue-Fri, 10am-6pm Sat, noon-5pm Sun; 12, 19, F, J, K, L, M, N; & Civic Center

Blind beading ambition will seize you when you're upstairs among the racks of bagged bulk beads, where visions of holiday gifts for the entire family appear like mirages: multi-tiered necklaces, sequined seascapes, beaded frames, lampshades even. To practice restraint, order smaller quantities downstairs from the bead-bedecked staff behind the counter, who will ring you up on bejeweled calculators.

GOODWILL 'AS IS' SHOP

Map pp110–11 Vintage Clothing & Accessories

☎ 415-575-2197; www.sfgoodwill.org; 86 11th St; 8am-3:30pm; & Civic Center

'Ooh, that wedding dress would look fierce with some blood on it!' Getting to the bottom of the bin before the regular crowds of emerging designers, vintage resellers, drag queens, serial costume-partiers and the rest of San Francisco's fashion rebels isn't always easy, but every item costs $2.50 and the commentary is priceless.

THE MISSION & POTRERO HILL

BLACK & BLUE TATTOO

Map pp116–17 Body Art

☎ 415-626-0770; www.blackandbluetattoo.com; 381 Guerrero St; noon-7pm; 14, 22, 26, 33; 16th St Mission

This women-owned-and-operated tattoo parlor gets it in ink with designs that range from graphic armbands to shoulder-to-shoulder spans of the Golden Gate Bridge. Check out the artists' work at the shop or online first for ideas, then book a consultation with the artist whose work interests you most. Once you've talked over the design, you can book your tattoo – you'll need to show up sober, well-fed and clear-headed for your transformation.

ADOBE BOOKS & BACKROOM GALLERY

Map pp116–17 Books, Art

☎ 415-864-3936; 3166 16th St; 11am-midnight; 14, 22, 33, 49; 16th St Mission

Come here for every book you never knew you needed – used and cheap. But first you'll have to navigate the obstacle course of sofas, cats, art books and German philosophy. Head to the tiny art gallery in back to discover emerging artists at reasonable prices.

CANDYSTORE COLLECTIVE

Map pp116–17 Clothing & Accessories

☎ 415-887-7637; www.candystorecollective.com; 3153 16th St; noon-7pm Mon-Sat, to 6pm Sun; 14, 26, 33, 49; 16th St Mission

Jars of Pixie Stix and tasty little numbers for men and women by indie designers. Slippery silk dresses in graphic prints by Corey Lynn Calter stand out in Mission bar crowds, while cozy motorcycle jackets made of grey sweatshirt fabric keep vegan bikers warm. Don't miss intoxicating Yosh perfumes, chunky aquamarine collars, and 70%-off sales bins.

DEMA

Map pp116–17 Clothing & Accessories, Local Designer

☎ 415-206-0500; www.godemago.com; 1038 Valencia St; 11am-7pm Mon-Fri, noon-7pm Sat, noon-6pm Sun; 14, 22, 26, 33, 49; 24th St Mission

BART from Downtown lunches to Mission art openings in vintage-inspired chic by San Francisco's own Dema Grimm. House specialties are nostalgic bias-cut dresses and tie-top blouses with buttons that look like gumdrops. Like any original designer, Dema's not dirt-cheap, but you get what you pay for here in squealed compliments; check bins and sales racks for deals up to 80% off.

FABRIC8

Map pp116–17 Clothing & Accessories, Local Designer

☎ 415-647-5888; www.fabric8.com; 3318 22nd St; 5-7pm Mon-Fri, 11am-7pm Sat & Sun; 14, 26, 33, 49; 24th St Mission

Pull into this Astro-turfed-garage-turned-indie-design-boutique for a Mission hipster style overhaul. Rings sprout tiny volcanic geodes, local DJs remix '80s one-hit-wonders into hyphy jams, and just to be contrarian, you'll find Oakland-cityscape tees.

GOOD VIBRATIONS

Map pp116–17 Clothing & Accessories, Local Designer

☎ 415-522-5460; www.goodvibes.com; 603 Valencia St; noon-7pm Mon-Wed, noon-8pm Thu, noon-9pm Fri, 11am-9pm Sat, 11am-7pm Sun; 14, 22, 33, 49; 16th St Mission

'Wait, I'm supposed to put that where?' The understanding salespeople in this worker-owned cooperative are used to giving rather, um, explicit instructions, so don't hesitate to ask – Margaret Cho is on the board, so you know they're not shy here. Check out the antique vibrators on the back wall, and imagine getting up close and personal with the one that looks like a floor waxer – then thank your stars for modern technology.

MISSION SKATEBOARDS

Map pp116–17 Clothing & Accessories, Sporting Goods

☎ 415-647-7888; www.missionsk8boards.com; 3045 24th St; 11am-7pm; 14, 26, 33, 49; 24th St Mission

Street creds come easy with locally designed decks, tees to kick-flip over, and Toms canvas shoes, where for every pair sold, one is gifted to kids in need (140,000 pairs donated to date). This shop is handy to Potrero del Sol/La Raza Skatepark (p120), and for newbies too cool for kneepads, SF General.

MISSION STATEMENT

Map pp116–17 Clothing & Accessories, Local Designer

☎ 415-255-7457; www.missionstatementsf.com; 3458 18th St; noon-8pm; 14, 22, 33, 49; 16th St Mission

Finally: locally designed, fashion-forward clothing and accessories that keep real people, real bodies and real budgets in mind. Sofie Ølgaard's drop-waisted silk sheaths are drop-dead gorgeous, Vanessa Gade's circle-chain necklaces bring a touch of infinity to your neckline, and Estrella Tadao's reconstructed '70s men's jackets revive radical-chic Maoist placket pockets. The counter staff at this collective are designers, so if that yellow bamboo-fiber wrap cardigan doesn't fit just so, they'll get one made to order for you on the spot.

SECESSION ART & DESIGN

Map pp116–17 Clothing & Accessories, Arts & Crafts

☎ 415-279-3058; www.secessionsf.com; 3361 Mission St; noon-7pm Tue & Thu-Sat; 14, 26, 49; 24th St Mission

Every weekend is an open studio event at this local designer/artist collective. Permanent installations include Colleen Mauer's loop-de-loop earrings and Heather Robinson's mysterious paintings of spoons and hammers poking through ornate wallpaper; recent gallery shows featured Anna Simson's abstract, color-blocked cityscapes and graffiti artist FuryOne's gritty, dreamy spray-paint portraits.

SUNHEE MOON

Map pp116–17 Clothing & Accessories, Local Designer

☎ 415-355-1800; www.sunheemoon.com; 3167 16th St; noon-7pm Mon-Fri, to 6pm Sat & Sun; 14, 22, 33, 49; 16th St Mission

Minding your girlish figure so you don't have to, Sunhee Moon creates svelte shirt-dresses and flattering tree-print tunics to make those curves work for you. You'll never need to wait for a sale, since there's always a rack with 20% to 50% off – yet another excuse to splurge on locally designed, free-form hoop earrings.

NEEDLES & PENS

Map pp116–17 DIY, Local Designer

☎ 415-255-1534; www.needles-pens.com; 3253 16th St; noon-7pm; 14, 22, 33, 49; 16th St Mission

Do it yourself or DIY trying: this scrappy zine/craft/how-to/art gallery delivers the inspiration to create your own magazines, rehabbed T-shirts or album covers. Nab Sara Thustra's silkscreened zines with drawings of every household purchase for a year, Maria Forde's 'advice portraits' of neighbors and their wisdom (eg 'don't wax on what you can't wax off') and recycled T-shirts screen-printed with portraits of famous suffragists.

SCRAP (SCROUNGERS' CENTER FOR RE-USABLE ART PARTS)

off Map pp116–17 DIY

☎ 415-647-1746; www.scrap-sf.org; 801 Toland St; 9am-5pm Tue-Sat

Renew, recycle and rediscover your creativity with post-industrial salvage arts and crafts from SCRAP – you'd be shocked what perfectly good raw materials San Francisco throws out. Take a workshop at SCRAP for inspiration, and make your very own Tupperware lamp, necklace from Barbie parts or Joseph Cornell–inspired diorama. Classes are held in the city (see website for locations); the entrance to SCRAP is at the confluence of Hwy 101 and Hwy 280, south of SoMa.

LITTLE OTSU

Map pp116–17 Gifts, Local Designer

☎ 415-255-7900; www.littleotsu.com; 849 Valencia St; 11:30am-7:30pm; 14, 22, 33, 49; 16th St Mission

Finally, organizational tools for the artistically inclined: a 'Film Diary' so you can keep track of your SF Film Festival favorites, Keri Smith's free-form 'Daily Non-Planner' so you can make dates and capture ideas when so moved, and a Simon Evans airplane bookmark that ominously declares its destination as 'TERMINAL EXCESSIVE SENSIBILITIES.' Stationery with jellyfish printed in vegetable inks on 100% post-consumer recycled paper makes an eco-smart gift, and everyone deserves a wombat button.

PAXTON GATE

Map pp116–17 Gifts, Flowers & Gardens

☎ 415-824-1872; www.paxton-gate.com; 824 Valencia St; noon-7pm Mon-Fri, 11am-7pm Sat & Sun; 14, 22, 33, 49; 16th St Mission

Salvador Dali probably would've shopped here for all his taxidermy and gardening needs. What with puppets made with animal skulls, a stuffed mouse dressed like the Pope, a vast selection of pruning shears and lollipops with actual worms in them, this place is beyond surreal. The new kids shop down the street is worthy of Lemony Snickett, with volcano-making kits, sea-monster mobiles and solar-powered dollhouses.

CLAUDIA KUSSANO

Map pp116–17 Jewelry, Local Maker

☎ 415-671-0769; www.claudiakussano.com; 591 Guerrero St; noon-7pm Mon-Fri, to 6pm Sat & Sun; 14, 22, 33, 49; 16th St Mission

Meteorites, dewdrops, eucalyptus buds and other natural wonders inspire delicate, fascinating jewelry by San Francisco designer Kussano. Fiddlehead fern earrings evoke the California Academy of Science's rainforest dome, and pod necklaces look like rare specimens from Crissy Field's marshlands.

ADS HATS

Map pp116–17 Millinery, Local Designer

☎ 415-503-1316; www.adshats.com; 418 Valencia St; noon-7pm Wed-Sat, to 5pm Sun; 14, 26, 33, 49; 16th St Mission

Hats come in handy in SF almost year-round, and this local hat-maker collective sells super-fly lids to keep the fog from chilling your scalp: distressed-leather newsboys, unisex bowlers, svelte 1920s cloches and floppy numbers that would do Janis Joplin proud.

AQUARIUS RECORDS

Map pp116–17 Music

☎ 415-647-2272; www.aquariusrecords.org; 1055 Valencia St; 10am-9pm Mon-Wed, to 10pm Thu-Sun; 14, 26, 33, 49; 16th St Mission

When pop seems played out, this is the dawning of the age of Aquarius Records, featuring Armenian blues, rare 1970s recordings by SF's Moog-powered punk rockers The Units, and new releases of blissed-out trance on – get this – cassette. Recent staff favorites include Ethiopian funkmaster Mahmoud Ahmed, groovy Brazilian garage rockers Bango and aluminum records of sci-fi synth by Finnish band Aavikko.

DISCOLANDIA

Map pp116–17 Music

☎ 415-826-9446; 2964 24th St; 11:30am-6:30pm Mon-Sat, noon-4pm Sun; 48; 24th St Mission

The oldest Latin-music store in the Bay Area and as funky as ever, making passersby step in time with merengue, salsa and Tejano blasting out the door. Get yours on CD or vintage vinyl, and stock up on Spanish-language mags, adult comics and pulp fiction.

COMMUNITY THRIFT

Map pp116–17 Vintage Clothing & Accessories

☎ 415-861-4910; www.communitythriftsf.org; 623 Valencia St; 10am-6:30pm; 14, 22, 33, 49; 16th St Mission

When local collectors and retailers have too much of a good thing, they donate it to Community Thrift, where proceeds go to community organizations – all the more reason to gloat over your $6 ikebana vase, $7 '80s mohair cardigan and that $35 art deco cigar humidor you found out back by the furniture. Donate your own unused stuff and show some love to the Community.

ROOM 4 Map pp116–17 Vintage Clothing & Accessories, Housewares

☎ 415-647-2764; www.room4.com; 904 Valencia St; noon-7pm; 14, 22, 33, 49; 16th St Mission

Spare yourself years of arduous thrifting, and head to this tiny treasure-box boutique for the good stuff: trippy green and orange enamel dishes; a pair of pearlescent dewdrop-shaped lamps; creepy portraits of big-eyed toddlers in the rain; and locally designed underwear made of vintage T-shirt fabric that is styled for boys, but cute enough for girly-girls.

THE CASTRO & NOE VALLEY

OMNIVORE Map p123 Books

☎ 415-282-4712; www.omnivorebooks.com; 3885a Cesar Chavez St; 11am-6pm Mon-Sat, noon-5pm Sun; 24, 48, J

Salivate over signed cookbooks by chef-legend Alice Waters, A16's James Beard Rising Star Chef Nate Appelbaum, and signed copies of *Omnivore's Dilemma* by Michael Pollan. Check the in-store events calendar for standing-room-only events with star chefs, and don't miss the collection of vintage cookbooks and such rarities as a Civil War–era recipe-book, written longhand.

AMBIANCE Map p123 Clothing & Accessories

☎ 415-647-7144/5800; www.ambiancesf.com; 3985 & 3989 24th St; 11am-7pm Mon-Fri, 10am-7pm Sat, 11am-7pm Sun; 24, 48, J

The splashy prints reel you in, and the sales pitch works every time: 'Oh. My. God. That looks so *key-oot* on you!' Expect to emerge clutching some little number requiring you to hit the town: swingy skirts for Lindy-hopping in Golden Gate Park, or DNA-pattern jackets for biotech lectures. The shoe-and-sale store next door encourages you to keep the retail rush going, while the sister store at 1458 Haight St features teen-appropriate prom dresses, and 1858 Union St in the Marina offers cocktail attire.

ISSO Map p123 Clothing & Accessories, Local Designer

☎ 415-920-9149; www.issosf.com; 3789 24th St; 11am-7pm Mon-Sat, noon-6pm Sun; 24, 48, J

'Made, found or designed in the Bay Area' is the motto of this purveyor of swingy, organic jersey dresses by SF designer SheBible, T-shirts with linocut portraits of Chaka Khan and Fela Kuti by Oakland's Nopal Apparel, and mod '60s white vinyl purses – all at sample-sale prices.

SUI GENERIS Map p123 Clothing & Accessories

☎ 415-436-9661; www.myspace.com/suigeneris_sfo; 2265 Market St; noon-7pm Wed & Thu, to 8pm Fri & Sat, to 4pm Sun; 24, F, K, L, M, Castro St

Even guys who thought they'd never go back in the closet crowd into this walk-in wardrobe of a boutique, with its streamlined Costume National jackets and crisp, slim-fit Filippa K shirts in front and deadstock rock tees in back. The selection is best for men who fit runway-model sizes, yet have relatively fat wallets – don't think of them as clothes but collectibles, and auction them off on eBay next year.

CLIFF'S VARIETY Map p123 DIY, Housewares

☎ 415-431-5365; www.cliffsvariety.com; 479 Castro St; 8:30am-8pm Mon-Fri, 9:30am-8pm Sat, 11am-6pm Sun; 24, 33, F, K, L, M, Castro St

None of the hardware maestros at Cliff's will raise an eyebrow if you express a dire need for a 4x4 beam, a jar of rubber nuns, non-toxic silver paint and more cocktail toothpicks than anyone can safely use in a lifetime, though they might angle for an invitation. The window displays at Cliff's, a community institution since 1936, are a local landmark.

GIVEN Map p123 Gifts

☎ 415-865-0353; www.givenonline.com; 575 Castro St; 11am-7pm Sun-Thu, to 8pm Fri & Sat; 24, 33, F, K, L, M, Castro St

Have no fear of birthdays: it's a Given that you'll find worthy gifts for all ages in this emporium of offbeat design, from Kimochi the cuddly cloud to a wallet disguised as a memo-pad. If this storefront seems familiar, you're right: this was once Harvey Milk's camera shop (p35), and the shop closed for six weeks so that the Academy Award–winning *Milk* could be filmed here.

GLOBAL EXCHANGE FAIR TRADE CRAFT CENTER Map p123 Gifts, Housewares

☎ 415-648-8068; www.globalexchangestore.org; 4018 24th St; 11am-6pm Sun-Thu, 11am-7pm Fri, 10am-7pm Sat; 24, 48, J

Consumerism with a heart of gold: wild splurges on splashy Rwandan laptop bags, fair-trade chocolate, sweatshop-free sneakers from Pakistan and crates of smiling, organic-Egyptian-cotton carrots seem somehow noble, since the proceeds go right back to the community cooperatives that made them via nonprofit Global Exchange.

HUMAN RIGHTS CAMPAIGN ACTION CENTER & STORE Map p123 Gifts

☎ 415-431-2200; www.hrc.org; 600 Castro St; 10am-7pm; 24, 33, F, K, L, M, Castro St

Make more than a fashion statement in a Heatherette 'Love is Real' tank or signature HRC tees designed by Marc Jacobs, Kenneth Cole and other fashion-forward thinkers, with proceeds supporting civil rights initiatives. Hopeful romantics head here to sign marriage-equality petitions and pop the question with rings inscribed on the inside with *Aequalitas* (Equality).

UNDER ONE ROOF
Map p123 Gifts, Housewares

☎ 415-503-2300; www.underoneroof.org; 518a Castro St; 10am-9pm; 24, 33, F, K, L, M, Castro St

All the fabulous gift ideas under this roof are donated by local designers and businesses, so AIDS service organizations get 100% of the proceeds from your indispensable elephant tape dispenser, etched San Francisco skyline martini glasses and adorable Jonathan Adler vase. Those sweet sales clerks are volunteers, so show them some love for raising – get this – $11 million to date.

KENNETH WINGARD
Map p123 Housewares, Local Designer

☎ 415-431-6900; www.kennethwingard.com; 2319 Market St; 10am-7pm Mon-Sat, noon-6pm Sun; 24, 33, F, K, L, M, Castro St

Upgrade from ho-hum IKEA with mod housewares priced for mass consumption that are positively scrumptious: glossy tangerine bud vases, vintage tiki-fabric cushions and mood-setting, ecofriendly cork-shaded lamps.

MABEL CHONG
Map p123 Jewelry, Local Designer

☎ 415-550-1665; www.mabelchong.com; 1311 Church St; noon-6pm; 24, 48, J

Sparkling wit is the specialty of local jewelry designer Mabel Chong, who combines painstaking craft with a touch of San Francisco whimsy: 'Pinot Gris' earrings are clusters of tiny seed pearls, while an asymmetrical chalcedony drop necklace is dubbed 'Formula for the Hypotenuse.'

PHOTOWORKS Map p123 Photo Processing

☎ 415-626-6800; www.photoworkssf.com; 2077a Market St; 10am-7pm Mon-Fri, 11am-6pm Sat, noon-5pm Sun; F, N

Quick, pro-quality photo processing and printing for film and digital shooters, plus bonus creative services: digital pics can be printed on classic Ilford black-and-white paper or on canvas, so you can make it into a pillow.

DE LA SOLE Map p123 Shoes

☎ 415-255-3140; www.delasole.com; 549 Castro St; 11am-7pm Sun-Fri, to 8pm Sat; 24, 33, F, K, L, M, Castro St

SF gets its kicks at De La Sole, from mod Ryan Rowe white wing-tips to radiator-vented sandals by Montreal brand Industry. Says the sales rep to a customer squeezing into a 60%-off gold ankleboot: 'Don't worry, it won't always be so tight.' Chimes in a fellow customer, without missing a beat: 'That's what they all say.'

THE HAIGHT

BRAINDROPS Map pp126–7 Body Art

☎ 415-621-4162; www.braindrops.net; 1324 Haight St; noon-7pm Sun-Thu, to 8pm Fri & Sat; 6, 7, 33, 37, 43, 71

New Yorkers and Berliners fly in for original custom designs by top tattoo artists here – bring design ideas to your consultant, or trust them to make suggestions. Piercings are done here gently without a gun, with body jewelry ranging from pop-star opal belly-button studs to mondo jade ear spools.

BOUND TOGETHER ANARCHIST BOOK COLLECTIVE Map pp126–7 Books

☎ 415-431-8355; www.boundtogetherbooks.com; 1369 Haight St; 11:30am-7:30pm; 6, 7, 33, 37, 43, 71

Given the state of the economy lately, an anarchist bookstore seems like the go-to place for answers. Since 1976, this volunteer-run, nonprofit bookstore has kept free thinkers supplied with organic farming manuals, prison literature and radical comics, while coordinating the **Anarchist Book Fair** (p21) and restoring its 'Anarchists of the Americas' storefront mural – makes us tools of the state look like slackers.

AQUA SURF SHOP

Map pp126–7 Clothing & Accessories, Sporting Goods

☎ 415-876-2780; www.aquasurfshop.com; 1742 Haight St; 🕑 11am-7pm; rental per day board/wetsuit $25/15; 🚌 6, 7, 33, 37, 43, 71

No locals-only attitude here: this laid-back, tiki-themed surf shop has sex wax for your board, Bantu's fair-trade African-print bikinis, and signature hoodies to brave chilly Ocean Beach. Even kooks (newbies) become mavericks with Aqua's wetsuit rentals, tide updates and lesson referrals.

DOE

Map pp126–7 Clothing & Accessories, Local Designer

☎ 415-558-8588; 629a Haight St; 🕑 noon-7pm Mon-Sat, to 6pm Sun; 🚌 6, 7, 22, 71, N

Upgrade from the 'I escaped from Alcatraz' shot-glasses to Doe's signature belts featuring the fogged-in Sutro Tower on the buckle, Jill Bliss stationery with unruly California poppies and mushrooms in the margins, or a gold outline of the state of California with a gem inset in (of course) San Francisco.

LOYAL ARMY CLOTHING

Map pp126–7 Clothing & Accessories, Local Designer

☎ 415-221-6200; www.loyalarmy.com; 1728 Haight St; 🕑 10am-8pm Mon-Sat, 11am-7pm Sun; 🚌 6, 7, 33, 37, 43, 71

Food with high self-esteem is a recurring theme on this San Francisco designer's cartoon-cute tees, totes and baby clothes: California rolls brag to nigiri sushi, 'That's how we roll!,' smiling custard declares 'Girls just wanna have flan!' and a grumpy bran muffin surrounded by uber-adorable pink cupcakes protests, 'Muffins are cute on the inside.' But the most popular character is the San Francisco fogbank: most of the clouds are silver and smiling, but there's always one that has fangs.

TRUNK

Map pp126–7 Clothing & Accessories, Local Designer

☎ 415-861-5310; www.trunksf.com; 544 Haight St; 🕑 11am-8pm Wed-Mon; 🚌 6, 7, 22, 71, N

The Burning Man aesthetic rages on year-round at this cooperative boutique, where most items are locally designed and eco-conscious, from Miranda Caroligne's radically reconstructed patchwork sweaters, mesmerizing Dida glass-globe earrings, and high-drama flower barrettes with veils.

UPPER PLAYGROUND

Map pp126–7 Clothing & Accessories, Local Designer

☎ 415-861-1960; www.upperplayground.com; 220 Fillmore St; 🕑 noon-7pm Mon-Fri, 11am-7pm Sat & Sun; 🚌 6, 7, 22, 71, N

Blend into the SF scenery with locally designed Fillmore neighborhood hoodies, Barbary Coast pirate tees and knit Muni caps. Men's gear dominates the main store, but there's an even more impressive selection of locally designed tees in the women's annex, and slick graffiti art in Fifty24SF Gallery next door.

PIEDMONT BOUTIQUE

Map pp126–7 Costumes & Fetish Wear, Local Designer

☎ 415-864-8075; www.piedmontsf.com; 1452 Haight St; 🕑 11am-7pm; 🚌 6, 7, 33, 37, 43, 71

'No food, no cell phones, no playing in the boas,' says the sign at the door, but inside, that last rule is gleefully ignored by cross-dressers, cabaret singers, strippers and people who take Halloween dead seriously. All the getups are custom-designed in-house and built to last – so, like certain escorts, honey, they're not as cheap as they look.

COCO-LUXE

Map pp126–7 Food & Drink, Local Maker

☎ 415-367-4012; www.coco-luxe.com; 1673 Haight St; 🕑 noon-8pm; 🚌 6, 7, 33, 37, 43, 71

The Gold Rush may be over, but the sugar rush is definitely on at this SF chocolate maker reinventing American dessert classics like devil's food cake, malted milkshakes and banana splits as truffles. Cinnamon-candied almonds dunked in chocolate and dusted with cocoa make Block Party Almonds the kind of treat

top picks

LOCAL DESIGNERS

- **Dema** (p152)
- **Loyal Army Clothing** (left)
- **Mabel Chong** (opposite)
- **Delilah Crown** (p147)
- **Upper Playground** (above)

you might not be inclined to share with neighbors.

GOORIN BROTHERS HATS
Map pp126–7 Millinery, Local Designer
☎ 415-436-9450; www.goorin.com; 1446 Haight St; 11am-7pm Sun-Fri, to 8pm Sat; 6, 7, 33, 43, 71
Peacock feathers, high crowns and locally designed embellishments make it easy for SF hipsters to withstand the fog while standing out in a crowd. Straw fedoras with striped tie-silk bands bring the shade in style, and flat-brim baseball caps go high-culture with embroidery of Sumerian hero Gilgamesh destroying the demon Humbaba.

AMOEBA MUSIC Map pp126–7 Music
☎ 415-831-1200; 1855 Haight St; 10:30am-10pm Mon-Sat, 11am-9pm Sun; 6, 7, 33, 37, 43, 71
Enticements are hardly necessary to lure the masses to the West Coast's most eclectic collection of new and used music and video, but Amoeba offers listening stations, a free music zine with uncannily accurate reviews, a free concert series that recently starred Elvis Costello and the Breeders, and a foundation that's saved over 950 acres of rainforest.

SFO SNOWBOARDING & FTC SKATEBOARDING
Map pp126–7 Sporting Goods, Local Maker
☎ 415-626-1141; www.sfosnow.com; 1630 Haight St; 11am-7pm; 6, 7, 33, 37, 43, 71
Big air and big style are the tip at this local snowboard and skateboard outfitter. Show some local style as you grab air on a Western Edition deck tricked out with drawings of Fillmore jazz greats and ramshackle Victorian houses, or hit the slopes with Tahoe-tested gear. Check the website for upcoming SF street games and current Tahoe snow conditions.

BLUEBIRD Map pp126–7 Vintage Clothing & Accessories, Local Designer
☎ 415-206-1107; www.bluebirdcollection.com; 214 Pierce St; 11am-7pm Thu-Sun; 6, 7, 66, 71, N
Even tiny terrors look adorable in Bluebird's flouncy, fun frocks and shoulder-tie sundresses inspired by the 1940s and '50s, when kids weren't expected to strut around like baby Britney Spears. Designer/owner Stephanie Scarpulla is also a vintage clotheshound, so you'll find striped '60s mod minis and dreamy 1970s Gunne Sax maxidresses for women here, too.

WASTELAND
Map pp126–7 Vintage Clothing & Accessories
☎ 415-863-3150; www.wastelandclothing.com; 1660 Haight St; 11am-8pm Mon-Sat, noon-7pm Sun; 71
The catwalk of thrifting, this vintage superstore adds instant style with funky bell-sleeved Custo shirts, Pucci maxi-skirts and a steady supply of go-go boots. Hip occasionally verges on hideous with acrylic sweaters and patchwork suede jackets, but at these prices, you can afford to take fashion risks.

HAYES VALLEY

FLAX Map p133 Art Supplies, DIY
☎ 415-552-2355; www.flaxart.com; 1699 Market St; 9:30am-7pm Mon-Sat; 6, 7, 71, J, K, L, M, N;
People who swear they lack artistic flair suddenly find it at Flax, where an entire room of specialty papers, racks of plump paint tubes in luscious colors, and a wonderland of hot glue guns practically make the collage for you. Kid-art projects start here, and the vast selections of pens and notebooks are novels waiting to happen.

POLANCO Map p133 Arts & Crafts
☎ 415-252-5753; 393 Hayes St; 11am-7pm Tue-Sat, 1-6pm Sun; 6, 7, 21, 71
Contemporary folk art by Mexican and Chicano artists mix traditional techniques and new ideas at Polanco, from Artemio Rodriguez's woodcuts of Day of the Dead skeletons sporting Mohawks to a traditional *ex voto* painting on tin showing before and after portraits of a transgendered friend by Fernando Guevara. Don't miss the Oaxacan devil masks embedded with actual goat's horns and teeth, or the Frida Kahlo–esque earrings of silver hands cupping tiny hearts.

NANCY BOY
Map p133 Beauty Products, Local Maker
☎ 415-552-3802; www.nancyboy.com; 347 Hayes St; 11am-7pm Mon-Fri, to 6pm Sat & Sun; 5, 21, 42, 47, 49
All you closet pomaders and after-sun balmers: wear those products with pride, without feeling like the dupe of some

cosmetics conglomerate. Clever Nancy Boy knows you'd rather pay for the product than for advertising campaigns featuring the starlet du jour, and delivers locally made products with effective plant oils that are tested on boyfriends, never animals.

GREEN ARCADE Map p133 Books

☎ 415-431-6800; www.thegreenarcade.com; 1680 Market St; 🕑 11am-7pm Tue-Sun; 🚌 6, 7, 21, 71

Everything you always wanted to know about foraging for mushrooms, composting with worms and running for office on an environmental platform, but were afraid to ask. This bookstore emphasizes helpful how-to books over eco-apocalypse treatises, so you'll leave with a rosier outlook on how you can make the world a greener place.

ISOTOPE Map p133 Books

☎ 415-621-6543; www.isotopecomics.com; 326 Fell St; 🕑 11am-7pm Tue-Fri, to 6pm Sat & Sun; 🚌 6, 7, 21, 71;

The toilet seats signed by famous cartoonists over the front counter show just how seriously Isotope takes comics. Newbies tentatively flip through Daniel Clowes and Chris Ware in the graphic-novel section, while fanboys load up on Berkeley's Adrian Tomine or the latest from SF's Last Gasp Publishing and head upstairs to lounge with local cartoonists.

DARK GARDEN

Map p133 Clothing & Accessories, Local Designer

☎ 415-431-7684; www.darkgarden.com; 321 Linden St; 🕑 11am-5pm Sun-Tue, to 6pm Wed-Sat; 🚌 6, 7, 21, 71

Not sure what to wear to your Victorian-theme wedding or your Marilyn Manson tribute band's debut? Dark Garden might have your answer, as long as you don't need to take any deep breaths and can get help with the lacing (not exactly a cinch, no matter what they tell you). Corsets are made to order and surprisingly comfortable, especially the va-va-voom velvet numbers.

MAC Map p133 Clothing & Accessories

☎ 415-863-3011; 387 Grove St; 🕑 11am-7pm Mon-Sat, noon-6pm Sun; 🚌 5, 21, 42, 47, 49

'Modern Appealing Clothing' is what they promise, and what they deliver with structured looks from Belgian minimalist Dries Van Noten, pop-art patterns from Van Beirendonck and silk dresses with midnight-blue forest silhouettes by Tsumori Chisato. The staff are on your side, rooting for you to rock these designs, steering you away from looks that don't quite click and enjoying the contact retail high when you find something from the 40%-to-75%-off sales rack.

RESIDENTS APPAREL GALLERY

Map p133 Clothing & Accessories, Local Designer

☎ 415-621-7718; www.ragsf.com; 541 Octavia Blvd; 🕑 noon-7pm Mon-Sat, to 6pm Sun; 🚌 6, 7, 21, 71

Local designers at design-school prices make eclectic SF chic easy at this certified-green cooperative boutique. Take your pick of limited-edition screen-printed tees, locally made designer dark denims (no sweatshops here, thank you), clever reconstructed vintage dresses and designer jewelry in silver, gemstones and recycled comics.

MIETTE Map p133 Food & Drink

☎ 415-626-6221; www.miettecakes.com; 449 Octavia Blvd; 🕑 11am-7pm; 🚌 6, 7, 21, 71, F

Pure candy heaven: racks of licorice twists, a table of artisan chocolate bars and a fully stocked cupcake counter. Tots load up on Pixie Stix and chocolate fire trucks, while adults ogle salty French caramels and dark chocolates spiked with chili. Ask for help first, so that you don't get caught with your hand in the candy jar.

LAVISH Map p133 Gifts, Clothing & Accessories

☎ 415-565-0540; www.shoplavish.com; 540 Hayes St; 🕑 11am-7pm Mon-Sat, to 6pm Sun; 🚌 6, 7, 21, 71, F

Baby shower gifts are a done deal here with teensy superhero capes, eensy unisex pink dumptruck onesies, and weensy moon boots. Splurge on your favorite mom while you're at it, with pin-tucked Plume organic peasant tops and screen-printed hipster hoodies that look nothing like standard-issue momswear.

ECOLOGIQUE

Map p133 Housewares, Local Designer

☎ 415-621-2431; www.shopecologique.com; 141 Gough St; 🕑 noon-8pm Tue-Sat, to 5pm Sun; 🚌 6, 7, 21, 71

Draped bamboo-fleece tops go from office weekdays to redwood-forest weekends effortlessly, and reconstructed vintage bags get upgraded from auntie to avant-garde at this green boutique. Helpful staff help you find your size in locally produced designs and provide precise sourcing info, from fair-traded cotton to the photo-biodegradable packaging.

LOTUS BLEU

Map p133 Housewares, Local Designer

☎ 415-861-2700; www.lotusbleudesign.com; 327 Hayes St; 11am-6pm Tue-Fri, to 7pm Sat, noon-5pm Sun; 5, 21, 42, 47, 49

French whimsy, Vietnamese design and a San Franciscan love of splashy color keeps eyes open wide in this tiny design boutique packed from basement to rafters with linen pillows with psychedelic blooms, French striped canvas totes, and pop-art lacquer breakfast trays.

PEACE INDUSTRY

Map p133 Housewares, Local Designer

☎ 415-255-9940; www.peaceindustry.com; 539 Octavia Blvd; 10am-6pm Mon-Fri, 11am-6pm Sat, 11am-5pm Sun; 6, 7, 21, 71

Persian carpets usually take credit for grand entrances, but Peace Industry's cooperative-made Iranian felted wool rugs offer graphic appeal and a deliciously spongy, ticklish texture. Get back to nature with a dewdrop pattern in off-white and brown wool, go arty with Ruth Asawa–inspired orbs, or opt for a single flower underfoot.

GIMME SHOES

Map p133 Shoes

☎ 415-864-0691; www.gimmeshoes.com; 416 Hayes St; 11am-7pm Mon-Sat, noon-6pm Sun; 6, 7, 21, 71

Don't let SF hills become your arch-rivals: head to Gimme Shoes and kick up those high-end heels. Bide your time and those coral Dries Van Noten kitten heels might hit the 40%-to-60%-off rack alongside Chie Mihara acid-yellow-and-eggplant slingbacks. Men have their pick of limited-edition exoskeleton Pumas by Alexander McQueen and pewter Converse by Varvatos.

FLIGHT 001

Map p133 Travel Accessories

☎ 415-487-1001; www.flight001.com; 525 Hayes St; 11am-7pm Mon-Sat, to 6pm Sun; 6, 7, 21, 71

Having a nice flight in the zero-legroom era is actually a possibility with the in-flight assistance of Flight 001. Clever carry-ons built to fit international size regulations come with just the right number of pockets for rubber alarm clocks, travel Scrabble sets and the first-class Jet Comfort Kit with earplugs, sleep mask, booties, neck rest, candy and cards.

GOLDEN GATE PARK & THE AVENUES

PARK LIFE

Map pp136–7 Art, Books

☎ 415-386-7275; www.parklifestore.com; 220 Clement St; noon-8pm Mon-Thu, 11am-9pm Fri & Sat, 11am-7pm Sun; 1, 2, 33, 38, 44;

Is Park Life a design store, an art gallery or an indie publisher? All of the above, with limited-edition scores that include flashlight-shaped candles, Styrofoam coffee cups recast in sustainable ceramic, and Park Life's own publications on graffiti artist Andrew Schoultz. The back gallery shows rising art stars such as Alexis McKenzie, whose surreal collages show animals spelling out the words 'Never Be Sad.'

GREEN APPLE BOOKS

Map pp136–7 Books

☎ 415-387-2272; 506 Clement St; 10am-10:30pm Sun-Thu, to 11:30pm Fri & Sat; 1, 2, 33, 38, 44;

Blissed-out booklovers emerge blinking into the sunset after an entire day browsing three floors of new releases, used titles and staff picks more reliable than *New York Times* reviews. Local favorites are easy to spot in the local interest section – look for the local author tag. You can sell your books here, but be prepared for rejection – they can afford to be picky. Don't miss the annex two doors down.

NEW MAY WAH

Map pp136–7 Food & Drink

☎ 415-221-9826; 719 Clement St; 7:30am-7pm; 1, 2, 28, 38, 44

No truly adventurous eater should leave town without a trip here. Flavored tapioca tea kits and stinky, acquired-taste durian are just the beginning: sharpen your stir-fry tasting skills with an array of fish sauce and bean pastes, and work your way through the shelves of chili sauce and *soju* (Korean rice wine) if you dare.

WISHBONE

Map pp136–7 Gifts

☎ 415-242-5540; www.wishbonesf.com; 601 Irving St; 11:30am-7pm Mon-Sat, to 6pm Sun; N, 44, 71;

Certain gifts never fail to please: explode-in-your-mouth Pop Rocks candy, smiling toast coin purses, candy-colored jewelry, and a stuffed toy called 'Yes, a Cat Named Marty Cohen.' Baby gear here is bound to please hipster parents, from baby Ramones T-shirts to Tiny Tyrant striped ensembles.

KAMEI RESTAURANT SUPPLY

Map pp136–7 Housewares

☎ 415-666-3699; 547 Clement St; 9am-7pm; 1, 2, 28, 38, 44

The human brain was not built to comprehend this broad a selection of ceramics, with three precariously stacked aisles ranging from basic geometric white to spectacular high-end raku platters that would make fried eggs look gourmet. But wait, there's more: enough industrial steel pots to open 50 restaurants simultaneously, and scouring pads to suit the most discerning dishwashers – all at bargain-basement prices.

MOLLUSK

Map pp136–7 Sporting Goods, Local Designer

☎ 415-564-6300; www.mollusksurfshop.com; 4500 Irving St; 10am-6:30pm; N

The high-impact store sign by renowned artist Tauba Auerbach is the first hint that this is the source of West Coast surfer cool. Visits by celebrity shapers (surfboard makers) yield limited-edition boards that you won't find anywhere else, and the signature Mollusk T-shirts and hoodies by local artists buy you nods of surfer recognition. Surf books and sculpture installations by the likes of the Society of Driftwood Enthusiasts give non-surfers vicarious surf-subculture thrills.

EATING

top picks

- **Jardinière** (p172)
- **Tataki** (p177)
- **La Taqueria** (p183)
- **Aziza** (p188)
- **Namu** (p188)

What's your recommendation? www.lonelyplanet.com/san-francisco

EATING

Other US cities boast bigger monuments, but San Francisco packs more flavor. Two secret ingredients have transformed this small city into a global culinary capital: dirt and competition. Almost anything can and does grow in California's fertile Central Valley, south of San Francisco; coastal pastures to the north are prime grazing territory for livestock; and rocky hillsides and volcanic *terroir* yield fine wines in nearby Sonoma and Napa (p282). Add local, sustainable seafood to the mix, and it might seem like a no-fail recipe for success. But what a chef does with those ingredients can make or break a restaurant in San Francisco, where there's about one restaurant for every 28 people – that's 10 times more restaurants per capita than any other city in North America.

For even a $10 meal, San Franciscans expect inventive combinations of fresh, seasonal ingredients; for $20 and up, they demand to know where those organic dry-farmed tomatoes were farmed, when that fish was caught, and everything but the pet nickname of that cow. Some menus include the generic disclaimer 'We use organic ingredients whenever possible' – but, increasingly, that's not enough to placate San Francisco diners, who buy organic, seasonal produce at home and expect the same from their favorite restaurants. Many San Francisco restaurant menus are meticulously detailed and heavily footnoted, sharing credit with the farms that grew key ingredients, and noting which ingredients are organic and sustainably sourced. Mock if you must, but people have been known to move here for the food (ahem).

HISTORY

Fresh, fusion cooking isn't a fad but a fine art in San Francisco, where the local palate has been constantly refined by imported flavors and local innovations for the past 150 years. Before San Francisco became part of the US it belonged to Mexico, which established NorCal ranching and farming traditions. California's Gold Rush attracted people from all over the world, and the influx of immigrants brought with it a range of culinary traditions and talents. Most '49ers were men not accustomed to cooking for themselves, so cooks found a ready market for their skills.

As the money poured in, San Francisco restaurants started catering to a multi-culti nouveau riche, and makers of specialty foods like Ghirardelli (p167) hit the mother lode with culinary risk-takers. French cuisine became all the rage, even though the French names of dishes and restaurants were unpronounceable to the city's mostly non-Francophone population.

Once the gold dust settled and panic set in, cooking began to seem a much wiser occupation than gold mining – sooner or later, everyone has to eat. San Francisco became the gastronomic oasis of the West with an unrivalled variety of novelties and cuisines. Chinese culinary traditions date from the Gold Rush, and the first Italian restaurant in the USA was opened in North Beach in 1886. The 1942–64 US Bracero program importing Mexican agricultural labor brought local variations on Mexican staples, including 'super' tacos loaded with toppings and mega-meals wrapped in flour tortillas known as burritos.

As the turbulent 1960s wound down, many disillusioned idealists concluded that the revolution was not about to be delivered on a platter, but in the Bay Area, chefs weren't about to give up on the idea. In 1971 Alice Waters opened Chez Panisse (p274) in a converted house in Berkeley, with the then-radical notion of making the most of the Bay Area's seasonal, all-natural, sustainably produced bounty. Waters combined French flourishes with California attention to craft and San Franciscan innovation, and diners tasted the difference for themselves. Today, Waters' credo of organic, seasonal, locally grown, pasture-raised cuisine has become a mantra for chefs worldwide and a rallying call for Bay Area chefs like Traci Des Jardins (see the boxed text, p172).

ETIQUETTE

San Francisco restaurants are thronged with people passing around food family-style, picking bites from one another's plates, and discussing their food with their mouths full. Rude? Not in this town, where dining is an experience discussed scene by scene and play by play, like a movie or a basketball game. Dining companions often plot out their orders together, and if you're not sharing plates family-style, it's considered good form to offer dining companions a taste of your dish. If there's something off about your dish, send it back – you can get your server's attention with a polite 'excuse me' (*garçon* is considered pretentious, even in a French place).

San Franciscans tend to split the bill when dining out, so if you're watching your cash flow, order modestly (ie skip the wine and dessert) and offer to cover your share when the bill comes (don't forget to factor in tax and tip, which together tack on 25% to 30% to your bill). Otherwise, the bill is usually divided equally among diners.

SPECIALTIES

California Cuisine

Even though it's 150 years in the making, the Bay Area's signature culinary tradition holds no ingredients sacred, and refuses to observe any strict canon of recipes. Dishes are prepared with a light touch in unexpected combinations, often using cooking techniques and kitchen craft borrowed from neighbors across the Pacific in East Asia and the distant Mediterranean (where the climate and soil are similar to the Bay Area's). Cheeses, breads and meats are often provided by local artisans, and fruits and vegetables typically come from small family farms. Over the past two decades, SF restaurants have increasingly sourced ingredients from local organic producers practicing sustainable agriculture, bringing California cuisine to new, all-natural highs.

Ethnic Taste Treats

Anyone attempting to leave the city of San Francisco without trying dim sum and burritos should be turned back at the airport for their own good – though once you try them, you might not want to leave. Dim sum is Cantonese for what's known in Mandarin as *xiao che* (small eats); some also call it *yum cha* (drink tea), and there are dozens of places in San Francisco where you'll call it delicious. Waitstaff roll carts past your table with steaming baskets of dumplings, platters of garlicky sautéed greens and, finally, plates of sweet crispy sesame balls and creamy egg custard. Bring friends along to share the bounty at venerable Ton Kiang Restaurant (p188) or the stylish City View (p174), or organize a dim-sum crawl to explore the counter-service joints lining Clement St between 5th and 9th Sts or Stockton St between Clay and Jackson Sts.

The most hotly debated local dish is the SF burrito, which is nothing like the imposters you'll find elsewhere. Your choice of beans (pinto, black or refried), meats (grilled or stewed) and salsas (fresh chopped *pico de gallo*, tangy green tomatillo, smoky mesquite or spicy mango) are loaded onto a flour tortilla and rolled into a foodstuff the approximate length and girth of a forearm. To contribute an informed opinion to the debate over who does burritos best, head to the Mission District, take your pick of busy taquerias (taco restaurants), then compare notes online with the admittedly obsessed **Burrito Eater** (www.burritoeater.com).

Seafood

The Pacific offers a haul of seafood to San Francisco diners, but there's trouble in those waters: some species have been overfished, and their extinction could throw the local aquaculture off balance. Monterey Bay Aquarium has been monitoring local fish stock for decades, and its Seafood Watch program helps diners identify best options, good choices and items to avoid on local seafood menus – find out which of your seafood favorites are on the best list at www.montereybayaquarium.org/cr/seafoodwatch.aspx.

Delicious, sustainable, local seafood choices found almost year-round include wild Dungeness crab, locally farmed oysters and locally farmed caviar. From late fall through spring you'll find Dungeness crab on virtually any San Franciscan menu, but locals make a ritual of the season's arrival with a trip out to PPQ Dungeness Island (p188) in outer Richmond or a steaming bowl of cioppino (cho-*pee*-noh) seafood stew, served by the vat at Catch (p183). Freshly shucked raw oysters have been a bar-top staple in the city from Gold Rush days, and the happy hour tradition continues at El Rio (p243). The most venerable purveyor is Hog Island Oyster Company (p168), where you can taste-test a few different variations for $1 each at happy hour. Tsar Nicoulai sustainably produces America's most sought-after ostetra caviar, and you can taste what the fuss is about at Tsar Nicoulai Caviar Cafe (p168).

Sourdough Bread

San Francisco is famous for its sourdough bread, although the pucker-inducing aftertaste can be an acquired taste. The most famous 'mother dough' in town dates back to 1849, when baker Isidore Boudin hit on a combination of wild yeast and bacteria that's been kept alive and getting a rise out of Boudin Bakery's bread ever since. You'll see people eating Boudin sourdough bowls filled with clam chowder down at Fisherman's Wharf, but be warned: the combination of starchy, salty glop, crusty carbs and the very occasional clam has yet to be proven digestible.

VEGETARIANS & VEGANS

To all you beleaguered vegetarians, accustomed to eating out in places where the only non-animal dish is some unspeakable vegetarian lasagna: you're in San Francisco now. Your needs are not an afterthought in California cuisine, which revolves around seasonal produce instead of the usual American meat and potatoes. Vegan fine dining is not an oxymoron here, with inventive menus at Millennium (p172) and the legendary Greens (p177). On the cheaper side, vegetarian options abound at taquerias, pizzerias, Japanese noodle joints, Thai restaurants, Ethiopian eateries and Middle Eastern places, plus bakeries and groceries.

PRACTICALITIES

Opening Hours

Most places to eat are open seven days a week, though some close Sunday and/or Monday night. To provide for caffeine needs, cafes open as early as 6am or 7am and tend to stay open until 8pm daily. Lunch starts at noon and runs through to 3pm. Evening dining starts at about 7pm or 7:30pm, with restaurants opening around 5:30pm and last service around 9:30pm during the week or past 10pm on weekends. Where opening hours are listed with a review in this chapter, the venue's opening hours vary from the norm.

How Much?

Even when you eat cheaply in San Francisco, you're spoiled for choice: for under $3 you can enjoy a gourmet taco, a plump, filling *pupusa* (Salvadoran stuffed, fried dough), an order of three-shrimp dumplings or a tasty roast beef *banh mi* (Vietnamese sandwich). At the other end of the spectrum are tasting menus at the city's top restaurants, which can easily run over $100 per person with wine pairings. The US recession has brought more daily and prix-fixe specials to local menus – see individual reviews for noteworthy standing offers.

If you're planning a dining-out celebration, bringing in your own bottle of bubbly and homemade cake may seem like a good value until you tack on the $10 to $30 corkage charge and per-plate cake-cutting fee of $2 to $5. Just so there are no surprises, call ahead and inquire.

Booking Tables

Most restaurants take reservations for lunch and dinner, so call ahead if you can – even if it's the same day. Many restaurants that take reservations also set seats aside for walk-ins, so you could try your luck if you're willing to wait. Restaurants that don't take reservations may subject customers to long waits (20 minutes or more), so get your name on the waiting list and make yourself comfy at the bar, or duck out and find another place.

At a few perennially popular restaurants, reservations need to be made well in advance. French Laundry (p285) and Chez Panisse (p274) often require reservations months in advance, and a few days or weeks lead time can be helpful at Gary Danko (opposite), Slanted Door (p168) and some of the more intimate restaurants such as Kabuto (p188) or Jai Yun (p173). If you call for prime-time same-day reservations at some in-demand restaurants, they might claim they're fully booked as a matter of principle, but you might be able to make a booking by asking if they have any 'last-minute cancellations.' Many in-demand restaurants also have counter or bar seating available on a first-come, first-served basis, with the same or a slightly limited menu.

Tipping

As elsewhere in the USA, tipping is customary in restaurants. Servers expect at least 15% of the check total before tax, unless something went horribly wrong with the service; you might give up to 10% more if the service is exceptional. Keep in mind that servers get paid a minimal wage, often without health benefits, and tips are what make their wages livable. Many restaurants add an automatic service charge for parties of six or more, so if you're traveling with an entourage, check before you tip. Tipping is optional at coffee bars and places where you place your own order at the counter, but a $1 tip is always well received.

Groceries

A grocery store may sound like the last place you'd want to have lunch or dinner, but wait until you see some of the gourmet goodies made locally or on the premises at SF's specialty markets. *Bento* boxes are prepared by sushi chefs behind the scenes at Nijiya Supermarket (p177); Sunrise Deli (p189) serves up arguably the city's best *baba ghanoush* (eggplant dip) and stuffed grape leaves; *kim bap* (Korean rolls) and *kimchee* (spicy fermented vegetables) are made in-house at First Korean Market (p190); and you can buy housemade salsa and fresh, still-warm tortillas at La Palma Mexica-tessen (p183). If you'd rather whip up something from scratch, hit a farmers market (see the boxed text, p169), and in case of misadventure, keep enough wine on hand to wash it all down from Ferry Plaza Wine Merchant (p142) or PlumpJack Wines (p150).

EMBARCADERO & THE PIERS

The piers used to be the seafood stop of last resort for picky locals who prefer their Dungeness crab with sides besides fries, and chowder without the sourdough bowl, but now the waterfront is regaining its gourmet footing along the Embarcadero. The temple to local food known as the Ferry Building Marketplace (p64) puts several foodie shrines under one roof, and features high-class take-out and a bustling farmers market. Swanky celebrity-chef eateries now shore up the waterfront alongside diners and the seafood shacks favored by sailors for a century.

PRICE GUIDE

In this chapter, the following price symbols apply, exclusive of drink, tax and tip:

$$$	over $30 a meal
$$	$15-30 a meal
$	under $15 a meal

FISHERMAN'S WHARF

GARY DANKO Map p63 — Californian $$$

☎ 415-749-2060; www.garydanko.com; 800 North Point St; dinner; 10, 19, 30, 47; Powell-Hyde

Smoked-glass windows prevent passersby from tripping over their tongues at the sight of exquisite roasted lobster with trumpet mushrooms, blushing duck breast with rhubarb compote, trios of crème brûlée and the lavish cheese cart. Take your server's seasonal recommendations of two to six small courses for $44 to $98, and prepare to be impressed. Gary Danko has won multiple James Beard Awards for providing an impeccable dining experience, from inventive salad courses like oysters with caviar and lettuce cream to the casually charming server who hands you tiny chocolate cakes as a parting gift.

FORBES ISLAND Map p63 — Grill $$$

☎ 415-951-4900; www.forbesisland.com; Pier 41; 5-10pm Wed-Sun; 15, 37, 49, F

No man is an island, except for an eccentric millionaire named Forbes Thor Kiddoo. A miniature lighthouse, thatched hut, waterfall, sandy beach and swaying palms transformed his moored houseboat into the Hearst Castle of the bay. Today this bizarre domicile is a restaurant strong on grilled meats and atmosphere. Reserve in advance and catch boat shuttles from Pier 39; landlubbers dining below deck should bring their motion-sickness meds.

CROWN & CRUMPET Map p63 — Cafe $$

☎ 415-771-4252; www.crownandcrumpet.com; 207 Ghirardelli Sq; 10am-9pm Mon-Fri, 9am-9pm Sat, 9am-6pm Sun; 10, 19, 30, 47; Powell-Hyde

Designer style and rosy cheer usher teatime into the 21st century: girlfriends rehash hot dates over scones with strawberries and champagne, and dads and daughters clink porcelain teacups with crooked pinkies and 38 kinds of tea. Reservations recommended on weekends.

GHIRARDELLI ICE CREAM Map p63 — Ice Cream $

☎ 415-474-3938; www.ghirardellisq.com; 900 North Point St, West Plaza; 10am-11pm Sun-Thu, to midnight Fri & Sat; 10, 19, 30, 47; Powell-Hyde

Gee, Mr Ghirardelli, you sure make a swell sundae. Chocolate milkshakes are for sharing and making moony eyes over, and the legendary Cable Car comes with Rocky Road ice cream, marshmallow topping and enough hot fudge to pave Jack Kerouac Alley.

IN-N-OUT BURGER Map p63 Burgers $

☎ 800-786-1000; www.in-n-out.com; 333 Jefferson St; 10:30am-1am Sun-Thu, to 1:30am Fri & Sat; 10, 30, 47, J; Powell-Hyde;

Gourmet burgers have taken SF by storm, but In-N-Out has had a good thing going for 60 years: prime chuck beef it processes itself, plus fries and shakes made with ingredients you can pronounce, all served by employees paid a living wage. Ask for yours off the menu 'wild style,' cooked in mustard with grilled onions.

EMBARCADERO & FERRY BUILDING

LA MAR CEBICHERIÁ

Map p63 Peruvian, Seafood $$$

☎ 415-397-8880; www.lamarcebicheria.com; Pier 1 1/2 Embarcadero; 11:30am-2:30pm Mon-Fri, noon-2:30pm Sat & Sun, 5:30-10pm Mon-Thu, 5:30-10:30pm Fri & Sat, 5:30-9pm Sun; 7, 21, 71, F, J, K, L, M, N; & Embarcadero

Business lunches here could lead to some very untoward office behavior: the key ingredient in these collaged plates of Peruvian *cebiche* is *leche de tigre,* the 'milk of the tiger,' a marinade of lime, chili and brine that 'cooks' the fish without a fire, and is said to have aphrodisiac properties. Sunny days are prime for seats by the bay and a plate of pristine, spicy *cebiche clasico* of California halibut, habañero, Peruvian corn and yam – or go with the Pacific Rim flair of *cebiche chifa*, with peanuts, daikon, ginger and mango.

SLANTED DOOR

Map p63 Vietnamese $$

☎ 415-861-8032; 1 Ferry Bldg; lunch & dinner; 2, 7, 21, 71, F, J, K, L, M, N; & Embarcadero

San Francisco's most effortlessly elegant restaurant harmonizes California ingredients, Continental influences and Vietnamese flair. Owner/chef Charles Phan enhances top-notch ingredients with bright flavors, heaping local Dungeness crab atop cellophane noodles and garlicky Meyer Ranch 'shaking beef' on watercress. The wildly successful venture is still a family establishment, with 20 Phan family members serving multistar meals for here and to go at Out the Door.

HOG ISLAND OYSTER COMPANY

Map p63 Seafood $$

☎ 415-391-7117; www.hogislandoysters.com; 1 Ferry Bldg; 11:30am-8pm Mon-Fri, 11am-6pm Sat & Sun; 2, 7, 21, 71, F, J, K, L, M, N; & Embarcadero

Slurp down the bounty of the North Bay with a view of the East Bay. Take yours au naturel, with *caper beurre blanc*, spiked with bacon and paprika, or perhaps classic lemon and shallots… oh, go on, try some of each. Mondays and Thursdays between 5pm and 7pm are happy hours indeed for shellfish fans, with $1 oysters and $3.50 beer.

BOULETTE'S LARDER

Map p63 Californian $$

☎ 415-399-1155; www.bouletteslarder.com; 1 Ferry Bldg; 9am-3pm Mon-Fri, noon-3pm Sat, 11am-3pm Sun; 2, 7, 21, 71, F, J, K, L, M, N; & Embarcadero

Dinner theater doesn't get better than brunch here at the communal table, strategically placed inside a working kitchen, amid a swirl of chefs preparing for dinner service. Inspired by their truffled eggs and beignets? Get spices and mixes to go at the pantry counter.

TSAR NICOULAI CAVIAR CAFE

Map p63 Seafood $$

☎ 415-288-8630; www.tsarnicoulai.com; 1 Ferry Bldg; 11am-7pm Mon-Thu, 11am-8pm Fri, 9am-7pm Sat, 11am-5pm Sun; 2, 7, 21, 71, F, J, K, L, M, N; & Embarcadero

Indulge champagne tastes and caviar dreams with a West Coast twist: grassy, sprightly Sonoma sparkling wine and sustainably farmed California ostetra caviar. Pair bubbly by the glass with the Infused Sampler: caviar with traces of brandy, kaffir lime, wasabi, truffle and ginger. Better yet: samplers are half-price on Mondays and Tuesdays. But the most deliciously perverse bar snack ever has to be the ahi and sturgeon sashimi, served in a glass inserted into a fishbowl, with fish flitting around the base.

NOW EAT THIS: SF FARMERS MARKETS

Year-Round Markets

- Daily: Island Earth (Map pp110–11; www.islandearthfarmersmarket.org; Yerba Buena Gardens entrance, lower level, Metreon; 10am-7pm or 8pm) has local produce, food artisans and wine tasting; it's indoors, occasionally with a live DJ. There are some organics, and prices are moderate.
- Saturday: Ferry Plaza (Map p63; www.cuesa.org; Market St & the Embarcadero; 8am-2pm Sat) has California-grown produce, meat, seafood and eggs, plus local artisan cheeses, chocolates, olive oils and other gourmet-prepared foods; there's an excellent range of organics and sustainably harvested foods at moderate-to-premium prices. Since 1945, city-run Alemany (www.sfgov.org/site/alemany; 100 Alemany Blvd; 6am-4pm Sat) has flowers, fish and eggs, and stalls with ready-to-eat foods, plus bargain prices and a good range of organics and sustainably harvested foods. The Fillmore Center Plaza (www.pcfma.com; O'Farrell at Fillmore; 9am-1pm Sat) has local produce, food vendors, live jazz and moderate prices.
- Sunday and Wednesday: Heart of the City (Map p77; United Nations Plaza, Market St btwn Hyde & Leavenworth Sts; 7am-4pm Wed, to 5pm Sun) has local produce (some organics), including an excellent selection of lesser-known varietals, plus prepared-food stalls. Bargain prices.
- Thursday: Crocker Galleria (50 Post St; 11am-3pm) has local fruit and vegetables and some organics; premium prices.

Seasonal Markets

Seasonal markets usually run from May to November.

- Sunday: Inner Sunset (parking lot btwn 8th & 9th Ave, off Irving St; 9am-1pm) has local produce and artisan foods, live music, some organics and bargain-to-moderate prices. There's also a seasonal market at the Ferry Plaza (Map p63; Market St & the Embarcadero; 10am-2pm).
- Tuesday and Thursday: the Ferry Plaza (10am-2pm Tue, 4-8pm Thu) offers seasonal produce.
- Wednesday: Castro farmers market (Market St at Noe St; 4-8pm) has local produce and artisan foods, some organics and moderate prices.

MIJITA Map p63 Mexican $

415-399-0814; www.mijitasf.com; 1 Ferry Bldg; 10am-7pm Mon-Wed, to 8pm Thu-Sat, to 4pm Sun; 2, 7, 21, 71, F, J, K, L, M, N; & Embarcadero; V

Owner/chef Traci Des Jardins puts her signature twist on her Mexican grandmother's standbys, using fresh local produce for tangy-savory jicama and grapefruit salad with pumpkin seeds, and sustainably harvested fish cooked with the minimum of oil in seriously addictive Baja fish tacos. Wash it all down with melon *agua frescas* (fruit-flavored drinks) bayside, with envious seagulls circling overhead.

DOWNTOWN

Whether you're in an economic boom or slump on any given day, there's a place for you to dine Downtown. From chef-operated lunch take-out to upscale destination dining at Aqua, Fleur de Lys and Restaurant Michael Mina, Downtown eateries aim to please your palate. The Financial District can seem desolate at night and Union Square can get rough around the peripheries west of Powell St and south of Sutter St, but as always in San Francisco, superior dining rewards the adventurous.

FINANCIAL DISTRICT

AQUA Map pp70–1 Californian $$$

415-956-9662; www.aqua-sf.com; 252 California St; 11:30am-2:30pm Mon-Fri, dinner nightly; F, J, K, L, M, N; & Montgomery St; California

Prix-fixe dinners here are major FiDi investments, but the $36 three-course business lunch delivers tiny, jewel-like dishes so fresh and delicately handled, you can almost taste the sun in a cherry-tomato sorbet and stormy seas in the geoduck clam ceviche. Trust your savvy server to recommend wine pairings and provide spot-on assessments of a dish, including where that tomato or clam comes from (most ingredients are sustainably sourced) and how it was prepared. Aqua has been justly famed as one of the city's finest for years now – this is where star chefs Traci Des Jardins and Michael Mina got their starts, among others – so be sure to book well ahead if you're planning a very special dinner here. Swinging singles, be warned that marriage proposals happen here at an alarming rate – could be something in the water, or more likely on the extensive California and French wine list.

GITANE

Map pp70–1 Basque, Mediterranean $$

☎ 415-788-6686; www.gitanerestaurant.com; 6 Claude Lane; 5:30pm-midnight Tue-Sat, bar to 1am; 1, 15; California; V

Slip out of the Financial District and into something more comfortable at this opulent new bistro with a wandering eye and a gypsy spirit. The decor and menu wink at Basque, Spanish and Moroccan traditions, but pure decadence is the real draw, with flirting co-workers in the bar feeding one another bacon bon-bons (goat-cheese-stuffed prunes wrapped in bacon and doused in cinnamon-port sauce). Serious canoodlers should get a room in the restaurant upstairs to share fragrant free-range chicken *tagines* (stews) on low divans.

MIXT GREENS

Map pp70–1 Salads $

☎ 415-433-6498; www.mixtgreens.com; 120 Sansome St; 10:30am-3pm Mon-Fri; F, J, K, L, M, N; & Montgomery St; V

No, they're not getting the Grateful Dead back together – those ponytailed stockbrokers lined up out the door are here for generous organic salads with humanely raised, herb-marinated chicken and chipotle dressing or mango, jicama and roasted peanuts with tangy Thai vinaigrette. Grab a stool or get yours to go in a compostable corn container to enjoy bayside at the Ferry Building.

BOXED FOODS

Map pp70–1 Sandwiches, Salads $

☎ 415-981-9376; www.boxedfoodscompany.com; 245 Kearny St; 8am-3pm Mon-Fri; 1, 15; California; V

Organic, local, seasonal ingredients make outrageously flavorful lunches, whether you choose the zesty strawberry salad with mixed greens, walnuts and tart goat cheese, or the Boxed BLT with crunchy applewood smoked bacon. Get yours to go to the Transamerica Pyramid & Redwood Park, or grab one of the two-top tables in back.

MURACCI'S CURRY

Map pp70–1 Japanese $

☎ 415-773-1101; www.muraccis.com; 307 Kearny St; 11am-6pm Mon-Thu, to 5pm Fri; 1, 15; California; V

On blustery days when the fog barrels down Kearny, warm up from the inside out with a steaming curry-topped *katsu* (breaded cutlet) or grilled chicken atop rice or noodles. Chipper counter staff take your order, and within minutes call you to pick up classic Japanese comfort-food curry – not spicy or sharp, but gently tingling, only faintly sweet, and powerfully savory.

BREAD AND COCOA

Map pp70–1 Cafe, Sandwiches $

☎ 415-956-7200; www.breadandcocoa.com; 199 Sutter St; 7am-6pm Mon-Fri, 8:30am-5pm Sat & Sun; 1, 15; California; V

When's the last time you actually craved a sandwich? Local, artisanal ingredients add a fresh zing to roast chicken panini with pesto, and tangy Humboldt Fog cheese works similar magic with prosciutto, organic tomato and arugula. These sandwiches may not be huge for $8 to $10, but their flavor sure is.

UNION SQUARE

RESTAURANT MICHAEL MINA

Map pp70–1 American $$$

☎ 415-397-9222; www.michaelmina.net; 335 Powell St; 5:30-9pm Tue-Thu, to 9:30pm Fri & Sat; 38, F, J, K, L, M, N; & Powell St

Involuntary shudders can be induced in most San Franciscan foodies by uttering the words 'hotel restaurant,' but chef Michael Mina's exception to the rule at the Hotel St Francis proved so successful, he's expanded his empire to 15 other restaurants. Mina takes a three-dimensional approach to dining, where each dish is actually three variations on one key ingredient. Though the signature triple tuna tartare starter and lobster pot pie mains have inspired raves and legions of copycats, the seasonal menu showcases innovation and ripe flavors – butter-poached lobster with melon laced with red curry, or foie gras terrine with pickled strawberries. Consultations with your well-versed servers and sommelier to navigate the complex menu options should come with a certificate of completion, especially at $105 to $135 for a full three-course menu, or $60 for three smaller plates in the lounge.

FLEUR DE LYS Map pp70–1 French $$$

☎ 415-673-7779; www.fleurdelyssf.com; 777 Sutter St; 🕑 dinner Mon-Sat; 🚌 38, F, J, K, L, M, N; 🚌 & Ⓜ Powell St

Long before celebrity chef Hubert Keller took his show on the road to Vegas and *Top Chef Masters,* this was the ultimate over-the-top SF destination. There's nothing subtle about the swanky sultan's tent interiors, but it's oddly suited to princely repasts involving gnocchi graced with chanterelles and hazelnut-encrusted scallops and halibut crowned with rhubarb coulis and truffle, and a king's ransom of foie gras on every other dish. Prix-fixe options for omnivores begin at $70 for three courses, while vegetarians are entitled to a five-course feast for a surprisingly reasonable $68.

FARMERBROWN

Map pp70–1 New American $$

☎ 415-409-3276; www.farmerbrownsf.com; 25 Mason St; 🕑 5-11pm Sun-Thu, to midnight Fri & Sat, weekend brunch bar to 2am; 🚌 5, 6, 7, 21, 31, F, J, K, L, M, N; 🚌 & Ⓜ Powell St

Half of SF has a crush on this rebel from the wrong side of the block, which dishes up a mean seasonal watermelon margarita with a cayenne salt rim (genius), ribs that stick to yours, and coleslaw with a kick that'll leave your lips buzzing like an everlasting game of spin the bottle. Chef-owner Jay Foster works with local organic and African American farmers to provide food with actual soul, in a setting that's rusted and cleverly repurposed as a shotgun shack, with harried service (it's always busy) and a band banging away in a corner some nights.

KATANA-YA Map pp70–1 Japanese $

☎ 415-771-1280; 430 Geary St; 🕑 11:30am-2am Mon-Fri, noon-2am Sat & Sun; 🚌 38, F, J, K, L, M, N; 🚌 & Ⓜ Powell St

A glorified closet of a restaurant, Katana-ya is the late-night place for a bite after a show at ACT across the street, or anytime you're willing to brave a couple of sketchy Tenderloin blocks for steaming bowls of udon and ramen with broth so savory it's almost dense. Avoid the bland sushi, but if you're coming here after Tenderloin dive bars, the curries seem to have curative properties.

JACKSON SQUARE

KOKKARI Map pp70–1 Greek $$$

☎ 415-981-0983; www.kokkari.com; 200 Jackson St; 🕑 lunch Mon-Fri, 5:30-10pm Mon-Thu, 5:30-11pm Fri, 5-11pm Sat; 🚌 41, 45, F; Ⓥ

This is one Greek restaurant where you'll want to lick your plate instead of break it, with starters like grilled octopus with a zing of lemon and oregano, and a signature lamb, eggplant and yogurt moussaka as rich as the Pacific Stock Exchange. Reserve ahead to avoid waits, or make a meal of hearty Mediterranean apps at the bar.

BOCADILLOS Map pp70–1 Basque $

☎ 415-982-2622; www.bocasf.com; 710 Montgomery St; 🕑 7am-10pm Mon-Wed, 7am-10:30pm Thu & Fri, 5-10:30pm Sat; 🚌 15, 30, 41, 45

Meals so cute you'll want to pinch them. Forget the suburban sprawl of multi-page menus and SUV-sized portions, and tuck into a North Beach studio–sized choice of two small sandwiches on dinner rolls served with a green salad for $7 to $9. The juicy lamb-burgers, snapper ceviche with Asian pears, and Catalan sausages are just-right Basque bites with wine by the glass.

PICKLES Map pp70–1 Burgers $

☎ 415-421-2540; 42 Columbus Ave; 🕑 11am-3pm Mon, to 10pm Tue-Thu, to 2:30am Fri & Sat; 🚌 15, 30, 41, 45

In a fancier joint, you could pay twice as much for a burger half as good as Pickles' mighty half-pound slab of humanely raised, antibiotic-free chuck for $8 (or a 6oz version for $6). This spiffed-up fast-food place has a fireplace on the patio and some foodie nerve, too: who would've thought that fried Brussels sprouts would make such a welcome alternative to French fries?

CIVIC CENTER & THE TENDERLOIN

This neighborhood's blustery avenues and sketchy blocks weed out timid diners, leaving more *pho* (Vietnamese noodles), inventive seasonal dishes and succulent vegan morsels for everyone else. The proximity to the opera, symphony and theaters make local restaurants prime date destinations, and chefs bring plenty of drama and romance to the plate.

JARDINIÈRE Map p77 Californian $$$

☎ 415-861-5555; www.jardiniere.com; 300 Grove St; 5-10:30pm Tue-Sat, to 10pm Sun & Mon; 5, 21, 42, 47, 49

Iron Chef and James Beard Award–winner Traci Des Jardins has a way with organic vegetables, free-range meats and sustainably caught seafood that's slightly naughty, topping succulent octopus with crispy pork belly, and drizzling Sonoma lavender honey over squash blossoms bursting with molten sheep's cheese. Leave room for operatic desserts with simple, sensational ingredients: polenta-almond cake becomes a platform for blackberries to sing duets with brown-sugar ice cream. Go Mondays, when $45 scores three decadent courses with wine pairings. Downstairs in the mood-lit lounge, an affordable bar menu pairs well with adventurous, seasonal cocktails – the Summer of St George with local Hangar vodka, basil spirits, ginger liqueur and aromatic lemon is a drink that takes the heat off spicy harissa fries.

MILLENNIUM Map p77 Vegetarian $$$

☎ 415-345-3900; www.millenniumrestaurant.com; 580 Geary St; 5:30-9:30pm Sun-Thu, 5-10pm Fri & Sat; 38; & Powell St; Powell-Hyde; V

If all vegan food could be this satisfying and opulent, there could be cattle roaming the streets of SF and no one would give them a second glance. Seasonal first courses include grilled semolina flatbread topped with caramelized onions, wilted spinach and a flourish of almond romesco, followed by a peppery pastry roulade that opens with a fork's touch to reveal a creamy center of golden potatoes and smoky achiote (chili) chard, and a saffron-scented rice pudding with mango sorbet. Book ahead for aphrodisiac dinners and vegetarian Thanksgiving.

FISH & FARM Map pp70–1 Californian $$

☎ 415-474-3474; www.fishandfarmsf.com; 339 Taylor St; 5-10pm Tue & Wed, to 11pm Thu-Sat; 38; Powell-Mason

Eco comfort food bound to improve your mood and the planet, featuring organic produce, sustainable seafood and humanely raised meats sourced within 100 miles of San Francisco. White Brentwood corn and organic sweet onions make a silky, sensational soup, while local cod gets soused on Liberty Ale batter, and fried, and topped with malted salt for fish and chips that would make an Englishman weep. Housemade pickles, preserves and condiments keep the menu lively even in winter, and cocktails with organic fruit help the conversation keep pace.

TRACI DES JARDINS: CHEF & RESTAURATEUR

What's so special about the food here? You'll notice a lot of Bay Area restaurants proudly name their producers on menus, like we do (at Jardinière; above). Sometimes farmers introduce chefs to new flavors; sometimes we see an ingredient on our travels we ask them to grow. I grew up on a farm, and I really appreciate that creative partnership with producers.

With such abundance, why the focus on sustainability? In the past five years a growing awareness among consumers has driven the market for organics. If people are paying attention to what they eat at home, they're going to bring that awareness into restaurants, and demand different choices: organics, fair-trade products, free-range meats, seafood that's not at risk. This makes our collaboration with producers even more important.

What's new on the SF menu? There's been an evolution in the Bay Area style of cooking around local, seasonal produce that Alice (Waters, of Chez Panisse, p274) started. Our food has evolved to be much more simple, with ingredients starring on the plate – it's more of the Italian school of combining five or six ingredients perfectly, instead of an overly layered French style.

Unusual items spotted at local farmers markets? Lately I've seen a lot of Jerusalem artichokes, gem lettuces and all kinds of heirloom carrots – red, white and thumb carrots. We're lucky that almost anything can grow in California, and because there's such a high demand for specialties, some items that used to be hard to find are now really easy to come by.

Where do you take foodie friends? The Ferry Building (p64), followed by a trip to the MH de Young Memorial Museum (p139) and Golden Gate Park (p138), and Crissy Field (p105) for spectacular views of the Golden Gate Bridge (p104).

Traci Des Jardins is a James Beard Award–winning chef and a restaurateur at Jardinière (above).

CAFÉ ASIA Map p77 Asian $

☎ 415-581-3630; 200 Larkin St; 10am-4:30pm Tue-Wed & Fri-Sun, to 8pm Thu; 5, 6, 7, 21, 31, 71, F, J, K, L, M, N; & Civic Center;

Rest those museum legs on the sunny outdoor balcony, and let your tastebuds do the trekking. You might pause at the green-tea soba-noodle base camp, or head for the spicy Korean pork sandwich. Adventurous eaters attack hearty Tibetan lamb and lentil stew, nibblers chill out with Thai green papaya salad, and dawdlers refresh with green tea and Pocky.

DOTTIE'S TRUE BLUE CAFÉ

Map p77 American $

☎ 415-885-2767; 522 Jones St; 7:30am-3pm Wed-Mon; 19, 38; & Powell St; Powell-Hyde

Consider yourself lucky if you stand in line less than an hour and get hit up for change only once – but fresh baked goods come to those who wait at Dottie's. Cinnamon pancakes, grilled cornbread, scrambles with whiskey fennel sausage and anything else off the griddle are tried and true blue.

PAGOLAC

Map p77 Vietnamese $

☎ 415-776-3234; 655 Larkin St; 5-9:30pm Tue-Sun; 5, 19, 31, 38, 42, 47;

Right in the hard heart of the Tenderloin is this inviting nook that's all warm wood and candlelight. The seven courses of beef may be overkill for anyone who's not a famished gaucho from the pampas, but the sugarcane shrimp and barbecued chicken are sublime. Pagolac also does a good *pho* with meatballs and *bo tai chanh,* lemon-marinated rare steak slices as extravagantly beefy as a Polk St men's bar.

SHALIMAR

Map p77 Indian $

☎ 415-928-0333; www.shalimarsf.com; 532 Jones St; noon-midnight; 2, 3, 4, 27, 38

Follow your nose to tandoori chicken straight off the skewer and naan bread still bubbling from the oven; vegetables are leaden, so don't hold back on the succulent tandoori chicken that jumpstarted the whole fluorescent-lit Pakistani restaurant scene. Watch and learn as foodies who demand five-star service elsewhere meekly fetch their own water pitchers and tamarind sauce from the fridge.

LAHORE KARAHI

Map p77 Pakistani $

☎ 415-567-8603; 612 O'Farrell St; 11am-10pm; 2, 3, 4, 27,38

Only one thing could induce relatively sane San Franciscans to brave merciless fluorescent lighting and risky business propositions in the gritty Tenderloin: succulent tandoori chicken with a grill's kiss of seared smokiness. Of all the linoleum-floored Pakistani tandoori joints this side of Geary, Lahore Karahi wins the loyalty of theatergoers and streetwalkers alike for consistency, cleanliness and cheerful cheapness.

SAIGON SANDWICH SHOP

Map p77 Vietnamese $

☎ 415-474-5698; 560 Larkin St; 6:30am-5:30pm; 5, 19, 31

Consider it frontier justice for the indecisive: order your $3 to $3.50 *banh mi* (Vietnamese sandwich) when the ladies of the Saigon call you, or you'll get skipped. Act fast, and you'll be rewarded with a baguette piled high with your choice of roast pork, chicken, pâté, meatballs and/or tofu, plus pickled carrots, cilantro, jalapeño and thinly sliced onion.

CHINATOWN

Ordering off the menu is overrated in Chinatown, where the best dishes are pushed past your table on a dim sum cart or listed in Chinese. Don't be shy about pointing at a promising dish on a neighboring table or ordering a mysterious dumpling on aroma alone. Try out the dim sum places and noodle joints along Stockton St, and wander along side streets off Grant Ave to find basement eateries where starving artists can afford to order in bulk, just like Jack Kerouac, Allen Ginsberg and the Beats did. But it's worth splashing out on local delicacies too – a feast in the Hong Kong indie-film atmosphere of Jai Yun, House of Nanking or Yuet Lee could be the highlight of your trip.

JAI YUN

Map p82 Shanghai-Style Chinese $$$

☎ 415-981-7438; www.menuscan.com/jaiyun; 680 Clay St; 6:30-9:30pm by reservation only; 30; California, Powell-Mason, Powell-Hyde

'Hello? When? How many? $55, $65, $75 per person? OK, see you!' That's how the reservation system works at Jai Yun, where chef Nei serves 15- to 20-course Shanghai-style market-fresh feasts by reservation only. There's no menu, since the chef creates the bill of fare based on what's fresh that day – but fingers crossed, your menu will include tender abalone that drifts across the tongue like a San Francisco fog, housemade rice noodles with cured pancetta, and seemingly lowly yet truly opulent mung beans with sesame oil. Never mind that the restaurant has more mirrors than a Bruce Lee movie and Christmas tinsel wrapped around dining-room surveillance cameras – the sophisticated, fascinating flavors will leave you smugly assured in your impeccable taste. One caution is the limited wine selection: bring your own pinot and pay $20 corkage.

YUET LEE

Map p82 Chinese, Seafood $$

☎ 415-982-6020; 1300 Stockton St; 11am-3am Wed-Mon; 1, 9, 15, 30, 45; Powell-Mason, Powell-Hyde; V

With a radioactive green paint job and merciless fluorescent lighting, this so-hideous-it's-cool seafood diner isn't for first dates, but for drinking buddies and committed couples who have nothing to hide and are willing to share outstanding batter-dipped salt-and-pepper calamari and tender roast duck.

HOUSE OF NANKING

Map p82 Shanghai-Style Chinese $$

☎ 415-421-1429; 919 Kearny St; 11am-10pm Mon-Fri, noon-10pm Sat, noon-9pm Sun; 15

Meekly suggest an interest in seafood, nothing deep-fried, perhaps some greens, and your no-nonsense server nods, snatches the menu and, within minutes, returns with meltaway scallops, fragrant sautéed pea shoots, minced squab lettuce cups, and a tea ball that blossoms in hot water. For bright, clean flavors at a price you'd expect to pay for food half this good, you can put up with bossy service, a strict cash-only policy and the inevitable wait for a table.

CITY VIEW

Map p82 Dim Sum $

☎ 415-398-2838; 662 Commercial St; 11am-2:30pm Mon-Fri, 10am-2:30pm Sat & Sun; 1, 10, 15, 30; California

Dim sum aficionados used to cramped quarters and surly service are wowed by impeccable shrimp and leek dumplings, tangy, tender asparagus and crisp Peking duck, all dished up from carts with a flourish in a spacious, sunny room. Try to come on the early or late side of lunch, when your server has the time to recommend that day's best dishes and you don't have to sit in the downstairs dining area contemplating the surreal Astroturf Zen garden beneath the stairs.

GOLDEN STAR Map p82 Vietnamese $

☎ 415-398-1215; 11 Walter Lum Pl; 10am-9pm; 1, 9, 30, 45

Elementary school cafeterias could outclass the Golden Star for atmosphere – but if you know *pho*, you know this is the place to go. Five-spice chicken *pho* is the house specialty that warms the bones on a foggy day, but on a hot day, branch out and get the *bun* (rice vermicelli) topped with thinly sliced grilled beef, imperial rolls, mint and ground peanuts. Except in understandable cases of extreme noodle gluttony, your bill will be under $8.

NORTH BEACH

When choosing an Italian restaurant in North Beach, use this rule of thumb: if a host has to lure you in with 'Ciao bella!' on the sidewalk, keep walking. Try smaller neighborhood Italian American restaurants on side streets off Grant Ave and Washington St, where staff are gossiping in Italian. Whether you're after pasta and Chianti or something with a lighter Cal-Med twist, you'll find it here, with heartfelt welcomes and reluctant goodbyes.

CAFÉ JACQUELINE

Map p87 French $$$

☎ 415-981-5565; 1454 Grant Ave; 5:30-11pm Wed-Sun; 20, 30, 39, 41, 45, 91

The secret terror of top chefs is the classic French soufflé: only when the ingredients are in golden-mean proportions, whipped into perfect peaks, baked at the right temperature and removed from the oven not a second too early or late will a soufflé rise to the occasion. Chef Jacqueline's soufflés float across the tongue like the fog over the Golden Gate Bridge, and with the right person across the tiny wooden table to share that seafood soufflé, dinner could hardly get more romantic – until you order the chocolate for dessert.

RISTORANTE IDEALE Map p87 Italian $$

☎ 415-391-4129; 1309 Grant Ave; ⌚ dinner; 🚌 15, 30, 41, 45

Italian regulars are stunned that a restaurant this authentic borders the Pacific, with *bucatini ammatriciana* (Roman tube pasta with savory tomato-pancetta-pecorino sauce) served properly *al dente,* creamy seafood risotto made with superior Canaroli rice, and a well-priced selection of robust Italian wines, served by wisecracking Tuscan waitstaff and a Roman chef. The portions are lavishly American, but seafood and meat preparations remain strictly Italian to highlight flavors released in cooking – unlike North Beach's many goat-cheese-and-sundried-tomato-pesto-on-everything imposters.

CINECITTÁ Map p87 Pizza $

☎ 415-291-8830; 663 Union St; ⌚ 11am-10pm Sun-Thu, to midnight Fri & Sat; 🚌 15, 30, 41, 45; 🚋 Powell-Mason; V 🚸

That tantalizing aroma you followed from down the block into this 18-seat eatery is thin-crust Roman pizza, probably the crowd-pleasing Capricciosa: artichoke hearts, olives, fresh mozzarella, prosciutto and egg. Vegetarians prefer Funghi Selvatici, with wild mushrooms, zucchini and sundried tomato, but that saliva-prompting aroma escaping the wood-fired oven is the ever-popular Travestere (fresh mozzarella, arugula and prosciutto), served with sass and a generous pint of draft Anchor Steam by Roman owner Romina. Save room for housemade tiramisu, hands down the best in North Beach.

MOLINARI Map p87 Italian, Deli $

☎ 415-421-2337; 373 Columbus Ave; ⌚ 9am-5:30pm Mon-Sat; 🚌 15, 30, 41, 45

Grab a number and a crusty roll, and when your number rolls around, the guys behind the counter will stuff it with translucent sheets of prosciutto di Parma, milky buffalo mozzarella, tender marinated artichokes or slabs of the legendary house-cured salami (the city's best). While you wait, load up on essential Italian groceries for later, like truffle-filled gnocchi, seasoned *pecorino* (sheep's cheese) and aged balsamic vinegar.

BAONECCI Map p87 Sandwiches, Bakery $

☎ 415-989-1806; www.caffebaonecci.com; 516 Green St; ⌚ 9am-5pm Tue-Sun; 🚌 20, 30, 39, 41, 45, 91

Recharge for the Coit Tower climb with panini turbo-loaded with bold Southern Italian flavors on house-baked ciabatta or focaccia. Tastebuds sit up and pay attention to the Studente, a ham and cheese sandwich slathered with hot Calabrese red-pepper paste and green olive spread for $6.50.

LIGURIA BAKERY

Map p87 Italian $

☎ 415-421-3786; 1700 Stockton St; ⌚ 8am-2pm Mon-Fri, 7am-2pm Sat, 7am-noon Sun; 🚌 15, 30, 41, 45; 🚋 Powell-Mason

Bleary-eyed art students and Italian grandmothers are in line by 8am for the cinnamon-raisin focaccia hot out of the 100-year-old oven, leaving 9am dawdlers a choice of tomato or classic rosemary, and 10am stragglers out of luck. Take what you can get, and don't kid yourself that you're going to save it for lunch.

BRIOCHE BAKERY Map p87 Bakery $

☎ 415-765-0412; 210 Columbus Ave; ⌚ 7am-8pm Mon-Sat; 🚌 15, 30, 41, 45

When Gold Rush miners found gold, they treated themselves to 'Frenchy food' here on what was once San Francisco's Barbary Coast – and now you too can start your day striking it rich with flaky cinnamon twists, not-too-sweet *pain au chocolat* (chocolate croissants), and namesake brioches golden with butter.

GELATERIA NAIA Map p87 Ice Cream $

☎ 415-677-9280; www.gelaterianaia.com; 520 Columbus Ave; ⌚ 11am-11pm Sun-Thu, to midnight Fri & Sat; 🚌 15, 30, 41, 45

Chinatown and North Beach cross-pollinate with creamy concoctions that improve on the ordinary, elevating the usual Chinese green tea or Italian pistachio ice cream options to a decadent choice of Kyoto maccha tea or locally roasted California pistachio gelato. Local, seasonal flavors and constant experimentation introduce entirely new sorbet and gelato obsessions with flavors ranging from white peach to black sesame.

RUSSIAN & NOB HILLS

Along Hyde and Polk Sts, at the western edge of Russian and Nob Hills, you'll be glad you made the climb to prime picnic spots and neighborhood bistros. These hilltops add romantic views to the bill of fare – and if the walk afterwards seems anticlimactic, try leaping aboard a cable car.

RUSSIAN HILL

ACQUERELLO

Map p92 Californian, Italian $$$

☎ 415-567-5432; www.acquerello.com; 1722 Sacramento St; 5:30-9:30pm Tue-Sat; 1, 19, 47, 49, 76; California

A converted chapel is a fitting location for a meal that'll turn Italian culinary purists into true believers in Cal-Italian cuisine. 'Oh…my…God…' is the obvious reaction to chef Suzette Gresham's generous pastas and ingenious seasonal meat dishes, including heavenly quail salad, devilish lobster *panzerotti* (stuffed dough pockets in a spicy seafood broth), and venison loin chops. Order a la carte, or a prix-fixe of three/four/five courses for $60/72/82. An anteroom where brides once steadied their nerves is now lined with limited-production Italian vintages, which the sommelier will pair by the glass.

1550 HYDE

Map p92 Californian, Italian $$

☎ 415-775-1550; www.1550hyde.com; 1550 Hyde St; 6-9:30pm Tue-Thu, 6-10pm Fri & Sat, 5:30-9:30pm Sun; 12, 19; Powell-Hyde; V

'Clang clang clang went the trolley, zing zing zing went my heartstrings…' That Judy Garland tune 'The Trolley Song' finally makes sense after an evening at this romantic hilltop restaurant, with dark wood, candles everywhere, and big bay windows to watch the cable cars pass. Go Sunday to Thursday for the $29.95 three-course dinner and $15 wine flights, and be seduced.

SWAN OYSTER DEPOT

Map p92 Seafood $$

☎ 415-673-1101; 1517 Polk St; 8am-5:30pm Mon-Sat; 1, 19, 27, 47, 49; California

Superior flavor without the superior attitude of most seafood restaurants. The downside is an inevitable wait for the few counter seats, but the upside of the high turnover is unbelievably fresh seafood. On sunny days, place an order to go, browse Polk St boutiques, then breeze past the line to pick up your crab salad with Louie dressing and the obligatory top-grade oysters with mignonette (wine/shallot) sauce. Hike or take a bus up to Sterling Park for superlative seafood with ocean views.

CHEESE PLUS

Map p92 Deli $

☎ 415-921-2001; www.cheeseplus.com; 2001 Polk St; 10am-7:30pm Mon-Sat, to 7pm Sun; 12, 19, 27, 47, 49, 76, 90

Foodies, rejoice: here's one deli where they won't blink an eye if you say you'd rather have the aged, drunken goat cheese than the plastic provolone on your sandwich. For $8, you can get a salad loaded with oven-roasted turkey and sustainable Niman Ranch bacon, but the specialty is the classic $7 grilled cheese, made with the artisan cheese du jour.

NOB HILL

ZA Map p92 Pizza $

☎ 415-771-3100; www.zapizzasf.com; 1919 Hyde St; noon-10pm Sun-Wed, to 11pm Thu-Sat; 41, 45; Powell-Hyde

Sit down and savor that slice, already. You don't get a gourmet, cornmeal-dusted, thin-crust slice like this every day. Pizza lovers brave the uphill climb for pizza slices piled with fresh ingredients, a pint of Anchor Steam, and a cozy bar setting with flirtatious pizza-slingers – all for under 10 bucks.

SWENSEN'S

Map p92 Ice Cream $

☎ 415-775-6818; www.swensensicecream.com; 1999 Hyde St; noon-10pm Tue-Thu, to 11pm Fri-Sun; 41, 45; Powell-Hyde

Bite into your ice-cream cone, and you'll get instant brain-freeze and a hit of nostalgia besides. Oooh-ouch, that peppermint stick really takes you back, doesn't it? The 16-ounce root beer floats are the 1950s version of Prozac, but the classic hot fudge sundae is pure serotonin with sprinkles on top.

JAPANTOWN & PACIFIC HEIGHTS

The Japan Center is packed with restaurants but some of the more intriguing Japanese restaurants can be found along Post St and in the Buchanan Mall, across Post St. Nearby Fillmore St is lined with restaurants that emphasize style over flavor – it's a nice place to shop, but you wouldn't necessarily want to eat there.

TATAKI Map p96 Japanese, Sushi $$

☎ 415-931-1182; www.tatakisushibar.com; 2815 California St; 11:30am-2pm & 5:30-10:30pm Mon-Thu, 11:30am-2pm & 5:30-11:30pm Fri, 5:30-11:30pm Sat, 5-9:30pm Sun; 1, 2, 4, 24

Pioneering sustainable-sushi chefs Kin Lui and Raymond Ho rescue dinner and the oceans with sustainable delicacies: silky Arctic char drizzled with yuzu-citrus and capers happily replaces at-risk wild salmon, and the Golden State Roll is a local hero, featuring spicy, line-caught scallop, Pacific tuna, organic-apple slivers and edible 24-karat gold leaf. Compliment your chefs on their sumptuous creations, and they'll demurely compliment you back on your eco-smart good taste.

NIJIYA SUPERMARKET

Map p96 Japanese, Sushi $

☎ 415-563-1901; www.nijiya.com; 1737 Post St; 10am-8pm; 2, 3, 4, 22, 38

Picnic under the Peace Pagoda with sushi or teriyaki *bento* boxes fresh from the deli counter and a swig of Berkeley-brewed Takara Sierra Cold sake from the drinks aisle, and you'll have change from a $20 for mango-ice-cream-filled *mochi* (chewy Japanese cakes with savory or sweet fillings).

WHOLE FOODS MARKET

Map p96 Groceries $

☎ 415-674-0500; www.wholefoodsmarket.com; 1765 California St; 8am-10pm; 1, 3, 22

Watch as locals wise to Whole Foods' Chilean imports of organic asparagus demand the local stuff instead, inquire after the care and feeding of cattle at the meat counter, and make a meal of free samples of fair-trade chocolate: this is luxury grocery shopping, San Francisco style.

BENKYODO Map p96 Japanese $

☎ 415-922-1244; www.benkyodocompany.com; 1747 Buchanan St; 8am-5pm Mon-Sat; 2, 3, 4, 22, 38

Everything you really need in life is within reach of your stool at Benkyodo. The perfect retro lunch counter cheerfully serves an old-school egg-salad sandwich or pastrami for $3.50. Across the aisle are glass cases featuring teriyaki-flavored pretzels and $1 *mochi* made in-house daily – come early for popular green tea and chocolate-filled strawberry varieties, but don't be deterred by the savory, nutty lima bean paste.

THE MARINA & THE PRESIDIO

The usual Marina dining destinations are on Chestnut St from Fillmore to Divisadero Sts, and Union St between Fillmore St and Van Ness Ave, but some fun, funky fare is found on Lombard St, and Greens makes the hike to Fort Mason worthwhile.

A16 Map pp100–1 Italian $$

☎ 415-771-2216; www.a16sf.com; 2355 Chestnut St; 11:30am-2:30pm Wed-Fri, 5-10pm Sun-Thu, 5-11pm Fri & Sat; 2, 3, 4, 22, 38

Like a high-maintenance date, this Neapolitan pizzeria demands reservations and then haughtily makes you wait in the foyer. The 2009 James Beard Rising Star Chef Nate Appleman's housemade mozzarella burrata and chewy-but-not-too-thick-crust pizza makes it worth your while, especially the kicky calamari. Skip the spotty desserts and concentrate on adventurous house-cured salumi platters, including the delectably spicy pig's ear terrine (no, really).

ROSE'S CAFÉ Map pp100–1 Californian $$

☎ 415-775-2200; www.rosescafesf.com; 2298 Union St; 7am-10pm Mon-Thu, 8am-10pm Fri & Sat, 8am-9:30pm Sun; 22, 41, 45; V

Follow your salads and housemade soups with rich organic polenta with gorgonzola and thyme, then linger over your espresso or grenadine-and-vanilla Monk's Blend tea. Shop if you must, but return to this corner cafe from 4pm to 6pm for half-price wine by the glass.

GREENS

Map pp100–1 Vegetarian, Californian $$

☎ 415-771-6222; www.greensrestaurant.com; Fort Mason Center, Bldg A; restaurant lunch Tue-Sat, dinner Mon-Sat, brunch Sun; take-out 8am-8pm Mon-Thu, 8am-5pm Fri & Sat, 9am-4pm Sun; 22, 28, 30; V

Career carnivores won't realize there's no meat in the hearty black bean chili with crème fraîche and pickled jalapeños, or that roasted eggplant *panino* (sandwich), packed with hearty flavor from ingredients mostly grown on a Zen farm in Marin. On sunny days, get yours to go so you can enjoy it on a wharfside bench, but if you're planning a sit-down weekend dinner or Sunday brunch you'll need reservations.

BLUE BARN GOURMET

Map pp100–1 Sandwiches, Salads $

☎ 415-441-3232; www.bluebarngourmet.com; 2105 Chestnut St; 11am-8:30pm Sun-Thu, to 7pm Fri & Sat; 22, 28, 30, 43, 76, 91

Toss aside thoughts of ordinary salads. Here for $8.50 you can build a mighty mound of organic produce from Sonoma's Oak Hill Farm, topped with your choice of six fixings: artisan cheeses, caramelized Copra onions, heirloom tomatoes, candied pecans, pomegranate seeds, even Meyer grilled sirloin. For a hot meal, try the toasted panini oozing with Manchego cheese, fig jam and chorizo.

WARMING HUT

Map pp100–1 Cafe, Sandwiches $

☎ 415-561-3040; 983 Marine Dr; 9am-5pm; 29

Wetsuited windsurfers and Crissy Field kite fliers thaw out with fair-trade coffee, organic pastries and organic hot dogs at the Warming Hut, while browsing an excellent selection of field guides and sampling honey made by Presidio honeybees. This eco-shack below the Golden Gate Bridge has walls ingeniously insulated with recycled denim and a heartwarming concept: all purchases fund Crissy Field's ongoing conversion from US Army air strip to wildlife preserve.

LA BOULANGE

Map pp100–1 Sandwiches, Bakery $

☎ 415-440-4450; www.baybread.com; 1909 Union St; 7am-6pm; 22, 41, 45, 47, 49, 76; V

Even the most die-hard boutique trawler needs to refuel sometime, and La Boulange offers caffeine and house-baked carbo-loading in the middle of the Union St strip. La Combo is a $7 lunchtime deal to justify your next Union St boutique purchase: half a tartine (open-faced sandwich) with soup or salad, plus all the Nutella and pickled cornichons (gherkins) you desire from the condiment bar.

REAL FOOD Map pp100–1 Groceries $

☎ 415-567-6900; www.realfoodco.com; 3060 Fillmore St; 8am-9pm; 22, 41, 45

Pacing the acres of deli counter packed with appealing foods prepared in-house and sandwiches in the making doesn't make choosing any easier, but may eventually qualify as a gastronomic Olympic sport. Go with respectable nigiri sushi, freshly roasted eggplant and tomato salad, free-range herb turkey on focaccia, organic gingerbread and fair-trade coffee, and on less windy days, grab a seat on the front patio. If you like what you taste, sign up for a cooking class here – see the website for details.

KARA'S CUPCAKES

Map pp100–1 Bakery, Dessert $

☎ 415-563-2253; www.karascupcakes.com; 3249 Scott St; 10am-8pm Mon-Sat, to 6pm Sun; 22, 28, 30, 43, 76, 91

Stand back and watch Proustian nostalgia wash over fully grown adults as they bite into the carrot cake with cream-cheese frosting, or babble excitedly about magician birthday parties over the chocolate-marshmallow. While the flavors seem simple, they are meticulously calculated for maximum glee.

SOMA

Back in the dot-com days, innovative new restaurants opened up almost weekly in South of Market, and only the standouts managed to survive both boom and bust. New ventures are again beginning to open in the area, once more raising the bar for creativity. Now's the time to taste-test, and place your bets on who the next round of SoMa survivors will be.

BOULEVARD Map pp110–11 Californian $$$

☎ 415-543-6084; www.boulevardrestaurant.com; 1 Mission St; lunch & dinner; F, J, K, L, M, N; & Embarcadero

The 1889 Belle Epoque styling of the quake-surviving Audiffred Building is a fitting locale for Boulevard, which remains one of San Francisco's most consistently creative and widely respected restaurants. Chef Nancy Oakes has a light, easy touch with juicy pork chops, enough local soft-shell crab to satisfy a sailor, and chocolate ganache cake with housemade bourbon ice cream.

WATERBAR Map pp110–11 Seafood $$$

☎ 415-284-9922; 399 The Embarcadero; 11:30am-9:30pm Sun-Tue, to 10pm Wed-Sat; F, N, T; & Embarcadero

The giant glass column aquariums in the dining room and the splendid vista of the bay beyond give you some idea just how fresh and local the sustainably sourced seafood is here. Leave the dining room to Silicon Valley strivers trying hard to impress dates and investors, and make a beeline for the oval bar, where the plates and prices are smaller, and oyster shells and corks are popping to keep pace with orders of local mollusks with shallot/wine mignonette and local champagne by the glass.

SALT HOUSE

Map pp110–11 Californian $$$

☎ 415-543-8900; www.salthousesf.com; 545 Mission St; lunch & dinner Mon-Sat, to midnight Fri & Sat; 6, 7, 10, 14, 21, 31, 71, F, J, K, L, M, N; & Montgomery St

For a business lunch that feels more like a spa getaway, take your choice of light fare such as duck confit or yellowfin tuna with beets. Forget the ice tea, and unwind with wine by the glass and refreshing ginger juleps instead. Service is leisurely, so order that carrot cake with cream-cheese ice cream now.

DELANCEY STREET

Map pp110–11 New American $$

☎ 415-512-5179; 600 Embarcadero St; 11am-11pm Tue-Fri, 10am-11pm Sat & Sun; 12, N, T

There's an explanation for the eclectic comfort-food menu and your server's tattoos: this restaurant is nonprofit Delancey St's job-retraining program for ex-cons, and everything from the menu to the service is provided by participants supervised by acclaimed restaurant professionals. Brunch is best, and the entire tab for your gingery pumpkin pancakes or poached eggs with crabcakes goes right into the program, tips included.

TROPISUEÑO Map pp110–11 Mexican $

☎ 415-243-0299; www.tropisueno.com; 75 Yerba Buena Lane; 11am-10:30pm; 6, 7, 10, 14, 21, 31, 71, F, J, K, L, M, N; & Powell St

Last time you enjoyed casual Mexican dining this much, there were probably balmy ocean breezes and hammocks involved. Instead, you're steps away from SFMOMA, savoring an *al pastor* (marinated pork) burrito with mesquite salsa and grilled pineapple, and sipping a margarita with a chili-salted rim. The organic rustic decor and the location are upscale, but the prices are about what you'd pay in the Mission, give or take a buck and a BART ride.

SENTINEL Map pp110–11 Sandwiches $

☎ 415-284-9960; www.thesentinelsf.com; 37 New Montgomery St; 7:30am-2:30pm Mon-Fri; 6, 7, 10, 14, 21, 31, 71, F, J, K, L, M, N; & Montgomery St

Rebel SF chef Dennis Leary is out to revolutionize lunchtime take-out, taking on the classics with top-notch seasonal ingredients. Tuna salad gets radical with chipotle mayo and the snap of crisp summer vegetables, and roast beef does an about-face with horseradish cream cheese. Menus change daily; come prepared for about a 10-minute wait, since every sandwich is made to order.

BUTLER & THE CHEF

Map pp110–11 French $

☎ 415-896-2075; www.thebutlerandthechefbistro.com; 155a South Park St; 8am-3pm Tue-Sat, 10am-3pm Sun; 12, N, T

All the French classics you'd never expect to find among SoMa warehouses are here, from the *croque monsieur* (pressed ham and cheese) with Niman Ranch ham, Emmenthal cheese and béchamel on organic bread, to light, flaky-crusted quiche Lorraine studded with crisp Niman Ranch bacon. The cafe tables are tiny: mind your elbows or they'll wind up in your French onion soup, made with rich beef stock and a proper *crouton* topped with melting Gruyère.

SPLIT PEA SEDUCTION

Map pp110–11 Soups, Sandwiches $

☎ 415-551-2223; www.splitpeaseduction.com; 138 6th St; 7am-3:30pm Mon-Fri; 5, 6, 7, 21, 31, F, J, K, L, M, N; & Civic Center

Right off Skid Row are unexpectedly healthy, homey $8.50 gourmet soup-and-sandwich combinations, including seasonal soups like potato and housemade pesto with a signature *crostata* (open-faced sandwich), such as cambozola cheese and nectarine drizzled with honey.

PATISSERIE PHILIPPE

Map pp110–11 Bakery $

☎ 415-558-8016; www.patisseriephilippe.com; 655 Townsend St; 8am-6pm Mon-Fri, to 5pm Sat; 19, 42, N, T

Pastries lighter than air that won't leave a dent in your wallet. Come for the impeccable ham-and-cheese croissant or classic quiche Lorraine, but ignore that European glass counter or you'll skip straight to dessert of *tarte tatin* loaded with caramelized sweet-tart apples. The secret is top-quality local ingredients, with Meyer lemon delivering tang to tarts and premium butter making that $1 bag of cookies a decadent investment.

TU LAN

Map pp110–11 Vietnamese $

☎ 415-626-0927; 8 6th St; 11am-9:30pm Mon-Sat; 5, 6, 7, 21, 31, F, J, K, L, M, N; & Civic Center

Sidewalks don't get skankier than the one you'll be waiting on, but try complaining after your heap of velvety Vietnamese chicken curry or tangy tomato-onion prawns. One dish under $10 easily fills two starving artists.

RAINBOW GROCERY

Map pp110–11 Groceries $

☎ 415-863-0620; www.rainbowgrocery.org; 1745 Folsom St; 9am-9pm; 12

The legendary cooperative attracts masses to buy eco/organic/fair-trade products in bulk, drool over the bounty of local cheeses, and flirt in the hemp-based skincare aisle. To have your questions about where to find what in the Byzantine bulk section answered, ask a fellow shopper – staff can be elusive.

THE MISSION & POTRERO HILL

There's more to the Mission than burrito wars and naked California culinary ambition. Between Mission and Dolores Sts, 16th St is bustling with affordable restaurants, from Pakistani to Vietnamese. Other eclectic dining awaits discovery around Valencia and Guerrero Sts at the corners of 21st and 22nd Sts, and along Mission St between 16th and 24th. For authentic Mexican taquerias and tamale parlors off the beaten path, head into *el corazon del Mission* (the heart of the Mission), east of Mission St along 24th St.

DELFINA Map pp116–17 Californian $$$

☎ 415-552-4055; www.delfinasf.com; 3621 18th St; dinner; 14, 26, 33, 49, J; 16th St Mission; V

Simple yet sensational seasonal California cuisine: Sonoma duck with Barolo-roasted cherries, wild nettle tagliatelle pasta, profiteroles with coffee gelato and candied almonds. Since this is the one California-cuisine restaurant all of SF's picky eaters agree on, it's always packed; make reservations and arrive prepared to wait, or settle for next-best Delfina Pizza next door.

FOREIGN CINEMA

Map pp116–17 Californian $$$

☎ 415-648-7600; www.foreigncinema.com; 2534 Mission St; dinner nightly, brunch Sat & Sun, bar to 2am; 14, 26, 48, 49; 24th St Mission; V

Reliably tasty dishes like seared scallops with pancetta or pork tenderloin with tart cherries and olives are the main attractions, but Luis Buñuel and François Truffaut provide an entertaining backdrop with movies screened in the courtyard, and subtitles you can follow when the conversation lags.

RANGE Map pp116–17 Californian $$

☎ 415-282-8283; www.rangesf.com; 842 Valencia St; dinner; 14, 26, 33, 49, J; 16th St Mission; V

Fine American dining is alive and well within Range. Lowly pork shoulder becomes an eye-opener rubbed with coffee and served with bafflingly smooth grits, and bread pudding becomes a main event baked to velvety perfection with local radish sprouts and gooey Gruyère. Although the beer fridge is a repurposed medical cabinet ominously emblazoned with the words 'Blood Bank,' no resuscitation will be necessary after you get the check – mains are priced around $20, with desserts and drinks under $10.

BAR BAMBINO

Map pp116–17 Californian, Italian $$

☎ 415-741-8466; www.barbambino.com; 2931 16th St; 11am-11pm Tue-Thu, 11am-midnight Fri & Sat, 5-10pm Sun & Mon; 14, 22, 26, 33, 49, 53; 16th St Mission

Rustic Italian fare at communal tables, right off the freeway. The olive-oil tasting is a bit much at $3 to $5 an ounce, but otherwise there's no denying the appeal of this Southern Italian menu highlighting Californian produce: pasta with Mission figs and pancetta, fresh squash blossoms stuffed with sheep's milk ricotta, and pine-nut-studded eggplant *polpette* (meat balls), each for under $15, plus a well-priced, adventurous Italian wine list.

LIBERTY CAFÉ

Map pp116–17 Bakery, Californian $$

☎ 415-695-1223; www.thelibertycafe.com; 410 Cortland Ave; ⌚ lunch Tue-Fri, dinner Tue-Sun, brunch Sat & Sun (bakery), 5:30-9:30pm Thu-Sat (wine bar); 🚌 24

Chicken pot pies are still the culinary calling card of Liberty Café, baked to order with fresh, organic ingredients and served piping hot. The cozy Bernal Heights institution isn't exactly cheap or always mindful of how long customers wait for brunch to arrive, but fresh-baked treats and light meals in the wine cottage still make it a find. No reservations; expect a wait.

MISSION BEACH CAFE

Map pp116–17 Californian $$

☎ 415-861-0198; www.missionbeachcafesf.com; 198 Guerrero St; ⌚ 7am-10pm Mon-Thu, 7am-11pm Fri, 9am-11pm Sat, 9am-6pm Sun; 🚌 22, 26, 37, 53, J, F

Brunch gets an upgrade to first class, with soufflé pancakes, *huevos rancheros* (ranch-style eggs) with sustainably raised pulled pork, eggs with caramelized onions and English muffins made by the in-house pastry chef – all whipped up with farm-fresh organic ingredients.

GOAT HILL PIZZA

Map pp116–17 Italian $$

☎ 415-641-1440; www.goathillpizza.com; 300 Connecticut St; ⌚ 11:30am-10pm Sun-Thu, to 11pm Fri & Sat; 🚌 22

Thin-crust sourdough pizza served with pitchers of Anchor Steam lures hungry crowds uphill from Bottom of the Hill (p212) and other downhill bars. When other restaurants are closed on Monday nights, here you can load up on all the pizza you can eat for $10.

WEIRD FISH

Map pp116–17 Seafood $

☎ 415-863-4744; www.weirdfishsf.com; 2193 Mission St; ⌚ 11am-4pm Mon-Fri, 9am-4pm Sat & Sun, 5-10:30pm Sun-Thu, 5-11:30pm Fri & Sat; 🚌 14, 26, 33, 49; Ⓑ 16th St Mission; Ⓥ

Jerked, blackened, almond-encrusted, tossed in a tortilla: get your fish as you like

SF'S BEST NONTRADITIONAL DINING VENUES

- Roving restaurants: visiting chefs use existing restaurants or cafes to prepare prix-fixe meals, sometimes with a theme, eg foraged foods or winemaker dinners. Downsides: often costs the same as a restaurant, but without advance menus, quality control or assurances of fair working conditions and tax receipts to support city initiatives. Best bets: Radio Africa Kitchen (www.radioafricakitchen.com; Coffee Bar at 1890 Bryant St; dishes $6-9; ⌚ Tue-Sat evenings), run by chef Eskender Aseged, serves inspired Mediterranean-African small plates with organic, local ingredients; and Kitchenette (Map pp116–17; www.kitchenettesf.com; 958 Illinois St; meals $9-10; ⌚ 11:30am-1:30pm Mon-Fri) is a Dogpatch catering company serving mean sandwiches with sustainable Fatted Calf cured meats, and *bento* boxes.
- Food carts: look for mobile carts dishing out surprisingly gourmet goods – curry, crème brûlée, amuse-bouches, wraps with sustainable rotisserie meats – at farmers markets and in the Mission, and track movements via Twitter @streetfoodsf. Downsides: recent crackdowns have eliminated some unlicensed carts, but look for a prominently displayed permit as your guarantee of proper food preparation, refrigeration, fair working conditions and tax-paying. Best bets: the Tamale Lady at Zeitgeist (p200) and Let's Be Frank hot dogs at the Warming Hut (p178).
- Community cooking groups: gourmet dinners taste better when you have a hand in making them with the Bay Area's passionate foodie community. Downsides: spots fill up fast, sometimes within an hour of an event notification email, so subscribe to the list and act fast. Nonprofit La Cocina (☎ 415-824-2729; www.lacocinasf.org; 2948 Folsom St) offers culinary and tasting classes, with proceeds providing training and professional kitchen space for low-income culinary entrepreneurs. Cook Here and Now (www.cookhereandnow.com) hosts free, multiculti community cooking events and food/wine pairings based around local, seasonal ingredients; sign-up is on a first-come, first-served basis. Not-for-profit 18 Reasons (☎ 415-252-9816; www.18reasons.org; 593 Guerrero St) is affiliated with Bi-Rite (p182) and hosts small potlucks ($5), educational dinners with local winemakers ($25 to $50) and food-prep demos with tastings ($50 to $75).
- Bar bites: catering companies sweeten cocktail hour with gourmet goods. Downsides: food sits out until it's gone, so arrive early to get the best choice while it's fresh. Since it's usually cheap food served to heavy drinkers, the ingredients probably aren't top quality. Best bets: Ichi Sushi (www.ichisushi.com) serves $6 to $8 sushi rolls made with sustainably sourced fish at Annie's Social Club (p212) and 111 Minna (p215).

it at this tiny restaurant. (It's also sustainably farmed and under $10.) Adventurous eaters can't resist the lure of the Suspicious Fish dish, made with the catch of the day and the chef's inspiration. But the vegan yam, guacamole, and spinach tacos with spicy pumpkin seeds are mighty tasty too – how very Weird and wonderful.

TARTINE Map pp116–17 Bakery $

415-487-2600; www.tartinebakery.com; 600 Guerrero St; breakfast, lunch & dinner; 14, 26, 33, 49, J; 16th St Mission; V

Riches beyond your wildest dreams: butter-intensive *pain au chocolat*, cappuccino with dense foam, and *croque monsieurs* turbo-loaded with ham, two kinds of cheese and béchamel. Lolling in Dolores Park is the only possible post-Tartine activity, and operating heavy machinery ill-advised without a shot of the organic espresso.

BI-RITE Map pp116–17 Groceries $

415-241-9760; www.biritemarket.com; 3639 18th St; 9am-9pm; 14, 26, 33, 49, J; 16th St Mission

Nemesis of grocery budgets and ally of gourmands whose cooking repertoire is limited to reheating, Bi-Rite is a San Francisco foodie's version of breakfast at Tiffany's. Local artisan cheeses and chocolates, organic, seasonal dishes whipped up on the premises, and organic local fruit are displayed like jewels, and the selection of Californian wines is downright dazzling. Across the street is organic Bi-Rite Creamery (415-626-5600; 3692 18th St; 9am-9pm), where the salted caramel ice cream and house-made hot fudge are worth the wait in line.

UDUPI PALACE

Map pp116–17 Indian $

415-970-8000; www.udupipalaceca.com; 1007 Valencia St; 11:30am-10pm Mon-Thu, to 10:30pm Fri-Sun; 14, 26, 33, 49; 24th St Mission

Tandoori in the Tenderloin is for novices – SF foodies swoon over the bright, clean flavors of South Indian *dosa*, a light, crispy pancake made with lentil flour dipped in mildly spicy vegetable *sambar* (soup) and coconut chutney. Don't miss the *medhu vada* (savory lentil donuts with *sambar* and chutney) or *bagala bhath* (yogurt rice with cucumber and nutty toasted mustard seeds).

OLD JERUSALEM

Map pp116–17 Middle Eastern $

415- 642-5958; www.oldjerusalemsf.com; 2976 Mission St; 11am-10pm Sun-Thu, to 11pm Fri & Sat; 14, 26; 24th St Mission

Foodies scouring the Mission for the ultimate taco shouldn't overlook this outpost of Middle Eastern authenticity, complete with Dome of the Rock poster and pristine hummus – they don't overdo the tahini or garlic, or put roasted red peppers where they don't belong. Get the classic felafel, *shwaerma* (marinated, roasted lamb) or *shish taouk* (marinated grilled chicken) with all the fixings: hummus, onion, eggplant, potato and tangy purple sumac, with optional hot-pepper paste.

HUMPHRY SLOCOMBE

Map pp116–17 Ice Cream $

415-550-6971; www.humphryslocombe.com; 2790 Harrison St; noon-9pm Tue-Sun; 24th St Mission

Indie-rock ice cream may permanently spoil you for Top 40 flavors: once balsamic-vinegar caramel and olive oil have rocked your tastebuds, cookie dough seems so obvious, and ice cream sandwiches can't compare for decadence to foie gras ice cream between ginger snaps.

TORTAS LOS PICUDOS

Map pp116–17 Mexican $

415-824-4199; 2969 24th St; 7:30am-8pm; 14, 26, 33, 49; 24th St Mission

Mexico City's signature street food reinvented to satisfy famished Potrero del Sol skateboarders: sandwiches ($6 to $8) stuffed with farm-fresh veggies and healthy poached chicken or tangy marinated pulled pork, with optional pickled jalapeños. Wash it down with a strawberry smoothie or fresh-squeezed OJ, and you can skip dinner.

MISSION PIE

Map pp116–17 American, Bakery $

415-282-1500; www.missionpie.com; 2901 Mission St; 7am-9pm Mon-Thu, 7am-10pm Fri, 8am-10pm Sat, 9am-9pm Sun; 14, 26, 48; 24th St Mission

Like mom used to make, only better: from savory quiche to all-American apple, all pie purchases here support a nonprofit sustainable farm where city kids find out where their food comes from, and learn about nutrition and cooking.

LA TAQUERIA Map pp116–17 Mexican $

☎ 415-285-7117; 2889 Mission St; ⏲ 11am-9pm Mon-Sat, to 8pm Sun; 🚌 14, 26, 48, 49; Ⓑ 24th St Mission; Ⓥ 👶

Rabble-rouser, are you? Ask a group of San Franciscans where to get the best burrito in town, then as voices rise, quietly slip off to La Taqueria. There's no debatable saffron rice, spinach tortilla or mango salsa here – just perfectly grilled meats, flavorful beans and classic tomatillo or mesquite salsa wrapped in a flour tortilla. Add spicy pickled vegetables and *crema* (Mexican crème fraîche), and you'll discover true burrito bliss.

PANCHO VILLA Map pp116–17 Mexican $

☎ 415-864-8840; www.panchovillasf.com; 3071 16th St; ⏲ 10am-noon; 🚌 14, 26, 33, 49; Ⓑ 16th St Mission

The hero of the downtrodden and burrito-deprived, delivering a worthy condiments bar and tinfoil-wrapped meals the girth of your forearm. The line moves fast going in, and as you leave, the door is held open for you and your newly acquired Pancho's paunch.

MITCHELL'S ICE CREAM
Map pp116–17 Ice Cream $

☎ 415-648-2300; www.mitchellsicecream.com; 688 San Jose Ave; ⏲ 11am-11pm; 🚌 14, 24, 26, 49

An otherwise nondescript Mission block is thronged with grinning grown-ups and kids doing happy dances as they make their Mitchell's selections: will it be a classic like Kahlua mocha cream or the toasted almond-peanut-butter indulgence, or a tropical flavor like *macapuno* (a coconut variation) or mango? The avocado and purple yam are acquired tastes, but aficionados claim they're hard to shake – and hard to find anywhere but here.

BALOMPIE CAFÉ Map pp116–17 Salvadoran $

☎ 415-648-9199; 3349 18th St; ⏲ 8am-9:30pm; 🚌 14, 26, 33, 49; Ⓑ 16th St Mission; Ⓥ

Loyal taco lovers, prepare to be tempted by *papusas*, Salvadoran pockets of corn *masa* (aka taco dough) filled with cheese and beans or meat and topped with 'slaw and hot sauce. *Papusas* run $2.50 to $3.50 if you eat them here (minimum order of two per person) or $1.99 if you get them to go for a Dolores Park picnic.

EL TONAYENSE TACO TRUCK
Map pp116–17 Mexican $

☎ 415-550-9192; parked near 16th St & S Van Ness Ave; ⏲ from 10am; 🚌 14, 22, 33; Ⓑ 16th St Mission

The best meal on wheels in SF. Burritos and quesadillas are generous to a fault, but the $2 tacos are an easy gourmet meal on the go – especially the *al pastor* (marinated roast pork) and *lengua* (beef tongue).

LA PALMA MEXICA-TESSEN
Map pp116–17 Mexican, Groceries $

☎ 415-647-1500; 2884 24th St; ⏲ 8am-6pm Mon-Sat, to 5pm Sun; 🚌 14, 48; Ⓑ 24th St Mission

Follow the hand-slapping sound of tortilla-making in progress to La Palma, and hit the take-out counter for still-hot tortillas, handmade tamales, hunks of *carnitas* (slow-roasted pulled pork) by the pound, *queso fresco* (Mexican cheese) and La Palma's own tangy tomatillo sauce. Now all you need is a small army to finish off that meal you've assembled…

THE CASTRO & NOE VALLEY

The stretch of Market St between Church and Castro Sts is notoriously tough on restaurants; the trick to passing the test of time here seems to be good value and late hours, not thumping club music or lavish decor (though many still try). Noe Valley along 24th St and on Church St from 24th to 30th is more forgiving – maybe too forgiving, since the restaurants in the area tend to be just nice enough to visit once and not again. But the Mission culinary powerhouse is too close by for Noe Valley and Castro eateries to slack off too much, and a few notable spots may yet give the Mission a run for its money.

CATCH
Map p123 Seafood $$

☎ 415-431-5000; www.catchsf.com; 2362 Market St; ⏲ lunch Mon-Fri, dinner nightly, brunch Sat & Sun; 🚌 24, 33, F, K, L, M, Castro St

As in, 'of the day' – Dungeness crab, oysters, sole – not necessarily a reference to that silver fox by the fireplace. The crowd consists almost entirely of men in turtlenecks and leather jackets accessorized with same, but, like the menu, the conversation can get unexpectedly saucy. Try the vat-sized cioppino, and maneuver away from the piano to hear the hot dish being served by fellow diners.

ANCHOR OYSTER BAR

Map p123 Seafood $$

☎ 415-431-3990; www.anchoroysterbar.com; 579 Castro St; 11:30am-10pm Mon-Fri, noon-10pm Sat, 4-9:30pm Sun; 24, 33, F, K, L, M, Castro St

Since its founding in 1977, Anchor has gone sleek, with shiny steel surfaces and men serious about their gym memberships, but it's never strayed far from foodie classics: local oysters on the half-shell, crab cakes, Boston clam chowder and Bloody Marys. It only seats 20, so you may wind up sitting in your neighbor's lap – not that that's such a bad thing.

HOME Map p123 American $$

☎ 415-503-0333; www.home-sf.com; 2100 Market St; 11am-midnight daily, brunch Sat & Sun; 22, 33, 37, F, J, K, L, M, Church St; V

There's no place like it, especially if you enjoy your comfort food fireside with a gaggle of gym-fresh men and a $4 Homegirl (aka Cosmo plus champagne) or margarita during the 4pm to 7pm happy hour. Midwestern favorites come with a twist: mac-n-cheese gets sneaky cayenne zing, roasted chicken is spiked with rosemary, and pot roast is slow-cooked, SF foodie style.

LOVEJOY'S TEA ROOM

Map p123 Bakery $$

☎ 415-648-5895; www.lovejoystearoom.com; 1351 Church St; 11am-6pm Wed-Sun; 24, J

All the chintz you'd expect from an English tea room, but with a San Francisco point of view: art curators talk video-installation art over Lapsang souchong, scones and clotted cream, while dual dads take their daughters and dolls out for the 'wee tea' of tiny sandwiches, a petit four and hot chocolate.

SUSHI TIME Map p123 Japanese, Sushi $

☎ 415-552-2280; www.sushitime-sf.com; 2275 Market St; 5:30-10:30pm Mon-Sat; 22, 24, 37, F, J, K, L, M, N, Castro St; V

Barbie, GI Joe and Hello Kitty make cameos on the *maki* (sushi roll) menu at this surreal sushi spot downstairs from a bookstore and gym, Tokyo-style. Devour sashimi in the tiny glassed-in patio like a shark in an aquarium, and notice how your munching mysteriously synchronizes with the J-pop on the stereo and exercise bikers pumping away upstairs.

LA MÉDITERRANÉE

Map p123 Middle Eastern $

☎ 415-431-7210; www.lamediterranee.net; 288 Noe St; 11am-10pm Sun-Thu, to 11pm Fri & Sat; 22, 24, 33, 37, F, K, L, M, Castro St; V

Zesty, lemon-laced Lebanese fare at friendly prices make La Méd the Castro's neighborhood meet-up spot. The chicken kebab over rice pilaf is pleasingly plump and juicy, the *kibbe* is a harmonious blend of pine nuts, ground lamb and cracked wheat, and the smoky eggplant in the baba ghanoush was roasted for hours and isn't the least bit bitter about it.

SPARKY'S DINER

Map p123 American $

☎ 415-626-8666; www.sparkysdinersf.com; 242 Church St; 24hr; 22, 37, F, J, K, L, M, N, Church St

By day it's a family-friendly burger joint, but around midnight Sparky's becomes the unofficial drunk tank of the Mission and Castro, with regulars stumbling through the door in their leather chaps (ouch, that step gets everyone), divas trailing boas demanding home fries and omelettes with Tabasco and 'extra grease,' and the occasional impromptu sing-along.

NOE VALLEY BAKERY

Map p123 Bakery $

☎ 415-550-1405; www.noevalleybakery.com; 4073 24th St; 7am-7pm Mon-Fri, to 6pm Sat & Sun; 24, J

Raspberry croissants beckon at breakfast; seasonal sandwiches on housebaked crusty bread under $6 are just right for boutique-blown budgets come lunchtime; and sympathetic chocolate éclair purchases are in order for friends and family who could use some Noe Valley cheer.

CASA MEXICANA

Map p123 Mexican $

☎ 415-551-2272; 180 Church St; 11am-10pm; 22, 37, F, K, L, M, N, Church St

No one remembers the name, but everyone knows the one taqueria that lures Missionites away from their home turf. Load up with *carne asada* (grilled beef) or *al pastor* and fresh beans on tortillas made without lard, and choose from six salsas and hot pickles at the condiment bar, and this Casa will become your home away from home-cooking.

DINNER & A MOVIE, SF STYLE

- Dim sum at Ton Kiang (p188) and a Hong Kong action flick at Four Star Theater (p221)
- A hot slice from Escape from New York Pizza (p186) and a cult hit at the Red Vic Movie House (p221)
- Classic seafood at Catch (p183) and a silver screen classic at Castro Theatre (p220)
- California-Vietnamese fusion from Slanted Door (p168) and a best-foreign-film Oscar contender at Embarcadero Center Cinema (p221)
- The sustainable catch of the day at Tataki (p177) and a Sundance winner at ecofriendly Sundance Kabuki Cinema (p221)

HOT COOKIE

Map p123 Bakery $

☎ 415-621-2350; 407 Castro St; 🕒 11am-11pm Mon-Thu, to 1am Fri & Sat, to 11:30pm Sun; 🚌 24, 33, F, K, L, M, Castro St

If this place seems familiar, that says something about your taste in cookies and entertainment. After a couple of adult film scenes were shot here, Hot Cookie became the place to be seen and photographed for porn stars – hence the wall of signed Hot Cookie underwear, and customers eating chocolate chip cookies with a certain gusto.

THE HAIGHT

The Upper and Lower Haight have mural-covered eateries that are easy on the wallet and great for people-watching, but Divisadero St between Fell and Fulton Sts offers more trendy, sexy options for hot dates. When the folks are in town and in the mood for upscale dining, try Cole Valley.

BAR CRUDO

Map pp126–7 Seafood $$

☎ 415-409-0679; www.barcrudo.com; 655 Divisadero St; 🕒 5-11pm Mon-Sat, to 10pm Sun; 🚌 5, 21, 24

An international idea that's pure California: choice morsels of local seafood served raw Italian-style, with pan-Asian condiments and Belgian beers. Stick to the pilsners with delicate raw Hawaiian kampachi served with Asian pear and mustard oil, and graduate to darker ales with gingery yellow-fin tuna served with Thai fish sauce and spring onion.

UVA ENOTECA

Map pp126–7 Californian, Italian $$

☎ 415-829-2024; www.uvaenoteca.com; 568 Haight St; 🕒 5-11pm Sun-Thu, to 11:30pm Fri & Sat; 🚌 6, 7, 22, 71

Boys with shags and girls with bangs discover the joys of Bardolino and Barbera by the tasting glass, served with inventive small plates of local veggies, cheese and charcuterie boards by a sassy staff of tattooed Lower Haight hotties.

ZIRYAB Map pp126–7 Middle Eastern $$

☎ 415-522-0800; www.ziryabgrill.com; 528 Divisadero St; 🕒 5-11:30pm Mon-Thu, 11:45am-11:30pm Fri, 9am-11:30pm Sat, 10am-3pm Sun, brunch Sat & Sun; 🚌 5, 6, 7, 21, 24, 71

Banish all traumatic memories of dry chicken *shwarmas* with this succulent, organic poultry rolled in flatbread and sealed by hummus with a tantalizing whiff of curry. The lentil soup is so robust it'll make your voice drop an octave, and the hookahs on the front porch provide solace to smokers rendered furtive by SF's antismoking laws.

LITTLE STAR PIZZA

Map pp126–7 Italian $$

☎ 415-441-1118; www.littlestarpizza.com; 846 Divisadero St; 🕒 dinner Mon-Sat; 🚌 5, 21, 24; V

Midwest weather patterns reveal that Chicago's thunder has been stolen by Little Star's deep-dish pie, with California additions of cornmeal crust, fresh local veggies and just the right amount of cheese. The all-meat pizza is a Chicago stockyard's worth of meat – not for the faint of heart.

MAGNOLIA BREWPUB

Map pp126–7 Californian, American $

☎ 415-864-7468; www.magnoliapub.com; 1398 Haight St; 🕒 noon-midnight Mon-Thu, noon-1am Fri, 10am-1am Sat, 10am-midnight Sun; 🚌 6, 7, 33, 37, 43, 71; V

Organic pub grub and samplers of homebrews keep the conversation flowing at communal tables, while grass-fed Prather Ranch burgers satisfy stoner appetites in the side booths – it's like the Summer of Love all over again, only with better food. Magnolia smells vaguely like a brewery because it is one, which can be a problem at brunch but is definitely an asset otherwise, with seasonal microbrew ales and wheat beers you won't find elsewhere.

AXUM CAFE Map pp126–7 Ethiopian $

415-252-7912; www.axumcafe.com; 698 Haight St; dinner; 6, 7, 22, 71, N; V

When you've got a hot date with a vegan, the hunger of an athlete, and/or the salary of an activist, Axum's vegetarian platter for two with spongy *injera* bread is your saving grace. Dig in with your bare hands, and try not to hog the lip-tingling red lentils and mellow yellow chick peas.

LITTLE CHIHUAHUA

Map pp126–7 Mexican $

415-255-8225; www.thelittlechihuahua.com; 292 Divisadero St; 11am-10pm Mon-Wed, 11am-11pm Thu & Fri, 10am-11pm Sat, 10am-10pm Sun; 6, 7, 24, 71

Who says sustainable, organic food has to be chi-chi and French? Charbroiled tomatillos, sustainable fish, Niman Ranch meats and organic veggies add up to sensational fresh flavor, packed into $4 tacos and $6 burritos.

ROSAMUNDE SAUSAGE GRILL

Map pp126–7 Sausages $

415-437-6851; 545 Haight St; 11:30am-10pm; 6, 7, 22, 71, N

Impress a dinner date with $10: load up classic Brats or duck-fig links with complimentary roasted peppers, grilled onions, whole-grain mustard and mango chutney, and enjoy with your choice of 100 beers at Toronado (p202) next door.

COLE VALLEY CAFE

Map pp126–7 Cafe $

415-668-5282; www.colevalleycafe.com; 701 Cole St; 6:30am-8pm Mon-Fri, 7am-8:30pm Sat & Sun; 6, 7, 33, 37, 43, 71, N; V

Powerful coffee, free wi-fi, and hot gourmet sandwiches that are a bargain at any price – let alone $6 for lipsmacking thyme-marinated chicken with lemony avocado spread, or the smoky roasted eggplant with goat cheese and sundried tomatoes. Chef/owner Jawad knows the entire neighborhood by name and lunch order, and has a kind word for everyone.

ESCAPE FROM NEW YORK PIZZA

Map pp126–7 Pizza $

415-668-5577; www.escapefromnewyorkpizza.com; 1737 Haight St; 11:30am-midnight Sun-Thu, to 2am Fri & Sat; 6, 7, 33, 37, 43, 71, N; V

The Haight's obligatory mid-bender stop for a hot slice. Pesto with roasted garlic and potato will send you blissfully off to carbo-loaded sleep, but the sundried tomato with goat cheese, artichoke hearts and spinach will recharge you to go another round.

HAYES VALLEY

Shoe-shoppers and Sunday brunchers throng Hayes Valley at weekends, but during the week you might have your choice of tables – at least until the opera or symphony let out. The blocks of Market St between Van Ness Ave and Octavia Blvd are included in this section as well.

ZUNI CAFE

Map p133 Californian $$$

415-552-2522; www.zunicafe.com; 1658 Market St; 11:30am-11pm Tue-Thu, 11:30am-midnight Fri & Sat, 11am-11pm Sun; 6, 7, 71, F

Gimmickry is for amateurs – Zuni has been turning basic menu items into gourmet staples since 1979. Reservations and fat wallets are necessary, but the see-and-be-seen seating is a kick and the food is beyond reproach: organic-beef burgers on focaccia, Caesar salad with house-cured anchovies, crispy roasted free-range chicken with horseradish mashed potatoes, and impeccable chocolate pudding.

DESTINO

Map p133 Nuevo Latino $$

415-552-4451; www.destinosf.com; 1815 Market St; dinner; 6, 7, 71, F;

Your tastebuds will think tectonic plates have shifted at this Peru-meets-California bistro, starring ahi ceviche with organic mango and achiote oil, duck breast with bacon-plantain cakes and passionfruit Pisco sour cocktails.

BAR JULES

Map p133 Californian $$

415-621-5482; www.barjules.com; 609 Hayes St; dinner Tue-Sat, lunch Wed-Sat, brunch Sun; 5, 21

Small, local and succulent is the credo at this corridor of a neighborhood bistro. The short daily menu thinks big with flavor-rich, sustainably minded pairings like local duck breast with farro, an abbreviated but apt local wine selection and the dark, sinister 'chocolate nemesis.' There are no reservations, and waits are a given – but so is simple, tasty food.

SUPPENKÜCHE Map p133 German $

☎ **415-252-9289; www.suppenkuche.com; 525 Laguna St; dinner daily, brunch Sun; 6, 7, 21, 71**

Feast on housemade Bratwurst sausages and spaetzle oozing with cheese, and toast your new friends at the unvarnished communal table with a 2L glass boot of draft beer – then come back tomorrow to cure inevitable hangovers with Sunday brunches of inch-thick 'Emperor's Pancakes' studded with brandied raisins.

STACKS Map p133 American $

☎ **415-241-9011; www.stacksrestaurant.com; 501 Hayes St; 7am-2:30pm Mon-Fri, to 3:30pm Sat & Sun; 6, 7, 21, 71**

The kitschy urns of artificial flowers and faux-garden decor are more Branson-Missouri motel than Cali cafe, but the fluffy-crispy wheat germ pancakes and crepes stuffed with pesto, portobello and roast chicken are fresh California takes on brunch. The prices may seem high until you get your loaded plate, and realize that you could use it for a boogie board.

PAULETTE MACARONS

Map p133 Dessert $

☎ **415-864-2400; www.paulettemacarons.com; 437 Hayes St; 11am-7pm Tue-Sat, noon-6pm Sun & Mon; 5, 21**

Sorry, Oreo: the competition for the ultimate sandwich cookie is down to Paulette's Sicilian pistachio and passionfruit French macarons. Declare a winner from your seat on a macaron-shaped pouf, or go for a second championship round: caramel *fleur-de-sel* salt and violet cassis.

GOLDEN GATE PARK & THE AVENUES

The best value for authentic ethnic foods and intriguing California variations on them is found out in the Avenues. Should you find your way to a spot serving delicious eats, you might be sworn to secrecy, since SF foodies protect their neighborhood joints as fiercely as California surfers defend their favorite breaks. Key foodie destinations include Clement St east of Park Presidio for Taiwanese, French, Thai and more, and Geary Blvd west of Park Presidio for Cal-Moroccan, dim sum, sushi, Polish delis and then some. The Sunset District has budget ethnic eating places along Irving St from 5th Ave all the way to 25th Ave, and along the last blocks of Judah St near the Ocean Beach. Come early if you want a spot, since service often winds down by 9pm.

SPRUCE

Map pp136–7 Californian $$$

☎ **415-931-5100; www.sprucesf.com; 3640 Sacramento St; 11:30am-2:30pm Mon-Fri, 5-10pm Mon-Sun, bar & lounge 11:30am-10pm Mon-Fri; 1, 2, 4, 33**

VIP all the way, with studded ostrich-leather chairs, mahogany walls and your choice of 1000 wines. Expense-accounters forget business and feast on pork tenderloin with crispy pork belly, and ladies who lunch dispense with polite conversation and tear into lavish salads of warm duck confit, plums, and greens grown on the restaurant's own organic farm.

BEST STREETS FOR EATS

The perennial question of where to go out for dinner only gets more complicated with the vast variety and quality of choices in San Francisco, but there is an upside. Instead of booking a table weeks in advance for a Friday night, you can just head to a major culinary strip and take your pick of restaurants with appealing menus. The obvious places to try this approach would be Columbus Ave in North Beach for Italian or Grant St in Chinatown for Chinese, but actually there are better choices available elsewhere.

- In North Beach (p86), try the Italian restaurants to the east and west of Washington Square Park and upper Grant Ave.
- For memorable Chinese options, venture beyond Chinatown to the outer Richmond and inner Sunset (p134), especially along upper Geary Blvd between 15th and 30th Aves and around 9th Ave and Irving St.
- For even more eclectic dining choices, Clement St in the inner Richmond (p134) offers standout Singaporean, French, Burmese and Vietnamese options, and Irving St between 19th and 28th Aves in the outer Sunset (p138) spoils you for choice, with memorable Middle Eastern, Hawaiian and Japanese dining.
- There's more than Mexican food to Mission St (p115), with organic Japanese, high-end Californian, cheap-o Thai and authentic Peruvian tucked in among the taquerias (taco restaurants) between 16th and 30th Sts.

PPQ DUNGENESS ISLAND

Map pp136–7 Seafood $$$

☎ 415-386-8266; 2332 Clement St; 11am-10pm Wed-Mon; 1, 2, 29, 38;

Dungeness crab season lasts most of the year in San Francisco, which means now is a fine time to enjoy one whole atop garlic noodles or dredged in peppercorn-laced flour and lightly fried, for a typical market price of about $20 per person (depending on weight and season). Ignore everything else on the menu, and put that bib to work.

KABUTO

Map pp136–7 Californian, Sushi $$

☎ 415-752-5652; www.kabutosushi.com; 5121 Geary Blvd; lunch Tue-Sat, dinner Tue-Sun; 38

Even doubting sushi-traditionalists and Japanese-food agnostics find themselves worshipping at the sushi bar of Kabuto, a former hot-dog place that's become a temple of sushi innovation. Every night there's a line out the door to witness sushi chef Eric top nori-wrapped sushi rice with foie gras and ollalieberry reduction, *ono* (Hawaiian wahoo fish) with grapefruit and crème fraîche, and the most religious experience of all: the 49er oyster with sea urchin, caviar, a quail's egg and gold leaf, chased with rare sake.

AZIZA Map pp136–7 Moroccan, Californian $$

☎ 415-752-2222; www.aziza-sf.com; 5800 Geary Blvd; dinner Wed-Mon; 2, 29, 38; V

Mourad Lahlou's inspiration is Moroccan and his produce organic Californian, but his flavors are out of this world: quail is a major sensation with huckleberries and cumin-orange glaze, and the prawn *tagine* with Meyer lemons is pizzazz in a pot. Glitz is kept to a minimum and lighting low, so as not to distract you from desserts of pecan tartlets with sea-salt caramel ice cream.

NAMU Map pp136–7 Korean, Californian $$

☎ 415-386-8332; www.namusf.com; 439 Balboa St; 5-10:30pm Mon-Fri, 10am-3pm & 5:30-10:30pm Sat & Sun; 5, 21, 31, 38

SF's unfair culinary advantages – top-notch organic ingredients, Silicon Valley inventiveness, and deep roots in Pacific Rim cuisine – are elegantly showcased in Korean-inspired small plates ($9 to $15) of buttery kampachi fish with chili oil and *fleur de sel*, bacon-wrapped enoki mushrooms, and Niman Ranch Kobe beef and organic vegetables in a sizzling stone pot.

TON KIANG RESTAURANT

Map pp136–7 Chinese, Dim Sum $$

☎ 415-387-8273; www.tonkiang.net; 5821 Geary Blvd; 10am-9pm Mon-Thu, 10am-9:30pm Fri, 9:30am-9:30pm Sat, 9am-9pm Sun; 2, 29, 38;

The reigning champion of dim sum runs laps around the competition, pushing trolleys laden with fragrant, steaming bamboo baskets. Don't bother asking for an explanation: choose some on aroma alone, and ask for the *gao choy gat* (shrimp and chive dumplings), *dao miu gao* (pea tendril and shrimp dumplings) and *jin doy* (sesame balls) by name. A running tally is kept at your table, so you could conceivably quit while you're ahead of the $20 mark – but wait, here comes another cart…

DRAGONFLY Map pp136–7 Vietnamese $$

☎ 415-661-7755; www.dragonfly420.com; 420 Judah St; lunch & dinner; 44, 66, 71, N;

You'd think this place was high-end from the sunken dining room, garlic noodles with lavish heapings of Dungeness crab, and shaking beef that threatens to steal the crown from Slanted Door's (p168) version – but prices and service are plenty friendly. Desserts and starter pâté aren't standouts, so load up on mains served family-style.

HALU Map pp136–7 Japanese $$

☎ 415-221-9165; 312 8th Ave; 5-10pm Tue-Sat; 2, 38, 44

Entering Halu is like wandering into a scene from Yellow Submarine: rare Beatles memorabilia plasters this five-table yakitori joint, where the ramen is reliably toothsome and your choice of chicken parts comes skewered on a stick.

BURMA SUPERSTAR

Map pp136–7 Burmese $$

☎ 415-387-2147; www.burmasuperstar.com; 309 Clement St; lunch & dinner; 1, 2, 38, 44

Yes, there's a wait, but do you see anyone walking away? Blame it on creamy, fragrant catfish curries and *la pat,* a traditional Burmese green-tea salad tarted up with lime and dried shrimp. Reservations aren't accepted, so ask the host to call you at the cafe across the street, and enjoy a glass of wine while you wait.

BE MY GUEST THAI BISTRO

Map pp136–7 Thai $

415-386-1942; www.bemyguestthaibistro.com; 951 Clement St; lunch & dinner Tue-Sun, dinner Mon; 1, 2, 28, 38, 44;

For mod orange and white decor, a full cocktail bar, and clever variations of Thai themes, there's only one thing to say: Be My Guest. The marinated Volcano Chicken is served flaming and melts in your mouth, while Mango Tango Prawns and Sea Bass Edamame bring surf to California turf with tangy, earthy flavors.

ROADSIDE BBQ

Map pp136–7 American $

415-221-7427; www.roadside-bbq.com; 3751 Geary Blvd; 11:30am-10pm Sun-Thu, to 11pm Fri & Sat; 2, 33, 38

Generous $8 pulled-pork sandwiches and $10 racks of ribs are slow-cooked in a smoker, and their baked beans, sweet-potato fries and coleslaw 'roadsides' are made fresh from scratch – diets are definitely roadkill here.

LOUIS

Map pp136–7 American $

415-387-6330; 902 Point Lobos Ave; 6:30am-4:30pm Mon-Fri, to 6pm Sat & Sun, to 8pm in summer; 5, 18, 31

The newfangled and sadly soulless Cliff House can't compare to old-school Louis just up the street, with its Pacific views, '70s brown-and-orange decor, and hearty diner fare confidently slapped down in front of you by waitstaff who know you'll be back for more. At brunch on weekends, get your name on the list, then explore Sutro Baths until your 20-minute wait is up.

SPICES

Map pp136–7 Szechuan, Chinese $

415-752-8884; 294 8th Ave; 11am-11pm; 1, 2, 28, 38, 44

The menu reads like an oddly dubbed Hong Kong action flick, with dishes labeled 'explosive!!' and 'stinky!' But the chefs can call zesty pickled Napa cabbage with chili oil, silky ma-po tofu, and brain-curdling spicy chicken whatever they want – it's definitely worthy of exclamation. When you head towards the kitchen for the bathroom, the chili aroma will make your eyes well up – or maybe that's just gratitude. Cash only.

TAIWAN RESTAURANT

Map pp136–7 Chinese, Taiwanese $

415-387-1789; 445 Clement St; 11am-9:30pm Mon-Fri, 10am-10pm Sat & Sun; 1, 2, 33, 38, 44;

Feast for days on heaping, housemade, sesame hot-sauce noodles, dumplings made fresh to order, smoky dry braised green beans, and feisty black bean chicken. The pink and chrome '80s decor just goes to show that the Taiwan is single-minded in its pursuit of the most lavish banquet for four you'll ever get this cheap.

YUM YUM FISH

Map pp136–7 Japanese, Sushi $

415-566-6433; www.yumyumfishsushi.com; 2181 Irving St; 10:30am-7:30pm; 71, N;

Watch and learn as Yum Yum's sushi chef lovingly slices generous hunks of fresh sashimi, preparing a platter to order with your special *maki* needs in mind. Rolls can be made specially for vegans for as little as a dollar per order, and if you want sustainable sushi, bring your Seafood Watch Card (p165) and order accordingly.

TROUBLE COFFEE

Map pp136–7 Cafe $

415-682-4732; www.troublecoffee.com; 4033 Judah St; 7am-8pm Mon-Fri, 8am-8pm Sat, 8am-5pm Sun; N

Coconuts are an unlikely find by blustery Ocean Beach, but Trouble Coffee happens to like unlikelihood. Hence the 'Build Your Own Damn House' breakfast special: coffee, thick-cut cinnamon-laced toast, and an entire young coconut. Surfers, stoners and surrealists in need of a snack, you must be looking for Trouble.

SUNRISE DELI

Map pp136–7 Middle Eastern $

415-664-8210; 2115 Irving St; 9am-9pm; 71, N;

A hidden gem in the fog belt, Sunrise dishes up what is arguably the city's best smoky baba ghanoush, *mujeddrah* (lentil-rice with crispy onions), garlicky *foul* (fava bean spread) and crispy falafel, either to go or to enjoy in the old-school cafe atmosphere. Local Arab American hipsters confess to passing off the Sunrise's specialties as their own home cooking to older relatives.

SAN TUNG Map pp136–7 Chinese, Dim Sum $

☎ 415-242-0828; 1031 Irving St; 11am-9:30pm Thu-Tue; 29, 44, 71, N

When you arrive at 5:30pm on a Sunday and already the place is packed, you might think you've hit a family dinner rush – but no, it's this crowded *all* the time. Blame it on the dry braised chicken wings – tender, moist morsels that defy the very name – and the housemade dumplings and noodles. You'll be smacking your lips with the memory when the bill comes: a three-course meal for two for $20. Next time you'll be in line by 5pm.

GENKI Map pp136–7 Dessert, Groceries $

☎ 415-379-6414; www.genkicrepes.com; 330 Clement St; 10:30am-10:30pm; 1, 2, 33, 38, 44

Life is always sweet at Genki, with aisles of packaged Japanese gummy candies nonsensically boasting of flavors 'shining in the cheeks of a snow-country child,' a dozen tropical fruit variations on tapioca bubble tea, and French crepes by way of Tokyo with green-tea ice cream and Nutella. Stock up in the beauty supply and Pocky aisle to satisfy sudden snack or hair-dye whims.

FIRST KOREAN MARKET

Map pp136–7 Korean $

☎ 415-221-2565; 4625 Geary Blvd; 9am-8pm; 1, 2, 33, 38, 44

Kimchee and *kimbap* cravings are well and truly satisfied at First Korean, where you'll find entire rows of the spicy fermented veggies (better than pickles) and sesame-oil-laced Korean seaweed, vegetable and rice rolls (not to be confused with sushi) at bargain prices.

UNDERDOG Map pp136–7 Sausages $

☎ 415-665-8881; 1634 Irving St; 11am-9pm; 28, 29, 44, 71, 91, N; V

For $4 to $5 organic meals on the run in a bun, Underdog is the clear winner. The roasted garlic and Italian pork sausages are USDA certified–organic, and the smoky veggie chipotle hot dog could make dedicated carnivores into fans of fake meat.

DRINKING

top picks

DRINKING

The word 'bar' loosely describes any establishment in San Francisco where you can have drinks: from the seediest dives to the swankiest lounges. Horn-rimmed hipsters and Mohawked hotties generally head to the Mission and Lower Haight; dancey girls and bi-curious boys trawl SoMa; and sorority gals with blond boyfriends populate the totally hetero pick-up joints of Union and Fillmore Sts. Gay/lesbian/bi/trans favorites are the Castro and SoMa (particularly Thursday to Sunday). Bars on Geary Blvd and Clement St, way out in the Richmond, are worth a 30-minute Muni ride from Downtown for their authentic Irish and faux tiki.

Count on the Castro and Lower Haight for a cheap buzz; pricier trend-conscious spots are North Beach, SoMa, some bars in the Tenderloin (aka the Trendy-loin) and, increasingly, the Mission. San Franciscans express outrage at nonhappy-hour cocktails hitting two digits and pints over $5 – hence the reduced-price happy 'hour' that actually runs from about 4pm until about 7pm.

The cafe scene is thriving in SF. Even on a Tuesday afternoon you'll see crowds of locals at the best spots, prompting many visitors to ask, 'Does anyone work in this town?' Actually, yes – cafes are de facto workplaces in SF: expect to see hardcore telecommuters and freelancers hunched over laptops anywhere there's wi-fi. Listen in on conversations and you'll also learn that cafes are the preferred meeting place for the full spectrum of locals, from clean-and-sober teens, to transgender poets, to harried moms taking time out for a caffeine jolt. For the best, head to North Beach, the Castro, the Mission and Haight.

This chapter lists bars of all stripes, but we've put some other bars in the Nightlife chapter (p206), particularly DJ-driven lounges and bars where you'll hear live music. If you're out and about and just want drinks, use this chapter to find a nearby bar. If you're planning a night on the town, read the Nightlife chapter as well, which is divided by genre, not by neighborhood.

ETIQUETTE

Unlike in NYC or LA, people won't usually wait in lines to get into SF bars – they just move on to the next one. Don't bother schmoozing the bartender (there aren't many VIP areas to weasel into), but do tell them if you want to start a tab with a credit card. Most aren't all that chatty anyway, and that's how locals like it: SF prefers surly bartenders who mix such a mean drink they don't have to be nice. Smoking's not allowed, but some bars have patios or special rooms. See the Top Picks box on p196.

If you're staying awhile with a small group of friends, buy a round for everyone – someone will get the next one, at least in theory. It's not impolite to decline a drink if it's offered, and bartenders are usually accommodating with creative nonalcoholic drinks if you're not boozing. At fancy lounges and clubs, those tempting little cocktail tables with seating are usually reserved for groups who buy overpriced bottles of champagne or vodka (think $300), and you might be reminded of this if you so much as lean on the armrest. Oh, and don't take your drink to the dance floor; nobody likes a splasher.

SPECIALTIES

Beer

Blowing off steam took on new meaning during the Gold Rush, when entrepreneurs trying to keep up with the demand for drink started brewing beer at higher temperatures, like ales. The result was a full, rich flavor and such powerful effervescence that when a keg was tapped, a mist would rise like steam. The much-beloved local Anchor Brewing Company has made its signature Anchor Steam amber ale this way, using copper distilling equipment since 1896. Other favorite local brews include Trumer Pils, and Speakeasy and Boont Amber ales, which are among the many beers on tap at Toronado (p202) and the 30-plus options at Zeitgeist (p200). Beer lovers look forward to the holidays for the arrival of locally microbrewed seasonal beers and ales. When it comes down to it, SF drinkers can be just as snobby about their beer as their wine. Head to the City Beer Store & Tasting Room (p200) for a drinkable education, and leave a tipsy connoisseur.

FREE BEER

Beer-lovers: Anchor Brewing Company (Map pp116–17; ☎ 415-863-8350; www.anchorbrewing.com; 1705 Mariposa St; 🚌 19, 22) offers weekday public tours, but you have to make reservations by phone at *least* a month in advance (three in summer). It's worth the wait for the 45-minute tour of Anchor's historic facilities and shiny-copper brewhouse, the crash course in beer-tasting, and six half-pints of different Anchor brews at the end. For free. 'Nuf said.

Irish Coffee

The Buena Vista Café (p194) is often mistakenly credited for the invention of this sweet concoction of whisky, coffee, sugar and foamy cream that renders drinkers warm, slightly toasted and oddly alert. At this Victorian-era bar near the cable-car turnaround, the cry of 'Make one!' from a server is understood to be an order for the 'Irish'. But for all that, it was not invented in San Francisco.

Mixology

A recent proliferation of 'mixology' bars in SF has revived the classic tradition of handcrafted drinks. Mixologists (aka bartenders) at these joints take their work very seriously indeed, crushing fistfuls of mint, zesting citrus, grating ginger, pulverizing plant leaves and carefully tasting for balance. Expect to wait – perfection takes time. The best mixologists are unearthing long-since-forgotten Prohibition-era drinks (Sazeracs are back) and learning how to make them the old-fashioned way. Among our favorite places are Cantina (p194), Rye (p196), Alembic (p202) and Beretta (p200). Even the speakeasy is back in style: at a small handful of bars, such as Bourbon & Branch (see the boxed text, p198), you'll need a password to get in.

The Martini

First mentioned in an 1887 bartending guide by Professor Jerry Thomas, the martini was supposedly invented when a boozehound walked into an SF bar and demanded something to tide him over until he reached Martinez across the bay. The original was made with vermouth, gin, bitters, lemon, maraschino cherry and ice, but the recipe has since been refined to gin and vermouth vapors with an olive or a twist. Today, order a martini in any SF bar and the bartender will probably await further instruction. It seems there are all kinds of ways to prepare (or butcher) a martini, so choose carefully.

Soju/Sake Cocktails

Grain alcohols from Korea and Japan (*soju* and sake, respectively) have lately become key mixers in SF bars, partly because they're not yet restricted by SF liquor license laws. It's like back in the day when LSD was still legal. More than two sake cocktails at Noc Noc (p202) will knock-knock you right off your stool.

Wine

SF is lucky enough to be near the Sonoma and Napa Valleys, aka Wine Country (p282). Some of the USA's best wines are produced within two hours of the city. Cabernet, pinot, zinfandel, syrah and sparkling wines are big in these parts. These days, it seems everyone's sworn off chardonnay in favor of riesling.

SF is inhabited by some of the USA's biggest wine snobs. To ensure complete satisfaction, the wine lists in fine restaurants commonly outsize the menus, and a sommelier visits each table to help diners make sense of it all.

PRACTICALITIES

Opening Hours

Bars typically open in the late afternoon on weekdays for happy hour (between 4pm and 7pm) and stay open until 11pm or midnight. On weekends, many open in the late morning and remain open until 2am. Last call is always a half-hour before close. That said, bar hours depend on what neighborhood you happen to be in, and whether the bar serves food, in which case the alcohol might flow earlier.

How Much?

Bar-pulled microbrews run from $4 to $7 a pint, depending on where you are and what brew you're having, and well-mixed drinks cost somewhat more, especially if you're into top-shelf hooch.

A slopped-together martini of Gordon's vodka and watermelon liquor might seem like a good deal at $6 to $7, until you discover it tastes like a Jolly Rancher candy and delivers an on-the-spot headache. The classic

ID, PLEASE...

If you can't show proof you're over 21 at bars and clubs, even if you're well over 30, you won't get in. Best is a government-issued ID, preferably your driver's license; otherwise carry a color photocopy of your passport – but if you look young, some bartenders won't serve you without seeing your actual passport, which we never recommend carrying around when you're drinking, unless you're the most together person we've never met.

or experimental gourmet choices with premium booze can cost a tenner or more, but be warned they pack a lot of bang for the buck. A small cup of regular American coffee averages $1.75, while a cappuccino or latte might be upwards of $3.

Tipping

Tips are most appreciated in cash. A dollar for every one or two beers will keep the drinks rolling along nicely, and if you want the bartender to remember you, tip more – or less.

Be sure to generously acknowledge any extra labor that went into a cocktail (like that fresh-pureed fruity number or perfect martini) and you'll be subtly rewarded on your next round. A note to foreigners from countries where alcohol is strictly measured: California bartenders are allowed to pour liberally, without using a state-controlled measuring spout. If you tip well, bartenders often pour heavier, meaning that your generosity may end up getting you drunk after the second cocktail.

EMBARCADERO & THE PIERS

BUENA VISTA CAFÉ

Map p63 Bar

415-474-5044; www.thebuenavista.com; 2765 Hyde St; 9am-2am Mon-Fri, 8am-2am Sat & Sun; Powell-Hyde

Warm your cockles with a prim little goblet of bitter-creamy Irish coffee, introduced to the US at this destination bar that once served sailors and cannery workers. The creaky Victorian floor manages to hold up carousers and families alike, served community-style at round tables overlooking the wharf.

DOWNTOWN

BUBBLE LOUNGE

Map pp70–1 Bar

415-434-4204; www.bubblelounge.com; 714 Montgomery St; 5:30pm-1am Tue & Wed, to 2am Thu & Fri, 6:30pm-2am Sat; 1, 10, 12, 20

Though its aesthetic went out of fashion with the recession, the velvet-draped Bubble Lounge remains Downtown's top spot for champagne by the glass. Suburbanites throng the place on weekends, but on weeknights it's perfect for a swanky date or girls' night out. When a sofa opens up, snag it immediately. Wear nice shoes.

CANTINA

Map pp70–1 Bar

415-398-0195; www.cantinasf.com; 580 Sutter St; 5pm-2am Mon-Sat; 2, 3, 4

All the Latin-inspired cocktails (think tequila, cachaça and pisco) are made with fresh juice – there's not even a soda gun behind the bar – at this mixologist's dream bar that's mellow enough on weeknights for quiet conversation. The all-local crowd includes many off-duty bartenders – always a good sign. DJs spin on weekends.

CLOCK BAR

Map pp70–1 Bar

415-397-7000; www.michaelmina.net/clockbar; Westin St Francis Hotel, 335 Powell St; 4pm-2am; & Powell St; Powell-Mason & Powell-Hyde

If it's in season, it goes into the glass at this top-end mixology bar, brainchild of celeb-chef Michael Mina. Ooh and ah over lobster corn dogs and truffled popcorn while sampling knockout cocktails in cozy leather-and-wood snugs. Arrive early or reserve ahead, or expect to stand. Cocktails are over $10.

GOLD DUST LOUNGE

Map pp70–1 Bar

415-397-1695; 247 Powell St; 7am-2am; & Powell St

Precarious Victorian brass chandeliers hover over a bar full of visitors and a twangy rockabilly band at this Union Square anachronism, where the gold paint has lost its glitter and pints are no longer cheap. But there's something of a time-machine effect in the swinging doors, coat stands and nude paintings – you almost expect someone to beckon you to a brothel upstairs.

IRISH BANK

Map pp70–1 Bar

☎ 415-788-7152; www.theirishbank.com; 10 Mark Lane; 11:30am-2am; 1, 15, 30, 45; California

Perfectly pulled pints and thick-cut fries with malt vinegar, plus juicy burgers, brats and anything else you could possibly want with lashings of mustard are staples at this cozy Irish pub. There are tables beneath a big awning in the little alley out front, ideal for smokers even on rainy nights.

JOHN'S GRILL

Map pp70–1 Bar

☎ 415-986-0069; 63 Ellis St; 11am-10pm Mon-Sat, noon-10pm Sun; & Powell St; Powell-Mason, Powell-Hyde

It could be the martinis, the low lighting, or the *Maltese Falcon* statuette upstairs, but something about Dashiell Hammett's favorite bar lends itself to hard-boiled tales of lost love and true crimes, confessed while chewing toothpicks. That is, until the tourists filling the joint snap you back into the present.

PIED PIPER BAR

Map pp70–1 Bar

☎ 415-512-1111; www.sfpalace.com; 2 New Montgomery St; 11:30am-11pm; & Montgomery St

Deep within the opulent Palace Hotel, the Pied Piper's mahogany walls and plush seating up the swank factor, but what sets it apart is the creepy-gorgeous 1909 Maxfield Parrish mural behind the bar. Prices are steep but include munchies. Good for a classic martini.

REDWOOD ROOM

Map pp70–1 Bar

☎ 415-775-4700; www.clifthotel.com; 495 Geary St; 5pm-2am Sun-Thu, 4pm-2am Fri & Sat; 2, 3, 4, 27, 38; Powell-Mason, Powell-Hyde

We love the landmark Redwood Room, with its walls paneled from a single ancient redwood tree. For years it was San Francisco's most iconic bar, inside one of its most storied hotels. Then Philippe Starck got hold of the place, making it horrifically trendy, mounting plasma screens on the walls (sin of sins), installing his now-tired-looking signature furniture, and raising cocktail prices through the roof. Still, it's worth seeing the room on a quiet weeknight, but never on weekends, when Carrie Bradshaw wannabes jam the place and aggressive bouncers fail to remember they exist in service of guests, not the other way round.

top picks

DIVES

- **Specs'** (p197)
- **Ha-Ra** (p196)
- **Saloon** (p197)
- **Doc's Clock** (p201)
- **House of Shields** (p200)

TUNNEL TOP BAR

Map pp70–1 Bar

☎ 415-722-6620; www.tunneltop.com; 601 Bush St; 5pm-2am Mon-Sat; 1, 2, 3, 4, 30, 45

You can't tell who's local and who's not in this happening, chill two-story bar with exposed beams, beer-bottle chandelier, and rickety balcony that always seems about ready to give out. The owners are French, and their Gallic friends throng the place, tapping their toes to conscious hip-hop (think Common, not Little Wayne) and boom-boom house music, the SF soundtrack. Cash only.

CAFFE AMICI

Map pp70–1 Cafe

☎ 415-391-3241; www.caffeamiciespresso.com; 155 Montgomery St; 5am-7pm Mon-Fri, 7am-5pm Sat & Sun; 1, 15, 30, 45; & Montgomery St;

Amici serves excellent coffee in hand-painted Italian cups, and draws hearts in cappuccino foam, warming the spirits of Downtown office workers.

CIVIC CENTER & THE TENDERLOIN

BAMBUDDHA LOUNGE

Map p77 Bar

☎ 415-885-5088; www.bambuddhalounge.com; 601 Eddy St; 5:30-10pm Wed-Thu, to 2am Fri & Sat; 5, 19, 31, 38

Vinyl beds, *mojitos* and occasional glimpses of B-grade rock stars through bamboo thickets – Bambuddha is SF's

top picks

FOR SMOKERS

- **Phone Booth** (p201)
- **Amber** (p202)
- **Edinburgh Castle** (below)
- **Rye** (right)
- **Zeitgeist** (p200)
- **Irish Bank** (p195)
- **Mars Bar** (p200)
- **Hemlock Tavern** (right)
- **Rosewood** (opposite)
- **Medjool Sky Terrace** (p201)

answer to Miami. We dig the hot bartenders and cool poolside happy hour (5:30-7pm Wed-Fri) on sunny afternoons, but evenings can go either way, when the pool closes and well-scrubbed 20-to-30-somethings flirt with each other inside the minimalist concrete space and groove to club-dance music.

EDINBURGH CASTLE

Map p77 Bar

415-885-4074; www.castlenews.com; 950 Geary St; 5pm-2am; 19, 38, 47, 49

SF's finest old-school monument to drink comes complete with dart boards, pool tables, rock bands, occasional literary readings and locals acting out (as is our habit). Photos of bagpipers, the *Trainspotting* soundtrack on the jukebox and a service delivering vinegary fish and chips in newspaper are all the Scottish authenticity you could ask for, short of haggis.

HA-RA

Map p77 Bar

415-673-3148; 875 Geary St; 3:30pm-2am Mon & Tue, 9:30am-2am Wed-Sun; 19, 38, 47, 49

If you're alone with your journal, or need a place for a tête-à-tête that may end in tears, bring a fiver for the jukebox, select Miles Davis, and cozy up in this often-empty vintage-1947 classic dive. Take note of the flashback-to-the-1950s black-and-white photo of the couple dancing, then look at the wall sconces and you'll realize you're standing in the exact same spot – only now it's filled with ghosts, not bee-boppers.

HEMLOCK TAVERN

Map p77 Bar

415-923-0923; www.hemlocktavern.com; 1131 Polk St; 4pm-2am; 2, 3, 4, 19, 38, 47, 49

When you wake up tomorrow with peanut shells in your hair (weren't they all over the floor?), a stiff neck from rocking entirely too hard to the Family Curse (weren't they good?) and someone else's mascara on your armpit (should we even ask?), you'll know it was another successful night at the Hemlock. Weekday nights, stand-up comedy and literary readings are anything but staid among this motley crowd of raucous, party-hardy San Franciscans.

KOKO COCKTAILS

Map p77 Bar

415-885-4788; www.kokococktails.com; 1060 Geary St; 5pm-2am; 2, 3, 4, 19, 38, 47, 49

Our favorite place to start a Polk St pub crawl is a retro-cool cocktail lounge that looks like a gussied-up rumpus room from the 1970s. Seven bucks gets you a fancy, hand-muddled cocktail, which you can sip at handmade tables of reclaimed oak. DJs spin reggae, soul and sometimes hip-hop, but never rap.

LUSH LOUNGE

Map p77 Bar

415-771-2022; www.thelushlounge.com; 1100 Polk St; 4pm-2am; 2, 3, 4, 19, 47, 49

Portraits of jazz luminaries and long-forgotten Hollywood stars line the walls at this mellow storefront bar that marks the line on Polk St where grit ends and hip begins. Martinis are the specialty (15 different varieties), but we also love the lemon drops, cosmos and anything in stemware. Ideal for couples and small groups; all sexual persuasions welcome.

RYE

Map p77 Bar

415-474-4448; www.ryesf.com; 688 Geary St; 5:30pm-2am Mon-Fri, 7pm-2am Sat & Sun; 27, 38

Rye's high-style design mixes concrete, steel and polished wood, and its leather sofas are a sexy spot for a basil gimlet or anything else made with herb-infused spirits or fresh-squeezed juice. The smokers' patio is actually a cage overlooking the sidewalk, and offers a glimpse of who's inside. It packs after 10pm; arrive early.

CHINATOWN

EZ5 Map p82 Bar

☎ 415-362-9321; www.ez5bar.com; 682 Commercial St; 4pm-2am Mon-Fri, 6pm-2am Sat; 1, 10, 41

Don't worry if you're not looking your best – EZ5's lighting is dim, with blue and red strings of Christmas lights that are reminiscent of a long-since-over New Year's Eve party. But the '80s-ish cherry-red vinyl seating isn't sticky, the disco ball still turns, and crowds show up at happy hour and on weekends after 11pm for DJ beats (house and hip-hop) to kick-start the otherwise dead room. If nobody's here, console yourself with Ms Pac Man.

LI PO Map p82 Bar

☎ 415-982-0072; 916 Grant Ave; 2pm-2am; 45

A fave of the Beat poets, Li Po's fake-grotto decor comes with lurid 1960s-era plush red booths, bartenders shouting in Cantonese and an unexpected Chinese-meets-hipster clientele. On slow nights, it may be just you and the barkeep watching TV.

NORTH BEACH

CHURCH KEY

Map p87 Bar

☎ 415-986-3511; 1402 Grant Ave; 5pm-2am; 20, 30, 41, 45

If there's a connoisseur's beer from Belgium, Japan, Canada or New Zealand that you've been dying to try, chances are you'll find it at this sparsely furnished hole-in-the-wall, with a little upstairs mezzanine, off North Beach's main strip. The local crowd means good conversation about all things SF. Beer, wine and cash only.

ROSEWOOD

Map p87 Bar

☎ 415-951-4886; 732 Broadway; 5:30pm-2am Wed-Fri, 7pm-2am Sat; 12, 30, 45

This unmarked bar delivers on its name with sleek floor-to-ceiling rosewood-paneled walls, dim lighting and low-slung tufted black-leather sofas. It's a cool first-drink spot and there's a bamboo-enclosed smokers' patio, but too many hard surfaces make conversation nearly impossible once crowds arrive and the music amps up.

CASH ONLY

Some small mom-and-pop bars don't take credit cards, so start the night with $40 in pocket. When you're trawling the streets hungry after bar shut-off at 2am, you'll be glad for that leftover five-spot when you espy a sausage vendor on the corner.

SALOON

Map p87 Bar

☎ 415-989-7666; 1232 Grant Ave; weekend cover $2-5; noon-2am; 20, 30, 45

A stalwart North Beach dive, the Saloon survived the 1906 fire when its loyal patrons brandished buckets of beer and wine to quench the flames. Today it's the oldest bar in SF, dating from 1861, and hasn't had a coat of paint in decades, which is exactly why disheveled old-timers and local hipsters love it. Blues and rock bands perform nightly and from 4pm weekend afternoons.

SPECS'

Map p87 Bar

☎ 415-421-4112; 12 William Saroyan Pl; 5pm-2am; 1, 20

Hidden on a tiny pedestrian alley, cave-like Specs' draws barflies in the afternoon and hipsters, literary radicals and other colorful local characters in the evening. It's also a sort of museum, packed with weird ephemera culled from ports around the globe – nobody's sure which species' desiccated penis hangs behind the bar, but everyone agrees it's from a marine mammal.

TONY NIK'S

Map p87 Bar

☎ 415-693-0990; 1534 Stockton St; 4pm-2am; 30, 45

Think Rat Pack lounge, c 1956, and you'll conjure retro-cool Tony Nik's, a tiny cocktail lounge with glass bricks, vintage granite floors and period wood-paneling. Good acoustics make for easy conversation. Aim for the cocktail tables in back, or hang with old-timers at the bar.

TOSCA CAFE Map p87 Bar

☎ 415-391-1244; 242 Columbus Ave; 5pm-2am Tue-Sun; 1, 20

If Francis Ford Coppola had filmed *The Godfather* in San Francisco, he would surely have set an operatic bloodbath or quiet strangling in Tosca. Coppola, Sean Penn, Robert DeNiro or Bono might be lurking in the VIP room, but we'd rather hang at one of the round red-vinyl booths, Irish coffee or retro-classic cocktail in hand. The place has that self-assured Italian American brusqueness, with a smoke-stained ceiling, a worn linoleum floor and an all-opera jukebox (with genuine 45rpm platters).

VESUVIO

Map p87 Bar

☎ 415-362-3370; 255 Columbus Ave; 6am-2am; 1, 20

Guy walks into a bar, roars and leaves. Without missing a beat, the bartender says to the next customer, 'Welcome to Vesuvio, honey – what can I get you?' It takes a lot more than a barbaric yawp to get Vesuvio's regulars to glance up from their microbrewed beers. Kerouac blew off Henry Miller to go on a bender here, and after knocking back a couple with neighborhood characters, you'll get why.

CAFFE TRIESTE

Map p87 Cafe

☎ 415-392-6739; 601 Vallejo St; 6:30am-11pm Sun-Thu, to midnight Fri & Sat; 20, 30, 41, 45;

Poetry on the bathroom walls, opera on the jukebox, monthly Saturday accordion concerts, and occasional sightings of poet laureate Lawrence Ferlinghetti: this is North Beach at its best, as it's been since the 1950s. Linger over a legendary espresso, join aging anarchists debating how best to bring down the government, or just sit with your sketchpad and watch the world go by outside.

HUSH-HUSH HOOCH

Psst...can you keep a secret? Speakeasies, those Prohibition-era underground gin joints, still exist in SF. We're not telling how, but once you've found the phone number or website for **Bourbon & Branch**, you can make a reservation to get the location (an unmarked door in the Tenderloin) and password for entry. Inside, studded leather banquettes, mirrored oak tables, and red velvet walls evoke the roaring 1920s, and the original speakeasy basement – complete with bullet holes and secret escape routes – and room hidden behind the fake bookcase are perfect for private parties. Don't tell anyone.

RUSSIAN & NOB HILLS

BIGFOOT LODGE

Map p92 Bar

☎ 415-440-2355; www.bigfootlodge.com; 1750 Polk St; 3pm-2am; 1, 19; California

Log-cabin walls, antler chandeliers, taxidermy animals everywhere you look – you'd swear you were at a state-park visitors center, but for all the giggly-drunk 20-somethings. If you're looking for your gay boyfriend, he's wandered across the street to the Cinch.

TONGA ROOM

Map p92 Bar

☎ 415-772-5278; www.fairmont.com; lower level, Fairmont Hotel, 950 Mason St; 6-11:45pm Sun-Thu, to 12:45am Fri & Sat; 1, 27; California

Tonight's San Francisco weather: 100% chance of tropical rainstorms every 20 minutes, but only around the top-40 band playing on the island in the middle of the indoor pool – you're safe in your grass hut. For a more powerful hurricane, order one in a plastic coconut. Note: at this writing, the future of the city's most famous tiki bar was uncertain; call ahead.

TOP OF THE MARK

Map p92 Bar

☎ 415-616-6916; www.topofthemark.com; 999 California St; cover $5-10; 5pm-midnight Sun-Thu, 4pm-1am Fri & Sat; California

So what if it's touristy? Nothing beats twirling in the clouds to a full jazz orchestra in your best cocktail dress on the city's highest dance floor. Check the online calendar to ensure a band is playing the night you're coming. Expect $15 drinks.

JAPANTOWN & PACIFIC HEIGHTS

BUTTERFLY BAR

Map p96 Bar

☎ 415-441-1280; www.cafemajesticsf.com; 1500 Sutter St; 5-11pm, sometimes later weekends; 2, 3, 4

The Hotel Majestic's intimate 20-seat lounge resembles an elegant library bar in an English manor house, with a gorgeous collection of rare butterflies adorning the walls. Great martinis. Bring a date.

top picks

DATE NIGHT

- Top of the Mark (opposite)
- Hôtel Biron (p203)
- Lush Lounge (p196)
- Butterfly Bar (opposite)
- Dosa (below)

DOSA Map p96

Bar

☎ 415-441-3672; http://dosasf.com; 1700 Fillmore St; ⏰ 5:30pm-midnight; 🚌 2, 3, 4, 22, 38

Baubled glittering chandeliers hang from high ceilings at Dosa, an otherwise overpriced Indian restaurant with a happening bar scene of sexy, non-snooty locals. It's a good spot for snazzy cocktails, but if you're wearing dumpy clothes, you'll feel out of place.

HARRY'S BAR

Map p96 Bar

☎ 415-921-1000; 2020 Fillmore St; ⏰ 11:30am-2am Mon-Fri, 10am-2am Sat & Sun; 🚌 1, 2

Cap off your upper Fillmore St shopping raid at Harry's mahogany bar with kick-ass Bloody Marys (made properly with horseradish) or freshly muddled *mojitos*. A Pac-Heights mainstay, Harry's appeals largely to aging debutantes who love getting politely hammered.

THE MARINA & THE PRESIDIO

BUS STOP Map pp100–1

Bar

☎ 415-567-6905; 1901 Union St; ⏰ 10am-2am; 🚌 45

Bus Stop has 18 flickering TV screens and a manly crowd that roars when their team scores. If your girlfriend wants to shop, but you must watch the game, wait here as she trawls through surrounding Union St boutiques.

CALIFORNIA WINE MERCHANT

Map pp100–1 Bar

☎ 415-567-0646; www.californiawinemerchant.com; 2113 Chestnut St; ⏰ 10am-midnight Mon-Wed, 10am-1:30am Thu-Sat, 11am-11pm Sun; 🚌 30

Part wine store, part wine bar, this little shop on busy Chestnut St caters to grey-at-the-temples professionals and neighborhood wine aficionados, and serves half-glasses as well as flights. Arrive early to score a table, or stand and gab with the locals.

MATRIXFILLMORE

Map pp100–1 Bar

☎ 415-563-4180; www.matrixfillmore.com; 3138 Fillmore St; ⏰ 6pm-2am; 🚌 22, 45

The neighborhood's most notorious up-market pick-up joint provides a fascinating glimpse into the lives of single, white Marina swankers. Treat it as a comic sociological study, while enjoying the stellar cocktails, blazing fireplace and sexy lounge beats. Bring your credit card.

SOMA

83 PROOF

Map pp110–11 Bar

☎ 415-296-8383; www.83proof.com; 83 1st St; ⏰ 2pm-midnight Mon & Tue, 2pm-2am Wed-Fri, 8pm-2am Sat; 🚌 F; 🚌 & Ⓜ Montgomery St

High ceilings and a mezzanine add visual drama to this happening Financial District bar, which is popular with an unpretentious mixed crowd of 20- and 30-something after-work drinkers, who swill sexy cocktails (think basil gimlets) as if tomorrow wasn't a work day.

BLOODHOUND

Map pp110–11 Bar

☎ 415-863-2840; www.bloodhoundsf.com; 1145 Folsom St; ⏰ 4pm-2am; 🚌 12, 19, 27, 47

Our favorite SoMa bar feels vaguely Nordic, with white wood, antler chandeliers and fantastic art, including a murder of crows painted on the ceiling. Top-shelf ingredients, but no drink is over-intellectualized. Best Sunday to Thursday, or before midnight on weekends. Killer jukebox.

BUTTER

Map pp110–11 Bar

☎ 415-863-5964; www.smoothasbutter.com; 354 11th St; ⏰ 6pm-2am Tue-Sun; 🚌 47

Butter satirizes trailer trash – think cocktails mixed with Tang – providing a refreshing contrast to the VIP clubs across the street. Best of all, you'll never pay $10 for a drink at this tiny, always-jumpin' bar, leaving you extra cash for Tater Tots and Spaghettios – cooked, of course, in a microwave.

CITY BEER STORE & TASTING ROOM

Map pp110–11 Bar

☎ 415-503-1033; www.citybeerstore.com; 1168 Folsom St; noon-10pm Tue-Sat, to 6pm Sun; 12, 19

Sample exceptional local and Belgian microbrewed beer (6oz to 22oz, depending how thirsty you are) at the city's top beer store, then assemble your own six-pack to go.

HOUSE OF SHIELDS

Map pp110–11 Bar

☎ 415-975-8651; www.houseofshields.com; 39 New Montgomery St; 2pm-2am Mon-Fri, from 7pm Sat; & Montgomery St

Flash back a hundred years at this classic high-ceilinged bar, with tiled floors and a huge mahogany backbar. The odd mix of slumming debutantes and bike-messengers seems weirdly anachronistic in this once-fancy bar; $5 cocktails explain why they're here. And everyone looks good: half the red bulbs in the original c 1908 chandeliers are usually burned out.

MARS BAR

Map pp110–11 Bar

☎ 415-621-6277; www.marsbarsf.com; 798 Brannan St; 6pm-midnight Thu, 9pm-2am Fri & Sat; admission $5-15; 12, 19, 27, 47

Cool urban cats hang at Mars Bar, a raw space defined not by its design (think beach shack), but by its happening crowd of locals who wear denim, not dresses. Dance on the little floor to bangin' house music, or hang on the big outside patio with the smokers. Check the online calendar for DJs.

MEDICI LOUNGE

Map pp110–11 Bar

☎ 415-863-8334; www.medicisf.com; 299 9th St; 11am-2pm Tue-Sat; 12, 27, 47

When you're wandering South of Market and just want a damn cocktail, Medici is a welcome sight. It's a dimly lit bar that serves great mixed drinks made with fresh-squeezed juices, including killer lemon drops. DJs sometimes spin down-temp beats. Good pizzas, too.

ZEITGEIST

Map pp110–11 Bar

☎ 415-255-7505; 199 Valencia St; 9am-2am; 26; 16th St Mission

Social headquarters for the city's motley crew of bikers (motorized and pedal-powered), Zeitgeist is always a happening scene – whether it's yours may be a different story. You've got two seconds flat to order from tough-gal barkeeps who are used to putting macho bikers in their place. When it's warm, regulars head straight to the bar's huge graveled back patio to sit at long picnic tables and smoke out.

BRAINWASH

Map pp110–11 Cafe

☎ 415-431-9274; www.brainwash.com; 1122 Folsom St; 7am-10pm Mon-Thu, 7am-11pm Fri & Sat, 8am-10pm Sun; 12, 19;

The coolest place to do laundry is also a happening cafe with coffee, beer and live performances most nights. Last wash is at 8:30pm.

THE MISSION & POTRERO HILL

ARGUS LOUNGE

Map pp116–17 Bar

☎ 415-824-1447; www.arguslounge.com; 3187 Mission St; 4pm-2am Mon-Sat, 5pm-2am Sun; 14, 26; 24th St Mission

This young locals' hangout named for a mythical monster that never slept supplies jukebox beats, occasional DJs and killer Bloodys in a moody-dark room festooned with peacocks and cattle skulls; there's a competitive pool table.

BERETTA

Map pp116–17 Bar

☎ 415-695-1199; www.berettasf.com; 1199 Valencia St; 5:30pm-1am Mon-Fri, 11am-1am Sat & Sun; 26

After a busy day shopping on Valencia St, nothing hits the spot like Beretta's lip-smacking seasonal cocktails, made with fresh everything. But consider avoiding this place during peak dinner hours, when the small storefront restaurant-and-bar gets packed and deafeningly loud. Good cracker-crust pizzas.

CONNECTICUT YANKEE
Map pp116–17 Bar

☎ 415-552-4440; www.theyankee.com; 100 Connecticut St; ⌚ from 11:30am; 🚌 22

Odd choice of name, because the owner has a shrine devoted to the Red Sox inside his neighborhood watering hole. Pony up to the old wooden bar and you'll know everyone by name before finishing your pint. Live music on weekends ($5 to $15 cover), TV sports, a sunny patio and decent pub grub attract mellow, hardworking ex-hippies.

DOC'S CLOCK
Map pp116–17 Bar

☎ 415-824-3627; www.docsclock.com; 2575 Mission St; ⌚ 6pm-2am Mon-Sat, 8pm-midnight Sun; 🚌 14, 49

Dig the dazzling neon sign at this happy-mellow, green-certified dive that's always good for a few pints, shuffleboard and conversation. Every second and fourth Tuesday is local-filmmaker night, with screenings of indie shorts and $2 draft PBR.

ELIXIR
Map pp116–17 Bar

☎ 415-552-1633; www.elixirsf.com; 3200 16th St; ⌚ 3pm-2am Mon-Fri, noon-2am Sat & Sun; Ⓑ 16th St Mission

SF's first certified-green bar uses organic spirits and fresh fruits to mix knockout drinks for an always appreciative, unpretentious crowd of Bacchanalian revelers, who throng this cozy, vintage-1907 saloon – some bring their dogs. Great habañero-chili cosmos.

MEDJOOL SKY TERRACE
Map pp116–17 Bar

☎ 415-550-9055; www.medjoolsf.com; 2522 Mission St; ⌚ 5-11pm Sun-Thu, to 2am Fri & Sat; 🚌 14, 26; Ⓑ 24th St Mission

SF's only open-air rooftop bar has knockout views, a party crowd, Mediterranean small plates and tasty (cash-only) cocktails, but as of this writing, noise-sensitive neighbors were pressing the city to pull its permit. Great on a warm evening, but call ahead.

PHONE BOOTH
Map pp116–17 Bar

☎ 415-648-4683; 1398 S Van Ness Ave; ⌚ 2pm-2am; Ⓑ 24th St Mission

Twenty-something sexually ambiguous art-school students squeeze around tiny cocktail tables to get wasted on cheap drinks, shoot pool, munch free popcorn, feed a killer jukebox, smoke cigs indoors (shh!) and – on a good night – make out in the dim red light.

top picks
FOR BILLIARDS

- **Zeitgeist** (opposite)
- **Argus Lounge** (opposite)
- **Edinburgh Castle** (p196)
- **Bitter End** (p204)
- **Hemlock Tavern** (p196)

YIELD
Map pp116–17 Bar

☎ 415-401-8984; www.yieldsf.com; 2490 3rd St; ⌚ 5pm-midnight Tue-Sat; 🚌 22

It's easy being green at Yield, a storefront wine bar with a rotating list of sustainably farmed vintages served at rough-hewn wood tables surrounded by low-slung ottomans. Order a bottle or glass, along with some tasty nibbles, and kick it with the convivial crowd of locals.

ATLAS CAFE
Map pp116–17 Cafe

☎ 415-648-1047; www.atlascafe.net; 3049 20th St; ⌚ 6:30am-10pm Mon-Fri, 8am-8pm Sat & Sun; Ⓑ 16th St Mission; wi-fi

A bohemian magnet for SF artists, some of whose works hang on the walls, Atlas has a big sunny patio, occasional weekend bluegrass jams, and a menu of exemplary coffees, full breakfasts, sandwiches, soups and small pizzas. Packed weekends.

FARLEY'S
Map pp116–17 Cafe

☎ 415-648-1545; www.farleyscoffee.com; 1315 18th St; ⌚ 6:30am-10pm Mon-Fri, 7:30am-10pm Sat, 8am-10pm Sun; 🚌 22; wi-fi

Retro-Americana down to the whitewashed slat-board walls and soda-shop-style counter, Farley's is Potrero Hill's unofficial gathering place, and has a big community newsboard and stellar magazine selection. Neighbors while away entire afternoons at sunny sidewalk tables. If you want to meet locals, this is the place.

RITUAL COFFEE ROASTERS

Map pp116–17 Cafe

☎ 415-641-1024; www.ritualroasters.com; 1026 Valencia St; 6am-10pm Mon-Fri, 7am-10pm Sat, 7am-9pm Sun; 14, 26; 24th St Mission;

Blue Bottle and Ritual Roasters are the two big names in SF's 'Third Wave' coffee movement, which esteems coffee as highly – and artfully – as fine chocolate and grand cru wine. We love bringing our laptop to Ritual's Mission location to get jacked and eavesdrop on tattooed bikers, internet pros and coffee aficionados, but lament the loss of electrical outlets at some tables.

THE CASTRO & NOE VALLEY

AMBER

Map p123 Bar

☎ 415-626-7827; 718 14th St; 6pm-2am; Church St

Amber's retro stylings are matched by its old-fashioned tolerance of smokers. You're free to light up here on one of the sleek, mid-century-modern couches or right at the bar. Nonsmokers flock here to hang with the giggling, mixed, 20-something crowd.

SAMOVAR TEA LOUNGE

Map p123 Cafe

☎ 415-626-4700; www.samovartea.com; 498 Sanchez St; 10am-10pm; 24, 33, F, K, L, M

Styled in soothing Zen-chic, Samovar's sunny Castro location specializes in organic, fair-trade teas, and provides a cozy alternative to the neighborhood's ubiquitous bars. *Bento* boxes, cheese plates and tea cookies give reason to linger.

top picks

CAFES

- Caffe Trieste (p198)
- Farley's (p201)
- Momi Toby's Revolution Café (opposite)
- Atlas Cafe (p201)
- Café Flore (p245)

THE HAIGHT

ALEMBIC Map pp126–7 Bar

☎ 415-666-0822; www.thealembicbar.com; 1725 Haight St; 4pm-2am Mon-Thu, noon-2am Fri-Sun; 6, 7

Haight St's spiffiest bar has hammered tin ceilings, rough-hewn wood floors and an impressive array of whiskeys and mixology drinks, appealing to bon-vivant 30-somethings who jam the tiny space every night. If you're not ordering dinner, expect to stand shoulder to shoulder. Great bar nibbles include *za'atar* potato chips.

AUB ZAM ZAM Map pp126–7 Bar

☎ 415-861-2545; 1633 Haight St; 3pm-2am; 6, 7

Arabesque arches, a gorgeous *Arabian Nights*–style mural, blues on the jukebox and top-shelf cocktails at low-shelf prices keep poets and musicians happy for the night at this Haight St mainstay. Ask about Bruno, the legendary now-deceased owner, who'd throw you out for ordering a vodka martini. Seriously.

MADRONE Map pp126–7 Bar

☎ 415-611-6838; www.madronelounge.com; 500 Divisadero St; 6pm-2am Tue-Sat, to midnight Sun & Mon; 5, 21, 24

A changing roster of DJs and giggling cuties come as a surprise in a goth-Victorian bar decorated with animal skulls, creepy murals of uprooted madrone trees and art suggesting untimely demises, but nothing surprises us as much as the jaw-dropping mashups at the Saturday-monthly Prince vs Michael Jackson party, when the place packs.

NOC NOC Map pp126–7 Bar

☎ 415-861-5811; www.nocnocs.com; 557 Haight St; 5pm-2am; 6, 7, 22, 71

Who's there? Nearsighted graffiti artists, anarchist bike messengers moonlighting as electronica DJs, and other characters straight out of an R Crumb comic, that's who. The sake cocktails will knock you off your stool.

TORONADO Map pp126–7 Bar

☎ 415-863-2276; www.toronado.com; 547 Haight St; 11:30am-2am; 6, 7, 22, 71

Glory hallelujah, beer-lovers: your prayers have been heard. Be humbled before the chalkboard altar listing 50-plus beers on tap and hundreds more bottled, including spectacular seasonal microbrews. Bring cash, come early and stay late, with a sausage from Rosamunde (p186) next door to accompany ale made by Trappist monks.

COFFEE TO THE PEOPLE
Map pp126–7 Cafe

☎ 415-626-2435; www.coffeetothepeople.com; 1206 Masonic Ave; 6am-9pm Mon-Fri, 7am-9pm Sat & Sun; 6, 7;

This utopian coffee shop hosts folksy Tuesday open-mic, and serves enough fair-trade coffee to revive the Sandinista movement. Five percent of your purchase goes to support community organizations, and baristas donate 3% of their tips to send children in coffee-growing regions to school.

HAYES VALLEY

CAV WINE BAR Map p133 Bar

☎ 415-437-1770; www.cavwinebar.com; 1666 Market St; 5pm-midnight Mon-Sat; 5, 6, F

If Hôtel Biron (below) is packed, fret not: nearby Cav serves 40 wines by the glass (most under $10), available in flights or 2.5oz pours, in a concrete-and-metal industrial space. Tasty small plates keep your palate zinging.

HÔTEL BIRON Map p133 Bar

☎ 415-703-0403; www.hotelbiron.com; 45 Rose St; 5pm-2am; 5, 6, F

Our favorite SF wine bar has an outstanding selection strong on French, Spanish and Portuguese vintages. The vibe is French underground, with cool art, moody lighting and little nooks, but it's hard to score a table. Once you do, barkeeps let you keep tasting until you find what you like. Great cheese plates.

MINT Map p133 Bar

☎ 415-626-4726; www.themint.net; 1942 Market St; noon-2am; 22, F, J

Die-hard singers comb through giant books for the perfect song at this mixed-straight-gay karaoke bar, where show tunes are serious stuff. Best with a big posse.

SUGAR LOUNGE Map p133 Bar

☎ 415-255-7144; www.sugarloungesf.com; 377 Hayes St; 4-11:30pm Mon-Thu, to 2am Fri & Sat; 21

Cozy low-slung velvet snugs, chill down-tempo beats, red lights and rock-candy-like wall sconces set a sexy mood at this tiny Hayes Valley bar, ideal after the symphony or opera, or for catching a buzz after shopping for strappy sandals up the street.

MOMI TOBY'S REVOLUTION CAFÉ
Map p133 Cafe

☎ 415-626-1508; 528 Laguna St; 7:30am-10pm Mon-Thu, 7:30am-11pm Fri, 8am-10pm Sat & Sun; 6, 7, 21, 71

For once, a cafe that's not an internet port. Dig the boho scene, with artists on both sides of the counter, swilling coffee and wine. Take sun at outdoor tables, or snag a window seat inside and meet the locals. There's another location in the Mission that hosts Classical Revolution (p222) on Sundays.

top picks
FOR BEER

- Toronado (opposite)
- Church Key (p197)
- Edinburgh Castle (p196)
- Zeitgeist (p200)
- Beach Chalet Microbrewery (below)

GOLDEN GATE PARK & THE AVENUES

540 CLUB
Map pp136–7 Bar

☎ 415-752-7276; www.540-club.com; 540 Clement St; 11am-2am; 2, 44

Regulars love to party at this neighborhood bar inside a former bank with two-story-high coffered ceilings, dusty red velvet curtains and cool pop art. Bartenders pull 12 brews on tap, and everyone seems to know each other – you will too after a couple of games of darts.

BEACH CHALET MICROBREWERY
Map pp136–7 Bar

☎ 415-386-8439; www.beachchalet.com; 1000 Great Hwy; 9am-10pm Sun-Thu, to 11pm Fri & Sat; 5, 18, 31, 38, N

Gaze over the Pacific with microbrewed beer at the Beach Chalet. There's always

top picks

FOR WINE

- **Hôtel Biron** (p203)
- **Cav Wine Bar** (p203)
- **California Wine Merchant** (p199)
- **Yield** (p201)
- **Bubble Lounge** (p194)

a long wait here, but that's OK because it gives you time to admire the downstairs 1930s Works Project Administration (WPA) frescoes, showing a condensed history of San Francisco and the development of Golden Gate Park.

BITTER END
Map pp136–7 Bar

☎ 415-421-7033; 441 Clement St; 4pm-2am Mon-Fri, 11am-2am Sat & Sun; 1, 2, 33, 38, 44
Tuesday-night trivia is big at this beat-up pub with worn wood floors, big tables for six, two pool tables and an overlit dart board. Pretty good pub grub makes it a good spot to start the night.

PLOUGH & THE STARS
Map pp136–7 Bar

☎ 415-751-1122; www.theploughandstars.com; 116 Clement St; 3pm-2am Mon-Thu, 2pm-2am Fri-Sun; 1, 2, 33, 38
Rumor has it the owners here are celebrities back in the Emerald Isle, which would explain how they manage to pull in top Celtic talent with little fanfare or advance warning. Other nights, shoot pool, throw darts and make merry with neighborhood locals.

TRAD'R SAM'S
Map pp136–7 Bar

☎ 415-221-0773; 6150 Geary Blvd; 11am-2am; 2, 29, 38
Snag a rattan island-themed booth at this threadbare faux-tiki gem. Classic-kitsch lovers order the Hurricane, which comes with two straws to share for a reason: drink it by yourself and it'll blow you away.

JAVA BEACH CAFÉ
Map pp136–7 Cafe

☎ 415-665-5282; www.javabeachcafe.com; 1396 La Playa St; 6am-11pm; 18, N;
Fearless surfers fuel up on coffee and carbs at the last stop on the N Judah, right before the beach. If it's not foggy, score an outdoor table, but we prefer to sit inside and cruise the dudes.

NIGHTLIFE

top picks

- **Yoshi's** (p211)
- **Qoöl** (p209)
- **Triple Crown** (p215)
- **Cafe Cocomo** (p214)
- **Beach Blanket Babylon** (p206)

NIGHTLIFE

If you've been misled to believe there's such a thing as a clubbing 'strip' in SF, think again. This city spreads its wealth across all neighborhoods, dropping gems into tiny dives, behind unmarked doors, in warehouse basements and garden patios, and it expects you to do the legwork to find them. Of course, there are thump-thump dance clubs with agro bouncers, but you can find those anywhere – better to go deep into SF's kaleidoscope of neighborhoods to find what's really going on.

For post-rave electronic, hip-hop and chill art lounges, head to SoMa. For gritty hipster and punk dives, pick through the buried treasures in the off-streets of the Mission, and on Divisadero and Haight Sts. Gay-friendly clubs are by no means quarantined in the Castro (see the Gay/Lesbian/Bi/Trans SF chapter, p241). Seedy Polk St, running from the Civic Center to Russian Hill, had the most historic gay-club scene in town, but new hipster garage-rock clubs like the Hemlock Tavern (p196) now draw everyone to Polk Gulch. If you're looking for 100% straight, you'll find it in the preppy, upscale Marina; for real Irish bars, head to the Richmond. North Beach has old-timey classics and neon-lit strip joints mixed with trendy martini lounges that morph into nightclubs, and out-of-the-way Bottom of the Hill (p212) is serious about live rock and punk. Jazz turns up just about anywhere, as does a very danceable and authentic Latin scene (check out www.salsacrazy.com for nightly action). Comedy clubs are also a pretty big deal; celeb funnies love to test their material here.

To find the hot spots, don't just check *SF Weekly*, the *San Francisco Bay Guardian*, www.nitevibe.com or www.sfstation.com; chat up the people you meet who seem to be in the know, and stay flexible – be ready to hop into a cab to Union Square or the Mission if the scene's a little flat in SoMa. Note that most regulars don't show up to clubs until after 10pm and, unlike New York or LA, many clubs close at 2am, with a few exceptions like the EndUp (p208).

COMEDY

San Francisco is among the USA's top cities for comedy, and well-known comics often try out their new material here, which can make for a great evening or an excruciating experience. The best guaranteed laughs are at Beach Blanket Babylon and Teatro Zinzanni.

BATS IMPROV Map pp100–1

Bay Area Theatersports; ☎ 415-474-8935; www.improv.org; 3rd fl, bldg B, Fort Mason Center; shows usually $15, admission depends on class/event; 🕑 weekend shows 8pm; 🚌 22, 28, 30

Bay Area Theatersports explores all things improv, from audience-inspired themes to wacked-out musicals at completely improvised weekend shows. Or take center stage yourself at an improv-comedy workshop (held on weekday nights and weekend afternoons). Think fast: classes fill quickly.

BEACH BLANKET BABYLON Map p87

☎ 415-421-4222; www.beachblanketbabylon.com; 678 Green St; admission $25-80; 🕑 shows 8pm Wed & Thu, 6:30pm & 9:30pm Fri & Sat, 2pm & 5pm Sun; 🚌 45

San Francisco's longest-running musical-cabaret spoofs current events with content that changes so often that stagehands giggle along with the audience. Some personalities seem a little dated (Richard Simmons?), but they're in and out so fast the overall effect is hilarious. And oh! those hats – legendary. If you see only one show, make it BBB. Reservations essential; arrive one hour early for best seats. Under-21s admitted only at matinees.

COBB'S COMEDY CLUB Map p87

☎ 415-928-4320; www.cobbscomedyclub.com; 915 Columbus Ave; admission $10-35 plus 2-drink minimum; 🕑 shows 8pm & 10pm; 🚌 15, 45; 🚋 Powell-Mason

There's no room to be shy at Cobb's, where bumper-to-bumper shared tables make for an intimate (and vulnerable) audience. The comfy little club loves its local talent, but sometimes hosts big-name national acts. Check the website for shows.

PUNCH LINE Map pp70–1

☎ 415-397-4337; www.punchlinecomedyclub.com; 444 Battery St; admission $12-23 plus 2-

drink minimum; shows 8pm Sun, Tue-Thu, 8pm & 10pm Fri & Sat; 1, 2, 7, F, J, K, L, M, N; & Embarcadero
Known for launching promising talent (think Robin Williams, Chris Rock, Ellen DeGeneres and David Cross), this historic standup venue is small enough for you to see into performers' eyes. Strong drinks keep you laughing, even when jokes sometimes bomb.

PURPLE ONION Map p87

415-956-1653; www.caffemacaroni.com; 140 Columbus Ave; admission $10-15; call for show times; 15, 30, 41, 45
Such legendary comics as Woody Allen and Phyllis Diller clawed their way up from underground at this grotto nightclub. Recently, comics took back the stage from lackluster lounge acts, and the club's been rejuvenated – Robin Williams has even stopped by to test material. Bookings are sporadic; call ahead.

TEATRO ZINZANNI Map p63

415-438-2668; http://zinzanni.org; Pier 29, Embarcadero; admission $145-195; 7:30-11pm; F
Inside a 19th-century Spiegeltent (an opulent Belgian traveling-circus tent), top circus talent flies overhead, a celeb-diva croons, and clowns pull wacky stunts as you dig into a surprisingly good five-course dinner. This ain't no B-grade dinner theater: a 'clown-wrangler' seeks out world-class talent in Europe and Asia, and the acts, menu and performers are refreshed quarterly. Former stars have included Joan Baez and Broadway's Liliane Montevecchi. Dress for dinner, and arrive early to see the over-the-top harmonium and boutique selling tiaras and ostrich-feather opera gloves (ideal if you're underdressed). Be prepared for audience participation – especially if you're a looker.

CLUBBING

SF is a city of DJs – the closest American equivalents are Detroit and Chicago – and it's often the DJ, more than the venue, that determines the crowd at nightclubs. House is the dominant paradigm, with variations including techno-house, techno, electronic, progressive, funky-house, gospel-house, breaks and drum-and-bass. Hip-hop is also big, but it often gets mixed with house.

You won't get into clubs wearing flip-flops, shorts or T-shirts (unless they're fancy). You'll usually only wait 10 minutes to get in anywhere, except at the city's biggest club, Ruby Skye, depending on the night. Groups of men are sometimes turned away, unless they're on the guestlist (see the boxed text, p208). Groups of women are never turned away, unless they're drunk. Couples usually get in everywhere. The following places have thumping sound systems and dance floors, but because

GETTING TICKETS

Major events often sell out the day tickets go on sale, but you can often find tickets for sold-out events on Craigslist (www.craigslist.org) – sometimes for the original face value. Tickets are also sold on eBay (www.ebay.com), and not necessarily at bidding-war prices. The mainstream ticket-sales agencies include Tickets.com (www.tickets.com), which has walk-up locations at Giants Dugout Stores in SF (including 4 Embarcadero Center and AT&T Park); Ticketmaster (800-745-3000; www.ticketmaster.com); and Ticketweb (www.ticketweb.com).

The following ticket agents distribute tickets to a wide range of events and add a service charge.

Brown Paper Tickets (800-838-3006; www.brownpapertickets.com) Our favorite ticketing agency has transparent business practices and low fees, and 5% of profits go to community organizations; it's the preferred vendor of many indie-arts organizations.

City Box Office (415-392-4400; www.cityboxoffice.com) Another top local ticketing agency for arts organizations, and other quality music, dance and comedy performances, as well as sports and events.

Mr Ticket (Map p92; 415-292-7328, 800-424-7328; www.mrticket.com; 2065 Van Ness Ave; 9am-5:30pm Mon-Fri, 10am-2pm Sat) A ticket broker that charges whatever price the market can bear; ideal when you're desperate.

TIX Bay Area (Map pp70–1; 415-433-7827; www.tixbayarea.org; Union Square; 11am-6pm Tue-Fri, 10am-6pm Sat, 10am-3pm Sun; Powell-Mason, Powell-Hyde) Offers discount theater tickets on the day of each performance at a sidewalk booth on the Powell St side of Union Square. Half-price tickets (cash only) are available for selected events. You can also order advance tickets at full price. For theater venues, see p224.

GET ON THE LIST

Most clubs charge $10 to $20 at the door – a lot of money to spend, especially if you walk in and determine you don't like the place. You can often get around this by logging onto the club's site and signing up for the guest list, usually indicated by an RSVP or VIP link. If it's not immediately clear, send the club an email. When this works, it cuts admission to about $5, but you may have to arrive before 11pm.

of the flexible definition of club, we've placed some venues where you can dance under Lounges (p215) and in the Drinking chapter (p192). For live music, also check out p210 and the Gay/Lesbian/Bi/Trans SF chapter (p241). For the best up-to-date information about SF's DJ-club culture and what's happening now, check out Nite Vibe (www.nitevibe.com), which is updated every Tuesday afternoon with well-filtered listings.

1015 FOLSOM Map pp110–11

☎ 415-431-1200; www.1015.com; 1015 Folsom St; admission $10-20; 🕑 8pm-4am Fri, to 7am Sat; 🚌 27

One of the city's biggest clubs, 'Ten-Fifteen' has been eclipsed by Temple and Ruby Skye, but still draws huge crowds, primarily Asian. Its main hall is enormous, and four other dance floors mean you'll lose your posse if you're not paying attention. If you're a sound purist, 1015's basement has one of the best systems in the city. Be prepared for a pat-down before you enter; there's a serious no-drugs (or weapons) policy after some problems with the SFPD. Free before 10:15pm.

CAT CLUB Map pp110–11

☎ 415-703-8965; www.catclubsf.com; 1190 Folsom St; admission $5 after 10pm; 🕑 9pm-3am Tue & Thu-Sat; 🚌 12, 19, F, J; 🚌 & Ⓜ Civic Center

The Cat Club's long-running Thursday-night dance party, 1984, packs the place every week for New Wave and '80s pop. Two grungy, sweaty rooms fill with a crowd that dances hard to one-hit wonders. Other nights rotate and vary from goth to lesbian; check the calendar.

CLUB SIX Map pp110–11

☎ 415-863-1221, 415-531-6593; www.clubsix1.com; 60 6th St; admission $5-15; 🕑 9pm-2am Thu, to 4am Fri & Sat; 🚌 & Ⓜ Civic Center

Bi-level Club Six defines casual cool, with lumpy sofas and worn hardwood floors. Weekly parties delve into hip-hop, house, world and dancehall reggae, drawing a mixed crowd with an up-for-anything attitude. Hang in the street level lounge or dive into the thick of it on the basement dance floor.

DNA LOUNGE Map pp110–11

☎ 415-626-1409; www.dnalounge.com; 375 11th St; admission $5-25; 🕑 9pm-late Fri & Sat, other nights vary; 🚌 12, 47, F, J

One of SF's last mega clubs hosts live bands and big-name DJs. Two floors of late-night dance action are just seedy enough to be interesting. As of this writing, the state's alcohol-licensing bureau was trying to close DNA for being 'injurious to the public welfare and morals' – the very reason we like it. Second-and-fourth Saturdays are Bootie, the kick-ass original mashup party (now franchised worldwide); Monday's 18-and-over night is goth. Check the website for events.

ENDUP Map pp110–11

☎ 415-646-0999; www.theendup.com; 401 6th St; admission $5-20; 🕑 10pm-4am Mon-Thu, 11pm-11am Fri (into Sat), 10pm Sat to 10pm Sun; 🚌 12, 27, 47

Anyone left on the streets of San Francisco after 2am on weekends is subject to the magnetic force of the EndUp's marathon dance sessions. It's the only club with a 24-hour license and remains best known for its Sunday tea dances, in full force since 1973, though the club has branched out with reggae and other changing parties (check the web). You're not a local till you've seen sunrise at the EndUp. Expect lots of gnashing teeth and saucer-sized eyeballs by night's end.

MEZZANINE Map pp110–11

☎ 415-625-8880; www.mezzaninesf.com; 444 Jessie St; admission $10-40; 🕑 call for details; 🚌 5, 26

With possibly the best sound system in SF, behemoth Mezzanine hosts electro-funk disco, house, hip-hop, classic alt bands like the Psychedelic Furs and electronic shows by the likes of Wyclef Jean, to keep you dancing all night inside its awesome brick-walled former-industrial space. Check the calendar.

MIGHTY

Map pp110–11

☎ 415-626-7001; www.mighty119.com; 119 Utah St; admission $10-20; 🕓 10pm-4am Fri, Sat & occasional weeknights; 🚌 9

In a former warehouse sequestered in a no-man's land between SoMa, the Mission and Potrero Hill, Mighty packs a no-bullshit wallop with its awesome sound system, underground dance music, urban vibe, graffiti-esque art, and cool local crowd that doesn't fuss about dress codes. Always-good weekend DJs (occasionally big names) veer towards electronic, dance-house and hip-hop. Call ahead or check the website for weeknight opening hours and to find out what's on.

PARADISE LOUNGE

Map pp110–11

☎ 415-252-5018; www.paradisesf.com; 1501 Folsom St; admission $5-25; 🕓 9pm-4am Fri & Sat, to 2am Sun; 🚌 19, 27

The stalwart Paradise is good on Fridays and Saturdays when you're wandering around 11th St undecided about where to go, but a recent remodel rendered it like a soap-opera set-designer's vision of what a club should be – by the time you arrive, we hope it's beat up. Sound is good on both dance floors, and the upstairs-downstairs layout is fun for running around. Verify Sunday opening times online.

QOÖL

Map pp110–11

☎ 415-974-1719; www.qoolsf.com; 111 Minna St; admission $5; 🕓 5-10pm Wed; 🚌 10, 14; 🚌 & Ⓜ Montgomery St

SF's coolest weekly dance party is a Wednesday-evening techno happy hour, with a progressive theme, inside a huge window-lined art gallery. It's been going strong for over a decade, and never fails to attract the cool cats. Afterwards, follow the crowd to Satellite, at Anu (p215), for more techno-dance till 2am.

RUBY SKYE

Map pp70–1

☎ 415-693-0777; www.rubyskye.com; 420 Mason St; admission $10-25; 🕓 9pm-late Fri & Sat, sometimes Thu & Sun; 🚌 2, 3, 4, 38; 🚌 & Ⓜ Powell St

The city's premier-name nightclub occupies a vintage theater reminiscent of classic NY clubs, with reserveable balcony boxes above the floor. The who's-who of the world's DJs play here – think Danny Tenaglia, Dimitri from Paris, Christopher Lawrence and Paul Van Dyk. The very-mainstream crowd sometimes gets messy (hence the gruff security), but when your fave DJ's playing, who cares? The Funktion-One sound system is state-of-the-art. Ruby Skye is sometimes open Thursday and Sunday (check the website).

SUPPERCLUB

Map pp110–11

☎ 415-348-0900; www.supperclub.com; 657 Harrison St; admission $15; 🕓 10pm-2am Tue-Sat; 🚌 10, 12, 30, 45

Supperclub titilates with the promise of ooh-la-la exotic – beds line the all-white dance floor – but whether it delivers depends on that night's crowd of snappily dressed, straight 20-to-40-somethings, who arrive after 10pm when the restaurant becomes a club. Best nights are the quarterly Suppervision, a pan-sexual bash when the beds actually get good use.

TEMPLE

Map pp110–11

☎ 415-978-8853; www.templesf.com; 540 Howard St; admission $20; 🕓 10pm-3am Fri & Sat, sometimes weeknights; 🚌 10, 14; 🚌 & Ⓜ Montgomery St

The city's greenest club is a restaurant before 10pm, when it turns into a nightclub, serving drinks in biodegradable cups. The sleek-looking, all-white upstairs room has huge Thai statuary and slick stone floors;

NO PARKING OFF THE DANCE FLOOR

A new law passed in 2009 disallows loitering outside SF nightclubs between 9pm and 3am to cut back on violence, particularly South of Market and along the Broadway strip in North Beach. Our guess is that the cops will mostly be hanging around the usual problem spots: 1015 Folsom (opposite), the 11th St strip between Folsom and Harrison Sts, Broadway around Columbus Ave, and City Nights (which we chose not to review because of, uh...a loitering problem). So where are you supposed to smoke? Find the smokers' patio, but if there isn't one, wander up the block if you see an unmarked black Ford Crown Victoria parked outside, especially if you're lighting up anything other than tobacco.

downstairs are two smaller rooms with midsized dance floors that get packed. Occasional big-name DJs spin the gamut from house to trance to techno; Fridays are consistently good for house. It's $5 before 11pm if you're on the guestlist. Check the website for weeknight openings. Dress hot.

VESSEL

Map pp70–1

☎ 415-433-8585; www.vesselsf.com; 85 Campton Pl; admission free-$20; 9pm-2am Wed-Sat; 2, 3, 4, 30, 38, 45; & Powell St

The crowd looks sharp at Vessel, a midsized subterranean club-lounge with kick-ass sound and mesmerizing lighting, which, because of its affiliation with Cielo in NYC, sometimes books big-name DJs (think Louie Vega). We prefer the more-local Wednesday to Thursday scene over the sometimes-suburban weekend crowd, which takes longer to get its drink on and dance. And hallelujah for polite bouncers. Get on the list.

LIVE MUSIC

Anything goes on SF's music scene. A single club may host funk, reggae, gospel and hardcore all in the same week. We've done our best to subdivide venues by category, but some clubs could fall under both Jazz and Rock, so if a particular place sounds appealing, check its online calendar.

We especially love SF's small, intimate venues, such as the Red Poppy Art House (opposite), Red Devil Lounge (p213) and Bottom of the Hill (p212); these places put you up close and personal with the performers. Of the big halls, we can't get enough of Yoshi's (opposite), and we love the Fillmore (p212) and Bimbo's 365 Club (p212) for their ghosts of musicians past. For classical music, see p221.

JAZZ, BLUES & FUNK

AMNESIA

Map pp116–17

☎ 415-970-0012; www.amnesiathebar.com; 853 Valencia St; admission free-$10; 5:30pm-2am; 16th St Mission

Amnesia's swinging scene is reminiscent of the jazz era, but in ragtag-hipster style. Red-hot jazz plays half the time in the dim, red-walled dive, attracting a boho crowd looking the part. Other nights run the gamut from bluegrass and burlesque to Argentinean gypsy guitar and psychedelic rock (the latter every Thursday).

BISCUITS & BLUES

Map pp70–1

☎ 415-292-2583; www.biscuitsandblues.com; 401 Mason St; admission $5-20; music 8-11:30pm Wed-Sat; & Powell St

With a steady lineup of top-notch blues and jazz talent, Biscuits & Blues has rightly earned a reputation as one of America's best blues clubs. And the name isn't a gimmick – the joint serves hot biscuits, catfish and chicken for the full Southern experience. Acts sometimes perform Tuesdays; big names fetch up to $35.

BOOM BOOM ROOM

Map p96

☎ 415-673-8000; www.boomboomblues.com; 1601 Fillmore St; admission $5-15; 4pm-2am Tue-Sun; 22, 38

Cooking continuously since the '30s, the Boom Boom Room is an authentic relic from the jumping post-WWII years of Fillmore St. Blues, soul and New Orleans funk (and sometimes even gospel) are performed six nights a week, and top touring talent makes frequent stops here. A large dance floor, killer cocktails and cool old photos lining the walls may encourage lingering until 2am. Shows usually start at 9pm.

ENRICO'S

Map p87

☎ 415-982-6223; www.enricossf.com; 504 Broadway; admission free; music 7:30-10:30pm; 12, 20, 30, 45

The last old-school swank joint on Broadway has a big, heated sidewalk patio (ideal for smokers) opening into a white-tablecloth restaurant and bar with swoop-back booths, high cocktail tables, and a baby grand piano. Musical bookings run the gamut from classical guitar to R&B, with local chanteuses singing the Great American Songbook other nights. Shine your shoes.

LOU'S PIER 47 Map p63

☎ 415-771-5687; www.louspier47.com; 300 Jefferson St; admission $5-10; shows 4pm-midnight Sun-Thu, 4pm-1am Fri, noon-1am Sat; F

Though we generally avoid the touristy Wharf in the evening, we're glad for stalwart Lou's, which presents live blues seven nights a week and on Saturday afternoon (when there's no cover). Good backup if you're staying nearby and don't want to travel.

PIER 23 Map p63

☎ 415-362-5125; www.pier23cafe.com; Pier 23; admission free-$10; shows 5-7pm Tue, 6-8pm Wed, 7-10pm Thu, 10pm-midnight Fri & Sat, 4-8pm Sun; F

It looks like a surf shack, but this old waterfront restaurant on Pier 23 regularly features R&B, reggae, Latin bands, mellow rock and the occasional jazz pianist. Wander out to the bayside patio to soak in views. The dinner menu features pier-worthy options like batter-fried oysters and whole roasted crab.

RASELLA'S Map p96

☎ 415-346-8696; www.rasellasjazzclub.com; 1534 Fillmore St; 2-drink minimum; 8pm-midnight Sun-Thu, to 1am Fri & Sat; 22, 38

Doubling as an Ethiopian restaurant, Rasella's big storefront windows let you look inside to see (and hear) who's playing before you commit. Live jazz seven nights a week (and occasionally salsa on Fridays) make this our favorite Upper Fillmore backup when we're wishy-washy about where to go.

RED POPPY ART HOUSE Map pp116–17

☎ 415-826-2402; www.redpoppyarthouse.org; 2698 Folsom St; suggested donation $12-15; generally Thu-Sun; 24th St Mission

By day an open artists studio, by night an all-volunteer-artist-run intimate coffeehouse featuring local jazz talent. It feels like a house party you've stumbled upon by accident, with tables crammed into a tiny, art-filled space. Other nights feature indie-film screenings. Arrive when doors open for best seats. Beer and wine available. Great spot to meet local artists. Check the lineup on the website, and call ahead to confirm opening times.

SAVANNA JAZZ

Map pp116–17

☎ 415-285-3369; www.savannajazz.com; 2937 Mission St; live music cover $5-10; 6pm-2am Wed-Sun, shows around 8pm; 14; 24th St Mission

The carpets are sticky, the lights dim, the drinks strong and the music hot at this midsized black-box showroom and bar. It's mostly swing and bebop, and the wooden dance floor packs with cats dressed to the nines on Wednesday evenings for ever-popular Lindy-hop parties. (Other nights the dance floor is covered with tables.) Open-mic Thursdays and Sundays are catch-as-catch-can.

YOSHI'S Map p96

☎ 415-655-5600; www.yoshis.com; 1300 Fillmore St; shows 8pm & sometimes 10pm; 22, 38

San Francisco's definitive jazz club draws the world's top talent and hosts occasional rare appearances by the likes of Nancy Wilson. We suggest advance tickets – if you're with a group, we like the round, high-back booths (table numbers 30 to 40), but there's not a bad seat in the house. Make a night of it by showing up early for pretty good sushi in the adjoining restaurant.

DANCIN' THE NIGHT AWAY

Couples-dancing has never gone out of style here. SF was at the forefront of the swing revival, and salsa and tango remain perennial favorites. The following host dance nights in most genres, from chacha and swing to tango and waltz. Admission ranges between $5 and $10; when bands perform, the price goes to about $25. Swing events tend to move venues; check www.oldtimey.net and www.lindylist.com for the latest.

Cheryl Burke Dance Center (Map pp116–17; ☎ 415-252-9000; www.cherylburkedance.com; 1830 17th St; 1-9pm Mon-Thu, 1-11pm Fri, 11am-7pm Sat, 10am-4pm Sun; 22) Always wished you could swing or tango? This dancing-school-cum-ballroom has one of the largest floors in the city. Classes in all kinds of couples-dancing happen daily, and dances are held every night. No need for a partner in most classes. There are same-sex events, too.

Verdi Club (Map pp116–17; ☎ 415-861-9199; www.verdiclub.net; 2424 Mariposa St; hrs vary; 33) Thursday night's *milonga* (Spanish dance) at the Verdi is an eyepopper, with *bandoneón* (free-reed instrument) players and sharply dressed tango dancers circling the floor. Wear silk or a pencil-thin moustache, and blend right in. Lindy-hoppers take over Tuesday nights. Other nights vary; check the website.

PUNK & METAL

Check who's playing in the tiny Tuesday-through-Sunday showroom at the Hemlock Tavern (p196), and see what's on at Thursday Night Live at the Eagle (p214) and Bottom of the Hill (below).

ANNIE'S SOCIAL CLUB Map pp110–11

415-974-1585; www.anniessocialclub.com; 917 Folsom St; admission $5-10 Fri & Sat; 4pm-2am Mon-Fri, 9pm-2am Sat; 12, 27, 30, 45; & Powell St

Wear your shit-kickers and spike your hair: you're going to Annie's. Nights vary. At Tuesday's 'Drunken Monkey' party, you'll hear everything from Johnny Cash to Ministry; Wednesday to Saturday live bands tend towards punk and metal; and Monday, Friday and Saturday, you can sing punk-rock-and-schlock karaoke (free Monday) in the back room. Best of all, drinks cost $5.

ROCK

Also see Thursdays at Amnesia (p210). Tuesday through Sunday, there are shows at Hemlock Tavern (p196).

BIMBO'S 365 CLUB

Map p87

415-474-0365; www.bimbos365club.com; 1025 Columbus Ave; tickets from $20; check calendar; 30; Powell-Mason

Rita Hayworth (aka Rita Casino) kicked up her heels in the chorus line at this vintage-1931 club, and Bimbo's still plays it fast and loose with strong drink and live shows by the likes of Zap Mama and Sandra Bernhard. It's not always open, so check the calendar.

BOTTOM OF THE HILL

Map pp116–17

415-621-4455; www.bottomofthehill.com; 1233 17th St; admission $5-12; shows after 8:30pm Tue-Sat, other nights vary; 19, 22

Top of the list for seeing fun local bands, like punk-polka Polkacide and goth-psychedelic Bellavista, Bottom of the Hill is out of the way – literally at the bottom of Potrero Hill – but worth the trek for indie-rockers. Big smokers' patio. Check the website for lineup and ticket info (if necessary).

CAFÉ DU NORD/SWEDISH AMERICAN HALL Map p123

415-861-5016; www.cafedunord.com; 2170 Market St; admission price varies; 7pm or 8pm-2am; 22, 37, J, K, L, M

You never know what's doing at Café du Nord, a former basement speakeasy, with bar and showroom. Rockers, chanteuses, comedians, raconteurs and burlesque acts perform nightly, and the joint still looks like it must've in the '30s. The hall upstairs features bigger acts, balcony seating and Scandinavian woodworking, but no booze. Tickets are available online. It's sometimes closed for private events; check out the calendar online.

ELBO ROOM Map pp116–17

415-552-7788; www.elbo.com; 647 Valencia St; admission $5-20; 5pm-2am; 14, 26, 33, 49; 16th St Mission

The Elbo Room draws a diverse indie crowd and showcases diverse acts in its upstairs black-box performance space, including rockabilly, salsa and reggae, with emphasis on funk and soul. Come any night for the (free) chill downstairs bar. There are $2 pints from 5pm to 9pm.

FILLMORE AUDITORIUM Map p96

415-346-6000; www.thefillmore.com; 1805 Geary Blvd; admission $20-40; box office 10am-4pm Sun, 7:30-10pm show nights; 2, 3, 4, 22, 38

Jimi Hendrix, Janis Joplin, the Doors – they all played the Fillmore. Now you might catch the Indigo Girls, Duran Duran or Tracy Chapman in the historic 1250-capacity standing-room theater (if you're polite and lead with the hip, you might squeeze up to the stage). Don't miss the priceless collection of psychedelic posters in the upstairs gallery.

GREAT AMERICAN MUSIC HALL

Map p77

415-885-0750; www.musichallsf.com; 859 O'Farrell St; admission $12-35; box office 10:30am-6pm Mon-Fri & on show nights; 19, 38

Once a bordello, the rococo Great American Music Hall is one of SF's coolest places for shows. A balcony with table seating rims the main standing-room floor area, the sound system is top-notch, and there are food and drinks. Music ranges from rock, alt-rock and country, to jazz and blues.

HOTEL UTAH Map pp110–11

☎ 415-546-6300; www.hotelutah.com; 500 4th St; bar admission free, shows $7-12; ⌚ 11:30am-2am Mon-Fri, 6pm-2am Sat & Sun; 🚌 27, 30, 45, N

Whoopi Goldberg and Robin Williams broke in the stage on the ground floor of a Victorian residence hotel in the '70s, and now it's a sure bet for indie-label favorites and acts you may only see in SF. The nonconformist streak goes deep here: back in the '50s the bartender graciously served Beats, grifters and Marilyn Monroe, but snipped the ties of businessmen when they leaned across the bar.

INDEPENDENT Map pp126–7

☎ 415-771-1421; www.theindependentsf.com; 628 Divisadero St; tickets $15-100; ⌚ box office 11am-6pm Mon-Fri, to 9:30pm show nights, doors 7:30pm or 8:30pm; 🚌 5, 21, 24

One of the city's coolest live-music venues, the Independent showcases damn-good up-and-coming acts, big names like Green Day, old bands like Erasure, and wacky events like the US Air Guitar Championships. The box-shaped room gets sweaty as hell when the crowd jumps.

MAKE-OUT ROOM Map pp116–17

☎ 415-647-2888; www.makeoutroom.com; 3225 22nd St; live music cover $5-10; ⌚ 6pm-2am; 🚌 14, 26, 48, 49; Ⓜ 24th St Mission

Velvet curtains and round booths add dusty swank to the evening's entertainment, which ranges from improv to punk-rock fiddle to occasional minor celebs – sometimes on the same night. For lovers of the indie underground, the Make-Out's a must.

RED DEVIL LOUNGE Map p92

☎ 415-921-1695; www.reddevillounge.com; 1695 Polk St; cover varies; ⌚ from 8pm or 9pm, usually closed Sun & Mon; 🚌 19, 47

The up-and-coming and formerly famous (think Vanilla Ice and Sugar Hill Gang) play this narrow, intimate club. Your once-fave stars may have lost its luster, but console yourself with strong drinks.

RICKSHAW STOP Map p77

☎ 415-861-2011; www.rickshawstop.com; 155 Fell St; admission $5-35; ⌚ 6pm-2am Wed-Sat; 🚌 40

Finally a club where 18-to-21-year-olds can (sometimes) get in for the high-school prom they wish they'd attended. Other nights the shabby-at-the-edges, nothing-fancy space and its changing lineup appeals to alterna-20-somethings. Friday it's Blowup, big with the electro-indie crowd, when 18-and-over kids feature their hottest looks. Check the website for one-off shows and other parties.

RITE SPOT CAFE Map pp116–17

☎ 415-552-6066; www.ritespotcafe.net; 2099 Folsom St; admission free; ⌚ 4pm-2am; Ⓜ 16th St Mission

Possibly so-called because it's the only spot for drinks around here, the Rite Spot is a tiny dive-bar and restaurant. You never

STRIP JOINTS

City oligarchs feign shame over the highly visible strip clubs, but in reality SF seems proud of its historically seedy amusements. In the '60s, Carol Doda took the tease out of stripping by slinking out of her G-string before astonished audiences at the Condor Club in North Beach. San Francisco's Mitchell Brothers gave the world *Deep Throat* and the O'Farrell Theater. A few local establishments bring more to the table than the usual sleaze:

Lusty Lady (Map p87; ☎ 415-391-3991; 1033 Kearny St; admission per min 25¢; ⌚ 11am-3am; 🚌 15) It's owned by women, the strippers are unionized, and it operates like an old-fashioned peep show. Drop quarters into a slot in a private booth, and a nekkid woman dances behind glass till your quarters run out.

Mitchell Brothers O'Farrell Theater (Map p77; ☎ 415-776-6686; www.ofarrell.com; 895 O'Farrell St; admission $20-40; ⌚ 11:30am-1:30am Mon-Thu, 11:30am-2:30am Fri & Sat, 5:30pm-1:30am Sun; 🚌 38) This infamous strip joint remains open, long after one of the founding brothers murdered the other. Jim and Artie Mitchell opened the theater in 1969 and began making porno, including the legendary *Deep Throat,* starring Marilyn Chambers. At its prime, the Mitchells' multimillion-dollar empire included a production company and 11 California theaters. But the Mitchell brothers went the way of Cain and Abel, when Jim shot and killed Artie in 1991. He was convicted of voluntary manslaughter and served six years; a heart attack killed him in 2007. Despite its tawdry background, the O'Farrell Theater is generally regarded as a classy place (with a capital k). Even if you don't go inside, ask to see the little porn museum by the door.

know who'll perform at the nightly music shows (think quirky lounge, burlesque piano and classic jazz), but it won't be mainstream, and won't be too loud for conversation.

SLIM'S Map pp110–11

☎ 415-255-0333; www.slims-sf.com; 333 11th St; tickets $11-28; 🕑 5pm-2am; 🚌 9, 12, 47, F, J
Big acts like Prince and Elvis Costello have played this midsized club owned by R&B star Boz Skaggs, and usually you'll find damn good touring and local bands. Shows are all-ages, though shorties may have a hard time seeing from the floor. Come early for burgers and fries.

THURSDAY NIGHT LIVE AT THE EAGLE Map pp110–11

☎ 415-626-0880; www.sfeagle.com; 398 12th St; admission $5-10; 🕑 from 9pm Thu; 🚌 9, 12, 47
It may be dead or packed, depending on the band, but there's always music here on Thursdays, the only time you'll see purses at the Eagle, an otherwise gay-only bar in a former light-industrial space, with a huge patio and big bar. Don't come other nights unless you're a motorcycle-riding leather-daddy.

WARFIELD Map pp70–1

☎ 415-775-7722; tickets www.livenation.com; 982 Market St; cover varies; 🕑 box office at the Fillmore 10am-4pm Sun, show nights 7:30-10pm; 🚌 6, 7, F; 🚌 & Ⓑ Powell St
Famous names play this former vaudeville theater, including the Beastie Boys, PJ Harvey and the Dead. Get tickets at the Fillmore (p212) box office.

SALSA & SWING

Salsa clubs enforce dress codes. Designer jeans are fine, but wear good shoes (never tennies) and a sexy top, or you won't get in. High heels and skimpy dresses guarantee admission. For swing, also consider Wednesdays at Savanna Jazz (p211).

CAFE COCOMO Map pp116–17

☎ 415-824-6910; www.cafecocomo.com; 650 Indiana St; admission $10-15; 🕑 7pm-midnight Mon, 6pm-midnight Thu, 6pm-2am Sat; 🚌 22
Hundreds fill the dance floor on Thursday and Saturday nights, when big bands play *muy caliente* Cocomo, a cavernous space with a mezzanine overlooking the dance-floor action and a big patio garden outside. Mondays are quieter, when there's no band, but those who come dance hard. Lessons precede parties.

CLUB HAVANA AT JELLY'S Map pp110–11

☎ 415-495-3099; www.jellyscafe.com; 295 Terry Francois St, Pier 50; admission $10; 🕑 4-9:30pm Sun; 🚌 T
Down on the docks, this club is the other Sunday spot for live-band salsa (El Rio, p243, is our top choice), but be warned: if you can't salsa, you'll be snubbed on Jelly's crowded floor. Console yourself with Cuban barbecue and *mojitos* on the bay-front patio.

ROCCAPULCO SUPPER CLUB Map pp116–17

☎ 415-648-6611; www.roccapulco.com; 3140 Mission St; admission $10-15; 🕑 8pm-2am; 🚌 14, 26; Ⓑ 24th St Mission
Get your salsa and merengue on at this high-ceilinged, stadium-sized Latino fave

NIGHTLIFE ACROSS THE BAY

Oakland and Berkeley have a wealth of unpretentious, often-unadvertised talent with die-hard local followings. Everyone knows famous Yoshi's (p271), but there are many lesser-known live-music hubs that put you smack in the middle of the East Bay's raw, soulful scene:

Cafe Van Kleef (p271) Bebop, jazz, R&B, rock, funk – you name it, it plays in this narrow bar full of junky collectibles.

Freight & Salvage Coffeehouse (p275) An all-ages, alcohol-free coffeehouse and performance venue for traditional, regional and ethnic music.

Paramount Theatre (p271) A gorgeous deco theater featuring everything from the symphony to big-name comedy and rock acts such as Morrissey.

Stork Club (p272) Punk, funk, rockabilly and reggae are showcased here.

Uptown (p271) You can converse at the 30ft-long mahogany bar, or slip into the adjoining room for the full sound experience of blues, folk or metal.

that books fantastic touring acts like El Grupo Niche. This is a straight bar, full of musk and hormones, and single women may feel overwhelmed: come with a group.

STARLIGHT ROOM Map pp70–1

☎ 415-395-8595; www.harrydenton.com; 21st fl, 450 Powell St; cover varies, often free; 8:30pm-2am Tue-Sat; & Powell St; Powell-Mason, Powell-Hyde

Views are mesmerizing from the 21st floor of the Sir Francis Drake Hotel, where khaki-clad tourists and bimbo blondes let down their hair and dance to live bands on weekends and DJs on weekdays. Safe space for tipsy dorks and conservative parents – except on Sundays, when there's a kooky drag-show brunch (make reservations).

LOUNGES

111 MINNA Map pp110–11

☎ 415-974-1719; www.111minnagallery.com; 111 Minna St; admission $5-15, free Tue; hrs vary; 10, 14; & Montgomery St

Window-lined gallery by day, rockin' lounge space and bar by night, 111 Minna hosts a wild array of events, from monthly free Sketch Tuesdays, when artists make work for sale to the audience, to SF's best techno-dance party Qoöl (p209), to live acoustic performances and disco-house nights. Best of all, you can look in the windows and see if it's your scene. Check the calendar.

ANU Map pp110–11

☎ 415-543-3505; www.anu-bar.com; 43 6th St; admission free; 5pm-2am Tue-Fri, 7pm-2am Sat; & Powell St

Funky-cool Anu draws a local crowd of techno-lovers, who crowd the tiny dance floor. But for its DJ music, which drifts into drum-and-bass and occasionally house, it's just a shotgun bar with a cool crowd. Wednesdays' party, Satellite, packs the joint when Qoöl (p209) lets out.

HARLOT Map pp110–11

☎ 415-777-1077; www.harlotsf.com; 46 Minna St; admission free 5-9pm Wed-Fri, $10-20 otherwise; 5pm-2am Wed-Fri, 9pm-2am Sat; & Montgomery St

Back when SoMa was the stomping ground of sailors, alleys were named for working girls, to whom Harlot pays homage. Velvet curtains glow purple under intense red lighting, rendering the brick-walled space a sort of goth-erotic-chic vampire's den. Before 9pm it's a lounge, after 9pm it's a club. The killer sound system pumps house on Thursdays and indie-rock on Wednesdays – our fave nights. Weekends get suburban, but everyone cuts loose, so who cares? Dress funky to get past doormen.

POLENG LOUNGE Map pp126–7

☎ 415-441-1710; www.polenglounge.com; 1751 Fulton St; admission free; 10pm-2am Tue-Sat; 5, 21, 43

Tea-infused cocktails and *soju* (grain alcohol) drinks are specialties at this Filipino-street-food restaurant that becomes a cool DJ lounge after 10pm, drawing scenester locals for underground hip-hop, rooted in late-'80s, top-40, not gangster. Black Eyed Peas used to do a free weekly jam at Poleng years ago. Now it's a hive of industry insiders – Rza, leader of the Wu-Tang Clan, hangs here. The front room is way sexier, with Asian statuary and water trickling down textured-concrete walls; the back room is for dancing (when it happens), but it's little more than a box with kick-ass sound. No need to dress fancy.

SHINE Map pp110–11

☎ 415-255-1337; www.shinesf.com; 1337 Mission St; admission free-$10; 9pm-2am Wed-Sat; 14, 26, Van Ness

We love the indie B-grade swank at tiny Shine, decorated with disco balls and fabric wall panels that look totally homemade. Seating is squishy, but no matter when there's a good DJ because you'll wind up dancing. Dig the photo booth. Cool spot to chill with local DJs. Check the online calendar.

TRIPLE CROWN Map p133

☎ 415-863-3516; www.triplecrownsf.com; 1760 Market St; admission varies; 5:30pm-2am; F

A storefront bar with adjoining black-box rooms – one with glittering chandeliers, another with a disco-ball dance floor – Triple Crown hosts DJs spinning everything from '60s-soul and '80s-pop to down-tempo funk and hip-hop. Expect an upbeat crowd of happy locals that love to dance and schmooze. Tuesdays are gay; see Chilidog Disco p242). Call ahead or check website to confirm opening times.

THE ARTS

top picks

- **San Francisco Symphony** (p223)
- **Oberlin Dance Collective** (p218)
- **Magic Theatre** (p225)
- **Commonwealth Club** (p224)
- **Midnight Mass** (p220)

What's your recommendation? www.lonelyplanet.com/san-francisco

San Franciscans are an arty crowd. The Bureau of Labor Statistics and the US Census rate SF the fourth-largest US city for 'creative density,' meaning the number of creative types per square mile. Californians are responsible for nearly 30% of US ticket sales in performing arts and sports, and the California Arts Council regularly recognizes many Bay Area arts organizations for their outstanding contributions. The scene here is not all about big names: though the city has a world-famous symphony orchestra, opera company and ballet troupe, it's equally known for its experimental avant-garde theater and dance – and many such organizations charge remarkably low ticket prices.

DANCE

Dance has a long history in San Francisco – Isadora Duncan once performed in the courtyard of the Palace of the Legion of Honor. Today, the city has the country's longest-running ballet company and multiple independent troupes specializing in genre-melding forms.

For a comprehensive calendar of dance events in the Bay Area, check with Dancers' Group (www.dancersgroup.org). It also pays to keep an eye out for one-off ethnic-dance performances, particularly around the time of Carnaval (p22), and during the San Francisco Ethnic Dance Festival (☎ 415-474-3914; www.worldartswest.org) in June. Definitely check what's on at Counterpulse (Map pp110–11; ☎ 415-626-2060; www.counterpulse.org; 1310 Mission St), a performance space for cultural innovators. Also look for whip-smart Chris Black/Potrzebie Dance Project (www.potrzebie.com), which performs sporadically.

Dance Mission (Map pp116–17; ☎ 415-826-4441; www.dancemission.com; 3316 24th St) always has something going on, from contact improv to dance jams and classes. There's a lot of 'extreme dance' in the Bay Area, experimental forms combining aerial performance, site-specific work, circus arts and dance. For these we particularly like Kunst Stoff (☎ 415-863-3040, ext 286; www.kunst-stoff.org) and Zaccho Dance Theater (☎ 415-822-6744; www.zaccho.org).

ALONZO KING'S LINES BALLET

☎ 415-863-3040; www.linesballet.org

Alonzo King's long, lean dancers perform complicated, angular movements that showcase their impeccable technical skills. Recent shows have included a knockout kung-fu-meets-ballet joint work with Shaolin monks, which explored a synthesis of Eastern and Western forms, pairing dance with martial arts. King also offers classes and workshops.

JOE GOODE PERFORMANCE GROUP

☎ 415-561-6565; www.joegoode.org

An early adaptor of narrative performance art into dance, maverick Joe Goode is known worldwide and performs nationally. His dancers are phenomenal exponents of their craft – and they're not kept silent: in Joe Goode works, the dancers use their voices as well as their bodies.

OBERLIN DANCE COLLECTIVE

Map pp116–17

☎ 415-863-9834; www.odctheater.org; 3153 17th St; Ⓜ 16th St Mission

For nearly 40 years, Oberlin Dance Collective (ODC) has continually wowed audiences with its risky and raw modern-dance performances, which irreverently explore the joy of movement. The ODC's season runs from September through to December, and its stage presents year-round shows, which feature local and international artists. Its Dance Commons is a hub and hangout for the local dance community and offers 200 classes a week; all ages and all levels are welcome to participate.

SAN FRANCISCO BALLET

Map p77

☎ 415-861-5600, tickets 415-865-2000; www.sfballet.org; War Memorial Opera House, 301 Van Ness Ave; tickets $10-120; 🚌 21, 47, 49; 🚌 & Ⓜ Civic Center

The San Francisco Ballet is the USA's oldest ballet company, and the first to premier the *Nutcracker,* which it performs annually. In San Francisco, its home is the War Memorial Opera House, but it also appears at other venues now and then; check the website.

SCOTT WELLS & DANCERS

☎ 415-931-8648; www.scottwellsdance.com

Thrilling, contemporary and smart, Scott Wells' contact-improvisation dance pieces dig deep into the male psyche and pack a hell of a punch. The athleticism is spellbinding. Performances usually take place in spring, but they pop up around town year-round.

SMUIN BALLET

☎ 415-495-2234; www.smuinballet.org

Smuin riled the local dance world in 2009 when it dubbed its work 'Ballet, but Entertaining' – as if the form wasn't – but the tag line captures the popular spirit of this 15-year-running dance company. Though always balletic in form, the works are at times wacky and humorous, or poignant and touching, and always have mass appeal – ideal for those who like dance performances but don't want to be challenged by experimental concepts.

YERBA BUENA CENTER FOR THE ARTS

Map pp110–11

☎ 415-978-2787; www.ybca.org; 700 Howard St; tickets $15-50; 30, 45; & Powell St

Rock stars regularly have their thunder stolen by YBCA openings, which draw hipper crowds willing to brave lines and coat-check their skateboards for contemporary art by the likes of filmmaker Isaac Julien, cartoonist R Crumb and satirist William Pope. The center also fosters fresh, inspiring local talent that has mounted everything from an aerial circus to a dance piece set entirely on bicycles. Most touring companies perform here.

FILM

Dinner-and-a-movie remains the classic way to spend a Friday night in SF, and the city's many cinemas present everything from the latest Hollywood blockbusters to indie foreign features that would never succeed at suburban shopping malls. Discerning local film buffs support multiple art-house venues, as well as several world-class annual film festivals. Movie tickets typically cost about $10, and weekday matinees, no longer the great bargain they once were, now cost about $8. Check online for schedules.

If you object to sitting through 20 minutes of corporate commercials preceding a film, you'll find plenty of independent theaters in SF. We particularly love the Bridge (p220), the Roxie (p221), the Red Vic (p221), the Four Star (p221) and the grandest movie palace of all, the Castro Theatre (p220). Nobody would dream of answering a cell phone at these places, and the crowd is often as stimulating as the film.

GO NOIR

Don your trench coat and slip into a darkened art-house theater for one of these classics, set in SF and still shown here. Or discover other long-since-forgotten noir films at the Noir City Film Festival (www.noircity.com) in late January – the definitive event for noir buffs.

- *The Maltese Falcon* (1941) – Dashiell Hammett penned the series in 1928 for a pulp magazine, *Black Mask*, from his apartment at 891 Post St. Later, Peter Lorre and Humphrey Bogart starred in the classic film, in which a private detective gets involved in a murderous hunt for a prized statuette. The working title was *The Gent from Frisco*.
- *Dark Passage* (1947) – A wrongly accused San Quentin inmate (Humphrey Bogart) escapes, wreaking revenge through nocturnal San Francisco. The camera makes a point of focusing on the city, at least until Lauren Bacall makes her appearance.
- *Born to Kill* (1947) – An SF socialite gets involved with her sister's husband, who's a sociopathic killer. Scenes pan the city, from Nob Hill to the Ferry Building to Ocean Beach.
- *The Lady from Shanghai* (1948) – Orson Welles not only wrote the script, but also played the hero in this classic femme fatale story that weaves through the Golden Gate and makes surreal use of SF sights like Chinatown and Steinhardt Aquarium, as well as some very unfortunate makeup.
- *The House on Telegraph Hill* (1951) – A Polish survivor of a Nazi death camp takes the identity of her deceased best friend and leaves for a new, privileged life in SF. But in the mansion by the bay, things turn sinister when suspicions begin to mount.

PEACHES CHRIST: DRAG DEITY, MOVIE MUSE & HOSTESS

What's so special about movies in SF? I've traveled all over Europe and the US to present movies, and we have the best audiences in the world here. The audiences don't just sit there: they're gonna hiss at the screen, and tell you how it is. We're hitting our 11th anniversary for Midnight Mass at the Bridge (below), and really, no other city would have nurtured Peaches Christ. You have to see a film at the Gay & Lesbian Film Fest (p22) at the Castro, too, so just book your plane ticket already.

Events worth dragging yourself out of bed and into drag for? On Easter weekend there are the Sisters of Perpetual Indulgence events (p21), though personally I don't recommend daytime drag. Folsom Street Fair (p23) never fails to shock new arrivals.

Any tips for drag novices? Give yourself a night to practice before your debut. Most people don't realize that there's a lot of trial and error, and it can go devastatingly wrong – there's good-bad, and then there's bad-bad. You can do crooked lipstick like Courtney Love, or decide you're going to have blood or spit-up on your dress – but really commit to it, have a blast.

Most underrated SF attractions? Cable cars get so much attention, but I love the vintage F Market streetcars. When you head down Market and see rainbow flags lining the city's major thoroughfare, it really makes you well up with pride. Alcatraz (p62) is perfect if you're a little sick-minded. I find it amazing that families go to that island, which is so dark and twisted and surrounded by the most beautiful views – I love that juxtaposition of evil wickedness with natural beauty and happy families.

Peaches Christ is the Midnight Mass hostess at the Bridge Theater (below).

AMC LOEWS METREON 16

Map pp110–11

☎ 415-369-6201; www.amctheatres.com; 101 4th St; adult/child/senior & matinee $10.50/7.50/8.50; 🚌 30, 45; 🚌 & Ⓜ Powell St

Housed in a mega-entertainment complex, the 16-screen Metreon has stadium reclining seats, digital projection screens and an IMAX theater. Downstairs are multiple shops and restaurants, but the wandering packs of loud teenagers are annoying to mellow types.

AMC VAN NESS 14

Map p77

☎ 415-674-4630; www.amctheatres.com; 1000 Van Ness Ave; adult/child/senior/matinee $10.75/6/7.75/8.75; 🚌 42, 47, 49

An enormous multiplex (14 screens) in a former Cadillac dealership, 1000 Van Ness mostly shows mainstream Hollywood releases, and has state-of-the-art theaters with surround sound and incredibly comfy high-backed stadium seating.

BRIDGE THEATER Map pp136–7

☎ 415-267-4893; www.landmarktheatres.com; 3010 Geary Blvd; adult/senior, child & matinee $10.50/8; 🚌 18, 38

One of the city's few remaining single-screen theaters, the Bridge shows an international lineup of independent films. Weekends in summer, at midnight, the Bridge hosts Midnight Mass, featuring camp, horror and B-grade movies, such as *Showgirls* and *Mommie Dearest,* with each screening preceded by a drag show spoofing the film. Local celeb Peaches Christ (see the boxed text, above) wrangles the always-raucous crowd; reserve ahead.

CASTRO THEATRE Map p123

☎ 415-621-6120; www.thecastrotheatre.com; 429 Castro St; adult/senior, child & matinee $9.50/7; 🚌 24, 33, K, L, M, Castro St

The Mighty Wurlitzer organ rises from the orchestra pit before the evening performance, and the audience cheers and whistles as the organist plays classics from the Great American Songbook. If there's a gay cult classic on the bill, such as *Whatever Happened to Baby Jane,* expect full audience participation. Otherwise, the crowd is well behaved and rapt. San Franciscans are wary of the seat beneath the giant chandelier, but film fests and Fellini tributes fill every available chair. Note: sound is echoey in the balcony.

CLAY THEATER Map p96

☎ 415-267-4893; www.landmarktheatres.com; 2261 Fillmore St; adult/senior, child & matinee $10.50/8; 🚌 22

In business since 1913, the single-screen Clay regularly screens a mix of both independent and foreign films. The crowd is quite civilized: the Clay is in fancy Specific Whites…err, Pacific Heights. On Saturdays (and occasionally Fridays) at midnight, look for classics like *Rocky Horror Picture Show*.

EMBARCADERO CENTER CINEMA

Map pp70–1

☎ 415-267-4893; www.landmarktheatres.com; top fl, 1 Embarcadero Center; adult/senior, child & matinee $10.50/8; 🚌 & Ⓜ Embarcadero

Blockbusters do nothing for the cinephile crowds at the Embarcadero – instead, people queue up for the latest Almodóvar film and whatever won best foreign film at the Oscars. The snack bar caters to discerning tastes with good local coffee, fair-trade chocolate and popcorn with real butter. Spoiler alert: aficionado audiences discuss reviews before and after films.

FOUR STAR THEATER

Map pp136–7

☎ 415-666-3488; www.hkinsf.com/4star; 2200 Clement St; single & double feature/matinee $9/7; 🚌 1, 2, 29, 38

Long before John Woo, Ang Li and Wong Kar-wai hit multiplex marquees, they brought down the house in the Four Star's postage-stamp-sized screening rooms. This diminutive cinema is still the audience testing ground for emerging Hong Kong and Taiwan cinema, and also shows double features.

LUMIERE THEATER Map p92

☎ 415-267-4893; www.landmarktheatres.com; 1572 California St; adult/senior, child & matinee $10.50/8; 🚌 19; 🚋 California

Right off Polk St, the rough-at-the-edges Lumiere has one large screening room and two smaller rooms, all with seats that need replacing. But we love the programming – a mix of first-run art-house, foreign and documentary films.

RED VIC MOVIE HOUSE

Map pp126–7

☎ 415-668-3994; www.redvicmoviehouse.com; 1727 Haight St; adult/senior & child/matinee $9/6/7; 🚌 6, 7, 33, 37, 43, 71, N

Collectively owned and operated for decades, the Red Vic has preserved a funky '70s vibe right down to the dilapidated couch seating and popcorn served in faux-wood snack bowls with optional brewer's yeast. Surfer flicks, punk rockumentaries and movies by local filmmakers pack the place, so get in line if you hope to avoid the too-deep seats with busted springs.

ROXIE CINEMA

Map pp116–17

☎ 415-863-1087; www.roxie.com; 3117 16th St; admission prices vary, generally around $10; 🚌 14, 22, 33, 49; Ⓜ 16th St Mission

The Roxie carries major clout with cinemaniacs for helping distribute and launch Hong Kong films Stateside, and for showing controversial films and documentaries banned elsewhere in the US. You never can predict the Roxie. Matt Groenig may show up to introduce a Simpsons film festival, and the audience will likely throw popcorn during the screening of the Academy Awards.

SUNDANCE KABUKI CINEMA

Map p96

☎ 415-929-4650; www.sundancecinemas.com/kabuki.html; 1881 Post St; adult/child/senior $11/8/8.75; 🚌 22, 38

Cinema-going at its best. Reserve a stadium seat, belly up to the bar, and order from the bistro, which serves everything from rib-eye steak to mac 'n' cheese. A multiplex initiative by Robert Redford's Sundance Institute, Kabuki features big-name flicks, festivals and exclusives – and it's a green venture, with recycled-fiber seating, reclaimed-wood decor and local chocolates and booze. Note: expect a $1 to $3 surcharge for the privilege of seeing a movie not preceded by commercials. Validated parking available.

OPERA & CLASSICAL MUSIC

You gotta love a city whose symphony conductor has rock-star status. Look for free summertime concerts at Stern Grove (see the boxed text, p222) and check the events calendar of **KDFC** (www.kdfc.com), the local classical music station (102.1FM).

CHANTICLEER

☎ 415-252-8589; www.chanticleer.org

The *New Yorker* called them 'the world's reigning male chorus,' and we have to agree. Twelve male voices blend in luxurious polyphony; the repertoire ranges from

Renaissance to gospel. The Grammy-winning ensemble makes its home in SF, and often performs at venues around town, when not touring internationally.

CLASSICAL REVOLUTION

Map pp116–17

☎ 415-642-0474; www.classicalrevolution.org; Revolution Cafe, 3248 22nd St; admission free; 8pm Sun; 24th St Mission

Young up-and-coming chamber musicians – usually recent grads from conservatories around the country – perform live on Sunday evenings at Momi Toby's Revolution Cafe (p203) in the Mission. If you're a formally trained musician in your 20s, find your tribe here. Arrive early (by 7pm latest) to snag a table.

POCKET OPERA COMPANY

☎ 415-972-8930; www.pocketopera.org; tickets adult/child/senior $34/20/31

The Pocket Opera was founded in 1978 by local character Donald Pippin, who translates librettos into English but remains faithful to original scores. The idea is to convey the story with clarity for contemporary audiences, and he's great at his craft. The company performs around the Bay Area from February to June. In San Francisco, performances are usually at the Legion of Honor (p135).

SAN FRANCISCO OPERA Map p77

☎ 415-864-3330; www.sfopera.com; War Memorial Opera House, 301 Van Ness Ave; tickets $10-350; 21, 47, 49; & Civic Center

SF has been obsessed with opera since the Gold Rush, and it remains a staple on the social calendar. Bluebloods like Ann Getty *always* book the Tuesday A-series – the best nights to spot fabulous drag. The gorgeous 1932 hall is cavernous and echoey, but there's no more glamorous seat in SF than the velvet-curtained boxes, complete with champagne service. The best midrange seats for sightlines and sound are in the front section of the dress circle. The balcony has the best sound but you'll need binoculars to see the stage, unless you come on 'Opera Vision' nights, when a huge screen shows the action on stage (don't sit directly beneath the flickering high-def monitors; if you come to the opera to get away from TV, you'll hate the balcony during these performances).

Hang in the back of the hall with die-hard opera buffs with standing-room-only tickets: starting at 10am, the box office sells 150 standing-room spots ($10, cash only); two hours before curtain, they release 50 more. Snag an empty seat after intermission, when somnambulant seniors go home – though all bets are off for Rossini and Mozart. Pre-order intermission cocktails at reserved tables in the lower-lobby cafe. Smokers and thrill-seekers: head to the Grand Tier outdoor terrace to overlook City Hall and Downtown's twinkling lights – one of SF's best nighttime views. If you're walking by during a performance, wander into the box-office lobby and watch the stage monitors for a teaser.

SAN FRANCISCO PERFORMANCES

☎ 415-677-0325; www.performances.org; tickets $32-50

SF Performances hosts excellent shows, from vocalists and solo classical pianists to

STERN GROVE FESTIVAL: SF'S BEST FREE CONCERTS

San Francisco may exist in a bubble, but its artists do not. The opera, symphony, ballet and celebrated touring acts take their gigs directly to the people in a series of free outdoor Sunday summer concerts at Stern Grove Festival (☎ 415-252-6252; www.sterngrove.org; Sun mid-Jun–Aug). You may see the symphony's first-chair trumpeter blowing jazz, Joan Baez strumming her guitar, Bollywood superstar Kailash Kher performing funked-out Sufi music, or the SF ballet showcasing highlights from its season. The setting is gorgeous – a wooded dell surrounded by fragrant eucalyptus trees that whoosh in the wind. Granted, the sound isn't as good as in a silent concert hall, but here you can chat up the locals sitting beside you, sharing picnics on blankets. Shows start at 2pm, but we recommend arriving by 11am (or earlier) to snag a good spot on the grass. Don't come late: once the lawn fills, it closes. You can enter a lottery for six seats at a picnic table (www.sterngrove.org/picnictableseats) – the deadline for entries is the Monday preceding a show. Bring a picnic and warm clothing: it may be sunny and warm downtown, but the grove will likely be foggy and cold. Stern Grove (Map pp60–1) is located at 19th Ave and Sloat Blvd. (Note: it is not in Golden Gate Park.) Take Muni bus 28 or 23, or take the K or M streetcar to the St Francis Circle Muni stop. There's also a free bicycle valet. Don't drive: parking is (nearly) impossible.

FREE & OUTDOORS

Free outdoor entertainment abounds in summer, when the city's dance, theater and music companies mount performances in parks.

Hardly Strictly Bluegrass Festival (www.strictlybluegrass.com; Speedway Meadow, Golden Gate Park; 3-7pm Fri, 11am-7pm Sat & Sun, early Oct; 33) Sip wine out of paper cups (BYO) and listen to lefty political commentary between front-porch hillbilly gospel and traditional bluegrass, with headliners like Aimee Mann and Marianne Faithful.

Levi's Plaza Park (Map p63; www.sfjazz.org; 1270 Battery St; from noon Wed, Sep–mid-Oct; 10, F) Presents jazz styles from post-bebop jazz to blues and sometimes a little klezmer.

Old St Mary's Noontime Concerts (Map p82; 415-777-3211; www.noontimeconcerts.org; 660 California St; from 12:30pm Tue; 1, 15, 30, 45; California, Powell-Mason, Powell-Hyde) Features a varied repertoire of free classical performances (sometimes indoors).

Opera in the Park (415-864-3330; www.sfopera.com/park; Sharon Meadow, Golden Gate Park; 1:30-3:30pm 2nd Sun in Sep; 33) This noncostumed concert heralds the start of opera season, drawing close to 50,000. Arrive early. Also see p23.

San Francisco Mime Troupe (415-285-1717; www.sfmt.org) A roving theater troupe that performs at parks throughout SF and the East Bay. Don't expect silent, white-faced mimes – this is strong political-musical theater in the *commedia dell'arte* tradition. Donations appreciated.

San Francisco Shakespeare Festival (415-558-0888; www.sfshakes.org; Sat & Sun Jul-Sep; 33) Among the city's most popular outdoor events. Each year one play is performed some 20-odd times at various Bay Area parks; in SF it's around Labor Day. Check online for location – either Golden Gate Park or the Presidio. Arrive two hours early.

Stern Grove Festival See the boxed text, opposite.

jazz ensembles, a guitar series and family matinees. Most take place at the Herbst Theater (Map p77), where the UN Charter was signed in 1945.

SAN FRANCISCO SYMPHONY Map p77

415-864-6000; www.sfsymphony.org; tickets $30-125; Davies Symphony Hall, 201 Van Ness Ave; 21, 47, 49; & Civic Center

The SF Symphony often wins Grammys, thanks to celeb-conductor and musical-director Michael Tilson Thomas, the world's foremost Mahler impresario. When he's not on the podium, other famous conductors take the baton. The orchestra is joined by the Grammy-winning Symphony Chorus for serious choral works, such as Beethoven's *Missa solemnis*. During festivals over summer and at Christmas, look for stars like Bernadette Peters, Pink Martini and Peabo Bryson. During intermission, head all the way upstairs and stand on the flying-saucer-like balconies for bird's-eye views of City Hall.

The best sound is in the cheap seats in the center terrace, but the loge is most comfy and glam and has the best sightlines. If you're on a budget, sit in the front section of AA, BB, HH or JJ; or sit behind the stage in the center terrace – the sound doesn't blend evenly, but you get the musicians' perspective and look into the conductor's eyes (likewise in pricier side terrace seats). Call the rush-ticket hotline (415-503-5577) after 6:30pm to find out whether the box office has released $20 next-day tickets, which you must pick up in person the day of performance: choose the side terrace over the front orchestra – unless you want to be 10ft from the strings, but the sound is uneven so close to the stage.

READINGS

The spoken word – and sometimes the shouted word – get top billing in literary-minded San Francisco, especially during the annual Litquake Festival (p23). The San Francisco Main Library (Map p77; 415-557-4400; http://sfpl.lib.ca.us; 100 Larkin St) hosts near-daily readings; we particularly love Michelle Tea's gay-focused Radar series – she's hysterical. For a literary throw down that's somewhere between *American Idol* and *American Gladiators*, look for the occasional appearance of Literary Death Match (www.literarydeathmatch.com).

BOOKSMITH

Map pp126–7

☎ 415-863-8688; www.booksmith.com; 1644 Haight St; 10am-10pm Mon-Sat, to 8pm Sun; 6, 7, 33, 37, 43, 71

SF is one of the country's top book markets, and authors often swing through town on tours. They sometimes read at Booksmith's Author Series. Past readings have included the likes of Kazuo Ishiguro, Ursula Le Guin and Jeanette Winterson. Check the online calendar.

CAFÉ ROYALE Map p77

☎ 415-441-4099; www.caferoyale-sf.com; 800 Post St; admission free; 10am-midnight Sun-Thu, to 2am Fri & Sat; 2, 3, 4

A Parisian tiled floor and semicircular fainting couches lend atmosphere and acoustics to this laid-back lounge, which hosts film screenings, open-mic poetry slams and jazz. Walk by during the day and you'll sometimes hear musicians rehearsing in the basement studio.

CITY ARTS & LECTURES

Map p77

☎ box office 415-392-4400; www.cityarts.net; Herbst Theater, 401 Van Ness Ave; 21, 47, 49; & Civic Center

The city's foremost lecture series hosts an all-star lineup of today's most celebrated artists, writers and intellectuals, from Joan Didion to David Sedaris and Madeline Albright to Michael J Fox. Lectures take place at the Herbst Theater, and most interviews are broadcast on local public-radio station KQED-FM (88.5); check the website for broadcast schedules.

COMMONWEALTH CLUB

Map pp70–1

☎ 415-597-6700; www.commonwealthclub.org; 595 Market St; 71, F; & Montgomery St

You know you've arrived when the Commonwealth Club asks you to speak. Every US president since Teddy Roosevelt has spoken at the club, the longest-running, most-influential public-affairs forum in the US. Intellectual luminaries and other important figures speak at over 400 annual events. Topics range from politics and economics to culture and society. Many programs are broadcast on public-radio stations nationwide, including local affiliate KQED-FM (88.5).

PORCHLIGHT

☎ 415-571-0998, 510-848-6328; www.porchlightsf.com

This monthly event is no ordinary reading series. Each month six interesting people are invited to recount a 10-minute story, without notes or memorization. The lineup is downright wacky, with people from all walks of life – from school-bus drivers to sex-workers. At this writing, Porchlight had moved to a new venue that serves alcohol, making it inappropriate for anyone under 21; verify current location and ticket information online.

THEATER

Since the days when Shakespeare companies soliliqued their way around the goldfields, San Franciscans have been diehard theatergoers. Although some historic theaters have since been converted into nightclubs and gyms, the city had 20 major theaters c 1900. Today, San Francisco has more than a hundred companies listed as members of Theatre Bay Area (www.theatrebayarea.org), an organisation with a comprehensive calendar of what's playing now. Touring Broadway shows regularly stop in SF; for details check with the production company SHN (☎ 415-512-7770; www.shnsf.com).

It's experimental theater that sets SF apart from other US cities. Pulitzer Prize–winning *Angels in America* got its wings here before moving on to Broadway. If you're here early September, catch a performance at Exit Theater's San Francisco Fringe Festival (http://theexit.org) for a glimpse of the scene. Also check out Beach Blanket Babylon (p206).

For its relatively small size, Berkeley has great theater, particularly at UC Berkeley's Zellerbach Hall (p275) and at the well-established, award-winning Berkeley Repertory Theatre (p275), which is possibly the Bay Area's best company. Also excellent are shows at Berkeley's Aurora Theatre (p275) and Shotgun Players (p275).

Ticket prices run the gamut – anyone should be able to enjoy a play or two while visiting the city. At larger houses, depending on seats and production, prices range from $35 to $150. Small, independent companies usually charge between $10 and $30. Same-day discount tickets can be purchased through TIX Bay Area or Gold Star Events (see the boxed text, opposite).

SCORE!

Going to a cultural event doesn't have to break the bank. There are lots of things to do in SF each week, and many events are free. Check the KQED Community Calendar (http://events.kqed.org/events) for a good list. The following three options let you take in a show and still have enough cash in pocket for dinner:

Dolores Park Movie Night (Map pp116–17; www.doloresparkmovie.org; 20th & Dolores St; admission free; dusk, 2nd Thu of the month, mid-Apr–mid-Oct; 33, J) At Mission Dolores Park, free outdoor screenings of new films and cult classics are made better by the appearance of beloved SF icon the Tamale Lady (say yes to the hot sauce – it's not that strong). Donations accepted. Bring a blanket and warm coat, and arrive early.

Gold Star Events (www.goldstarevents.com) Sign up for free and you'll get regular emails offering discounts for whatever's playing that week. In addition to comedy, theater, rock concerts and opera, you'll also find last-minute deals on local spas and other fun stuff.

TIX Bay Area (Map pp70–1; 415-433-7827; www.tixbayarea.org; Union Square; Powell-Mason, Powell-Hyde) Line up at the half-price ticket booth to score cheap seats for unsold day-of or next-day shows. Check the website first, if you can, because some tix are available only online, others only at the booth.

A TRAVELING JEWISH THEATER

Map pp116–17

415-292-1233; www.atjt.com; 470 Florida St; tickets $20-34; 27

Founded in 1978, this theater presents a variety of genres focusing on Jewish and American cultural issues. Borscht Belt comedy, music, storytelling, and serious and comic drama appear on the company's main stage in the Mission, but sometimes elsewhere too; check with the box office to confirm locations.

AMERICAN CONSERVATORY THEATER

Map pp70–1

415-749-2228; www.act-sf.org; 415 Geary St; 2, 3, 4, 27, 38; Powell-Mason, Powell-Hyde

Breakthrough shows destined for the big time in London or New York sometimes pass muster at the turn-of-the-century Geary Theater, which has hosted ACT's landmark productions of Tony Kushner's *Angels in America* and Robert Wilson's *Black Rider,* with a libretto by William S Burroughs and music by the Bay Area's own Tom Waits.

CLIMATE THEATER

Map pp110–11

415-263-0830; www.climatetheater.com; 285 9th St; 12, 27, 47

You never know what's doing at the Climate, a tiny black-box experimental theater, which is a testing ground for new works, from comedy improv to small plays pulled together on a shoestring.

EXIT THEATER

Map pp70–1

415-673-3847; http://theexit.org; 156 Eddy St; admission $15-20; 31; & Powell St

Experimental theater in this tiny venue provides an escape from the musical-and-melodrama treadmill. It's also home to the annual San Francisco Fringe Festival, a mass exodus from the norm.

INTERSECTION FOR THE ARTS

Map pp116–17

415-626-2787; www.theintersection.org; 446 Valencia St; admission $5-20; 16th St Mission

Alterna-theater, jazz, literary readings and an upstairs gallery are all part of this non-profit arts space, the oldest in SF (opened 1965). Intersection has lots going on, including a literary series, workshops and an 'open process' series, which explores the craft of making art; check the website for details.

MAGIC THEATRE

Map pp100–1

415-441-8822; www.magictheatre.org; 3rd fl, Bldg D, Fort Mason Center; 22, 28, 30

The Magic Theatre is well known for taking risks and staging provocative plays by such playwrights as Bill Pullman, Terrence McNally, Edna O'Brien, David Mamet and longtime playwright-in-residence Sam Shepard. Watch the next generation of playwrights and provocateurs break through in professionally staged works written by teenagers as part of the Young California Writers Project.

MARSH Map pp116–17
☎ 415-641-0235; www.themarsh.org; 1062 Valencia St; tickets $8-35; 🕑 8pm Thu-Sun; 🚌 14, 26, 49
The Marsh is a hive of creativity. One-acts and one-off stagings of works-in-progress involve the audience in the creative process. This is San Francisco experimental theater at its most exciting. A sliding-scale pricing structure allows all to participate. Also offers workshops.

RED POPPY ART HOUSE Map pp116–17
☎ 415-826-2402; www.redpoppyarthouse.org; 2698 Folsom St; Ⓜ 24th St Mission
It feels like a house party you've stumbled upon by accident, where guests are instead performers still in rehearsal mode. The little corner storefront is open to passersby; inside you'll find art in progress, musical performances and occasional film screenings. Check the lineup on the website, or just wander in. If you dig open studios, this is a very cool concept and a great way to meet local artists.

SPORTS & ACTIVITIES

top picks

- **San Francisco Giants game** (p228)
- **Kabuki Springs & Spa** (p237)
- **Lindy in the Park** (p235)
- **Midnight Rollers** (p231)
- **Sunday bicycling in Golden Gate Park** (p229)

SPORTS & ACTIVITIES

San Franciscans love the outdoors, and with good reason. The low-rise city's topography perfectly lends itself to exploration, with lots of open space, parks, beaches and woodlands. Locals hike to remote hilltops to find the perfect picnic spot, sail the bay's glittering grey waters and stroll arm-in-arm down foggy beaches. On Sundays, Golden Gate Park is ground zero for outdoor fun, with Lindy dancing, roller boogie, and all manner of human-powered vehicles gliding down the park's wide boulevard, John F Kennedy Dr. You'll never be at a loss for something to do outdoors, even during winter's rains when the Pacific positively thunders – a thrilling sight.

Mountain-biking got its start in nearby Marin County, and every weekend thousands of cyclists cross the Golden Gate to explore the Marin Headlands (p277). Inline skaters make a sort of commando raid every Friday night along the waterfront, and cyclists jam city streets on the last Friday of the month for the controversial Critical Mass – locals love to mix politics with fun. Spectator sports are big too, especially when the Giants make it to the World Series, but even then don't expect the post-championship riots that happen elsewhere (with the notable exception of the infamously wacked Oakland Raiders fans across the bay). When SF teams win, you spot an occasional band of happy, screaming fans. When they lose, most shrug their shoulders and shift their attention to the beauty that surrounds them.

SPECTATOR SPORTS

There are two types of sports-viewers in San Francisco: those in stadiums, and those in bars. Much as we love catching a Giants game at awesome AT&T Park (right), we'd be remiss not to point you to local gin mills such as Bus Stop (p199), where you can get into the psyche of local sports fanatics. When you want the real deal, book tickets through team websites, or try Ticketmaster (www.ticketmaster.com); if games are sold out, search the 'tickets' category on craigslist.org. For the latest sports stats and predictions, pick up the *San Francisco Chronicle,* which has a long history of good sports-writing, or check *The Examiner* online (www.examiner.com/san_francisco).

BASEBALL

OAKLAND A'S

☎ 510-568-5600; http://oakland.athletics.mlb.com; Oakland-Alameda Coliseum, Oakland; tickets $9-55; Ⓑ Coliseum

When the Giants are away, the A's are usually home, which expands the possibilities for those desperate for a summer baseball fix. BART stops just outside the ballpark. The A's most recent championship came at the Giants' expense in the quake-addled 1989 series, and they remain fierce contenders. If you want to catch them in an interleague-play game, get your tickets early.

SAN FRANCISCO GIANTS

☎ 415-972-2000; http://sanfrancisco.giants.mlb.com; AT&T Park; tickets $5-135; N; ♿

April to October, you can catch one of the 81 home games of SF's National League baseball team in this intimate ballpark, which changes its name with every telecom merger. The Giants pack in huge crowds and often make the playoffs, but haven't won the baseball big tomato, the World Series, since 1954 (the team called New York home in those days). Games are frequently sold out, but season-ticket holders often sell unwanted tickets through the team's Double Play Ticket Window on the website; it's also worth checking internet auctions like eBay.com and craigslist.org.

A behind-the-scenes tour (☎ 415-972-2400; tickets $12.50; nongame days at 10:30am & 2:30pm) includes visits to the clubhouse, dugout and field. There's also a kids' play structure in a giant Coca-Cola bottle, a mini-replica of the field and the world's largest baseball glove. Bonus: on the east side of the park, you can stand at the archways along the waterfront promenade and watch a few innings for free.

BASKETBALL

GOLDEN STATE WARRIORS

☎ 510-986-2200, 888-GSW-HOOP; www.warriors.com; Oakland Arena; tickets $15-450; Ⓑ Coliseum

If it's hoops you must have, then it's the Warriors for you. This team has a long history, starting in Philadelphia in 1947. In 1962 it moved to San Francisco and played in the Cow Palace as the San Francisco Warriors. In 1971 the team moved across the bay and has played at the Oakland Arena (next to the Coliseum) ever since, as the Golden State Warriors. After a decade-plus slump, the Warriors advanced to the playoffs in 2007 and caused quite a commotion when they beat the top-ranking Dallas Mavericks. Alas, still no trophy.

FOOTBALL

OAKLAND RAIDERS

☎ 510-762-2277, 888-447-2433; www.raiders.com; Oakland-Alameda Coliseum, Oakland; tickets $30-100 at www.ticketmaster.com; Ⓑ Coliseum

With three Super Bowl championship wins, the notorious bad boys of the NFL have had their ups and downs over the years, but they have the staunchest, rowdiest fans in the western US. The team ungratefully moved to Los Angeles for 12 years, but returned in 1995, the prodigal football club, to Oakland's open arms. It's been football bliss in Oakland ever since, unlike in SF, where in 2009 the 49ers were in final negotiations with Santa Clara County to build a new stadium and leave SF behind. Given the choice between a 20-minute BART ride to Oakland and a 40-mile drive to Santa Clara…well, we wish the 49ers luck.

SAN FRANCISCO 49ERS

☎ 415-656-4900; www.sf49ers.com; Monster Park; tickets $25-100 at www.ticketmaster.com; 🚌 T; shuttle buses

The 49ers were the dream team of the National Football League (NFL) during the 1980s and early '90s, but the team has been in a sorry state of late, finishing at the very bottom of the heap in the 2004 season and not making the playoffs since. Clearly, these five-time Super Bowl champs will be rebuilding for some years to come, but fan loyalty has not flagged – although that may change: as of this writing the team was in serious negotiations with nearby Santa Clara County to leave San Francisco.

OUTDOOR ACTIVITIES

Come the weekend, it seems every local is strolling, kite-flying, surfing or biking. SF's fog keeps temps perfect for exercising, but layer on the sunscreen even when it's cloudy: UV rays penetrate the deceptively thin cloud layer.

BICYCLING

Road-biking on skinny tires is big in SF. On any given day, expect to see Lycra-clad cyclists huffing and puffing up the city's most excruciating hills en route to the hilly coastal roads of the Presidio. In neighborhoods like the Mission, Downtown and South of Market, you'll spot commuters on hybrids and mountain bikes – their only mode of transportation. Local bikers pride themselves on knowing every flat route across town, and feature their street cred with an elastic-banded pant leg. To get the inside track on the biking scene in SF, check out the **San Francisco Bicycle Coalition** (www.sfbike.org), a clearinghouse of bicycling-related resources and information; contact it for the *San Francisco Biking/Walking Guide*, which shows how to avoid traffic and hills. The map is also available at local bike shops and Rainbow Grocery (p180) or online in PDF at the coalition's site.

The best places to cycle are Golden Gate Park, the Embarcadero and the wooded Presidio. Check out our biking tour on p106, which takes you from the waterfront to Golden Gate Bridge. The classic Sunday ride runs through

SAVE YOUR LEGS: HOW TO AVOID HILLS ON FOOT OR BIKE

San Francisco's hills are lovely, but they're a bitch to climb on foot or bicycle. Formerly you had to carry a specialized paper map, one showing street grades, such as the excellent *San Francisco Biking/Walking Guide* by Rufus Graphics. But what if you didn't get it together in time to order it online or pick up a copy at **Rainbow Grocery** (p180)? Take heart: you can use your smart phone to call up the perfect route using the San Francisco Bike Route Planner. (Google it on the fly, or pre-program your phone with the following address: http://amarpai.com/bikemap/bikemap.html.) You enter your starting address and destination, tick a box stating whether you want the most direct route or the most bike-friendly route, hit enter and – voilà! – a map appears showing you the optimal route, along with each street's grade listed in an accompanying chart. While nothing replaces the convenience of a proper paper map, we're glad to have a backup in pocket.

Golden Gate Park, along John F Kennedy Dr (which is car-free on Sundays, east of Crossover Dr) to Ocean Beach (best when it's not too windy).

Many streets have bicycle lanes (check the PDF map on the Bicycle Coalition's website), and major parks have bike paths. To prove your right of way in this bicycling city, pedal with the renegade mob Critical Mass (Google it) on the last Friday of the month. Bicyclists are legally allowed to 'take the lane,' as in ride down the center of the street, if hazards make riding on the shoulder unsafe. Some motorists get angry about this, so use caution and stand down if someone flips you off from a passing car.

Hardcore mountain-bikers cross the Golden Gate for the trails of the Marin Headlands (p277) and Mt Tamalpais (p281), the birthplace of mountain-biking. The first off-road races in the '70s kicked up dirt on Mt Tam, which remains the Bay Area's supreme mountain-biking challenge. The Headlands is a quick ride over the Golden Gate; Mt Tam is further and most Bay Area bikers strap their knobby tires to their cars to get there.

Good books for Bay Area cyclists include *Bay Area Bike Rides,* by Ray Hosler, and *Cycling the San Francisco Bay Area: 30 Rides to Historic Sites and Scenic Places,* by Carol O'Hare. Also check the resources page of the Bicycle Coalition's site for tips. In addition to the following bike-rental shops, see the Running, Walking & Skating section, opposite, for other places that rent bicycles.

AMERICAN CYCLERY

Map pp126–7

☎ 415-664-4545; www.americancyclery.com; 510 Frederick St; 🕑 11am-7pm Mon-Fri, 10am-6pm Sat, 10am-5pm Sun; 🚌 71

If you've been lusting after a banana-seat Stingray, you might find one here. The oldest indie bike shop in SF, American Cyclery carries contemporary mountain and hybrid bikes as well as the occasional vintage model (the owner's a collector). Though the shop hosts events and rides, alas, there are no rentals.

AVENUE CYCLERY

Map pp126–7

☎ 415-387-3155; www.avenuecyclery.com; 756 Stanyan St; bikes per hr/day $8/30; 🕑 10am-7pm Mon-Sat, to 6pm Sun; 🚌 21, 33; ♿

In one of the more bike-friendly parts of the city, Avenue has an extensive selection of bikes for rent and for sale. It also does repairs, fittings and cycle clinics. Rental includes a helmet.

BLAZING SADDLES Map p92

☎ 415-202-8888; www.blazingsaddles.com; 1096 Columbus Ave; bikes per hr $7-11, per day $28-68; 🕑 8am-sunset; 🚌 30; 🚋 Powell-Mason; ♿

Blazing Saddles is tailored to visitors, with a main shop on Columbus Ave and rental stands along Fisherman's Wharf. It has the most convenient locations for biking the Embarcadero or along the bay to the Golden Gate Bridge and Marin County. You can reserve a bike online for a 10% discount, and it includes all the extras (bungee cords, packs etc). But beware the after-hours return: it's a hassle to find the locker Downtown in the dark, and return instructions are complicated.

GOLF

If you like smooth, clipped greens, mild weather and gorgeous views, you'll love playing in SF. If you're economizing, most of the following have twilight fees.

GOLDEN GATE MUNICIPAL GOLF COURSE

Map pp136–7

☎ 415-751-8987; www.goldengateparkgolfcourse.com; 47th Ave & Fulton St; Mon-Thu $14, Fri-Sun $19; 🕑 6am-8pm; 🚌 5

Golden Gate Park has a challenging nine-hole, par-27 course with a variety of holes, from 100yd drop-offs to 180yd elevated greens. Peaceful and with some nice views of the Pacific, it's busiest before 9am weekdays and after school. On weekend afternoons, prepare for an hour-long wait. No reservations.

HARDING PARK MUNICIPAL GOLF COURSE

Map pp60–1

☎ 415-664-4690; www.harding-park.com; 99 Harding Rd at Skyline Blvd; 9-hole course Mon-Thu $25, Fri-Sun $30, 18-hole course Mon-Thu $135, Fri-Sun $155; 🕑 6:30am-7pm; 🚌 18

San Francisco's premier public course is a verdant 18-hole course partially shaded by cypress trees beside the ocean; call to reserve a tee-time. Also on the site is the Jack Fleming nine-hole course, where walk-ins are welcome. Cart included.

SKATE CITY

In skate circles, SF is known not for its sourdough bread, but as the home of roller disco and the skate magazine *Thrasher* (www.thrashermagazine.com). Get with the locals at these prime spots:

Boards

- Haight St – urban skating at its obstacle-course best, especially the downhill slide from Baker to Pierce. Get geared up at Shoe Biz and Upper Playground (p157).
- Potrero del Sol/La Raza Skatepark (p120) – pop ollies with local dudes at the city's newest and most rad skate park. Drawback: distance from Downtown; sketchy neighborhood after sunset.

Inline

- Midnight Rollers Friday Night Skate (http://web.cora.org/friday.phtml) – every Friday at 8:30pm at the Ferry Building, the Rollers bust out boom boxes, and at 9pm they're off to Pier 39, the Palace of Fine Arts, and back through Chinatown and Union Square to the Ferry Building.
- Golden Gate Park roller-skaters – roller skaters have converged at Golden Gate Park since 1891, and in the 1970s heyday of roller disco, up to 20,000 Sunday skaters cruised the park, and each other. You can still boogie down on Sundays at the blacktop known as 'Roller Village,' off John F Kennedy Dr, near 6th Ave.

LINCOLN PARK GOLF COURSE

Map pp136–7

☎ 415-221-9911; www.lincolnparkgc.com; 34th Ave & Clement St; Mon-Thu $34, Fri-Sun $38; ⏲ sunrise-sunset; 🚌 1, 18, 38

For game-sabotaging views, the hilly, 18-hole Lincoln Park course wraps around the Palace of the Legion of Honor and graces the coast west of the Golden Gate Bridge. This one has the most iconic SF vistas; it's the number-two public course after Harding.

PRESIDIO GOLF COURSE Map pp100–1

☎ 415-561-4661; www.presidiogolf.com; Arguello Blvd & Finley Rd; Mon-Thu resident/non-resident $69/125, Fri $85/145, Sat & Sun $99/145; ⏲ sunrise-sunset; 🚌 28

Whack balls with military-style precision on the course once reserved exclusively for US forces. The Presidio course, now operated by the Arnold Palmer company, runs along the bay and is considered one of the country's best. You can book up to 30 days in advance on the website, where you can sometimes find rate specials, too. Cart is included in the price.

RUNNING, WALKING & SKATING

Marina Green has a 2.5-mile jogging track and fitness course, and trails abound in Golden Gate Park, including a 400m synthetic track in Kezar Stadium at the park's southeast corner. A couple of routes run all the way from the Panhandle to the ocean, covering about 3 miles, and on Sunday cars are banned from John F Kennedy Dr, east of Crossover Dr. The Presidio, with its eucalyptus forests and fresh ocean air, is another runners' paradise. Lake Merced Park, a 368-acre island of country trails at the southwest end of the city, is made for long inspiring sessions of elevated heart rates. Some of SF's major races, like Bay to Breakers (p21), are more festive than serious.

Walking the city's undulating hills combines excursion with exertion, challenging even the fittest tourist. Golden Gate Park is the place for promenading, while SF's windswept beaches are best for long romantic strolls.

CALIFORNIA OUTDOOR ROLLERSKATING ASSOCIATION MIDNIGHT ROLLERS

☎ 415-752-1967; www.cora.org; ⏲ 8:30pm Fri

A posse of thrill-seeking skaters gathers Friday nights at the Ferry Building (p64) to skate away the evening, heading up the Embarcadero to the Marina and back again. There are usually a couple dozen skaters, but past jaunts have included as many as 150 people, rolling in an amorphous mob. They may stop for drinks or snacks; carry some cash, as well as a helmet and some extra layers. Check the CORA website for route information and more on local skater events.

DOLPHIN SOUTH END RUNNING CLUB

☎ 415-978-0837; www.dserunners.com; per person $5

'Start slowly and taper off' is the Dolphins' motto. While these guys do conduct some more serious runs, most weekend runs are given over to the tortoise, and the hare is sent packing. About 50 'racers' assemble and mostly they just jog along merrily, chatting, joking and relaxing. All are welcome; call or check the website for the week's rendezvous point.

GOLDEN GATE PARK BIKE & SKATE

Map pp136–7

☎ 415-668-1117; 3038 Fulton St; skates per hr/day $6/24, bikes $5/25, discs $5/20; 10am-6pm (closed when raining); 5

In addition to bikes and skates (both quad-wheeled and inline), this little rental shop just outside the park also rents saucer-shaped putters and drivers for the nearby free disc golf course. Call ahead to confirm it's open if the weather looks iffy.

HASH HOUSE HARRIERS

☎ 415-566-4274; www.sfh3.com; per person $5-10; 6:15pm Mon

Hash House Harriers – an atypical athletic organization by any stretch – is loosely based on the English game Hare and Hounds. Members of 'the Hash' say they are drinkers with a running problem: their goal is to work up thirst and appetite. One member is designated as the Hare, and lays out a paper chase – a route marked with paper or chalk full of devious detours, false leads and dead ends. All others are Harriers, who find their way through bad neighborhoods, muddy fields, rubbish heaps – the wackier, the better. At run's end, expect lots of beer and munchies. All are welcome; call or check the website for the week's rendezvous place.

KENNEDY DRIVE FREESTYLE ROLLER DANCE

6th Ave at John F Kennedy Dr, Golden Gate Park; Sun;

Roller boogie is alive and kicking – at least on Sundays in Golden Gate Park. Fearless skaters leap, twirl and pirouette to blaring house music and classic disco, much to the delight of crowds gathered on the adjacent grassy hill. Kids' eyes positively light up. If you're brave enough to join the dance, rent skates at nearby Golden Gate Park Bike & Skate (left).

WHEEL FUN RENTALS Map pp136–7

☎ 415-668-6699; www.wheelfunrentals.com; 50 Stow Lake Dr; skates per hr/day $6/20, bikes $8/25; 9am-7pm; 44

Achy feet slowing you down? Problem solved at this rental shop in the heart of Golden Gate Park. Dip into the Sunset (the neighborhood to the south), roll westward to Ocean Beach's promenade for a glimpse of the kite-boarders, or just glide around the park. Cheaper cruiser bikes cost the same price as skate rentals. If you want to hit Stow Lake, hop aboard a surrey (tandem paddleboat) with a baguette and feed the geese. To cruise the waterfront, head to its second location in the Marina, at Fort Mason (call for directions; it's in a parking lot).

SAILING & WINDSURFING

Sailboats dot the bay nearly any given day in SF, prompting many to ask, doesn't anyone work in this town? It *is* work to sail the bay: currents are strong, winds erratic and cold, and tidal currents ferocious. Head out in a small craft at ebb tide and you may find yourself kissing San Francisco goodbye as you're sucked out to sea. Know what you're doing, or else hit the water aboard a skippered sailboat cruise, cocktail in hand. Sailing is best from April through August, when the westerlies are most reliable, but diehards sail year-round.

ADVENTURE CAT Map p63

☎ 415-777-1630; www.adventurecat.com; Pier 39; cruises from $30; F;

There's no better view of San Francisco than from the water, especially at twilight on a fogless evening aboard a sunset cruise. Adventure Cat uses catamarans, with a windless indoor cabin for grandmums and a trampoline between the hulls for bouncy kids. There are three daily cruises in March through October; weekends only from November through February.

BOARDSPORTS KITEBOARDING & WINDSURFING

☎ 415-385-1224; www.boardsportsschool.com; Crown Beach, Alameda; 2-day windsurfing class $50, 90min kiteboard intro class $165; call for lesson times & seasonal rental hrs; 12th St (Oakland), then 51 to Alameda

Boarding school is never dull at Boardsports, where you can learn to fast tack and pivot jibe in a weekend. The Bay Area has prime wind conditions, and the sweet-spot for lessons is in Alameda, just across the bay. Instructor-student ratio is almost 1:1, and knowledgeable, fun-loving staff will keep you laughing even when you fall off your board. Gear and wetsuit included; bring a towel, snack and change of clothes. If you already know what you're doing, rentals are available.

SPINNAKER SAILING Map pp110–11

☎ 415-543-7333; www.spinnaker-sailing.com; Pier 40; lessons $375; 10am-5pm; N, T

Do luff, cringle and helms-a-lee mean anything to you? If yes, captain a boat from Spinnaker and sail into the sunset. If no, charter a skippered vessel, or take classes and learn to talk like a sailor – in a good way. The website is packed with everything you need to know.

SWIMMING & SURFING

The Beach Boys hail from the other California. To get your head around the Northern California beach scene, think Hitchcock. Wind and fog, not sun, are the dominant summer weather patterns, and the waters around SF are frigid and riddled with currents. If you love swimming in the ocean, we first recommend Santa Cruz (p296) for its warmer beaches, but if you're determined to brave SF's waters, you have options. There's a tiny patch of beach at Aquatic Park (p67), just west of Fisherman's Wharf, where you often see hardy swimmers in the chilly waters. Baker Beach (p105), on the ocean just south of the Golden Gate, is popular with sunbathers, walkers, surf fishers and nudists (at the northern end); swimming is feasible close to shore when the tide is coming in. Four-mile-long Ocean Beach (p138) is best for romantic walks: its currents render it dangerous for swimming, unless you really know what you're doing; we don't recommend it.

Surfing is best in winter, when storms churn up swells 12ft or higher. Santa Cruz is the top destination, followed by Stinson Beach in Marin. SF's Ocean Beach sees its share of local surfers, who mostly come at daybreak in winter, but SF's waters are not for beginners. **Aqua Surf Shop** (Map pp60–1; ☎ 415-242-9283; http://aquasurfshop.com; 2830 Sloat Blvd; 10am-5:30pm Sun-Tue, to 7pm Wed-Sat) rents boards and wetsuits and tells you the best breaks. Also check the **surf report** (☎ 415-273-1618).

If you prefer calm waters, the city operates a number of pools that are clean, if you can get past the surly staff and grungy facilities: Hamilton Pool in Lower Pacific Heights, Garfield Pool in the Mission/Bernal Heights, and North Beach Pool; all are heated. City pool schedules are listed at www.parks.sfgov.org. On a sunny day we most love the outdoor Mission Pool. Also consider the Embarcadero YMCA (p237). Otherwise, try one of the following.

BAKAR FITNESS & RECREATION CENTER Map pp110–11

☎ 415-514-4545; http://mbfitness.ucsf.edu; 1675 Owens & 16th Sts; day pass $15; 5:30am-10pm Mon-Fri, 7:30am-8pm Sat & Sun; 22, T

As outdoor pools go, the view from the dizzyingly high 25yd rooftop pool is enough to make you forget you came here to swim. Located at the UCSF Mission Bay campus, it's lovely and modern, with six lanes and an adjacent patio, and you can get a fresh perspective on everything from the ballpark to the Bay Bridge. A second pool, one level below, offers water-based exercise classes. Both are available for private parties.

KORET POOL

Map pp126–7

☎ 415-422-6821; www.usfca.edu/koret; Parker Ave & Turk St; adult/senior & child under 17yr $15/10; 6am-9pm Mon-Fri, 8am-6pm Sat & Sun; 5, 31

For a serious lap swim, head to this Olympic-sized pool, at the University of San Francisco, with 40ft ceilings and oversized windows. Admission includes use of the full gym as well.

TENNIS

There are free public tennis courts all over San Francisco – the courts at Mission Dolores Park (p118) are especially popular. For other free public courts, contact the **San Francisco Recreation & Park Department** (☎ 415-831-2700; www.parks.sfgov.org; 9am-4pm). The 21 courts in Golden Gate Park (p139) charge $4 to $6 for adults, and kids under 18 are free. Call for weekend **reservations** (☎ 415-753-7131; 4-6pm Wed, 9am-5pm Thu & Fri), ideally at 4pm on the Wednesday before.

WHALE-WATCHING

Whale-watching season peaks mid-October through December, when gray whales migrate from the Bering Sea to Baja California – the longest annual mammal migration in the world. Because the whales tend to cruise along the coastline, they're easy to spot from land. Point Reyes (p291), north of the city, is the prime whale-watching spot. The whales pass again on their way home in March, but they're further from shore on the northbound journey.

OCEANIC SOCIETY EXPEDITIONS

Map pp100–1

☎ 415-474-3385; www.oceanic-society.org; Bldg A, Fort Mason Center; per person $100-120; office 9am-5pm Fri-Mon, trips Sat & Sun; 22, 28, 30

The Oceanic Society runs ocean-going boat trips – sometimes to the Farallon Islands – during both whale-migration seasons, with top-notch naturalists providing keen insight. Cruises depart from Fort Mason and last all day. Kids must be 10 years or older. Reservations required.

INDOOR ACTIVITIES

ICE SKATING & BOWLING

When the weather's not cooperating, San Franciscans in search of fun – especially local parents – keep bowling and skating in their back pocket. At this writing, the fate of the old Presidio Bowl was up in the air; do an internet search to see if it's still operating when you're here.

YERBA BUENA CENTER ICE SKATING & BOWLING Map pp110–11

☎ 415-820-3532; www.skatebowl.com; 750 Folsom St; skating adult/child/senior $8/5.50/6.25 plus $3 skate rental, bowling per game $4.50-6, per hr $25-35; bowling 10am-10pm Sun-Thu, to midnight Fri & Sat, check website or call for skating times; & Powell St;

Built on the rooftop of the Moscone Convention Center, the ice and bowling centers are a huge draw for families. Unlike most rinks, this one is bright and naturally lit with walls of windows; the bowling alley is small but serves beer.

YOGA

You'll never see so many people walking around with rolled-up blue yoga mats as you will in San Francisco. Some locals are pushing for yoga competitions in the Olympics, while others are appalled, saying this defeats the purpose entirely. Regardless of your viewpoint, you'll find hundreds of studios in SF to support it. If you're a serious devotee of a particular tradition, you'll find it in SF with a quick internet search. Many local gyms also offer classes.

IT'S YOGA Map pp110–11

☎ 415-543-1970; www.itsyoga.net; 307a 5th St; drop-in classes $15-18; & Powell St

Some call it a factory, but we like It's Yoga for its big classes – ideal for shy types who don't like being singled out for adjustments of posture. It's all about Ashtanga here, which focuses on breath, flow and power. Classes are held in large rooms with big windows with lots of light. Reserve online for the busiest late-afternoon classes from Monday to Friday.

YOGA TREE Map pp116–17

☎ 415-647-9707; www.yogatreesf.com; 1234 Valencia St; drop-in classes $17; 10am-10pm; 24th St Mission

Yoga-lovers will find instant community in this clean, warm, colorful studio, which has personable, high-quality instructors, great deals on introductory classes (three sessions for $20) and drop-in classes, primarily in Hatha yoga. Massage and private lessons are available too, and there are three other locations to choose from: the Castro, Hayes Valley and Stanyan St.

JAILHOUSE SWIM

Once each summer, SF's hardiest swimmers participate in the Alcatraz Sharkfest Swim. They ferry to Alcatraz, then dive into the bay's icy water to swim 1.5 miles back to Aquatic Park. Entry costs $175. Reserve *at least* three months in advance by calling Envirosports (☎ 415-868-1829; www.envirosports.com; PO Box 1040, Stinson Beach, CA, 94970), which also provides race information. In October, you can join the 1.5-mile Treasure Island to YMCA (ti2Y) swim, organized by the Embarcadero YMCA (☎ 415-957-9622; www.ymcasf.org/embarcadero; 169 Steuart St; & Embarcadero). The cost is $85 if you register before July 31, $95 after.

OTHER ACTIVITIES

SF rebels against the mainstream in just about every way possible, and its sporting and leisure activities are no exception. The following are a smattering of alternative options, from circus arts to hang-gliding. If you like a bit of hand-holding or enjoy group activities, such as kayaking, surfing and camping, contact the University of California San Francisco's Outdoors Programs (☎ 415-476-2078; www.outdoors.ucsf.edu), which are open to the public and a great way to meet people.

CIRCUS CENTER TRAPEZE

Map pp136–7

☎ 415-759-8123, ext 810 for trapeze enrolment; www.circuscenter.org; 755 Frederick St; 2hr workshop $42; 🚌 71, N; ♿

If you've ever dreamed of running away and joining the circus, indulge your fantasy at this serious circus-arts school, where students learn everything from Chinese acrobatics to the flying trapeze. Neophytes can arrange one-off courses in trapeze, but be warned: if you fall in love, you may end up enrolling in the school's Clown Conservatory – the only clown-training school in the US.

CITY KAYAK Map pp110–11

☎ 415-357-1010; http://citykayak.com; South Beach Harbor; kayak rentals per hr $14-26, 3hr lesson & rental package $49, tours $59-69; 🚌 N, T

We can't say enough about the view of San Francisco from the water, and one of the best ways to see it is from a kayak. If you're new to paddling, it's best to stick to the waters near the Bay Bridge; if you've some experience, opt for a trip to the choppy waters beneath the Golden Gate Bridge, or for a moonlight tour. Adventurers can set out alone with all-inclusive rentals; aspiring newbies can take lessons and get their sea arms, then head out alone or with an escorted tour – check the website for details.

FLYCASTING CLUB Map pp136–7

www.ggacc.org; McLaren Anglers' Lodge & Casting Pools, John F Kennedy Dr, Golden Gate Park; 🚌 5, 9

Across from the buffalo paddock in Golden Gate Park, sheltered from the breeze by tall cypress and eucalyptus trees, there's an impressive set of casting pools, complete with targets, for the general public to use. You can stroll in and watch flycasters out in their waders, gracefully setting a fly from a thin line that looks about a mile long. Check the website for dates and times of free casting lessons.

LAWN BOWLING CLUB Map pp136–7

☎ 415-487-8787; http://sflb.filesforfriends.com; Bowling Green Dr, Golden Gate Park; 🚌 7, 44, N

Pins seem ungainly and bowling shirts unthinkable once you've stepped onto Golden Gate Park's spongy lawn-bowling green in your classic sweater-and-slacks combo. Free lessons are available on Wednesday at noon, Wednesday evenings in summer, or by appointment. Flat-soled shoes are mandatory, as is all-white clothing at its social events.

LINDY IN THE PARK

Map pp136–7

www.lindyinthepark.com; John F Kennedy Dr btwn 8th & 10th Aves, Golden Gate Park; admission free; 🕑 11am-2pm Sun, weather permitting; 🚌 5, 38, 44; ♿

Start your Sunday right with swing-dancing in Golden Gate Park. In the classic SF tradition, this party is open to everyone: the point is to have fun. You'll spot amazing dancers as well as giggling first-timers, so no need to worry if you've two left feet. Free half-hour lessons begin at noon. Or just come watch. If you can't make it Sunday, there's a monthly Wednesday party at Union Square from May to October.

MISSION CULTURAL CENTER FOR LATINO ARTS Map pp116–17

☎ 415-643-2785; www.missionculturalcenter.org; 2868 Mission St; 🕑 10am-5pm Tue-Sat; 🚌 14, 26, 48, 49; Ⓜ 24th St Mission; ♿

Join a class in flamenco, salsa or Latin belly-dancing; make arts and crafts with the kids; or create a poster at the printmaking studio at this happening cultural center. Teachers are friendly, and participants range from *niños* to *abuelos* (kids to grandpas). Great place to meet locals on a rainy day. Check the online calendar.

PLANET GRANITE Map pp100–1

☎ 415-692-3434; www.planetgranite.com; Glass Palace, 924 Old Mason St, Crissy Field; day use adult/child $18/10; 🕑 6am-11pm Mon-Fri, 8am-8pm Sat, 8am-6pm Sun; 🚌 29

Take in spectacular bay views through a wall of glass as you ascend false-rock structures in this kick-ass 25,000-sq-ft climbing center – the ideal place to train for a hiking expedition to Yosemite. Master top ropes as high as 45ft or test your strength ascending giant boulders and vertical-crack climbing walls, then finish your workout in the full gym, or stretch in a yoga session. Check the web for class schedules.

SAN FRANCISCO CROQUET CLUB

Map pp60–1

☎ 415-928-5525; www.croquetworld.com/sfcc.html; Stern Grove, 19th Ave & Wawona St; admission free; 🚌 28;

Think croquet is a thing of childhood, backyard parties and Sunday picnics? Think again. These folks are hardcore about their wickets, but manage not to take themselves too seriously. Nonmembers can join free sessions on the first three Saturdays of the month; kids are always welcome.

SAN FRANCISCO DISC GOLF

Map pp136–7

www.sfdiscgolf.org; Marx Meadow Dr at Fulton St btwn 25th & 30th Aves; admission free; 🚌 5, 28, 29, 31

If you love to throw Frisbees, head to the tranquil woods of Golden Gate Park to find a permanent 18-hole disc-golf course, enjoyed by cultish veterans and reckless beginners. You can rent a bag of flying saucers at Golden Gate Park Bike & Skate (p232). Tournaments happen Sundays from 8:30am to 10am.

SAN FRANCISCO HANG GLIDING CENTER

☎ 510-528-2300; www.sfhanggliding.com; Mt Tamalpais; 2hr intro lesson $160, per person $295-325

Soar above the Marin Coast from the Bay Area's highest peak for spectacular views over Bolinas Lagoon and Point Reyes. But first you have to get yourself to Mt Tamalpais (p281). The thrilling 2-mile flight from Mt Tam to Stinson Beach includes instruction, and lasts anywhere from seven to 30 minutes, depending on the winds. Alternatively, try paragliding, which is similar but you float beneath parachute-like material not attached to a fixed wing. Location and times vary; be sure to call ahead for details.

SAN FRANCISCO MODEL YACHT CLUB

Map pp136–7

☎ 415-386-1037; www.sfmyc.org; Spreckels Lake, Golden Gate Park; 🚌 5;

Kids go nuts for the impeccable scale-model yachts that sail on little Spreckels Lake. The parade of tiny ships is serious business for collectors, who lovingly build and maintain their crafts in the adjacent clubhouse, and occasionally throw mini-

BEST PLACES TO BE NAKED IN SF

Yep, it's legal: in September 2004, a California appellate court ruled public nudity OK in SF. Should the mood strike, you can strip down bare-ass-nekkid and not end up in jail. The Golden Gate National Recreation Area allows nudity on Land's End Beach and North Baker Beach as long as there's no lewd behavior and nobody complains (only out-of-towners ever do); rangers patrol, so keep an eye out if you get cuddly on the sand. Check the *San Francisco Bay Guardian's* (sfbg.com) annual nude-beach reviews for more. You'll also spot the occasional odd streaker at some parades and protests.

You'd look out of place if you were dressed while scrubbing down with salt at Kabuki Springs & Spa (opposite). Alas, bathing suits are required on coed Tuesdays.

Tourists straying down the trails and cliffs near the Cliff House are often stunned to find nude sunbathers at Lands End and Baker Beaches, in a tiny and often windy quarter-mile-long cove. Better to choose North Baker Beach, SF's most popular nude beach. Take the 29 bus to Lincoln Blvd, turn right and take the second left onto Bowley St, a right on Gibson Rd and right again once you're on the sand. Gay boys prefer Marshall's Beach (aka Marcia's Beach), immediately south of the Golden Gate Bridge. Ask around, if you're gay. No gawkers, please.

World Naked Bike Ride (www.sanfrancisco.worldnakedbikeride.org) takes place in early June to protest US dependence on fossil fuel. A clever compromise for shy types: body paint. When the city threatened to ban nudity at the annual Bay to Breakers (p21) race in May, everyone freaked out, demanding it continue. And so it does.

September's Folsom Street Fair (p23) is not for the faint of heart. Some horrified out-of-towners have complained to the SF Police Dept about the ubiquitous public sex at the fair, which is not legal; we'll see if they do anything about it. Honorable mention for unmentionables goes to Berkeley for its clothing-optional controversies: perhaps the most famous is the sad story from the early '90s of UC Berkeley student Andrew Martinez (Google it); more recent displays, such as 'Boobs Not Bombs' protests, push at the city's anti-nudity ordinance. Score one for San Francisco values.

ature regattas (check the website). While you're here, look for tortoises on shore: Spreckels Lake is where many locals dump their unwanted turtles.

HEALTH & BEAUTY

San Francisco is among the top 10 fittest cities in the US. And where there's fitness, there are aching muscles: massage therapy is big business in SF. Independent salons and spas are sprinkled around town, with the highest concentrations at Union Square, the Upper Fillmore and the Marina. Most top-end hotels also have in-house spas; for maximum swank, we recommend the St Regis Hotel (p259). The following list includes spas, salons and gyms. Women: San Francisco men are generally polite in gyms, but if you're squeamish about working out with guys, opt for a gay gym, where you'll be totally ignored (see p246).

BARBER LOUNGE Map pp110–11

☎ 415-934-0411; www.barberlounge.com; 854 Folsom St; services $10-80; 10am-8pm Tue-Fri, 9am-6pm Sat; 12, 27; & Powell St

Kick back in an ultra-comfortable, art deco–style leather barber's chair for a classic straight-razor shave, haircut or moustache trim. A spin on the classic barbershop, Barber Lounge caters primarily to men, but also offers services for women, from makeup to mani-pedis. We love the masculine vibe and clean, high-ceilinged urban-design setting – a great alternative to prissy salons.

BELLA PELLE SKIN STUDIO Map pp70–1

☎ 415-362-6384; www.bellapelle.com; 9 Maiden Lane; facials $65-150, waxing $20-155; 8am-8pm Mon-Fri, 9am-5pm Sat, 11am-5pm Sun; & Powell St

This cheery-bright spa is a chic treat, with lovely details like free mimosas and muffins on Sundays. The down-to-earth staff pampers, whether you're braving a wax job (they do 'em all here) or lying back for a top-notch facial, the spa's specialty. They also make their own high-quality scrubs, balms, custom-blended makeup, and even a numbing cream.

DIPIETRO TODD SALON Map p96

☎ 415-674-4366; www.dipietrotodd.com; 2239 Fillmore St; haircuts about $100; 10am-4pm Mon, to 6pm Tue-Fri, to 5pm Sat; 22

When you need a fabulous haircut to go with your spiffy new outfit, book Chad (or Eva) at this Upper Fillmore salon. If they're not available, fret not: all the stylists are top-notch. There's another, bigger location at Union Square.

EMBARCADERO YMCA Map pp110–11

☎ 415-957-9622; www.ymcasf.org/embarcadero; 169 Steuart St; day pass $15; 5:30am-9:45pm Mon-Fri, 8am-7:45pm Sat, 9am-5:45pm Sun; & Embarcadero

Downtown professionals flock to this clean, modern YMCA, with complete gym equipment, swimming pool, basketball court and massage services. Each locker room has a steam room. Bring a lock for your locker, or else use the tiny penny lockers by the swimming pool.

KABUKI SPRINGS & SPA Map p96

☎ 415-922-6000; 1750 Geary Blvd; admission Mon-Fri $22, Sat & Sun $25; 10am-9:45pm, coed Tue, women only Sun, Wed & Fri, men only Mon, Thu & Sat; 2, 3, 4, 22, 38

Our favorite urban retreat is a spin on communal Japanese baths. Scrub yourself down with salt in the giant steam room or sauna, then soak in the lovely hot pool before taking a cold plunge. Afterwards, doze off on wooden chaise longues. Quiet is the order of the day: if people get chatty, you need only tap the gong on the water-and-tea table, and all will fall silent. The look is sleek and modern, with wood, tile and low lighting that's soothing after a stressful day. Men and women alternate days, except on Tuesday, when bathing suits are required. Plan two hours minimum; expect a 30-to-60-minute wait at peak times. Communal baths cost $15 with massages (book ahead of time, and come on the gender-appropriate day).

TRUE MASSAGE & WELLNESS Map pp70–1

☎ 415-677-9461; www.true-massage.com; 760 Market St; 60/90min massage $90/130; by appointment; & Powell St

When you want a massage, but don't want the buzz of a spa or salon, book an appointment at this quiet Downtown studio, which offers a full range of styles, from acupressure to reflexology. Look online for special discounts.

GAY/LESBIAN/BI/TRANS SF

top picks

- Sunday afternoon at **Eagle Tavern** (p243)
- **Café Flore** (p245)
- Hot Boxxx Girls at **Aunt Charlie's** (p241)
- **Ladies Night** (p243)
- **Sundance Saloon** (p247)
- **Baker Bmetric converseach** (p240)
- **Parker Guest House** (p248)
- **LGBT Pride Parade** (p247)

GAY/LESBIAN/BI/TRANS SF

The mothership of gay culture, San Francisco is America's pinkest city, the easiest place in the US to be gay, where 'mos are accepted as part of mainstream society. (Remember, this is where gay marriage first became legal in the US.) New York Marys may label SF the retirement home of the young – indeed, the sidewalks roll up early – but when it comes to sexual outlaws and underground weirdness, SF kicks New York's ass.

The intersection of 18th and Castro Sts is the heart of the gay scene, and there are bars a go-go, but most are predictably middlebrow. Dancing queens and slutty boys head South of Market (SoMa), the location of most thump-thump clubs and sex venues. Cruise Castro by day, SoMa by night. On sunny days, Speedo-clad gay boys colonize the grassy hill at 20th and Church Sts, in Mission Dolores Park, overlooking Downtown. Be prepared for pot smoke: SF is stoner central. Weeknights, most guys stay home – those looking for dates jockey their keyboards – and it's trickier to find the party: check out the boxed text, p242.

So where the sexy ladies at? They're busy scamming on their exes' exes at the Lexington Club (p243), screening documentaries at **Artists' Television Access** (www.atasite.org) or raising kids in Noe Valley and Bernal Heights. Your best bet is Valencia St – the funkier outer fringe where Castro hits the Mission – the preferred 'hood of bad-ass dykes, alt-chicks and cute femmes.

If you're giving aggressive gaydar, expect direct come-ons at thrift shops, activist cafes and back patios of neighborhood bars. The boys definitely beat the girls for mass socializing, but expect grrrls galore at Les Ladiez on Thursday nights at the Lookout (p243), power gals at Ladies Night at Orson (p243), and various weekly or monthly events. Check **Go Get Your Girl On** (http://gogetyourgirlon.com) for concerts and parties, or plug into the A-ladies' scene on **Betty's List** (www.bettyslist.com).

To get the latest on the current GLBT conversation, pick up the *San Francisco Bay Times* (www.sfbaytimes.com), which also has good resources for transsexuals, and read the *Bay Area Reporter* (aka BAR; www.ebar.com) for news and listings.

SIGHTS & ACTIVITIES

BAKER BEACH Map pp100–1

Presidio; sunrise-sunset; 28, 29

Down craggy bluffs, past wind-sculpted Monterey pines and cypress trees, beckons a mile-long stretch of sandy beach, with fishing spots galore and full-frontal nudity at the north end (gay men and straight girls). The views of the Golden Gate are spectacular, but huge crowds come weekends. The all-gay local beach is further north, at Marshall's Beach (aka Marcia's Beach), immediately before the bridge. Ask around for directions, but *never* climb the dangerous rugged cliffs north from Baker to reach it. Take pathways, and find the stairs.

GLBT HISTORICAL SOCIETY

Map pp110–11

415-777-5455; www.glbthistory.org; Suite 300, 657 Mission St; suggested donation $4; 1-5pm Tue-Sat; 6, 7, 14, 21, 31, 71, F, J, K, L, M, N; & Montgomery St

The little nonprofit that could, the GLBT HS mounts historical exhibits that rotate every nine months – a must for any gay historian. Recent well-curated exhibitions have included iconic objects such as the sewing machine that stitched the first rainbow flag. Note: it's tricky to find; take the elevator in back to the 3rd floor.

SHOPPING

A DIFFERENT LIGHT BOOKSTORE

Map p123

415-431-0891; www.adlbooks.com; 489 Castro St; 10am-11pm; 24, 33, F, Castro St

This long-standing literary venue is struggling to reinvent itself, and has caved to commercial pressure (eg lube by the register), but it still carries some good titles and merits a look, especially for pictorials. Check the bulletin board in back for schedules of occasional readings. Serious book shoppers: also check nearby **Books Inc** (415-864-6777; www.booksinc.net; 2275 Market St; 10am-10pm).

HUMAN RIGHTS CAMPAIGN ACTION CENTER & STORE Map p123

☎ 415-431-2200; www.hrc.org; 600 Castro St; 🕑 10am-7pm; 🚌 24, 33, F, K, L, M, Castro St
The Human Rights Campaign (HRC) keeps the Civil Rights movement charging gaily forward, lobbying for GLBT causes and candidates and protecting hard-won freedoms. Stop by to see what's next on the agenda, or pick up signature condoms and a limited-edition designer HRC tee. Great spot to get the latest on Prop 8.

WORN OUT WEST Map p123

☎ 415-431-6020; 582 Castro St; 🕑 noon-7pm Mon-Fri & Sun, 11am-7pm Sat; 🚌 24, 33, F, Castro St
Left your gear at home? Pick up leathers, original-cut Levi's 501s, cock rings and tanks tops at this old-school-Castro, used-clothing store, and dress like a local. Good fetish wear at great prices. Not much for gals, alas.

DRINKING & NIGHTLIFE

BARS & CLUBS

For the latest, pick up the free rag *Gloss Magazine*, and community newspapers *Bay Area Reporter* and *San Francisco Bay Times*, available at kiosks, bars and A Different Light Bookstore (opposite). Juanita More (www.juanitamore.com) throws fierce parties (especially on Gay Pride), and they're always attended by sexy-hot boys. Cockblock (www.cockblocksf.com), at the Rickshaw Stop (p213), draws a happening gay-boy-and-girl crowd on the second Saturday of the month. Fresh (http://freshsf.com), at Ruby Skye (p209), is the monthly Sunday-night circuit party. There's gay salsa every third Friday at Cafe Cocomo (p214).

Ladies: log on to Craigslist (www.craigslist.org) and click on women-seeking-women to search for monthly parties or post a query. Mango, from 3pm to 9pm on the fourth Saturday of the month at El Rio (p243), is blazing hot. Hit the Lexington Club (p243) and inquire about the roving party Flourish – when dykes dress up. Hipster gals pack Stay Gold on the last Wednesday of the month at the Make-Out Room (p213).

CALL A SPADE A SHOVEL

You know you're a local when you refer to bars by their nicknames.

- Midnight Sun: Midnight Scum
- Badlands: Sadlands
- The Cinch: The Stench
- Powerhouse: Powerblouse
- Hole in the Wall: Hole in the Head
- Lone Star: Go-Home-Alone Star
- Café Flore: Cafe Floor Show
- Daddy's/440: Debby's/220

440 CASTRO Map p123

☎ 415-621-8732; www.the440.com; 440 Castro St; 🕑 noon-2am; 🚌 Castro St
The most happening bar on the street, 440 Castro (aka Daddy's) draws bearded 30-something dudes in tight T-shirts, and an odd mix of Peter Pans for Monday's underwear night.

AUNT CHARLIE'S Map p77

☎ 415-441-2922; www.auntcharlieslounge.com; 133 Turk St; admission $3; 🕑 9am-2am; 🚌 31; 🚌 & Ⓜ Powell St
On one of Downtown's worst blocks, divey-chic Aunt Charlie's brings vintage pulp-fiction covers to life with the Hot Boxxx Girls, the city's best classic drag show, Friday and Saturday nights at 10pm (call for reservations). Thursday is Tubesteak Connection ($5), when bathhouse anthems, vintage porn and early '80s disco draw throngs of art-school gay boys. Other nights, it's the classic old-school dump.

BADLANDS Map p123

☎ 415-626-9320; www.badlands-sf.com; 4121 18th St; 🕑 2pm-2am; 🚌 24, 33, Castro St
The Castro's primary dance bar gets packed with gay college boys, their screaming straight girlfriends and a few chicken hawks. If you're over 30, you'll feel old. Weekends, expect a line, which no self-respecting local would ever wait in.

BLACKBIRD Map p123

☎ 415-503-0630; www.blackbirdbar.com; 2124 Market St; 🕑 3pm-2am Mon-Fri, noon-2am Sat & Sun; 🚌 22, F, J, K, L, M, N, Church St
The latest addition to the Castro lounge-bar scene draws a happening local crowd of guys in tight T-shirts and their gal-pal admirers. The look is sleek and clean, but not overstyled; cocktails are strong; and there's a good selection of wines and craft beers by the glass. Bartenders provide delicious eye candy. Ideal spot to begin a Castro pub crawl.

BLOW BUDDIES

Map pp110–11

☎ 415-777-HEAD; www.blowbuddies.com; 933 Harrison St; admission $12, plus $8 membership fee; Thu-Sun nights, call about Wed-night fetish parties; 27, 47

When it's time to get laid, head to the Disneyland of cock. The original owner was a Disney fetishist and set out to recreate, with exacting detail, Disneyland-like attractions, with mazes and specialty-fetish rooms spread over 6000 sq ft of indoor-outdoor warehouse space. New owners aren't detail-oriented, and rarely put money back into the club (the outdoor camouflage-berm tore away years ago, and the play area under the stairs closed eons ago when the barber's chair broke), but for a sex club it's the best in town. Some nights are positively dreary: count coats in the coat-check through the barred window by the entrance; if fewer than 30, don't go in unless it's early. Note: no cologne, or they won't let you in. Sweat – and spilled poppers – are the preferred scents.

CHAPS II Map pp110–11

☎ 415-255-2427; www.chapsbarsanfrancisco.com; 1225 Folsom St; Mon-Thu 7pm-2am, Fri & Sat 3pm-2am; 12, 19

Chaps II promises what its eponymous 1970s predecessor delivered: leather, kink, gear and cruising. Black walls, vintage-'70s leather-porn posters and red lighting provide sexy visuals, but the place rarely fills. SF needs a hard-cruise bar in these days of online hook-ups, but will men really leave their keyboards? We remain hopeful. Best between 9pm and midnight, Thursday to Saturday, after which everyone goes to Powerhouse.

CHILIDOG DISCO Map p133

☎ 415-863-3516; www.triplecrownsf.com; Triple Crown, 1760 Market St; admission $3; 10pm-2am Tue; F

If anybody's out on a Tuesday night, chances are they're at super-cool Chilidog, a disco-house party for hedonistic, arty gay boys and gals, hosted by oh-so-sexy DJ Stanley.

CINCH Map p92

☎ 415-776-4162; www.thecinch.com; 1723 Polk St; 9am-2am Mon-Fri, 6am-2am Sat & Sun; 19, 47, 49

The last of the old-guard Polk St bars is best on Friday nights, when Anna Conda hosts Charlie Horse, the every-mess-was-there drag party. Pool, pinball and free popcorn lure locals from surrounding 'hoods other nights. Smokers patio.

DECO LOUNGE Map p77

☎ 415-346-2025; www.decosf.com; 510 Larkin St; 10am-2am Sun-Thu, to 4am Fri & Sat; 5, 19, 31

There's usually a party at this indecorous dive club, where the all-male clientele rocks into the wee hours. Theme nights range from disco-queen to shirtless-bear extravaganzas, and drink specials embolden patrons to enter occasional wet-jockstrap contests. Sports queens watch Giants games off hours.

THE WEEKNIGHT SCENE

Going out on weeknights and Sunday nights can be boom or bust – but you have to know where to start. Many spots are dead midweek. Ask around for the latest, and read posters at the gym and on lampposts in the Castro.

- Sunday: Beer Bust at the Eagle (opposite), the definitive SF bar party, especially in summer. Afterwards, Truck (p245) for burgers and socializing, Lone Star (opposite) for bears or Powerhouse (p245) for hook-ups. For dancing, Honey Soundsystem (opposite) or Sundance Saloon (p247).
- Monday: Underwear Night at 440 Castro (p241) is hit or miss – it can be very strange. Kids dance at Badlands (p241).
- Tuesday: Chilidog (above) for DJ beats; Pink Slip (confirm it's still happening) at the Stud (p245); and C U Next Tuesday at Qbar (p245). Get the password for Truck (guys only; p245).
- Wednesday: Booty Call at Qbar (p245) for 20-somethings. Powerhouse (p245) goes either way; check the online calendar. At 440 Castro (p241) there's Frat House for college dudes in tight T-shirts. Blow Buddies (above) hosts hit-or-miss fetish parties.
- Thursday: most bars are busy. Troll Folsom St, from Cat Club (p208) to Hole in the Wall (opposite). The Eagle (opposite) hosts bands on Thursdays for a mixed crowd. At 440 Castro (p241) its CDXL – go-go boys and hot messes. Women first hit Ladies Night (opposite) at Orson, then Les Ladiez at the Lookout (opposite).

EAGLE TAVERN

Map pp110–11

☎ 415-626-0880; www.sfeagle.com; 398 12th St; ⏲ noon-2am; 🚌 9, 12, 47

The place on Sunday afternoons, SF's long-standing boots-and-cigar bar serves all-you-can-drink beer ($10) from 3pm to 6pm. Wear leather – or act like a whore – and blend right in. The enormous open-air back patio gets packed with a mishmash of biker-daddies, hipsters, art boys, shirtless drunks, bears, gay softball teams and the occasional politician working the pack (SF's version of kissing babies); conspicuously absent is the khakis crowd. Leave your straight girlfriends at home. The Tamale Lady shows up around 5pm; say yes when she asks if you want hot sauce. Other nights are (much) quieter, except the mixed-straight-gay Thursday Night Live (p214).

EL RIO Map pp116–17

☎ 415-282-3325; www.elriosf.com; 3158 Mission St; admission $3-8; ⏲ 5pm-2am Mon-Thu, 3pm-2am Fri-Sun; 🚌 14, 26; 🚌 & Ⓑ 24th St Mission

El Rio likes its music and patrons eclectic and mixed, funky and pansexual. The club rightly boasts about the back garden, its 'Totally Fabulous Happy Hour' from 4pm to 9pm Tuesday to Friday, and free oysters on the half shell on Fridays at 5:30pm. Sunday afternoons are busiest (though mostly straight), when salsa bands rock (lessons at 3pm) and everyone shimmies and shakes. Drawback: distance from other bars if it's dead.

GANGWAY Map p77

☎ 415-776-6828; 841 Larkin St; ⏲ 8am-2am; 🚌 19, 38

The Tenderloin's longest-running gay dive, the Gangway draws toothless drunks and merry hipsters. We love the gritty authenticity of the place and the chance to meet old-guard drag performers out of face.

HOLE IN THE WALL

Map pp110–11

☎ 415-431-4695; www.holeinthewallsaloon.com; 1369 Folsom St; ⏲ noon-2am; 🚌 19, 27

When the Hole moved from 8th St in 2008, it lost its legendary filthiness because it would otherwise have lost its license. It still has the best sex-poster-art in SF (but now it's behind Plexiglass) and remains ground zero for weirdos (in a good-ish way).

HONEY SOUNDSYSTEM

Map pp110–11

☎ 415-252-5018; www.honeysoundsystem.com; Paradise Loft, 1501 Folsom St; ⏲ 9pm-2am Sun; 🚌 19, 27

If you dance, hunt down Honey Soundsystem's Sunday-night party, when DJs spin everything from German techno to obscure disco B-sides, celebrating gay culture as if AIDS and Reagan never happened. Confirm location on website.

LADIES NIGHT

Map pp110–11

☎ 415-777-1508; http://bettyslist.com; Orson Restaurant, 508 4th St; ⏲ 5:30pm-10-ish; 🚌 30, 45

A-list ladies who eschew Doc Martins for Jil Sander gather for Thursday cocktails and networking at Orson, the restaurant helmed by local power-dyke Liz Faulkner. To meet lesbian society, there's no faster track. Confirm location online. Join its Facebook group for the latest.

LEXINGTON CLUB

Map pp116–17

☎ 415-863-2052; 3464 19th St; ⏲ 3pm-2am; 🚌 14, 26, 33, 49

To get past the cliquishness at SF's long-standing grrrrl bar, don't just think you can get a crew cut, don a black T-shirt, shout 'Power to the Pussy!' and buy everyone $4 beers. Be strategic: compliment someone on her skirt (she made it herself) or tattoo (she designed it herself) and casually mention you're undefeated at pinball, pool or thumb-wrestling. When she wins (because she's no stranger to the Lex) pout just a little, and maybe she'll buy you a beer.

LONE STAR Map pp110–11

☎ 415-863-9999; www.lonestarsaloon.com; 1354 Harrison St; ⏲ noon-2am Mon-Fri, 9am-2am Sat & Sun; 🚌 19, 27

Ground zero for bears who go 'Woof!' like dogs, the Lone Star is dedicated to big guys with fur. Don't miss the back patio. Busiest Thursday through Sunday.

LOOKOUT Map p123

☎ 415-431-0306; www.lookoutsf.com; 3600 16th St; ⏲ 3:30pm-2am Mon-Fri, 12:30pm-2am Sat & Sun; 🚌 F, Castro St

To hook up with locals, attend one of Lookout's drag or sports-team fundraisers.

Hot rugby players come Sunday afternoons for Jock; happening dykes come Thursday nights for Les Ladiez ($2).

MARTUNI'S Map p133

☎ 415-241-0205; www.martunis.citysearch.com; 4 Valencia St; 2pm-2am; F

Slip behind the velvet curtains to see who's tickling the ivories at the city's last piano bar, where gay and straight, graying regulars seem to have committed the Great American Songbook to memory.

MIDNIGHT SUN

Map p123

☎ 415-861-4186; 4067 18th St; 2pm-2am Mon-Fri, 1pm-2am Sat & Sun; 33, F, Castro St

A favorite of khaki-clad suburbanites who aren't entirely comfortable socializing unless there's something specific to divert attention, Midnight Sun is a video bar. The *Dynasty* era marked its heyday, but crowds still come for *American Idol*, and it remains a reliable place to…well, watch TV. Neighborhood gay boys sometimes anagram the velcro letter-board sign outside the club (management hates this).

MIX

Map p123

☎ 415-431-8616; www.sfmixbar.com; 4086 18th St; 6am-2am; 33, F, Castro St

The last Castro bar to open at 6am, the Mix is a must on a pub crawl. We like the low-ceilinged pool and bar area, but prefer the open-air back smokers' patio (no joints or they'll throw you out). Expect gal-next-door baby dykes, 20-something gay boys, trannie pals (more FTM than MTF) and the odd stumbling drag-queen mess. Wednesday is chick night, Monday free pool.

MOBY DICK

Map p123

☎ 415-861-1199; www.mobydicksf.com; 4049 18th St; 2pm-2am Mon-Fri, noon-2am Sat & Sun; 33, F, Castro St

The name overpromises, but not for the giant fish tank behind the bar, which provides a focal point for shy boys who would otherwise look at their shoes. A&F types get their weekend drink on here, then keep moving. Weekdays it's a mellow spot for pool, pinball and meeting neighborhood 20-to-40-somethings.

DRAG ROYALTY

The SF drag scene is at the leading edge of contemporary performance art – for a taste of local talent, search YouTube for 'Silencefiction Lipstique.' To find what's happening now, look for these names on posters, flyers and gutters outside clubs.

Anna Conda (on Facebook) Think coked-up sorority girl; see Cinch, p242.

Downie ('Tiara Sensation' on Facebook) High-concept and stupid at once.

Fauxnique (www.fauxnique.net) Ballerina for Bauhaus, in toe shoes.

Gina LaDivina (www.thehotboxxxgirls.com) The $65,000 Silicone Wonder.

Glamamore ('David-Glamamore' on Facebook) Legendary – the Queen.

Heklina (heklina.org) SF's best emcee, of Trannyshack fame.

Juanita More (juanitamore.com) Kick-ass parties; Latina glam.

Kiddie (www.myspace.com/badkiddie) Looks like she'll cut you but won't.

Metal Patricia (www.myspace.com/metalpatricia) Hot rocker-bitch drag.

Mrs Vera (www.queer-arts.org/johnstone/) In a comic-book world alone; the drag queen you want your children to meet.

Peaches Christ (peacheschrist.com) See the boxed text, p220.

Precious Moments (www.partywithprecious.com) Aka pornstar Michael Soldier.

Putanesca (Google her) Siouxsie Sioux meets Shiela E.

Suppositori Spelling (on Facebook) Aka Spaz; see Truck, opposite.

Vickie Marlane (www.thehotboxxxgirls.com) World's oldest living drag queen.

Vinsantos (www.vinsantosmusic.com) Tattooed goth macabre snob.

PILSNER INN Map p123
☎ 415-621-7058; www.pilsnerinn.com; 225 Church St; 10am-2am; F, Church St
A long-standing fave of gay-softball leagues, the Pilsner is the classic neighborhood bar, with a big smokers' patio, pinball and pool. Good meeting point if your group is splitting in two directions, SoMa and Castro.

POWERHOUSE Map pp110–11
☎ 415-552-8689; www.powerhouse-sf.com; 1347 Folsom St; 4pm-2am; 12, 19
Thursdays through Sundays are best at Powerhouse, an almost-rough-trade SoMa bar for leathermen, shirtless gym queens and the occasional porn star. Draft beer is cheap, and specials keep the crowd wasted. Smokers feel each other up on the (too-smoky) back patio, while oddballs lurk in the corners. Don't bring girls.

QBAR Map p123
☎ 415-864-2877; www.qbarsf.com; 456 Castro St; 4pm-2am Mon-Fri, 2pm-2am Sat & Sun; 24, 35, F, Castro St
Baby 20-somethings pack shoulder-to-shoulder to shout over ear-splitting pop and dance on a tiny dance floor. Occasional go-go boys add spice; smokers pack the front room. Wednesday's Booty Call is a staple. 'Too many girls!' declare old-timers, who stay far away.

STUD Map pp110–11
☎ 415-252-7883; www.studsf.com; 399 9th St; admission $5-8; 5pm-3am; 12, 19, 47
The Stud has rocked the gay scene for over 40 years, but it's hit-and-miss and as of this writing had few weekly parties worth writing about, except Monday-midnight's weird drag show Tiara Sensation, and Tuesday's Pink Slip, a gay-kids' dance party. Check the website.

TRUCK Map pp116–17
☎ 415-252-0306; www.trucksf.com; 1900 Folsom St; 11am-2am Mon-Fri, 4pm-2am Sat, 2pm-2am Sun; 12, 14, 47
Truck is relentlessly clique-ish, with local artists, out-of-face drag queens, off-duty DJs and underground celebs, but draws a happy crowd and serves burgers and fries. Suppositori Spelling hosts Sunday's always-odd drag show. Other nights vary: think neighborhood bar. Dirty boys: get the password for Tuesday's speakeasy (no girls).

TWIN PEAKS TAVERN
Map p123
☎ 415-864-9470; www.twinpeakstavern.com; 401 Castro St; noon-2am Mon-Fri, 8am-2am Sat & Sun; 24, 33, F, Castro St
Don't call it the glass coffin. Show some respect: Twin Peaks was the first gay bar in the world with windows opening to the street. The jovial crowd skews (way) over 40, but they're not chicken hawks (or they wouldn't hang here), and they love it when happy kids show up and join the party. Ideal for a tête-à-tête after a film at the Castro, or for cards, Yahtzee or backgammon (BYO). Expect impromptu sing-alongs if Judy Garland starts playing. Learn, child, learn…

WILD SIDE WEST Map pp116–17
☎ 415-647-3099; 424 Cortland Ave; 1pm-2am Mon-Sat, to midnight Sun; 14, 24, 67
Grrrlfriends make out in the overgrown garden, while others pony up to the noisy saloon bar. The paint's peeling, but to fix it would ruin the place. Dig the pin-up-girl art, then flirt with the crafty gals at the sewing-machine table by the fireplace. Best on weekends.

CAFES

CAFÉ FLORE Map p123
☎ 415-621-8579; www.cafeflore.com; 2298 Market St; 7am-midnight Sun-Thu, to 2am Fri & Sat; 24, 33, F, Castro St
You haven't done the Castro till you've lollygagged on the sun-drenched patio at the Flore – everyone winds up here sooner or later. Weekdays present the best chance to meet neighborhood regulars, who colonize the tables outside. Weekends get packed. Great happy-hour drink specials, like two-for-one-margarita Tuesdays. Pretty-good food, too. Wi-fi is available on weekdays only.

JUMPIN' JAVA Map p123
☎ 415-431-5282; 139 Noe St; 7am-8pm; N
Alterna-dorks hunch over MacBooks and trade passing glances at the Castro's quietest café, nicknamed 'Laptop Library.' Nobody talks. Bring a computer or be bored. Packed weekends. Fun fact: this chapter was penned here.

THE ARTS

BRAVA THEATER Map pp116–17

☎ 415-641-7657; www.brava.org; 2781 24th St; 🚌 9, 27, 33, 48

Brava's been producing women-run theater for 20 years, and it's the nation's only company whose sole purpose is to produce original works by women of color and lesbians. Nodding to the neighborhood's Mexican heritage, Brava posts hand-painted billboards like the kind you'd see in old Mexico – see some in the lobby.

FEMINA POTENS Map p123

☎ 415-864-1558; www.feminapotens.org; 2199 Market St; 🕐 noon-6pm Thu-Sun; 🚌 F, Castro St

SF's showcase for women's talents is a tiny storefront gallery by day, performance and workshop venue at night. Check the web for current offerings, ranging from the Crafty Bitches, a knitting-and-crafts night, to seminars on BDSM for queers and trans.

NEW CONSERVATORY THEATER Map p77

☎ 415-861-8972; www.nctcsf.org; 25 Van Ness Ave; tickets $10-30; 🚌 47, 49, Van Ness

This respected gay company draws playwrights like Terrance McNally and continually shows new works. There's usually a boy partially naked on stage, earning it the nickname 'Nude Conservatory Theatre,' but it's never a strip show. Shows range from camp to dead serious. Worth investigating.

SF LESBIAN GAY BISEXUAL TRANSGENDER COMMUNITY CENTER Map p133

☎ 415-865-5555; www.sfcenter.org; 1800 Market St; 🚌 6, 7, 71; ♿

When the center opened up, the entire community grew excited with the possibility of finally having a gathering place, but because of poor endowment, too-high rental rates and weak programming, it hasn't panned out. Still, it's worth a look to see if something's on.

THEATRE RHINOCEROS Map pp116–17

☎ 415-861-5079; www.therhino.org; 2926 16th St; tickets $10-30; Ⓜ 16th St Mission

By turns edgy, bawdy, serious and experimental, the Rhino mounts noteworthy shows on a shoestring. Despite being a small, no-frills black-box studio, it's the nation's longest-running GLBT company. Check the calendar.

GYMS

GOLD'S GYM Map p123

☎ 415-626-4488; www.goldsgym.com; 2301 Market St; admission $15; 🕐 5am-midnight Mon-Thu, 5am-11pm Fri, 7am-9pm Sat, 7am-8pm Sun; 🚌 24, 33, F, K, L, M, Castro St

The definitive gay gym draws a neighborhood crowd of chatty muscle-Marys and quiet straight gals who appreciate being left alone. Full selection of equipment; packed after work. Notorious steam room. Testosterone-y daddies prefer the SoMa location (Map pp110–11; ☎ 415-552-4653; 1001 Brannan St; 🚌 10, 19), a vast warehouse space with twice the equipment, a sauna and a steam room. Both have classes – Body Pump to yoga – but the Castro has a proper dance studio instead of a gymnasium.

FESTIVALS & EVENTS

SAN FRANCISCO INTERNATIONAL LESBIAN & GAY FILM FESTIVAL

☎ 415-703-8650; www.frameline.org; Castro Theatre, Roxie Cinema & other local movie theaters; 🕐 mid-Jun to end of Jun

GLBT-themed cinema is showcased at this two-week extravaganza with intensive scheduling (250 to 300 films) that reveals the best of queer filmmaking. Films by John Waters and Gus Van Sant, and crossover programs like the British *Queer as Folk* TV series premiered here. A word to the wise: if you can afford a festival pass, get one. Passholders avoid the interminable queues.

DYKE MARCH

☎ 415-241-8882; www.dykemarch.org; Dolores Park through the Mission to the Castro; 🕐 last Sat in Jun

The annual Dyke March, the Saturday-night event preceding Pride, got its start by a single rallying call. At the 1993 LGBT March, a group called the Lesbian Avengers set forth to Washington, protesting what they saw as the control of Gay Pride by white gay men and corporate sponsors. Armed with one bullhorn and word-of-mouth, the Avengers announced the first-ever Dyke March and, to their shock, thousands swarmed the White House. The same gals organized San Francisco's first Dyke March the following year. The event draws 50,000 lesbian, bi and transgender women. (Men are welcome as supporters but not necessarily as marchers.)

The march kicks off at 7:45pm, led by the Women's Motorcycle Contingent (Dykes on Bikes). Wrapping up on Castro, it joins Pink Saturday – the Castro's best annual street party. Castro and upper Market Sts close to traffic, punk bands mouth off, and dancing goes till midnight.

LESBIAN, GAY, BISEXUAL & TRANSGENDER PRIDE PARADE

☎ 415-864-3733; www.sfpride.org; Downtown from Embarcadero, up Market St; ⌚ last Sun in Jun

Hands down, the year's biggest party. Pirates in pink and giant-winged fairies toss candy and condoms from overflowing fanny packs, while pit bulls in rainbow-hued tutus trot alongside. Stilt-walkers in glitter, trannies on unicycles, queens on roller skates – anything goes. Crowds pour from BART and Muni, climbing streetlight posts for better views, and float-dancers strut atop moving stages. Growing almost every year since 1971, Pride draws about a million participants and sidewalk supporters, running the gamut from sweater queens to granola dykes, bondage masters to GLBT seniors. Afterwards there's an all-afternoon festival at Civic Center. Hotels fill; book early. The night before the parade, don't miss Pink Saturday on Castro St (6pm to midnight). Ongoing controversy reigns about Pride's aggressive corporate presence. To avoid it, head to Faerie Camp, the only advertising-free zone of the party, where Radical Faeires gather naked on blankets and smoke out.

FOLSOM STREET FAIR

☎ 415-861-3247; www.folsomstreetfair.com; SoMa (Folsom St & 7th to 11th Sts); ⌚ last Sun in Sep

Bondage and fetish enthusiasts emerge from dungeons across the world for San Francisco's wildest street party. Expect leather chaps, restraints and latex skirts, and blown-away tourists with videocams. This is the third-largest event in the entire state, trailing only the Tournament of Roses in So Cal and San Francisco's Pride Parade. It's one of the kinkiest, most-insane parties anywhere, with free spankings (donations to charities accepted) and fully equipped dungeons inside tents. For tamer paraders and observers, there's a poster-art competition, national bands, cheap beer and eye-candy galore. But be warned: you'll see some people naked who you'll wish you hadn't.

CASTRO STREET FAIR

☎ 415-841-1824; www.castrostreetfair.org; the Castro (Castro St to Sanchez St, 17th to 19th Sts along Castro); ⌚ first Sun in Oct

The yin to the Folsom Street Fair's yang happens the following weekend, when white sweaters replace black leathers. The fair was founded by gay political icon and city supervisor Harvey Milk in 1974 to put the nascent community on the map. Now an estimated 150,000 people come to the all-day event, with bands, emcees and speakers, and endless cruising and shopping at booths set up in the streets. The coolest place to hang out: Sugar Valley, on 18th St just east of Castro St. Look for Mrs Vera, local legend (Google 'Mrs Vera's Daybook').

DANCE-ALONG NUTCRACKER

☎ 415-255-1355; www.sflgfb.org/show.html; Yerba Buena Center for the Arts; ⌚ first weekend in Dec

The Lesbian/Gay Freedom Band does the Nutcracker Suite, with tutu and fairy-wand rentals, a costumed Sousa band and an audience of Sugar Plum wannabes, at Yerba Buena Center for the Arts (p219) on the first weekend in December. Look for ever-popular 'lipstick thespian' Trauma Flintstone.

WORTH THE TRIP

Pull on your cowboy boots at Sundance Saloon (Map pp116–17; ☎ 415-820-1403; http://sundancesaloon.org; 550 Barneveld Ave; ⌚ 6:30-10:30pm with lessons 7-8pm Thu, 5-10:30pm with lessons 5:30-7:15pm Sun; admission $5; 🚌 24) and two-step Texas-style to country music with moustached daddies and their cowpoke admirers. Show up early for lessons. The happy, loyal crowd thins by 10pm: daddies need their rest. It's in the middle of nowhere, but the bus stops a few blocks away and runs till midnight, long after the party ends.

SLEEPING

All SF hotels welcome gays and lesbians, but all-gay lodgings are few. Rates skyrocket during popular GLBT events. Also consider Beck's Motor Lodge (p261) and Belvedere House (p260).

PARKER GUEST HOUSE

Map p123 $$

☎ 415-621-3222, 888-520-7275; www.parkerguesthouse.com; 520 Church St; r $139-229; J;

The Castro's most stately digs occupy two side-by-side hundred-year-old Edwardian mansions. Details are elegant and formal, but never froufrou. Rooms feel more like a swanky hotel than a B&B, with super-comfortable beds and down comforters. Bathroom fixtures gleam. The garden is ideal for a lovers' tryst, as is the steam room.

INN ON CASTRO Map p123 $$

☎ 415-861-0321; www.innoncastro.com; 321 Castro St; ste $155-185, r $135-165, without bathroom $115-125, breakfast incl; 24, F;

A portal to the Castro's disco heyday, this Edwardian townhouse is decked out with top-end '70s-mod furnishings. Rooms are retro-cool and spotlessly kept. Our fave: the patio suite with its flower-festooned deck. Exceptional breakfasts – the owner is a chef.

WILLOWS Map p123 $$

☎ 415-431-4770; www.willowssf.com; 710 14th St; r $110-145; 22, F, Church St;

Willows has the homey comforts of a B&B, without any fuss. None of the 12 rooms has a private bathroom, though all have sinks. Shared kitchenette. Rooms on Church St are noisy: book one in the back. The better bathroom is upstairs.

24 HENRY Map p123 $$

☎ 415-864-5686, 800-900-5686; www.24henry.com; 24 Henry St; r $149, without bathroom $105-110; F;

A converted Victorian on a quiet side street, 24 Henry's rooms are simply decorated with cast-off antiques and utilitarian furniture. Great value for no-fuss gay travelers. Ask about the nearby, slightly fancier **Village House** (4080 18th St; r $149, without bathroom $106-110;), though it's not as quiet.

SLEEPING

top picks

- **Hotel Bohème** (p257)
- **Hotel Vitale** (p259)
- **Hotel Triton** (p253)
- **Orchard Garden Hotel** (p253)
- **Hotel des Arts** (p255)

SLEEPING

San Francisco has many convention hotels, several good four-stars with predictable comforts, and three palatial five-stars with top-flight luxuries. But it's the unexpected gems that stand out. This is the birthplace of the boutique hotel, and you'll find elegant Victorians on neighborhood side streets, artsy hotels with intimate bars, and small inns that smell of freshly baked cookies. The broade*st hotel selection is Downtown, near Union Square, conveniently near all public transportation and within walking distance of many major sights, but the area is densely urban and dedicated to chain-store shopping, theaters and restaurants. At nighttime it's dead. Union Square also abuts the Tenderloin on its southwest side, a 'hood of drug-addled panhandlers – though it's also home to artists, who lend an up-and-coming vibe to the grit. (The worst area extends roughly three blocks in all directions from Eddy and Jones Sts.) Staying in other districts provides a glimpse of how the locals live. We particularly like the Cali-chic low-rise Marina, the gay-ghetto Castro and the Latino-meets-hipster Mission.

Tipping housekeepers in US hotels is standard practice; leave a couple of dollars on your pillow each morning, and be guaranteed excellent housekeeping service.

All lodging in San Francisco is by definition gay-friendly, but also check our chapter devoted to GLBT San Francisco (p248).

If you're planning on staying for a few months, subletting an apartment or room is a good way to go. Scan the classified ads on **Craigslist** (www.craigslist.org).

RESERVATIONS

Hotels routinely overbook, especially when there's a convention in town. 'City-wide sellouts' happen several times a year. If you haven't chosen dates for your trip, check the SF Convention & Visitors Bureau's convention calendar (www.sfcvb.org/convention/calendar.asp), which shows the expected bed count each convention requires. The city has a total of 33,000 rooms; if the calendar says a convention (such as the annual Oracle meeting) will require over 10,000 beds, choose other dates or expect to pay a premium.

Always reconfirm your reservation the day of arrival, and ask if the hotel is oversold. If it is, make clear that you don't want to be 'walked.' ('Walking a guest' means that when the hotel is oversold, management books you into another hotel and pays your first-night's stay at the other hotel, which may be as far away as the airport or Oakland.) If you're planning to arrive after 4pm, guarantee with a credit card or your reservation may automatically cancel. Ask about the hotel's cancellation policy, and if you do cancel, get the cancellation code, which ensures that the agent has properly entered your cancellation into the reservations system. Finally, get the names of the people you speak with on the telephone; not only will this bolster your

RESERVATION SERVICES & DISCOUNTS

Hotel-reservation services provide a convenient way to shop for a hotel room, simplifying what would otherwise require multiple phone calls. Some also serve as clearinghouses for hotel bookings during low-occupancy periods, when they can offer lower rates than the hotel would quote. If you're flexible, you can save big bucks on rooms that would otherwise blow your budget. Services are free to customers, but prepayment is sometimes required and cancellation fees may apply.

Hostels.com (www.hostels.com) General information about hostels in San Francisco and elsewhere, plus a link to online reservations.

Priceline (www.priceline.com) A clearinghouse for upscale lodging; you can often find a room for as little as $75 a night in highly rated Union Square hotels. You don't get to choose the hotel, though.

Topaz Hotel Services (☎ 510-628-4450, 800-677-1570; www.hotelres.com) A locally based booking agent that can get you great prices in the city or elsewhere in the Bay Area and Wine Country.

www.bbsf.com Find Bay Area B&Bs and great deals.

PRICE GUIDE

$$$ over $200 a night
$$ $100-200 a night
$ under $100 a night

Reviews list the average high-season rates for a standard room.

argument if you get conflicting information on arrival, it's also nice to thank the people who helped you on the phone. Kindness often scores upgrades, especially on sold-out nights.

If you can't find a room, the Visitors Information Center (☎ 800-637-5196, 415-391-2000; www.onlyinsanfrancisco.com) helps with reservations.

ROOM RATES

Rates in SF fluctuate wildly. To get the best prices at chains, call the hotel directly and speak with in-house reservations, rather than the central reservations, for the most up-to-date information about room inventories and specials. Some hotels have internet specials not available by telephone. When booking online, know that 'best rate' does not necessarily mean the lowest-available rate. When in doubt call the hotel directly.

Although bright, friendly hostels and budget hotels have opened up in Downtown, the Mission and the Marina, rooms are never truly cheap in SF: expect to pay at least $65 at a budget hotel or for a private hostel room, and over $100 at any midrange hotel. Note the hefty 15% room tax on top of the quoted rates (hostels are exempt), and that local telephone calls may cost $1 and wi-fi an extra $10. Ask about parking: it's rarely included (when it is, we've noted it with a Ⓟ). Prices run higher June to August, and drop between September and May. If you're staying awhile, ask about weekly rates. The rates we quote are for high season (summer); you can sometimes do better, unless there's a convention in town (see Reservations, opposite). On weekends, business hotels' rates drop and tourist hotels' go up.

EMBARCADERO & THE PIERS

The proximity to the waterfront is fun for kids, but you'll be surrounded exclusively by tourists.

ARGONAUT HOTEL

Map p63 Hotel $$$

☎ 415-563-0800, 866-415-0704; www.argonauthotel.com; 495 Jefferson St; r $205-325; F;

The top hotel at Fisherman's Wharf was built as a cannery in 1908, and has century-old wooden beams and exposed brick walls. Rooms sport an over-the-top nautical theme, with porthole-shaped mirrors and plush deep-blue carpets. Though they've amenities of an upper-end hotel – ultra-comfy beds, stereo CD players – some rooms are tiny and get limited sunlight. Pay extra and you'll get light and a mesmerizing bay view. Kids love the playful aesthetic and meet other kids in the big lobby.

TUSCAN INN

Map p63 Hotel $$

☎ 415-561-1100, 800-648-4626; www.tuscaninn.com; 425 North Point St; r $169-229; 47;

Just because you want to stay at touristy Fisherman's Wharf, it doesn't mean you have to settle for a plain-Jane chain, such as the nearby Marriott or Hilton. The Tuscan Inn – managed by fashion-forward Kimpton Hotels – is just as comfortable, but has way more character, with spacious rooms done in bold colors and mixed patterns. Who says stripes and checks don't match? Kids love the in-room Nintendo; parents love the afternoon wine hour.

WHARF INN

Map p63 Motel $$

☎ 415-673-7411, 800-548-9918; www.wharfinn.com; 2601 Mason St; r $139-189; F; Ⓟ

This standard-issue, two-story motor lodge has clean, simple rooms, ideal for kids who make a mess. Rates fluctuate wildly with the tourist tide. Free parking.

DOWNTOWN

MANDARIN ORIENTAL

Map pp70–1 Hotel $$$

☎ 415-276-9888, 800-622-0404; www.mandarinoriental.com; 222 Sansome St; r $295-375, ste from $875; 1; & Montgomery St; California;

Occupying the top 11 floors of the third-tallest building in SF, the Mandarin has sweeping, unobstructed views from every room. There's nothing risky about the classical decor, but we love the luxurious beds and bold Asian-accented color schemes – gold with cinnamon-red – and oh, those vistas. If you can swing it, book a 'Mandarin King' room (from $500), which has an oversized bathtub surrounded by floor-to-ceiling windows with views of either the Golden Gate or Bay Bridge. Alas, there's no spa or pool (hence the four-star designation). But the service, particularly at the concierge desk, equals or betters the service you'll receive at any of the city's three five-star hotels.

PALACE HOTEL

Map pp70–1 Historic Hotel $$$

☎ 415-512-1111, 800-325-3535; www.sfpalace.com; 2 New Montgomery St; r $199-329; & Montgomery St;

The 1906 landmark Palace stands as a monument to turn-of-the-20th-century grandeur, aglow with century-old Austrian crystal chandeliers. The cushy (if staid) accommodations cater to expense-account travelers, but prices drop on weekends. Even if you're not staying here, see the opulent Garden Court, where you can sip tea beneath a translucent glass ceiling in one of Northern California's most beautiful rooms. There's also an on-site spa; kids love the big indoor pool.

HOTEL MONACO

Map pp70–1 Boutique Hotel $$$

☎ 415-292-0100, 866-622-5284; www.monaco-sf.com; 501 Geary St; r $199-269; 38;

The Monaco maintains its playful spirit, though the vintage-1990s rooms are starting to look dated. Still, we love the opulent lobby, the guestrooms' bold colors and fabrics, and the goldfish available on request to keep you company in your room. Front-desk reception could be warmer, but evening wine hour and free wi-fi compensate for occasionally lackluster service. Don't miss the lobby's walk-in fireplace, a cool place to sit with a book.

HOTEL PALOMAR

Map pp70–1 Boutique Hotel $$$

☎ 415-348-1111, 866-373-4941; www.hotelpalomar-sf.com; 12 4th St; r $199-299; & Powell St;

The chic and stylin' Hotel Palomar is decked out with crocodile-print carpets, stripy persimmon-red chairs, chocolate-brown wood and cheetah-print robes in the closet. Hugh Hefner would definitely approve. Beds are sumptuous, with feather-light down comforters and Frette linens, and there's plenty of floor space to stretch out for in-room yoga (ask at the front desk for a mat and yoga DVD). Though the hotel sits smack in Downtown, rooms have soundproof windows so you can sleep late. Don't miss drinks at the swank on-site Fifth Floor restaurant.

> **BOOK ACCOMMODATIONS ONLINE**
>
> For more accommodation reviews and recommendations by Lonely Planet authors, check out the online booking service at www.lonelyplanet.com. You'll find the true, insider lowdown on the best places to stay. Reviews are thorough and independent. Best of all, you can book online.

SIR FRANCIS DRAKE HOTEL

Map pp70–1 Historic Hotel $$$

☎ 415-392-7755, 800-795-7129; www.sirfrancisdrake.com; 450 Powell St; r $199-279; & Powell St; Powell-Mason, Powell-Hyde;

The city's most famous doormen, clad like clownish Beefeaters, stand sentinel at this vintage-1920s classic. Rooms have less flair and their intentionally mismatched colors feel forced, but 16th-to-20th-floor rooms have expansive city views. All have great beds. Ask about the secret room, between elevator platforms, where during Prohibition the hotel operated a speakeasy. Pop into the top-floor touristy-swank Starlight Room (p215) for cocktails.

WESTIN ST FRANCIS HOTEL

Map pp70–1 HIstoric Hotel $$$

☎ 415-397-7000, 800-228-3000; www.westin.com; 335 Powell St; r $209-369; & Powell St; Powell-Mason & Powell-Hyde;

This is one of SF's most storied hotels – Gerald Ford was shot right outside. Tower rooms have stellar views, but feel generic. We prefer the original building's old-fashioned charm, with its high ceilings and crown moldings. Though Westin beds set the industry standard for comfort, service is decidedly business-class, not first. Don't miss the glass elevators, even if you're not staying here.

HOTEL ADAGIO

Map pp70–1 Boutique Hotel $$

☎ 415-775-5000, 800-228-8830; www.thehotel adagio.com; 550 Geary St; r $149-229; 🚌 38; wi-fi

Huge rooms and a super-snappy aesthetic set the Adagio apart. The hotel's designers placed a premium on style, blending chocolate-brown and off-white leather furnishings with bright-orange splashes. Beds are sumptuous, with Egyptian-cotton sheets and feather pillows, but bathrooms are disappointing. Still, it's a hot address for a reasonable-ish price. Great bar downstairs.

ORCHARD GARDEN HOTEL

Map pp70–1 Eco Hotel $$

☎ 415-399-9807, 888-717-2881; www.theorchard gardenhotel.com; 466 Bush St; r $179-249; 🚌 2, 3, 4, 30, 45; wi-fi

San Francisco's first all-green-practices hotel opened in 2006, and uses sustainably grown wood, chemical-free cleaning products and recycled fabrics in its soothingly quiet rooms. Don't think you'll be trading comfort for conscience: rooms have unexpectedly luxe touches like flat-screen TVs, iPod docking stations, high-end down pillows and Egyptian-cotton sheets. The rooftop terrace is open to the public – an ideal spot for a Downtown tryst.

WHITE SWAN INN

Map pp70–1 Inn $$

☎ 415-775-1755, 800-999-9570; www.jdvhotels .com; 845 Bush St; r $159-199; 🚌 27; wi-fi

In the tradition of English country inns, the romantic White Swan is styled with cabbage-rose wallpaper, red-plaid flannel bedspreads and polished Colonial-style furniture. Each oversized room has a gas fireplace – a cozy touch on a foggy night. Hipsters may find it stifling, but if you love Tudor style, you'll feel right at home.

top picks

HOTEL VIEWS

- **Hotel Vitale** (p259)
- **Seal Rock Inn** (p262)
- **Sir Francis Drake Hotel** (opposite)
- **Westin St Francis Hotel** (opposite)
- **W Hotel** (p259)

HOTEL FRANK

Map pp70–1 Boutique Hotel $$

☎ 415-986-2000, 800-553-1900; www.hotelfrank sf.com; 386 Geary St; r $169-269; 🚌 38; wi-fi

Redone in 2008, the Frank (formerly the Maxwell) has a snappy, vaguely Austin Powers black-and-white design aesthetic, with big houndstooth checks and faux-aligator headboards. The bathrooms are tight and few have tubs (request one, if it matters), but extras like plasma-screen TVs and the just-off Union Square location compensate.

HOTEL REX

Map pp70–1 Boutique Hotel $$

☎ 415-433-4434, 800-433-4434; www.jdv hospitality.com; 562 Sutter St; r $149-279; 🚌 2, 3, 4; 🚋 Powell St; wi-fi

Strains of French gramophone music fill the intimate lobby and the adjoining dimly lit lounge, intended to conjure New York's Algonquin in the 1920s. The Rex exudes a sexy broodiness: rooms are done in chocolate-brown and brick-red, with antique rotary telephones, hand-painted lampshades, and works by local artists. Great beds, too, with top-notch mattresses, crisp linens and down pillows. One caveat: most rooms have limited natural light – great for late sleepers, bad for sufferers of SAD.

LARKSPUR HOTEL

Map pp70–1 Boutique Hotel $$

☎ 415-421-2865, 800-919-9779; www.larkspur hotelunionsquare.com; 524 Sutter St; r $169-199; 🚌 2, 3, 4; 🚋 Powell St; wi-fi

Built in 1915 and overhauled in 2008, the understatedly fancy Larkspur has a monochromatic, earth-tone color scheme and clean lines. Bathrooms are tiny, but have fab rainfall showerheads. There's nothing risky about the Spartan aesthetic, but it's smartly done and presents a soothing alternative to Union Square's splashier boutique hotels.

HOTEL TRITON

Map pp70–1 Boutique Hotel $$

☎ 415-394-0500, 800-800-1299; www.hotel -tritonsf.com; 342 Grant Ave; r $169-239; 🚌 & Ⓜ Montgomery St; wi-fi

The Triton's lobby thumps with high-energy music, and pops with color like the pages of a comic book. This was one of SF's first boutique hotels, and every room is different. Some are tiny, but all have an aggressively whimsical design, ecofriendly amenities and shag-worthy beds. Bathrooms have massaging shower heads, but limited space. Suites are decorated in honor of celebs like Carlos Santana and Jerry Garcia. Don't miss the tarot-card readings and chair massages during the nightly wine hour.

WARWICK REGIS

Map pp70–1 Boutique Hotel $$

☎ 415-928-7900, 800-203-3232; www.warwicksf.com; 490 Geary St; r $149-249; 38;

If you prefer high heels to hiking boots but can't afford the Ritz, the Warwick Regis presents a (way) less-expensive alternative. Conveying discrete tastefulness, with European antiques and Chinese porcelain, it's an ideal choice for debutantes and royalty on a budget. Beds are remarkably comfortable, and even have triple-sheeting, but you'll have to request feather pillows.

PETITE AUBERGE

Map pp70–1 Inn $$

☎ 415-928-6000, 800-365-3004; www.jdvhospitality.com; 863 Bush St; r $169-219; 27

Petite Auberge feels like a French country inn, with floral-print fabrics, a sunny yellow color scheme, and fireplaces in many rooms. Though cheerfully decorated, several rooms are dark (especially tiny number 22) and face an alley where rubbish collectors rattle cans early in the morning (request a quiet room). Nonetheless, Petite Auberge remains one of Downtown's most charming mid-price B&B inns, and we'd happily stay here ourselves. Breakfast and afternoon wine are served fireside in the cozy salon.

HOTEL DIVA

Map pp70–1 Boutique Hotel $$

☎ 415-885-0200, 800-553-1900; www.hoteldiva.com; 440 Geary St; r $159-229; 38;

Favored by mid-budget fashionistas and traveling club kids, the industrial-chic Diva's stainless-steel and black-granite design aesthetic feels like a dot-com-era holdover, but still conveys a sexy urban look. Beds are comfy, with good sheets and feather pillows, but poly-fill duvets (a small reminder that this is a mid-budget property). Some find it cold, but if you like hard edges and you're here to party, you'll dig it.

HOTEL ABRI

Map pp70–1 Boutique Hotel $$

☎ 415-392-8800, 866-823-4669; www.hotel-abri.com; 127 Ellis St; r $149-229; & Powell St;

Totally renovated in 2008, the Abri has an up-to-the-minute design sensibility. Each snazzy room has a bold black-and-tan motif, a pillow-top bed with feather pillows, double-pane glass, an iPod docking station, flat-screen TV and a big desk with cordless phone. Few bathrooms have tubs, but big rainfall showerheads compensate. Best of all, everything looks fresh and clean, and staff are friendly and accommodating.

ANDREWS HOTEL

Map pp70–1 Hotel $$

☎ 415-563-6877, 800-926-3739; www.andrewshotel.com; 624 Post St; r incl breakfast $99-189; 2, 3, 4; Powell St;

Just two blocks west of Union Square, this 1905 hotel has friendly, personable staff, small but comfortable rooms (the quietest are in back) and a romantic Italian restaurant downstairs, where continental breakfast is served. Though it's nothing fancy, we love the Andrews' hominess – it's like staying at your aunt's house, without having to pet the cat.

HOTEL UNION SQUARE

Map pp70–1 Hotel $$

☎ 415-397-3000, 800-553-1900; www.hotelunionsquare.com; 114 Powell St; r $160-220; & Powell St;

Renovated in 2008, the Hotel Union Square looks sharp, with swank design touches complementing the original brick walls. The main drawbacks are lack of sunlight and small rooms, but designers compensated with cleverly concealed lighting, mirrored walls and plush fabrics. The location is convenient and near major public transport – never mind the panhandlers outside.

HOTEL CALIFORNIA

Map pp70–1 Boutique Hotel $$

☎ 415-441-2700, 800-227-4223; www.thesavoyhotel.com; 580 Geary St; r $149-169; 38;

Alas, no pink champagne on ice, but it does provide frosted tequila shots upon check-in. This bay-windowed vintage-1920s mainstay of the theater district has fresh-looking rooms with cheery yellow walls, hardwood floors, flat-screen TVs, fluffy beds, and double-pane windows that are great for blocking street noise (request a quiet room). Wine and cheese each evening.

GOLDEN GATE HOTEL

Map pp70–1 Hotel $$

☎ 415-392-3702, 800-835-1118; www.goldengatehotel.com; 775 Bush St; r with/without bathroom $165/105; 2, 3, 4; Powell St

Like an old-fashioned pensione, the Golden Gate has kindly owners and simple rooms with mismatched furniture, inside a 1913 Edwardian hotel safely up the hill from the Tenderloin. Rooms are small, clean and comfortable, and most have private bathrooms (some with antique claw-foot tubs). Enormous croissants, homemade cookies and a resident kitty-cat provide TLC after a long day's sightseeing.

METROPOLIS HOTEL

Map pp70–1 Hotel $

☎ 415-775-4600, 800-553-1900; www.hotelmetropolis.com; 25 Mason St; r $89-125; & Powell St;

Never mind the streetwalkers outside, the Metropolis has fresh-looking rooms with standard-issue Ikea-like furniture, cushioned windowsills, and good amenities in the tiny bathrooms. If you're timid, you'll hate the neighborhood, but if you're an intrepid traveler, these are good digs at great prices.

HOTEL DES ARTS

Map pp70–1 Art Hotel $$

☎ 415-956-3232, 800-956-4322; www.sfhoteldesarts.com; 447 Bush St; r $139-199, without bathroom $99-149; & Montgomery St;

Finally a mid-budget hotel for art freaks. Specialty rooms are painted with jaw-dropping murals by underground street artists. The linens are thin and some sinks have separate hot and cold taps (ask when you book), but the art is incredible – it's like sleeping inside a painting. Standard rooms are less exciting but are clean and great value, with a few smart design touches.

DAKOTA HOTEL

Map pp70–1 Hotel $

☎ 415-931-7475; 606 Post St; dm $30-35, r $98-110; 2, 3, 4; & Powell St;

Upgrade from hostel to hotel at this 42-room, vintage-1920s, sunlight-filled property that has clean, basic rooms and claw-foot bathtubs. The carpeting is relatively new, as is the mass-market furniture, and there's a microwave and fridge in every room. Alas, street noise is loud (bring earplugs) and the elevator temperamental. Still, it's great value. There are also unisex dorms with six to eight beds.

STRATFORD HOTEL

Map pp70–1 Hotel $

☎ 415-397-7080, 888-504-6835; www.ctwohotels.com; 242 Powell St; r incl breakfast $89-149; & Powell St;

A great value at Union Square, the eight-story Stratford has clean, simple and smallish rooms. Bathrooms are gleaming and have thirsty towels and rainfall shower-heads, but no tubs. Rooms on Powell St are loud; book a room in back.

ADELAIDE HOSTEL

Map pp70–1 Hostel $

☎ 415-359-1915, 877-359-1915; www.adelaidehostel.com; 5 Isadora Duncan Lane; dm $31, r $55-90, incl breakfast; 38;

Down a mysterious little alley, the 18-room Adelaide sets the standard for San Francisco hostels, with personal service, surprisingly well-done decor, thick carpeting, up-to-date furnishings and sparkling bathrooms with shiny chrome fixtures. The big kitchen even has granite countertops. And the place is blissfully quiet. Dinner costs a mere $5.

USA HOSTELS

Map pp70–1 Hostel $

☎ 415-440-5600, 877-483-2950; www.usahostels.com; 711 Post St; dm $30-34, r $73-83; 2, 3, 4; Powell St;

Built in 1909, this former hotel was recently converted into a spiffy hostel that draws an international crowd. Private rooms sleep three or four, and you can usually save a few bucks by reserving through the website. The basic cafe serves inexpensive cafeteria-style dinners every night.

AMSTERDAM HOSTEL

Map pp70–1 Hostel $

☎ 415-673-3277; www.hostelworld.com; 749 Taylor St; dm/r $30/80; 2, 3, 4; Powell St;

Busy, young and fun, the Amsterdam's dorms have ensuite bathrooms with gleaming new fixtures – there are even hairdryers. All have either four or six beds, so there's no over-crowding. Private rooms include TV, microwave and fridge. Great service.

CIVIC CENTER & THE TENDERLOIN

All of the following are in safe areas, but when walking to Market St, walk east to Powell St, or west to Polk St (or Van Ness Ave), then cut south. The less-safe area extends roughly three blocks in all directions from Eddy and Jones Sts.

HOTEL VERTIGO

Map p77 Boutique Hotel $$

☎ 415-885-6800, 800-553-1900; www.hotelvertigosf.com; 940 Sutter St; r $169-219; 🚌 2, 3, 4, 19, 27; wi-fi

Scenes from Hitchcock's *Vertigo* were shot here, and the refurb of the former York Hotel (the Empire Hotel, in the film) nods to the master with Spirograph-like artwork reminiscent of the opening sequence. The snappy aesthetic mixes burnt-orange, cocoa-brown and bright-white, with low-slung wingchairs beside platform beds with down duvets. It's a 10-minute walk to anywhere noteworthy, but with extras like 32in flat-screen TVs, iPod docking stations and sound-proof windows, you get more bang for your buck than right at Union Square – and bragging rights to a bit of movie history.

PHOENIX HOTEL

Map p77 Motel $$

☎ 415-776-1380, 800-248-9466; www.jdvhospitality.com; 601 Eddy St; r $119-169 incl breakfast; 🚌 5, 19, 31, 38; P wi-fi swimming pool

The city's rocker crash pad draws minor celebs and Dionysian revelers to a vintage-1950s motor lodge with basic rooms dolled up with tropical decor. Check out the cool shrine to actor-director Vincent Gallo, opposite room 43. The sometimes-happening Bambuddha Lounge occupies the former coffee shop. One complaint: noise. Bring earplugs. Parking is free, as is weekday admission to Kabuki Springs & Spa (p237).

STEINHART HOTEL & APARTMENTS

Map p77 Apartment Hotel $

☎ 415-928-3855, 800-533-1900; www.steinharthotel.com; 952 Sutter St; studio per week $455-595, 1-bedroom apt from $875; 🚌 2, 3, 4, 27; wi-fi

If you're staying for a week or longer, the Steinhart is a great address, a glorious early-20th-century building with high ceilings and swank art deco furnishings. Small studios have galley-style kitchenettes; larger studios and one-bedroom apartments have full kitchens. Rates include weekly housekeeping, free wi-fi and local calls, and use of the backyard patio and grill.

HI SAN FRANCISCO CITY CENTER

Map p77 Hostel $

☎ 415-474-5721; www.sfhostels.com; 685 Ellis St; dm $24-29, r $82-100; 🚌 19; wi-fi

A converted seven-story hotel, this better-than-average hostel sports 262 beds and 11 private rooms at the edge of the Tenderloin, with cheap eats nearby. The opera, symphony and Asian Art Museum are a quick walk away.

CHINATOWN

SW HOTEL

Map p82 Hotel $$

☎ 415-362-2999, 888-595-9188; www.swhotel.com; 615 Broadway; r $109-149; 🚌 45; P wi-fi

The legendary flophouse known as the Sam Wong underwent a late '90s overhaul that included earthquake retrofitting and updated decor. Now it's simple and respectable, with bland pastel decor. Parking is first-come, first-served and not always available. The hotel's number-one selling point is location – on the Broadway axis dividing North Beach and Chinatown.

GRANT PLAZA

Map p82 Hotel $

☎ 415-434-3883, 800-472-6899; www.grantplaza.com; 465 Grant Ave; r $69-129; 🚋 California; wi-fi

Many rooms overlook the blinking neon and exotic street scene of Grant Ave, which is the best reason to stay here. Rooms are generally clean (never mind the heavy air-freshener), but blandly decorated with generic furniture. If you want to be in the heart of Chinatown, this is the place.

PACIFIC TRADEWINDS HOSTEL

Map p82 Hostel $

☎ 415-433-7970, 888-734-6783; www.san-francisco-hostel.com; 680 Sacramento St; dm $24-26; 🚌 1; wi-fi

San Francisco's smartest-looking all-dorm hostel has a blue-and-white nautical theme, fully equipped kitchen and spotless glass-brick showers. The nearest BART station is Embarcadero. Alas, you'll have to haul your bags up three flights, but it's worth it. Great service, fun staff.

NORTH BEACH

WASHINGTON SQUARE INN

Map p87 Inn $$$

415-981-4220, 800-388-0220; www.wsisf.com; 1660 Stockton St; r $179-329 incl breakfast; 30, 45;

On leafy, sun-dappled Washington Square, the inn looks decidedly European and caters to the over-40 set, with tasteful rooms and a few choice antiques, including carved-wooden armoires. The least expensive rooms are tiny, but what a stellar address. Wine and cheese each evening, and optional breakfast in bed sweeten the deal.

HOTEL BOHÈME

Map p87 Boutique Hotel $$

415-433-9111; www.hotelboheme.com; 444 Columbus Ave; r $174-194; 30, 45;

Our favorite boutique hotel is a love letter to the jazz era, with moody orange, black and sage-green color schemes that nod to the 1950s. Inverted Chinese umbrellas hang from the ceiling, and photos from the Beat years decorate the walls. Rooms are smallish, and some front on noisy Columbus Ave (the quietest are in back), but the hotel is smack in the middle of North Beach's vibrant street scene.

SAN REMO HOTEL

Map p87 Hotel $

415-776-8688, 800-352-7366; www.sanremohotel.com; 2237 Mason St; d $55-85; 30, 45;

One of the city's best values, the San Remo dates to 1906 and is long on old-fashioned charm. Rooms are simply done, with mismatched turn-of-the-century furnishings, and all share bathrooms. Think reputable, vintage boarding house. Note: the least-expensive rooms have windows onto the corridor, not the outdoors.

GREEN TORTOISE HOSTEL

Map p87 Hostel $

415-834-1000; www.greentortoise.com; 494 Broadway; dm/d $29/70 incl breakfast; 15;

An international crowd of young party-scene backpackers flocks to the Green Tortoise. It's on Broadway, North Beach's seedy (though safe) strip-joint strip. If you're into rowdy hostels, look no further. Bars, restaurants and cafes are right around the corner. No curfew.

RUSSIAN & NOB HILLS

FAIRMONT SAN FRANCISCO

Map p92 Historic Hotel $$$

415-772-5000, 800-441-1414; www.fairmont.com; 950 Mason St; r $199-329; California;

One of the city's most storied hotels, the Fairmont's enormous lobby is decked out with crystal chandeliers, marble floors and towering yellow-marble columns. Rooms sport traditional business-class furnishings, but lack the finer details of a top-end luxury hotel. For maximum character, book a room in the original 1906 building. Tower rooms have stupendous views, but look generic.

MARK HOPKINS INTERCONTINENTAL

Map p92 Historic Hotel $$

415-392-3434, 800-327-0200; www.markhopkins.net; 999 California St; r $169-319; California;

Glistening marble floors reflect glowing crystal chandeliers in the lobby of the 1926 Mark Hopkins, a San Francisco landmark. Detractors call it staid, but its timeless elegance is precisely why others love it. Rooms are done with tasteful furnishings and fabulous beds with Frette linens. The top-floor Top of the Mark (p198) lounge has knockout views and live jazz.

NOB HILL INN

Map p92 Inn $$

415-673-6080; www.nobhillinn.com; 1000 Pine St; r $125-165, ste $195-275; California;

Situated in a genteel old Edwardian house one block below the top of Nob Hill, the 21 rooms at this inn are classically decorated with antiques, armoires and (some) four-poster beds. It's predominantly a time-share-hotel, popular with an older crowd (read: quiet). Web specials drop rates as low as $99. Suites sleep four to six and have kitchenettes.

NOB HILL HOTEL

Map p92 Hotel $

415-885-2987; www.nobhillhotel.com; 835 Hyde St; r $95-135; 2, 3, 4;

Rooms in this 1906 hotel have been dressed up in Victorian style, with brass beds and floral-print carpet. The look borders on grandma-lives-here, but it's definitely not cookie cutter and service is warm and personable. Rooms on Hyde St are loud; book in back. Wi-fi in lobby.

JAPANTOWN & PACIFIC HEIGHTS

KABUKI HOTEL

Map p96 Theme Hotel $$

☎ 415-922-3200, 800-333-3333; www.jdvhotels.com/hotels/kabuki; 1625 Post St; r $129-249; 🚌 4; wi-fi

The Kabuki nods to Japan, with *shoji* (rice-paper) screens on the windows and bright-orange silk dust ruffles beneath platform beds. The boxy 1960s architecture is plain, but rooms are spacious and we love the deep Japanese soaking tubs and adjoining showers – perfect for a classic Nippon bathing ritual with your lover. Don't miss the lovely bonsai garden off the '60s-modern glass lobby.

HOTEL TOMO

Map p96 Theme Hotel $$

☎ 415-922-3200, 800-333-3333; www.jdvhotels.com/tomo; 1800 Sutter St; r $109-179; 🚌 4; wi-fi; family-friendly

Japanese pop culture informs the look of the Tomo, with big-eyed anime characters blinking on the lobby's TV screens. The blond minimalist room furniture and fatboy beanbags make it feel a bit like a college dorm, but it's great fun for families and anime nuts – if not high-heeled sophisticates.

QUEEN ANNE HOTEL

Map p96 Historic Hotel $$

☎ 415-441-2828, 800-227-3970; www.queenanne.com; 1590 Sutter St; r $99-179, ste $145-229; 🚌 4; wi-fi

The Queen Anne occupies a lovely 1890 Victorian mansion, formerly a girls' boarding school. Though the decor borders on frilly and twee (what's with the compact fluorescents in the brass chandeliers?), we love the stately house. Rooms are comfy (some are tiny) and have a mishmash of antiques; some have romantic wood-burning fireplaces. There's wi-fi in the lobby.

HOTEL MAJESTIC

Map p96 Historic Hotel $

☎ 415-441-1100, 800-869-8966; www.thehotelmajestic.com; 1500 Sutter St; r $95-125; 🚌 2, 3, 4; wi-fi

The 1902 Hotel Majestic holds a torch for traditional elegance – even if its edges are fraying. Rooms are done in dusty-rose and sage-green, with Chinese porcelain lamps beside triple-sheeted beds, and while they're showing signs of wear, we like the stalwart old-school vibe. Standard rooms are small but better value than comparable Union Square hotels. The lobby has wi-fi, and the clubby lobby bar is ideal for a clandestine meeting with your paramour.

top picks

HOTEL BARS

- **Tonga Room** (p198)
- **Top of the Mark** (p198)
- **Pied Piper Bar** (p195)
- **Redwood Room** (p195)
- **Starlight Room** (p215)

THE MARINA & THE PRESIDIO

HOTEL DEL SOL

Map pp100–1 Theme Motel $$

☎ 415-921-5520, 877-433-5765; www.thehoteldelsol.com; 3100 Webster St; d $149-199; 🚌 28, 43; P wi-fi; pool; family-friendly

The kid-friendly del Sol is a riot of color with its tropical-themed decor. A quiet, revamped 1950s motor lodge with a palm-lined central courtyard, it's also one of the few San Francisco hotels with a heated outdoor pool. Family suites have bunks and board games.

MARINA MOTEL

Map pp100–1 Motel $$

☎ 415-921-9406, 800-346-6118; www.marinamotel.com; 2576 Lombard St; r $105-145; 🚌 76; P wi-fi

Established in 1939 to accommodate visitors arriving via the new Golden Gate Bridge, the Marina has an inviting, vintage Spanish-Mediterranean look, with a quiet bougainvillea-lined courtyard. Rooms are homey, simple and well maintained (never mind the occasional scuff mark); some have full kitchens (an extra $10). Rooms on Lombard St are loud; request one in back.

COVENTRY MOTOR INN

Map pp100–1 Motel $

☎ 415-567-1200; www.coventrymotorinn.com; 1901 Lombard St; r $95-145; 76;

Of the scores of motels lining Lombard St (Hwy 101), the generic Coventry has the highest overall quality-to-value ratio, with spacious, well-maintained (if plain) rooms and extras like air-con (good for quiet sleeps) and covered parking. Parents: there's plenty of floor space to unpack the kids' toys, but no pool.

MARINA INN

Map pp100–1 Inn $

☎ 415-928-1000, 800-274-1420; www.marinainn.com; 3110 Octavia Blvd; r $69-99; 28, 30;

A good deal in the Marina, this pretty, white turn-of-the-century inn has a little parlor lobby and 40 clean, straightforward and comfortable rooms with cabbage-rose decor, offering a cozier alternative to a generic motel. Rooms facing Lombard St are loud, and there's no on-site parking, but the inn is close to Union St shopping and bars.

HI SAN FRANCISCO FISHERMAN'S WHARF

Map pp100–1 Hostel $

☎ 415-771-7277; www.hihotels.com; Bldg 240, Fort Mason; dm $26-30, r $75-125; 30, 47, 49;

The hostel trades Downtown convenience for a lush-green, parklike setting within spitting distance of the bay. Dorms range from a manageable four beds to a whopping 24 beds; some are coed. There's no curfew, but daytime access to the dorms is limited. Groups of three or four should opt for a private room. There's limited free parking.

SOMA

ST REGIS HOTEL

Map pp110–11 Hotel $$$

☎ 415-284-4000, 877-787-3447; www.stregis.com/sanfrancisco; 125 3rd St; r from $399; 30, 45; & Montgomery St;

The pinnacle of luxury, the St Regis is one of SF's three five-star hotels (the others are Four Seasons and Ritz-Carlton), and it's our favorite for its art collection, which nods to the neighboring Museum of Modern Art. Rooms have all the latest bells and whistles, including magnificent beds dressed with Pratesi linens. Bathrooms sport travertine floors and two-person tubs. Alas, the recession has affected service standards (we wonder how long St Regis will hold its fifth star), but we still love the oversized rooms, despite their too-beige monochromatic color scheme. (Note: the giant plate-glass windows don't open; if that bothers you, choose the Four Seasons.)

top picks

HOTELS FOR KIDS

- **Hotel del Sol** (opposite)
- **Americania Hotel** (p260)
- **Hotel Tomo** (opposite)
- **Argonaut Hotel** (p251)
- **Seal Rock Inn** (p262)

W HOTEL

Map pp110–11 Hotel $$$

☎ 415-777-5300, 877-946-8357; www.whotel.com; 181 3rd St; r from $259; & Montgomery St;

Sexy doormen stand sentinel, looking like bouncers at a disco, and club-kids-turned-conventioneers crowd the lobby, which blares with thump-thump music. Though forced in its cool, the look is sexy – wear black and blend right in. Every room in the 31-story tower has unobstructed city views (request a Bay Bridge view), upholstered window seats, stereos with chill music and sumptuous beds. Though the concept is definitely corporate, W does a stellar job capitalizing on sex and rock-and-roll – the drugs are your business.

HOTEL VITALE

Map pp110–11 Design Hotel $$$

☎ 415-278-3700, 888-890-8688; www.hotelvitale.com; 8 Mission St; d $239-339, ste $669-799; & Embarcadero;

The ugly exterior disguises a fashion-forward shagadelic-chic hotel, with echoes of mid-century-modern design enhanced by up-to-the-minute luxuries and a soothing spa theme. Beds are dressed with silky-soft 450-thread-count sheets. On the roof are two big hot tubs. Suites have extras like waterfall showerheads, limestone-tile bathrooms, two-person soaking tubs, and – best of all – semi-circular glass walls with stunning bay views.

AMERICANIA HOTEL

Map pp110–11 Design Motel $$

☎ 415-626-0200; www.jdvhotels.com; 121 7th St; r $129-169; 🚌 & Ⓜ Civic Center; 📶 🏊 👶

Rooms at this restyled motor lodge face a central courtyard and look sharp, with a retro-'70s aesthetic incorporating black-and-teal-checked carpeting, white-vinyl headboards, pop art and playful extras like Yahtzee dice. Kids love the outdoor heated pool. Parents love the microbrews at the excellent downstairs burger joint.

GOOD HOTEL

Map pp110–11 Design Motel $$

☎ 415-621-7001; www.jdvhotels.com; 112 7th St; r $109-169; 🚌 & Ⓜ Civic Center; 📶

A revamped motor lodge attached to a restyled apartment hotel, Good Hotel places a premium on green, with reclaimed wood headboards, light fixtures made from reused glass bottles, and fleece bedspreads made of recycled soda bottles and cast-off fabrics. The candy-color paint jobs, two-sided window-shade art, and low-slung platform beds make rooms look like the dorm you wish you'd had in college. Rooms on Mission St are loud; book in back. Also has bikes for rent and a good pizza parlor downstairs.

MOSSER HOTEL

Map pp110–11 Hotel $

☎ 415-986-4400, 800-227-3804; www.themosser.com; 54 4th St; r $109-149, with shared bathroom $69-89; 🚌 & Ⓜ Powell St; 📶

A tourist-class hotel with stylish details, the Mosser has tiny rooms and tinier bathrooms, but rates are a bargain. Service can be lackluster and the building is old, but it's close to Union Square shops, Yerba Buena museums and the Moscone Convention Center – and rooms are half the price of the neighboring Marriott, a boon for conventioneers on a budget.

top picks

HOTELS WITH POOLS

- St Regis Hotel (p259)
- W Hotel (p259)
- Palace Hotel (p252)
- Phoenix Hotel (p256)
- Hotel del Sol (p258)
- Americania Hotel (above)

THE MISSION & POTRERO HILL

INN SAN FRANCISCO

Map pp116–17 Inn $$

☎ 415-641-0188, 800-359-0913; www.innsf.com; 943 S Van Ness Ave; r $175-285, with shared bathroom $120-145, cottage $335, all incl breakfast; 🚌 49; 📶

The stately Inn San Francisco occupies an elegant 1872 Italianate Victorian mansion, impeccably maintained and packed with period antiques. All rooms have fresh-cut flowers and sumptuous beds with fluffy featherbeds; some have Jacuzzi tubs. There's also a freestanding garden cottage that sleeps up to six. Outside there's an English garden and redwood hot tub open 24 hours (a rarity). Full breakfast.

SAN FRANCISCO ELEMENTS

Map pp116–17 Hostel $

☎ 415-647-4100, 866-327-8407; www.elementssf.com; 2524 Mission St; dm/d $29/60; 🚌 14; 📶

If you're 21 to 30 and love to party, the Mission is your 'hood. At the heart of the nightlife scene, Elements has clean, up-to-date, good-looking (if institutional) rooms with noise-blocking double-pane windows. Dorms are coed or segregated, and all have in-room baths. The rooftop bar, Medjool Sky Terrace (p201), is a happening weekend hangout. Other extras include comfy lounges, movie nights and rooftop barbecues.

THE CASTRO & NOE VALLEY

BELVEDERE HOUSE

off Map p123 B&B $$

☎ 415-731-6654, 877-226-3273; www.belvederehouse.com; 598 Belvedere St; r incl breakfast $130-190; 🚌 6, 33, 37, N; 📶

Its location on a leafy residential street, up a steep hill from the Castro, makes this B&B one of the city's best-kept secrets. Six cozy rooms have eclectic art and vintage chandeliers, and the living room is packed with treasures from the owner's world travels. Though primarily for gay guests, all are welcome – kids get child-sized bathrobes. For other gay-friendly digs, see p248.

BECK'S MOTOR LODGE

Map p123 Motel $

☎ 415-621-8212, 800-227-4360; www.becksmotorlodgesf.com; 2222 Market St; r $95-135; Ⓜ Castro St;

Though technically not gay, its placement at the center of the Castro makes it the defacto gay favorite for a bang-the-headboard romp. We don't recommend bringing the kids, especially during big gay events, when rooms reserve months ahead. Book a rear-facing unit for quiet, a room in front to cruise with your blinds open.

THE HAIGHT

STANYAN PARK HOTEL

Map pp126–7 Historic Hotel $$

☎ 415-751-1000; www.stanyanpark.com; 750 Stanyan St; r $135-225, ste $275-350, incl breakfast; 🚌 71;

On the eastern edge of Golden Gate Park, a block from Haight St, this stately Victorian hotel is completely up-to-date, with nary a drafty window or creaky floor. There's nothing risky about the traditional American decor – Queen Anne and Chippendale-style chairs, floral-print wallpaper and dusty-green and pale-pink color schemes – but that's also its charm: soothing familiarity and timelessness. Though junkies congregate at the nearby McDonald's at nighttime, fret not: the 'hood is generally safe and the hotel secure.

RED VICTORIAN BED, BREAKFAST & ART

Map pp126–7 B&B $$

☎ 415-864-1978; www.redvic.net; 1665 Haight St; r $149-229, without bathroom $89-129, incl breakfast; 🚌 43;

The year 1968 lives on at the tripped-out Red Vic. Each individually decorated room in the 1904 landmark building pays tribute to peace, ecology and global friendship, with themes like Sunshine, Flower Children and, of course, the Summer of Love. Only four of the 18 rooms have bathrooms; all come with breakfast in the (naturally) organic Peace Café. Reduced rates available for longer stays. There's wi-fi in the lobby.

CHATEAU TIVOLI

Map pp126–7 Historic Inn $$

☎ 415-776-5462; www.chateautivoli.com; 1057 Steiner St; r $140-170, r without bathroom $100-130, ste $250-290; 🚌 5, 22;

This imposing, glorious chateau on a secondary thoroughfare near Alamo Sq has somewhat faded since the time when Isadora Duncan and Mark Twain were guests. Still, you can't pass by without gawking at the two-toned gabled roofs, domed turrets and cornices – all painted maroon and blue with gold accents. The guestrooms are more modest, with no TVs, but the place is full of soul, character and, rumor has it, the ghost of a Victorian opera diva.

INN 1890

Map pp126–7 Historic Inn $

☎ 415-386-0486; www.inn1890.com; 1890 Page St; r $129, r without bathroom $99-119, ste $169; 🚌 33;

This stately 16-bedroom Victorian mansion sits on a residential street just one block from the action on Haight St. Every room is different, with eclectic furniture and nothing frou-frou to get in your way. Most rooms only have a shower, but all have robes, slippers and down comforters. You can reserve one of the four parking spaces.

METRO HOTEL

Map pp126–7 Hotel $

☎ 415-861-5364; www.metrohotelsf.com; 319 Divisadero St; r $76-120; 🚌 24;

On a thoroughfare bisecting the Upper and Lower Haight districts, this straightforward no-frills hotel provides cheap, clean rooms with private bathroom and an outdoor garden patio. Its location is largely residential, but you can easily walk to the Haight's bars and restaurants.

HAYES VALLEY

EDWARDIAN SAN FRANCISCO HOTEL

Map p133 Hotel $$

☎ 415-864-1271, 888-864-8070; www.edwardiansfhotel.com; 1668 Market St; r $119-189; 🚌 F, Van Ness;

An unassuming brick-faced inn, the Edwardian has an ideal middle-of-the-city location between the Castro/Mission and Downtown, close to the symphony and opera. Rooms are well kept, but tiny – note that images on its website are shot with a fish-eye lens. The excellent Cav Wine Bar (p203) is downstairs, as is Zuni Cafe (p186) and the Hôtel Biron (p203).

AIRPORT ACCOMMODATIONS

Staying near San Francisco International Airport (SFO) is cheaper than in town, and ideal if you've an early flight. There are direct-dial phones to many hotels in the baggage-claim area, and free shuttle buses run to the terminals. There are over 20 hotels around the airport, and competition is fierce. Millbrae and Burlingame, just south of the airport, and South San Francisco, immediately north of the airport, have multiple chain hotels with midrange rates. Here are a few to consider:

Clarion Hotel (☎ 650-692-6363; www.choicehotels.com; 401 E Millbrae Ave; r $90-125;) By the bay, a mile from SFO, the Clarion has generic rooms, an exercise room, laundry facilities, and 24-hour airport shuttle. Parking is $10.

Embassy Suites (☎ 650-589-3400, 800-362-2779; www.embassy-suite.com; 250 Gateway Blvd; r from $129;) Two miles north of SFO, this suites-only hotel is good for families, with laundry, a pool and free airport shuttle.

Motel 6 (☎ 650-877-0770, 800-466-8356; www.motel6.com; 111 Mitchell Ave; r $59-79) Two miles north of SFO, this is your basic, cheap, cookie-cutter motel with lackluster service. There's no shuttle, but car-rental agencies are nearby, so plan to drop off your vehicle and catch the rental-firm's shuttle. A cab to SFO costs about $12.

SLEEP OVER SAUCE

Map p133 B&B $

☎ 415-252-1423; www.sleepsf.com; 135 Gough St; r $110-185; 21;

We like the homey vibe of this vintage-1906 inn, set upstairs from Sauce, a pretty-good dinner house. In late 2009 new owners renovated the former Albion House Inn, determined to remove all the little-old-lady furnishings left by the previous owners. Now the look borders on Ikea, with muted earth tones, mass-market furnishings and a big common room with leather sofas. We wish there were feather pillows, but at these rates we're not complaining. Some rooms have baths across the halls; ask when you book if yours has en-suite facilities. The best reason to stay here is easy access to Hayes Valley shopping, the opera and the symphony.

HAYES VALLEY INN

Map p133 Inn $

☎ 415-431-9131; www.hayesvalleyinn.com; 417 Gough St; s $76-94, d $84-105, incl breakfast; 21;

Like a European pension, this amazingly reasonable find is surrounded by Hayes Valley shops and has simple, small rooms with shared bathrooms, a cocker spaniel panting in the parlor and staff who want to mother you. Many guests are long-term, repeat visitors. This is a good place to stay if you're looking for an apartment.

GOLDEN GATE PARK & THE AVENUES

SEAL ROCK INN

Map pp136–7 Inn $$

☎ 415-752-8000, 888-732-5762; www.sealrockinn.com; 545 Point Lobos Ave; s $110-142, d $120-152; 38;

Hunter S Thompson used to stay at this vintage-1950s ocean-side motel to listen to the seals, which have since migrated to Fisherman's Wharf. Rooms need updating (think 1970s rumpus-room style), but they're big and most sleep up to four people. All have refrigerators; some have kitchens. It's good for families who want to spend time at the beach and hiking the coastal trails. Reserve way ahead for the upgraded 3rd-floor fireplace rooms. A heated pool (summer only) and Ping-Pong keep the kids from getting antsy. There's wi-fi in the lobby.

EXCURSIONS

EXCURSIONS

Cross the Golden Gate into Marin County and you would never know you were in the USA's fifth-largest metropolitan area. Within an hour's drive you'll discover primordial redwood groves, long rocky beaches, fragrant eucalyptus groves, fern-laced waterfalls and sweeping hilltop vistas of the Pacific Ocean. Head east and you'll reach the culture centers of Berkeley and Oakland. And then there's Wine Country – provenance of some of the world's greatest vintages – where rolling hills turn the color of lion's fur in summer, and lazy rivers cut serpentine paths to the sea. Take our advice: get out of town.

The East Bay is inextricably linked with San Francisco, and Oakland and Berkeley feel almost like boroughs of SF. But don't be deceived: they're cities in their own right, each with its own character and soul. Around the time of the dot-com boom (1996 to 2000), working-class Oakland benefited from a huge influx of San Franciscans prospecting for cheaper rents, and these days its formerly depressed art deco downtown is looking pretty spiffy. Berkeley remains as contradictory and politically complex as its reputation suggests. Liberal and elitist all at once, the little city derives its vibrant energy from its famous university; North Berkeley's skirt-and-sweater matrons provide a counterpoint to the hippie-grunge around campus. Marin County, on the other hand, goes to great lengths to remain separate. Its citizens successfully blocked both a freeway up the coast and BART trains from infiltrating its borders. As a result, Marin looks pretty much as it always has, with small towns, dense woodlands and rolling hills.

It's a quick ferry, bus, train or car ride to the East and North Bay regions. Though not all destinations listed in this chapter are easily accessible without a car, you'll find plenty of nearby opportunities to muddy your hiking boots, bone up on your Shakespeare, get sand in your shorts, and purple your tongue with the latest vintages.

METROPOLITAN LIFE

Just a few BART stops from San Francisco, downtown Oakland (p266) has a prominent African American community, much larger than anywhere else in the Bay Area. The city has a gritty, atmospheric Chinatown, elegant art deco architecture along Broadway (the main downtown street) and excellent restaurants within blocks of Lake Merritt. BART also accesses the city's more affluent Rockridge neighborhood – on the Berkeley–Oakland border – known for top-notch shopping and dining. To reach Berkeley (p272), hop back on BART and transfer trains to the Richmond line. Berkeley's compact downtown is worth a stroll, but the adjacent university campus is most compelling. Students spill off campus onto Telegraph Ave, the location of some of the Bay Area's best book and record stores – but be prepared for panhandlers, drug-addled former hippies and grunge. North Berkeley, up Shattuck Ave, couldn't be more different: locals call it the 'Gourmet Ghetto,' and you'd be hard-pressed to spot a tattooed skateboarder within eyeshot of legendary Chez Panisse (p274).

NATURE

For a quick dose of stunning Northern California scenery, most visitors head to Muir Woods (p277), an old-growth redwood stand on the Marin coast, 30 minutes north of the Golden Gate. If you've a day to explore, continue north to Point Reyes National Seashore (p291). Via Shoreline Hwy (Hwy 1), you can get there in an hour from the Golden Gate. Hwy 1 over Mt Tamalpais (p281) is winding and slow, but if you love woods, you'll hardly notice. To explore Wine Country (p282), you'll need one full day, but we recommend staying at least one night to immerse yourself in the local culture and drink with nary a care about the 90-minute drive back to SF.

PICTURESQUE TOWNS

Woodsy-chic Marin County is home to some of the Bay Area's loveliest towns, but you'll need a car to reach the further-flung villages of West Marin, such as Point Reyes Station and Stinson Beach. However, it's an easy half-hour ferry ride (p302) from San Francisco to pretty little Tiburon (p280) and arty Sausalito (p280).

38°30'N
123°W
To Healdsburg/ Russian River (10mi)
122°30'W
St Helena
Lake Berryessa
122°W
38°30'N
To Sacramento (25mi)
Forestville
Monte Rio
Sugarloaf Ridge State Park
Rutherford
Oakville
Yountville
Dixon
Santa Rosa
Occidental
Sebastopol
Annadel State Park
Kenwood
Mt Vaca (2819ft)
Vacaville
Bodega Bay
Bodega
Glen Ellen
Wine Country (p282)
Rohnert Park
Sonoma Mtn (2295ft)
Valley Ford
Napa
Sonoma
Penngrove
Bodega Bay
Tomales
Tomales Point
Napa River
Fairfield
Suisun City
Petaluma
Petaluma River
Tomales Bay
Hicks Mtn (1532ft)
Burdell Mtn (1558ft)
Tomales Bay State Park
Grizzly Bay
Inverness
Novato
Vallejo
Point Reyes National Seashore (p291)
Point Reyes National Seashore
Point Reyes Station
Nicasio
San Pablo Bay
Mare Island
Crockett
Suisun Bay
Olema
Samuel P Taylor State Park
China Camp State Park
Rodeo
Benicia
Bay Point
Pittsburg
38°N
Drakes Beach
Drakes Bay
Forest Knolls
Pinole
Hercules
Martinez
38°N
Point Reyes
Fairfax
San Anselmo
San Rafael
El Sobrante
Concord
San Pablo
Wildcat Canyon Regional Park
Briones Regional Park
Pleasant Hill
Richmond
Larkspur
Muir Woods National Monument
Mill Valley
El Cerrito
Tilden Regional Park
Alamo
Walnut Creek
Mt Diablo (3849ft)
Bolinas
Duxbury Point
Albany
Tiburon
Berkeley
Lafayette
Marin County (p276)
Angel Island
Oakland & Berkeley (p266)
Mount Diablo State Park
Sausalito
Golden Gate
SAN FRANCISCO
Oakland
Redwood Regional Park
Danville
Blackhawk
Point Lobos
San Ramon
Farallon National Wildlife Refuge
Alameda
San Francisco Bay
San Leandro
Anthony Chabot Regional Park
To I-5; Tracy
Farallon Islands
Oakland International Airport
Castro Valley
Dublin
Daly City
Brisbane
South San Francisco
San Lorenzo
Hayward
Pleasanton
San Bruno
San Francisco International Airport
Union City
Pacifica
Point San Pedro
Burlingame
San Mateo
Sunol
Foster City
Fremont
Point Montara
Montara
Moss Beach
Newark
37°30'N
Princeton-by-the-Sea
Pillar Point
Miramar
Redwood City
37°30'N
Half Moon Bay
San Carlos
East Palo Alto
Half Moon Bay
Palo Alto
Milpitas
Woodside
Mountain View
Norman Y Mineta San Jose International Airport
Portola Valley
Sunnyvale
The Road South (p293)
San Gregorio
Santa Clara
San Jose
La Honda
Cupertino
Campbell
PACIFIC OCEAN
Pescadero Point
Pescadero
Portola Redwoods State Park
Saratoga
Pigeon Point
Butano State Park
Castle Rock State Park
Los Gatos
Pigeon Point Lighthouse
Big Basin Redwoods State Park
Redwood Estates
Loma Prieta (3806ft)
Año Nuevo Point
Boulder Creek
Ben Lomond
Henry Cowell Redwoods State Park
Felton
Scotts Valley
The Forest of Nisene Marks State Park
37°N
Davenport
Soquel
37°N
Sand Hill Bluff
Santa Cruz
Wilder Ranch State Park
Capitola
Aptos
Point Santa Cruz
Monterey Bay
To Monterey Bay Aquarium (25mi)
0 20 km
0 10 miles
123°W
122°30'W
122°W

SNOW BOUND: TAHOE SKI TRIPS

It's a mere four hours to Lake Tahoe and the Sierra Nevada mountains for some of the USA's premier skiing and riding. Though champagne-powder days are a rarity in California (they call the snow Sierra cement for a reason), temps are usually above freezing midday, and an average-annual 300 sunny days means you may get a tan as you shoosh down majestic granite peaks, some with drop-dead vistas of cobalt-blue Lake Tahoe (especially at Heavenly and Homewood resorts). If you don't want to deal with the drive, contact the Bay Area Ski Bus (☎ 925-680-4386; www.bayareaskibus.com), which offers one-day and overnight trips.

To reach Tiburon and Sausalito, cross the Golden Gate (Hwy 101), then exit onto Paradise Dr. The winding road hugs the bay and leads to Tiburon, a good spot for a stroll and lunch. Take Hwy 131 (Tiburon Blvd) back to Hwy 101, then head south to Sausalito for drinks while overlooking the bay.

BEACHES

South of the city is where those classic California clichés – long beaches, convertible cars, lazy living – become reality (but this is the Bay Area, so bring a sweater as well as a bikini). The beaches at **Half Moon Bay** (p293) are good for family excursions. **Santa Cruz** (p296) has great people-watching and surfing (winter is best). State beaches line the coast between SF and Santa Cruz, and each has its own flavor (for detailed descriptions, see the San Mateo Coast page of www.71miles.com). If you don't have a car, it's easiest to head south. Take the bus to Half Moon Bay, Santa Cruz or Monterey.

OAKLAND & BERKELEY

By 'East Bay,' San Franciscans generally mean Oakland and Berkeley. While many SF residents rarely cross the bay, the city would be incomplete without the East Bay. This is where the ports are located and the transcontinental railroad ends; lose Oakland and SF loses its supply line – as happened in the 1906 earthquake. Vital communities in their own rights, Oakland and Berkeley are more than suburbs. With museums, celebrity restaurants and universities, the East Bay has surprisingly great culture – and much warmer summertime weather.

Orientation

Oakland is connected to San Francisco by the Bay Bridge and the underwater Transbay Tube, which BART trains use. The city slopes gently from its eastern hills down to the industrial zone by the bay. In the middle, College Ave snakes northward to couple with Berkeley in the gastronomic Rockridge area (head for the 6300 block). Commercial Broadway runs west through downtown and Chinatown till its terminus at Jack London Sq. The jewel of Oakland, immediately east of downtown, is Lake Merritt, with jogging paths and paddleboats. Beyond it, 14th St becomes International Blvd, the axis of a significant Vietnamese enclave and, further out, an even larger Latino district.

Just north of Oakland, Berkeley is bisected vertically by Shattuck Ave and horizontally by University Ave. One or the other will get you within striking distance of almost anyplace in the People's Republic of Berkeley. Just south of Shattuck and University Aves' intersection is the Downtown Berkeley BART station. From here, you can walk nearly anywhere. With the exception of the eastern hills, the town is flat and easy to walk or bike. I-80 runs along the town's western edge, next to the marina.

OAKLAND

Scrappy Oakland's got attitude, and shouts it out at every chance. It's got the Oakland A's and deep African American roots that emerge artfully in world-celebrated music, literature and art. It has the USA's fourth-largest port: arriving ferry passengers are greeted by sky-high cranes plucking freight containers from the ground. But best of all, Oakland has stellar summer weather – it's usually 10°F warmer than SF. Oaktown has less than half San Francisco's population, but more urban grit. It also has a lovely downtown: many architectural gems survive from the early 20th century and a little saltwater lake sits right in the heart of downtown. Oakland is a city of neighborhood joints, local groceries and small clusters of clubs and restaurants.

Hop on BART to downtown Oakland (an easy 15-minute ride), or drive over the Bay Bridge. Oakland's downtown is best visited on a weekday, when it's lively with action (at night it's dead). Wander past historic buildings and poke into colorful local shops. With easy access from San Francisco via BART and ferry, you can comfortably spend a half day exploring downtown, nearby Chinatown and Jack London Sq on foot.

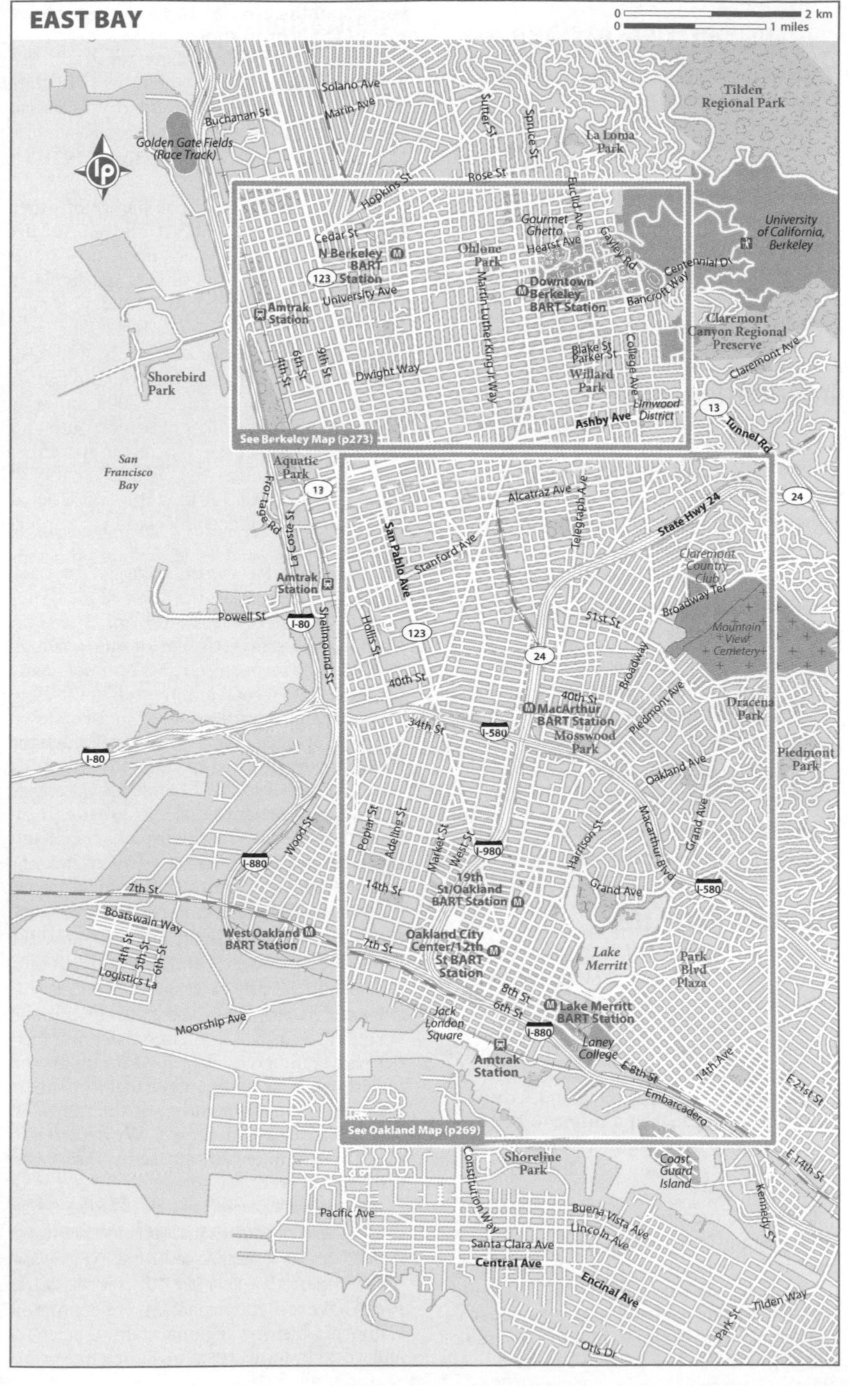
EAST BAY
0 2 km
0 1 miles
Tilden Regional Park
Solano Ave
Marin Ave
Buchanan St
Golden Gate Fields (Race Track)
Sutter St
Spruce St
La Loma Park
Rose St
Hopkins St
Euclid Ave
Gourmet Ghetto
Hearst Ave
Gayley Rd
University of California, Berkeley
Cedar St
N Berkeley BART Station
Ohlone Park
Centennial Dr
Downtown Berkeley BART Station
Bancroft Way
University Ave
Amtrak Station
Martin Luther King Jr Way
Claremont Canyon Regional Preserve
4th St
6th St
9th St
Dwight Way
Blake St
Parker St
College Ave
Willard Park
Claremont Ave
Shorebird Park
Elmwood District
Ashby Ave
Tunnel Rd
See Berkeley Map (p273)
San Francisco Bay
Aquatic Park
Frontage Rd
Alcatraz Ave
Telegraph Ave
State Hwy 24
La Coste St
San Pablo Ave
Stanford Ave
Claremont Country Club
Broadway Ter
Amtrak Station
Powell St
Shellmound St
51st St
Hollis St
Mountain View Cemetery
Broadway
40th St
40th St
MacArthur BART Station
Piedmont Ave
Dracena Park
34th St
Mosswood Park
Piedmont Park
Oakland Ave
Poplar St
Adeline St
Market St
West St
Harrison St
MacArthur Blvd
Grand Ave
Wood St
19th St/Oakland BART Station
14th St
Grand Ave
7th St
Boatswain Way
West Oakland BART Station
7th St
Oakland City Center/12th St BART Station
4th St
5th St
6th St
Logistics La
Lake Merritt
Park Blvd Plaza
8th St
6th St
Lake Merritt BART Station
Jack London Square
Moorship Ave
Laney College
Amtrak Station
E 8th St
14th Ave
E 21st St
Embarcadero
See Oakland Map (p269)
Constitution Way
Shoreline Park
Coast Guard Island
E 14th St
Kennedy St
Pacific Ave
Buena Vista Ave
Lincoln Ave
Santa Clara Ave
Central Ave
Encinal Ave
Tilden Way
Park St
Otis Dr

TRANSPORTATION: OAKLAND

Distance from San Francisco 16 miles from downtown to downtown

Direction East

Travel time 25 minutes

Car Bay Bridge to I-880; take the Broadway exit to downtown

BART The Richmond and Pittsburg/Bay Point lines run through downtown Oakland. Get off at the 12th St or 19th St exits. Pittsburg/Bay Point trains stop in Rockridge and on College Ave.

Information

The *Oakland Tribune* is Oakland's daily newspaper. The free weekly *East Bay Express* has good Oakland and Berkeley listings, though the restaurant reviews are often overrated.

Diesel (☎ 510-653-9965; 5433 College Ave; Ⓑ Rockridge) One of Oakland's fine new-and-used bookstores.

Marcus Bookstore (☎ 510-652-2344; 3900 Martin Luther King Jr Way; Ⓑ MacArthur) Specializes in African American literature and history.

Oakland Convention & Visitors Bureau (☎ 510-839-9000; www.oaklandcvb.com; 463 11th St; 8:30am-5pm Mon-Fri; Ⓑ Oakland City Center) Near the Oakland Marriott Hotel.

Post office (1446 Franklin St; Ⓑ Oakland City Center) There's another branch at 201 13th St.

Walden Pond Bookstore (☎ 510-832-4438; 3316 Grand Ave; 12 AC Transit) An excellent bookstore.

Sights & Activities

The pedestrianized **City Center** (Broadway & Clay St, 12th & 14th Sts; Ⓑ Oakland City Center) forms the heart of downtown Oakland. The twin towers of the Ronald Dellums Federal Building are on Clay St, just behind it. Highlighting the skyline on 13th and Franklin Sts is the 1923 Tribune Tower, an Oakland icon with a cool red neon clock and home to the *Oakland Tribune*. The beautiful, refurbished 1914 Beaux Arts City Hall, on 14th and Clay Sts, is another beauty.

Old Oakland (Washington St, btwn 8th & 10th Sts; Ⓑ Oakland City Center), immediately west of Broadway, is lined with historic buildings dating from the 1860s to 1880s. The buildings have been restored and new, upscale restaurants have begun to make this a hub of evening activity. The area also hosts a lively Chinese-influenced **farmers market** every Friday morning – a great time to visit.

North of the center, where Telegraph Ave angles off Broadway, stands the 1913 flatiron **Cathedral Building**. The nearby **Paramount Theatre** (☎ 510-465-6400; www.paramounttheatre.com; 2025 Broadway; Ⓑ 19th St) is a restored 1931 art deco masterpiece.

Downtown Oakland has plenty of other buildings adorned with art nouveau or art deco details; unfortunately, many now stand empty and are in need of care, particularly those further out from City Center. One success story is the 1928 **Fox Oakland Theatre** (www.thefoxoakland.com; Telegraph Ave & 19th St; Ⓑ 19th St), once the largest cinema west of Chicago. A two-year renovation ended in 2009, and now the theater hosts the likes of Sonic Youth and Kylie Minogue (see the website for upcoming shows); it also houses the Oakland School of the Arts. Also look for the **I Magnin Building**, at 2001 Broadway, gracefully clad in green terracotta tiling.

Jack London Square (www.jacklondonsquare.com; Broadway; 51 AC Transit) bears the name of the writer who raised hell on the waterfront. The sanitized marina strip feels like an outdoor mall with many vacant storefronts and not many people, but it's a good jumping-off point. Here you can catch a ferry to San Francisco, down a pint at lopsided **Heinold's First & Last Chance Saloon** (p271), wander downtown along Broadway, or visit **Yoshi's** (p271) for sushi and top-class jazz. For organic produce, artisan breads, fresh flowers and tasty free samples, check out the Oakland **farmers market** (10am-2pm Sun). Franklin Delano Roosevelt's official yacht, the **Potomac** (Floating White House; ☎ 510-627-1215; www.usspotomac.org), is usually moored beside the ferry landing and is definitely worth a look.

Oakland's **Chinatown** (downtown Oakland, immediately east of Broadway; Ⓑ Oakland City Center) is much smaller than its San Francisco sister, but bustles with commerce. English is infrequent and tourists few. Oaklanders argue that its Chinese restaurants are more authentic than those in San Francisco's Chinatown. We'd prefer to take this argument on a case-by-case basis; otherwise it's a draw.

The **Oakland Museum of California** (☎ 510-238-2200; www.museumca.org; 1000 Oak St; adult/child/senior & student $8/free/5, 2nd Sun of month admission free; 10am-5pm Wed-Sat, noon-5pm Sun, 10am-9pm 1st Fri of month; Ⓑ Lake Merritt) has excellent permanent collections on California history, regional natural sciences and works by local artists, including fine prints

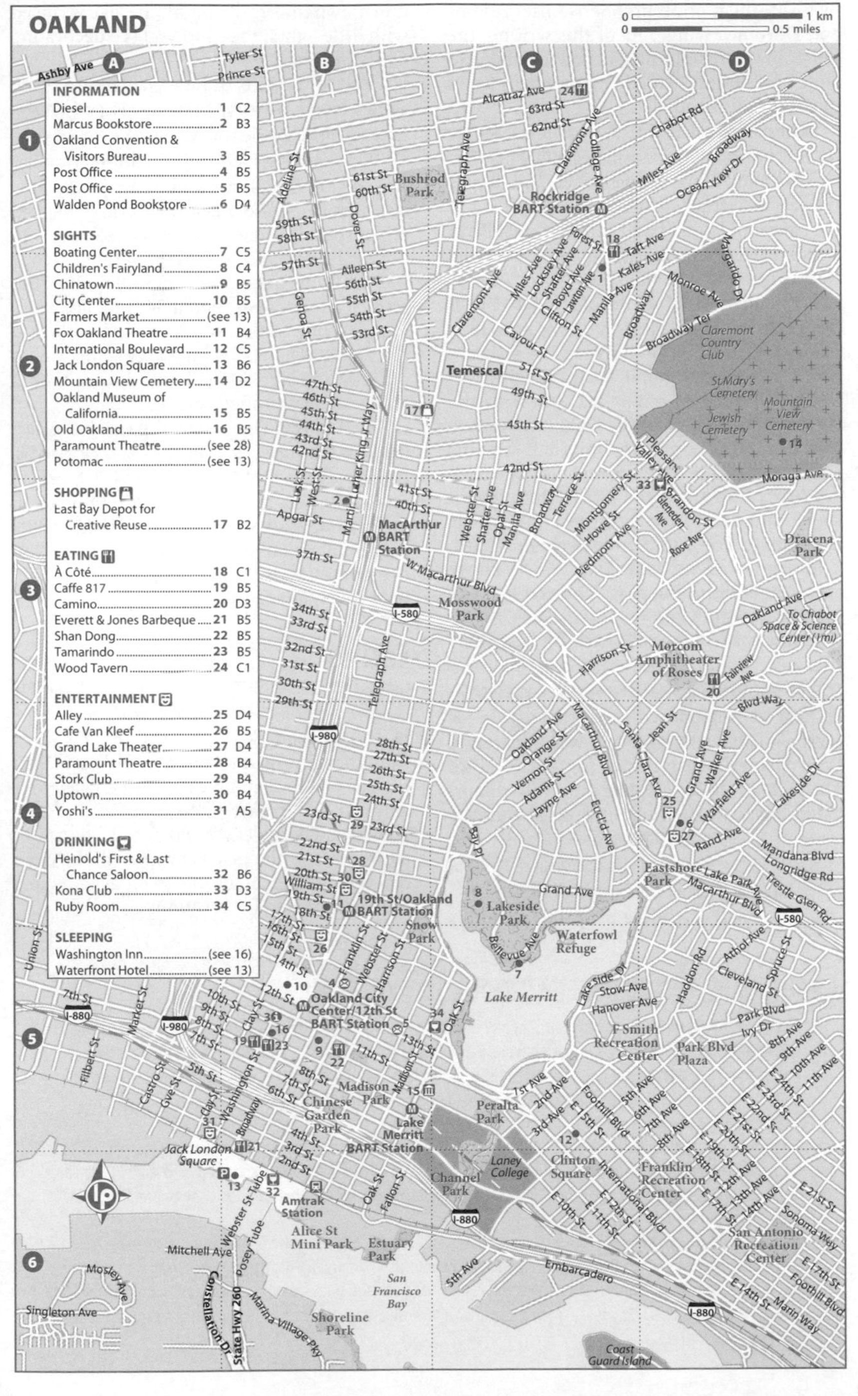

OAKLAND
0 1 km
0 0.5 miles
INFORMATION
Diesel 1 C2
Marcus Bookstore 2 B3
Oakland Convention & Visitors Bureau 3 B5
Post Office 4 B5
Post Office 5 B5
Walden Pond Bookstore 6 D4
SIGHTS
Boating Center 7 C5
Children's Fairyland 8 C4
Chinatown 9 B5
City Center 10 B5
Farmers Market (see 13)
Fox Oakland Theatre 11 B4
International Boulevard 12 C5
Jack London Square 13 B6
Mountain View Cemetery 14 D2
Oakland Museum of California 15 B5
Old Oakland 16 B5
Paramount Theatre (see 28)
Potomac (see 13)
SHOPPING
East Bay Depot for Creative Reuse 17 B2
EATING
À Côté 18 C1
Caffe 817 19 B5
Camino 20 D3
Everett & Jones Barbeque 21 B5
Shan Dong 22 B5
Tamarindo 23 B5
Wood Tavern 24 C1
ENTERTAINMENT
Alley 25 D4
Cafe Van Kleef 26 B5
Grand Lake Theater 27 D4
Paramount Theatre 28 B4
Stork Club 29 B4
Uptown 30 B4
Yoshi's 31 A5
DRINKING
Heinold's First & Last Chance Saloon 32 B6
Kona Club 33 D3
Ruby Room 34 C5
SLEEPING
Washington Inn (see 16)
Waterfront Hotel (see 13)
Ashby Ave
Bushrod Park
Rockridge BART Station
Temescal
Claremont Country Club
St Mary's Cemetery
Jewish Cemetery
Mountain View Cemetery
MacArthur BART Station
Mosswood Park
Dracena Park
To Chabot Space & Science Center (1mi)
Morcom Amphitheater of Roses
19th St/Oakland BART Station
Snow Park
Lakeside Park
Waterfowl Refuge
Lake Merritt
Eastshore Park
Oakland City Center/12th St BART Station
F Smith Recreation Center
Park Blvd Plaza
Madison Park
Chinese Garden Park
Lake Merritt BART Station
Peralta Park
Laney College
Channel Park
Clinton Square
Franklin Recreation Center
San Antonio Recreation Center
Jack London Square
Amtrak Station
Alice St Mini Park
Estuary Park
San Francisco Bay
Shoreline Park
Coast Guard Island
Webster St Tube
Posey Tube
State Hwy 260
Embarcadero
I-580
I-980
I-880

by Californian photographers Ansel Adams and Dorothea Lange. As of this writing, the museum was rebuilding and had scheduled to close until spring 2010, then potentially again in 2012. Call ahead.

International Boulevard (14th St east of Lake Merritt; 82 AC Transit) is a three-mile carnival of Vietnamese and Mexican businesses. You'll find the best taco trucks along Fruitvale Ave or at the corner of High St and International Blvd. The Bay Area's best *pho* (Vietnamese noodle soup) joints are just blocks away.

Oakland's visual centerpiece, Lake Merritt (along Lakeside Dr; Lake Merritt) is a gorgeous place to stroll, jog or lollygag on a sunny day. Once a tidal marsh teeming with waterfowl, it became a lake in 1869 with the damming of an arm of the Oakland estuary. It still supports migratory birds and remains connected to the estuary, but its 155 acres are briny and unfit for swimming. You'll spot hundreds of Canada geese (and their droppings) along a 3.5-mile perimeter path. You can also rent boats (see below). Those crew teams whipping past? They're the Lake Merritt Rowing Club.

In oak-shaded Lakeside Park, on Lake Merritt's eastern shore, Children's Fairyland (510-452-2259; www.fairyland.org; Grand & Bellevue Aves; admission $7; 10am-4pm daily summer, Wed-Sun spring & fall, Fri-Sun winter; 12 AC Transit; 19th St) was apparently Walt Disney's inspiration for Disneyland. Through adult eyes, it has a weirdly dilapidated charm; little kids love it. The boating center (510-238-2196; 568 Bellevue Ave in Lakeside Park; boats per hr $8-15; 10:30am-4pm daily summer, 10:30am-4:30pm Sat & Sun winter, hr vary spring & fall; 12 AC Transit) lets you sail or paddle beneath Oakland's downtown towers. At night, the lake is ringed with little lights, the kind you see decorating Christmas-tree lots.

Head to the hills of East Oakland to Chabot Space & Science Center (510-336-7300; www.chabotspace.org; 10000 Skyline Blvd; adult/child & senior $15/11; 10am-5pm Wed & Thu, 10am-10pm Fri & Sat, 11am-5pm Sun; 53 AC Transit), a hands-on science museum in Redwood Regional Park, which no self-respecting science geek should miss. On fogless Friday and Saturday evenings, scope out far-flung nebulae through 8in and 20in refractor telescopes, and a 36in reflector telescope – one of the largest in the US open to the public. Tickets include access to a stellar planetarium and Megadome theater with a 70ft, seamless domed screen.

OK, it's not your typical park, but Mountain View Cemetery (510-658-2588; www.mountainviewcemetery.org; 5000 Piedmont Ave; 59 AC Transit) was designed by Frederic Law Olmstead, the man behind NYC's Central Park, and its gardens and statuary are gorgeous. Once you overcome (or indulge) the macabre aspect, it's a lovely place for a picnic.

Eating

Camino (510-547-5035; www.caminorestaurant.com; 3917 Grand Ave; mains $20-25; dinner Wed-Mon, brunch Sat & Sun; 12 AC Transit) Kick-back-chic Camino's short daily-changing menu showcases the best of local organic produce and meats, most cooked over an open fire in slow-food-meets-California-now style. The tables are of recycled old-growth redwood, and the place buzzes with the city's bon vivants, high on European biodynamic and organic vintages. Reservations essential.

FOUR OAKLAND-BERKELEY 'HOODS TO EXPLORE

- Piedmont Ave – in Oakland, between 51st and Broadway. This is where the locals shop. Key-makers, cobblers, cafes, tea houses, yoga studios – not boutique-y, but lots of one-of-a-kind shops. Not as upscale as Rockridge.
- Rockridge – College Ave connects Oakland and Berkeley; the 6300-block marks the line. The Berkeley side is fancier, with upscale boutiques. The Oakland side (south of Rockridge BART) has more eclectic shopping and is heavily influenced by the nearby California College of the Arts.
- Telegraph Ave – in Berkeley, south of campus. Not for everyone. Expect students, left-over hippies, panhandlers, tattooed skateboarders, Irish pubs that reek of last night, and *great* record shops and used bookstores. Only Santa Cruz can top it as the land of the great unwashed. Seventeen-year-olds in their Jim Morrison phase dig it, but suburban moms run screaming.
- Temescal – Oakland, around 51st and Telegraph. Up-and-coming but not quite up-and-running, Temescal is where artists moved when they got priced out everywhere else. We predict it's the next hot spot. Find good new restaurants, Korean BBQ joints, cafes and a way-cool artists' salvage shop called the East Bay Depot for Creative Reuse (510-547-6470; www.east-bay-depot.org; 4695 Telegraph Ave; 11am-6pm) – a must for teachers and arts-and-crafters.

top picks

EAST BAY EATS

- Chez Panisse (p274)
- Camino (opposite)
- Wood Tavern (below)
- Vik's Chaat Corner (p275)
- Cheese Board Pizza Collective (p274)

Wood Tavern (☎ 510-654-6607; http://woodtavern.net; 6317 College Ave; lunch $10-20, dinner mains $19-26; 11:30am-10pm; Rockridge) The daily-changing New American brasserie-style menu features what's in season, with earthy, soulful dishes like pan-roasted lemon-rosemary chicken, chopped salads, cheese boards, charcuterie plates and a damn good burger. Very local, happening crowd. Make reservations.

À Côté (☎ 510-655-6469; http://acoterestaurant.com; 5478 College Ave; dishes $5-16; dinner; Rockridge) Small plates are the specialty at this foodie-scenester restaurant, and they're deliciously creative – our favorite is the knock-out lobster-corn fritters. Great cocktails. Women can sport high heels without standing out; men can wear jeans and blend in.

Tamarindo (☎ 510-444-1944; www.tamarindoantojeria.com; 468 8th St; dishes $5-12; lunch Tue-Sat, dinner Mon-Sat; 12th St) The carefully crafted *antojitos* (Mexican tapas) aren't your usual Mexican fare. Expect flavor-packed spins on familiar dishes, like tostadas and tacos (try the shrimp), served in a stylish brick-walled space. No reservations.

Caffe 817 (☎ 510-271-7965; www.cafe817.com; 817 Washington St; breakfast $4-9, lunch $7-8; 7:30am-3pm Mon-Fri, 8:30am-3pm Sat; 12th St) Bowls of steaming café au lait, poached eggs *en croute* (in pastry) and crunchy baguette sandwiches – if you're looking for Paris in Oakland, you'll find it at this deliciously unpretentious sidewalk cafe.

Everett & Jones Barbeque (☎ 510-663-2350; www.eandjbbq.com; 126 Broadway; lunch $7-9, dinner $12-20; 11am-10pm Sun-Thu, to midnight Fri & Sat; 12th St) The smoked pork ribs are damn good at this simple, family-run spot with plastic red-checked tablecloths, occasional live music and slow service (stick around, it's worth it).

Shan Dong (☎ 510-839-2299; http://sd.222.to; 328 10th St; dishes $8-12; 10am-9:30pm Mon-Thu, to 10pm Fri-Sun; 12th St) Hand-cut sesame noodles, giant pork buns, fresh dumplings – you can't go wrong at this authentic Mandarin hole-in-the-wall with plastic chairs and fluorescent lighting. This is the real deal, so don't expect fortune cookies, which are American in origin.

Drinking

Heinold's First & Last Chance Saloon (☎ 510-839-6761; 56 Jack London Sq; 3-10pm Mon-Thu, to 1am Fri & Sat, from 10am Sun; 12th St) Heinold's is tilted from age and earthquakes (hold onto your beer), but its real claim to fame is that author Jack London was a regular – he even brought his school books to study here when he was a kid.

Ruby Room (☎ 510-444-7224; 132 14th St; 5pm-2am Mon-Sat, from 9pm Sun; Lake Merritt) Two red flood-lights are the only clues that this dive exists. Bartenders pour wicked-strong drinks, DJs spin pop to punk, and the red lighting makes everyone look hot.

Kona Club (☎ 510-654-7100; 4401 Piedmont Ave; 2pm-2am; 59 AC Transit) Despite the tiki bar's return to vogue, there ain't many around, which is why we love Kona. Think low-fi tiki – no pineapple-shaped glasses or torches, but rattan walls, a good pool table and paper cocktail umbrellas compensate.

Entertainment

Cafe Van Kleef (☎ 510-763-7711; www.cafevankleef.com; 1621 Telegraph Ave; 4pm-2am Mon-Fri, 6pm-2am Sat; 19th St) Every square inch of wall space is covered with knickknacks and garage-sale leftovers at this Oakland staple, which has live music on weekends, lip-smacking freshly squeezed Greyhounds (gin and grapefruit) and a party-down crowd.

Yoshi's (☎ 510-238-9200; www.yoshis.com; 510 Embarcadero West; shows $15-30; lunch & dinner; 12th St) The Bay Area's leading jazz club books a full calendar of talent from around the world. There's a pretty good sushi restaurant and full bar, but the real draws are the cavernous jazz lounge, awesome acoustics and top-flight acts.

Uptown (☎ 510-451-8100; www.uptownnightclub.com; 1928 Telegraph Ave; admission varies; 19th St) Local rock bands and occasional celebs play this mammoth bar with a big outdoor smoking patio. You never know who might appear – Green Day came unannounced in 2009. Schedule varies; call ahead.

Paramount Theatre (☎ 510-465-6400; www.paramounttheatre.com; 2025 Broadway; 19th St) This gorgeously restored art deco theater is fabulous from every angle; check out the gentlemen's smoking room and the ladies' chamber. In any given month there'll be rock concerts (Morrissey, Nelly Furtado), the Oakland Symphony or stand-up comedy. Tours ($5, starting at 10am) are on the first and third Saturdays of the month.

Grand Lake Theater (☎ 510-452-3556; www.renaissancerialto.com; 3200 Grand Ave; adult/child $9.50/6.50; 12 AC Transit) One of the last remaining 1920s movie palaces to show first-run films. On Friday and Saturday evenings, certain films are preceded by performances on the mighty Wurlitzer organ (check the website).

Stork Club (☎ 510-444-6174; http://storkcluboakland.com; 2330 Telegraph Ave; admission $5; shows 9pm; 59 AC Transit) It seems every budding Bay Area indie-rock band plays the Stork at least once. The crowd skews young and loves loud bands.

Alley (☎ 510-444-8505; 3325 Grand Ave; 11am-2am; 58 AC Transit) The Alley draws a wacky mix of hams and crooners, who come to sing by the piano (Tuesday to Saturday evenings). No beer on tap, but cocktails are stroooong.

Sleeping

Waterfront Hotel (☎ 510-836-3800; www.waterfronthoteloakland.com; Jack London Sq; r $129-199; 12th St;) Best rooms overlook the bay at this spiffy nautical-themed hotel, with granite baths, big-screen TVs and ultra-comfy beds with feather pillows. Kids love the outdoor heated pool. Excellent service.

Washington Inn (☎ 510-452-1776; www.thewashingtoninn.com; 495 10th St; r $99-169; 12th St;) A 1913 Victorian hotel with up-to-date amenities, spotless baths and good beds. The website makes it look (much) fancier than it is, but it's clean, safe, inexpensive and friendly.

BERKELEY

With over 30,000 students and enough Nobel Prize winners to give the Swedish Academy its reason for being, the University of California is what makes Berkeley more than a picturesque bedroom community. Intellectual inquiry and political discourse are part of everyday conversation. For an idea of what Berkeley stands for (or doesn't), get stuck in the town's maddening traffic, tune in to KPFA 91.4FM (Berkeley's 'free-speech radio') and scope out the parade of bumper stickers. Some are the usual rallying calls, like 'If You're Not Outraged, You're Not Paying Attention,' but you'll occasionally spot counter-counterculture knee-slappers, like 'If We're Not Supposed to Eat Animals, Why Are They Made of Meat?' You're nothing in Berkeley without an opinion. Much of the student culture concentrates on a few grungy blocks of Telegraph Ave, immediately south of the university campus.

The number one reason to visit Berkeley is hedonistic: some plan their entire California trip around dinner at Chez Panisse (p274) in the 'Gourmet Ghetto' at the northern end of Shattuck Ave – the counterpoint to Telegraph Ave's grunge.

Cesar Chavez Park and the Berkeley Marina sit side by side at the western end of University Ave, and provide panoramic water-level bay views. Unleashed dogs sniff the grass, while shorebirds squawk overhead, defending their airspace against kites.

Information

Berkeley Convention & Visitors Bureau (☎ 510-549-7040, 800-847-4823; www.visitberkeley.com; 2015 Center St; 9am-5pm Mon-Fri; Downtown Berkeley) This friendly bureau has free visitors' packets and also sells the useful book *41 Walking Tours of Berkeley* ($7.50).

Moe's (☎ 510-849-2087; 2476 Telegraph Ave; Downtown Berkeley) Founded at the height of the beatnik era, this bookstore provides four packed floors of new and used books.

Visitor Services Center (☎ 510-642-5215; www.berkeley.edu/visitors; 101 University Hall, 2200 University Ave; 8:30am-4:30pm Mon-Fri; Downtown Berkeley) Pick up campus maps and information. Provides free 90-minute campus tours at 10am Monday to Saturday, and 1pm Sunday – from Monday to Friday meet at the Visitor Services Center, on Saturday and Sunday meet at the Campanile (see below).

Sights

The campus of the **University of California, Berkeley** – aka 'Cal' – is California's oldest university. The college was founded in 1866, and the first students arrived in 1873. Today UCB has over 30,000 students and more than 1000 professors. From Telegraph Ave, enter the campus via Sproul Plaza and Sather Gate, ground zero for people-watching, soapbox oration and pseudo-tribal drumming. Alternatively, enter from Center and Oxford Sts, near the Downtown BART station.

The **Campanile** (elevator rides $2; 10am-4pm Mon-Fri, to 5pm Sat, to 1:30pm & 3-5pm Sun; Downtown

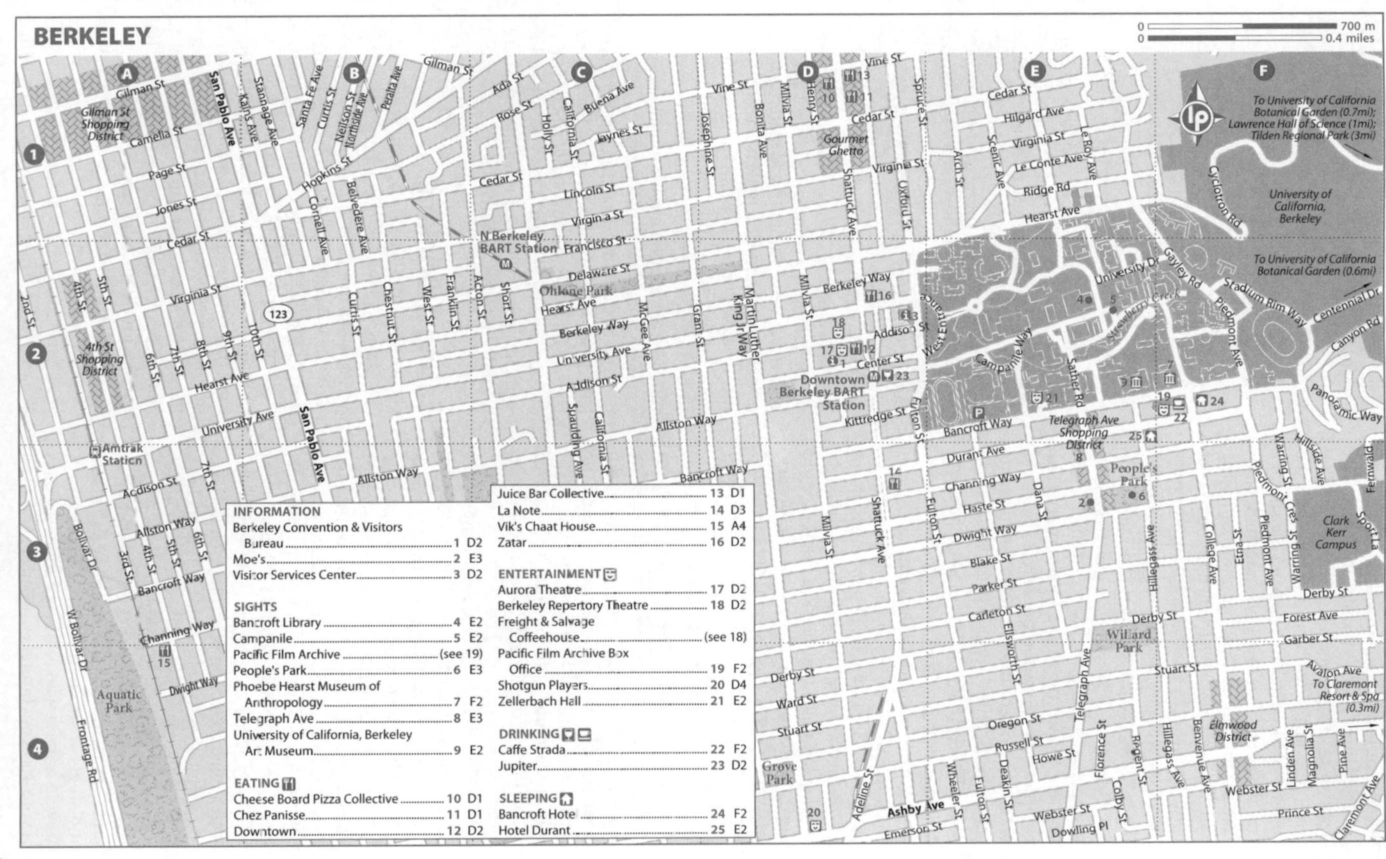
BERKELEY
0 700 m
0 0.4 miles
To University of California Botanical Garden (0.7mi); Lawrence Hall of Science (1mi); Tilden Regional Park (3mi)
University of California, Berkeley
To University of California Botanical Garden (0.6mi)
To Claremont Resort & Spa (0.3mi)
Gilman St Shopping District
4th St Shopping District
Gourmet Ghetto
Telegraph Ave Shopping District
Elmwood District
N Berkeley BART Station
Downtown Berkeley BART Station
Amtrak Station
Ohlone Park
People's Park
Willard Park
Grove Park
Aquatic Park
Clark Kerr Campus
Gilman St
Camelia St
Page St
Jones St
Cedar St
Virginia St
Hearst Ave
University Ave
Addison St
Allston Way
Bancroft Way
Channing Way
Dwight Way
San Pablo Ave
Kains Ave
Stannage Ave
Santa Fe Ave
Curtis St
Neilson St
Northside Ave
Peralta Ave
Hopkins St
Cornell Ave
Belvedere Ave
Chestnut St
West St
Franklin St
Acton St
Short St
Ada St
Rose St
Holly St
California St
Buena Ave
Jaynes St
Lincoln St
Francisco St
Delaware St
Berkeley Way
McGee Ave
Spaulding Ave
Grant St
Martin Luther King Jr Way
Josephine St
Bonita Ave
Milvia St
Henry St
Vine St
Shattuck Ave
Oxford St
Spruce St
Arch St
Scenic Ave
Hilgard Ave
Le Conte Ave
Le Roy Ave
Ridge Rd
Cyclotron Rd
University Dr
Gayley Rd
Stadium Rim Way
Centennial Dr
Canyon Rd
Piedmont Ave
Panoramic Way
Strawberry Creek
West Entrance
Campanile Way
Sather Rd
Center St
Kittredge St
Fulton St
Durant Ave
Haste St
Blake St
Parker St
Carleton St
Derby St
Ward St
Stuart St
Oregon St
Russell St
Howe St
Ellsworth St
Dana St
Telegraph Ave
Florence St
Regent St
Colby St
Hillegass Ave
Benvenue Ave
College Ave
Etna St
Warring St
Piedmont Cres
Hillside Ave
Fernwald
Sport La
Forest Ave
Garber St
Avalon Ave
Webster St
Linden Ave
Magnolia St
Pine Ave
Prince St
Claremont Ave
Ashby Ave
Adeline St
Wheeler St
Deakin St
Emerson St
Dowling Pl
2nd St
3rd St
4th St
5th St
6th St
7th St
8th St
9th St
10th St
Bolivar Dr
W Bolivar Dr
Frontage Rd
123
INFORMATION
Berkeley Convention & Visitors Bureau 1 D2
Moe's 2 E3
Visitor Services Center 3 D2
SIGHTS
Bancroft Library 4 E2
Campanile 5 E2
Pacific Film Archive (see 19)
People's Park 6 E3
Phoebe Hearst Museum of Anthropology 7 F2
Telegraph Ave 8 E3
University of California, Berkeley Art Museum 9 E2
EATING
Cheese Board Pizza Collective 10 D1
Chez Panisse 11 D1
Downtown 12 D2
Juice Bar Collective 13 D1
La Note 14 D3
Vik's Chaat House 15 A4
Zatar 16 D2
ENTERTAINMENT
Aurora Theatre 17 D2
Berkeley Repertory Theatre 18 D2
Freight & Salvage Coffeehouse (see 18)
Pacific Film Archive Box Office 19 F2
Shotgun Players 20 D4
Zellerbach Hall 21 E2
DRINKING
Caffe Strada 22 F2
Jupiter 23 D2
SLEEPING
Bancroft Hotel 24 F2
Hotel Durant 25 E2

Berkeley), officially named Sather Tower, was modeled on St Mark's Basilica in Venice. The 328ft spire offers knockout views of the Bay Area, and at the top you can stare into the carillon of 61 bells, ranging from the size of a cereal bowl to that of a Volkswagen. Recitals take place daily at 7:50am, noon and 6pm, with a longer piece performed on Sunday at 2pm. The University of California, Berkeley Art Museum (☎ 510-642-0808; www.bampfa.berkeley.edu; 2626 Bancroft Way; adult/child, student & senior $8/5; 🕑 11am-5pm Wed-Sun; Ⓜ Downtown Berkeley) has 11 galleries showcasing a wide range of works, from ancient Chinese to cutting-edge contemporary. The complex also houses a bookstore, cafe and sculpture garden, and the much-loved avant-garde Pacific Film Archive (opposite).

The Bancroft Library (☎ 510-642-3781; http://bancroft.berkeley.edu; 🕑 9am-5pm Mon-Fri; Ⓜ Downtown Berkeley) houses, among other gems, a copy of Shakespeare's First Folio and the records of the Donner Party. Its small public exhibits of historical California include the surprisingly small gold nugget that sparked the 1849 Gold Rush. You must register to use the library, be over 18 (or a high-school graduate) and present two forms of identification (one with photo). Visit the registration desk on entering. In Kroeber Hall, the Phoebe Hearst Museum of Anthropology (☎ 510-643-7648; http://hearstmuseum.berkeley.edu; admission free; 🕑 10am-4:30pm Wed-Sat, noon-4pm Sun; Ⓜ Downtown Berkeley) showcases the diversity of human cultures from around the world, with artifacts from ancient Peru, Egypt and Africa, among others. There's also a large collection highlighting native California cultures.

Uphill from the campus, the University of California Botanical Garden (☎ 510-643-2755; http://botanicalgarden.berkeley.edu; 200 Centennial Dr; adult/child/senior $7/2/5, first Thu of month admission free; 🕑 9am-5pm, closed 1st Tue of month) has one of the most varied collections in the USA. Pick up a self-guided tour at the gift shop. Further up the same road, Lawrence Hall of Science (☎ 510-642-5132; http://lhs.berkeley.edu; Centennial Dr; adult/child 3-4yr/senior & student $11/6/9; 🕑 10am-5pm) educates and entertains with a huge collection of displays, from lasers to earthquakes to a climbable 60ft model of a DNA molecule.

Telegraph Ave is the throbbing heart of Berkeley's studentville, with a constant flow of shoppers, vagrants and vendors, brisk walkers and sluggish strollers. Expect an odd mix of greying hippies who reminisce about the days of yore, too-cool hipsters who sneer at tie-dyed nostalgia, ponytailed panhandlers pressing you for change, and street vendors hawking everything from crystals to bumper stickers to self-published books. It's not for everyone – some find it trashy and obnoxious – but when you're on the hunt for books, maps and CDs, this is the place. Amoeba and Rasputin carry some of the Bay Area's most diverse collections of music.

TRANSPORTATION: BERKELEY

Distance from San Francisco 14 miles

Direction Northeast

Travel time 20 to 30 minutes

Car Bay Bridge to I-80 East; take the University Ave exit

BART Downtown Berkeley BART station is most convenient

Just east of Telegraph Ave, People's Park (btwn Haste St & Dwight Way; 🚌 1 AC Transit) rose to fame in the late '60s as the epicenter of political battles between students and state-and-local law enforcement. The park has since served mostly as an unofficial day room for Berkeley's homeless. A publicly funded restoration somewhat spruced it up, and occasional festivals still happen here, but really it's just a mangy patch of trampled grass.

For a better park, head to Tilden Regional Park (☎ 510-562-7275; www.ebparks.org), in the Berkeley hills, which has hiking trails, picnic areas, swimming at Lake Anza, and plenty of kids stuff, like pony rides and a steam train. There's a small fee for most activities.

Eating & Drinking

Chez Panisse (☎ 510-548-5525; www.chezpanisse.com; 1517 Shattuck Ave; cafe $18-25, prix-fixe restaurant $65-95; 🕑 cafe lunch & dinner Mon-Sat, restaurant dinner Mon-Sat; 🚌 7, 9, 43 AC Transit) The temple of Alice Waters – doyenne of California cuisine – remains at the pinnacle of Bay Area dining. Book one month ahead for the legendary prix-fixe meals downstairs in the cozy Craftsman-style dining room. Note: there are no variations to the daily restaurant menu. If you'd prefer to choose, book a table at the less-expensive but equally lovely upstairs cafe.

Cheese Board Pizza Collective (☎ 510-549-3055; www.cheeseboardcollective.coop; 1512 Shattuck Ave; pizza slice $2.50; 🕑 11:30am-3pm & 4:30-8pm Tue-Sat; 🚌 7, 9, 43 AC Transit) A Gourmet Ghetto mainstay, with a fantastic variety of artisanal cheeses and killer goat-cheese pizzas.

Vik's Chaat Corner (☎ 510-644-4432; 2390 4th St; meals under $8; 🕒 11am-6pm Tue-Fri, to 8pm Sat & Sun; 🚌 9, 19, 51 AC Transit) Our favorite Berkeley cheap-eats serves all freshly made Indian classics (no tikka masala here) that you order at the counter. Daily specials include chicken, fish and lamb curries served with all the trimmings for a mere $6 to $8.

La Note (☎ 510-843-1535; www.lanoterestaurant.com; 2377 Shattuck Ave; mains $10-13; 🕒 8am-2:30pm; Ⓑ Downtown Berkeley) A good spot to fuel up before exploring, La Note serves a French-cafe menu of omelettes and pancakes at breakfast, and *croques monsieurs*, Niçoise salads and baguette sandwiches at lunch.

Juice Bar Collective (☎ 510-548-8473; http://thejuicebar.org; 2114 Vine St; dishes $3-6; 🕒 10am-4:30pm; 🚌 7, 9, 43 AC Transit) A tiny storefront cafe, Juice Bar makes tasty polenta pizzas, quiches, sandwiches and dee-lish smoothies.

Downtown (☎ 510-649-3810; www.downtownrestaurant.com; 2102 Shattuck Ave; dishes $8-16, mains $17-26; Ⓑ Downtown Berkeley) Smack in downtown, this is an ideal spot to start an evening. While the California fare is solidly good, it's not particularly innovative, but the bar makes great cocktails and the tasty appetizers appeal to peckish eaters who don't want to fill up before a performance.

Caffe Strada (☎ 510-843-5282; 2300 College Ave; 🕒 7am-midnight; 🚌 7, 51 AC Transit) University students get wired on caffeine on the giant outdoor patio and study, ardently talk philosophy or make eyes at each other. Good pastries.

Zatar (☎ 510-841-1981; www.zatarrestaurant.com; 1981 Shattuck Ave; lunch mains $8-14, dinner mains $22-26; 🕒 lunch Fri, dinner Wed-Sat; 🚌 51 AC Transit) Zatar's mishmash Mediterranean–Middle Eastern cooking spans Morocco to Iran. We like the bold spicing, homemade Iranian bread and fresh ingredients – many from the restaurant's own organic garden – but the food's pricey and a tad precious.

For the best social introduction to Berkeley's bar scene, head to the back patio at Jupiter (☎ 510-843-8277; 2181 Shattuck Ave; Ⓑ Downtown Berkeley).

Entertainment

Aurora Theatre (☎ 510-843-4822; www.auroratheatre.org; 2081 Addison St; Ⓑ Downtown Berkeley) The audience surrounds the stage on three sides, putting you close to the actors. Expect classics by playwrights such as Edward Albee and new works by up-and-coming artists.

Berkeley Repertory Theatre (☎ 510-845-4700; www.berkeleyrep.org; 2025 Addison St; Ⓑ Downtown Berkeley) Some San Franciscans cross the bay for only one reason: top-notch professional theater at Berkeley Rep.

Shotgun Players (☎ 510-841-6500; www.shotgunplayers.org; 1901 Ashby Ave; Ⓑ Ashby) The first solar-powered theater in the US mounts innovative new plays by leading Bay Area playwrights and classics by Shakespeare and Stoppard.

Freight & Salvage Coffeehouse (☎ 510-548-1761; www.freightandsalvage.org; 2020 Addison St; admission $5-22; Ⓑ Downtown Berkeley) Smart programming explores the regional styles of traditional, acoustic world music. Think fiddle, folk, strings and soul. No alcohol.

Pacific Film Archive (☎ 510-642-1124; www.bampfa.berkeley.edu; 2575 Bancroft Way; adult/child & senior $8/5; Ⓑ Downtown Berkeley) The PFA is internationally renowned for daily screenings that explore the art of film-making, including rare, new and historic prints from around the globe. The box office (☎ 11am-5pm) is at 2621 Durant Ave.

Zellerbach Hall (☎ 510-642-9988; www.calperfs.berkeley.edu; UC campus; Ⓑ Downtown Berkeley) The concrete-box acoustics inside this vintage-1970s hall are terrible for non-amplified classical, but Zellerbach is the premier East Bay stage, and it showcases top-flight dance and music performances by international ensembles.

Sleeping

Basic and midrange motels are clustered west of campus along University Ave. The Berkeley & Oakland Bed & Breakfast Network hotline (☎ 510-547-6380; www.bbonline.com/ca/berkeley-oakland) provides information on private homes for rent, from garden cottages to grand houses.

Claremont Resort & Spa (☎ 510-843-3000, 800-551-7266; www.claremontresort.com; 41 Tunnel Rd; r $229-420, ste from $369; 🚌 9 AC Transit; 📶 🏊 👶) The grand 1915 Claremont sits perched on the sunny Oakland hills and has gorgeous views. Rooms are upmarket business-class. The full-service spa merits a special trip.

Hotel Durant (☎ 510-845-8981, 800-238-7268; www.hoteldurant.com; 2600 Durant Ave; r $135-180; 🚌 7, 51 AC Transit; 📶) A 2008 renovation of this 140-room, 1920s hotel makes it downtown's spiffiest, with fabulous beds and fun details like bong lamps – and it's green-certified.

Caveats: some rooms are tiny; request a large one. Upper-floor '05 rooms have bay views. Corners have the best air circulation. There's a great bar downstairs, but ensure your room isn't above it.

Bancroft Hotel (☎ 510-549-1000, 800-549-1002; www.bancrofthotel.com; 2680 Bancroft Way; r $149; 🚌 51 AC Transit) Traditional Berkeley at its best. This lovely 1928 Craftsman hotel has 22 simple, homey rooms that need updating, but they're comfy. No elevator.

MARIN COUNTY

Majestic redwoods cling to coastal bluffs while the thundering surf bludgeons new shapes into the cliffs. Miles of verdant trails crisscross the county's west side, from Point Reyes National Seashore, through Muir Woods and up Mt Tamalpais State Park. Wine Country (p282) is a few freeway exits away, and even the furthest reaches of the county are within an hour's drive of San Francisco. In the 1950s, a small group of Marinites blocked freeway construction up the coast and over Mt Tamalpais, and in doing so, preserved the spectacular landscape from development. Today, Marinites pride themselves on living the good life – Marin is the USA's 11th-wealthiest county. Old-timers who got in before the booms of the 1970s and 1990s are a mishmash of ranchers, country folk and aging back-to-the-landers; newcomers pay a million or more for the privilege of settling here. On their surfaces the small towns look like idyllic hamlets, but shops cater to cosmopolitan tastes – no sane Marin restaurateur would dream of serving conventionally farmed produce. Marin's main drawback is traffic: rush-hour traffic is s-l-o-w over the Golden Gate. But it takes more than traffic to stop us from visiting every chance we get.

Orientation

Busy Hwy 101 heads north across the Golden Gate Bridge ($6 toll, southbound only), connecting the well-to-do communities of Sausalito, Larkspur and San Rafael. Bucolic Hwy 1 twists through sparsely populated West Marin, passing beauty spots like Muir Woods and Stinson Beach on its way to Point Reyes. (If you get carsick, beware Hwy 1. Eat crystalized ginger and wear motion-sickness pressure-point bracelets, or take Dramamine). Fuel up before heading towards the coast: once beyond Mill Valley, you won't find gas before Stinson Beach, then Point Reyes Station. Hwy 580 connects Marin with the East Bay via the Richmond–San Rafael Bridge ($4 toll, westbound traffic only) and meets Hwy 101 at Larkspur. Avoid freeways during rush hour.

Information

Marin County Convention & Visitors Bureau (☎ 866-925-2060, 415-925-2060; www.visitmarin.org; Suite B, 1 Mitchell Blvd, San Rafael; 🕑 9am-5pm Mon-Fri) Handles tourist information for the entire county.

Sausalito Visitors Center (☎ 415-332-0505; 780 Bridgeway Blvd; 🕑 11:30am-4pm Tue-Sun) Offers local information and great historical exhibits.

TRANSPORTATION: MARIN COUNTY

Distance from San Francisco Marin Headlands 10 miles; Sausalito 12 miles; Mt Tamalpais 14 miles

Direction North

Travel time 20 minutes to Marin Headlands; 30 minutes to Sausalito; 40 minutes to Mt Tamalpais

Car Take the Alexander Ave exit immediately after the Golden Gate Bridge. For Marin Headlands, cut left under the freeway. Turn right on Conzelman Rd, immediately before the southbound bridge entrance. For Muir Woods and Mt Tamalpais, continue north on Hwy 101 to the Hwy 1 exit (to Mt Tam follow signs to Panoramic Hwy, then exit on Pan Toll Rd and follow signs to Mt Tamalpais). For Sausalito, take the Alexander Ave exit and bear right.

Bus Muni bus 76 operates a Sunday service to Marin Headlands. Golden Gate Transit bus 10 runs from downtown SF to Sausalito, but take the ferry.

Bicycle Cross the Golden Gate Bridge and head uphill on Conzelman Rd for Marin Headlands, down Alexander Ave into Bridgeway for Sausalito.

Ferry Golden Gate Ferries run between the Ferry Building in SF to Sausalito and Larkspur in Marin County. Blue & Gold Ferries run from Pier 39 to Sausalito, Angel Island and Tiburon.

MARIN HEADLANDS

Immediately northwest of the Golden Gate Bridge, the rugged natural beauty of the Marin Headlands stands in stark contrast to downtown San Francisco's towers, visible across the bay. Once you're hiking atop the rolling hills, beyond earshot of cars, you'll hear only the ocean crashing on craggy beaches and the wind whooshing through tall grass. With winter's rains, the hills turn vibrant green; in summer they dry up and turn golden brown. The headlands make an ideal day trip. Plan to hike, picnic, walk or mountain bike; there's also limited camping.

Administered by the Golden Gate National Recreation Area, the headlands are free of development, except for the occasional fort and bunker, known as batteries, left over from a century of US military occupation. Some have been turned into park buildings. Immediately northwest of the bridge, explore the remains of the never-completed **Battery Spencer** (Conzelman Rd; admission free) and take snapshots of the famous view through the bridge cables towards downtown San Francisco. Pick up trail maps, field guides and historical information at the **Marin Headlands Visitors Center** (☎ 415-331-1540; www.nps.gov/goga; Bldg 948, Fort Barry; 9:30am-4:30pm).

Every fall, migratory birds and raptors – including hawks, falcons and eagles – soar overhead at **Hawk Hill** (www.ggro.org; Conzelman Rd; admission free). Because open water doesn't support the thermals that birds need to stay aloft, they use the headlands to gain altitude for the 2-mile crossing of the Golden Gate. Bring binoculars. Go 1.8 miles up Conzelman Rd, park along the road and walk up the west side of the hill; for a map and details on which birds are there now, see www.ggro.org. Near the end of Conzelman Rd is the still-operating 1855 **Point Bonita Lighthouse** (12:30-3:30pm Sat-Mon, free tours at 12:30pm), a breathtaking half-mile path from the parking area, ending at a suspension footbridge above the churning surf (acrophobes: beware). Looking west from the tip of Point Bonita, with the Pacific roiling around you, the distant city skyline looks out of place.

Marine Mammal Center (☎ 415-289-7325; www.tmmc.org; 4 Bunker Rd; admission free, donation suggested; 10am-5pm), on the hill above Rodeo Lagoon, is the largest marine mammal hospital in the world. In 2009 the center opened its all-green, solar-powered hospital, with observation decks for visitors to get close to the recovering patients (mostly seals and sea lions) before they're released back into the wild. Spring brings oh-so-cute new pups – and the most visitors. Kids love the hands-on exhibits and see-through glass walls to the science labs and animal rooms.

At the end of Bunker Rd sits black-sand **Rodeo Beach** (ro-*day*-oh), protected from the wind by cliffs.

Sleeping

HI Marin Headlands Hostel (☎ 415-331-2777; www.norcalhostels.org/marin; Bldg 941, Fort Barry; dm/r $24/66) Set amid towering eucalyptus trees, this friendly, ecosensitive hostel has two parts: the main building (formerly a military infirmary), location of 76 dorm beds; and the cozier annex (formerly officers' housing), location of most private rooms. Picture windows overlook the lush landscape. Good game room. Easy access to hiking.

There are four small campgrounds in the Marin Headlands; all require a short hike from the nearest parking. Note: bring waterproof gear to counter the nighttime fog. **Kirby Cove Campground** (☎ 800-365-2267; campsites $25; Apr-Oct) occupies a spectacular shady dell on the Golden Gate's west side, near the mouth of the bay; there's a small beach. Hawk, Bicentennial and Haypress campgrounds are inland; camping is free but must be reserved through **Marin Headlands Visitors Center** (☎ 415-331-1540; www.nps.gov/goga; Bldg 948, Fort Barry; 9:30am-4:30pm).

MUIR WOODS & MUIR BEACH

Coastal redwoods are the tallest living things on earth, and exist only on the California coast, from Santa Cruz to just over the Oregon border. Only 4% of the original forest remains, but you can explore a glorious old-growth stand at **Muir Woods National Monument** (☎ 415-388-2595; adults/under 16 $5/free; 8am-sunset, call ahead), 12 miles north of the Golden Gate Bridge. It gets crowded weekends, so come midweek if you can. Otherwise arrive in early morning or late afternoon, when tour buses leave. Even at busy times, a short hike gets you beyond the densest crowds, onto trails with mammoth trees and stunning vistas.

The 1-mile **Main Trail Loop** is easy, leading alongside Redwood Creek to 1000-year-old trees at **Cathedral Grove**; it returns via **Bohemian Grove**, where the park's tallest tree stands at 254ft. The **Dipsea Trail** is a strenuous 2-mile hike to the top of aptly named **Cardiac Hill**, but it's possibly the most beautiful hike for views – a half-mile steep grade through lush,

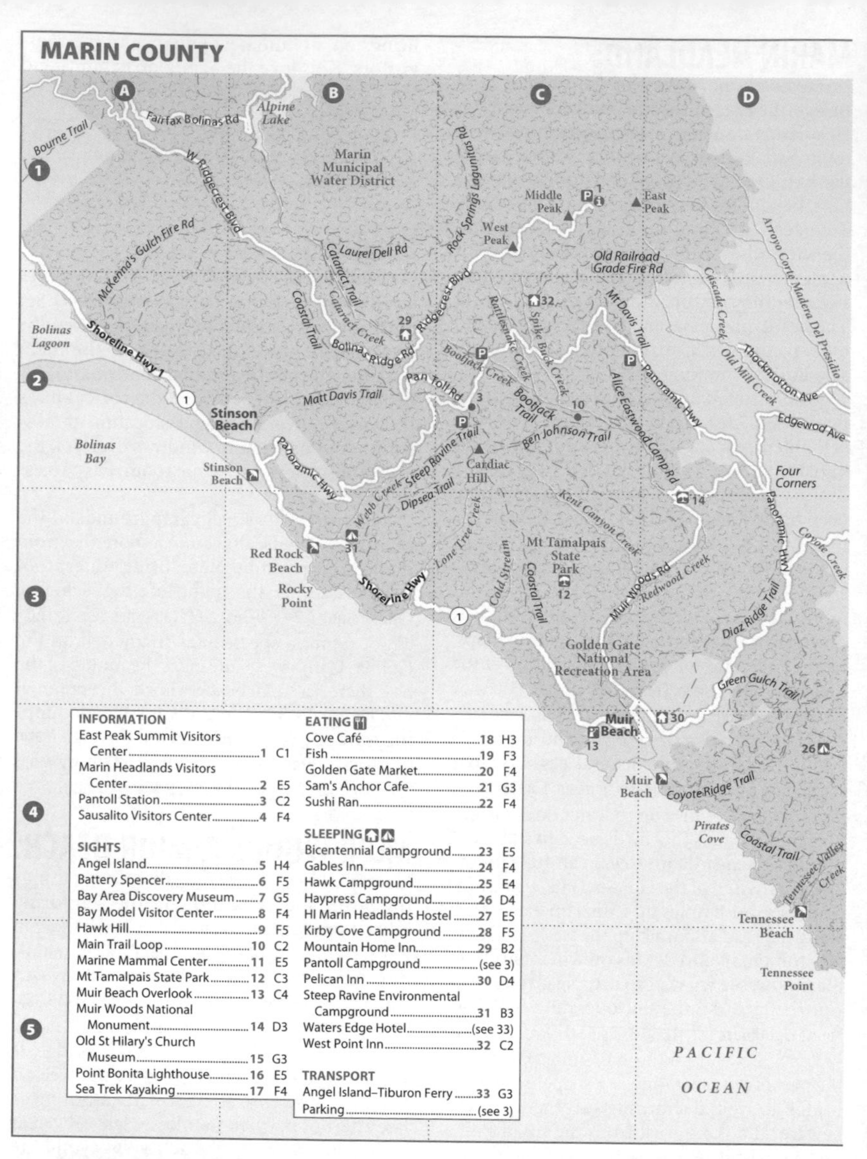

fern-fringed forest leads from the canyon to an exposed ridge, from which you can see Mt Tamalpais, the Pacific and San Francisco. Gorgeous. You can trek to Stinson Beach if you're up for a longer stint.

You can also walk down into Muir Woods via trails from Panoramic Hwy (such as Bootjack Trail, from Bootjack picnic area) or from Mt Tam's Pantoll Station campground (via Ben Johnson Trail).

The turnoff to **Muir Beach** from Hwy 1 is marked by the north coast's longest row of mailboxes (mileage-marker 5.7, just before Pelican Inn). Immediately north there are superb coastal views from the **Muir Beach Overlook**; during WWII scouts kept watch from the surrounding concrete lookouts for invading Japanese ships.

The oh-so-English Tudor-style **Pelican Inn** (☎ 415-383-6000; www.pelicaninn.com; 10 Pacific Way;

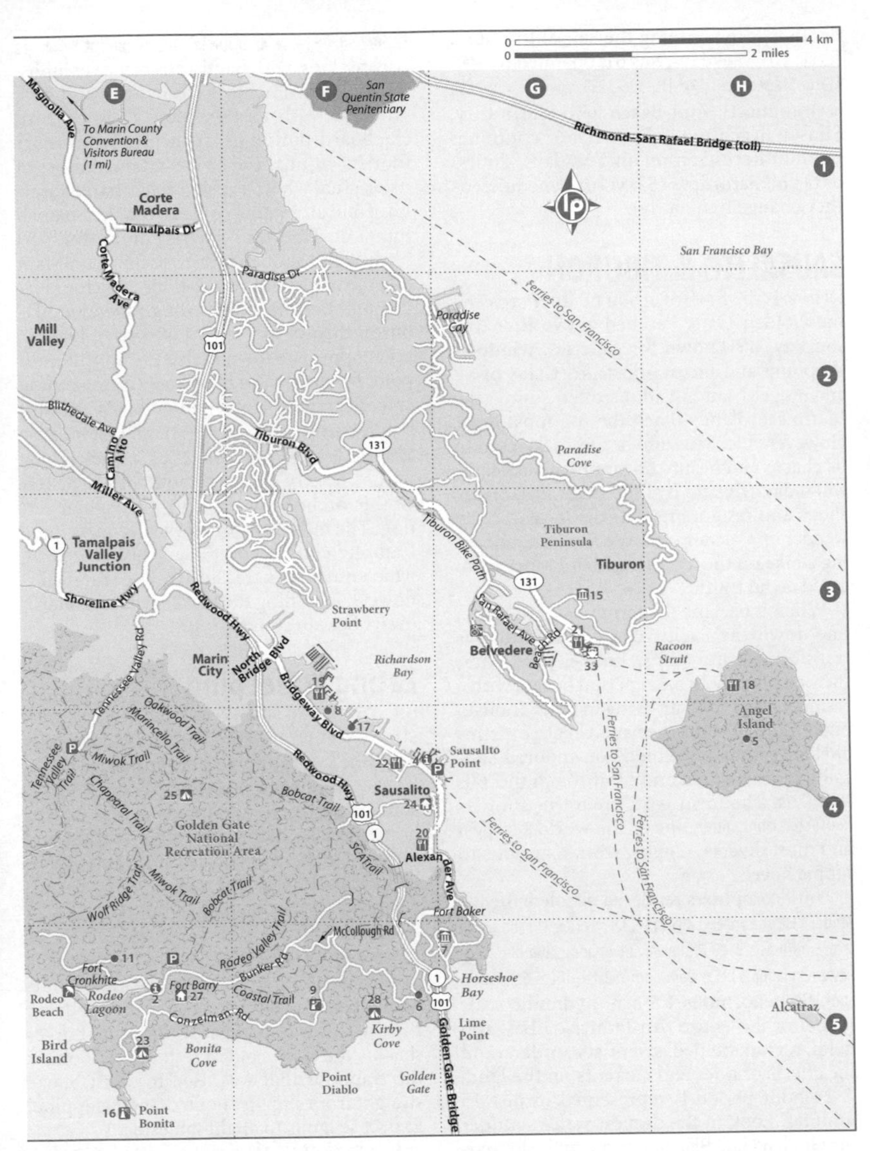

lunch $10-17, dinner $15-29) is Muir Beach's only commercial establishment. Hikers, cyclists and families come for pub lunches inside its timbered restaurant and cozy bar, perfect for a pint, a game of darts and warming up beside the open fire. The British fare is respectable, but nothing mind-blowing – it's the setting that's magical. Upstairs are seven luxe rooms (from $190), each individually decorated in Tudor style, with cushy half-canopy beds.

To get to Muir Woods, drive north on Hwy 101, exit at Hwy 1 and continue north along Hwy 1/Shoreline Hwy to the Panoramic Hwy (a right-hand fork). Continue for about 1 mile to Four Corners, where you turn left onto Muir Woods Rd (look for signs). In summer, Golden Gate Transit offers a daily shuttle service from the ferry in Sausalito to Muir Woods (adults $3, youth and seniors $1); purchase tickets at the SF ferry ticket booth before boarding the Sausalito-bound ferry. On weekdays, bus 61, operated by West Marin Stagecoach (☎ 415-526-3239; www.marintransit.org), connects Muir Beach with Marin City, Stinson Beach and Bolinas; bus 62 continues to Point Reyes Station on Tuesdays, Thursdays and Saturdays ($2; verify schedules, as they change frequently).

SAUSALITO & TIBURON

Sausalito is the first town you hit after crossing the Golden Gate. Perched above Richardson Bay, it's known for galleries, window-shopping and picture-postcard vistas of SF and Angel Island. And it's often sunny: the Marin Headlands block the fog most days. However cute, Sausalito becomes a victim of its charm and beauty on summer weekends, when day-trippers jam the sidewalks, pricey shops and restaurants. For the locals' scene, wander up Caledonia St. We recommend taking a bike on the ferry from San Francisco to avoid awful traffic.

When it became the terminus of the train line down the Pacific coast, Sausalito was transformed into a busy lumber port. After the war a new bohemian period began, with a resident artists colony living in 'arks' (houseboats moored along the bay). Creative genius Shel Silverstein lived on a non-moored Sausalito houseboat on and off through the '60s and '70s. The town is still renowned for its houseboat community, one of the world's largest and most diverse, ranging from mansions to hippie hovels.

Until computers rendered obsolete the Bay Model Visitor Center (☎ 415-332-3871; www.spn.usace.army.mil/bmvc; 2100 Bridgeway Blvd; admission free, suggested donation $3; 9am-4pm Tue-Fri, 10am-5pm Sat & Sun), this enormous 1.5-acre hydraulic scale model of the entire San Francisco Bay and delta region helped scientists understand the effects of tides and currents on the land. A 24-hour period is represented in just 15 minutes. Look in the deepest water – under the Golden Gate Bridge – to grasp the incredible force of tidal movement. To explore the actual bay yourself, consider renting a kayak with Sea Trek Kayaking (☎ Mon-Fri 415-332-8494, Sat & Sun 415-332-4465; www.seatrekkayak.com; 85 Liberty Ship Way, Sausalito; s/d for 1hr $20/35; 9am-5pm), which also guides monthly summertime trips ($85) to Angel Island. At Fort Baker, the Bay Area Discovery Museum (☎ 415-339-3900; www.baykidsmuseum.org; 557 McReynolds Rd, Sausalito; adult/child to 17yr $8.50/7.50; 9am-4pm Tue-Fri, 10am-5pm Sat & Sun) is cool for kids, with hands-on science exhibits, musical instruments, festivals and camps.

Tiburon, with its tiny Main St lined with clapboard buildings, is further from most tourists' minds, and so has retained more of its original wharf-rat character than Sausalito. Tiburon's name comes from the Spanish Punta de Tiburon – Shark Point – but you likely won't spot any. Browse shops on Main St, grab a bite and you've done Tiburon. Friday nights from May through October, Tiburon throws its Main St block party, kicking off at 6pm. The town is also the jumping-off point for nearby Angel Island. Commanding splendid views from its perch, Old St Hilary's Church Museum (☎ 415-435-1853; 201 Esperanza St; admission free; 1-4pm Wed & Sun, Apr-Oct) is one of the country's last examples of Carpenter Gothic architecture still in its original setting. The hillsides around the deconsecrated Catholic church comprise St Hilary's Preserve, which nurtures a treasure trove of rare wildflowers, including the black jewel and Marin dwarf flax. Best in spring.

Eating & Sleeping

Fish (☎ 415-331-3474; 350 Harbor Dr, Sausalito; mains $12-30; 11:30am-8:30pm;) This kid-friendly dockside joint at the end of Harbor Dr hooks locals with sustainable, line-caught fish – some from their own boats – and down-home details, like picnic-table seating and Mason-jar glasses. Sustainability and organics have their price: the Saigon salmon sandwich will set you back $22 – but it's worth it. No credit cards.

Sam's Anchor Cafe (☎ 415-435-4527; 27 Main St, Tiburon; dishes $10-25;) Everyone wants an outdoor table, but you can't reserve the bay-front patio at this way-popular seafood and burger shack – the town's oldest restaurant (look for the trapdoor that was used to spirit booze straight from ship to saloon). Good cioppino. Expect seagulls to alight tableside.

Sushi Ran (☎ 415-332-3620; www.sushiran.com; 107 Caledonia St, Sausalito; dishes $5-17; lunch Mon-Fri, dinner daily) One of the Bay Area's top sushi spots. A wine and sake bar ease the pain of long waits – and perhaps the bill.

Golden Gate Market (☎ 415-332-3040; 221 2nd St, Sausalito; 8am-9pm Mon-Sat, 9am-7pm Sun) Grab deli sandwiches, cheese and wine for picnics at this grocery/deli/liquor store on the town's south side.

Gables Inn (☎ 415-289-1100, 800-966-1554; www.gablesinnsausalito.com; 62 Princess St, Sausalito; r $155-495; 📶) All nine cozy B&B rooms in this swank historic home have massive baths; the more expensive have Jacuzzis, fireplaces and balconies with spectacular views. Breakfast and evening wine included.

Waters Edge Hotel (☎ 415-789-5999; www.marinhotels.com/waters.html; 25 Main St, Tiburon; r $159-499; 📶) This smart 23-unit hotel extends over the bay, with a variety of room types and amenities. All have crisp white bedspreads and balconies (limited views, except in suites), and some have fireplaces. Those with wood ceilings are most atmospheric. Complimentary in-room breakfast and evening wine and cheese.

MT TAMALPAIS

Though officially pronounced *ta*-mul-*pie*-us, everyone calls it 'Mt Tam.' To get here, head north along Hwy 1. You can ascend the summit by car, but hiking or biking is the best way to see it.

A popular recreational area since the mid-1800s, the mountain got a now-defunct rail line in 1907 for easy access from Mill Valley to Mt Tam's highest point, **East Peak** (2571ft). The track's 281 curves earned it the reputation of being the crookedest railroad in the world. Now it's long gone, but hikers can still walk 2 miles to the railway's westernmost point to stay at the rustic 1904 West Point Inn (right). On a clear day the view sweeps the East Bay, parts of SF, the Marin Headlands, one tower of the Golden Gate Bridge, and the Pacific – big payoff for your hike.

The 6300 hill-and-dale acres of **Mt Tamalpais State Park** (☎ 415-388-2070; www.mttam.net; 801 Panoramic Hwy) were formed in 1928 from land donated by naturalist William Kent; deer, foxes and bobcats rustle deep in the trees and scurry over the trails. Multitudes of hikers, bikers and horseback riders traverse the park's 50 miles of paths, including the old railroad grade, but the park is so expansive it doesn't feel crowded. You may find yourself wandering secluded unmarked trails or accidentally hiking up towards West Peak, an abandoned air-force radar facility. The trails connect with a larger 200-mile trail system on adjacent parklands.

Get information and pick up the free park map at **Pantoll Station** (☎ 415-388-2070; 801 Panoramic Hwy), the state park's headquarters, just past Mt Home Inn and Bootjack on Panoramic Hwy (watch carefully or you'll miss the turnoff). Overnight parking is available. You can day-hike from here – it's a beautiful 8.5-mile climb to East Peak Summit and back – or drive 4.2 miles along Ridgecrest Blvd to the East Peak Summit Visitors Center (parking $6), then climb the remaining quarter-mile to the summit.

From Pantoll Station, Steep Ravine Trail follows a wooded creek to the coast (about 2.1 miles each way). For a longer hike, veer right after 1.5 miles onto the Dipsea Trail, which meanders through woods for a mile before ending at Stinson Beach.

Mountain-biking was made famous on Mt Tam in the '70s. When you kick up gravel flying downhill, though, know that strict speed limits of 15mph (5mph around blind curves) are enforced, and access is limited to fire roads – no single-track riding allowed. Violations cost up to $250.

Sleeping

Mountain Home Inn (☎ 415-381-9000; www.mtnhomeinn.com; 810 Panoramic Hwy; r $195-345; 📶) Set atop a ridgeline amid redwood, spruce and pines, Mountain Home is perfect for a romantic, woodsy retreat. All 10 rooms face east and most have balconies and fireplaces. Some are tiny, but cozy nonetheless. No TVs. Full breakfast. Its restaurant serves brunch ($10 to 20) and dinner (prix fixe $38) from Wednesday to Sunday.

West Point Inn (☎ 24hr reservations 415-646-0702, inn 415-388-9955; www.westpointinn.com; 1000 Panoramic Hwy; r adult/under 18yr $50/25) Pack your own food, sleeping bag and towels, and bring a flashlight – there's no electricity at this rustic, charming 1904 inn. Hike-in only. No same-day reservations.

Pantoll Campground (☎ 415-388-2070; 801 Panoramic Hwy; campsites $25) Eight trails depart from this forested campground, with 16 walk-in sites, 100yd from parking. Each has a fire pit and grill. Flush toilets and drinking water are nearby, and there's firewood for sale. Arrive early! First-come, first-served.

Steep Ravine Environmental Campground (☎ reservations 800-444-7275, info 415-388-2070; 801 Panoramic Hwy; campsites/cabins $25/100) One of the Bay Area's premier campgrounds lies 1 mile south of Stinson Beach, with drop-dead ocean views from a high promontory. Book rustic five-person cabins seven months ahead; campsites are easier to snag, but coveted nonetheless.

ANGEL ISLAND

Rising from the middle of the bay, Angel Island (☎ 415-435-5390; www.angelisland.org) was devastated by a 2008 fire that burned 300 of the park's 740 acres. As you explore this domed beauty, all around you'll spot signs of the land repairing itself. You can spread out a picnic in a protected cove overlooking the close but immeasurably distant urban surroundings, or explore the island on foot or bicycle. The island has served as a military base, immigration station, WWII Japanese internment camp and Nike missile site, leaving it some interesting and thought-provoking forts, exhibits and bunkers to explore.

There are 13 miles of hiking trails and 8 miles of bike paths around the island, including a hike to the summit of 781ft Mt Livermore (no bikes) and a 5-mile perimeter trail. Wednesday to Sunday, the Immigration Station and its detention barracks, which operated from 1910 through to 1940, are open for tours, but you must buy tickets (adult/child $7/5) in advance or on arrival, near the ferry dock at the Cove Café in Ayala Cove. Camp Reynolds, the East Garrison Chapel and the Guard House at Fort McDowell sometimes offer guided tours.

To get here, take the Angel Island–Tiburon Ferry (☎ 415-435-2131; www.angelislandferry.com; 21 Main St, Tiburon; round-trip adult/child/bike $13.50/11.50/1). It runs from Tiburon four times daily midweek and eight times on weekends.

Eating & Sleeping

Cove Café (☎ 415-435-3392; Ayala Cove; 🕒 during ferry-operating hrs, roughly 10:30am-3pm, to 4pm summer weekends) This snack bar sells hot dogs, ice cream and barbecued oysters. Rent bicycles for $10 per hour or $35 per day. Cash only.

Book campsites through www.angelisland.org or Reserve America (☎ 800-444-7275; www.reserveamerica.com). All are walk-in only, so be prepared to lug your stuff a mile from the ferry. The camping fee is $30.

ALERT: PARKS MAY BE TERMINATED

To balance California's catastrophic budget mess, Governor Arnold Schwarzenegger has twice proposed the closure of California state parks that don't turn a profit – among them Mt Tamalpais and Angel Island. As of this writing, the California State Parks Foundation (www.calparks.org) was again spearheading a letter-writing campaign to block the closures. It worked once, and we hope it will work a second time. Before visiting a state park, call or refer to the state park website at www.parks.ca.gov to ensure the park is open to visitors. Fingers crossed…

WINE COUNTRY

For 150 years the West has gone wild for the spas, the gourmet grub and the almighty grape in the patchwork of vineyards stretching from sunny Napa to coastal Sonoma. Napa has art-filled tasting rooms by big-name architects with prices to match; in down-to-earth Sonoma, you'll drink in sheds and probably meet the vintner's dog. Tastings usually cover four to six different wines; Napa Valley wineries typically charge $10 to $30 per flight, while tastings in Sonoma generally run from $5 to $10, which is refundable with purchase. You're never obliged to buy, though you might consider picking up a bottle wherever you picnic – sunshine is free, but maintenance isn't.

Orientation

Wine Country is about 90 minutes north of San Francisco by car via Hwy 101 or I-80; see the Transportation box (p284) for alternative transport options. Skinny Napa Valley stretches from Carneros in the southwest to Howell Mountain in the northeast; most wineries are clustered along Hwy 29 and Silverado Trail. Sonoma County sprawls from Sonoma Valley along Hwy 12 north to Healdsburg and Dry Creek Valley and west to Russian River Valley. Wineries are listed south to north, unless otherwise noted.

NAPA VALLEY

Brace your senses for impact: Napa awaits with 220 standard-setting wineries, a constellation of star chefs, and sleek new spa-hotels. When Napa wines took top honors at a 1976 blind tasting in Paris, the wine-drinking world was shocked – except Napa, which has been growing grapes since the Gold Rush. But cowboys who grabbed a bite, bunk and tub at Napa's dusty stagecoach stops a century ago would now find their options upgraded to humanely raised steaks with truffled potatoes, luxury sheds with high-end linens and aromatherapy mudbaths.

Information

Napa Library (☎ 707-253-4241; www.co.napa.ca.us/library; 580 Coombs St; ⏰ 10am-9pm Mon-Thu, 10am-5pm Fri & Sat, 2-9pm Sun) Check work email before wine-tasting.

Napa Valley Visitors Bureau (☎ 707-226-7459; www.napavalley.com; 1310 Napa Town Center; ⏰ 9am-5pm) Spa deals, wine-tasting passes and the free *Preiser Key to Napa Valley*, which has comprehensive winery maps.

Wineries

Ditch the car and mellow out in downtown Napa at the **Vintners' Collective** (☎ 707-255-7150; www.vintnerscollective.com; 1245 Main St; tasting $25; ⏰ 11am-6pm Wed-Mon) with a sampling of six wines from 20 boutique wineries in a former 19th-century brothel, then discover affordable pinot blends in the spiffy mural-lined tasting room of **Ceja** (☎ 707-226-6445; www.cejavineyards.com; 1248 First St; tasting $10; ⏰ noon-6pm Sun-Thu, to 10pm Fri & Sat).

Blue-chip art and big red wines are the pride of the **Hess Collection** (☎ 707-255-1144; www.hesscollection.com; 4411 Redwood Rd; ⏰ 10am-4pm), a winery/gallery northwest of downtown Napa that pairs monster cabs with art by mega-modernists like Francis Bacon and Robert Motherwell.

Head northeast of Napa for boutique wineries along the **Silverado Trail**, starting with super-Tuscan-style sangiovese at **Luna Vineyards** (☎ 707-255-5862; www.lunavineyards.com; 2921 Silverado Trail; ⏰ 10:30am-4pm). Stone bulls glower from atop pillars lining the driveway of **Darioush** (☎ 707-257-2345; www.darioush.com; 4240 Silverado

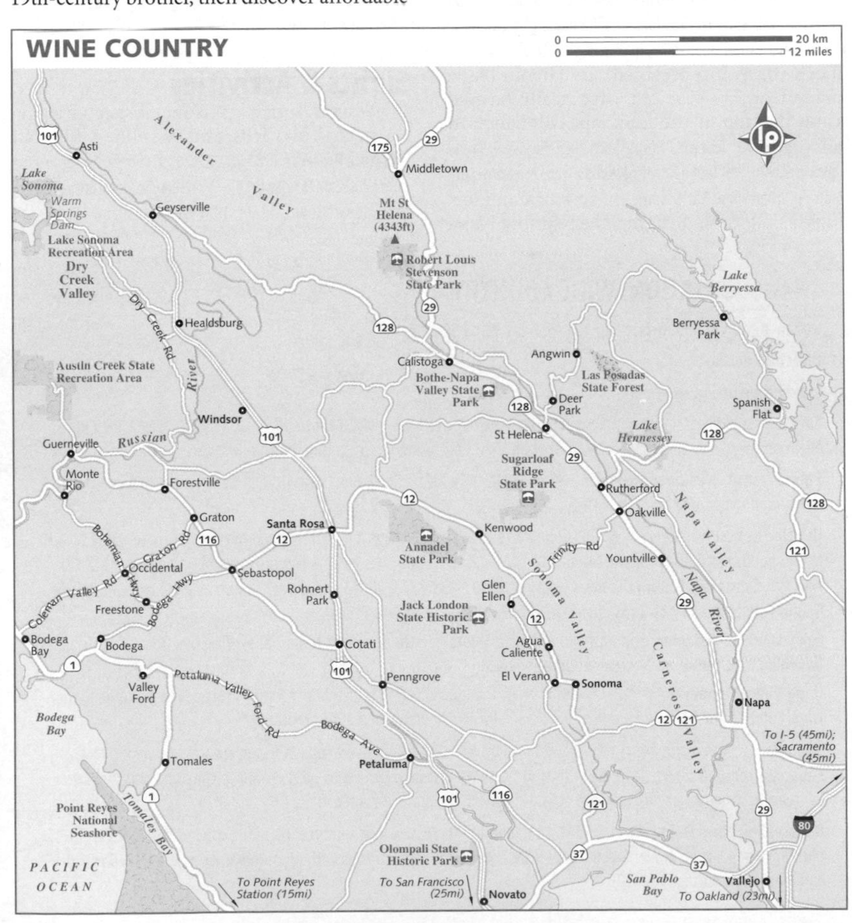

Trail; tasting $25; 10:30am-5pm), a jaw-dropping new winery styled after the ancient Persian temples of Persepolis that offers monumental merlots. Oenophiles (aka wine geeks) need no introduction to Stag's Leap Wine Cellars (☎ 707-261-6441; www.cask23.com; 5766 Silverado Trail; tasting $15-30; 10am-4:30pm), which produced the first California cab to beat French competitors in 1976. Pull off Silverado towards Rutherford to Frog's Leap (☎ 707-963-4704; www.frogsleap.com; 8815 Conn Creek Rd, Rutherford; tours with tasting $25; by appointment 10am-4pm Mon-Thu) for affordable, organically grown cabs and irreverent tours of its ecofriendly, LEED-certified winery – limber up for basketball free-throws to win free wine.

Further up Silverado, you'll spot the tasting barn and pet goats of laid-back, solar-powered Casa Nuestra (☎ 866-844-9463; www.casanuestra.com; 3451 Silverado Trail, St Helena; tastings $5, refundable with purchase; by reservation 10am-4:30pm Mon-Sat), ideal for picnics with melon-accented, dry chenin blanc made from 50-year-old, organically farmed vines. Try top-of-the-line Napa cult wines off Silverado at Joseph Phelps (☎ 800-707-5789; www.jpvwines.com; 200 Taplin Rd, off Silverado Trail; 9am-5pm Mon-Fri, 10am-4pm Sat & Sun), makers of complex, highly collectible Insignia, the reigning Napa Meritage red blend reinvented every year since 1974 with a simple recipe: 'five grapes, no rules.'

On the west side of Napa Valley, you can't miss the faux-Tuscan towers of Castello di Amorosa (☎ 707-967-6272; www.castellodiamorosa.com; 4045 Hwy 29, Calistoga; tasting $10-15, tour adult $25-30, tour ages 5-20yr $15-20, tour child under 5yr free; 9:30am-6pm), a new 121,000-sq-ft stone castle where you can tour wine dungeons, taste tangerine-tinged late-harvest gewürztraminer and occasionally catch jousting matches. For authentic Napa history, turn off Hwy 29 to Schramsberg (☎ 707-942-2414; www.schramsberg.com; 1400 Schramsberg Rd, off Peterson Dr; tour & tasting $35; by reservation 10am, 11:30am, 12:30pm, 1:30pm, 2:30pm). Tours of the landmark 1862 winery dive into historic caves and end at the bar, with signature bubbly that eased international relations between Nixon and Zhou Enlai in 1972.

Sights & Activities

When you notice scrap-metal sheep grazing Carneros vineyards, you've spotted di Rosa Art + Nature Preserve (☎ 707-226-5991; www.dirosapreserve.org; 5200 Carneros Hwy 121; gallery 9:30am-3pm Wed-Fri, tours depart 10am, 11am, 1pm Wed-Fri, 10am, 11am, noon

TRANSPORTATION: WINE COUNTRY

Distance from San Francisco Sonoma 45 miles; Napa 50 miles

Direction Northeast

Travel time One to two hours

Car From San Francisco to Napa/Sonoma take Hwy 101 to Hwy 37 east. At the split take Hwy 121 north, then north again on Hwy 12 to Sonoma. For Napa, stay on Hwy 121, turning east, to Hwy 29 and turn north.

Public Transit Take the scenic route to Napa via ferry (p302), or go by bus with Golden Gate Transit to Santa Rosa or Greyhound to Sonoma Plaza (p304).

Bicycle The best way to explore Wine Country's scenic back roads. Bring your own via ferry or bus, or rent one for $30 to $45 per day at Calistoga Bike Shop (☎ 707-942-9687, 866-942-2453; www.calistogabikeshop.com; 1318 Lincoln Ave, Calistoga), Sonoma Valley Cyclery (☎ 707-935-3377; 20093 Broadway, Sonoma Valley) or Healdsburg's Spoke Folk (☎ 707-433-7171; www.spokefolk.com; 201 Center St).

Enjoy sunshine and wine without parking hassles by taking the ferry and Napa Valley Vine bus from SF (p302), and switching to adventurous alternative transportation:

Napa Valley Hoppers (☎ 707-224-4677; www.nvhoppers.com) Motorized rickshaw excursions make three to four winery stops from 10am to 2pm ($89 per person for five hours); reservations required.

Napa Valley Adventure Tours (☎ 707-259-1833, 877-548-6877; www.napavalleyadventuretours.com; Oxbow Public Market, 610 1st St, Napa; 6.5hr tour $139) Wine-tasting bicycle trips with organic picnics and personal introductions to winemakers, artisans and organic farmers along the Silverado Trail.

Napa Valley Wine Train (☎ 707-253-2111, 800-427-4124; www.winetrain.com; adult/child under 12yr $49.50/25, plus lunch $44.50/25, dinner $49.50/30) Cushy, touristy three-hour trips with an optional winery stop ($25 extra) and a bar car (four tastings $10).

Sat). Reserve ahead for tours covering everything from Tony Oursler's grimacing video projections in the wine cellar to million-dollar Robert Bechtel abstracts hung on the living-room ceiling.

Northeast in downtown Napa, graze at Oxbow Public Market (below) and get an eyeful of intriguing local art at Nest (☎ 707-255-7484; www.napanest.com; 1019 Atlas Peak Rd; 10am-6pm Thu-Sun), such as Kana Tanaka's indoor thunderstorm of blown-glass raindrops.

Small towns with outsize reputations line Hwy 29, from tiny Yountville, home to the most Michelin-starred eateries per capita in the US, to charming historic St Helena, where Napa congregates at the Farmers' Market (☎ 707-486-2662; www.sthelenafarmersmkt.org; Crane Park, off Grayson Ave; 7:30am-noon Fri May-Oct) for first dibs on heirloom tomatoes.

Calistoga is the down-to-earth north end of Napa, where for centuries native Wappo headed for rejuvenating rolls in the volcanic mud. Today, Indian Springs (☎ 707-942-4913; www.indianspringscalistoga.com; 1712 Lincoln Ave; 9am-8pm) offers volcanic mud baths ($85) with free access to its hot-springs pool, while vintage-1950s Dr Wilkinson's Hot Springs (☎ 707-942-4102; www.drwilkinson.com; 1507 Lincoln Ave; 8:30am-5:30pm) features wallows in volcanic mud and peat moss, mineral whirlpools, steam rooms and blanket wraps ($89). Couples prefer Lavender Hill Spa (☎ 707-942-4495; www.lavenderhillspa.com; 1015 Foothill Blvd; 10am-6pm Sun-Thu, to 8pm Fri & Sat) for private cottages ($70 per person) with side-by-side clawfoot Jacuzzi tubs filled with lavender-infused mud.

Eating

French Laundry (☎ 707-944-2380; www.frenchlaundry.com; 6640 Washington St, Yountville; fixed-price menu $240; dinner 5:30-9.30pm daily, 11am-1pm Sat & Sun by reservation) The definition of California fine dining: inspired and seasonal, setting international trends with extraordinary ingredients plucked from the organic garden out back. A culinary experience worthy of lifetime achievements – a 40th birthday, say, or a Nobel Prize. Book one to six months ahead; call at 10am sharp.

Ad Hoc (☎ 707-944-2487; www.adhocrestaurant.com; 6476 Washington St, Yountville; 5-9pm Mon, Wed, Thu-Sun, 10:30am-2pm Sun) Don't bother asking for a menu at Thomas Keller's most innovative restaurant since French Laundry: chef Dave Cruz dreams up his four-course, $48 market menu daily. No substitutions are offered unless you mention dietary restrictions when making reservations, but none are needed – every dish is comforting, garden-fresh and fabulous.

Ubuntu (☎ 707-251-5656; www.ubuntunapa.com; 1140 Main St, Napa; small plates $6-14; 5:30-9pm Mon-Thu, 11:30am-2:30pm & 5:30-10pm Fri & Sat, 11:30am-2:30pm & 5:30-9pm Sun) Chef Jeremy Fox's seasonal, vegetarian menu features natural wonders from the biodynamic kitchen garden, satisfying hearty eaters with four to five inspired small plates and eco-savvy drinkers with 100-plus sustainably produced wines.

Jolé (☎ 707-942-5938; www.jolerestaurant.com; 1457 Lincoln Ave, Calistoga; small plates $6-14; 5-10pm Sun & Tue-Thu, to 11pm Fri & Sat) Here seasonal small plates are responsible for the biggest sensations this side of top-chef flagships, at a fraction of the price: local sole with tiny, tangy Napa grapes, caramelized Brussels sprouts with capers, and organic Baldwin apple strudel with house-made burnt caramel ice cream.

Oxbow Public Market (☎ 707-226-6529; www.oxbowpublicmarket.com; 610 & 644 First St, Napa; 9am-7pm Mon-Sat, 10am-5pm Sun) A gourmet food court, featuring Hog Island's sustainably harvested oysters (six for $15), Pica Pica's Venezuelan cornbread sandwiches ($6.99) and Three Twins certified-organic ice cream ($3.65 for a single waffle cone).

Paninoteca Ottimo! (☎ 707-945-1229; www.napastyle.com; 6525 Washington St, Yountville; sandwiches $7-9; 10am-6pm Mon-Sat, to 5pm Sun) Sandwiches with organic veggies and top-notch Italian cured meats and cheeses come with a side of celebrity at this gourmet deli, right behind the organic wine bar at celebrity chef Michael Chiarello's NapaStyle gourmet emporium.

Oakville Grocery (☎ 707-944-8802; www.oakvillegrocery.com; 7856 Hwy 29, Oakville; 8am-6pm) Gourmet meals on the go: serious espresso, crusty bread, Sonoma goat cheese, Willie Bird smoked duck breast, and decadent desserts.

Entertainment

Napa Valley Opera House (☎ 707-226-7372; www.nvoh.org; 1000 Main St, Napa) This was the first respectable music hall west of the Mississippi – divas have belted out their best here since 1879. But since the Opera House's 2003 restoration, the house is just as likely to be brought down by Portuguese *fado* singer Mariza or Grammy-winning banjo sensation Béla Fleck.

Cameo Cinema (☎ 707-963-9779; www.cameocinema.com; 1340 Main St, Napa) First-run movies share billing with 3D flicks and art-house favorites at this 1915 vintage cinema, with artisan gelato at the glitzy snack bar and a red-velvet-swagged theater perfect for Saturday late-night horror flicks.

Sleeping

Carneros Inn (☎ 707-299-4900; www.thecarnerosinn.com; 4048 Sonoma Hwy (Hwy 121/12), Carneros; r Mon-Fri $435-595, Sat & Sun $475-655;) The corrugated-metal buildings among the vineyards look like a winery from afar, but luxury guest-sheds feature kingly beds, wood-burning fireplaces and private patios with outdoor showers.

Bardessono (☎ 707-204-6000; www.bardessono.com; 6526 Yount St, Yountville; ste Mon-Fri $330-525, Sat & Sun $425-699) Luxury comes naturally inside the reclaimed-wood walls of this LEED-certified green hotel, which opened in 2009. It features sleekly modern rooms awash with natural light, spa bathrooms with soaking tubs or outdoor showers, and vineyard views from plush beds with organic linens.

Napa Valley Railway Inn (☎ 707-944-2000; www.napavalleyrailwayinn.com; 6523 Washington St, Yountville; r $125-210) Rest tired cabooses in revamped railcars with cushy beds, skylights, flat-screen TVs and gym access, right in downtown Yountville.

Hotel St Helena (☎ 707-963-4388; www.hotelsthelena.net; 1309 Main St, St Helena; r with shared bathroom $95) Period-furnished rooms in the heart of historic St Helena.

Bothe-Napa Valley State Park (☎ 707-942-4575, reservations 800-444-7275; www.parks.ca.gov; campsites $15-25;) Hillside campsites with gorgeous hiking beneath redwoods to the historic Bale Grist Mill.

Calistoga Inn (☎ 707-942-4101; www.calistogainn.com; 1250 Lincoln Ave, Calistoga; r with shared bathroom midweek/weekend $89/139) Snug rooms lack phones and TVs, but a lively brewery-restaurant is downstairs and spas are within walking distance.

SONOMA VALLEY

So what if it's not noon yet? Relax and enjoy your white port and chocolate ice cream drizzled with organic olive oil; now that you're in Sonoma, conventions need not apply. Sonoma belonged to Mexico in 1846, when American settlers of varying sobriety declared an independent 'California Republc' [sic] with a homemade flag featuring a blotchy, porcine bear. Today, Sonoma showcases its independent thinking in adventurous farm-to-table menus, pioneering green wineries, and 'vinotherapy' spa treatments.

Information

Sonoma Valley Visitors Bureau (☎ 707-996-1090; www.sonomavalley.com; 453 1st St E; 9am-5pm) Arranges accommodations (no fee) and offers walking-tour maps and festival and event info.

Wineries

More casual and less commercial than Napa, Sonoma Valley has 70 wineries clustered around Hwy 12 – and unlike Napa, most welcome picnicking. Down a country road from downtown, Gundlach-Bundschu (☎ 707-938-5277; www.gunbun.com; 2000 Denmark St) is a solar-powered castle perched above a reclaimed-water lake producing legendary tempranillo. GunBun also runs nearby Bartholomew Park Winery (☎ 707-939-3026; www.bartpark.com; 1000 Vineyard Lane; tasting $5-10, museum & park entry free; tasting room & museum 11am-4:30pm), a 400-acre preserve with vineyards originally cultivated in 1857 and now certified-organic, yielding citrus-sunshine sauvignon blanc and smoky-midnight merlot.

Picnic like a rock star at BR Cohn (☎ 707-938-4064; www.brcohn.com; 15000 Sonoma Hwy; tasting $10, applicable to purchase; 10am-5pm), whose founder Bruce Cohn managed '70s superband the Doobie Brothers before moving onto organic olive oils, his Doobie Red Bordeaux blend, and throwing an annual November benefit concert amid the vineyards and olive groves. Another maverick is Demeter-certified biodynamic behemoth Benziger (☎ 800-989-8890; www.benziger.com; 1883 London Ranch Rd, Glen Ellen; tasting $10-15, tram tour adult incl tasting/under 21 $15/5; 10am-5pm;), where educational tram tours explain environmentally savvy, esoteric winegrowing methods that yield sensational truffled-cranberry cabs.

West off Hwy 12, many of Sonoma Valley's best buys await at Wellington (☎ 800-816-9463; www.wellingtonvineyards.com; 11600 Dunbar Rd, Glen Ellen; tastings $5; 10am-5pm), where under $30 gets you hazelnutty white port or award-winning, white-peppery zins produced by 100-year-old vines that miraculously survived Prohibition. Swerve off Hwy 12 near Kenwood to Kaz Winery (☎ 707-833-2536; www.kazwinery.com; 233 Adobe Canyon Rd, Kenwood; tasting $5-10, applicable to purchase; 11am-5pm Fri-Mon), where members of the Kasmier family proudly serve offbeat, organically grown wines like Nebbiolo blush port and cabernet franc on the barrel-top bar in the barn.

Sights & Activities

Downtown Sonoma was once the capital of a rogue nation, and though Sonoma Plaza looks stately with its stone mission revival City Hall (1906–08), it gets plenty lively during balmy summer nights and spring–fall farmers markets (9am-noon Fri, 5:30-8pm Tue Apr-Oct). See where Sonoma settlers surprised Mexican soldiers in 1850 and declared an independent Bear Flag Republic at the Adobe Barracks (707-935-6832; www.parks.ca.gov; 20 E Spain St; adult/child under 17yr $2/free, entry fee covers same-day admission to Mission Solano; 10am-5pm;). Across the street, adobe Mission Solano San Francisco (707-938-9560; 114 E Spain St; adult/child under 17yr $2/free, entry fee covers same-day admission to Adobe Barracks; 10am-5pm;) was founded in 1823 and once included 10,000 acres farmed by 900 conscripted Native Californian workers; the East Spain St wing remains largely intact, with a reconstructed chapel.

Northwest of downtown Napa is Morton's Warm Springs (707-833-5511; 1651 Warm Springs Rd; admission adult/child under 3yr/senior & child $8/free/7, reserved picnic & BBQ sites per person $11; 10am-6pm Sat & Sun May & Sep-Oct, to 6pm Tue-Sun Jun-Aug), long believed to have healing properties by native Wappo, with three geothermal mineral pools, hiking trails, volleyball nets and BBQ facilities. For true decadence, Kenwood Inn & Spa (707-833-1293; www.kenwoodinn.com; 10400 Sonoma Hwy, Kenwood; r incl breakfast $400-495;) offers complimentary bubbly with 'vinotherapy' antioxidant red-wine body wraps ($175 for 80 minutes) that go straight to your head. Spa treatments start from $125.

Obey the call of the wild up Hwy 12 at Jack London State Historic Park (707-938-5216; www.jacklondonpark.com; 2400 London Ranch Rd; 10am-5pm Oct-Apr, 9:30am-7pm May-Sep), where adventure-novelist Jack London brought Sonoma's slashed-and-burned hillsides back to life. Hike to the lake to overlook London's pristine 129-acre farmstead or ride through fragrant redwood groves with Triple Creek Horse Outfit (707-887-8700; www.triplecreekhorseoutfit.com; 2400 London Ranch Rd; group rides 1/2/3hr with lunch $60/90/250; by reservation).

Eating

Vineyards Inn Bar & Grill (707-833-4500; www.vineyardsinn.com; 8445 Sonoma Hwy 12, Sonoma; mains $8-20; 11:30am-9:30pm) If you try only one Wine Country burger, make it the Jake Steak: a half-pound of succulent certified-organic chuck on ciabatta. Seafood is fresh, wild and line-caught, and most produce comes from chef Esteban's certified-organic and biodynamic Rose Ranch.

Café la Haye (707-935-5994; www.cafelahaye.com; 140 E Napa St, Sonoma; mains $17-25; from 5:30pm Tue-Sat) In an open kitchen, this tiny bistro whips up big-city cuisine from ingredients grown within a 60-mile radius.

Fig Cafe (707-938-2130; www.thefigcafe.com; 13690 Arnold Dr, Glen Ellen; mains $15-20; 5:30-9pm daily, 10am-2:30pm Sat & Sun) Sonoma's take on comfort food: organic salads, Sonoma duck cassoulet and free corkage on Sonoma wines, served in a converted living room.

El Dorado Kitchen (707-996-3030; www.eldoradosonoma.com; 405 1st St W, Sonoma; mains $7-15; 11:30am-2:30pm & 5:30-9pm; V) Biodynamic salads and gargantuan pastrami sandwiches with parmesan-dusted truffle fries are big enough to split in this sunny corner kitchenette, but get your own soft-serve ice cream topped with BR Cohn olive oil and sea salt.

Red Grape (707-996-4103; www.theredgrape.com; 529 1st St W, Sonoma; pizzas $10-16; 11:30am-10pm; V) Thin-crust pizza with local cheeses and cured meats, plus small-production Sonoma wines by the half-bottle.

Sonoma Market (707-996-3411; 500 W Napa St, Sonoma; sandwiches $6-9; 6am-9pm) Superior deli with hot pressed panini created by the in-house chef.

WINE COUNTRY CHEFS REVEAL ALL

Ramekins Culinary School (707-933-0450; www.ramekins.com; 450 W Spain St, Sonoma) is Wine Country's premier workshop venue for home chefs, with hands-on cheesemaking seminars, knife-skills boot camps and demos by Sonoma's award-winning Mediterranean cookbook author Paula Wolfert. At the Culinary Institute of America (707-967-1100; www.ciachef.edu; 2555 Main St, St Helena; cooking demonstration $15, mains $21-34; cooking demonstrations at 1:30pm & 3:30pm Mon & Fri, 10:30am & 1:30pm Sat & Sun, restaurant 11:30am-9pm Sun-Thu, to 10pm Fri & Sat), set in an 1889 stone chateau, you can watch acclaimed chefs do demos and chef-trainees impress instructors in an open kitchen.

Drinking & Entertainment

Sebastiani Theatre (☎ 707-996-9756; www.sebastianitheatre.com; 1021 Central Ave, Sonoma; adult/senior & child under 12yr $9/6;) Sonoma's single-screen art deco movie palace spots Oscar contenders early and runs them longer than multiplexes, along with film festivals, concerts and musicals.

Wine Exchange of Sonoma (☎ 800-938-1794; www.wineexsonoma.com; 452 1st St E, Sonoma; 10am-6pm Mon-Fri, to 7pm Sat & Sun) Come for the wine, but stay for the four microbrews on draft in the speakeasy-style rear tasting bar, plus another 250 beers 'at last count' along the wall.

Sleeping

At the northern end of Sonoma Valley, **Santa Rosa** offers affordable chain motels along Cleveland Ave, west of Hwy 101.

Beltane Ranch (☎ 707-996-6501; www.beltaneranch.com; 11775 Hwy 12; r incl breakfast $150-220; P) The graceful yellow 1890s homestead once belonged to Mary Ellen Pleasant, daughter of slaves, former brothel owner and California pioneer. Now guests enjoy ranch-raised meals and can hike trails, play tennis and sit on the porch swing and watch horses graze.

Gaige House Inn (☎ 707-935-0237, 800-935-0237; www.gaige.com; 13540 Arnold Dr, Glen Ellen; r $229-289, ste $359-459;) Sonoma's sleekest inn, with Zen-chic rooms in the historic main house and spa suites with hewn-granite tubs and pebbled meditation courtyards near the pool.

Sonoma Hotel (☎ 707-996-2996, 800-468-6016; www.sonomahotel.com; 110 W Spain St, Sonoma; r incl breakfast midweek/weekend Nov-Mar $140/170, Apr-Oct $170/198) Stylish 1880 landmark hotel on happening Sonoma Plaza, with larger/smaller rooms for $30 more/less; two-night minimum on weekends.

Hillside Inn (☎ 707-546-9353; www.hillside-inn.com; 2901 4th St, Sonoma; s/d Nov-Mar $70/78, Apr-Oct $74/82; P) Downtown Sonoma's best-kept motel is close to wine-tasting action; add $4 for kitchens.

Sugarloaf Ridge State Park (☎ 707-833-5712, reservations 800-444-7275; www.parks.ca.gov; Adobe Canyon Rd; campsites $15-20) North of Kenwood wineries, 50 sites without hookups are nestled in two mellow meadows.

RUSSIAN RIVER VALLEY

The West preserves its wild ways in Russian River, two hours north of San Francisco (via Hwys 101 and 116) in western Sonoma County. Here ancient redwoods tower over independent wineries, and the aptly named 10-mile **Bohemian Highway** is lined with resorts for rebels, hippie craft galleries and gay-friendly honky-tonks.

> **top picks**
>
> **WINE COUNTRY SPAS**
>
> - **Indian Springs** (p285)
> - **Osmosis** (opposite)
> - **Kenwood Inn & Spa** (p287)
> - **Spa at Hotel Healdsburg** (p290)
> - **Lavender Hill Spa** (p285)

Information

Guerneville Visitor Center (☎ 707-869-9000; www.russianriver.com; 16209 1st St, Guerneville; 10am-5pm) Offers maps and last-minute lodging info.

Sebastopol Area Chamber of Commerce & Visitors Center (☎ 707-823-3032, 877-828-4748; www.sebastopol.org; 265 S Main St, Sebastopol; 10am-noon & 1-5pm Mon-Fri) Provides maps and the free *Sonoma County Farm Trails Guide* (www.farmtrails.org), which lists Sonoma farms open to visitors.

Wineries

Pinot noir is a finicky grape that withers in sun and mildews in fog, yet it thrives in Russian River Valley, delivering autumn-spiced pinot noir at solar-powered **Moshin** (☎ 707-433-5499; www.moshinvineyards.com; 10295 Westside Rd; 11am-4:30pm). At organic, certified-biodynamic **Porter Creek Vineyards** (☎ 707-433-6321; www.portercreekvineyards.com; 8735 Westside Rd; tastings free; 10:30am-4:30pm), woodsy pinot noir is served in a shed on a bar made from a bowling alley lane. Near the coast, **Freestone** (☎ 707-874-1010; www.jpvfreestone.com; 12747 El Camino Bodega, Freestone; 11am-5pm Fri-Sun) grows grapes biodynamically and interferes minimally to yield pomegranate-bright Fogdog pinot noir.

But Pinot grapes also make respectable Champagne-style whites, as pioneer Francis Korbel discovered 120 years ago north of Guerneville at **Korbel Champagne Cellars** (☎ 707-887-2294; www.korbel.com; 13250 River Rd, Guerneville; 10am-5pm). Stop by for free tours of the champagne cellars, fragrant rose gardens and toasts of Korbel's bubbly. For sparkling wines served to US presidents, head 15 minutes south of

Guerneville to the splendid outdoor hilltop tasting bar at Iron Horse Vineyards (☎ 707-887-1507; www.ironhorsevineyards.com; 9786 Ross Station Rd; tasting $10-15; 🕒 10am-3:30pm).

Sights & Activities

Paddle down winding Russian River past herons and otters in Burke's Canoes (☎ 707-887-1222; www.burkescanoetrips.com; 8600 River Rd, Forestville; canoes per person $59; 🕒 9am-6pm May-Oct), or rent kayaks at King's Sport & Tackle (☎ 707-869-2156; www.guernevillesport.com; 16258 Main St, Guerneville; kayaks per day $30-50; 🕒 9am-5:30pm May-Oct) and launch off at Johnson's Beach (☎ 707-869-2022; www.johnsonsbeach.com; end of Church St, Guerneville; 🕒 10am-6pm May-Oct).

Towering old-growth redwoods at 805-acre Armstrong Redwoods State Reserve (☎ 707-869-2015; www.parks.ca.gov; 17000 Armstrong Woods Rd; parking $6, overnight camping $20; 🕒 8am-sunset) were saved by lumber baron Colonel James Boydston Armstrong, who bought these woods in 1874 and saved them from the axe, including the 308ft, 1400-year-old Colonel Armstrong tree.

Occidental is the heart of the Bohemian Hwy, with its organic farmers market (☎ 707-793-2159; www.occidentalfarmersmarket.com; 🕒 4pm-dusk Fri, Jun-Oct), clever crafts from reclaimed materials at Renga Arts (☎ 707-874-9407; www.rengaarts.com; 3605 Main St, Occidental; 🕒 11am-5pm Fri-Mon) and outlandish April Fool's Day Parade.

Three miles south in Freestone, get buried up to your neck in warm wood chips at Osmosis (☎ 707-823-8231; www.osmosis.com; 209 Bohemian Hwy, Freestone; 🕒 by appointment 9am-8pm), where redwood tubs filled with soft, slow-fermenting cedar and rice bran soothe weary muscles ($85 for 45 minutes). Sebastopol's Sumtime Spa (☎ 707-823-2053; www.sumbody.com; 118 N Main St, Sebastopol; 🕒 10am-7pm Tue-Sun) offers revitalizing Swedish massages ($75 for 60 minutes) and facials ($39 for 30 minutes) with the spa's own organic skincare line.

Eating

Zazu (☎ 707-523-4814; www.zazurestaurant.com; 3535 Guerneville Rd; dishes $19-26; 🕒 dinner Wed-Sun) Get fresh over farm-to-table feasts with house-made salumi, organic ingredients from the garden out back, delicate Liberty duck or whole roasted pig, and warm, honey-drizzled Sonoma cheese for dessert.

Bistro des Copains (☎ 707-874-2436; www.bistrodescopains.com; 3782 Bohemian Hwy, Occidental; mains $16-28; 🕒 5-9pm Sun-Thu, to 10pm Fri & Sat) Hearty, French-style classics hot from the wood-fired oven make dream pairings with local pinot; come weekdays for bargain three-course menus, Tuesdays for free corkage and Wednesdays for $1 oysters.

Wild Flour Bakery (☎ 707-874-2938; 140 Bohemian Hwy, Freestone; pastries under $5; 🕒 8:30am-6pm Fri-Mon) This bakery makes organic brick-oven breads, giant sticky buns and killer coffee.

East West Cafe (☎ 707-829-2822; www.eastwestcafesebastopol.com; 128 N Main St, Sebastopol; dishes $7-14; 🕒 8am-9pm; Ⓥ) Go global at this Mediterranean diner, with grilled eggplant and feta on pesto-slathered organic bread, and organic pancakes with real maple syrup.

Drinking & Entertainment

Rio Theater (☎ 707-865-0913; www.riotheater.com; 20396 Bohemian Hwy, Monte Rio; adult $8, senior, child & matinees $6; 🕒 Wed-Sun) Dinner and a movie, Russian River style: gourmet hot dogs ($7) in a converted 1940s army-shed cinema.

Hopmonk Tavern (☎ 707-829-7300; www.hopmonk.com; 230 Petaluma Ave) Serves tasty home brews in its beer garden with funky world beats, from sizzling salsa to New Orleans blues.

Sleeping

For longer stays, find vacation rental deals at www.rrgetaways.com, www.sonomacountyvacations.com and http://sfbay.craigslist.org/nby/vac.

Dawn Ranch (☎ 707-869-0656; www.dawnranch.com; 16467 River Rd; d incl breakfast $99-120; 🅟) Take your pick of vintage cabins with woodstoves among the redwoods, or poolside cabanas, and don't miss the historic roadhouse for killer cocktails and organic dining.

Boon Hotel & Spa (☎ 707-869-2721; www.boonhotels.com; 14711 Armstrong Woods Rd; d $185-205, tr $225-250) Guerneville's chic new eco-retreat has sleek cork-floored and solar-heated cabanas alongside the chlorine-free pool. There are fluffy organic cotton robes and onsite an organic bistro and a spa offering hot-stone massages.

Inn at Occidental (☎ 707-874-1047, 800-522-6324; www.innatoccidental.com; 3657 Church St; r incl breakfast $249-349) This gorgeously restored 1876 Victorian inn offers escapes from the ordinary, with folk art, bold colors, proper feather beds and gas fireplaces.

Vine Hill Inn (☎ 707-823-8832; www.vine-hill-inn.com; 3949 Vine Hill Rd, off Hwy 116; r incl breakfast $170; 🅟) Four guestrooms are tucked under the eaves of this 1897 Victorian farmhouse. There are gorgeous vineyard views and breakfasts with farm-fresh omelettes; two rooms have Jacuzzis.

HEALDSBURG & DRY CREEK VALLEY

More than 90 wineries are located within a 30-mile radius of Healdsburg, where upscale eateries, wine-tasting rooms and stylish inns ring the Spanish-style plaza. Just over Hwy 101 from downtown Healdsburg is Dry Creek, a dreamscape of lazily grazing sheep, fish leaping from glistening creeks, and gnarled old vineyards blooming with organic ground cover.

Information

Healdsburg Visitors Center (☎ 707-433-6935, 800-648-9922; www.healdsburg.org; 217 Healdsburg Ave; 🕑 9am-5pm Mon-Fri, 9am-3pm Sat, 10am-2pm Sun) Handy for tasting passes, maps and info.

Sonoma County Library (☎ 707-433-3772; www.sonoma.lib.ca.us; cnr Piper & Center Sts, Healdsburg; 🕑 9:30am-6pm) Features California's best public enology reference library.

Wineries

Natural beauty gets bottled in Dry Creek, beginning with zins served in caves at Bella Vineyards (☎ 707-473-9171, 866-572-3552; www.bellawinery.com; 9711 W Dry Creek Rd; tasting $5; 🕑 11am-4pm). Mosey over to the 19th-century homestead at Preston Vineyards (☎ 707-433-3327, 800-305-9707; www.prestonvineyards.com; 9282 W Dry Creek Rd; tasting $5, refundable with purchase) for picnics of certified organically grown Barbera and Viognier with home-baked bread, organic fruit, and Pug's Leap goat cheese, plus marathon bocce ball games.

Pull up an Adirondack chair creekside and stay awhile at Truett-Hurst (☎ 707-433-6913; www.truetthurst.com; 5610 Dry Creek Rd; 🕑 by appointment Mon-Thu, 11am-5pm Fri-Sun), Dry Creek's newest biodynamic winery, which is already producing stellar old-vine zins. Pristine biodynamic field blends are served inside a fluorescent-lit garage at Unti (☎ 707-433-5590; www.untivineyards.com; 4202 Dry Creek Rd; 🕑 Sat & Sun, by appointment Mon-Fri), but even under harsh lighting, everyone looks gorgeous after a glass of bodacious Brunello-style sangiovese and the voluptuous syrah.

Eating

Cyrus (☎ 707-433-3311; www.cyrusrestaurant.com; 29 North St, Healdsburg; fixed-price menu $102-130; 🕑 6-11pm Wed-Mon) Critics rave about the decadent truffle-laced dishes, but the local secret is the bar, where dishes are served a la carte with mad-scientist cocktails.

Bovolo (☎ 707-431-2962; www.bovolorestaurant.com; 106 Matheson St, Healdsburg; dishes $6-14; 🕑 9am-6pm Thu, Fri, Mon, Tue, to 9pm Sat & Sun) Fast food gets a slow-food spin at this bistro in the back of a bookstore, with locally grown salads, farm-fresh egg breakfasts and pizza topped with meats cured in-house.

Scopa (☎ 707-433-5282; www.scopahealdsburg.com; 109-A Plaza St, Healdsburg; mains $12-26; 🕑 5:30-10pm Tue-Sun) Call ahead for a spot at this converted barbershop for thin-crust pizza and Nonna's slow-braised chicken melting into a polenta pillow.

Dry Creek General Store (☎ 707-433-4171; www.dcgstore.com; 3495 Dry Creek Rd; sandwiches $8-10; 🕑 6am-6pm) When your stomach protests zin before lunch, make a pit stop here for a Toscano salami and manchego sandwich or the classic BLT, and a sunny spot on the porch.

Drinking

Flying Goat Coffee (☎ 707-433-9081; www.flyinggoatcoffee.com; 324 Center St, Healdsburg; 🕑 7am-6pm) Cappuccinos with fresh-roasted beans and ferns drawn by baristas in stiff foam are served in a restored storefront with lazy ceiling fans.

Bear Republic Brewing Company (☎ 707-433-2337; 345 Healdsburg Ave, Healdsburg; 🕑 11:30am-late) Handcrafted, award-winning ales, plus pub grub and live music on weekends.

Sleeping

Healdsburg Inn on the Plaza (☎ 707-433-6991, 800-431-8663; www.healdsburginn.com; 110 Matheson St, Healdsburg; Mon-Fri $200-250, Sat & Sun $220-325) Renovated in 2005 with a nod to Tuscany, sunny, high-ceilinged guestrooms have fine linens and gas fireplaces; hang out in the solarium or the cushy living room over full breakfasts, afternoon wine, cheese and cookies.

Hotel Healdsburg (☎ 707-431-2800, 800-889-7188; www.hotelhealdsburg.com; 25 Matheson St, Healdsburg; r incl breakfast $260-790; 🏊) Smack on the plaza, this polished-concrete chic hotel has soothing earth-toned guestrooms with vast beds, some with soaking tubs; leave rested and gleaming from a Crushed Zinfandel Body Polish ($115 for 50 minutes) in the garden spa.

Best Western Dry Creek Inn (☎ 707-433-0300, 800-222-5784; 198 Dry Creek Rd, Healdsburg; r $119-155; 🏊) Healdsburg's spiffiest motel, with remodeled rooms, free laundry and an outdoor hot tub.

L&M Motel (☎ 707-433-6528; www.landmmotel.com; 70 Healdsburg Ave, Healdsburg; r $75-99;) Vegas-kitschy and friendly, this family-owned motel is within walking distance of the town plaza. It has an Olympic-sized indoor swimming pool, a sauna and a Jacuzzi, and backyard barbecue grills.

Cloverdale Wine Country KOA (☎ 707-894-3337, 800-368-4558; www.winecountrykoa.com; 26460 River Rd, Cloverdale; tent/RV sites from $35/55, 1-/2-bedroom cabins $72/82;) Surrounded by vineyards six miles from Hwy 101 Central Cloverdale exit, this campground offers hot showers, a swimming pool and a hot tub, nature trails, a laundry, paddleboats and bicycles.

POINT REYES NATIONAL SEASHORE

Forty miles north of San Francisco, on an entirely different tectonic plate from the mainland, the windswept peninsula of Point Reyes juts 10 miles out to sea and lures marine mammals, migratory birds and whale-watching tourists. In 1579 Sir Francis Drake landed here to repair his ship, the *Golden Hind*. During his five-week stay he mounted a brass plaque (which has never been found) claiming this land for England; historians believe he was at Drakes Beach. In 1595 the *San Augustine* went down offshore, the first of scores of ships lost here. A Spanish treasure ship from Manila, she was laden with luxury goods, such as porcelain, and to this day bits of her cargo wash up on shore. Even now, despite GPS systems, the dangerous waters and treacherous rocks continue to claim the occasional vessel, adding to the peninsula's mystique.

Point Reyes National Seashore, established by President Kennedy in 1963, includes 110 sq miles of pristine ocean beaches, wind-tousled ridgetops and diverse wildlife. With excellent hiking and camping, Point Reyes is one of the Bay Area's top day-trip excursions, and its surrounding villages make a romantic spot for a quick overnight. Bring warm clothing: even the sunniest days can quickly turn cold and foggy. The West Marin Chamber of Commerce (☎ 415-663-9232; www.pointreyes.org) provides info on the Point Reyes region.

Start out at the Bear Valley Visitors Center (☎ 415-464-5100; www.nps.gov/pore; Bear Valley Rd; 9am-5pm Mon-Fri, 8am-5pm Sat & Sun), the park's headquarters (near Olema), which provides maps, information and worthwhile exhibits. This is the major trailhead for the park – the longest trail is Palomarin Trail at 11.5 miles. You can also get information at the Point Reyes Lighthouse (☎ 415-669-1534; 10am-4:30pm Thu-Mon) and the Ken Patrick Center (☎ 415-669-1250; Drakes Beach; 10am-5pm Fri-Tue summer, 10am-5pm Sat, Sun & holidays winter).

Other fun hikes are Arch Rock (4.1 miles one-way), Sky Camp (2.7 miles one-way), Wildcat Camp (6.3 miles one-way) and Coast Camp (8.9 miles one-way). Within easy walking distance you'll find Kule Loklo, which is a replica of a Miwok village. One of the coolest interpretive walks is the Earthquake Walk, smack dab on the San Andreas Fault. Point Reyes sits on the Pacific tectonic plate, the mainland on the North American plate, and the two grind against each other and occasionally trigger earthquakes. Along the Earthquake Walk, look for the fence that split and shifted a stunning 18ft during the 1906 earthquake. Amazing.

Limantour Rd, off Bear Valley Rd about 1 mile north of Bear Valley Visitors Center, leads to the Point Reyes Hostel and to Limantour Beach. The Inverness Ridge Trail heads from Limantour Rd up to 1282ft Mt Vision.

The Point Reyes Lighthouse (☎ 415-669-1534; 10am-4:30pm Thu-Mon) sits at the end of Sir Francis Drake Blvd. The wild, steep terrain here gets buffeted by ferocious winds, and offers the best whale-watching along the coast. The lighthouse sits 600ft below the headlands, down 308 steps, so that its light can shine below the fog that usually blankets the point. The lens room and clockworks are open as conditions permit.

Nearby Chimney Rock makes a lovely short hike, especially in spring when wildflowers are

TRANSPORTATION: POINT REYES NATIONAL SEASHORE

Distance from San Francisco 40 miles to park headquarters

Direction North

Travel time 60 minutes

Car Cross the Golden Gate and follow signs on Hwy 101 for Hwy 1 north. Just past Olema turn south on Bear Valley Rd to the park headquarters.

Bus Take bus 68 run by West Marin Stagecoach (☎ 415-526-3239; www.marintransit.org) from the San Rafael Transit Center to the Bear Valley Visitors Center. To reach San Rafael, take Golden Gate Transit bus 70 or 80 from downtown SF.

blossoming. Look for wild cucumber, purple thistle, bright-orange California poppies and wild grasses tenaciously clinging to the cliffs. A nearby viewing area lets you spy on the park's braying elephant-seal colony.

On weekends during good weather, from 9am to 5:30pm in late December through mid-April, the road to Chimney Rock and the lighthouse is closed to private vehicles. Instead, you must take a shuttle ($5; children under 16 free) from Drakes Beach. Buy tickets between 9am and 3pm at the Ken Patrick Center (p291). Shuttles run every 20 minutes from 9:30am to 3:30pm, weather permitting; for daily updates call ☎ 415-464-5100, ext 2, then press 1.

McClures Beach, near the north end, is a gem of a beach, with white sand, forceful surf and excellent tidepools at low tide. Start the steep half-mile trail down to the beach at the end of Pierce Point Rd, also the starting point of the stunning, mostly level 3-mile bluff-top walk to Tomales Point – through herds of Tule elk. (Keep your distance, lest they charge.)

You can also explore on horseback with Five Brooks Stable (☎ 415-663-1570; www.fivebrooks.com; 8001 Hwy 1, Olema; 1/2/3/6-hr rides $40/60/80/160; 9am-5pm), which also offers pony rides for kids ($15).

To explore the peninsula from the water, contact Point Reyes Outdoors (☎ 415-663-8192; www.pointreyesoutdoors.com; 11401 Hwy 1, Point Reyes Station; guided trips $85-110); or Blue Waters Kayaking (☎ 415-669-2600; www.bwkayak.com; rentals $40-120, guided trips $68-98), which has two locations, one in Inverness, the other in Marshall. Call to confirm opening hours. The bird-watching at Tomales Bay is superb mid-winter.

EATING

Nick's Cove & Cottages (☎ 415-663-1033; http://nickscove.com; 23240 Hwy 1, Marshall; mains $14-30; 8am-9pm) Celeb SF chef Mark Franz runs the kitchen at Point Reyes' only destination restaurant, a vintage-1930s roadhouse perched over Tomales Bay (20 minutes north of Point Reyes Station), with trophy heads mounted on knotty pine walls and a roaring fireplace. Book a window table to bird-watch while you sup on impeccable seafood, grilled meats and local oysters – all sustainably farmed. Reservations essential. The adjoining cottages are expensive ($355 to $700), but oh-so romantic.

Station House Cafe (☎ 415-663-1515; www.stationhousecafe.com; 11180 Hwy 1, Point Reyes Station; dishes $11-20; 11am-9pm Thu-Tue) The New American menu is a crowd-pleaser, with meatloaf, BBQ ribs, fish and chips, burgers and meat and seafood mains, but the food is just OK and service is slow. Still, we like the outdoor patio and convenient location before or after hiking. Full bar.

Cafe Reyes (☎ 415-663-9493; 11101 Hwy 1, Point Reyes Station; dishes $6-14; noon-9pm; V) The Latin-Asian wraps, stir-fries, sandwiches and salads are solidly good, but the best thing is the view from the big outdoor deck.

Priscilla's Pizza (☎ 415-669-1244; 12781 Sir Francis Drake Blvd, Inverness; pizzas around $10; 11am-8pm Wed-Mon; V) Good pizza (some soy); other dishes are so-so. In the morning there's coffee and pastries.

Perry's Delicatesen (☎ 415-663-1491; 2301 Sir Francis Drake Blvd, Inverness Park; sandwiches $6-8; 6:30am-8pm) The great vegetarian sandwiches are made greater with the addition of bacon. Pop one in your backpack and enjoy it mid-hike from a high promontory.

Tomales Bay Foods (☎ 415-663-9335; www.cowgirlcreamery.com; 10am-6pm Wed-Sun) Home of the famous Cowgirl Creamery cheese-makers (tours Friday mornings at 11:30am; reservations recommended), here you can gather stellar picnic fixings – fruit, bread and gooey-delicious cheese.

Hog Island Oyster Co (☎ 415-663-9218, ext 208; www.hogislandoysters.com; 20215 Hwy 1, Marshall; picnic fee Mon-Fri $5, Sat & Sun $8, 12 oysters $10-15, 50 oysters $32-52, 100 oysters $60-90; 9am-5pm) Picnic on fresh local oysters in a bayside cove at this renowned oyster farm, which provides tables, barbecues, lemons, hot sauce, trays of ice, shucking knives and instruction. Bring wine, beer and other food items. Bay Area families come every year, and book months ahead for summer weekends (but you can sometimes show up without reservations late afternoons on Saturday and Sunday); best to come weekdays. Make reservations. If you love oysters, don't miss it.

SLEEPING

Point Reyes has many small inns and B&Bs, from simple to luxe. The Point Reyes Lodging Association (☎ 800-539-1872, 415-663-1872; www.ptreyes.com) has a good list.

Motel Inverness (☎ 866-453-3839, 415-236-1967; www.motelinverness.com; 12718 Sir Francis Drake Blvd, Inverness; r $100-150;) This upmarket motel has wonderful service and spiffy rooms with good beds. Alas, it was built backwards: rooms face the parking lot, but behind there's gorgeous wetlands. No matter – enjoy the view from the lovely main room, with its roaring fire and board games.

Point Reyes Hostel (☎ 415-663-8811; www.norcalhostels.org/reyes; off Limantour Rd; dm from $22) The only lodging in the park lies in a secluded valley surrounded by hiking trails, 2 miles from the ocean – and it's green-certified. The one private room (from $64) is reserved for families traveling with a child under six.

Point Reyes has four campgrounds (☎ 415-663-8054; campsites $15) with pit toilets, untreated water and picnic tables (no fires). Permits are required; reserve at Bear Valley Visitors Center or by telephone three months ahead. Reaching the campgrounds requires a 2- to 6-mile hike. One word: wildcat.

THE ROAD SOUTH

The coastal road south of San Francisco is lined with craggy beaches, windswept coastal plains, grassy prairies and small towns straight out of a Norman Rockwell painting. Passengers are the lucky ones – heading south they get unobstructed views of the crashing surf. Drivers will be hard-pressed to keep their eyes on the double-yellow line.

Leave time to stop at vista points, and you may spot whales breaching offshore, windsurfers skimming waves like giant mosquitoes, flocks of shorebirds and the occasional nude sunbather. Half Moon Bay is an easy day trip from the city, but most beauty shots lie further south along the San Mateo Coast. Santa Cruz is good for a day trip or a quick overnight.

TRANSPORTATION: THE ROAD SOUTH

Distance from San Francisco Half Moon Bay 28 miles; Santa Cruz 70 miles

Direction South

Travel time 40 minutes to Half Moon Bay, 1½ hours to Santa Cruz

Car Take Hwy 1 south. The slow route: take Great Highway along Ocean Beach and keep heading south until it merges with Hwy 1. The faster option: take I-280 to the Hwy 1/Pacifica exit.

Bus SamTrans runs regular buses as far as Half Moon Bay during commute hours, with reduced schedules on weekends. Greyhound (☎ 831-423-1800) runs daily buses to Santa Cruz.

SAN FRANCISCO TO HALF MOON BAY

Head south on the coast and within 20 minutes the city feels far away. The urban landscape disappears behind hills, and suddenly you're on a lonely highway taking the great American road trip. The beauty shots begin south of not-so-pretty Pacifica as you approach infamous Devil's Slide, an unstable cliff zone that, after winter storms, often slides into the Pacific, taking the road with it. At this writing, a long-overdue tunnel bypass was under construction. If you're heading out in a big winter storm to see the Pacific roil and churn, first verify road conditions by calling ☎ 511.

State beaches line the coast; most charge $5 for parking. Lovely Gray Whale Cove State Beach is the most popular clothing-optional strand; bring a sweater. To get there, follow the steps that lead down from the parking lot, which is on the inland side. Montara State Beach is a half-mile south and the local favorite for pristine sand. Its Point Montara Lighthouse (p294), once a fog station in 1875, is now a popular lighthouse hostel. South of the lighthouse, Fitzgerald Marine Reserve (☎ 650-363-4020; www.fitzgeraldreserve.org) at Moss Beach has exquisite tidepools. The website has links to a tide guide, telling the best times to peer down at anemones and coralline algae.

At Pillar Point Harbor, there's a kinda cute assemblage of shops and eateries and a good brew pub in the hamlet of Princeton-by-the-Sea. If you're not hungry or don't want a beer, keep driving – unless you want to see giant waves and sexy surfers. When the wintertime surf rages, climb the dunes from Pillar Point Harbor to Mavericks, and watch death-defying surfers ride 40ft-plus swells past rocky cliffs. This is one of the most challenging breaks in the world and has claimed more than one life. The world-famous Quicksilver/Mavericks competition happens here – with only a day's notice – sometime between December and March.

The town of Half Moon Bay is an old Victorian beach resort and the main coastal town between SF and Santa Cruz. It's most famous for pumpkin patches, roadside fruit-and-vegetable stands and garden shops. The annual Half Moon Bay Art and Pumpkin Festival (www.miramarevents.com/pumpkinfest) culminates with a competition for the biggest pumpkin, which usually weighs upwards of 1500 pounds. (Yes, you read that right.) Up and down the coast in October, you'll spot pumpkin patches gussied up with bails of hay, corn mazes, giant scarecrows and huge stacks of pumpkins and gourds. This is *the* place for a pre-Halloween family outing.

Downtown HMB is good for a stroll and to refuel on sandwiches, but the shopping is nothing special. If you want to hit the water, contact Half Moon Bay Kayaking (☎ 650-773-6101; www.hmbkayak.com; Pillar Point Harbor; rentals s/d per hr $20/40, guided trips $65-150), which rents kayaks and leads stellar guided wildlife and sunset paddles. The main beach in town is OK if you have little kids who constantly have to go to the bathroom, but it gets way too crowded; keep going.

If you're here on a weekend, don't miss the Bach Dancing & Dynamite Society (☎ 650-726-4143; www.bachddsoc.org; 311 Mirada Rd, Half Moon Bay; admission $25-35) and its stellar salon-style jazz, classical and world-music concerts at Douglas Beach House. This is where locals hang. Performances start in the late afternoon. Kids welcome, but if they're fidgety sit outside. Drinks and finger foods are available, or bring a picnic.

Eating & Drinking

Sam's Chowder House (☎ 650-712-0245; www.samschowderhouse.com; 4210 North Cabrillo Hwy, Half Moon Bay; dishes $12-32; 11:30am-9pm) In the tradition of big Cape Cod waterside fish houses, Sam's makes a mean bowl of chowder, whole steamed crab (in season), traditional lobster-clambake with all the fixins, and a knockout lobster roll – to find better, fly to Maine. There's a full bar and great ocean views.

Barbara's Fish Trap (☎ 650-728-7049; 281 Capistrano Rd, Princeton-by-the-Sea; dishes $8-32; 11am-9pm Sun-Thu, to 10pm Fri & Sat;) Generations of families come to this ramshackle harborside seafood shack with checked tablecloths, fresh-fish specials, fish and chips and a near-constant line out the door. Always good, never great.

Flying Fish Grill (☎ 650-712-1125; 99 San Mateo Rd, Half Moon Bay; dishes $4-10; lunch & dinner;) This tiny fish shack makes delicious, inexpensive fish tacos and other seafood plates to eat in or to go.

San Benito House Deli (☎ 650-726-3425; www.sanbenitohouse.com; 356 Main St, Half Moon Bay; sandwiches $6; 10am-5pm;) Our favorite place to pick up homemade-bread sandwiches. Simple, straightforward, fast.

Cameron's Restaurant & Inn (☎ 650-726-5705; www.cameronsinn.com; 1410 S Cabrillo Hwy, Half Moon Bay; dishes from $9;) Eat pub grub, swill beer and shoot darts at Cameron's, a century-old, atmospheric English-style pub with more garage-sale junk pinned to the walls than you'll be able to take in.

Moss Beach Distillery (☎ 650-728-5595; 140 Beach Way, Moss Beach) During Prohibition illicit cargoes of whiskey were smuggled in here, and celebrities drank with local politicians, who ensured raids never happened. Today it's still best for drinks: snuggle beneath blankets on the waterview deck, but skip the food.

Sleeping

San Benito House (☎ 650-726-3425; www.sanbenitohouse.com; 356 Main St, Half Moon Bay; r without bathroom $70-100, r with bathroom $70-130) Folksy, modest, Americana-style rooms for rent above an old-fashioned bar and steakhouse. Breakfast not available.

Mill Rose Inn (☎ 650-726-8750, 800-900-7673; www.millroseinn.com; 615 Mill St, Half Moon Bay; r $175-360;) The Mill Rose is overdone with too much frilly fabric, but has some cushy touches and the town's most eye-popping gardens. Full breakfast.

Old Thyme Inn (☎ 650-726-1616, 800-720-4277; www.oldthymeinn.com; 779 Main St, Half Moon Bay; r $155-325;) This 1898 inn has cheerful B&B rooms, some with Jacuzzis and fireplaces. Full breakfast.

Point Montara Lighthouse (☎ 650-728-7177; www.norcalhostels.org/montara; Hwy 1 & 16th St, Montara; dm/r from $22/65;) The hostel is adjacent to a grand lighthouse, and has a living room, kitchen facilities and an outdoor hot tub. Guests run the gamut from international backpackers to local families. Book ahead in summer.

HALF MOON BAY TO SANTA CRUZ

From Half Moon Bay it takes about 20 minutes to reach San Gregorio State Beach, a driftwood-strewn beauty of a beach with a long, sandy strand. Note: the north end is private, charges a fee and is for gay and nude bathers. Families: stick to the state beach, where kids can build forts from branches washed down the little stream that meets the sand. For a flashback to the Old West, turn inland on Rte 84, and go 1 mile to the San Gregorio General Store (☎ 650-726-0565) on Stage Rd – watch carefully or you'll miss it. It's a classic old emporium catering to local farmers and ranchers, who drink booze at the counter. They'll stare when you walk in, but endure their glances to peruse cowboy hats, flannel shirts, crockery, woodstoves, odd books and sewing notions. It's also the local post office. The best reason to come is for local bluegrass and folk; call ahead for the schedule. (For food, head to Pescadero, below.)

South of the general store, the stately Pigeon Point Lighthouse rises 115ft – the tallest lighthouse on the Pacific coast. At the time of writing, the tower had closed to visitors because of damage sustained during a major storm in 2001, but you can wander the base and plunk down at the fantastic viewing deck to whale-watch, from March through May. Down below there's a little beach with small tidepools; in springtime gorgeous wildflowers bloom. The former lighthouse-keeper's quarters are a popular hostel (above).

Nearby Año Nuevo State Reserve (☎ 650-879-0227; www.parks.ca.gov; parking $10) is the breeding ground of hundreds of elephant seals that took over abandoned Año Nuevo Island; you can view them as they fight for dominance and submission, from December to March. Reservations are essential for the 2.5-hour, 3-mile guided walking tour ($7). The walk across the vast plateau passes through gorgeous grasslands with peerless views and zero highway noise. At trail's end, you emerge at a little beach, where from April to August you'll find yourself within spitting distance of belly-to-belly seals molting (shedding skin and hair) on the sand – thrilling. (Keep your distance.) Crowds come in winter, but we love it here in June and July, when the trail is lined with ollalieberries (similar to blackberries) and you can gorge yourself till you purple your hands and tongue. Arrive by 3pm to gather the necessary trail permit.

South of Año Nuevo on the inland side, look for Swanton Berry Farm (☎ 831-469-8804; www.swantonberryfarm.com; Hwy 1; strawberry-picking 8am-6pm, farmstand 8am-6pm spring, to 8pm summer), 2 miles north of Davenport, where in spring and summer you can pick the Bay Area's best organic strawberries or pop into an old-fashioned unmanned farmstand for flats of berries, berry pie, strawberry lemonade and hot chocolate – leave your money in the little box. Families gather at the picnic tables on the grassy lawns. This is old-school Northern California at its very best.

The San Mateo Coast is lined with side-by-side state beaches too numerous to detail here. For a complete rundown, check out the San Mateo Coast pages of www.71miles.com.

Sleeping

Costanoa (☎ 650-879-1100, 877-262-7848; www.costanoa.com; 2001 Rossi Rd; tents & RVs $40-65, tent cabins without bathroom $115-175, cabins without bathroom $185-195, lodge r with bathroom $210-270;) Four miles south

DETOUR: PESCADERO

The old farming village of Pescadero (www.pescaderovillage.com) is the perfect destination for a day trip from SF. Three miles east of Hwy 1, it's a tiny hamlet abutting mountainous parks and forest preserves, and it's only about an hour's drive from the city. The wind whooshes through open fields, picket fences line little gardens beside whitewashed houses, and the local church's tall steeple pokes at the fog. Locals gather at the general store and an aging hippie sometimes lays out his cache of curios in front of his trailer home. But the best reason to come is Duarte's Tavern (☎ 650-879-0464; www.duartestavern.com; 202 Stage Rd; dishes $16-23; 7am-9pm), a country-style diner in the heart of town, serving classic Americana blue-plate home cooking. The same family has run the place for three generations, and the James Beard Foundation named their little linoleum-floored restaurant an American Classic. The menu lists chops, steaks, deep-fried seafood, good sandwiches and the usual burgers, but it's the fresh-fish dishes (such as fried sand dabs and cioppino), homemade berry pies with flaky crusts, and rich meaty pan gravies that really win our vote. If you didn't make reservations and aren't up for the wait, you can score authentic tacos and hibiscus sodas at Taqueria y Mercado de Amigos (☎ 650-879-0232; 1999 Pescadero Creek Rd; snacks $2-9; lunch & dinner), an unassuming gas station minimart. Plan to poke around after lunch and discover antique stores, curiosity shops, a handmade-furniture studio, a blacksmith's shop and an old church. Half a day here away from the city, and you'll no doubt feel like you've hit the reset button. If you're compelled to stay, we love the one-room Pescadero Creekside Barn (☎ 650-879-0868; www.pescaderolodging.com; 248 Stage Rd; r $150, 2-night minimum weekends;), a turn-of-the-century, 2nd-floor hay loft that's been converted into a cozy, romantic hideaway for two, with a clawfoot soaking tub in the corner and big barn doors opening to the street below.

To reach Pescadero, take Pescadero Creek Rd from Hwy 1, south of San Gregorio State Beach.

of Pigeon Point, Costanoa is part ecolodge, part campground, tucked between three state parks. Great for outdoor enthusiasts, it feels like summer camp for former hippies turned moms and dads, with hiking on gorgeous, wide-open hillsides and weekend activities like yoga and horseback-riding. Accommodations range from comfy lodge rooms to our favorite retreat-like modern duplex cabins, to tiny tent cabins with heated mattresses (turn off your light when you have sex, lest you put on a shadow-puppet show). Every room comes with extras, such as robes and aromatherapy soap; shared bathhouses also have saunas. No TVs.

Pigeon Point Lighthouse (☎ 650-879-0633; www.norcalhostels.org/pigeon; 210 Pigeon Point Rd; dm $23-25, s $53-68, d $61-76, tr $84-104;) Let the sound of the ocean lull you to sleep at this former lighthouse-keeper's house. There's also a blufftop ocean-view hot tub.

SANTA CRUZ

Santa Cruz is counterculture central, a touchy-feely city famous for leftie-liberal politics and live-and-let-live ideology – except when it comes to dogs (not allowed off leash or downtown), parking (meters run seven days a week) and Republicans (shot on sight). Santa Cruz has a vibrant downtown. On the waterfront is the famous beach boardwalk, and in the hills, the University of California at Santa Cruz (UCSC). Plan to spend a day, but to fully appreciate the aesthetic of jangly skirts and waist-length dreadlocks, stay longer.

Orientation & Information

Hwys 1 and 17 are the main arteries into town; the former becomes Mission St, the latter Ocean St. To reach Main Beach and the boardwalk, head south on Front St (parallel to Ocean St) and turn left on Beach St. Pacific Ave is the town's main commercial strip. Carry quarters for parking meters: blue poles have 12-hour limits, others have two-hour limits.

The **Santa Cruz County Conference & Visitors Council** (☎ 831-425-1234, 800-833-3494; www.santacruz.org; 1211 Ocean St; 9am-5pm Mon-Fri, 10am-4pm Sat, 11am-3pm Sun) has brochures, maps, free internet and lodging information.

Bookstore Santa Cruz (☎ 831-423-0900; 1520 Pacific Ave; 9am-10pm Sun-Thu, to 11pm Fri & Sat) and **Logos Books & Records** (☎ 831-427-5100; 1117 Pacific Ave; 10am-10pm Sun-Thu, to 11pm Fri & Sat) are the town's leading independent booksellers.

Sights & Activities

The **Santa Cruz Beach Boardwalk** (☎ 831-426-7433; www.beachboardwalk.com; 400 Beach St; rides $2.25-4.50, all-day ticket $30; daily mid-April–mid-Nov, hrs vary Sat & Sun mid-Nov–mid-April;) dates from 1907 and is the oldest beachfront amusement park on the West Coast. The boardwalk has a glorious old-school Americana vibe, with the smell of cotton candy permeating the salt air, punctuated by the distant squeals of kids hanging upside down on carnival rides. Its most famous rides include the half-mile-long Giant Dipper, a vintage-1924 wooden roller coaster, and the 1911 Looff carousel – both National Historic Landmarks. For kids, the Cave Train is unexpectedly fun for its portrayal of cavemen in modern times. But the thing that's so great is its proximity to the beach, where parents can wait while teens explore. On Friday nights in summer look for free concerts by rock veterans you may have presumed dead.

SC is surfer central. Walk southwest from the wharf along West Cliff Dr. At the tip, **Lighthouse Point** overlooks **Steamers Lane**, one of the West Coast's best and most accessible surfing spots. The lighthouse houses the tiny **Surfing Museum** (☎ 831-420-6289; www.santacruzsurfingmuseum.org; admission free; noon-4pm Thu-Mon;). Tops for sunsets, **Natural Bridges State Beach** (☎ 831-423-4609;) is at the end of West Cliff Dr, 3 miles from the wharf. Explore tidepools and the state's only monarch-butterfly preserve, where monarchs roost from November to March.

Adjacent to the boardwalk, the long **municipal wharf** is lined with restaurants and take-away fish counters. Sea lions beneath the wharf bray in an echoing cacophony.

Downtown Santa Cruz centers on **Pacific Avenue**, with boutiques, chain stores and cool cafes. In the hills above town, the **University of California at Santa Cruz** (UCSC; ☎ 831-459-4008; www.ucsc.edu) has 13,000 liberal-leaning students, a redwood-studded campus, architecturally interesting buildings – many of recycled materials – two top-notch galleries and a beautiful **arboretum** (☎ 831-427-2998).

Seymour Marine Discovery Center (☎ 831-459-3800; www2.ucsc.edu/seymourcenter; near Delaware Ave & Swift St; adult/student & senior $6/4; 10am-5pm Tue-Sat, noon-5pm Sun;), west of town near Natural Bridges, is part of UCSC's famous Long Marine Laboratory. Interactive exhibits include aquariums and the world's largest blue-whale skeleton, which gets lighted at Christmas.

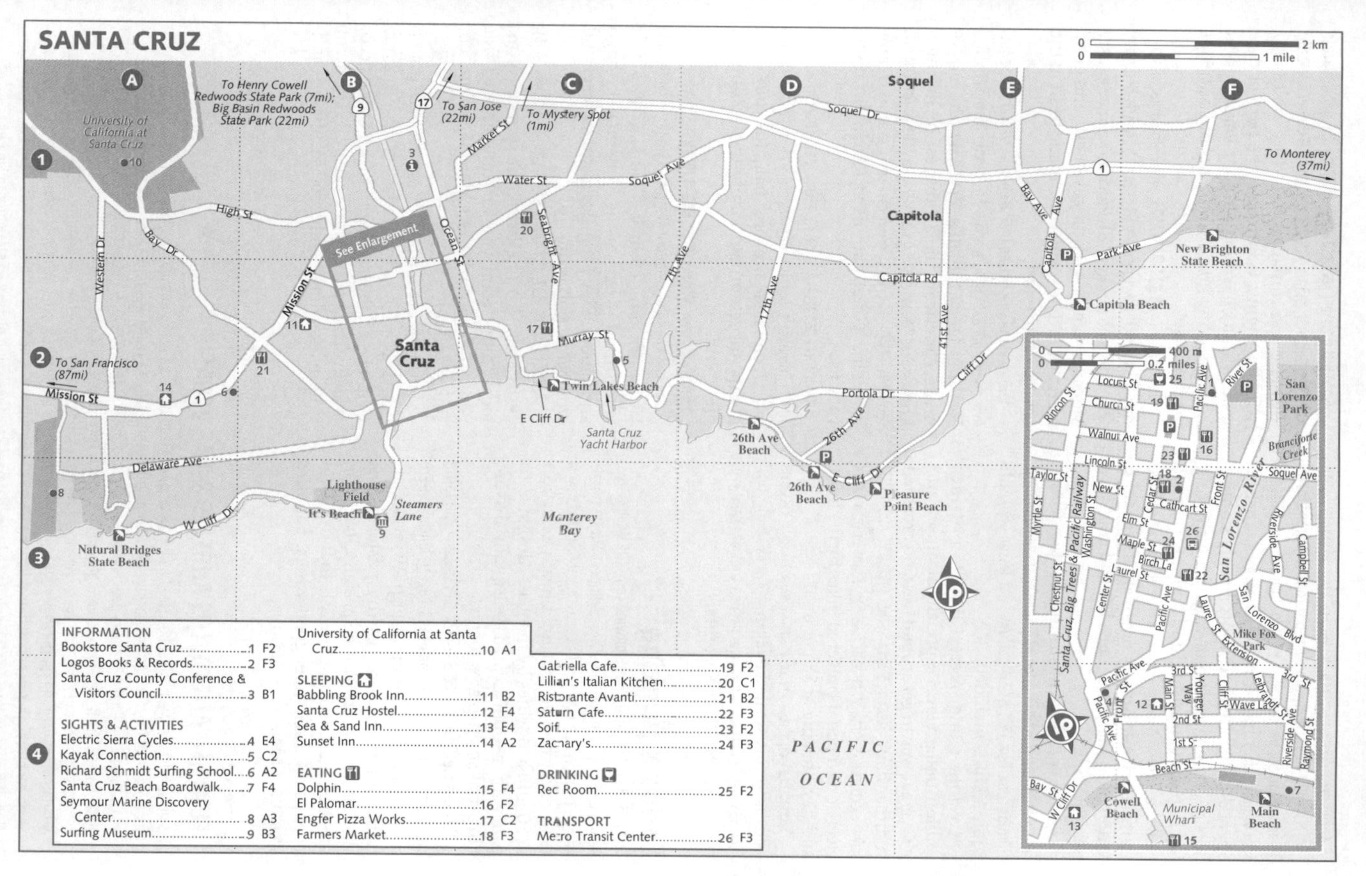
SANTA CRUZ
0 2 km
0 1 mile
To Henry Cowell Redwoods State Park (7mi); Big Basin Redwoods State Park (22mi)
To San Jose (22mi)
To Mystery Spot (1mi)
To San Francisco (87mi)
To Monterey (37mi)
University of California at Santa Cruz
Soquel
Capitola
Santa Cruz
See Enlargement
Soquel Dr
Soquel Ave
Water St
High St
Bay Dr
Western Dr
Mission St
Market St
Ocean St
Seabright Ave
Murray St
7th Ave
17th Ave
26th Ave
41st Ave
Capitola Rd
Capitola Ave
Bay Ave
Park Ave
Portola Dr
Cliff Dr
E Cliff Dr
W Cliff Dr
Delaware Ave
New Brighton State Beach
Capitola Beach
Twin Lakes Beach
Santa Cruz Yacht Harbor
26th Ave Beach
Pleasure Point Beach
Lighthouse Field
It's Beach
Steamers Lane
Natural Bridges State Beach
Monterey Bay
PACIFIC OCEAN
0 400 m
0 0.2 miles
Locust St
Church St
Walnut Ave
Lincoln St
Taylor St
New St
Cedar St
Cathcart St
Elm St
Maple St
Birch La
Laurel St
Myrtle St
Chestnut St
Center St
Washington St
Santa Cruz, Big Trees & Pacific Railway
Pacific Ave
Rincon St
River St
Front St
San Lorenzo Park
Branciforte Creek
Soquel Ave
San Lorenzo River
Riverside Ave
Campbell St
San Lorenzo Blvd
Mike Fox Park
Laurel St Extension
3rd St
Main St
Younger Way
Cliff St
Wave La
Leibrandt St
2nd St
1st St
Beach St
Raymond St
Bay St
W Cliff Dr
Cowell Beach
Municipal Wharf
Main Beach
INFORMATION
Bookstore Santa Cruz 1 F2
Logos Books & Records 2 F3
Santa Cruz County Conference & Visitors Council 3 B1
University of California at Santa Cruz 10 A1
SIGHTS & ACTIVITIES
Electric Sierra Cycles 4 E4
Kayak Connection 5 C2
Richard Schmidt Surfing School 6 A2
Santa Cruz Beach Boardwalk 7 F4
Seymour Marine Discovery Center 8 A3
Surfing Museum 9 B3
SLEEPING
Babbling Brook Inn 11 B2
Santa Cruz Hostel 12 F4
Sea & Sand Inn 13 E4
Sunset Inn 14 A2
EATING
Dolphin 15 F4
El Palomar 16 F2
Engfer Pizza Works 17 C2
Farmers Market 18 F3
Gabriella Cafe 19 F2
Lillian's Italian Kitchen 20 C1
Ristorante Avanti 21 B2
Saturn Cafe 22 F3
Soif 23 F2
Zachary's 24 F3
DRINKING
Rec Room 25 F2
TRANSPORT
Metro Transit Center 26 F3

Classic Americana kitsch, the Mystery Spot (☎ 831-423-8897; www.mysteryspot.com; off Branciforte Dr; admission $5, parking $5; 9am-7pm summer, 10am-5pm winter;) has scarcely changed since it opened in the 1940s. On this steeply sloping hillside, compasses point crazily, mysterious forces push you around and buildings lean at weird angles. Make reservations or be stuck waiting. Head 3 miles north of town: take Water St to Market St, turn left and continue into the hills.

To try your luck at surfing, contact Richard Schmidt Surfing School (☎ 831-423-0928; www.richardschmidt.com; Box 192, 849 Almar Ave; 2hr lesson $80); all equipment is included.

Cycling along West Cliff Dr provides million-dollar views, especially at sunset, and it's a great way to get around town on crowded summer days. Electric Sierra Cycles (☎ 831-425-1593; www.electricbikes.com; 302 Pacific Ave; 10am-6pm) rents electric and pedal-powered bikes by the hour and day, starting at $8 per hour.

You can occasionally spot sea lions, otters and dolphins while kayaking. Kayak Connection (☎ 831-479-1121; www.kayakconnection.com; 413 Lake Ave; kayak s/d per 4hr $35/50) has rentals.

Eating & Drinking

Soif (☎ 831-423-2020; www.soifwine.com; 105 Walnut Ave; small plates $4-7, mains $18-23; dinner) Part wine shop, part wine bar and restaurant, Soif draws food-savvy bon vivants for a heady selection of 50 unusual wines by the glass, designed to pair with a sophisticated, seasonally driven, Euro-Cal small-plates menu.

Ristorante Avanti (☎ 831-427-0135; www.ristoranteavanti.com; 1711 Mission St; mains $13-26; lunch Mon-Fri, dinner nightly;) Mom-and-pop Avanti's Cal-Italian menu features earthy pasta dishes; chicken cacciatore is the specialty, but look for seasonal knockout specials that use local produce. Casual vibe, good wines. Families welcome. Make reservations.

Gabriella Cafe (☎ 831-457-1677; www.gabriellacafe.com; 910 Cedar St; mains $15-25; lunch & dinner Tue-Sun) Intimate and romantic, with tiny tables and twinkling lights, Gabriella is the perfect date spot, with a charming outdoor garden for a long, lingering lunch. Dinner could be better for the price.

El Palomar (☎ 831-425-7575; www.elpalomarcilantros.com; 1336 Pacific Ave; meals $10-22; lunch & dinner;) Always-packed El Palomar serves tasty Mexican staples – try the ceviches – and good margaritas. The tortillas are made fresh in the covered courtyard.

Lillian's Italian Kitchen (☎ 831-425-2288; 1116 Soquel Ave; mains $8-23 lunch Tue-Fri, dinner Mon-Sat;) Nothing-fancy Lillian's serves terrific home-made American-Italian dishes, including a knockout 'Sunday gravy' – a slow-cooked, tomato-based meat sauce – using an old family recipe. Great paninis at lunch. No reservations.

Dolphin (☎ 831-426-5830; Municipal Wharf; mains $9-18; breakfast, lunch & dinner;) For fish on the wharf, you'll get the most bang for your buck at this unpretentious, family-owned diner at pier's end.

Engfer Pizza Works (☎ 831-429-1856; www.engferpizzaworks.com; 537 Seabright Ave; pizzas $8-17; 4-9:30pm Tue-Sun;) Engfer makes Santa Cruz's best wood-fired pizzas, using homemade dough and sauces. Play Ping-Pong and sip beer and wine while you wait.

Zachary's (☎ 831-427-0646; 819 Pacific Ave; dishes $6-11; breakfast;) The breakfast spot covetous locals don't want you to know about (hide your guidebook). 'Mike's Mess' is the kitchen-sink standout.

Saturn Cafe (☎ 831-429-8505; www.saturncafe.com; 145 Laurel St; dishes $6-9; 10am-3am; V) A Santa Cruz classic, the late-night Saturn Cafe's decor is an evolving pop-culture carnival. The menu is upmarket diner, with good salads and sandwiches and lots for vegetarians.

FURTHER AFIELD: LOS ANGELES & LAS VEGAS

San Franciscans live in a bubble. Need a new viewpoint? Heading to LA is like pushing the fast-forward button on the movie of your life. For muscle beaches, celebrity sightings and camera-ready wackiness, head south on coastal Hwy 1 to La La Land. It'll take 12 hours depending on traffic and how often you stop. A quicker jaunt is less-scenic Hwy 101 (nine hours); the fastest route is boring inland I-5, which takes about six hours.

Las Vegas, Nevada, is a nine-hour non-stop drive from San Francisco. Cross the Bay Bridge to 580 east, to I-5 south, veering off towards 99 south (at exit 278), to 58 east, then I-15 the last 160 miles. A slower, gloriously scenic option is to go east through Yosemite National Park on Hwy 120 (summer only; verify by calling 800-GAS-ROAD) and south on Hwy 395, east on Hwy 190 through Death Valley National Park then south on Hwy 95 straight into Sin City.

Farmers Market (☎ 831-454-0566; www.santacruzfarmersmarket.org; Cedar & Lincoln Sts; 2:30-6:30pm Wed) For organic fruits and vegetables and a taste of the local vibe, hit this oh-so-colorful farmers market.

Red Room (☎ 831-426-2994; 1003 Cedar St) Scenesters swill cocktails at Red. Upstairs is style-y, with moody lighting, big sofas and a fireplace; downstairs is grungier and looks like a vintage-50s mafia hangout. Signs say you can't smoke, but many do.

Sleeping

Santa Cruz doesn't have enough beds to satisfy demand: expect outrageous prices at peak times for nothing-special rooms. Prices listed below are for high season; winter is much cheaper. For straightforward motels, check Ocean St. Places near the boardwalk run from friendly to frightening.

Babbling Brook Inn (☎ 831-427-2437; www.babblingbrookinn.com; 1025 Laurel St; r $209-289;) Built around a running stream with meandering gardens, the inn has cozy rooms in small buildings, decorated in French-provincial style. Most have gas fireplaces, some have Jacuzzis; all have featherbeds and downy-soft pillows. There's afternoon wine and full breakfast.

Sea & Sand Inn (☎ 831-427-3400; www.santacruzmotels.com; 201 W Cliff Dr; r $199-249;) The spiffiest motel in town overlooks Main Beach and has grassy lawns at the cliff's edge – fall asleep to braying sea lions. Rooms are smallish and bathrooms could use updating (showers, no tubs), but they're clean, never mind that the tiles needs re-grouting. Stellar views explain the rates.

Sunset Inn (☎ 831-423-7500; www.sunsetinnsantacruz.com; 2424 Mission St; r $95-165;) On the outskirts of town, this single-story motel has big rooms with fridges and microwaves. It's plain Jane, but clean, well kept and one of town's best deals.

Santa Cruz Hostel (☎ 831-423-8304; www.hi-santacruz.org; 321 Main St; dm $25-28, d $55-75) This lovely hostel occupies several century-old cottages surrounded by flowering gardens. It's two blocks from the beach, five from downtown. Note: there's a three-night maximum and an 11pm curfew (bummer). Make reservations.

Pitch a tent and **camp** (☎ 800-444-7275; campsites $25) among the redwoods in nearby Henry Cowell Redwoods or Big Basin Redwoods State Parks, north of town off Hwy 9. Otherwise, there's New Brighton State Beach, 4 miles south of Santa Cruz, near Capitola. Call ahead, as these state parks may close under Governor Schwarzenegger's budget plan.

Getting Around

Santa Cruz Metropolitan Transit (☎ 831-425-8600; www.scmtd.com; ticket/day pass $1.50/4.50) operates from the Santa Cruz **Metro Transit Center** (920 Pacific Ave) and serves the greater Santa Cruz region, including San Jose ($4), where you can catch Caltrain to SF, or Amtrak to Oakland and Berkeley.

TRANSPORTATION

Back during the Gold Rush, prospectors would run, gallop and swim to get to San Francisco pronto. But since those days the city has mellowed out, and now being in a rush seems very un–San Francisco. Dude, this isn't Los Angeles or New York. When San Franciscans don't have somewhere else to be right quick – and even when they do – most people walk, bike or take Muni instead of a car or cab. Those slackers are smart: this is the best way to take in San Francisco, and helps preserve the city's many all-natural charms by curbing carbon emissions and other pollutants.

As Jack Kerouac says, the journey to San Francisco can blow your mind. That said, you don't have to endure months *On the Road* to make it memorable. Consider taking your sweet time getting here by train, boat or bicycle instead of a car or plane. That way, you can actually relax and enjoy the spectacular coastal scenery without all the wrong turns, traffic jams, flight delays, airport security hassles and excess carbon emissions. The hippies had it right: San Francisco isn't just a destination, it's a total trip.

AIR

Deals can be found year-round to San Francisco, where service from multiple domestic and international airlines in three Bay Area airports keeps prices competitive. Listed below are some of the major carriers serving the Bay Area. Check online for the best deals, and if you're flying into San Jose or Oakland instead of San Francisco, don't forget to factor in additional transit time and costs to get to SF. To take the scenic route to SF, consider taking the train instead (p306) – you'll be doing the environment a favor by cutting back on carbon emissions, too. Flights and rail tickets can be booked online at www.lonelyplanet.com/travel_services.

THINGS CHANGE...

The information in this chapter is particularly vulnerable to change. Check directly with the airline or a travel agent to make sure you understand how a fare (and ticket you may buy) works and be aware of the security requirements for international travel. Shop carefully. The details given in this chapter should be regarded as pointers and are not a substitute for your own careful, up-to-date research.

Airlines

Alaska Airlines (AS; ☎ 800-252-7522; www.alaskaair.com) Covers much of the western USA, Canada and Western Mexico; direct service to Hawaii, Alaska and Seattle.

British Airways (BA; ☎ 800-247-9297; www.britishairways.com) Offers nonstop flights to London.

Continental Airlines (CO; ☎ 800-523-3273; www.continental.com) Serves a wide range of domestic locations, including nonstop service to Chicago, New York and Houston (hub), and onward to major airports in Asia and Europe.

Delta Airlines (DL; ☎ 800-221-1212; www.delta.com) Serves domestic airports, with Atlanta the hub; international partners serve major European destinations.

Jet Blue (B6; ☎ 800-538-2583; www.jetblue.com) Flies from Oakland and San Francisco. Often has the cheapest flights to New York City, and has nonstop service to Boston, Austin, Long Beach (California) and Washington DC.

Northwest Airlines (NW; ☎ 800-225-2525; www.nwa.com) Partners with Dutch carrier KLM to serve 1000 cities in 160 countries.

Southwest Airlines (SW; ☎ 800-435-9792; www.southwest.com) Low rates on flights throughout the USA from Oakland, San Francisco and San Jose.

United Airlines (UA; ☎ 800-864-8331, international 800-538-2929; www.united.com) Serves a wide range of destinations to and from its hub at SFO, with direct service to Australia, London, Japan, Hong Kong, Beijing and Munich.

Virgin Airlines (VS; ☎ 800-821-5438; www.virgin-atlantic.com, www.virginamerica.com) Virgin Atlantic flies nonstop to London; Virgin America offers low-cost nonstop service to LA, San Diego, Seattle, New York and Boston.

Airports

SAN FRANCISCO INTERNATIONAL AIRPORT

One of the busiest airports in the country, San Francisco International Airport (SFO; Map p265; ☎ 650-821-8211; www.flysfo.com) serves over 40 million passengers annually on 45 airlines. Flights

CLIMATE CHANGE & TRAVEL

Climate change is a serious threat to the ecosystems that humans rely upon, and air travel is the fastest-growing contributor to the problem. Lonely Planet regards travel, overall, as a global benefit, but believes we all have a responsibility to limit our personal impact on global warming.

Flying & Climate Change

Pretty much every form of motor transport generates CO_2 (the main cause of human-induced climate change) but planes are far and away the worst offenders, not just because of the sheer distances they allow us to travel, but because they release greenhouse gases high into the atmosphere. The statistics are frightening: two people taking a return flight between Europe and the US will contribute as much to climate change as an average household's gas and electricity consumption over a whole year.

Carbon Offset Schemes

Climatecare.org and other websites use 'carbon calculators' that allow jetsetters to offset the greenhouse gases they are responsible for with contributions to energy-saving projects and other climate-friendly initiatives in the developing world – including projects in India, Honduras, Kazakhstan and Uganda.

Lonely Planet, together with Rough Guides and other concerned partners in the travel industry, supports the carbon offset scheme run by climatecare.org. Lonely Planet offsets all of its staff and author travel.

For more information check out our website: www.lonelyplanet.com.

to/from Asia, Europe and Latin America go through the International terminal; the North and South terminals handle domestic flights. The International terminal has racked up awards for food and architecture; Terminal 2 is currently undergoing reinvention as a LEED Silver-certified green building. The entire airport is nonsmoking.

There are information booths (8am-1:30am) and white courtesy phones (information 7-0018) on the lower (arrivals) level of all three terminals, Traveler's Aid information booths (9am-9pm) on the upper levels, and an airport ground transportation hotline (800-736-2008; 7:30am-5pm Mon-Fri).

A clinic (650-821-5600; 8:30am-5pm Mon-Fri, 9am-1pm Sat) can be contacted from white courtesy phones found on the lower level of the International terminal. Harmony Pharmacy (650-821-1313; www.harmonypharmacy.com; 9am-6pm) is available in Terminal 3's Boarding Area F, after you pass through security.

All terminals have ATMs, and there is a currency exchange in the International terminal. Lockers (per 24hr $2) are located at all boarding areas, and there is luggage storage in the travel agency area, in the upper-level connector between the South and International terminals.

SFO is on the bayside of the peninsula, 14 miles south of Downtown San Francisco. Highway 101 connects the airport directly to Downtown. If you're driving, the trip between the airport and the city can take as little as 20 minutes, but give yourself an hour during morning and evening rush hours. If you're headed to the airport via Hwy 101, take the San Francisco International Airport exit. Don't be misled by the Airport Rd exit, which just leads to parking lots and warehouses.

Transportation arrives and departs at the upper and lower levels, and color-coded zones identify the correct places to catch buses going to rental-car lots, long-term parking lots, other airports, and nearby hotels. This can be confusing, so read the terminal signs carefully before stepping outside. For transportation options to Downtown SF, see the boxed text, p302.

OAKLAND INTERNATIONAL AIRPORT

Travelers arriving at Oakland International Airport (OAK; Map p265; 510-563-3300; www.oaklandairport.com), 15 miles east of Downtown, will have a little further to go to reach San Francisco. The least expensive way from the Oakland airport is via BART train and the AirBART shuttle (510-569-8310; adult/child & senior $3/1; 5am-midnight Mon-Sat, 8am-midnight Sun). The AirBART shuttle leaves both terminals every 10 to 20 minutes for the BART Coliseum Station; buy your AirBART shuttle ticket from the ticket machine before exiting the airport. Upon arrival at Coliseum Station, purchase your BART ticket ($3.80) from the machine for the 30-minute trip to Downtown San Francisco.

NORMAN Y MINETA SAN JOSE INTERNATIONAL AIRPORT

Fifty miles south of Downtown San Francisco, Norman Y Mineta San Jose International Airport (SJC; Map p265; ☎ 408-501-0979; www.sjc.org) is a straight shot into the city by car via Highway 101. The VTA Airport Flyer (bus 10; tickets $1.75; from 5am to midnight) makes a continuous run between the Santa Clara Caltrain station (Railroad Ave and Franklin St) and the airport terminals, departing every 10 to 15 minutes. From Santa Clara station, Caltrain (one-way $7.75; 80 minutes) runs several trains every day to the terminal at 4th and King Sts in SF.

BICYCLE

San Francisco is fairly bike-friendly, but traffic Downtown can be dangerous; biking is best east of Van Ness Ave. For bike shops and rentals in SF, see p229; for bike rentals and tours in Wine Country, see p284. Bicycle rentals run $7 to $10 per hour, $28 to $50 per day, and over $100 per week. Bike prices start at about $200, with top-of-the-range models starting at $650; check shops and Craigslist (www.craigslist.org) for sales and used bikes. If you're bringing your own, bicycles can be checked in boxes on Greyhound buses for $20 to $30; bike boxes cost $10. On Amtrak, bikes can be checked as baggage for $5.

BOAT

The opening of the Bay Bridge in 1936 and the Golden Gate Bridge in 1937 spelled the near demise of ferry services across the Bay, but with the revival of the Embarcadero and reinvention of the Ferry Building as a gourmet dining destination, commuters and tourists alike are taking the scenic way across the bay after leisurely meals at Ferry Building eateries.

Alcatraz Cruises (Map p63; ☎ 415-981-7625; http://alcatrazcruises.com; day tour adult/child/senior $26/$16/$24.50, night tour $33/$19.50/$30.50; call center 8am-7pm) has ferries departing from Pier 33 for Alcatraz every half-hour from 9am to 3:55pm, and at 6:10pm and 6:45pm for night tours. For tour details, see p62.

Blue & Gold Fleet Ferries (Map p63; ☎ 415-705-8200; www.blueandgoldfleet.com) operates ferries from the Ferry Building, Pier 39 and Pier 41 at Fisherman's Wharf to Jack London Sq in Oakland (one-way $7.75), Tiburon or Sausalito (one-way $11) and Angel Island (p282). During the baseball season, a Giants ferry service runs directly from the landing at the Seals Plaza entrance to AT&T Park to Oakland and Alameda. Ticket booths are located at the Ferry Building and Piers 39 and 41 (Map p63).

Golden Gate Transit Ferries (Map p63; ☎ 415-455-2000; www.goldengateferry.org; 6am-9:30pm Mon-Fri, 10am-6pm Sat & Sun) runs regular ferry services from the Ferry Building to Larkspur and Sausalito (one-way adult/child under five years/senior and youth six to 18 years $7.85/free/3.90). Transfers are available to Muni bus services, and bicycles are permitted. Ferries from Larkspur to Giants games also run in baseball season; $8 one-way tickets are available at ferry terminal ticket windows.

Get to Napa car-free via Vallejo Ferry (Map p63; ☎ 877-643-3779; www.baylinkferry.com; adult/child under

GETTING INTO TOWN

- BART (Bay Area Rapid Transit; ☎ 415-989-2278; www.bart.gov; 6am-11pm) offers a cheap, direct 30-minute ride from the San Francisco airport to Downtown San Francisco for $8.10 one-way, and connects to Oakland via the AirBART shuttle (p301). The SFO BART station is connected to the International terminal; tickets can be purchased from machines inside the station entrance.
- Door-to-door shuttle vans pick up/drop off from any San Francisco location to/from SFO, and usually take some time circulating to different hotels to pick up more passengers. Call for a reservation for pick ups in SF; reservations aren't necessary from the airport, since vans leave frequently from the baggage claim level outside all terminals. Companies include Super Shuttle (☎ 415-558-8500; www.supershuttle.com), Lorrie's (☎ 415-334-9000; www.gosfovan.com), Quake City (☎ 415-255-4899; www.quakecityshuttle.com) and American Airporter Shuttle (☎ 415-202-0733, 800-282-7758; www.americanairporter.onsmartpages.com/services). Fares are $14 to $17 one-way.
- SamTrans (☎ 800-660-4287; www.samtrans.com) express bus KX ($4.50, 30 minutes) or the slightly slower local SamTrans bus 292 ($1.75) leave from the BART station at SFO, and drop you at San Francisco's Transbay Terminal (Map pp110–11) in the South of Market area.
- Taxis to Downtown San Francisco from SFO cost $30 to $45, plus tip, departing from the yellow zone on the lower level. Taxis at Oakland airport leave curbside and cost $60 to $70 to Downtown SF.

BIKING AROUND THE BAY AREA

- Within SF: Muni has racks that can accommodate two bikes on some of its community-service routes, including 17, 35, 36, 37, 39, 53, 56, 66, 76, 91 and 108.
- Marin County: bikes are allowed on the Golden Gate Bridge, so getting north to Marin County is no problem. You can transport bicycles on Golden Gate Transit buses, which usually have free racks available (first-come, first-served). Ferries also allow bikes aboard when space allows.
- Wine Country: to transport your bike to Wine Country, take Golden Gate Transit or the Vallejo Ferry. Within Sonoma Valley, take Arnold Dr instead of busy Hwy 12; through Napa Valley, take the Silverado Trail instead of Hwy 29, with manic drivers U-turning for wineries and swerving for photo-ops. The most spectacular ride in Wine Country – and pretty much anywhere else we can think of – is sun-dappled, tree-lined West Dry Creek Rd in Sonoma's Dry Creek Valley.
- East Bay: cyclists can't use the Bay Bridge, so you'll need to take your bike on BART. Bikes are allowed on BART at all hours, but during rush hours some limits apply. Between 6:30am and 9am, people with bikes are only allowed to travel in the 'reverse commute' direction from Embarcadero station in San Francisco to points in the East Bay. From 4pm to 6:30pm, people with bikes can travel only from points in the East Bay to San Francisco, and they must exit at Embarcadero station. During commute hours, you can also travel with your bike across the bay via the CalTrans Bay Bridge Bicycle Commuter Shuttle (☎ 510-286-0876; tickets $1; ⏲ 6:30-8:30am & 3:50-6:15pm Mon-Fri), which operates between San Francisco's Transbay Terminal and the MacArthur BART station in Oakland.

6yr/senior & child over 6yr $13/free/6.50) with departures from Ferry Building docks about every hour from 6:30am to 7pm weekdays and every two hours from 11am to 7:30pm on weekends; bikes are permitted. From the Vallejo Ferry Terminal, take Napa Valley Vine bus 10 to downtown Napa, Yountville, St Helena or Calistoga.

BUS, STREETCAR & CABLE CAR

The city's principal public transportation system Muni operates nearly 100 bus lines, the streetcar system, and the city's signature cable cars. Buses and streetcars are referred to interchangeably as Muni and marked in this book with 🚌, while cable cars are marked with 🚋.

Some areas are better connected than others, but public transport spares you the costly hassle of driving and parking in San Francisco, and is often faster than driving during rush hour (7:30am to 9:30am and 4:30pm to 6:30pm, Monday to Friday). Nighttime and weekend service is less frequent. For fastest routes and the most exact departure times, consult http://transit.511.org.

Tickets can be bought on board buses and streetcars, or at Muni stations for the underground streetcars. On most Muni lines, free transfer tickets are available at the start of your journey and you can then use them for two connecting Muni trips within 90 minutes or so (but not BART or cable cars). Hang onto your ticket or transfer even if you're not planning to use it again: if you're caught without one by the transit police, you're subject to a $75 fine (repeat offenders may soon be fined up to $500).

Discounts & Passes

Muni passes and discounts are available as follows:

One-day Muni Passport good for unlimited travel on buses, streetcars and cable cars $11

Three-day Passport $18

Week-long Passport $24

10-ride ticket book $20

Monthly Muni Fast Pass adult $55, senior, youth (five to 17 years) or disabled $15

Ticket books and Passports can be purchased at the Muni kiosk at the Powell St cable-car turnaround on Market St, at Montgomery station ticket booth, the half-price ticket kiosk on Union Square, and from a number of hotels. Fast Passes are available at the Muni kiosk at the Powell St cable car turnaround and from businesses that display the Muni Pass sign in their window.

Bus

Four public bus systems serve the Bay Area, and most leave from clearly marked bus stops; for transit maps, check out the website listed

MAGIC BUS

Ever since Ken Kesey and his Merry Pranksters boarded their bus with a declared destination 'Further' (see p34), buses have been the transport of choice for California hippies. It's not too late to get on the bus, and go further with these biofueled buses:

Green Tortoise (☎ 800-867-8647, 415-834-1000; www.greentortoise.com) Quasi-organized, slow travel on customized, biodiesel-fueled buses with built-in berths that run from San Francisco to points across California and beyond, including three-day trips to Yosemite or Death Valley; three-to-five-day jaunts to Burning Man and other festivals; and three-to-seven-day coastal trips south to Santa Cruz, Monterey and LA.

Transported SF (☎ 415-424-1058; www.transportedsf.com) The journey is the destination with these DJ-equipped buses bound for organic Sonoma wineries, East Bay food-foraging expeditions, and nowhere in particular in the Mission.

for each bus system. The main hub connecting San Francisco to points across the bay and beyond is the Transbay Terminal (Map pp110–11; 425 Mission St); this is the SF terminus for Greyhound.

WITHIN SF

Muni (☎ 415-701-2311; www.sfmuni.com; adult/child under 4yr/senior & child 5-17yr $2/free/75¢; 5am-late Mon-Fri, reduced schedules Sat & Sun) bus tickets are available on board, but you'll need exact change. Tickets are valid until the expiration time noted on your ticket. Arrival times can be viewed on digital displays or guesstimated by consulting schedules posted inside bus shelters. Owl service (1am to 5am) is offered on a limited number of lines, with departures about every half-hour. Buses display their route number and final destination on the front and side. If the number is followed by the letter A, B, X or L, then it's a limited-stop or express service.

The major bus routes are as follows:

5 Fulton From the Transbay Terminal, along Market and McAllister Sts to Fulton St, along the north side of Golden Gate Park to the ocean.

7 Haight From the Ferry Building, along Market and Haight Sts, through the Haight to the southeast corner of Golden Gate Park; daytime only.

14 Mission From the Transbay Terminal, along Mission St through SoMa and the Mission District.

15 Kearny From 3rd St in SoMa, through the Financial District on Kearny St, through North Beach on Columbus Ave, then along Powell St to the Fisherman's Wharf area.

22 Fillmore From Dogpatch (Potrero Hill), through the Mission on 16th St, along Fillmore St past Japantown to Pacific Heights and the Marina.

33 Stanyan From San Francisco General Hospital, through the Mission, Castro and Haight, past Golden Gate Park to Clement St.

BUS SERVICES TO/FROM SF

To travel both to and around the East Bay, AC Transit (☎ 510-891-4777; www.actransit.org) offers bus services from the Transbay Terminal. For public transport connections from BART in the East Bay, get an AC Transit transfer ticket before leaving the BART station and then pay an additional 75¢.

Golden Gate Transit (Map pp110–11; ☎ 415-455-2000; www.goldengatetransit.org), the main public transit company serving Marin and Sonoma counties, also connects to San Francisco, but be advised that service can be slow and erratic. Bus 70/80 runs from San Francisco to Petaluma ($8) and to Santa Rosa ($8.80); catch it at 1st and Mission Sts, across from the Transbay Terminal.

Greyhound (☎ 800-231-2222; www.greyhound.com; 425 Mission St) provides nationwide bus service from the Transbay Terminal and somewhat more limited service from its terminal in downtown Oakland (2103 San Pablo Ave). Regular services operate from San Francisco to Los Angeles ($39 and up, from eight hours) and Santa Rosa ($21 to $26); transfer for local buses.

Samtrans (☎ 800-660-4287; www.samtrans.com) runs buses up and down the peninsula between San Francisco and the South Bay, including two bus services to/from SFO. Buses pick up/drop off from the Transbay Terminal and other marked bus stops within the city; see the website for the transit map.

Streetcar

Muni Metro streetcars run both above and below ground, from 5am to midnight on weekdays, with limited schedules on weekends. The L and N lines operate 24 hours, but between 12:30am and 5:30am, 'Owl' buses replace the streetcars.

At underground Muni stations, you'll need $2 in coins for turnstiles; change bills using the BART ticket machines, and don't forget to grab your ticket as you pass through the turnstile. Above-ground, tickets can be bought on board in the front car, but you'll need exact change. Streetcar arrival times are indicated on digital displays in stations and on some street-level transit shelters.

The most scenic route is the F-Market line, which runs mint-condition antique streetcars along Market St from Castro St to the Embarcadero, where they turn north to Fisherman's Wharf. Other streetcars run below Market St Downtown, beginning at the Embarcadero. Beyond Van Ness Ave station, Muni lines split into five routes: J-Church, K-Ingleside, L-Taraval, M-Oceanview and N-Judah. The T line heads south along the Embarcadero through SoMa and Mission Bay, then down 3rd St past Dogpatch to Bayview.

KEY STREETCAR DESTINATIONS

F Fisherman's Wharf and Embarcadero to Castro

J Downtown to Mission/Castro

K, L, M Downtown to Castro

N Caltrain and SBC Ballpark to Haight and Ocean Beach

T Embarcadero to Caltrain, China Basin and Bayview

Cable Car

In this age of seat belts and air bags, a rickety cable-car ride is an anachronistic thrill. Cable cars are handy on hills, if you can find a spot on board. The Powell St cable-car turnaround (p74) can be crowded; locals usually head uphill along the line and leap on board instead. There are seats for about 30 passengers, but sitters are often outnumbered by passengers clinging to creaking leather straps.

Cable cars cost $10 to ride all day or $5 for a single trip (no transfers); kids under four years old ride free. Tickets can be purchased on board or at the Muni kiosks at Powell and Market Sts or Hyde St at Beach. Cable cars run from approximately 6am to 12:30am daily.

CABLE CAR LINES

California Runs east–west along California St, from the Downtown terminus at Market and Davis Sts through Chinatown and Nob Hill to Van Ness Ave.

Powell-Mason Runs from the Powell St cable-car turnaround past Union Square, turns west along Jackson St, and descends north down Mason St, Columbus Ave and Taylor St towards Fisherman's Wharf. On the return trip it takes Washington St instead of Jackson St.

Powell-Hyde Follows the same route as Powell-Mason until Jackson St, where it turns down Hyde St to terminate at Aquatic Park; coming back it takes Washington St.

CAR & MOTORCYCLE

If you can, avoid driving in San Francisco: traffic is a given, street parking is harder to find than true love, and meter readers are ruthless. Gas prices are rising steadily, and driving on these hills means shifting gears and applying brakes often – and contending with drivers who think they're Steve McQueen in *Bullitt*. For tips on living the care-free, car-free SF life, check out www.liveablecity.org.

Driving

San Francisco streets mostly follow a grid bisected by Market St, and are well marked with signs to tourist zones such as North Beach, Fisherman's Wharf and Chinatown. If you're driving a stick shift (manual transmission), you'd better have your hill-start technique down pat. Before heading to any bridge, airport or other traffic choke-point, call ☎ 511 toll-free for a traffic update.

Members of the American Automobile Association (AAA; Map p77; ☎ 415-773-1900, 800-222-4357; www.aaa.com; 160 Sutter St; 8:30am-5:30pm Mon-Fri) can call the 800 number any time for emergency road service and towing. AAA also provides travel insurance and free road maps of the region.

Parking

This is a tricky, often costly proposition, especially Downtown – ask your hotel about parking, and inquire about validation at restaurants and entertainment venues. The most convenient Downtown parking lots are at the Embarcadero Center, at 5th and Mission Sts, under Union Square, and at Sutter and Stockton Sts; for more public parking garages, see www.sfmta.com. Downtown parking garages charge from $2 to $6 per hour and around $25 to $40 a day, depending on how long you park and whether you require in-and-out privileges.

If you're looking for street parking, know that parking restrictions are indicated by the following color-coded sidewalk curbs:

Blue Disabled parking only; identification required.

Green Ten-minute parking zone from 9am to 6pm.

Red No parking or stopping.

White For picking up or dropping off passengers only.

Yellow Loading zone from 7am to 6pm.

Parking tickets can be expensive. Desperate motorists often resort to double-parking or parking in red zones or on sidewalks, but parking authorities are quick to tow cars. If this should happen to you, you'll have to retrieve your car at **Autoreturn** (Map pp110–11; ☎ 415-865-8200; www.autoreturn.com; 450 7th St; 24hr; 27, 42). Besides at least $73 in fines for parking violations, you'll also have to fork out a towing and storage fee ($244.25 for the first four hours, $43 for the rest of the first day, $51.50 for every additional day, plus a $24.25 transfer fee if your car is moved to a long-term lot). Cars are usually stored at 415 7th St, corner of Harrison St.

Rental

All the big rental-car operators can be found in the Bay Area, along with a host of small, local operators. Booking ahead usually ensures the best rates, and airport rates are generally better than those in the city. As part of SF's citywide green initiative, rentals of hybrid cars and low-emissions vehicles from rental agencies at SFO are available at a discount.

Typically, a small car might cost $40 to $60 a day or $175 to $300 a week, plus the 9.5% sales tax. Unless your credit card covers car-rental insurance, you'll need to add in $10 to $15 a day for a loss/damage waiver. Most rates include unlimited mileage; with cheap rates, there's often a per-mile charge above a certain mileage.

To rent a motorcycle, contact **Dubbelju** (Map pp110–11; ☎ 415-495-2774; www.dubbelju.com; 689a Bryant St; 27); rates start at $99 per day.

MAJOR CAR-RENTAL AGENCIES

Alamo Rent-a-Car (Map p92; ☎ 415-693-0191, 800-327-9633; www.alamo.com; 750 Bush St; 7am-7pm; 2, 3, 4, 76; Powell-Mason, Powell-Hyde)

Avis (Map pp70–1; ☎ 415-929-2555, 800-831-2847; www.avis.com; 675 Post St; 6am-6pm; 2, 3, 4, 76)

Budget (Map pp70–1; ☎ 415-292-8981, 800-527-0700; www.budget.com; 321 Mason St; 6am-6pm; 2, 3, 4, 38)

Dollar (Map pp70–1; ☎ 800-800-5252; www.dollarcar.com; 364 O'Farrell St; 7am-7pm; 2, 3, 4, 38)

Hertz (Map pp70–1; ☎ 415-771-2200, 800-654-3131; www.hertz.com; 325 Mason St; 6am-6pm Mon-Thu, to 8pm Fri & Sat; 2, 3, 4, 38)

Thrifty (Map pp70–1; ☎ 415-788-6906, 800-367-2277; www.thrifty.com; 350 O'Farrell St; 7am-7pm; 2, 3, 4, 38)

Car Share

Car-sharing is a handy alternative to rentals that spares you pick-up/drop-off and parking hassles: reserve a car online for just an hour or two or all day, and you can usually pick up/drop off your car within blocks of where you're staying. It also does the environment a favor: fewer cars on the road means less congestion and pollution, especially given the fuel-efficient and hybrid models.

Zipcar (☎ 866-494-7227; www.zipcar.com) rents Prius Hybrids and Minis by the hour for flat rates starting at $8.33 per hour, including gas and insurance, or by day for $62.10; a $25 application fee and $50 prepaid usage are required in advance. Drivers without a US driver's license should follow instructions at www.zipcar.com/apply/foreign-drivers. Once approved, cars can be reserved at www.zipcar.com or at 866-4ZIPCAR. Check the website for pick-up/drop-off locations.

TAXI

Fares start at $3.50 at the flag drop and run about $2.25 per mile. Add at least 10% to the taxi fare as a tip ($1 minimum). Cabs are easiest to hail along Downtown streets; elsewhere you may need to call. Credit cards are often accepted, but ask before getting into the cab, or stop at an ATM along the way. The following taxi companies have 24-hour dispatches.

Arrow Taxicab (☎ 415-648-3181)

DeSoto Cab (☎ 415-970-1300)

Green Cab (☎ 415-626-4733; www.greencab.com) Fuel-efficient hybrids; worker-owned collective.

Luxor Cab (☎ 415-282-4141)

Yellow Cab (☎ 415-333-3333)

TRAIN

Easy on the eyes and carbon emissions too, train travel is a good way to visit the Bay Area and beyond. Three major train lines serve San Francisco, offering relaxing, scenic transit alternatives to traffic snarls, airport hassles and air pollution.

Throughout this book, venues readily accessible by **BART** (Bay Area Rapid Transit; ☎ 415-989-2278; www.bart.gov; 4am-midnight Mon-Fri, 6am-midnight Sat, 8am-midnight Sun) are denoted by followed by the name of the nearest BART station. The fastest link between Downtown and the Mission District also offers transit to SF airport,

Oakland and Berkeley. Within SF, one-way fares start at $1.75.

BART tickets are sold in machines in BART stations, and you'll need your ticket to enter and exit. If your ticket still has value after you exit the station, it is returned to you with the remaining balance. If your ticket's value is less than needed to exit, use an Addfare machine and pay the appropriate amount. Bicycles can be carried on BART, but not in the commute direction during weekday rush hours.

Four of the system's five lines pass through SF before terminating at Daly City or SFO. At San Francisco BART stations, a 25¢ discount is available for Muni buses and streetcars; look for transfer machines before you pass through the turnstiles. A monthly Muni Fast Pass covers BART travel within San Francisco. Popular BART routes include San Francisco to Oakland ($3.10) or downtown Berkeley ($3.65).

From the depot at 4th and King Sts in San Francisco, Caltrain (☎ 800-660-4287; www.caltrain.com) heads south to Millbrae (connecting to BART and SFO, 30 minutes), Palo Alto (one hour) and San Jose (1½ hours). This is primarily a commuter line, with frequent departures during weekday rush hours and less often between non-rush hours and on weekends.

The train routes Amtrak (☎ 800-872-7245; www.amtrakcalifornia.com) runs with government support through the San Francisco Bay are some of the most scenic in the USA, so take advantage while government subsidies last. The Coast Starlight is a spectacular 35-hour run from Los Angeles to Seattle via Oakland, and the California Zephyr takes its sweet time (51 hours) traveling from Chicago through the ruggedly handsome Rockies and Sierra Nevada en route to Emeryville (near Oakland). Both have sleeping cars and dining/lounge cars with panoramic windows, and at $98 and $182 one-way respectively, these train journeys can be cheaper than air travel with far lower carbon emissions. For a modest fee, you can stop along the route and resume your journey in a day or two. Amtrak runs free shuttle buses to San Francisco's Ferry Building and Caltrain station from its terminals in Emeryville and Oakland's Jack London Sq.

BUSINESS HOURS

Standard business hours are as follows. Nonstandard hours are listed in specific reviews.

Banks 9am-4:30pm or 5pm Monday to Friday (occasionally 9am to noon Saturday)

Offices 8:30am to 5:30pm Monday to Friday

Restaurants Breakfast 8am to noon, lunch noon to 3pm, dinner 5:30pm to 10pm; Saturday and Sunday brunch 10am to 2pm

Shops 10am or 11am to 6pm or 7pm Monday to Saturday and noon to 6pm Sunday

CHILDREN

San Francisco has the fewest kids per capita of any US city, which translates to fewer playmates for your kids and lots of doting attention from grown-ups. Most venues listed in this book are kid-friendly, even some of the high-end restaurants. To find the best places for children, just look for the symbol. For more on traveling with kids, check out Lonely Planet's *Travel with Children*.

Most museums and parks in town are equipped to keep kids happy and hyperstimulated. Golden Gate Park has something for every kid: a butterfly-filled rainforest dome and penguins at the California Academy of Sciences (p140), miniature forests at the Japanese Tea Garden (p140), and paddleboats and tandem bikes at Stow Lake (p140). In the Marina, kids squeal their way through the Tactile Dome at the Exploratorium (p102) and fly kites at Crissy Field (p105). For vacation photo-ops, check out the charming old carousel and sea lions at Pier 39 (p66), historic ships (p65), and 19th-century arcade games at Musée Mécanique (p66).

Uphill journeys can become big adventures on cable cars (p305), and a ferry ride (p302) can make a grand day out. Alcatraz (p62) fascinates and creeps out kids, and keeps them on their best behavior for hours.

Other key entertainment options for wee ones are the Asian Art Museum (p76), Zeum (p113), Portsmouth Square (p83), St Mary's Park (p84), Mission Dolores Park (p118) and the Cartoon Art Museum (p109).

Being a cool auntie or uncle (or mom or dad) is easy when you're in the know about all the hip hot spots for teens in SF, which currently include the following:

Haight St SFO Snowboarding & FTC Skateboarding (p158), Amoeba Music (p158) and Loyal Army Clothing (p157).

Japantown Kinokuniya Books & Stationery (p148), Super7 (p149) and Sundance Kabuki Cinema (p221).

Clement St Genki (p190) and Park Life (p160).

Valencia St 826 Valencia (p118) and Ritual Coffee Roasters (p202).

Babysitting

Licensed childcare can be found through American Child Care (Map p82; ☎ 415-285-2300; www.americanchildcare.com; Suite 1600, 580 California St; California) for $20 per hour plus gratuity, and a four-hour minimum. Major hotels often offer childcare for $15 to $30 per hour through providers with solid references. Otherwise, you can choose from the dozens of nanny and babysitter listings daily on Craigslist (http://sfbay.craigslist.org/kid), but be sure to check references and credentials first.

CLIMATE

Don't believe the hype: Mark Twain never actually said 'The coldest winter I ever spent was a summer in San Francisco,' although legend has it that he caught a mean case of hypothermia here. To avoid a similar fate, always bring layers of clothes with you to brave wind whipping along Downtown streets at up to 30mph, fog in the Richmond and Sunset even when it's sunny in the Haight, and a clammy noir-novel chill that tends to settle over the city at night.

The best times to visit San Francisco are in spring (March to May) after the winter rains have ended, and in the late summer or early fall (August to November) when the city

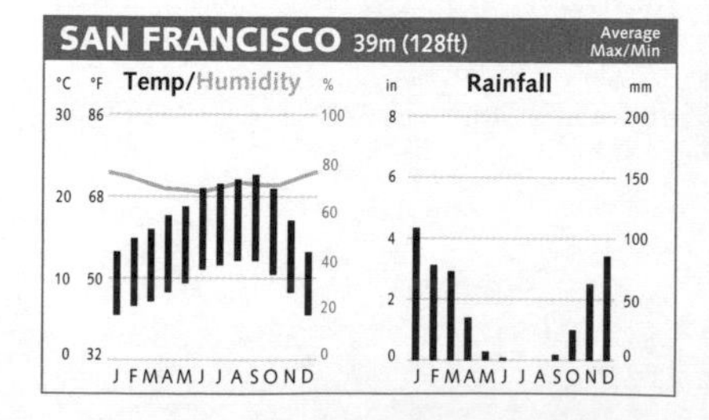

enjoys long stretches of warm, dry weather. The winter rainy season (December to February) can be wet and gloomy, but temperatures never go below freezing in town. For more on ideal times to visit SF, see p20, and for the latest forecast, see www.sfgate.com/weather.

COURSES

Inspiration is a given in San Francisco – the question is, what are you going to do about it? There's great raw material here for creative minds: farmers markets (see the boxed text, p169), Britex Fabrics (p144), industrial excess at SCRAP (p153) and art supplies at Flax (p158). To get schooled in SF, see the Sports & Activities chapter (p228) for classes in aquatic exercise, croquet, flamenco, fly casting, hang gliding, kite boarding, lawn bowling, Lindy hopping, printmaking, rock climbing, sailing, trapeze, windsurfing and yoga.

Museums and local universities also offer lecture series and short courses. The following venues are among those offering hands-on workshops:

Asian Art Museum (p76) Calligraphy, woodblock prints and other hands-on art demos.

California College of the Arts (p119) Fashion design, visual arts and art collecting.

Cav Wine Bar (p203) Wine tasting and pairings.

Cheese Plus (p176) Cheese tasting and pairings.

Real Food (p178) Cooking courses.

San Francisco Center for the Book (p119) Bookmaking and binding.

San Francisco School of Bartending (Map pp70–1; ☎ 415-362-1116; www.sfbartending.com; Suite 833, 760 Market St; 🚌 & Ⓜ Powell St) Cocktail making and shaking.

CUSTOMS REGULATIONS

Each person over the age of 21 is allowed to bring 1L of liquor and 200 cigarettes duty-free into the USA. Non-US citizens are allowed to bring in $100 worth of duty-free gifts. Should you be carrying more than $10,000 in US and foreign cash, traveler's checks or money orders, you need to declare the excess amount – undeclared sums in excess of $10,000 may be subject to confiscation.

DISCOUNTS & CARDS

The Go Card (☎ 800-887-9103; www.gosanfranciscocard.com; adult/child 1-day $49.99/39.99, 2-day $79.99/54.99, 3-day $89.99/71.99) offers unlimited access to the city's major attractions, including cable cars, the MH de Young Memorial Museum, Exploratorium, SFMOMA, Aquarium of the Bay and more, plus discounts on packaged tours and waterfront restaurants and cafes. Do the math on entry fees at your desired destinations, and think about how much you reasonably can do in a day; there's no sense tuckering yourself out just to sweeten your Go Card deal.

It pays to be green in SF, with special discounts on Bay Area green-friendly businesses from the Green Zebra guide (☎ 415-346-2361; www.thegreenzebra.org). Some green-minded venues also offer discounts for ticket-bearing Muni riders, including the MH de Young Memorial Museum, the California Academy of Sciences and the Legion of Honor. For public transit passes, see p303.

ELECTRICITY

Electric current in the USA is 110 to 115 volts, 60Hz AC. Outlets may be suited for flat two-prong or three-prong plugs. If your appliance is made for another electrical system, pick up a transformer or adapter at Walgreens (p312).

EMBASSIES & CONSULATES

Australia (Map pp110–11; ☎ 415-536-1970; www.australiaconsulate.org; Suite 200, 625 Market St, SoMa; 🕑 8:45am-1pm & 2-4:30pm Mon-Fri; 🚌 6, 7, 71, F, J, K, L, M, N, T; 🚌 & Ⓜ Embarcadero)

Canada (Map p82; ☎ 415-834-3180; www.sanfrancisco.gc.ca; 580 California St, 14th fl, Chinatown; 🕑 8:30am-4:30pm Mon-Fri; 🚌 & Ⓜ Embarcadero) For legal emergencies or visa questions call the Operations Centre toll-free ☎ 1-800-267-6788; outside Canada, call collect ☎ 613-996-8885.

France (Map pp70–1; ☎ 415-397-4330; www.consulfrance-sanfrancisco.org; 540 Bush St, Downtown; 🕑 9am-12:30pm Mon-Fri; 🚌 & Ⓜ Embarcadero)

Germany (Map p96; ☎ 415-353-0300; www.germanyinfo.org; 1960 Jackson St, Japantown; 🕑 9am-noon Mon-Fri; 🚌 1,38)

Ireland (Map pp70–1; ☎ 415-392-4214; 33rd fl, 100 Pine St, Downtown; 🕑 10am-noon & 2-3:30pm Mon-Fri; 🚌 & Ⓜ Montgomery St)

Japan (Map pp110–11; ☎ 415-777-3533; www.cgjst.org; Suite 2300, 50 Fremont St, SoMa; 🕑 9am-5pm Mon-Fri; 🚌 & Ⓜ Embarcadero)

Mexico (Map pp110–11; ☎ 415-354-1700; www.consulmexsf.com; 532 Folsom St, Downtown; 🕑 7:30am-1:30pm Mon-Fri; 🚌 & Ⓜ Powell St)

Netherlands (☎ 650-403-0073; www.ncla.org; 901 Mariners Isl Blvd, San Mateo; by appointment)

New Zealand (Map pp70–1; ☎ 415-399-1255; www.mft.govt.nz; Suite 700, 1 Maritime Plaza, Downtown; by appointment; & Embarcadero)

UK (Map pp70–1; ☎ 415-617-1361; www.ukinusa.fco.gov.uk; Suite 850, 1 Sansome St, Downtown; 8:30am-1pm & 2-5pm Mon-Fri; & Embarcadero)

EMERGENCY

If something is stolen from you, make sure you report it to the police; you'll need a police report to make a claim if you have a travel-insurance policy. If your credit cards or traveler's checks have been taken, notify your bank or the relevant company as soon as possible.

Drug treatment (☎ 415-362-3400)

Police, fire and ambulance (☎ emergency 911, non-emergency 311)

San Francisco General Hospital (Map pp116–17; ☎ emergency room 415-206-8111, main hospital 415-206-8000; www.sfdph.org; 1001 Potrero Ave; 9)

Suicide crisis line (☎ 415-781-0500)

Trauma Recovery & Rape Treatment Center (☎ 415-437-3000; http://traumarecoverycenter.org)

HOLIDAYS

A majority of shops are open on public holidays (with the exception of July 4, Thanksgiving, Christmas and New Year's Day). Conversely, banks, schools and offices are usually closed. For information on festivals and events, see p20. Holidays that may affect business hours and transit schedules include the following:

New Year's Day January 1

Martin Luther King Jr Day Third Monday in January

Presidents' Day Third Monday in February

Easter Sunday (and Good Friday and Easter Monday) in March or April

Memorial Day Last Monday in May

Independence Day July 4

Labor Day First Monday in September

Columbus Day Second Monday in October

Veterans Day November 11

Thanksgiving Fourth Thursday in November

Christmas Day December 25

WI-FI ACCESS

San Francisco's mayor Gavin Newsom has pledged to provide free wi-fi service to the entire city, although he hasn't yet struck a deal with a provider (a Google deal fell through). However, at latest count there are 370 free wi-fi hot spots citywide, so there's usually at least one wi-fi connection configured for open access in any given part of the city. Typically you can connect for free in Union Square, most cafes, some laundries, hotel lobbies and guestrooms. For a listing of the city's free wi-fi spots, check out www.wififreespot.com/ca.html.

INTERNET ACCESS

The easiest and cheapest ways to get online in San Francisco are available to travelers equipped with their own laptops (see the boxed text, above). All the major hotels (and many lesser ones) offer free wi-fi in the lobby and/or business centers that provide web access, fax, phone and savvy assistants. Places listed in this guide that offer wi-fi have a symbol.

If you don't have a computer to download images from your digital camera, Walgreens (p312) can burn digital photos onto a CD for $2.99. Those traveling without laptops can surf the internet for free at almost any public library, or the Downtown **Apple Store** (Map pp70–1; ☎ 415-392-0202; www.apple.com; 1 Stockton St; 10am-9pm Mon-Sat, 11am-7pm Sun; & Powell St;), which has high-speed wi-fi access and internet terminals. The **San Francisco Main Library** (Map p77; ☎ 415-557-4400; http://sfpl.lib.ca.us; 100 Larkin St; 10am-6pm Mon & Sat, 9am-8pm Tue-Thu, noon-6pm Fri, noon-5pm Sun; 5, 6, 7, 21, 31, 71, F, J, K, L, M, N; & Civic Center;) has 160 terminals, including some available to non-library-card-holding visitors on the 1st floor; internet access is available on a 15-minute basis, and there's spotty wi-fi access.

Brainwash laundromat (p200) offers pay internet terminals as well as food, coffee, beer and occasional live music.

LAUNDRY

Bernal Bubbles (Map pp116–17; ☎ 415-821-9530; www.bernalbubbles.com; 397 Cortland Ave, near Bocana St; 7am-10pm;) Free wi-fi, coin laundry, wash and fold service, video games and a bulletin board for stray socks. Mark your calendars for free-soap Tuesdays, half-price-dryer Wednesdays, and terrific free Soap Box Lectures on the first Saturday of the month.

Brainwash (Map pp110–11; ☎ 415-431-9274; www.brainwash.com; 1122 Folsom St; 🕑 7am-10pm Mon-Thu, 7am-11pm Fri-Sat, 8am-10pm Sun; 🚌 12, 19; 📶) Come with laundry, stay for breakfast all day, cheap beer, live entertainment, pinball, free wi-fi and pay internet terminals ($3 per 20 minutes).

LEGAL MATTERS

San Francisco police usually have more urgent business than fining you for picking a protected wild orange California poppy (up to $500), littering ($100 and up), jaywalking (ie crossing streets outside a pedestrian crosswalk, which can run from $75 to $125) or failing to clean up after your puppy ($30 in some places, plus shaming glares from fellow dog-owners). You may be let off with a warning for being caught taking a puff on a joint, but don't count on it – possessing marijuana for personal use is still a misdemeanor in this lenient city, though legal with a prescription inside a medicinal marijuana club. In recent years the police have cracked down on park squatters, so maybe you should change your plans if you were hoping to relive the Summer of Love in Golden Gate Park.

Americans are eligible to vote at 18, the legal age of consent is 17, and driver's licenses can be obtained by passing the necessary tests at age 16. Visitors old enough to drink back home might not be here, where the legal drinking age is 21. Drinking alcoholic beverages outdoors is not officially allowed, though drinking beer and wine is often permissible at street fairs and other outdoor events.

If you are arrested for any reason, it's your right to remain silent, but never walk away from an officer until given permission or you could be charged with resisting arrest. Anyone arrested gets the right to make one phone call. If you want to call your consulate, the police will give you the number on request.

MAPS

Besides the handy pull-out map included with this book, you might pick up the *San Francisco Street Map & Visitor Guide* for free at many of the city's hotels, and the *Muni Street & Transit Map*, which is free online (www.sfmta.com) or $3 in hard-copy form at the San Francisco Visitor Information Center (p315) or any large bookstore.

MEDICAL SERVICES

Before traveling, you should always contact your health-insurance provider to ascertain what types of medical care they will cover outside your home town (or home country). Overseas visitors should acquire travel insurance that covers medical situations in the US, where nonemergency care for uninsured patients can be very expensive. For nonemergency appointments at hospitals, you'll need proof of insurance or cash. Even with insurance, you will most likely have to pay for nonemergency care out of your own pocket up front, and then wrangle with your insurance company afterwards in order to get your money reimbursed. That said, San Francisco has reputable medical facilities as well as alternative medical practices and herbal apothecaries; see below for specific listings.

Clinics

American College of Traditional Chinese Medicine (Map pp116–17; ☎ 415-282-7600; www.actcm.edu; 455 Arkansas St; 🕑 8:30am-9pm Mon-Thu, 9am-5:30pm Sat; 🚌 22) Acupuncture, herbal remedies and other traditional Chinese medical treatments.

Haight Ashbury Free Clinic (Map pp126–7; ☎ 415-746-1950; 558 Clayton St; 🕑 call for appointment; 🚌 6, 7, 24, 66, 71, N) Services offered by appointment only, but once you're in, a doctor will see you for free and will offer advice if further medical attention is needed.

Lyon-Martin Women's Health Services (Map pp110–11; ☎ 415-565-7667; www.lyon-martin.org; Suite 201, 1748 Market St; 🕑 11am-7pm Mon & Wed, 9am-5pm Tue & Fri, noon-5pm Thu; 🚌 6, 7, 66, 71, F) Relatively affordable health services are available at this women's clinic; lesbian-friendly.

Emergency Rooms

Davies Medical Center (Map pp126–7; ☎ 415-565-6000; Noe St; 🕑 24hr; 🚌 6, 7, 24, 71, J, N) Has 24-hour emergency services.

San Francisco General Hospital (Map pp116–17; ☎ emergency room 415-206-8111, main hospital 415-206-8000; www.sfdph.org; 1001 Potrero Ave; 🕑 24hr; 🚌 9) Provides care to uninsured patients; no documentation required beyond ID.

University of California San Francisco Medical Center (Map pp136–7; ☎ 415-476-1000; www.ucsfhealth.org; 505 Parnassus Ave; 🕑 24hr; 🚌 6, 7, 24, 71, J, N) At the vanguard of medical advances.

Pharmacies

Pharmaca (Map pp126–7; ☎ 415-661-1216; www.pharmaca.com; 925 Cole St; 8am-8pm Mon-Fri, 9am-8pm Sat & Sun; 6, 43, N) Pharmacy plus naturopathic and alternative remedies, and weekend chair massage.

Walgreens (Map p123; ☎ 415-861-3136; www.walgreens.com; 498 Castro St at 18th St; 24hr; 24, 35, F, Castro St) Pharmacy and over-the-counter meds; dozens of locations citywide (see website).

MONEY

US dollars are the only accepted currency in San Francisco, though barter is sometimes possible on Craigslist (http://sfbay.craigslist.org) and for under-12s at 826 Valencia (p118). The dollar is divided into 100 cents, with coins of 1¢ (penny), 5¢ (nickel), 10¢ (dime), 25¢(quarter), the relatively rare 50¢ (half dollar), and the equally elusive one-dollar coin. Bills can be quite confusing to foreign visitors, because they are all the same size and color; get used to carefully checking the corners for amounts. They come in denominations of $1, $2, $5, $10, $20, $50 and $100.

Debit/credit cards are accepted widely, but bringing a combination of cash, cards and traveler's checks is always wise. Though there are exchange bureaus located at airports (p300), the best rates are generally at banks in the city. For exchange rates, see the inside front cover, and get the latest rates at www.xe.com, a handy currency converter site. For more on costs and money, see p24.

American Express (Map pp110–11; AmEx; ☎ 415-536-2600; www.americanexpress.com/travel; 455 Market St; 8:30am-5:30pm Mon-Fri, 9:30am-3:30pm Sat; 21, 71, F, J, K, L, M, N, T; & Embarcadero) Traveler's checks are still a handy cash backup in case your ATM and credit cards inexplicably stop working; the shop exchanges money as well.

Bank of America (Map pp70–1; ☎ 415-837-1394; www.bankamerica.com; downstairs, 1 Powell St; 9am-6pm Mon-Fri, to 2pm Sat; 5, 6, 7, 21, 31, 71 F, J, K, L, M, N; & Powell St) Though any bank can exchange currency, this branch of the Bank of America is the most centrally located and convenient.

ATMs

Most banks have ATM machines, which are open 24 hours a day, except in areas where street crime has proved a problem (such as near the BART stop at 16th and Mission Sts). For a nominal service charge, you can withdraw cash from an ATM using a credit card; check with your provider about applicable fees.

Credit Cards

Following is a list of phone numbers to report lost or stolen credit cards.

American Express (☎ 800-992-3404)

Diners Club (☎ 800-234-6377)

Discover (☎ 800-347-2683)

MasterCard (☎ 800-622-7747)

Visa (☎ 800-847-2911)

Traveler's Checks

In the US, traveler's checks in US dollars are virtually as good as cash; you don't have to go to a bank to cash them, as many establishments will accept them just like cash. The major advantage of traveler's checks in US dollars over cash is that they can be replaced if lost or stolen. For lost or stolen traveler's checks you can call the following numbers:

American Express (☎ 800-992-3404)

MasterCard (☎ 800-622-7747)

Thomas Cook (☎ 800-223-7373)

Visa (☎ 800-227-6811)

NEWSPAPERS & MAGAZINES

San Francisco Bay Guardian (www.sfbg.com) Free weekly; alternative news and entertainment listings.

San Francisco Chronicle (www.sfgate.com) Main daily newspaper; news, entertainment and event listings online (no registration required).

SF Weekly (www.sfweekly.com) Free weekly; local gossip and entertainment.

ORGANIZED TOURS

Magical mystery tours of San Francisco and beyond by bus can be found in the Transportation chapter (p304).

At the California Historical Society Museum (Map pp110–11; ☎ 415-357-1848; www.californiahistoricalsociety.org; 678 Mission St; adult/child under 5yr/senior & student $3/free/1; noon-4:30pm Wed-Sat; 6, 7, 14, 21, 31, 71, F, J, K, L, M, N; & Montgomery St), when eccentric urban planner Gary Holloway isn't dressing in monk's robes or rearranging his tea tin collection, he leads enlightening Historical Walkabouts through obscure San Francisco neighborhoods.

DIY TOURS

Follow your bliss with these handy self-guided tour tools:

- For a terrific literary map of San Francisco, go to 826 Valencia (p118); City Lights Bookstore (p146) sells literary guides to Northern California, plus volumes of poetry inspired by San Francisco locations.
- Match your interest to tours from San Francisco's nonprofit history goldmine at http://foundsf.org, with historical photos, oral history clips, and videos around San Franciscan themes such as Food, Dissent, Wilderness and more.
- The San Francisco League of Urban Gardens (☎ 415-285-7584) organizes Open Garden tours of private backyard beauties every June; call for meeting times and places.
- Follow the Ecology Trail through the Presidio with maps available from the Presidio Visitors Center (Map pp100–1; Officers' Club, 50 Moraga Ave; 9am-5pm; 43, 76), heading through Tennessee Hollow, site of a refugee camp after the 1906 earthquake and blooming with endangered pink clarkia flowers in summer, to Inspiration Point and *Spire*, Andy Goldsworthy's 100ft sculpture of reclaimed Presidio cypress logs.
- Artist Kate Pocrass collects odd things she and other locals have noticed around town into loosely organized Mundane Journeys (☎ 415-364-1465; www.mundanejourneys.com); call for a phone recording guiding you to some of these odd places.

Teens who grew up here lead two-hour Chinatown Alleyway Tours (☎ 415-984-1478; www.chinatownalleywaytours.org; adult/child 6-9yr/student $18/5/12; 11am-1pm Sat or by appointment) offering an up-close-and-personal peek into Chinatown's past. Hot stuff: Fire Engine Tours (☎ 415-333-7077; www.fireenginetours.com; Beach St at the Cannery; adult/child under 12yr/teen $50/30/40; 1pm Wed-Mon) takes you on a 75-minute ride in an open-air vintage fire engine over Golden Gate Bridge.

Precita Eyes Mission Mural Tours (☎ 415-285-2287; www.precitaeyes.org; adult $10-12, child under 17yr $5; 11am & 1:30pm Sat & Sun) offers two-hour walking tours by local artists covering 60-plus murals in a six-block radius of mural-covered Balmy Alley. Public Library City Guides (☎ 415-557-4266; www.sfcityguides.org; public tours free, donations accepted) are local historians who lead one-to-two-hour tours by neighborhood and theme: Art Deco Marina, Gold Rush Downtown, and Summer of Love Treasure Hunt in the Haight. See the website for times and locations.

The only way for true techies to cover the waterfront: on an electric Segway scooter with San Francisco Segway Tours (☎ 415-474-3130; www.sfelectrictour.com; tours depart from 757 Beach St; per person $70; tours depart 9am, 12:30pm & 4pm Apr-Oct, 10:30am & 1:30pm Nov-Mar). Tour price includes 35-minute training on operating the Segway.

PETS

Since San Franciscans have more pets than kids, this town is definitely pet-friendly – although dogs still have to stay on a leash in many parts of town, and you're required by law to clean up your dog's little gifts to nature. To check out the best locations for Rover to roam free, see http://sf.urbanhound.com, and bone up on local leash laws at www.sfdog.org.

To find SF hotels that allow dogs, check out www.dogfriendly.com. If you need to go away for a few days, you might check your pet into the swanky Wag Hotel (Map pp116–17; ☎ 415-876-0700; www.waghotels.com; 25 14th St). There are opportunities galore for pet lovers to connect in SF, including two SF-based websites: www.catster.com and www.dogster.com.

POST

You can buy stamps at post offices and some ATMs. Current rates for 1st-class mail within the US are 44¢ for letters up to 1oz (17¢ each additional ounce) and 28¢ for postcards. International airmail to locations other than Canada (75¢) and Mexico (79¢) is 98¢ for a 1oz letter or postcard. Post restante (general delivery) can be arranged at any US post office. Check out www.usps.com for post office locations throughout San Francisco. Following are the most convenient post offices for visitors.

Civic Center Post Office (Map p77; ☎ 415-563-7284; 101 Hyde St; & Civic Center)

Rincon Center Post Office (Map pp110-11; ☎ 800-275-8777, 415-896-0762; 180 Steuart St; 8am-6pm Mon-Fri, to 2pm Sat)

US Post Office (Map pp70–1; ☎ 415-397-3333; Macy's, 170 O'Farrell St; 5, 6, 7, 21, 31, 71, F, J, K, L, M, N; & Powell St; Powell-Mason & Powell-Hyde) Located in Macy's department store.

RADIO

For local listening in San Francisco and online via podcast and/or streaming audio, check out these local stations:

KALW 91.7 FM (www.kalw.org) Local NPR affiliate: news, talk, music, original programming.

KPFA 94.1 FM (www.kpfa.org) Alternative news and music.

KPOO 89.5 FM (www.kpoo.com) Community radio with jazz, R&B, blues and reggae.

KQED 88.5 FM (www.kqed.org) Local NPR affiliate: news, talk, music, original programming.

SAFETY

Keep your city smarts and wits about you, especially at night in the Tenderloin, SoMa and the Mission. The Bayview-Hunters Point neighborhood south of Potrero Hill along the water is plagued by a high crime rate and frequent violence, and not particularly suitable for wandering tourists. After dark, Dolores Park, Buena Vista Park and the entry to Golden Gate Park at Haight and Stanyan Sts host drug deals and casual sex hookups.

Expect to be asked for spare change often in San Francisco, but don't feel obliged – donations stretch further at the nonprofit Haight Ashbury Food Program (p128).

TAXES

SF's 9.5% sales tax is added to virtually everything, including meals, accommodations and car rentals. Groceries are about the only items not taxed. There's also a 14% hotel room tax to take into consideration when booking a hotel room. In response to city laws mandating healthcare benefits for restaurant workers, some restaurants are passing along those costs to diners by tacking an additional 4% charge onto the bill – a slippery business practice mentioned in the menu fine print that may eventually be eliminated, given widespread diner protest.

TELEPHONE

The US country code is ☎ 1, and San Francisco's city code is ☎ 415. To make an international call from the Bay Area, call ☎ 011 + country code + area code + number. When calling Canada, there's no need to dial the international access code ☎ 011. When dialing another area code, the code must be preceded by a 1. For example, to dial an Oakland number from San Francisco, start with ☎ 1-510.

Area Codes in the Bay Area

East Bay ☎ 510

Marin County ☎ 415

Peninsula ☎ 650

San Francisco ☎ 415

San Jose ☎ 408

Santa Cruz ☎ 831

Wine Country ☎ 707

Local calls from a pay phone usually start at 50¢. Hotel telephones will often add heavy surcharges. Toll-free numbers start with ☎ 800 or ☎ 888, while phone numbers beginning with ☎ 900 usually incur high fees.

Cell Phones

Most US cell phones besides the iPhone operate on CDMA, not the European standard GSM – make sure you check compatibility with your phone service provider. Most North American travelers can use their mobiles in San Francisco and the Bay Area, but should check with the carrier about roaming charges.

Operator Services

International operator (☎ 00)

Local directory (☎ 411)

Long-distance directory information (☎ 1 + area code + 555-1212)

Operator (☎ 0)

Toll-free number information (☎ 800-555-1212)

Phonecards

For international calls from a public pay phone, it's a good idea to use a phone card, available at most corner markets and drug stores. Otherwise, when you dial 0, you're at the mercy of the international carrier who covers that pay phone.

TIME

San Francisco is on Pacific Standard Time, three hours behind the East Coast's Eastern Standard Time and eight hours behind Greenwich Mean Time (GMT). In the summer, there's Summer Time in Britain and Daylight Saving Time in the United States, so the eight-hour difference is maintained.

TOILETS

Downtown, clean toilets and baby-changing tables can be found in the Westfield San Francisco Centre (p144) and in Macy's (p144). In the area around the Civic Center, the San Francisco Main Library (p79) has rest rooms, as do public library branches and parks throughout the city. Otherwise, try the green coin-operated sidewalk kiosk commodes, which cost 25¢ and can be found in North Beach, Fisherman's Wharf, the Financial District and the Tenderloin. The Haight-Ashbury and Mission District are woefully lacking in public toilets, and you may have to buy a coffee or a beer to gain access to locked bathrooms.

TOURIST INFORMATION

The helpful, centrally located **San Francisco Visitor Information Center** (Map pp70–1; ☎ 415-391-2000, events hotline 415-391-2001; www.onlyinsanfrancisco.com; lower level, Hallidie Plaza, Market & Powell Sts; 9am-5pm Mon-Fri, to 3pm Sat & Sun, closed Sun Nov-Apr; & Powell St) provides practical information for tourists, publishes glossy tourist-oriented booklets and runs a 24-hour events hotline.

For further tourist information, check out the following websites:

Lonely Planet (www.lonelyplanet.com)

SFGate.com (www.sfgate.com)

SFist (http://sfist.com)

TRAVELERS WITH DISABILITIES

All Bay Area transit companies offer travel discounts for the disabled, and wheelchair accessible service. Muni's *Street & Transit Map* (www.sfmta.com) details which bus routes and streetcar stops are wheelchair friendly. The *San Francisco Bay Area Regional Transit Guide* (http://tripplanner.transit.511.org) covers accessibility for people with disabilities. Major car-rental companies can usually supply hand-controlled vehicles with one or two days' notice.

For further information about wheelchair accessibility on public transit and in hotels and other facilities, contact the **Independent Living Resource Center of San Francisco** (☎ 415-543-6222; www.ilrcsf.org; 9am-4:30pm Mon-Thu, to 4pm Fri).

For visually impaired people, major intersections emit a chirping signal to indicate when it is safe to cross the street. For the hearing impaired, many local TV stations include subtitles.

VISAS

The USA Visa Waiver Program (VWP) allows nationals from 27 countries to enter the US without a visa, provided they are carrying a machine-readable passport. Citizens of VWP countries need to register with the government online (http://esta.cbp.dhs.gov/) three days before their visit. The registration is valid for two years.

If you do not have a machine-readable passport, you must obtain a visa to enter the USA, even if you come from one of the VWP countries. In addition, if your passport was issued between October 26, 2005, and October 25, 2006, your passport must have a digital photo on the information page or an integrated chip from the data page. (After October 25, 2006, the integrated chip is required on all machine-readable passports.) If your passport does not meet these requirements, you simply need to obtain a visa from a US embassy or consulate in your home country.

For the updated list of countries included in the program and current requirements, see the website of the **US Department of State** (http://travel.state.gov/visa). All other travelers will need a visitor's visa except for Canadian citizens, who currently need only proof of identity and citizenship – but check the US Department of State for updates, as requirements may change.

WOMEN TRAVELERS

Women should apply their street smarts in San Francisco as in any other US city, just to be on the safe side. In SF, women are safe to walk into a bar alone without encountering uninvited come-ons – no one is going to make presumptions about your availability, interest or sexual orientation.

The **Women's Building** (Map pp116–17; ☎ 415-431-1180; www.womensbuilding.org; 3543 18th St; 9am-6pm; 14, 26, 33, 49, J; 16th St Mission) has a Community Resource Room offering information on healthcare, domestic violence, childcare, harassment, legal issues, employment and housing. For more sites and venues geared specifically to women (biological and otherwise), see the Gay/Lesbian/Bi/Trans SF chapter (p240).

WORK

Foreign visitors are not legally allowed to work in the USA without the appropriate working visa. The type of visa you need depends on the type of work.

H visa For temporary workers.

L visa For employees in intra-company transfers.

O visa For workers with extraordinary abilities.

P visa For athletes and entertainers.

Q visa For international cultural-exchange visitors.

The most common, the H visa, can be difficult to obtain. It usually requires a sponsoring organization, ie the company you will be working for in the US. The company will need to demonstrate why you, rather than a US citizen, are most qualified for the job. If you'd like to line up a job before you go, monitor the extensive employment listings on Craigslist (http://sfbay.craigslist.org).

Doing Business

To help your meetings or convention run smoothly in San Francisco, check in with the San Francisco Convention & Visitors Bureau (Map pp70–1; SFCVB; ☎ 415-974-6900; www.sfcvb.org; 900 Market St; 8:30am-5pm Mon-Fri). If San Francisco's history of boom and bust doesn't scare you off, consult the San Francisco Chamber of Commerce (Map pp70–1; ☎ 415-392-4520; www.sfchamber.com; 12th fl, 235 Montgomery St; 9am-5pm Mon-Fri) for information about business climate, loans, leasing and other start-up essentials.

Fax machines are easy to find in the USA, at packaging outlets, photocopy services and hotel business service centers. The San Francisco Main Library (p79) also offers fax services.

Express Photo & Mail (☎ 415-551-1277; 1388 Haight St; 9am-7pm Mon-Fri, to 5pm Sat; 6, 7, 43, 71) offers fax machines and can take care of all your shipping needs.

Volunteering

To demonstrate your gratitude to San Francisco for showing you a good time, why not volunteer for a local nonprofit? Check out the online service VolunteerMatch (www.volunteermatch.org), which can set you up with a worthy local nonprofit that matches your interests, talents and availability, even if it's only a few hours. Craigslist (http://sfbay.craigslist.org/vol) also lists opportunities to make yourself handy in the community, from nonprofit fashion-show fundraisers to teaching English to new arrivals.

THIS BOOK

This 7th edition of *San Francisco* was written by Alison Bing and John A Vlahides. Alison also wrote the previous edition along with Dominique Channell. This guidebook was commissioned in Lonely Planet's Oakland, California, office and produced by the following:

Commissioning Editors Jennye Garibaldi, Suki Gear

Coordinating Editors Carolyn Boicos, Simon Williamson

Coordinating Cartographer Marc Milinkovic

Coordinating Layout Designers Jessica Rose, Kerrianne Southway

Senior Editors Helen Christinis, Katie Lynch

Managing Cartographers Alison Lyall, Adrian Persoglia

Managing Layout Designer Sally Darmody

Assisting Editor Gabrielle Stefanos

Assisting Cartographer Khanh Luu

Cover Paul Mosig, lonelyplanetimages.com

Project Managers Bronwyn Hicks, Craig Kilburn

Thanks to Shahara Ahmed, Lucy Birchley, Jessica Boland, Daniel Corbett, Melanie Dankel, Heather Dickson, Indra Kilfoyle, Wayne Murphy, Raphael Richards, Juan Winata

Cover photographs Living roof, California Academy of Sciences image gallery/Tim Griffith (top). Golden Gate Bridge engulfed in fog, Morton Beebe/CORBIS (bottom).

Internal photographs p9 (#3) Amy Snyder/The Exploratorium; p10 (#2) Ed Kashi/Corbis. All other photographs by Lonely Planet Images: p5 (#1), p13 (#3), p16 (#2), p16 (#3) Richard Cummins; p6 (#1), p6 (#2), p6 (#3), p7 (#1), p7 (#2), p8 (#1), p8 (#3), p9 (#2), p10 (#1), p10 (#3), p13 (#1), p13 (#2), p15 (#2) Sabrina Dalbesio; p5 (#3) John Elk III; p2, p4 (#1), p4 (#2), p16 (#1) Lee Foster; p5 (#2), p11 (#2), p14 (#1), p15 (#1) Rick Gerharter; p8 (#2), p14 (#3) Roberto Gerometta; p4 (#3) Johnny Haglund; p3 Holger Leue; p12 (#2) Curtis Martin; p9 (#1) Mark Newman; p11 (#1), p11 (#3), p14 (#2) Rachael Nusbaum; p7 (#3), p12 (#1) Anthony Pidgeon.

THANKS

ALISON BING

Many thanks and crushing California bear hugs to editorial superhero Suki Gear; delightful coauthor, co-conspirator, muse and raconteur John A Vlahides; fellow travelers Jennye Garibaldi and Carolyn Boicos; fearless leaders Brice Gosnell and Heather Dickson at Lonely Planet; cartographer Alison Lyall; editor Sasha Baskett; project manager Craig Kilburn; the Sanchez Writers' Grotto for steady inspiration; fellow foodies Dee Budney, Sahai Burrowes, Yosh Han, Luke Haas, Mini Kahlon, Dave Knox, Lisa Park, Raj Patel and Cook Here and Now; and above all to Marco Flavio Marinucci, whose powerful kindness and bracing espresso makes anything possible, including romance on a skeevy Muni bus.

JOHN A VLAHIDES

John A Vlahides is grateful to his coauthor Alison Bing, commissioning editor Suki Gear, cartographer Alison Lyall, editor

THE LONELY PLANET STORY

Fresh from an epic journey across Europe, Asia and Australia in 1972, Tony and Maureen Wheeler sat at their kitchen table stapling together notes. The first Lonely Planet guidebook, *Across Asia on the Cheap*, was born.

Travelers snapped up the guides. Inspired by their success, the Wheelers began publishing books to Southeast Asia, India and beyond. Demand was prodigious, and the Wheelers expanded the business rapidly to keep up. Over the years, Lonely Planet extended its coverage to every country and into the virtual world via lonelyplanet.com and the Thorn Tree message board.

As Lonely Planet became a globally loved brand, Tony and Maureen received several offers for the company. But it wasn't until 2007 that they found a partner whom they trusted to remain true to the company's principles of traveling widely, treading lightly and giving sustainably. In October of that year, BBC Worldwide acquired a 75% share in the company, pledging to uphold Lonely Planet's commitment to independent travel, trustworthy advice and editorial independence.

Today, Lonely Planet has offices in Melbourne, London and Oakland, with over 500 staff members and 300 authors. Tony and Maureen are still actively involved with Lonely Planet. They're traveling more often than ever, and they're devoting their spare time to charitable projects. And the company is still driven by the philosophy of *Across Asia on the Cheap*: 'All you've got to do is decide to go and the hardest part is over. So go!'

Carolyn Boicos and regional publisher Brice Gosnell for being so damn wonderful to work with. Many thanks to those who helped during research: Christine Murray, DJ Gray, Sam Khedr, Karl Soehnlein and Kevin Clarke, Paul Marchegiani, Monique Jenkinson and Marc Kate, Marianne Wong and Warren Longmire. And thanks to Jim Aloise for encouraging me to get out of my mind. But I'm most grateful to you, dear reader. Enjoy this book and have a blast in San Francisco. You'll see: it's a really fun town to sink your teeth into.

OUR READERS

Many thanks to the travelers who used the last edition and wrote to us with helpful hints, useful advice and interesting anecdotes:

Robert Douthit, Adam Gendell, Mikael Knutsson, Lawrence Mar, Victoria Mascord, Kirsty Moore, Hanne Munk Rasmussen, David Schnur, Allie Smith, Sharon Spencer

SEND US YOUR FEEDBACK

We love to hear from travelers – your comments keep us on our toes and help make our books better. Our well-traveled team reads every word on what you loved or loathed about this book. Although we cannot reply individually to postal submissions, we always guarantee that your feedback goes straight to the appropriate authors, in time for the next edition. Each person who sends us information is thanked in the next edition and the most useful submissions are rewarded with a free book.

To send us your updates – and find out about Lonely Planet events, newsletters and travel news – visit our award-winning website: lonelyplanet.com/contact.

Note: We may edit, reproduce and incorporate your comments in Lonely Planet products such as guidebooks, websites and digital products, so let us know if you don't want your comments reproduced or your name acknowledged. For a copy of our privacy policy visit lonelyplanet.com/privacy.

Notes

Notes

INDEX

000 map pages
000 photographs

Q

R

S

T

U

000 map pages
000 photographs

EATING

000 map pages
000 photographs

000 map pages
000 photographs

000 map pages
000 photographs

HOTELS

INNS

MOTELS

RANCHES

RESORTS & SPAS

THEME HOTELS

SPORTS & ACTIVITIES

BASEBALL

BASKETBALL

COOKING COURSES

CYCLING

FOOTBALL

GOLF

HEALTH & BEAUTY

ICE SKATING & BOWLING

OTHER ACTIVITIES

RUNNING, WALKING & SKATING

SAILING & WINDSURFING

SWIMMING

WHALE WATCHING

YOGA

TOP PICKS

000 map pages
000 photographs

GREENDEX

GOING GREEN

Lonely Planet is committed to good times had by all in San Francisco – that means you, your hosts and organizations keeping this city clean, green, fair and forward-thinking (see www.lonelyplanet.com/responsibletravel). GreenDexed organizations include the following:

- Museums, hotels and other buildings certified by the Leadership in Energy and Environmental Design (LEED) Green Building Rating System or working towards energy independence with alternative energy sources.
- Businesses certified green by the city of San Francisco for leadership in conservation.
- Organizations and businesses that preserve Bay Area cultural history and/or provide ongoing financial support for nonprofit community and cultural initiatives.
- Travel and transportation providers preserving the environment through biodiesel-fueled vehicles and conservation-focused programming.
- Restaurants, stores and other businesses that support local economies and reduce carbon footprints through well-established commitments to local and sustainable sourcing, including California-certified organic farms and vineyards and Bay Area designers and artisans.

If you note efforts that deserve acclaim or seem to have gone awry, please let us know via www.lonelyplanet.com/feedback.

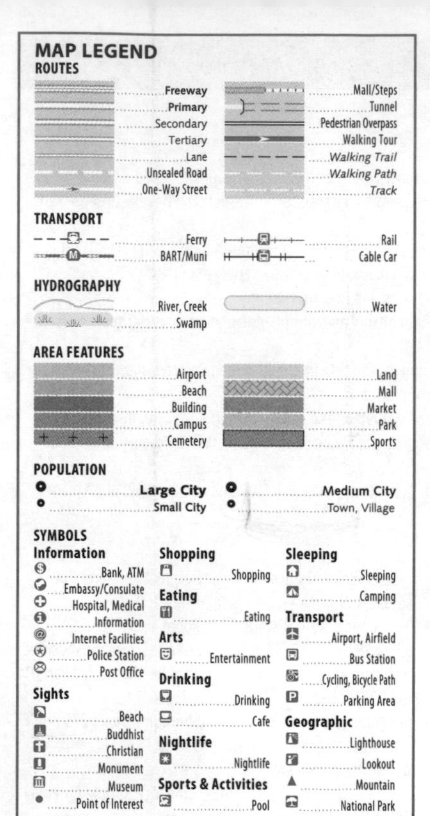

Published by Lonely Planet Publications Pty Ltd
ABN 36 005 607 983

Australia (Head Office)
Locked Bag 1, Footscray, Victoria 3011,
☎03 8379 8000, fax 03 8379 8111,
talk2us@lonelyplanet.com.au

USA 150 Linden St, Oakland, CA 94607,
☎510 250 6400, toll free 800 275 8555,
fax 510 893 8572, info@lonelyplanet.com

UK 2nd fl, 186 City Rd, London, EC1V 2NT,
☎020 7106 2100, fax 020 7106 2101,
go@lonelyplanet.co.uk

Printed through Colorcraft Ltd, Hong Kong.
Printed in China.